INTERNATIONAL FILM EX

Providing Specialized Distribution
for Independent Producers
Throughout the World

Theatrical
Non-Theatrical
Television

INTERNATIONAL FILM EXCHANGE LTD.

159 WEST 53 STREET
NEW YORK, NY 10019
TELEPHONE: (212) 582-4318

TELEX: 420748 RAPP UI
CABLE: IFEXREP NEW YORK

Jeannine Seawell

INTERNATIONAL SALES REPRESENTATIVE

J & M Film Sales Limited

9 Clifford Street,
London W.1.
Tel: 01-734 2181
Telex: 298538 (Filming)

Suite 402,
8899 Beverly Boulevard,
Los Angeles
California 90048
Tel: 213-271-7159
Telex: 674996

Foreign sales – producers' representatives
Contact Julia Palau or Michael Ryan

INTERNATIONAL FILM GUIDE 1983

EDITED BY PETER COWIE

ASSOCIATE EDITOR: DEREK ELLEY

London
THE TANTIVY PRESS
 **NEW YORK ZOETROPE** INC.
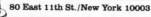 80 East 11th St./New York 10003

Twice a year!
April and October

MIFED

**The International
Film, TV film
and Documentary Market**

Do you have feature or TVfilms to sell?
Are you a buyer for television channels or for cinema circuits?

Copyright © 1982 by The Tantivy Press Ltd. U.S. Library of Congress Catalogue Card No. 64-1076.   ISBN 0-900730-00-5

Photoset, printed and bound in Great Britain at The Camelot Press Ltd, South-ampton.

Choice of Films 1981/82

1 *Yol*, Güney/Gören (Turkey/
   Switzerland)
2 *Shoot the Moon*, Parker (U.S.A.)
3 *Britannia Hospital*, Anderson
   (U.K.)
4 { *Missing*, Costa-Gavras (U.S.A.)
   Die Faelschung, Schlöndorff
   (West Germany)
6 *Gallipoli*, Weir (Australia)

7 *The Flight of the Eagle*, Troell
   (Sweden/Norway)
8 *Montenegro*, Makavejev
   (Sweden/U.K.)
9 *The Tree of Knowledge*,
   Malmros (Denmark)
10 *My Dinner with André*, Malle
   (U.S.A.)

20 Years, 20 Films

The Editor's Choice of Titles
(alphabetical order)

Annie Hall, Allen.
Belle de jour, Buñuel.
Cadaveri eccellenti, Rosi.
Chimes at Midnight, Welles.
Days and Nights in the Forest, Ray.
La Dentellière, Goretta.
Five Easy Pieces, Rafelson.
The Godfather, Coppola.
If . . ., Anderson.

Illumination, Zanussi.
Kagemusha, Kurosawa.
Last Tango in Paris, Bertolucci.
Man of Marble, Wajda.
Mephisto, Szabó.
Ma Nuit chez Maud, Rohmer.
La Nuit américaine, Truffaut.
8½, Fellini.
The Passenger, Antonioni.
Persona, Bergman.
2001: A Space Odyssey, Kubrick.

International Liaison

Afghanistan: Lyle Pearson
Argentina: Alberto Tabbia
Australia: David J. Stratton
Austria: Goswin Dörfler
Belgium: Paul Davay
Brazil: Luis Arbex
Bulgaria: Ivan Stoyanovich
Canada: Gerald Pratley
Chile: Malcolm Coad
Denmark: Claus Hesselberg
Eire: Liam O'Leary
Finland: Kari Uusitalo
France: Michel Ciment

Germany (FRG): Edmund Luft
Greece: Andreas Bellis
Iceland: Edda Kristjánsdóttir
India: Uma da Cunha
Indonesia: Fred Marshall
Israel: Dan Fainaru
Italy: Lorenzo Codelli
Japan: Naoki Togawa
Malaysia: Baharudin A. Latif
Mexico: Tomás Pérez Turrent
New Zealand: Lindsay Shelton
Norway: Jan E. Holst
Philippines: Agustin Sotto

Poland: Kjell Albin Abrahamson
Portugal: Fernando Duarte
Romania: Manuela Cernat
Senegal: Lyle Pearson
South Africa: Lionel Friedberg
Spain: José Luis Guarner
Sri Lanka: Amarnath Jayatilaka
Switzerland: Felix Bucher
Thailand: Michael Denison
Turkey: Vecdi Sayar
U.S.A.: Diane Jacobs
U.S.S.R.: Ronald Holloway
Yugoslavia: Ronald Holloway

Directors of the Year

1964	1965	1966	1967	1968
Visconti	Fellini	Kurosawa	Franju	Widerberg
Welles	Ray (S)	Rosi	Losey	Ivens
Truffaut	Buñuel	Demy	Polanski	Lumet
Wajda	Malle	Brooks	Frankenheimer	Němec
Hitchcock	Kubrick	Haanstra	Torre Nilsson	Antonioni

1969	1970	1971	1972	1973
Bondarchuk	Anderson	Donskoi	Bertolucci	Bergman
Forman	Chabrol	Kazan	Donner	Bresson
Jancsó	Ichikawa	Melville	Kozintsev	Makavejev
Penn	Pasolini	Oshima	Rohmer	Resnais
Tati	Skolimowski	Schorm	Troell	Schlesinger

1974	1975	1976	1977	1978
Boorman	Altman	Cacoyannis	Allen	Goretta
Gaál	Ferreri	Cassavetes	Cukor	Hu
Godard	Has	Coppola	Kobayashi	Minnelli
Huston	Lester	Fassbinder	Sautet	Ritchie
Ivory	Sjöman	Zanussi	Wertmüller	Saura

1979	1980	1981	1982	1983
Benegal	Ashby	Berlanga	Pialat	Güney
Herzog	Carlsen	Kieślowski	Reisz	Peries
Mészáros	Tavernier	Olmi	Schlöndorff	Rafelson
Rademakers	Weir	Roeg	Sen	Risi
Scorsese	Wenders	Yates	Szabó	Tarkovsky

Distribution of IFG

Outside the United Kingdom and the United States of America, *International Film Guide* is distributed through the following outlets:

AUSTRALIA
Space Age Books, 305–307 Swanston Street, Melbourne 3000, Victoria.

HONGKONG
Film Society of Hongkong Ltd., GPO Box 5169.

INDIA
Orient Longman Ltd., R. Kamani Marg, Ballard Estate, Bombay 400 038.

NETHERLANDS
Idea Books, Nieuwe Herengracht 35, Amsterdam.

SPAIN
Interlibro, Ronda Gral. Mitre 211–213, Barcelona 23.

SWEDEN
Proprius Förlag, Värtavägen 35, S–115 29 Stockholm.

WEST GERMANY
Filmland Presse, Aventinstr. 4, D–8000 Munich 5.

GUIDE TO CONTENTS

Staff

EDITOR:
Peter Cowie

ASSOCIATE EDITOR:
Derek Elley

ADVERTISING:
Jane Dudman
Anne Hall

EDITORIAL ASSISTANCE:
Beverley Norrie

Editorial and Business Offices:
THE TANTIVY PRESS LTD., MAGDALEN HOUSE, 136–148 TOOLEY STREET, LONDON SE1 2TT, ENGLAND. Tel: (01) 407 7566. Telegrams: TANTIVY LONDON SE1. Telex: 847303 ACTION G.

U.S.Academy Awards: 1981

Best Film: *Chariots of Fire*.
Best Direction: Warren Beatty for *Reds*.
Best Actor: Henry Fonda for *On Golden Pond*.
Best Actress: Katharine Hepburn for *On Golden Pond*.
Best Supporting Actor: John Gielgud for *Arthur*.
Best Supporting Actress: Maureen Stapleton for *Reds*.
Best Original Screenplay: Colin Welland for *Chariots of Fire*.
Best Adapted Screenplay: Ernest Thompson for *On Golden Pond*.
Best Cinematography: Vittorio Storaro for *Reds*.
Best Art Direction: Norman Reynolds, Leslie Dilley, and set director Michael Ford, for *Raiders of the Lost Ark*..
Best Costume Design: Milena Canonero for *Chariots of Fire*.
Best Editing: Michael Kahn for *Raiders of the Lost Ark*.

Best Score (original): Vangelis Papathanassiou for *Chariots of Fire*.
Best Original Song: "The Best That You Can Do" from *Arthur*, by Burt Bacharach, Carole Bayer Sager, Christopher Cross and Peter Allen.
Best Sound: Bill Varney, Steve Malsow, Gregg Landaker, Roy Charman for *Raiders of the Lost Ark*.
Best Foreign-Language Film: *Mephisto* (István Szabó, Hungary).
Best Documentary Feature: *Genocide*.
Best Documentary Short: *Close Harmony*.
Best Live-Action Short: *Violet*.
Best Animated Short: *Crac*.
Best Makeup: Rick Baker for *An American Werewolf in London*.
Jean Hersholt Humanitarian Award: Danny Kaye.
Irving Thalberg Award for Industry Achievement: Albert R. Broccoli.
Honorary Award: Barbara Stanwyck.

British Academy of Film and Television Awards: 1981

Best Film: *Chariots of Fire*.
Best Direction: Louis Malle for *Atlantic City*.
Best Screenplay: Bill Forsyth for *Gregory's Girl*.
Best Cinematography: Geoffrey Unsworth, Ghislain Cloquet for *Tess*.
Best Production Design/Art Direction: Norman Reynolds for *Raiders of the Lost Ark*.
Best Costume Design: Milena Canonero for *Chariots of Fire*.
Best Editing: Thelma Shoonmaker for *Raging Bull*.
Best Sound: Don Sharpe, Ivon Sharrock, Bill Rowe for *The French Lieutenant's Woman*.
Original Film Music: Carl Davis for *The French Lieutenant's Woman*.

Best Actress: Meryl Streep for *The French Lieutenant's Woman*.
Best Actor: Burt Lancaster for *Atlantic City*.
Most Promising Newcomer to Leading Film Role: Joe Pesti for *Raging Bull*.
Best Short Film: *Recluse* by Bob Bentley.
Best Animated Film: *The Sweater* by Sheldon Cohen.
Michael Balcon Award for outstanding British contribution to cinema: David Puttnam.
Robert Flaherty Award: *Soldier Girls* by Nick Broomfield and Joan Churchill.
Fellowship Award: Andrzej Wajda.

WORLD SURVEY

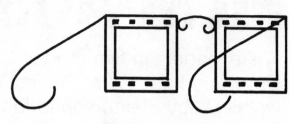

In Gratitude . . .

The companies and individuals listed below have advertised in each and every edition of INTERNATIONAL FILM GUIDE since we launched the book twenty years ago. We signal here both their endurance and their support.

Agfa-Gevaert
Berlin Film Festival
British Film Institute
La Cinémathèque Suisse
ETV Films
Film Polski
Hagens Anthony & Co.
John Halas

Hampton Books
Hungarofilm
Jauch & Hübener
Locarno Film Festival
MIFED
Le Minotaure
Hans Rohr Buchhandlung
Shell International
Swedish Institute
Triangle Films
TVC (London)
Richard Williams
A. Zwemmer

Introduction

Enormous changes have coursed through the film world since we launched the first, petite edition of our annual, some twenty years ago. Just as industrial technology has mutated with ferocious speed during these two decades, so the face of the cinema has altered beyond expectation. *Gone with the Wind* had by 1963 held sway as the box-office champion of all time for almost a quarter of a century. Since then, the race for the summit has produced a flow of ousted champions – *The Sound of Music, The Godfather, The Exorcist, Jaws, Star Wars . . .*

The great Hollywood studios have all been swallowed by other non-film conglomerates. One moment M-G-M appears to be on the edge of extinction, the next it has acquired United Artists. Fox, on its knees in the wake of *Cleopatra* when we published the initial IFG, has seen its coffers filled with the receipts from the *Star Wars* saga and at the same time succumbed to a takeover bid from a Colorado billionaire.

The movie palaces of yesteryear have been replaced with multiple complexes, emporia where the casual visitor may select as though from a menu the film that suits his taste. In the face of this supermarket attack, the "neighbourhood" art house survives perilously, if at all, sharing with the big chains a single imperative – to lure a dwindling audience away from the ever-more sophisticated paraphernalia of home video equipment. Video and cable TV are indeed the most dramatic novelties to enter the film world since 1963; yet the cinema may be able to assimilate their threat just as it did the menace of TV, learning to profit from the new technology instead of being stunned into defeat.

In Europe, traditionally the breeding ground of ideas, while the American cinema remains peerless master of the genre movie, governments have gradually recognised the need to support the film as an art form. Scandinavia has led the way in creating a system of subsidies that sustains the infra-structure of its national film industries without destroying their character.

A whole generation of talent has come, and in some cases (Fassbinder, Jarva, Huszárik . . .) tragically gone. The revolutionaries of the Fifties and Sixties have coalesced into the Establishment of the Eighties. Directors continue, alas, to be judged in a nationalistic context, and the fortunes of various countries have soared and fallen by turns. Twenty years ago, who could have predicted the renaissance of West German cinema? Or of the Czech, or Swiss, or Australian? Some revivals, like the Swedish, Dutch, and Yugoslav, have flattered to deceive. Others, like the Hungarian and Polish, improved so discreetly that they achieved a classic quality almost before the critics (and certainly the exhibitors) were aware of it.

Animation has made great strides. Today there are some thirty animated feature films in production throughout the world, while no fewer than 30,000 people are employed in the Japanese animated movie industry – more than in the live-action field in that country. The craft of the short film, however, has suffered, save in the educational field; TV has pre-empted the early phase of a film-maker's career, while the theatres have steadily eliminated shorts from their programmes. Film education, though, has leapt ahead, with courses being offered at nearly every university in the United States and at a respectable proportion of higher learning establishments in Europe. And the past twenty years has seen a prodigious crop of books on the movies – literally thousands of titles in an area of publishing previously neglected.

Forecasting the future is no less difficult than grasping the past. In two decades from now, cinema theatres will surely still exist, but in what quantity is hard to gauge. One suspects that enthusiasts will continue to patronise them for just two types of product: the extremely *recherché* foreign films, and those movies that rely on spectacular visual and sonic effects for their appeal. *Plus ça change . . .*

THE EDITOR

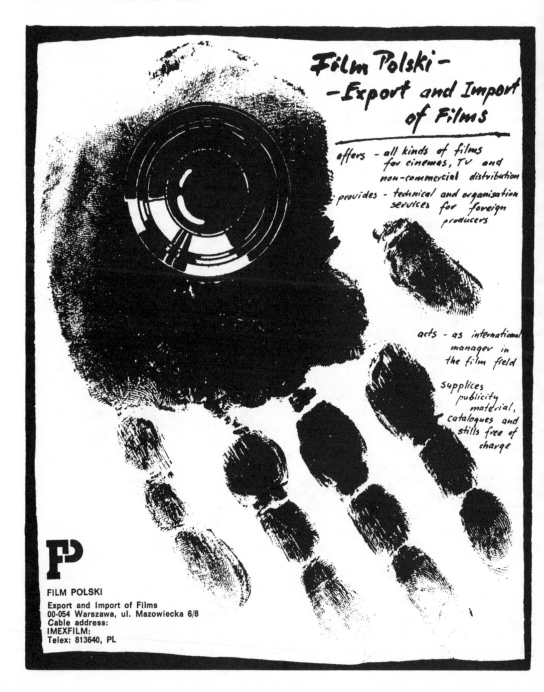

**Film Polski -
-Export and Import
of Films**

offers - all kinds of films
for cinemas, TV and
non-commercial distribution

provides - technical and organisation
services for foreign
producers

acts - as international
manager in
the film field

supplies
publicity
material,
catalogues and
stills free of
charge

FILM POLSKI
Export and Import of Films
00-054 Warszawa, ul. Mazowiecka 6/8
Cable address:
IMEXFILM:
Telex: 813640, PL

FIVE DIRECTORS OF THE YEAR

Yılmaz Güney

by Derek Elley

In his native Turkey, Yılmaz Güney has been many things to many different people – matinee idol, novelist, scriptwriter, left-wing activist, director, public hero, imprisoned martyr. To international audiences he simply represents the best of committed Turkish cinema, an enigma who has enjoyed most of his overseas fame from behind prison walls, speaking to the outside world through a small group of disciples. Güney's films show a Turkey poised between feudalism and capitalism, with the excesses of both; yet, despite their often bleak subject-matter, his pictures remain both accessible and hopeful. Güney has never forgotten his own roots and has not fallen into the trap of merely catering for an intellectual ghetto: his films build on his popular matinee image while at the same time expressing his most personal fears and grievances. And that, essentially, is the secret of his magic.

YILMAZ GÜNEY was born in 1937 in a small village near Adana in southern Turkey. The son of a Kurdish farm labourer, he grew up in a family of six and held a variety of jobs during his youth – water carrier, farm worker, cotton picker, butcher's apprentice. He started writing at secondary school, and developed a taste for cinema in his teens, but it was law that he went on to study (in

Ankara), followed by economics in İstanbul in 1957. At this time he also published his first short stories and in 1958 started work with director Atıf Yılmaz as scriptwriter, assistant director and actor. Yılmaz (b. Mersin, 1925) had, like Güney, originally studied law before turning to the cinema in the late Forties; a variable talent, equally adept at any genre, he nevertheless shared many of Güney's socio-national interests and in the late Fifties produced some of his best early works. After a more commercial spell during the Sixties, Yılmaz returned to more serious treatment of peasant and small-town life in the early Seventies, retaining the link with Güney (whose ill-starred *The Poor Ones* he co-wrote and co-directed).

In 1961, however, Güney had his first of many brushes with the authorities when he was arrested and sentenced to 18 months' jail and six months' exile for publishing a supposedly "communist" novel, *Equations with Three Strangers*. After his release in 1963 he embarked on a vigorous career in the commercial cinema, writing and/or starring in a vast number of the heroic melodramas which are a staple of the country's cinematic diet. Cast either as gangster or sturdy peasant, abused by either the authorities or landowners, Güney quickly built up a nationwide following as a

GÜNDÖR BAYRAK AND AYTAC ARMAN IN *THE ENEMY*, SCRIPTED BY GÜNEY AND DIRECTED BY ZEKI ÖKTEN

matinee idol, nicknamed "The Ugly King" (Çirkin kral). His life during the Sixties was delicately poised between that of a wealthy film star on the one hand and a left-wing sympathiser subject to discreet harassment from the authorities. In 1968 he set up his own company, Güney Film (Güney-Filmcilik), to make more personal works, while continuing to write and star in others' films.

In 1972 the bubble burst. In the midst of production of *The Poor Ones*, Güney was arrested on the charge of sheltering wanted anarchist students and imprisoned without trial. In 1974, after 26 months in jail, he was released under a general amnesty for political prisoners brought in by the new, more liberal government of Bulent Ecevit. It was a temporary freedom. After making *The Friend* he set to work on *Anxiety* in August of that year; but after less than a week's filming near his home town, fate intervened. One evening, in a crowded restaurant in Adana where the crew had been filming, Güney was repeatedly insulted by an inebriated judge of known right-wing sentiments; a shot rang out, the judge died and Güney – despite confessions by some of his associates and a string of suspicious legal tangles – was sentenced to 24 years' hard labour for homicide, later commuted to 18 years' imprisonment.

The most extraordinary part of Güney's career now began. Despite pressure for his release, he remained in jail – but with special privileges in deference to his status (his popularity, if anything, now greater for this "martyrdom"). Inside prison he was allowed both to screen films and continue writing scripts, the latter directed by the young Zeki Ökten (b. İstanbul, 1941) who had started as an assistant director for Atıf Yılmaz and later shown some promise, amid several routine commercial jobs, with *The Return of the Soldier*

(*Askerin dönüşü*, 1974). Ökten directed both *The Herd* and *The Enemy* from Güney scripts; and it was the success of these films which brought worldwide attention to the imprisoned writer/director.

Güney remained philosophic about his imprisonment. In 1978 he told visiting director Elia Kazan: "My wife [whom he married in 1970] has learnt to look on my imprisonment as natural. If I left, I'd be back here a week later anyway." And in the fragile political atmosphere of present-day Turkey, Güney is aware of his own dilemma. "I could have escaped from any of my prisons. But I am safer here. I have friends who protect me. Anyone who tried to kill me in here wouldn't last five minutes; but outside an assassin could kill me and escape easily." Until recently, Güney's dilemma seemed insoluble. In 1978, in the relatively relaxed confines of İstanbul's Toptaşı prison, he told Kazan. "The ruling class would like me to leave but I'll never do that. I'll fight for our cause till the finish – and on Turkish soil."

Perhaps the fall of the Ecevit government, his subsequent move to a different prison, and the takeover of the military in September 1980 convinced Güney that more could be achieved from outside. In any event, he "escaped" (or, more accurately, walked away) from prison in October 1981 and, as of early 1982 was working on post-production of *The Road* – directed from his script by long-time associate Şerif Gören, who had taken over the reins on *Anxiety* in 1974.

Güney's early films work solidly within the framework of his commercial image – that of the wronged outsider or vengeful lover, either in a semi-feudal setting or on the brink of society. In *My Name Is Kerim* (1967) an apparently peaceful man is driven to violence when both his pride and his girlfriend are threatened; and in *Nuri the Flea* (1968) a trio of thieves find their circle threatened when they agree to take on a girl pickpocket and one of them falls in love with her.

Sharper, and benefiting from its detailed portrait of Anatolian village life, is *Bride of the Earth* (1968), in which the conventions of the Italian western (much favoured in Turkish cinema) and mainstream melodrama are underscored by Güney's own obsessions. There is little new in the story of a young girl forced to marry a local rich man while her true love is away, but Güney sharpens the irony of the story, first by making the latter's absence due to his desire to find fame and riches in the big city and second by making his pride indirectly the cause of the girl's death. The marguerites which Seyyit Han plants for his *fiancée* are also his undoing: in a duel with the rich man, the target (a marguerite) hides the head of his *fiancée*, buried in sand up to her neck.

With *The Hungry Wolves* (1969) there are the first distinct signs of Güney building towards a personal style. The film was shot in rugged eastern Anatolia while he was doing his military service, and he was thus prevented from working on its post-production; but behind the dramatic imagery and music – both of which Güney has consistently used throughout his career – lies a solitariness and sense of desperation which is to dominate his work more and more. The tale of a mountain brigand hunted by police directly prefigures the later *Elegy* in its use of landscape and character, and already

YILMAZ GÜNEY   PHOTO: CACTUS FILM

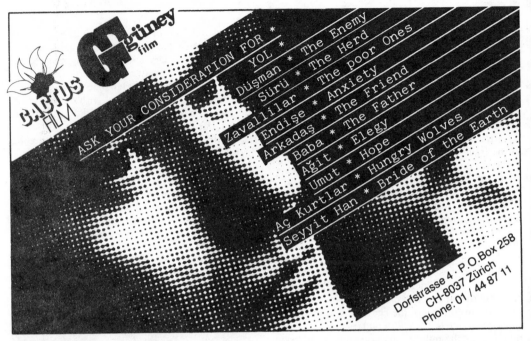

Güney shows that he is able to maintain an air of social realism without forfeiting either visual *élan* or narrative drive.

Yet nothing he had produced to that time quite forecast the accomplishment of *Hope* (1970). The title is ironic – the first of several evoking basic moods (*Elegy*; *Pain*; *Anxiety*) or relationships (*The Father*; *The Friend*; *The Poor Ones*; *The Enemy*) – but the view of the human condition is filled with immense warmth and not a little humour. The film is strongly autobiographical and the setting (Adana) full of personal associations, but the central character is a personality in his own right. Cabar (played by Güney himself with none of his usual glowering heroism) is the quintessential little man ground under society's heel but refusing to give up. When his horse is killed by a rich man's car, Cabar is put out of business and, unable to gain compensation, drifts relentlessly into poverty. Even crime is no help (the hapless Cabar has his pocket picked) and, with all possessions sold in the flea-market, he is finally left with only his fantasies: he and a friend, hearing of buried treasure in the desert, take along a *hodja*

(holy man) to help divine its whereabouts; but despite days of digging the dry earth yields nothing but dust.

Güney builds up his portrait of Cabar with unerring skill, from the first, bleak shots of Adana at dawn (recalling Antonioni's use of black-and-white in *La notte*), through the listless, claustrophobia of family life (with Cabar playing an increasingly unstable role of stern *paterfamilias*) to the final scenes of dementia beneath the blazing sun (Cabar caught in an overhead shot walking round in endless circles). The film has its moments of unsubtlety (notably the over-obvious portrayal of rich Adana at play) which jar in such a delicately textured film but *Hope* is still a magnificent achievement. While acknowledging the influence of Italian neo-realism, it works throughout in specifically Turkish terms (enhanced by the doleful sound of the clarinet-like *ney* playing the repetitive main theme) and – more importantly – defines for the first time Güney's universe with startling clarity.

After such an intensely personal film, Güney returned to a more outgoing subject in *Elegy*

(1971), one of a string of films made that year in a more commercially dramatic mould. Set like *The Hungry Wolves* in the unrelenting landscape of eastern Anatolia, it tells of a group of smugglers hunted by both a rival gang and the police. Here, as in so much of rural Turkish cinema (and not just Güney's films), time seems caught in some curious warp, with so-called civilisation massed against a way of life unchanged for centuries. *Elegy* is in many respects Güney's quintessential portrait of the noble savage – the bandit forced into a way of life by rigid social laws but unable to cross the line when challenged. Again, the title of the film is ironic: there is little that is elegiac in the bandits' way of life and famous sequences like the *ad hoc* operation performed amidst an avalanche of boulders have a gritty heightened realism. Yet Güney rarely judges: his "hero" Cobanoğlu, like the

simple Cabar, is no hero – merely an incomprehending puppet of the combined forces of tradition and stupidity.

In *The Father* (1971) Güney moves away from home territory to show the penumbra of big-city life. Again the central character is an essentially non-violent, incomprehending pawn in a greater game: Cemal, a Bosporus boatman, scraping a living for his wife and three children, has his application to work in Germany rejected because of imperfect teeth. To raise some money he agrees to take the blame for a rich client's murder on condition that on his release his family receives TL 200,000 – roughly what he would have saved during the same 8–10 years working in Germany. His sentence, however, turns out to be 24 years; and while he is in prison the rich man rapes his wife, who abandons their youngest child and runs

STILL FROM *THE HERD*

away in shame. When Cemal is released in 1971, he finds his son working as a gangster and his daughter as a prostitute. He takes the girl under his wing without telling her she is his daughter and, after shooting the rich man in revenge, is gunned down by his own son.

The story, and much of the direction, shows strong influences of the commercial Turkish cinema, with the gangster sequences shot (deliberately?) in a flashy, operatic style. However, *The Father* is remarkable for its portrait of downbeat family life, filmed with compassion and sensitivity, if photogenically. Güney cannot yet provide any answers but beneath the mood-painter throbs an angry soul, nowhere better caught than in the finely etched scenes of prison life.

In contrast, *The Poor Ones* (1972–75), also set in the underbelly of İstanbul, is a very openended, casual film. Its grey portrait of city life contains none of the lyrical views of the Bosporus which pepper *The Father*. Most of the film is taken up with flashbacks detailing the past misfortunes of the three main characters as they stroll the streets in winter, penniless and hungry. One stole money owed to him by an unscrupulous boss; another rescued, was cuckolded by and stabbed a prostitute; the third, Abu (played by Güney), began as a child thief breaking into flats for food and in his teens once had a fleeting hope of finding work at a girlfriend's factory. The uneasy camaraderie of the trio is nicely drawn in the many sequences of wandering through the city in their search for food. Again, Güney's central character finally ends up alone: in desperation the trio walk into a restaurant and order a meal (restraining their hunger with difficulty), but Abu is left to carry the can when his two comrades take flight.

Güney's prognosis, for both society and human relationships within it, seems outwardly bleak, but his films burn with an intense compassion. Each man is essentially his own master and should not rely on either the traditional bosom of the family or the authorities to provide succour or relief. The fatalistic atmosphere which hangs over so many of Güney's films is more than just a dramatic device; it is also an expression of the writer's sense of inadequacy at the twin forces of feudalism and capitalism in whose grip Turkish society seems caught. In only one film, *The Friend*

(1974), has Güney tried to confront the dilemma head on, virtually free of fictional trappings. It is an uneasy film, often awkwardly paced and acted, but is Güney's most polemic statement of his beliefs.

The action is set in the house of a rich architect in an exclusive resort suburb of İstanbul; one day he is visited by an old classmate, who has spent a term in prison for his political beliefs. Gradually the two former friends discover the political abyss that has grown between them. The architect's idealism has now gone; the friend's has remained, despite jail and a comfortable career. The latter also slowly opens the eyes of the architect's spoilt daughter to another, less luxurious Turkey. *The Friend* is the most didactic of Güney's films and, significantly, the weakest as cinema; but it is a clear reflection of his own anger after his two-year jail sentence and also an apologia for his own earlier life as a prosperous film star. Melike Demirağ, the actress playing the daughter, is herself the daughter of a wealthy producer and first met Güney under similar circumstances.

Anxiety (1974), the last film on which Güney has so far worked as a director, returns to the peasant life of his home district around Adana in southern Anatolia. Fate, in the form of the vendetta, hangs heavy over the community of cotton-pickers, one of whom must raise TL 15,000 or face the consequences. When his co-workers go on strike, Cevher starts his slow descent into a typical Güney maelstrom, enduring insults in the name of money and finally running away to a certain death. The film shows in great detail the day-to-day work of the cotton-pickers (with use of radio bulletins to sketch political developments in the big city) but *Anxiety* at no time approaches the field of documentary. Lyrically – and often elegiacally – filmed by Şerif Gören, it nevertheless lacks Güney's characteristic visual and editing intensity; one wonders whether Güney, had he completed the picture, would himself have played the central character and made him a stronger personality.

The same characteristics can be seen in both *The Herd* (1978) and *The Enemy* (1979). Both are quintessentially Güney subjects – the first a Kurdish herdsman's confrontation with a feud in his home district and later the different values of modern Ankara, the second a saga of an İstanbul labourer's attempts to find a decent job – but their

STILL FROM *YOL*

mise-en-scène is clearly Ökten's. His relative inexperience shows in the distended length of *The Enemy*, which loses much of its initial impulse in the final hour, and in controlling and resolving the various strands of *The Herd* once the film reaches Ankara. Güney himself is quite clear on the matter: "I allow a lot of leeway for inspiration and improvisation during shooting. I like to add a lot spontaneously on the set. But *The Herd* and *The Enemy* were different. The scripts were much more detailed, broken down into individual shots, covered with little notes alongside the dialogue to indicate my ideas about the shooting, the lighting or the performances. But despite all my notes, they are Zeki Ökten's films, not Yılmaz Güney's. Güney would have made them differently. Each of us makes a film in his own way. It can never be the same. . . ."

GÜNEY FILMOGRAPHY

Between 1958 and 1972 Güney appeared as an actor in more than 80 films, excluding his own. He worked as assistant director on the following films, all directed by Atıf Yılmaz: *Clum perdesi* (*The Screen of Death*, 1960), *Dolandırıcılar* (*The King of Thieves*, 1961), *Kızıl vazo* (*The Red Vase*, 1961) and *Seni kaybederesen* (*If I Lose You*, 1961). Sources differ on his writing credits but the following scripts are credited to him: *Bu vatanın çocukları* (*The Children of This Country*, 1958; co-scr.), *Alageyik* (*The Hind*, 1958; co-scr.), *Karacaoğlanın kara sevdası* (*Karacaoğlan's Mad Love*, 1959; co-scr.), *Yaban gülü* (*The Desert Laughs*, 1961; co-scr.), *Ölüme yalnız gidilir* (*The Dead Only Perish*, 1963), *Ikiside cesurdu* (*Two Brave Men*, 1964; co-scr.), *Hergün ölmektense* (1964), *Kamalı zeybek* (*Hero with a Knife*, 1964), *Prangasız mahkumlar* (*Condemned without Chains*, 1964), *Dağların kurdu Koçero* (*Koçero, Mountain Wolf*, 1964), *Kasımpaşalı* (1965), *Kasımpaşalı Recep* (1965), *Kanyakcı* (*The Drunkard*, 1965), *Krallar kralı* (*King of Kings*, 1965), *Burçak tarlası* (1966), *At avrat silah* (*The Horse, the Woman and the Gun*, 1966), *Hudutların kanunu* (*The Law of Smuggling*, 1966), *Yedi dağın aslanı*

ZEKI ÖKTEN, DIRECTOR OF VARIOUS FILMS WRITTEN BY GÜNEY

(*Seven Wild Lions/The Mountain King*, 1966), *Aslanarın dönüşü* (*Return of the Heroes*, 1966), *Tilki Selim* (*Crafty Selim*, 1966), *Eşrefpaşali* (1966), *Bana kurşun işlemez* (*Bullets Cannot Pierce Me*, 1967), *Çirkin kral afetmez* (*The Ugly King Does Not Forgive*, 1967), *Azrail benim* (*The Executioner*, 1968), *Kargacı Halil* (*Halil, the Crow-Man*, 1968), *Belanın yedi türlüsü* (*Seven Kinds of Trouble*, 1969), *Piyade Osman* (*Osman the Wanderer*, 1970), *İmzam kanla yazılır* (*I Sign in Blood*, 1970), *Onu Allah affetsin* (*May Allah Forgive Him*, 1970), *Sevgili muhafızın* (*My Dear Bodyguard*, 1970), *Yedi belalılar* (*The Seven No-Goods*, 1970), *Şeytan kayalıkları* (*Devil Crag*, 1970), *İbret* (*The Example*, 1971), *İzin* (*Leave*, 1975), *Bir gün mutlaka* (*One Day Certainly*, 1975), *Sürü* (*The Herd*, 1978), *Düşman* (*The Enemy*, 1979) and *Yol* (*The Way*, 1982). In some sources, Güney is also credited with co-direction of Hasan Kazankaya's *At avrat silah* (1966), Alaaddin Perveroğlu's *Bana kurşun işlemez* (1967), Şerif Gören's *Piyade Osman* (1970), İrfan Atasoy's *Yedi belalılar* (1970) and Şerif Gören's *İbret* (1971). The films listed below are those in which it is definitely known he played a decisive role. Güney is also the subject of Hans Stempel and Martin Ripkens's 45-minute documentary *Besuch auf İmralı* (*Portrait of Yılmaz*

Güney, 1979), as well as of a Swedish TV profile.

1967
BENİM ADIM KERİM / MY NAME IS KERIM. Script and direction: YG. Photography: Ali Yaver. Players: YG, Birsen Menekşeli, Yıldırım Gençer, Tuncer Necmioğlu. Produced by Şahinler Film.

1968
PİRE NURİ / NURI THE FLEA. Script: YG. Direction: YG, Şeref Gedik. Photography: Gani Turanlı. Players: YG, Nebahat Çehre, Nihat Ziyalan, Sami Tunç, Danyal Topatan. Produced by Güney Film.
SEYYIT HAN "TOPRAĞIN GELİNİ"/BRIDE OF THE EARTH/SEYYIT KHAN. Script and direction: YG. Photography: Gani Turanlı. Music: Ali Ekber Çiçek, Bin Ali Selman, Haceli Geçkiner, Can Etili, Mustafa Ceyhanlı. Musical direction: Nedim Otyam. Players: YG (*Seyyit Han*), Nebahat Çehre, Hayatı Hamzaoğlu, Sami Tunç, Nihat Ziyalan, Hüseyin Zan, Çetin Başaran, Enver Dönmez, İhsan Gedik, Selahettin Geçgel, Ahmet Koç, Yusuf Çağatay, Neclâ Akbaş, Osman Öğretmen, Ali Sudun, Hasan Kapılı, Seyfi Sudun. Produced by Erman Film. 78 mins.

1969
AÇ KURTLAR / THE HUNGRY WOLVES. Script and direction: YG. Photography: Ali Uğur. Music: Necip Saricioğlu. Assistant director: Savaş Eşici. Players: YG, Hayatı Hamzaoğlu, Sevgi Can, Enver Güney, Türkân Ağrak, Osman Oymak, Bahri Özkan, Hakki Kivanç, Çetin Dağdelen, Emine Hoş, Bilal İnci, İhsan Gedik, Yusef Sezer, Sirri Elilaş, Çino. Produced by İâle Film. 72 mins.
BİR ÇIRKIN ADAM/AN UGLY MAN. Script and direction: YG. Photography: Gani Turanlı. Players: YG, Hayatı Hamzaoğlu, Feri Cansel, Nihat Ziyalan, Süleyman Turan, Mümtaz Alparslan, Asim Nipton. Produced by Güney Film.

1970
UMUT / HOPE. Script: YG. Şerif Gören. Direction: YG. Photography: Kaya Ererez. Editing: Celâl Köse. Music: Arif Erkin. Assistant director: Erdinç Çöl. Players: YG (*Cabar*), Gülsen Alnıaçık (*Fatma, his Wife*), Tuncel Kurtiz (*Hasan*), Osman Alyanak (*Holy Man*), Sema Engin (*Cemile*), Sevgi Tatlı (*Hatice*), Kürsat Alnıaçık (*Mehmet Emin*), Hicret Gürson (*Hieret*), Nizam Ergüder (*Nizam*), Enver Dönmez (*Pickpocket*), Lütfü Engin (*Salesman*), Kemal Tatlı (*Commissioner*), Ahmet Koç (*Hand Worker*). Produced by Güney Film. 101 mins.

1971
KAÇAKLAR / THE FUGITIVES. Script and direction: YG. Photography (colour): Ali Yaver. Players: YG, Fatma Karanfil, Mehmet Büyükgüngör, Mümtaz Ener, Aysun Aybek. Produced by Alfan Film.
VURGUNCULAR / THE WRONGDOERS. Script and direction: YG. Photography (colour): Gani Turanlı. Players: YG, Fikret Hakan, Orhan Günşiray, Nazan Şoray, Erol Taş, Hayatı Hamzaoğlu, Bilâl İnci, Muzaffer

Tema, Danyal Topatan, Melek Görgün, Figen Han, Hüseyin Zan, Feridun Çölgeçen, Yılmaz Türkoğlu, Tarik Şimşek, Ayben. Produced by Güney Film.

YARIN SON GÜNDÜR / TOMORROW IS THE FINAL DAY. Script and direction: YG. Photography (colour): Ali Yaver. Players: YG, Fatma Girik, Süleyman Turan, Nihat Ziyalan, Erol Taş, Nükhet Egeli, Bilal Inci, Feridun Çölgeçen. Produced by Irfan Film.

UMUTSUZLAR / THE HOPELESS ONES. Script and direction: YG. Photography (colour): Gani Turanlı. Music: Yalçın Tura. Players: YG, Fatma Girik, Hayatı Hamzaoğlu, Mehmet Büyükgüngör, Menduh Un, Nihat Ziyalan, Kazim Kartal, Tuncer Necmioğlu, Refik Kemal Aduman, Sükriye Atav, Yesim Tan, Ceyda Karahan. Produced by Akin Film.

ACI / PAIN. Script and direction: YG. Photography (colour): Gani Turanlı. Music: Metin Bükey. Players: YG, Fatma Girik, Hayatı Hamzaoğlu, Oktay Yavuz, Osman Han, Dündar Aydinlı, Mehmet Büyükgüngör, Niyazi Gökdelen, Sahin Dilbas. Produced by Azleyis Film.

AGIT / ELEGY. Script and direction: YG. Photography (colour): Gani Turanlı. Music: Arif Erkin. Players: YG (*Cobanoğlu*), Hayatı Hamzaoğlu (*Mehmet Emin, the Doctor*), Bilâl Inci (*Ramazan, the Smuggler*), Atillâ Olgaç (*Bekir, the Policeman*), Yusuf Koç (*Sivasli*), Şahin Dilbaz (*Karga*), Selmin Hürmeriç (*Doctor*), Nizam Ergüder (*Nizamettin*), Ahmet Soner, Oktay Yavuz. Produced by Güney Film. 81 mins.

BABA / THE FATHER. Script: YG, based on a novella by Bekir Yıldız. Direction: YG. Photography (colour): Gani Turanlı. Editing: Şerif Gören. Music: Metin Bükey. Art direction: Nizam Ergüden. Assistant director: Sami Güçlü. Players: YG (*Cemal, the Boatman*), Müşerref Tezcan, Kuzey Vargın, Yıldırım Onal, Nedret Güvenç, Yeşim Tan, Ender Sonku, Nimet Tezer, Feridun Çölgeçen, Mehmet Büyükgüngör, Aytaç Arman, Muammer Gözalan, Guven Şengil, Faik Coşkun, Osman Han, Mehmet Yağmur, Ali Seyhan, Mustafa Yavuz, Ahmet Karaca, Cemal Tezer, M. Ali Güncör, Oktay Demiris, Saliha Demiris. Produced by Akün Film. 96 mins.

1974

ARKADAŞ / THE FRIEND. Script and direction: YG. Photography (colour): Çetin Tunca. Music: Şanar Yurdatapan, Atillâ Özdemiroğlu. Players: YG (*The Friend*), Kerim Afşar (*The Host*), Melike Demirağ (*The Girl*),

STILL FROM *THE ENEMY*

Azra Balkan, Abu Tuğnay, Civan Canova, Semra Özdamar, Nizam Ergüden. Produced by Güney Film. 103 mins.

ENDİŞE / ANXIETY. Script: YG. Ali H. Ozgentürk. Direction: Şerif Gören. YG. Photography (colour): Kenan Ormanlar. Editing: Şerif Gören. Music: Şanar Yurdatapan, Atillâ Özdemiroğlu. Players: Erkan Yücel (*Cevher*), Kâmuran Usluer (*Ramazan*), Aden Tolay (*Fate*), Emel Mesçi (*Aliye*), Nizam Ergüden (*Osman, the Manager*), Mehmet Eken (*Aga, the Peasant*), Insel Ardan (*Beyaz*), Yaşar Gökoğlu (*Sino*), Ahmet Bayrak (*Elci Mehmet, the Messenger*). Produced by Güney Film. 85 mins.

1975

ZAVALLILAR / THE POOR ONES. Script and direction: YG, Atıf Yılmaz. Photography (colour): Gani Turanlı, Kenan Ormanlar. Music: Şanar Yurdatapan, Atillâ Özdemiroğlu. Players: YG (*Abu*), Güven Şengil (*Arap*), Yıldırım Onal (*Haci*), Kâmuran Usluer (*Lawyer*), Hülya Şengül (*Fidan*), Seden Kızıltunç (*Naciye*), Göktürk Demirezen (*Abu, as a Boy*), Mehmet Sahiner, Hakkı Kıvanç. Produced by Güney Film. 85 mins.

Lester James Peries   by Derek Elley

Almost single-handedly during the past twenty-five years Lester James Peries has pioneered the establishment and development of a truly national Sri Lankan cinema beneath the mighty shadow of its Indian neighbour. His concerns are those of many other Third World film-makers – the conflict between town and country life, the legacy of colonial rule, the uneasy role of superstition in a modern age – but he has consistently related these concerns to everyday Sri Lankan life. The peculiar magic of his cinema is difficult to sum up in words: he lacks the polemic anger which motivates much Third World film-making and is clearly uninterested in large tableaux. His is the cinema of simple contrasts, subtle shades of feelings and emotions – in short, lives which reflect larger conflicts being played just out of view.

LESTER JAMES PERIES was born on April 5, 1919, in Colombo, Ceylon (renamed Sri Lanka in 1972). His upbringing reflected the island's cultural mixture of the time: brought up in "an aggressively middle-class Roman Catholic family" (his own words), he spoke Sinhala at home but English (under pain of punishment) in the Catholic

LESTER JAMES PERIES

priests' college where he was educated. His father was a doctor who had received his education in Scotland. In his teens he was pressed by one of the priests to take up the cloth but "escaped," left the college in 1938 and told his family he wanted to be a writer. For five years he stayed at home, studying and reading, and came under the influence of the photographer Lionel Wendt (narrator on Basil Wright's 1934 documentary *Song of Ceylon*) who told Peries he had heard the British army might start a film unit on the island. Nothing came of the matter but during the war years Peries gained experience in the theatre and on radio as a scriptwriter. In 1946 he was sent to London by his parents to see how his brother was faring and was asked by Frank Moraes (the new editor of "The Times" of Ceylon) to write articles for his newspaper. While there he made three amateur shorts (including the prize-winning *Soliloquy*) and returned to Ceylon in 1952 to join Ralph Keene at the Government Film Unit, directing two further shorts.

Peries had finally found his chosen medium to express himself in, but after three years at the unit the constraints became too great. The mid-Fifties was a time of revolutionary change in the theatre and arts in Ceylon. The island had gained its independence from the U.K. in 1948 but for the next eight years was ruled by a party more concerned with protecting the rights of the Tamil-speaking Hindus. It was left to the socialist Sri Lanka Freedom Party (SLFP), formed in 1951 by Solomon Banadaranaike, to emphasise the island's national heritage and fight for the recognition of Sinhala as the national language and Buddhism as the official religion.

Sinhalese films had been produced since 1946 but they were shot by Tamil directors mostly in Southeast Indian studios, mimicking the escapist song-and-dance romantic fantasies of the Indian film industry. When Peries, William Blake (a cameraman of Dutch descent) and editor Titus De Silva (who was to nationalise his name to Titus Thotawatte) resigned from the unit in 1955, they consciously set out to make the first authentically

Sinhalese film, shot on real locations and portraying a recognisable Sinhalese way of life.

Unbeknown to the trio at the time, Satyajit Ray was putting the finishing touches in Calcutta to a similar (Bengali) challenge to the established Hindu industry, *Pather panchali*. However, in Ceylon Peries and his small team were all alone, looked upon as "three lunatics" by the rest of the industry. They acquired an Arriflex from Germany, and some heavy magnetic sound equipment, and set off into the jungle for six months to make their film (at the time there were no post-synching facilities on the island). The result, *The Line of Destiny* (*Rekava*), was hailed by local critics as "at last a national Sinhalese film" but local audiences, long conditioned to Tamil-influenced fantasies, were horrified and the picture was a box-office failure. Peries remained out-of-work for several years afterwards and not until he had laboured over an epic potboiler, *The Message* (*Sandesaya*), which was a huge success, and waited another three years to make *Changes in the Village* (*Gameraliya*), did audiences begin to accept his location style of shooting.

Rekava (1956) is every bit as important a first film as Ray's *Pather panchali* (Peries has for too long laboured under comparisons with the Indian director, even if some of its technical inadequacies (notably the sound) often work against its delicate atmosphere. Peries' film is a far less structured work, far less consciously "cinematic," than Ray's, but the rough-hewn performances of the amateur local cast give the picture an extraordinary vitality. *Rekava* is an extended mood-portrait (the influences of the British documentary school and Italian Neo-realism on Peries' style are never more marked than here), set in a tiny village populated by stock components of rural life – a money-lender, a landowner, a boatman, a wandering minstrel, a village headman. Life is seen through the eyes of the boy Sena (Somapala Dharmapriya) and the young girl Anula (Myrtle Fernando) their perceptions of nature, of village tensions, of local superstitions. Events come and go: a colourful wedding, an argument over a swing at school, the visit of a traditional puppet theatre, the blindness and miraculous cure (attributed to Sena, from which his family tries to profit) of Anula. It is a film packed with ideas and spirit, very Fifties-positive

STILL FROM *THE LINE OF DESTINY*

(unlike *Pather panchali*), and summed up in its memorable opening of Miguel the minstrel leading the local children in song along the road. From the very first, Peries recognises the power of the allusive, rather than direct, image.

The production team on *Rekava* contained the seeds of Peries' repertory company that he slowly built over the years. Editor Titus De Silva was replaced in the Sixties by Peries' second wife Sumitra Gunawardena (now a director in her own right) but William Blake has continued to work on-and-off with him for the past twenty-five years. Even actor Gamini Fonseka started as a camera assistant on *Rekava*. Much the same technical crew assembled for Peries' next feature, *The Message* (*Sandesaya*, 1960), the first of three large-scale pictures he has so far made in his career. Each has dealt directly with major historical figures in Sinhalese history and each shows Peries' unease with tackling nationalism head-on rather than by implication – Hamlet figures rather than the Rosencrantz and Guildensterns of this world.

Sandesaya, made with a cast of over 130 in a gruelling six months on location, deals with the period of Portuguese occupation; *The God King* (1975), shot in English for the international market, is set in Fifth-century AD Ceylon and tells of the tyranny of King Dhatusena (Geoffrey Russell) and the rise and fall of Kassapa the God King (Leigh Lawson), raised to be a philosopher-ruler; *Rebellion (Veera Puran Appu*, 1979) details the anti-British uprising of 1848, led by a young 35-year-old adventurer who is finally captured and executed. The latter two were both made in scope but Peries is clearly unhappy handling the format and embarrassed during the action sequences by the paucity of his resources. *Rebellion* adopts a factual stance (paragraphed with captions) and despite flashes of technical brilliance (some multi-screen near the end) ends up merely dry and laboured. *The God King* is considerably better: the English dialogue is handled naturally and the film's celebratory air magnificently caught in William Blake's Eastmancolor compositions. Yet the best scenes are undoubtedly the more intimate "family" ones: here lies Peries' heart, rather than in the (albeit sumptuous) ceremonial/political set-pieces.

Peries' first film after *Sandesaya*, and the foundation of much future development, was *Changes in the Village (Gamperaliya*, 1964), part-financed by himself and Sumitra and originally intended as the first part of a trilogy based on Martin Wickremasinghe's famous novel. (Peries has only now managed to complete the trilogy with *Yuganthayo*.) *Gamperaliya* is perhaps Peries' quintessential examination of family tensions as a microcosm of wider issues and, despite the fact that it is adapted from another's work, fits easily into his own universe. The film spans several years and takes in a reversal of family fortunes: Nanda (Punya Heendeniya), younger daughter of a village chief, falls for the school teacher Piyal (Henry Jayasena) but is forced by her family to marry the approved Jinadasa (Gamini Fonseka). When hard times come, Jinadasa leaves to find work in Colombo but does not return; Nanda finally married Piyal, now a successful businessman, but both find their former days of romantic longing hard to recapture.

Gamperaliya is the first of Peries' films to show a recurrent structural device: exposition with false climax roughly two-thirds in (here, Jinadasa leaving for the big city), followed by development (often a reversal of earlier material, such as Piyal's changed personality in *Gamperaliya*) and open-ended conclusion. Despite some awkward editing, especially in dialogue sequences (a fault Peries was not to overcome until *Silence of the Heart*, some five years later), the performances win through, notably from Punya Heedeniya as the bruised Nanda and Trilica Gunwardena as her acerbic elder sister.

It was almost twenty years before Peries was able to film part two of the trilogy, *The Time of Kali (Kaliyugaya*, 1982), which advances the family's story to the point where Nanda and Piyal are now comfortably off and middle-aged with an estranged son studying in London. In line with its title (Kali is the Hindu goddess of destruction) the film is about a challenge to established values – here those of the parents by their embittered son. A letter from the son, recalling his childhood and youth, starts off a chain reaction leading to Nanda remembering her own youth. With great economy, Peries intercuts key moments from *Gamperaliya* as the present more and more begins to parallel the past – and the parents find they still have lessons to learn. Again, the village is seen as the *fons et origo* of Sri Lankan life: Anula tells Nanda that she should join her back in the countryside ("We were both born in the village and should go back there to die"). *Kaliyugaya* is a mature, ruminative film, secure in its own pace, which calmly chews over the problems, pains and joys of middle age – children, past affairs and loss of trust in relationships.

In the mid-Sixties Peries could clearly be seen working towards a finished, personal style from film to film. *Rekava* had stated his case; *Gamperaliya* focused in on his concerns. His next two films worked some technical weaknesses out of his system, while demonstrating most clearly his use of simple contrasts on which to peg his concerns. *Between Two Worlds (Delovak athara*, 1966) shows East vs. West, upper-class city values vs. simple country life. The latter is only implied, as the film is entirely set in Colombo society, but Peries has already made his sympathies clear in the earlier works. Nissanka (Tony Ranasinghe), with

STILL FROM *KALIYUGAYA*

his fast cars and night-clubs, is a familiar figure from Sixties European cinema, and his attempted cover-up of a motor accident (in which a peasant dies) stands for his class's wholesale betrayal of traditional values. However, the script fails to develop some of the edgier moments of class warfare and the ending, in which Nissanka repents of his moral cowardice, is too pat.

The Yellow Robe (Ran salu, 1967) is more open-ended in its conclusion, the atmosphere more delicately wrought. The contrasts are similar (simple Buddhist values vs. irresponsible Western influences), and the playing of actor Tony Ranasinghe subtler than in *Between Two Worlds*; the ever-present role of the elder generation in young peoples' lives is also better handled. However, it is the more fluid development of the central story (a girl's rejection of her upper-class life for the serenity offered by Buddhism) that marks *The Yellow Robe* as a significant advancement in Peries' career. A long, wordless sequence near the end, as the repentant Sarojini (Anula Karunatilleka) watches the graceful Sujatha (Punya Heendeniya) find tranquillity in the shrine room shows Peries to be a supreme visual stylist for whom words are almost superfluous adjuncts in depicting interior feelings.

After such a film, it came as no surprise that *Silence of the Heart (Golu hadawatha,* 1968) should be the first film to reveal Peries in full bloom. The plot is microscopic (a thwarted romance between a student and a schoolgirl) but the pacing and cutting is exemplary. It is a film of looks and gestures, superbly acted by Wickrema Bogoda and Anula Karunatilleka, and Peries uses his individual structure in an unexpected way: the later development section is a review of the first half, this time from the girl's point-of-view of the girl who, in a lengthy voice-over, explains her earlier, previously unspoken thoughts. The film unwinds like a seamless, lyrical poem, with Peries' recurrent images of windows, lattice-work and bars used to the same effect as at the end of *The Yellow Robe.*

Five Acres of Land (Akkara paha, 1969) shares with *Silence of the Heart* the pinnacle of Peries' middle period. Its story of family life is as detailed as that of *Gamperaliya* but the technique and style much more assured. Once again, Peries draws the best performances from his female characters, three of whom stand for the various city influences which are to shape the life of Sena (Milton Jayawardena), a young student sent to study in Kandy by his struggling peasant father. Sena's absorption and final rejection of city values (though not without a heavy price to pay) forms the core of the film, and Peries has learnt much since the more black-and-white conflicts of *Between Two Worlds.* The country scenes, especially, are sketched with a gritty lyricism (excellent monochrome work by M. S. Anandan, Peries' regular cameraman at this time) which hymns simple virtues without romanticising the plight of the poor.

In what in retrospect seems a natural pause for reassessment, Peries next made two works which turned to darker, more interior problems. *The Treasure (Nidhanaya,* 1970) is atypical of his work – a shadowy portrait of one man's obsession rather than a group portrait. Yet the theme of superstition (here in the central character's manic belief that a legendary treasure will save him from ruin) runs deep in Peries' work – if less darkly. The old colonial mansion, with its surrounding portico, assumes a presence of its own, echoing the moods of the central character – bright and sunny (for his new bride), dank and wet (his violent moods), dark and eerie (his impending suicide). Peries' use of music (astute in all his films) is here excellent, with Premasiri Khemadasa's melancholy, drooping theme, and the ending is neat and tidy: "Here my story ends. I am not interested in your judgement. But if I have made you feel anything of my pain, I shall have achieved my objective," relates the central character. And one senses that was Peries' own attitude to this off-beat exercise.

Though similarly obsessive, *The Eyes* (*Desa nisa*, 1972) at least returns to familiar Peries territory. In fact, the opening is among the most stunning passages in his entire corpus, as the unsightly Nirudaka (Joe Abeywickrema in unfamiliar guise) eyes some peasant girls wading in a luxuriant lake of lilies. Peries unites landscape, tradition and music into a resonant sexual metaphor for Nirudak's plight, the camera itself taking the voyeur's role as he looks through some holes in an upturned pot floating in the lake. Nirudaka's later marriage to a blind girl is marred by his own fear that she will desert him if Sundari ever regains her sight. Beneath the sumptuous monochrome photography echoing the words of Sundari ("We blind people have a sense of things. We have imagination") lurks the darker current of Nirudaka's fear. Their journey to a mountain hermit to cure Sundari's blindness thus becomes a direct challenge to Nirudaka's (perilous) manhood, especially when the hermit is revealed as a man with desires like any other. Yet the final conflict is played out between wife and hermit rather than between hermit and village fool; it is Sundari's strength that wins through in the end, and leads to the couple's lyrical reunion in the dappled forests below.

After the lengthy production of *The God King*, and all its attendant problems (including the complete recasting of the three English leads after 10 days' shooting), it was not until the mid-Seventies that Peries again returned to a more intimate subject. *Enchanted Island* (*Madol duwa*, 1976), from a story by veteran Martin Wickremasinghe, is a slight but charming tale of two children's battle to set up home on a deserted island. Lively performances from Joe Abeywickrema as a village teacher and Ajith Jinadasa as the boy Upali rescue a sometimes stilted children's tale.

The late Seventies was something of a trough in Peries' career. *Enchanted Island* was followed by *White Flowers for the Dead* (*Ahasin polawatha*,

STILL FROM *VILLAGE IN THE JUNGLE*

1978), a melodramatic tale of a husband's emotional coldness. Peries seems ill at ease here, and a modishly dissonant score by Nimal Mendis (previously responsible for the fine music to *The God King*), only heightens the cliches. Despite nice touches like the man's nagging old family servant, *White Flowers* is best left buried.

Following the equally uneasy *Rebellion*, Peries returned to form in *Village in the Jungle* (*Baddegama*, 1980), based on the novel by Leonard Woolf. The work is considered the best English novel on Ceylon and Peries sees in it dramatic parallels almost on a par with Greek Tragedy. Unlike in his earlier village films, he here opts for partial stylisation: the peasants' huts and homes are spotless, the action mostly limited to simple exchanges with few bursts of emotion – climaxing in the calm, deliberately anti-dramatic episode of the peasant Silindu confronting and later shooting the despotic headman, symbol of the tradition and superstition crushing village life. There is a cool ceremonial quality to *Baddegama* (heightened by Willie Blake's immaculate, cut-glass colour photography) which has not been seen in Peries' work since *The God King*. The film is perhaps too much of a connoisseur's piece, a distillation of previous exercises; and the final trial sequence is harmed by Arthur C. Clarke's flat delivery as the judge. But as an often terrifyingly cool treatment of a highly emotive subject, it is very effective.

As of summer 1982 Peries is at work on the third and final part of the Wickremasinghe trilogy.

End of an Era (*Yuganthayo*) builds on the influence of the West seen in *Kaliyugaya* in Nanda and Piyal's estranged son Alan. The main characters, however, are different and the time is now 1952, the beginning of Ceylon's maturity as an independent nation. A tea tycoon, Simon Kabalana (Gamini Fonseka) — based on a real-life Northcliffe-figure of journalism — sends his son to London for an education, only to find his own firm threatened when he returns radicalised from the West. As the son gains control of the firm's unions, the story predicts Ceylon's swing to the left under the SLFP in 1956. Peries is to use newsreel clips of the time but, like the flashbacks to *Gamperaliya* in *Kaliyugaya*, for emotional rather than political effect. As always, it is the human relationships which concern Peries — and the recognition that both the present and past must find a mutual respect if Sinhalese values are to be preserved for the future.

PERIES FILMOGRAPHY

Peries has also directed the following shorts: *Soliloquy* (1949; 12 mins.), *Farewell to Childhood* (1950; 14 mins.), *A Sinhalese Dance* (1950; 8 mins.), *Conquest in the Dry Zone* (1954; 14 mins.), *Be Safe or Be Sorry* (1955; 20 mins.), *Too Many Too Soon* (1961; 20 mins.), *Home from the Sea* (1962; 50 mins.), *Forward into the Future* (1964; 24 mins.), *Steel* (1969; 20 mins.), *Forty Leagues from Paradise* (1970; 27 mins.), *Kandy perahera* (*The Procession of Kandy*, 1971; 27 mins.), *Pinhamy* (1979; 42 mins.).

1956
REKAVA/THE LINE OF DESTINY/THE LINE OF LIFE. Script and direction: LJP. Photography: William Blake. Editing: Titus De Silva. Music: Sunil Santha, K. A. Dayaratne. Players: Somapala Dharmapriya (*Sena*), Myrtle Fernando (*Anula*), Sesha Paliyakkara (*Miguel*), Romulus De Silva (*Village Headman*), Mallika Pillapitiya (*Premawathie*), Iranganie Meedeniya (*Kathrina*), D. R. Nanayakkara (*Sooty*), N. R. Dias (*Podimahathaya*), Ananda Weerakoon (*Nimal*), Winston Serasinghe (*Kumetheris*). Produced by LJP for Chitra-Lanka. 89 mins.

1960
SANDESAYA/THE MESSAGE. Script: LJP, K. A. W. Perera, B. Dodampegama. Direction: LJP. Photography: William Blake. Editing: Titus De Silva. Songs: Sunil Santha. Players: Ananda Jayaratne, Kanthi Gunatunga, Eddie Jayamanne, Gamini Fonseka, Arthur Vanlangenburg. Produced by K. Gunaratnam for Cinemas Ltd. 120 mins.

LEIGH LAWSON AS KASSAPA IN *THE GOD KING*

1964
GAMPERALIYA/CHANGES IN THE VILLAGE. Script: Reggie Siriwardena, from the novel by Martin Wickremasinghe. Direction: LJP. Photography: William Blake. Editing: Sumitra Gunawardena. Music: W. D. Amaradeva. Art direction: A. S. Weerakkody. Players: Henry Jayasena (*Piyal Weliwela*), Punya Heendeniya (*Nanda*), Wickrema Bogoda (*Tissa*), Trilicia Gunawardena (*Anula*), Gamini Fonseka (*Jinadasa*), Shanti Lekha, David Dharmakirti, Tony Ranasinghe, Anula Karunatilleka. Produced by Anton Wickremasinghe for Cine Lanka. 108 mins.

1966
DELOVAK ATHARA/BETWEEN TWO WORLDS. Script: LJP, Reggie Siriwardena, Gamini Gunawardena, Tissa Abeysekara. Direction: LJP. Photography: William Blake. Editing: Sumitra Gunawardena. Music: W. D. Amaradeva. Players: Tony Ranasinghe (*Nissanka*), Subinitha Abeysekara (*Chitra*), Jeevaranee Kurukulasuriya (*Shiranee*), Iranganie Serasinghe (*Nissanka's Mother*), J. B. L. Gunasekara (*Nissanka's Father*), Winston Serasinghe. Produced by Anton Wickremasinghe for Cine Lanka. 103 mins.

1967
RAN SALU/THE YELLOW ROBE. Script: P. K. D. Seneviratne. Direction: LJP. Photography: Sumitta Amarasinghe. Editing: Sumitra Gunawardena. Music: W. D. Amaradeva. Players: Tony Ranasinghe

(*Cyril*), Punya Heendeniya (*Sujatha*), Anula Karunatilleka (*Sarojini Perera*), Dayananda Gunawardena (*Friend*), J. B. L. Gunasekara (*Sujatha's Father*), Iranganie Serasinghe (*Sujatha's Mother*), Subhasini Athukorala, D. R. Nanayakkara. Produced by Upasena Marasinghe, L. M. Simon for Chameekara Films. 106 mins.

1968
GOLU HADAWATHA/SILENCE OF THE HEART. Script: Reggie Siriwardena, from the novel by Karunasena Jayalath. Direction: LJP. Photography: M. S. Anandan. Editing: Sumitra Gunawardena, Edwin Leetin. Music: Premasiri Khemadasa. Players: Wickrema Bogoda (*Sugath Weerasekara*), Anula Karunatilleka (*Damayanthie Kariwayasa*), Wijeratne Warakagoda (*Sarath*), Sriyani Amerasena (*Champa*). Produced by P. E. E. Anthonipillai for Ceylon Studios. 125 mins.

1969
AKKARA PAHA/FIVE ACRES OF LAND. Script: Tissa Abeysekara, from the novel by Madawala S. Ratnayake. Direction: LJP. Photography: M. S. Anandan. Editing: Sumitra Gunawardena. Music: W. D. Amaradeva. Art direction: J. A. Vincent. Players: Milton Jayawardena (*Sena*), Malini Fonseka (*Kumari*), Janaki Kurukulasuriya (*Theresa*), Anoma Wattaldeniya (*Sandawathie*), Douglas Ranasinghe (*Samarasena*), Gamini Wijesuriya (*Sena's Father*), Shanti Lekha (*Sena's Mother*), Sriyani Perera. Produced by P. E. E. Anthonipillai for Ceylon Studios. 128 mins.

1970
NIDHANAYA/THE TREASURE. Script: Tissa Abeysekara, from a story by G. B. Senanayake. Direction: LJP. Photography: M. S. Anandan. Editing: LJP, Edwin Leetin, Gladwin Fernando. Music: Premasiri Khemadasa. Art direction: J. A. Vincent. Players: Gamini Fonseka (*Willie*), Malini Fonseka (*Irene*), Saman Bokalawala (*Julius*), Francis Perera (*Juwanis*), Mapa Gunaratne (*Doctor*), Shanti Lekha (*Irene's Mother*), Trilicia Gunawardena (*Dulcie*), Thilakasiri Fernando (*Diyonis*), J. B. L. Gunasekara (*Willie's Father*), Thalatha Gunasekara (*Nanny*), Kumarasinghe Appuhamy (*Gurunanse*), K. L. Coranelis Appuhamy (*Willie's Elder Brother*), Barry Whittington (*G.A.*), Wijeratne Warakagoda (*Silva*). Produced by P. E. E. Anthonipillai for Ceylon Studios. 108 mins.

1972
DESA NISA/THE EYES. Script: Gunasena Galappathi. Direction: LJP. Photography: Sumitta Amarasinghe. Editing: Gladwin Fernando. Music: Premasiri Khemadasa. Players: Joe Abeywickrema (*Nirudaka*), Sriyani Amarasena (*Sundari*), Ravindra Randeniya (*Hermit*). For Lester James Peries Productions/Northwestern Enterprises. 97 mins.

1975
THE GOD KING. Script: Anthony Greville-Bell. Direction: LJP. Photography (Eastmancolor/Todd-AO 35):

William Blake. Editing: Sumitra Peries, Russ Lloyd, Robert Richardson. Music: Nimal Mendis (arranged and conducted by Larry Ashmore). Production design: Herbert Smith. Players: Oliver Tobias (*Migara*), Leigh Lawson (*Kassapa – "The God King"*), Geoffrey Russell (*King Dhatusena*), Ravindra Randeniya (*Mogallana*), Iranganie Serasinghe (*Varuni*), Joe Abeywickrema (*Swami*), Anne Loos (*Leila*), Wijaya Kumaratunge (*Lalith*), Douglas Wickremasinghe (*Council Leader*), Mano Breckendridge (*Opposition Leader*). Produced by Dmitri de Grunwald. 99 mins. The film originally started shooting with Ben Kingsley as Kassapa and Mark Burns as Migara.

1976
MADOL DUWA/ENCHANTED ISLAND. Script: Philip Coorey, from the novel by Martin Wickremasinghe. Direction: LJP. Photography (colour): M. S. Anandan. Editing: Sumitra Peries, Gladwin Fernando. Music: Premalal Danwatte. Songs: W. D. Amaradeva. Art direction: Hamapala Dharmasena. Players: Ajith Jinadasa (*Upali*), Padmasena Attukorala (*Jinna*), Joe Abeywickrema (*Schoolteacher*), Somalata Subasinghe, Dhamma Jagoda, Shanti Lekha, David Dharmakirti, Deawaka Haminne, Punitha Mendis, S. A. James, Trilicia Gunawardena, Upali Attanayaka, Daya Alwis, Somaratne Dasanayaka, U. Mapa Gunaratne, Merlyn Gunaratne. Produced by Upasena Marasinghe for Laklooms Company. 92 mins.

1978
AHASIN POLAWATHA/WHITE FLOWERS FOR THE DEAD. Script: Tissa Abeysekara, from the novel by Eileen Siriwardena. Direction: LJP. Photography: Donald Karunaratne. Editing: Sumitra Peries. Music: Nimal Mendis. Players: Tony Ranasinghe (*Sarath*), Sriyani Amarasena (*Pushpa*), Wijaya Kumaratunge, Vasanthi Chathurani. Produced by U. W. Sumathipala. 90 mins.

1979
VEERA PURAN APPU/REBELLION. Script: Tissa Abeysekara. Direction: LJP. Photography (scope): Donald Karunaratne. Editing: M. Rupasena. Music: Premasiri Khemadasa. Players: Ravindra Randeniya (*Veera Puran Appu/Franciscu Fernando*), Malini Fonseka (*Bandara Menike*), Joe Abeywickrema (*Gongalegoda Banda/King David*), Tissa Abeysekara (*Kudapola Thero*), Robin Fernando (*Dinirala*), Jean-Pierre Hautin (*Captain Watson*), Alfred Berry (*Government Agent Bullen*), John Burgess (*Governor Torrington*), David Thackeray (*Sir Emerson Tennent*). Produced by Tyrone Fernando for Shalanka Films. 107 mins.

1980
BADDEGAMA/VILLAGE IN THE JUNGLE. Script: A. J. Gunawardena, LJP, from the novel "Village in the Jungle" by Leonard Woolf. Direction: LJP. Photography (colour): William Blake. Editing: Gladwin Fernando. Music: Nimal Mendis (arranged by Sarath Fernando). Art direction: Hamapala Dharmasena. Players: Joe

Abeywickrema (*Silindu*), Malini Fonseka (*Punchi Menika*), Tony Ranasinghe (*Babun*), D. R. Nanayakkara (*Old Man*), Henry Jayasena (*Head Man*), Arthur C. Clarke (*Judge*), Wijaya Kumaratunge, Nadika Gunasekara, Trilicia Gunawardena, Navanandana Wijesinghe. Produced by Wilfred Perera for Lester James Peries Productions. 121 mins.

1982
KALIYUGAYA/THE TIME OF KALI. Script: A. J. Gunawardena, from the novel by Martin Wickremasinghe. Direction: LJP. Photography (colour): Donald Karunaratne. Editing: Gladwin Fernando. Music: Premasiri Khemadasa. Players: Punya Heendeniya (*Nanda*), Henry Jayasena (*Piyal Weliwela*), Trilicia Gunawardena (*Anula*), Wickrema Bogoda (*Tissa*), Sanath Gunetileka (*Alan*), Anoma Weerasinghe (*Irene*), Asoka Peries (*Friend*), Tony Ranasinghe (*Doctor*). Produced by Wijaya Ramanayake for Tharanghe Films. 85 mins.

1983
YUGANTHAYO/END OF AN ERA. Script: A. J. Gunawardena, from the novel by Martin Wickremasinghe. Direction: LJP. Photography (colour): William Blake. Editing: Gladwin Fernando. Music: Premasiri Khemadasa. Players: Gamini Fonseka (*Simon Kabalana*), Richard Zoysa (*Malin Kabalana*), Mahal Wijewar-

STILL FROM *WHITE FLOWERS FOR THE DEAD*

dena (*Nalika*). Produced by Wijaya Ramanayake for Tharanghe Films. In production summer/autumn 1982.

Bob Rafelson

by Tom Milne

With five films in fourteen years, Bob Rafelson has taken over from Orson Welles as Hollywood's most distinguished maverick. Until *The Postman Always Rings Twice* proved otherwise, not too long after Rafelson had been fired from *Brubaker* amid a litter of unrealised projects, the assumption appears to have been that he could not "think" a movie in commercial terms. His intransigence, like that of Welles, translated as a mixture of intellectualism, incompetence and profligacy. And like Welles's recurring concern with the theme that power corrupts, Rafelson's perennial quest for ways to escape the American dream was perhaps felt to be an obscure threat.

Not that Rafelson's preoccupations were objectionable in themselves: after *Easy Rider*, the dropout dream of fleeing the pressures of success had become box-office. It was the terms in which they were expressed, the contexts that defined their exact drift. *Easy Rider*, after all, had enshrined an odyssey in search of the old pioneer America of tradition. *Stay Hungry* contemptuously dismissed the value of that, or indeed any, tradition. To an industry that has always sidestepped art but bowed in reverential homage to the Artist (just think of all those biopics of great composers, those sensitive souls starving in garrets, those Pulitzer prizewinners rewarded for the great crusade), there is something peculiarly perverse about the way Bobby Dupea, the hero of *Five Easy Pieces* played by Jack Nicholson, wilfully turns his back on a career as a concert pianist, preferring life as a redneck oil-driller. Audiences schooled by Hollywood might well respond to a hero who refused to Prostitute his Art for Money. But one like Bobby, who elects to drift rather than contemplate the splendours of music, constitutes a mystery.

To understand the drive behind Rafelson's seemingly disparate movies one has to go back to the beginning. BOB RAFELSON was born in New York City in 1935, and did his military service with the occupation forces in Japan, serving as disc jockey for a military radio station (where he dispensed rambling philosophical yarns in a manner echoed by Jack Nicholson in *The King of Marvin Gardens*), while acting on the side as adviser on American markets to Shochiku Films (where he became an Ozu admirer). Returning to America, he became the bright young television executive during the late Fifties, serving time as reader, script supervisor and story editor with David Susskind (*Play of the Week*), Desilu and Columbia Screen Gems. In 1966, for NBC, he prepared the way for a double-barrelled coup by creating, with Bert Schneider, a synthetic substitute for the Beatles. Hugely successful, the Monkees continued to churn out programmes for almost two years, mostly directed by unknowns like Rafelson himself and James Frawley.

Then in 1968, with Bert Schneider and Steve Blauner, Rafelson founded BBS Productions, and he made his first feature, *Head*. That BBS was conceived as a challenge to the status quo is now a matter of history. The record speaks for itself, with titles like *Easy Rider, Five Easy Pieces, The Last Picture Show, A Safe Place, Drive, He Said, The King of Marvin Gardens, Hearts and Minds*, and the influence continuing in such films as *Tracks, Goin' South, Days of Heaven*. *Head*, a sadly underrated film which was swept aside as just another tiresome slice of psychedelic fun climbing on the bandwagon set rolling by Dick Lester and the Beatles, has never really received its due as an act of provocation.

It opens, as Rafelson has pointed out, with the Monkees metaphorically committing suicide on their way to a concert. Indestructibly making their way to the auditorium (the fan hysteria brooks no denial), they are whisked through a Hollywood anthology of war movie, epic, Western, problem picture, musical and Gothic horror. Sometimes affectionate, always parodic, these episodes rudely turn the genres upside down and expose their seams. At the same time, the boys are seen to be manipulated by a gigantic and genial *deus ex machina* (Victor Mature), who demonstrates their insignificance by having them reduced to specks of dandruff in his hair for a shampoo commercial on TV. After which, as the studio in which they are trapped shrinks to a small black box lifted by helicopter and dropped from a great height, the god casually squashes both box and Monkees underfoot. A witty and wicked mousetrap, snapping the hands that had hitherto baited it, *Head* is deliberately designed to snare the giant hype that goes hand-in-glove with the film and television industries.

As though to demonstrate a difference, *Five Easy Pieces* and *The King of Marvin Gardens* are diffident, unassuming, elliptical. Instead of the flashy, darting hand-held style that marked *Head*, and which meant that the film *could* be appropriated as just another sample of pop fever, the camera is now stationary as often as not, inviting contemplation of meaning and motive. There is a sense of exploration here, an intellectual curiosity and cultural ease that invited immediate comparison with Ozu, Olmi, Godard or Rohmer. Not only are Rafelson's films built on philosophic rather than pragmatic foundations, but his use of classical music in *Five Easy Pieces*, or of the ambivalently horrible beauty of Atlantic City in *The King of Marvin Gardens*, is structural in a manner more usually associated with the European art house than with Hollywood.

Yet the films themselves are rooted in America. So deeply so that *Five Easy Pieces* is open to misreading as an archetypal road movie celebrating, like *Wanda* or *The Rain People*, the freedom of escape from responsibility and restraint. Actually, running away from the ready-made cultural outfit supplied by his family, Bobby Dupea dons a drifter's sloppy garb only because nothing tailor-made to his uncertain, questing inner self seems to be on offer. To correct this misapprehension, Rafelson's next film, his masterpiece to date, adds uncertainty of form to uncertainty of mind.

The King of Marvin Gardens opens, arrestingly, on a long, unwinking close-up of Jack Nicholson's face, picked out of the darkness as he confides a story of how he and his brother let their grandfather choke to death. We have no idea, for the moment, that he is a disc jockey in a studio hosting a late-night radio show. Once we do know, he promptly leaves the studio on an endless journey, ever downwards through nocturnal streets and stairways and into the depths of the subway, eventually to debouch in what is, in a sense, the interior of his childhood.

The technique employed here, as Rafelson has commented, is guaranteed to make audiences restless by withdrawing solid ground from under their feet: "Well, the subject of *Marvin Gardens* basically was instability . . . and I tried to find a way of rendering instability in the form of the movie." So we are unceremoniously tipped into a seesaw relationship between two brothers, neatly characterised by David Thomson as the depressive and the manic. One (Nicholson) has retreated into his own mind, hiding his sense of inadequacy within a literary ivory tower; the other (Bruce Dern), newly released from his own ivory tower of prison, is the eternal wheeler-dealer, ebulliently floating schemes that he knows will fail but hopes may not.

Both are dreamers, each in his own way, and their fatal encounter takes place in Atlantic City, the fantastic playground which provided the place names for the game of *Monopoly*, and whose crumbling decor of Xanadu palaces and white elephants is itself a mirage of dreams and paper wealth. What this encounter demonstrates, in an argument elaborated with incredible complexity as Nicholson is inexorably shunted by sex, society, heritage and ambition into his role as Cain causing the death of his brother, is that so long as competition persists and somebody wants to be king of the castle, there can be no escape even in dreams.

Stay Hungry, delightful for its quirkishly funny picture of professional body-builders, is a minor interlude in Rafelson's career. Working for the first time with material that was not his own, he nevertheless managed to shape it into another Q.E.D. of the theorem that there is no escape. Craig Blake (Jeff Bridges) is, like Bobby Dupea, expected to maintain tradition, this time by carrying on the family steel business after the sudden death of his parents. Instead, camping out in the ancestral home, oblivious to the decades of gracious living he is eroding through his hippie life style, he probes enviously but disastrously into the alternatives offered by some property speculators, a guru-like bodybuilder, and a backwoods community in moonshine territory. Fitting nowhere, unable to reconcile his inner self with the outer worlds he discovers, he ultimately opts for a solution that is an admission of defeat: he retreats,

as John Russell Taylor put it, "to the mindless, tasteless life of a Winnebago mobile home and the wonderful world of Polyester."

Also adapted from a literary source, much more faithful to Cain's novel than either the Visconti or the Garnett versions, *The Postman Always Rings Twice* is Rafelson's most accessible film to date, no doubt intentionally so. At first glance it seems sleekly impersonal, fringing the exploitation condemned by moralists offended by its lusty sex. Yet the film contains so much of Rafelson that the effect is rather as though Bobby Dupea, last seen hitching a lift at the fadeout of *Five Easy Pieces*, had ended his ride outside Nick's café, there to find whatever it was he had been seeking in the spontaneous combustion that occurs when Frank Chambers meets Cora.

Their first ecstatic mating on the kitchen table, sending dough and utensils flying, is awkward, ugly, bestial. Yet for them it becomes transcendent, because it is theirs, because it owes nothing to anybody, because it *is* spontaneous combustion. And Frank's tragedy is that he loses this thing of purity, cleansed into innocence by its own incandescent flame, precisely because convention raises its ugly head and he commits murder to protect his claim. Just before she dies in the accident that falls like retribution, the pregnant Cora suggests selling the café and moving out. The eternal drifter demurs: "It ain't bad out here for pets and kids." For the first time a Rafelson hero has made his gold strike and found a world where he could have coexisted in peace and fulfilment.

RAFELSON FILMOGRAPHY

Before making his first feature, Rafelson produced *The Wackiest Ship in the Army* (1965) and co-produced with Bert Schneider the TV series *The Monkees* (1966–68), three of whose episodes he also directed. Schneider and Rafelson have since produced *Easy Rider*, *The Last Picture Show* and *Drive He Said*. Rafelson also worked for ten days on *Brubaker* but was then replaced by Stuart Rosenberg.

1968
HEAD. Script: BR, Jack Nicholson. Direction: BR. Photography (Technicolor): Michael Hugo. Editing: Mike Pozer. Music: Ken Thorne. Art direction: Sydney Z. Liwack. Choreography: Toni Basil. Players: Peter Tork (*Peter*), David Jones (*Davey*), Micky Dolenz (*Micky*), Michael Nesmith (*Mike*), Victor Mature (*Big*

JESSICA LANGE IN *THE POSTMAN ALWAYS RINGS TWICE*

Victor), Annette Funicello (*Minnie*), Timothy Carey (*Lord High 'n' Low*), Logan Ramsey (*Officer Faye Laid*), Abraham Sofaer (*Swami*), Vito Scotti (*I. Vitteloni*), Charles Macauley (*Inspector Shrink*), T. C. Jones (*Mr. and Mrs. Ace*), Charles Irving (*Mayor Feedback*), William Bagdad (*Black Sheik*), Percy Helton (*Heraldic Messenger*), Sonny Liston (*Extra*), Ray Nitschke (*Private One*), Carol Doda (*Sally Silicone*), Frank Zappa (*Critic*), June Fairchild (*Jumper*), Terry Garr (*Testy True*), I. J. Jefferson (*Lady Pleasure*), BR, Jack Nicholson (*Themselves*), Terry Chambers (*Hero*), Mike Burns (*Nothing*), Esther Shepard (*Mother*), Kristine Helstoski (*Girlfriend*), John Hoffman (*Sex Fiend*), Linda Weaver (*Lever Secretary*), Jim Hanley (*Siderf*). Produced by BR, Jack Nicholson for Raybert Productions. 86 mins.

1970
FIVE EASY PIECES. Script: Adrien Joyce, from a story by BR, Adrien Joyce. Direction: BR. Photography (Technicolor): Laszlo Kovacs. Editing: Christopher Holmes, Gerald Sheppard. Music: Chopin (F minor Fantasy, op. 49; E minor Prelude, op. 28), Mozart (E flat major Piano Concerto; D minor Fantasy), J. S. Bach (Chromatic Fantasy and Fugue). Art direction: Toby Rafelson. Players: Jack Nicholson (*Robert Eroica Dupea*), Karen Black (*Rayette Dipesto*), Lois Smith (*Partita Dupea*), Susan Anspach (*Catherine Van Ost*), Billy "Green" Bush (*Elton*), Fannie Flagg (*Stoney*), Ralph Waite (*Carl Fidelio Dupea*), Helena Kallianiotes (*Palm Apodaca*), Toni Basil (*Terry Grouse*), Sally Ann Struthers (*Betty*), Marlena Macguire (*Twinky*), John Ryan (*Spicer*), Irene Dailey (*Samia Glavia*), Lorna Thayer (*Waitress*), Richard Stahl (*Recording Engineer*), William Challee (*Nicholas Dupea*). Produced by BR, Richard Wechsler for BBS. 98 mins.

1973
THE KING OF MARVIN GARDENS. Script: Jacob Brackman, from a story by BR, Jacob Brackman. Direction: BR. Photography (Eastmancolor): Laszlo Kovacs.

Editing: John F. Link II. Art direction: Toby Carr Rafelson. Players: Jack Nicholson (*David Staebler*), Bruce Dern (*Jason Staebler*), Ellen Burstyn (*Sally*), Julia Anne Robinson (*Jessica*), Benjamin "Scatman" Crothers (*Lewis*), Charles Lavine (*Grandfather*), Arnold Williams (*Rosko*), John Ryan (*Surtees*), Sully Boyar (*Lebowitz*), Joshua Mostel (*Frank*), William Pabst (*Bidlack*), Gary Goodrow (*Nervous Man*), Imogene Bliss (*Magda*), Ann Thomas (*Bambi*), Tom Overton (*Spot Operator*), Maxwell "Sonny" Goldberg (*Sonny*), Van Kirksey, Tony King (*Messengers*), Jerry Fujikawa (*Agura*), Conrad Yama (*Fujito*), Scott Howard, Henry Foehl (*Auctioneers*), Frank Hatchett, Wyetta Turner (*Dancers*). Produced by BR for BBS. 104 mins.

1977
STAY HUNGRY. Script: Charles Gaines BR, from the novel by Charles Gaines. Direction: BR. Photography (Deluxe Color): Victor Kemper. Editing: John F. Link II. Music: Bruce Langhorne, Byron Berline. Production design: Toby Carr Rafelson. Players: Jeff Bridges (*Craig Blake*), Sally Field (*Mary Tate Farnsworth*), Arnold Schwarzenegger (*Joe Santo*), R. G. Armstrong (*Thor Erickson*), Robert Englund (*Franklin*), Helena Kallianiotes (*Anita*), Roger E. Mosley (*Newton*), Woodrow Parfrey (*Craig's Uncle*), Scatman Crothers (*William*), Kathleen Miller (*Dorothy Stephens*), Fannie Flagg (*Amy Walterson*), Joanna Cassidy (*Zoe Mason*), Richard Gilliland (*Hal Foss*), Mayf Nutter (*Packman*), Ed Begley Jr. (*Lester*), John David Carson (*Halsey*), Joe Spinell (*Jabo*), Cliff Pellow (*Walter Jr.*), Dennis Fimple (*Bubba*), Garry Goodrow (*Moe Zwick*), Bart Carpinelli (*Laverne*), Bob Westmoreland (*M. Kroop*), Brandy Wilde (*Flower*), Laura Hippe (*Mae Ruth*), John Gilgreen (*Guard*), Murray Johnson (*Man*), Dennis Burkley (*Bones*), Autry Pinson (*Harry*). Produced by Harold Schneider, BR for Outov. 102 mins. (GB: 100 mins.).

1981
THE POSTMAN ALWAYS RINGS TWICE. Script: David Mamet, from the novel by James M. Cain. Direction: BR. Photography (Metrocolor): Sven Nykvist. Editing: Graeme Clifford. Music: Michael Small. Production design: George Jenkins. Players: Jack Nicholson (*Frank Chambers*), Jessica Lange (*Cora Papadakis*), John Colicos (*Nick Papadakis*), Michael Lerner (*Katz*), John P. Ryan (*Kennedy*), Anjelica Huston (*Madge*), William Traylor (*Sackett*), Tom Hill (*Barlow*), Jon Van Ness (*Motorcycle Cop*), Brian Farrell (*Mortenson*), Raleigh Bond (*Insurance Salesman*), William Newman (*Man from Home Town*), Albert Henderson (*Beeman*), Ken Magee (*Scoutmaster*), Eugene Peterson (*Doctor*), Don Calfa (*Goebel*), Louis Turenne (*Ringmaster*), Charles B. Jenkins (*Garage Attendant*), Dick Balduzzi, John Furlong (*Sign Men*), Sam Edwards (*Ticket Clerk*), Betty Cole (*Grandmother*), Joni Palmer (*Granddaughter*), Ron Flagge (*Shoeshine Man*), Christopher Lloyd (*Salesman*), James O'Connell (*Judge*), William H. McDonald (*Bailiff*), Elsa Raven (*Matron*), Kopi Sotiropulos (*Greek Mourner*). Produced by Charles Mulvehill, BR for Lorimar. 121 mins.

Dino Risi

by Lorenzo Codelli

The comic vein in Italy – from ancient Rome to Cinecittà – was always linked to the more popular forms of entertainment: the *vulgus* normally had the only power to laugh at their own misfortunes, and their only voice became the comedians' acting. In our century the lowbrow theatrical tradition is strictly interlaced with the growth of the cinema, since most of the comic film players sprang from stage shows like the "avanspettacolo," the "varietà," the "caffé-chantant." The Fascist censorship controlled and watered down for too many years the satirical genius of Petrolini, Totò, Macario, Aldo Fabrizi, and of their writers and directors. In the burst of freedom after the war, the Neorealist movement used many of them to communicate new political ideas. But other intellectuals like Dino Risi, Alberto Lattuada, Mario Monicelli, Steno, Raffaello Matarazzo, opted for retracing people's preferences and for reinventing the genres of this new era. Risi's smiling talent was revealed in the middle of the Fifties through a brilliant series of juvenile comedies that brought on the screen a new generation of appealing players; and he soon became the trendsetting originator of the "commedia all' italiana."

DINO RISI was born in Milan on December 23, 1917. He graduated in medicine and specialised in psychiatry. Thanks to his friendship with the young film-maker Alberto Lattuada, he started to work casually in the cinema; during the war he also attended some film lessons by Jacques Feyder in Geneva. He left hospital life and worked as a film journalist in some magazines. In 1946 he directed his first short, *I bersaglieri della signora*, a documentary on an old people's hospice. In his other shorts he followed the Neorealist path, reporting on beggars, workers, realistic painters, abandoned areas; his scientific interests – that have infused all his work – were displayed in his first two non-commercial features: *Il siero della verità* (1949) about a serum that allows patients to remember more than they would like, and *Seduta spiritica* (1949), about a medium talking with the spirits. One of his last shorts, *Buio in sala* (1950), told the story of a desperate man going into a

theatre and finding a new hope by seeing all kind of films that were shown just through the spectator's reactions.

The success of this short drove Risi into going to Rome, where he accepted to direct a film with and for children: *Vacanze col gangster* (*Vacation with a Gangster*), about a group of kids who liberate from prison a dangerous criminal and discover his real nature. After a pleasant comedy on the world of Cinecittà (*Viale della speranza/ Hope Avenue*), Risi was involved in the collective feature *Amore in città* (*Love in the City*), conceived by Cesare Zavattini and co-ordinated by Marco Ferreri; it was a kind of aesthetic manifesto for Fellini, Antonioni, Lattuada and particularly for Risi, who looked at the brief, illusory happiness of some young couples in a dancing hall. This motif of songs and fashionable music is used in many of his works to underline the cheap raptures of alienated people.

His first commercial successes were two unoriginal farces put together for the very popular couple of Sophia Loren and Vittorio De Sica, and exploiting the profitable model of *Pane, amore e fantasia* (directed by Luigi Comencini in 1953). In 1956 Risi declared in reply to a questionnaire to young film-makers that he wanted "seriously . . . to create entertainment from whatever material," and that the Neorealist style was no longer valid as a means of explaining reality.

Together with Pasquale Festa Campanile and Massimo Franciosa – an adroit pair of writers who would become themselves directors in the Sixties – he then designed *Poveri ma belli* (*Poor but Beautiful*), a low-budget comedy played by newcomers like Marisa Allasio, Renato Salvatori, Lorella De Luca, Maurizio Arena. These fresh faces animated the friendly entanglements of some young Romans looking for impending prosperity with an irresistible optimism. This enormously successful film saved the old major firm Titanus from going bankrupt, it paved the way to many follow-ups (by Risi and by others) and imitations, and moreover opened the field for other young directors.

Apparently detached and full of irony, Risi is

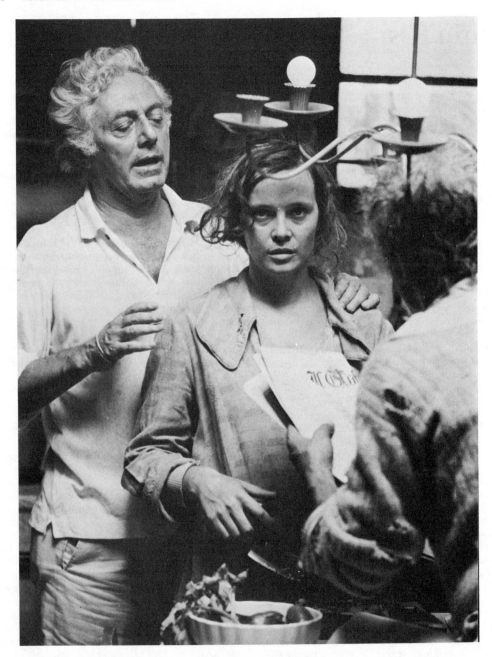

DINO RISI WITH THE ACTRESS LAURA ANTONELLI, ON THE SET OF *SESSOMATTO*

deeply involved in the not so frivolous misadventures of his characters, even when they are consciously inspired by Goldonian prototypes as in the classic *Venezia, la luna e tu (Venice, the Moon and You)*. Here he transforms into two Venetian gondoliers no less than Alberto Sordi and Nino Manfredi, two of the most Roman comics of the Italian cinema. His strength in directing confirmed players in the most unusual roles is a quality he later expands through the virtuosity of Sordi, Manfredi, Ugo Tognazzi and Vittorio Gassman, the four acknowledged "monsters" of the Italian Comedy.

After *Il vedovo (The Widower)*, a black comedy with Sordi, Risi met for the first time Vittorio Gassman – one of the greatest tragic actors of the stage who had recently switched to comic movies with *I soliti ignoti (Big Deal on Madonna Street)*, by Mario Monicelli. In twelve films he would become Risi's *alter ego*, starting from his various extraordinary disguises in *Il mattatore (Love and Larceny)*, about the swindles of a genial cheater.

As a pause in his career, Risi directed a dramatic love story in 1960, *Un amore a Roma (Love in Rome)*; its dark romanticism portended some of the themes he would approach only in the later years, but its commercial failure prompted him to return permanently to his lighter side.

Una vita difficile (A Difficult Life), one of his masterpieces, originated from a revival of works devoted to the Resistance against Fascism, mostly conceived to celebrate its glorious memory (like Rossellini's *Il generale Della Rovere*). Risi and his screenwriter Rodolfo Sonego, on the contrary, described the unconventional vicissitudes of a leftist journalist from his tepid involvement in the Resistance movement, to his quixotic struggles in the Fifties against corruption and despotic capitalists. Sordi played the perfect type of angry idealist often too inclined to give up, and finally reforming himself in a symbolic gesture. Twenty years of national life were sardonically narrated by Risi in this memorable picture – that was also appreciated by Italian critics, usually violently attacking Risi's humorous style.

He then directed *La marcia su Roma (The March to Rome)*, a Brechtian apologue on the birth of Fascism, co-written by two other famous teams of screenwriters, Age and Scarpelli, Maccari and Scola, basic pillars of the comic genre. Risi returned to contemporary themes with *Il sorpasso*, an on-the-road social satire whose American title *The Easy Life* was something more than an inspiration for *Easy Rider* and its spin-offs. Gassman played a lazy fellow, extrovert and cynical, who drives for a summer day with a naive young student, his opposite. Through their casual encounters Risi penetrates the deceptive appearances of the Italian economic "boom," where the rush to holidays at any cost leaves people deeply unsatisfied. His nihilist vision would be reaffirmed in other splendid comedies on frenetic vacations, like *L'ombrellone (The Parasol/Weekend Italian Style)*, or *Il giovane normale (The Normal Young Man)*.

I mostri (The Monsters/Opiate 67) was an instant classic in the copious genre of portmanteau films. Tognazzi and Gassman displayed their versatility in twenty bizarre episodes, some of them strikingly funny; like the one where a crowd is crying: "They arrested the monster at last!", and then you see a common small man surrounded by two monstrously ugly soldiers (Tognazzi and Gassman); or like the other – cut in many countries – where Tognazzi and his wife, sitting in a theatre, watch a bloody scene of an execution of partisans by Nazis, just to exclaim that they would like for their home a wall painted like that one on the screen! And the final segment of *I mostri* was a moving novelette about two ageing boxers, two desperate cretins not understanding each other, like Beckett's creatures, attempting an impossible comeback.

Risi's peculiar gusto for the paradoxical short story was sanctioned in some other episodes he directed for collective movies like *Le bambole (The Dolls)*, *I complessi (The Complexes)*, *I nostri mariti (Our Husbands)*. But when he could direct an actor or an actress for several episodes in a same picture, he cut loose with remarkable achievements. This was the case with Nino Manfredi in *Vedo nudo (I See Everybody Naked)*, playing successively an absent-minded doctor, a peasant in love with his hen, a frustrated transvestite, a short-seeing peeping tom, an idiot mistaken for a rapist, an engineer making love with running locomotives, and an advertising agent obsessed by visions of naked people. This formula was tailored again for Monica Vitti's twelve performances in *Noi donne siamo fatte così* (*Women: So We are Made*), a feminist comedy, then for Giancarlo Giannini and Laura Antonelli (two much weaker players) in *Sessomatto* (*How Funny Can Sex Be?*), then for Johnny Dorelli and Laura Antonelli in *Allegria* (*Happiness*). One should remember at least two *silent* episodes, the first from *Noi donne siamo fatte così*, in which we follow the strange day of a cymbal player, living and exercising herself just to play two notes in a big orchestra; the second, aptly called *Senza parole* (*No Words*), and one of Risi's contributions to *I nuovi mostri* (*The New Monsters*), in which Ornella Muti plays an air hostess falling in love with a beautiful stranger and taking his present when she leaves on a flight; we learn over the radio that he was a terrorist and that his bomb was concealed in the cassette-player he gave to her so romantically. Reversal of situations, vilification of "innocents," denouncement of stupidity, these are some of Risi's ethical tools.

His most personal comedies of the Sixties also include *Il giovedì* (*Thursday*), about the delicate relationship between a divorced father and his witty child; *Il gaucho* (*The Gaucho*), a jovial satire on Italians abroad, shot ex-tempore in Argentina with the creative freedom Risi holds dear; *Operazione San Gennaro* (*Treasure of San Gennaro*), a wild parody of American hold-up pictures; *Straziami ma di baci saziami* (*Tear Me But Satiate Me with your Kisses*), a sublime satire on proletarians living as in the rosy songs they love.

Risi's attitude grows darker during the Seventies. *In nome del popolo italiano* (*In the Name of the Italian People*) and *Mordi e fuggi* (*Bite and Run*) are two hard political indictments relieved by his nonchalant humour; he does not want to drum home messages, but simply to testify to the appalling decay of institutions.

The international success of *Profumo di donna* (*Scent of a Woman*) did not reveal the source of this pessimistic picture. Freely adapted from a novel by Giovanni Arpino (like Risi's later *Anima persa*), it allowed Gassman to play the exuberant blind officer travelling with his young attendant towards a tragic confrontation with destiny. More than an updated version of *Il sorpasso*, it seemed a pivotal adjustment for the

Italian comedy to these less laughable times. While Risi would still direct straight comedies, like *Telefoni bianchi* (*The Career of a Chambermaid*) – a brisk satire on movies under Fascism – or like *Sono fotogenico* (*I Am Photogenic*) – a bittersweet farce on a crazy aspiring actor – his inner anxieties were to be better expressed in some literary fictions.

Anima persa (*Lost Soul*) and *La stanza del vescovo* (*The Bishop's Room*) are two *kammerspiel* psychoanalytic dramas where Gassman and Tognazzi respectively impersonate two different old *bon vivants* who have lost their real self. The tendencies to self-destruction are also evident in the Sternbergian *Primo amore* (*First Love*), about an old actor's passion for a nymphet. And in *Caro papà* (*Dear Father*) Risi, helped by his own son, goes back to the conflict of generations that is a root of all his work, this time having Gassman little by little discovering that a scheme for his murder was concocted by his beloved son. *Fantasma d'amore* (*Ghost of Love*), one of Risi's better efforts, develops the Gothic bewitchment between a bourgeois lawyer and his dead lover. In these mature works Risi devotes more attention to the atmosphere and the decor, and his natural ambiguity unfolds greater levels of interpretation. Fortunately his unshakable playfulness serves as an undercurrent to avoid any ponderousness of thought. Risi is a genuine story-teller with an unwitting sociologist inside him, and may give us still more surprises.

RISI FILMOGRAPHY

Dino Risi started his career working as an assistant to Mario Soldati in *Piccolo mondo antico* (1941) and to Alberto Lattuada in *Giacomo l'idealista* (1942). He directed the following shorts professionally: *I bersaglieri della signora* (1946), *Barboni* (1946 – a winner at the Mostra of Venice), *Verso la vita* (1946), *Pescatorella* (1947), *Strade di Napoli* (1947), *Tigullio minore* (1947), *Cortili* (1947), *Costumi e bellezze d'Italia* (1948), *Cuore rivelatore* (1948), *1848* (1948), *La fabbrica del Duomo* (1948), *Segantini, il pittore della montagna* (1948), *La città dei traffici* (1949), *Caccia in brughiera* (1949), *La montagna di luce* (1949), *Vince il sistema* (1949), *Terra ladina* (1949), *L'isola bianca* (1950), *Il grido della città* (1950), *Buio in sala* (1950), *Fuga in città* (1950). He also directed two scientific features: *Il siero della verità* (1949) and *Seduta spiritica* (1949). Dino Risi co-wrote the following features: *Anna* (1951) by Alberto Lattuada,

DINO RISI WITH OLIVER REED DURING THE SHOOTING OF *MORDI E FUGGI*

Totò e i re di Roma (1951) by Steno and Mario Monicelli, *Gli eroi della domenica* (1952) by Mario Camerini, *Montecarlo* (1956) by Samuel Taylor.

1952
VACANZE COL GANGSTER / VACATION WITH A GANGSTER. Script: DR, Ennio de Concini. Direction: DR. Photography: Piero Portalupi. Editing: Eraldo Da Roma. Music: Mario Nascimbene. Art Direction: Flavio Mogherini. Players: Marc Lawrence (*Jack Minotti*), Giovanna Pala (*Amelia*), Lamberto Maggiorani, Mario Girotti, Antonio Macchi, Alfredo Baldieri, Gaetano Pessina, Luciano Caruso, Diana Perbellini, Magri Zacconi, Bianca Doria, Anna Arena, Silvio Bagolini, Aldo Alimonti, Mario Galli, Mario Cianfanelli, and the dog Doc. Produced by Antonio Mambretti for Mambretti Film.

1953
VIALE DELLA SPERANZA / HOPE AVENUE. Script: DR, Gino De Santis, Ettore Margadonna, Franco Cannarosso. Direction: DR, Photography: Mario Bava. Editing: Eraldo Da Roma. Music: Mario Nascimbene. Art Direction: Flavio Mogherini. Players: Marcello Mastroianni (*Mario*), Cosetta Greco (*Luisa*), Liliana Bonfatti (*Giuditta*), Maria Pia Casilio (*Concettina*), Piera Simoni (*Franca*), Nerio Bernardi (*Franzi*), Pietro De Vico (*Tonino*), Gisella Monaldi (*Titina*), Achille Majeroni,

Franco Migliacci, Carlo Hintermann, Nino Marchetti, Ettore Jannetti, Alessandro Fersen, Silvio Bagolini, Bianca Maria Fusari, Corrado Pani, Vincenzo Milazzo, Cesare Vieri, Clara Loy, Odoardo Girotti, Arrigo Basevi, Giulio Cali, Mario Raffi. Produced by Antonio Mambretti for Mambretti Film – ENIC. 100 mins.
AMORE IN CITTA' / LOVE IN THE CITY / Episode: **PARADISO PER QUATTRO ORE / PARADISE FOR FOUR HOURS.** Script: DR, Cesare Zavattini, Aldo Buzzi, Luigi Chiarini, Luigi Malerba, Tullio Pinelli, Vittorio Vetroni, Marco Ferreri. Direction: DR. Photography: Gianni Di Venanzo. Editing: Eraldo Da Roma. Music: Mario Nascimbene. Art Direction: Gianni Polidori. Players: non-professionals. Produced by Marco Ferreri for Foro Film. The other episodes were directed by Carlo Lizzani (*L'amore che si paga*), Federico Fellini (*L'agenzia matrimoniale*), Michelangelo Antonioni (*Tentato suicidio*), Francesco Maselli and Cesare Zavattini (*Storia di Caterina*), Alberto Lattuada (*Gli italiani si voltano*).

1955
IL SEGNO DI VENERE / THE SIGN OF VENUS. Script: Edoardo Anton, Ennio Flaiano, Franca Valeri, DR, Cesare Zavattini, from a story by Edoardo Anton, Luigi Comencini, Franca Valeri. Photography: Carlo Montuori. Editing: Mario Serandrei. Music: Renzo

Rossellini. Art Direction: Gastone Medin. Players: Sophia Loren (*Agnese*), Franca Valeri (*Cesira*), Vittorio De Sica (*Alessio Spano*), Raf Vallone (*Ignazio Bolognini*), Peppino De Filippo (*Mario*), Alberto Sordi (*Romolo Proietti*), Virgilio Riento (*Tirabassi*), Tina Pica (*Tina*), Lina Gennari, Eloisa Cianni, Leopoldo Trieste, Maurizio Arena, Franco Fantasia, Marcella Rovena, Mario Meniconi, Furio Meniconi, Anita Durante, Giuseppe Chinnici, Gustavo Giorgi, Marcello Ruffini. Produced by Marcello Girosi for Titanus.

PANE, AMORE E ... / BREAD, LOVE AND ... / SCANDAL IN SORRENTO. Script: Ettore Margadoona, from a story by Marcello Girosi, Ettore Margadonna, Vincenzo Talarico, DR. Direction: DR. Photography (Eastmancolor, Scope): Giuseppe Rotunno. Editing: Mario Serandrei. Music: Alessandro Cicognini. Art Direction: Gastone Medin. Players: Vittorio De Sica (*Maresciallo Carotenuto*), Sophia Loren (*Sofia*), Lea Padovani (*Donna Violante*), Antonio Cifariello (*Nicolino*), Mario Carotenuto (*don Matteo Carotenuto*), Tina Pica (*Caramella*), Virgilio Riento (*Priest*), Joka Berrety, Clara Crispo, Pasquale Misiano, Gaetano Audiero, Nino Imparato, Fausto Guerzoni, Attilio Torelli, Vittorio Pucci, and the dog Kitty. Produced by Marcello Girosi for Titanus. 100 mins.

1956
POVERI MA BELLI / POOR BUT BEAUTIFUL. Script: Pasquale Festa Campanile, Massimo Franciosa, DR, from a story by DR. Direction: DR. Photography: Tonino Delli Colli. Editing: Mario Serandrei. Music: Piero Piccioni. Art Direction: Piero Filippone. Players: Marisa Allasio (*Giovanna*), Maurizio Arena (*Romolo*), Renato Salvatori (*Salvatore*), Memmo Carotenuto (*Tram Driver*), Lorella De Luca (*Marisa*), Alessandra Panaro (*Anna Maria*), Mario Carotenuto (*Uncle Mario*), Virgilio Riento (*Giovanna's Father*), Ettore Manni (*Ugo*), Gildo Bocci (*Janitor*), Lina Ferri, Rosella Como, Erminio spalla, Carla Onofrio, Tina De Santis, Mario Ambrosino, Nino Vingelli, Sergio Cardinaletti, Maurizio Monticelli, Marcello Avallone, Luciano Basso, Luciano Berti. Produced by Silvio Clementelli for Titanus (Rome)/ Société Générale de Cinématographie (Paris). 102 mins.

1957
LA NONNA SABELLA / GRANDMOTHER SABELLA. Script: Pasquale Festa Campanile, Massimo Franciosa, DR, from the novel by Pasquale Festa Campanile. Direction: DR. Photography: Tonino Delli Colli. Editing: Mario Serandrei. Music: Michele Cozzoli. Art Direction: Piero Filippone. Players: Tina Pica (*Nonna Sabella*), Peppino De Filippo (*Emilio*), Sylva Koscina (*Lucia*), Renato Salvatori (*Raffaele Rizzullo*), Dolores Palumbo (*Carmelina*), Paolo Stoppa (*Evaristo Mancuso*), Rossella Como (*Evelina*), Renato Rascel (*Don Gregorio*), Gorella Gori, Gina Mascetti, Edoardo Guerrera, Fausto Guerzoni, Mario Ambrosino, Lina Ferri, Mimmo Billi, Mara Ombra, Eugenio Galadini, Agnes de Angelis. Produced by Silvio Clementelli for Titanus (Rome)/Franco-London Films (Paris). 90 mins.

BELLE MA POVERE / BEAUTIFUL BUT POOR / IRRESISTIBLE. Script: Pasquale Festa Campanile, Massimo Franciosa, DR. Direction: DR. Photography: Tonino Delli Colli. Editing: Mario Serandrei. Music: Piero Piccioni. Art Direction: Piero Filippone. Players: Marisa Allasio (*Giovanna*), Maurizio Arena (*Romolo*), Renato Salvatori (*Salvatore*), Lorella De Luca (*Marisa*), Alessandra Panaro (*Anna Maria*), Riccardo Garrone (*Franco*), Carlo Giuffré (*Marisa's Beau*), Memmo Carotenuto (*Tram Driver*), Gildo Bocci (*Janitor*), Marisa Castellani, Lina Ferri, Sergio Cardinaletti, Maurizio Moticelli, Roy Ciccolini, Giorgio Gangos, Mario Meniconi, Ughetto Bertucci, Giancarlo Zarfati. Produced by Silvio Clementelli for Titanus. 99 mins.

1958
VENEZIA, LA LUNA E TU / VENICE, THE MOON AND YOU. Script: Pasquale Festa Campanile, Massimo Franciosa, DR. Direction: DR. Photography (Eastmancolor): Tonino Delli Colli. Editing: Mario Serandrei. Music: Lelio Luttazzi. Art Direction: Alberto Boccianti. Players: Alberto Sordi (*Bepi*), Marisa Allasio (*Nina*), Nino Manfredi (*Toni*), Riccardo Garrone (*don Fulgenzio*), Inge Schoener (*Janet*), Nicky Dantine (*Nathalie*), Luciano Baracelli, Anna Campori, Jole Mauro, Ernesto Boni, Lila de Santis, Lilli Mantovani, Giulio Tomei, Giuliano Gemma. Produced by Silvio Clementelli for Titanus (Rome)/Société Générale de Cinématographie (Paris). 107 mins.
POVERI MILIONARI / POOR MILLIONAIRES. Script: Pasquale Festa Campanile, Massimo Franciosa, DR. Direction: DR. Photography: Tonino Delli Colli. Editing: Mario Serandrei. Music: Armando Trovaioli. Art Direction: Piero Filippone. Players: Maurizio Arena (*Romolo*), Renato Salvatori (*Salvatore*), Lorella De Luca (*Marisa*), Alessandra Panaro (*Anna Maria*), Sylva Koscina (*Alice*), Memmo Carotenuto (*Tram Driver*), Gildo Bocci (*Door-keeper*), Lina Ferri, Roberto Rey, José Jaspe, Miguel Jade, Fred Buscaglione and his Band. Produced by Silvio Clementelli for Titanus. 95 mins.

1959
IL VEDOVO / THE WIDOWER. Script: Rodolfo Sonego, Dino Verde, Sandro Continenza, Fabio Carpi, DR, from a story by Rodolfo Sonego, Fabio Carpi, DR. Direction: DR. Photography: Luciano Trasatti. Editing: Alberto Gallitti. Music: Armando Trovaioli. Art Direction: Piero Filippone. Players: Alberto Sordi (*Alberto Nardi*), Franca Valeri (*Elvira Nardi*), Livio Lorenzon (*Stucchi*), Nando Bruno (*Oncle Alberto*), Eleonora Ruffo (*Gioia*), Ruggero Marchi, Gastone Bettanini, Mario Passante, Enzo Petito, Nando Primavera, Rosita Pisano, Alberto Rabagliati, Mario Cianfarelli, Luigi Reder. Produced by Edgardo Cortese and Elio Scardamaglia for Paneuropa/Cino Del Duca. 100 mins.
IL MATTATORE / LOVE AND LARCENY. Script: Sandro Continenza, Ettore Scola, Ruggero Maccari, from a story by Age (Agenore Incrocci) and (Furio) Scarpelli, and from an idea by Sergio Pugliese. Direction:

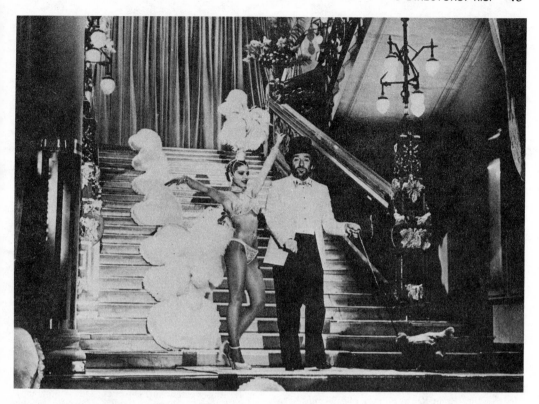

ORNELLA MUTI AND UGO TOGNAZZI IN *PRIMO AMORE*

DR. Photography (Totalscope, with a final sequence in colour): Massimo Dallamano. Editing: Eraldo Da Roma. Music: Pippo Barzizza. Art Direction: Giorgio Giovannini. Players: Vittorio Gassman (*Gerardo*), Dorian Gray (*Elena*), Anna Maria Ferrero (*Annalisa*), Peppino De Filippo (*Chinotto*), Mario Carotenuto (*Lallo*), Alberto Bonucci (*Gloria Patri*), Fosco Giachetti (*General Mesci*), Luigi Pavese (*Adolfo Rebuschini*), Mario Scaccia (*Jeweller*), Fanfulla (*Sor Annibale*), Armando Bandini (*Accountant*), Erminio Spalla (*Prisoner*), Gisella Sofio (*Doris*), Nando Bruno, Linda Sini, Piera Arico, Aldo Bufi Landi, Enrico Glori, Salvatore Cafiero, Mario Frera. Produced by Mario Cecchi Gori for Maxima Film, Cei Incom (Rome)/Société Générale de Cinématographie (Paris). 104 mins.

1960
UN AMORE A ROMA/LOVE IN ROME. Script: Ennio Flaiano from the novel by Ercole Patti. Direction: DR. Photography: Mario Montuori. Editing: Otello Colangeli. Music: Carlo Rustichelli. Art Direction: Piero Filippone. Players: Mylène Demongeot (*Anna Padoan*), Peter Baldwin (*Marcello Cenni*), Elsa Martinelli (*Fulvia*), Claudio Gora (*Curtatoni*), Maria Perschy (*Eleonora*), Jacques Sernas (*Tony Meneghini*), Armando Romeo (*Nello D'Amore*), Umberto Orsini (*Peppino Barlacchi*), Vittorio De Sica (*Film Director*), Laura Rocca, Anne White, Fanfulla, Renato Montalbano, Anna Glory, Enrico Glory, Gianni Musy. Produced by Mario Cecchi Gori for Fair Film, Cei Incom (Rome)/Laetitia Film, Les Films Cocinor (Paris)/Alpha Film (Berlin). 114 mins.

A PORTE CHIUSE/BEHIND CLOSED DOORS. Script: Marcello Coscia, Dino De Palma, Sandro Continenza, from a story by Fabio Carpi, DR. Direction: DR. Photography: Mario Montuori. Editing: Otello Colangeli. Music: Piero Umiliani. Art Direction: Piero Filippone. Players: Anita Ekberg (*Olga Dubovitch*), Claudio Gora (*Judge*), Ettore Manni (*Sailor*), Fred Clark (*Xatis*). Mario Scaccia (*Manning*), Gianni Bonagura (*Lawyer*), Alberto Talegalli (*Poseyon*), Hélène Rémy (*Marietta*), Beatrice Altariba (*Young Married*), Agostino Salvietti (*Polydette*). Leonardo Porzio (*Kinalis*), Vittorio Caprioli (*Police Chief*), Giampiero Littera, Carlo Di

Maggio. Produced by Mario Cecchi Gori for FaiR Film, Rire Cinematografica, Società, Generale Cinematografica. 103 mins.

1961

UNA VITA DIFFICILE / A DIFFICULT LIFE. Script: Rodolfo Sonego from his story. Direction: DR. Photography: Leonida Barboni. Editing: Tatiana Casini. Music: Carlo Savina. Art Direction: Mario Chiari. Players: Alberto Sordi (*Silvio Magnozzi*), Lea Massari (*Elena*), Franco Fabrizi (*Franco Simonina*), Lina Volonghi (*Amelia Pavinato*), Mino Doro (*Gino Laganà*), Daniele Vargas (*Marquis Cafferoni*), Loredana Cappelletti (*Elena's Friend*), Edith Peters (*Herself*), Paolino Vanni (*Paolino Magnozzi*), Norante Domizlaff, Valeria Manganelli, Brunno Perego, and with Silvano Mangano, Vittorio Gassman, Renato Tagliani, Alessandro Blassetti (all playing themselves). Produced by Dino De Laurentiis for Dino De Laurentiis Cinematografica. 118 mins.

1962

LA MARCIA SU ROMA / THE MARCH TO ROME. Script: Age, Ruggero Maccari, Furio Scarpelli, Sandro Continenza, Ghigo De Chiara, Ettore Scola. Direction: DR. Photography: Alfio Contini. Editing: Alberto Gallitti. Music: Marcello Giombini. Art Direction: Ugo Pericoli. Players: Vittorio Gassman (*Domenico Rocchetti*), Ugo Tognazzi (*Umberto Gavazza*), Roger Hanin (*Captain Paolinelli*), Angela Luce (*Peasant*), Gérard Landry (*Milziade Bellinzoni*), Mario Brega (*Mitraglia*), Giampiero Albertini (*Cristoforo*), Alberto Vecchietti, Claudio Peroni, Antonio Cannas, Howard Rubiens, Nino Di Napoli, Nando Angelini, Daniele Vargas, Edda Ferronao, Carlo Kecler. Produced by Mario Cecchi Gori for Fair Film (Rome)/Orsay Films (Paris). 94 mins.

IL SORPASSO / THE OVERTAKING / THE EASY LIFE. Script: DR, Ettore Scola, Ruggero Maccari, from a story by Rodolfo Sonego (uncredited). Photography: Alfio Contini. Editing: Maurizio Lucidi. Music: Riz Ortolani. Art Direction: Ugo Pericoli. Players: Vittorio Gassman (*Ugo Cortona*), Jean-Louis Trintignant (*Roberto Mariani*), Catherine Spaak *;(Lilly)*, Claudio Gora (*Bibi*), Luciana Angiolillo (*Bruno's Wife*), Luigi Zerbinati (*Commendatore*), Linda Sini, Franca Polesello, Bruna Simionato, Lilli Dorelli, Mila Stanic, Nando Angelini, Edda Ferronao. Produced by Mario Cecchi Gori for Fair Film, Incei Film, Sancro Film. 108 mins.

1963

IL SUCCESSO / THE SUCCESS. Script: Ettore Scola, Ruggero Maccari. Direction: Mauro Morassi (and DR. uncredited). Photography: Sandro D'Eva. Editing: Maurizio Lucidi. Music: Ennio Morricone. Art Direction: Ugo Pericoli. Players: Vittorio Gassman (*Giulio Ceriani*), Anouk Aimée (*Laura*), Jean-Louis Trintignant (*Sergio*), Maria Grazia Spina (*Diana*), Cristina Gajoni (*Maria*), Filippo Scelzo (*Francesco*), Annie Gorassini (*Marisa*), Franca Polesello (Carla), Armando Bandini (Romanelli), Riccardo Garrone, Umberto D'Orsi, Leopoldo Trieste, Daniele Vargas, Gastone Moschin,

Mino Doro. Produced by Mario Cecchi Gori for Fair Film, Incei Film, Montflour Film (Rome)/Cinetel (Paris). 106 mins.

I MOSTRI / THE MONSTERS / OPIATE '67 / 15 FROM ROME. Film in 20 episodes. Script: Age, Furio Scarpelli, Elio Petri, DR, Ettore Scola, Ruggero Maccari. Direction: DR, Photography: Alfio Contini. Editing: Maurizio Lucidi. Music: Armando Trovaioli. Art Direction: Ugo Pericoli. Players: Ugo Tognazzi (in 12 disguises), Vittorio Gassman (in 11 disguises), Ricky Tognazzi, Lando Buzzanca, Marisa Merlini, Michèle Mercier, Rica Dialina, Jacques Herlin, Marino Masè, Mario Brega, Lucia Modugno, Luisa Rispoli. Produced by Mario Cecchi Gori for Fair Film, Incei Film, Montflour Film. 118 mins.

IL GIOVEDI' / THURSDAY. Script: Castellano (Franco Castellano) and Pipolo (Giuseppe Moccia), DR. Direction: DR. Photography (Scope): Alfio Contini. Editing: Gisa Radicchi Levi. Music: Armando Trovaioli. Art Direction: Alberto Boccianti. Players: Walter Chiari (*Dino Versini*), Michèle Mercier (*Elsa*), Roberto Ciccolini (*Robertino*), Umberto D'Orsi (*Rigoni*), Alice and Ellen Kessler (*Themselves*), Emma Baron (*Dino's Mother*), Carol Walker (*Dino's Wife*), Silvio Bagolini, Milena Vukotich, Liliana Maccalè, Olimpia Cavalli, Else Sandom, Gloria Parri, Ezio Risi, Edy Biagetti, Salvo Libassi, Sara Simoni. Produced by Isidoro Broggi, Renato Libassi, Marcello Girosi for D.D.L., Center Films. 110 mins.

1964

IL GAUCHO / THE GAUCHO. Script: Ettore Scola, Ruggero Maccari, Tullio Pinelli, from a story by Ettore Scola, Ruggero Maccari. Direction: DR. Photography: Alfio Contini. Editing: Marcello Malvestiti. Music: Armando Trovaioli. Art Direction: Ugo Pericoli. Players: Vittorio Gassman (*Marco Ravicchio*), Nino Manfredi (*Stefano*), Amedeo Nazzari (*Marucchelli*), Silvana Pampanini (*Luciana*), Maria Grazia Buccella (*Mara*), Annie Gorassini (*Lorella*), Nelli Panizza, Guido Gorgari, Sanchez Calleja, Nora Carpena, Aldo Vianello, Nando Angelini. Produced by Mario Cecchi Gori for Fair Film (Rome)/Clemente Lococo (Buenos Aires). 110 mins.

LE BAMBOLE / THE DOLLS / BAMBOLE. Episode: **LA TELEFONATA / THE TELEPHONE CALL.** Script: Rodolfo Sonego. Direction: DR. Photography (colour): Ennio Guarnieri. Editing: Roberto Cinquini. Music: Armando Trovaioli. Art Direction: Gianni Polidori. Players: Nino Manfredi (*Giorgio*), Virna Lisi (*Luisa*), Alicia Brandet (*Armenia*). 20 mins. Produced by Gianni Hecht Lucari for Documento Film (Rome)/Orsay Films (Paris). The other episodes were directed by Luigi Comencini (*Il trattato di eugenetica*), Franco Rossi (*La minestra*), Mauro Bolognini (*Monsignor Cupido*).

1965

I COMPLESSI / THE COMPLEXES. Episode: **UNA GIORNATA DECISIVA / A DECISIVE DAY.** Script: Ettore Scola, Ruggero Maccari, Marcello Fondato, from

LAURA ANTONELLI IN *SESSO E VOLENTIERI*

a story by Ettore Scola, Ruggero Maccari, DR. Direction: DR. Photography: Giorgio Giovannini. Editing: Roberto Cinquini. Music: Armando Trovaioli. Art Direction: Luciano Fondato. Players: Nino Manfredi (*Quirino Raganelli*), Ilaria Occhini (*Gabriella*), Riccardo Garrone (*Alvaro*), Umberto d'Orsi (*Ernesto*), Leopoldo Valentini, Donatella Della Nora. Produced by Gianni Hecht Lucari for Documento Film (Rome)/S.P.C.E. (Paris). The other episodes were directed by Franco Rossi (*Il complesso della schiava nubiana*), Luigi Filippo D'Amico (*Guglielmo il dentone*).

L'OMBRELLONE / THE PARASOL / WEEKEND ITALIAN STYLE / WEEKEND WIVES. Script: Ennio De Concini, DR. Direction: DR. Photography (Eastmancolor): Armando Nannuzzi. Editing: Franco Fraticelli; Music: Lelio Luttazzi. Art Direction: Maurizio Chiari. Players: Enrico Maria Salerno (*Enrico Marletti*), Sandra Milo (*Giuliana*), Daniela Bianchi (*Isabella Dominici*), Trini Alonso (*Clelia Valdemari*), Alicia Brandet (*the Swedish*), Pepe Calvo (*Commendatore*), Pedro De Quevedo (*Gustavo Valdemari*), Lelio Luttazzi (*Count Antonio Bellanca*), Raffaele Pisu (*Pasqualino*), Lepoldo Trieste (*Franco Spotorri*), Veronique Vendell (*Giuliana*),

Jean Sorel (*Sergio*), Gianna Castor (*Mrs. Pellini*), Antonella Della Porta. Produced by Ultra Film (Rome)/Les Films du Siècle (Paris)/Altura Films (Madrid). 103 mins.

1966
I NOSTRI MARITI / OUR HUSBANDS. Episode: **IL MARITO DI ATTILIA** or **NEI SECOLI FEDELE / ATTILIA'S HUSBAND** or **FOREVER FAITHFUL.** Script: Age and Furio Scarpelli, Stefano Strucchi, from a story by Age and Scarpelli. Direction: DR. Photography: Carlo Carlini, Roberto Gerardi, Marco Scarpelli. Editing: Adriana Benedetti, Roberto Cinquini, Renato Cinquini. Music: Armando Trovaioli, Piero Piccioni. Art Direction: Elio Costanzi, Gianni Polidori. Players: Ugo Tognazzi (*Umberto Codegato*), Liana Orfei (*Attilia*), Giulio Rinaldi (*Ettore Rossi "Tantumergo"*). Produced by Gianni Hecht Lucari for Documento Film. The other episodes were directed by Luigi Filippo D'Amico (*Il marito di Roberta* or *Un matrimonio difficile*), Luigi Zampa (*Il marito di Olga* or **Il complesso di Angelotto**).
OPERAZIONE SAN GENNARO / OPERATION SAN GENNARO / TREASURE OF SAN GENNARO. Script:

Adriano Baracco, Nino Manfredi, Ennio De Concini, DR, from a story by Ennio De Concini, DR. Direction: DR. Photography (Eastmancolor): Aldo Tonti. Editing: Franco Fraticelli. Music: Armando Trovaioli. Art Direction: Luigi Scaccianoce. Players: Nino Manfredi (*Dudù*), Totò (*Don Vincenzo 'O' Fenomeno'*), Mario Adorf (*Sciascillo*), Senta Berger (*Maggie*), Harry Guardino (*Jack*), Claudine Auger (*Concettina*), Vittoria Crispo (*Mamma Assunta*), Ugo Fangareggi (*Agonia*), Jean Louis (*The Baron*), Dante Maggio (*The Captain*), Ralf Wolter (*Frank*), Pinuccia Ardia, Giovanni Druti, Solvi Stubing. Produced by Turi Vasile for Ultra Film (Rome)/Lyre Films (Paris)/Roxy Film (Münich). 104 mins.

1967
IL TIGRE / THE TIGER AND THE PUSSYCAT. Script: Age and Scarpelli, from a story by Age, Scarpelli, DR. Direction: DR. Photography (Eastmancolor): Sandro D'Eva, Editing: Marcello Malvestiti. Music: Fred Bongusto. Art Direction: Luciano Ricceri. Players: Vittorio Gassman (*Francesco Vincenzini*), Ann-Margret (*Carolina*), Eleanor Parker (*Esperia*), Fiorenzo Fiorentini (*Tazio Menichelli*), Antonella Steni (*Pinella*), Luigi Vannucchi (*Gianni Renzi Marasutti*), Caterina Boratto (*Delia*), Jacques Herlin (*Father Sartorelli*), Eleanor Brown (*Luisella Vincenzini*), Giambattista Salerno (*Luca Vincenzini*), Ruggero Orlando (*Himself*), Nino Segurini, Giovanni Scratuglia. Produced by Mario Cecchi Gori for Fair Film (Rome) and by Joseph E. Levine for Avco-Embassy (Hollywood). 110 mins.
IL PROFETA / THE PROPHET / MR. KINKY. Script: Ettore Scola, Ruggero Maccari, DR. Direction: DR. Photography (Technicolor): Sandro D'Eva. Editing: Marcello Malvestiti. Music: Armando Trovaioli. Art Direction: Piero Poletto. Players: Vittorio Gassman (*Piero Breccia*), Ann-Margret (*Maggie*), Oreste Lionello (*Puccio*), Liana Orfei (*Albertina*), Yvonne Sanson (*Carla Bagni*), Fiorenzo Fiorentini (*Guido Calacicchi*), Geoffrey Copleton (*Bagni*), Evi Rigano (*Tiziana*), Harry Stuart (*Magnus*), Franco Gulà, Enzo Robutti, Gianni Scratuglia, Giuseppe Lauricella, Anita Saxe, Nino Curcio, Renato Marzano, Tiziano Montagni. Produced by Mario Cecchi Gori for Fair Film. 94 mins.

1968
STRAZIAMI MA DI BACI SAZIAMI / TEAR ME BUT SATIATE ME WITH YOUR KISSES. Script: Age and Scarpelli, from a story by Age, Scarpelli, DR. Direction: DR. Photography (Technicolor): Sandro D'Eva. Editing: Antonietta Zita. Music: Armando Trovaioli. Art Direction: Luigi Scaccianoce. Players: Nino Manfredi (*Mario Balestrini*), Pamela Tiffin (*Marisa Di Giovanni*), Ugo Tognazzi (*Umberto Ciceri*), Moira Orfei (*Adelaide*), Livio Lorenzon (*Artemio Di Giovanni*), Gigi Ballista (*The Engineer*), Piero Tordi (*Priest Arduino*), Samson Burke (*Guido Scortichini*), Checco Durante, Edda Ferronao, Michele Cimarosa, Francesco Sormano, Mara Krupp, Donatella Della Nora, Antonietta Fiorito, Ettore Garofalo. Produced by Edmondo Amati pour Fida

Cinematografica (Rome)/Productions Jacques Roitfeld (Paris). 105 mins.

1969
VEDO NUDO / I SEE EVERYBODY NAKED. Film in 7 episodes. Script: Ruggero Maccari, from stories by DR, Ruggero Maccari, Fabio Carpi, Bernardino Zapponi. Direction: DR. Photography (Technicolor, Techniscope): Sandro D'Eva, Erico Menczer. Editing: Alberto Gallitti. Music: Armando Trovaioli. Art Direction: Luciano Ricceri. Players: Nino Manfredi (in 7 disguises), Sylva Koscina (*Herself*), Enrico Maria Salerno (*Carlo Alberto Ribaudo*), Veronique Vendell (*The Virgin*), Daniela Giordano (*Luisa*), John Karlsen, Umberto D'Orsi, Nerina Montagnani, Marcello Prando, Bruno Boschetti, Guido Spadea. Produced by Pio Angeletti and Adriano De Micheli for Dean Film, Jupiter Generale Cinematografica. 118 mins.
IL GIOVANE NORMALE / THE NORMAL YOUNG MAN. Script: Ruggero Maccari, from the novel by Umberto Simonetta, adapted by Umberto Simonetta, DR, Ruggero Maccari, Maurizio Costanzo. Direction: DR. Photography (Technicolor, Techniscope): Sandro D'Eva. Editing: Alberto Gallitti. Music: Armando Trovaioli. Art Direction: Luciano Ricceri. Players: Lino Capolicchio (*Giordano*), Janet Agren (*Diana*), Eugene Walter (*Nelson*), Jeff Morrow (*Professor Sid*), Umberto D'Orsi (*Car Driver*), Claudio Trionfi (*Mariolino*), Giuseppe Franco (*Claudio*), Gino Santercole (*Giorgio*), Dana Ghia, Giovanni Gianfelice. Produced by Franco Cristaldi for Vides, and by Pio Angeletti and Adriano De Micheli for Dean Film, Italnoleggio. 105 mins.

1970
LA MOGLIE DEL PRETE / THE PRIEST'S WIFE. Script: Ruggero Maccari, Bernardino Zapponi, from a story by Ruggero Maccari, Bernardino Zapponi, DR. Direction: DR. Photography (Eastmancolor, widescreen): Alfio Contini. Editing: Alberto Gallitti. Music: Armando Trovaioli. Art Direction: Lorenzo Baraldi. Players: Sophia Loren (*Valeria Billi*), Marcello Mastroianni (*Don Mario Carlisi*), Venantino Venantini (*Maurizio*), Pippo Starnazza (*Arduino Billi*), Miranda Campa (*Mrs. Billi*), Dana Ghia (*Lucia*), Jacques Stany (*Jimmy*), Anna Carena (*Don Mario's Mother*), Giuseppe Maffioli (*Davide Libretti*), Gino Cavalieri (*Don Filippo*), Augusto Mastrantoni (*Monsignor Caldana*), Brizio Montinaro, Paola Natale, Gino Lazzari. Produced by Carlo Ponti for Champion Film (Rome)/Editions Cinématographiques Françaises (Paris) 108 mins.

1971
NOI DONNE SIAMO FATTE COSI' / WOMEN: SO WE ARE MADE. Film in 12 episodes. Script: DR, Luciano Vincenzoni, Giuseppe Catalano, Age and Scarpelli, Ettore Scola, Rodolfo Sonego. Direction: DR. Photography (Technicolor): Carlo Di Palma. Editing: Alberto Gallitti. Music: Armando Trovaioli. Art Direction: Luigi Scaccianoce. Players: Monica Vitti (in 12 disguises), Enrico Maria Salerno (*The professor*),

Michele Cimarosa, ettore Manni, Pupo De Luca, Greta vaillant, Clara Colosimo, Jean Rougeul, Carlo Giuffrè. Produced by Edmondo Amati for International Apollo Film. 106 mins.

1972
IN NOME DEL POPOLO ITALIANO / IN THE NAME OF THE ITALIAN PEOPLE. Script: Age and Scarpelli. Direction: DR. Photography (Technicolor): Sandro D'Eva. Editing: Alberto Gallitti. Music: Carlo Rustichelli. Art Direction: Luigi Scaccianoce. Players: Ugo Tognazzi (*Mariano Bonifazi*), Vittorio Gassman (*Lorenzo Santenocito*), Yvonne Furneaux (*Lavinia Santenocito*), Agostina Belli (*Silvana Lazzarini*), Michele Cimarosa (*Marshal Casciatelli*), Enrico Ragusa (*Lorenzo's Father*), Rosella Bergamonti (*Flora*), Edda Ferronao (*Waitress*), Marcella Albani (*Silvana's Mother*), Salvo Randone (*Silvana's Father*), Alfredo Adami (*Del Tomaso*), Mario Maranzana (*Colombo*), Franco D'Adda (*Lipparini*), Claudio Trionfi (*TV Reporter*), Pietro Tordi (*Rivaroli*). Produced by Edmondo Amati for International Apollo Film. 101 mins.

1973
MORDI E FUGGI / BITE AND RUN. Script: Ruggero Maccari, DR, Bernardino Zapponi. Direction: DR. Photography (colour): Luciano Tovoli. Editing: Alberto Gallitti. Music: Carlo Rustichelli. Art Direction: Luciano Ricceri. Players: Marcello Mastroianni (*Giulio Borsi*), Oliver Reed (*Fabrizio*), Carole André (*Danda*), Lionel Stander (*The General*), Nicoletta Machiavelli (*Sylva*), Bruno Cirino (*Raul*), Marcello Mando (*Spallone*), Gianni Agus (*Sergio*), Renzo Marignano (*Franco*), Barbara Pilavin (*Norma*), Luigi Zerbinati (*Giulio's Father-in-law*), Regina Bissio (*Elsa*), Filippo Degara (*Waiter*), Gianfranco Barra, Gino Rocchetti, Giulio Baraghini, Alvaro Vitali, Lino Murolo, Jean Rougeul. Produced by Carlo Ponti for C. C. Champion (Rome)/Les Films Concordia (Paris). 105 mins.
SESSOMATTO / MAD SEX / HOW FUNNY CAN SEX BE? Film in 9 episodes. Script: Ruggero Maccari, from stories by DR, Ruggero Maccari. Direction: DR. Photography (Technicolor): Alfio Contini. Editing: Alberto Gallitti. Music: Armando Trovaioli. Art Direction: Lorenzo Baraldi. Players: Giancarlo Giannini (in 9 disguises), Laura Antonelli (in 8 disguises), Paola Borboni (*Esperia*), Cinzia Romanazzi (*Giovanna*), Dulio Del Prete (*Vittorio*), Carla Mancini (*Waitress*), Franca Scagnetti, Lorenzo Piani, Patrizia Mauro, Pippo Starnazza. Produced by Pio Angeletti and Adriano De Micheli for Dean Film, Cinetirrena. 116 mins.

1974
PROFUMO DI DONNA / SCENT OF A WOMAN / THAT FEMALE SCENT. Script: Ruggero Maccari, DR, from the novel *Il buio e il miele* by Giovanni Arpino. Direction: DR. Photography (Technicolor): Claudio Cirillo. Editing: Alberto Gallitti. Music: Armando Trovaioli. Art Direction: Lorenzo Baraldi. Players: Vittorio Gassman (*Captain Fausto*), Alessandro Momo

(*Giovanni Bertazzi*), Agostina Belli (*Sara*), Moira Orfei (*Mirka*), Franco Ricci (*Raffaele*), Elena Veronese (*Michelina*), Stefania Spugnini (*Candida*), Lorenzo Piani (*Don Carlo*), Sergio Dipinto (*Vincenzo's Attendant*), Marisa Volonnino (*Ines*), Torindo Bernardi (*Vincenzo*), Carla Mancini (*Natalina*). Produced by Pio Angeletti and Adriano De Micheli for Dean Film. 103 mins.

1975
TELEFONI BIANCHI / WHITE TELEPHONES / THE CAREER OF A CHAMBERMAID. Script: Ruggero Maccari, DR, Bernardino Zapponi, from a story by DR, Bernardino Zapponi. Direction: DR. Photography (colour, Technospes): Claudio Cirillo. Editing: Alberto Gallitti. Music: Armando Trovaioll. Art Direction: Luciano Ricceri. Players: Agostina Belli (*Marcella Valmarin alias Alma Doris*), Vittorio Gassman (*Franco Denza*), Ugo Tognazzi (*Adelmo*), Cochi Ponzoni (*Roberto Trevisan*), Renato Pozzetto (*Bruno*), Maurizio Arena (*Mr. Luciani*), William Berger (*Swiss Industrialist*), Lino Toffolo (*Goldrano Rossi*), Dino Baldazzi (*Mussolini*), Paolo Baroni, Carla Terlizzi, Alvaro Vitali, Toni Maestri, Renate Schmidt. Produced by Pio Angeletti and Adriano De Micheli for Dean Film. 108 mins.

1976
ANIMA PERSA / LOST SOUL. Script: Bernardino Zapponi, DR, from the novel by Giovanni Arpino. Direction: DR. Photography (colour, Technospes): Tonino Delli Colli. Editing: Alberto Gallitti. Music: Francis Lai. Art Direction: Luciano Ricceri. Players: Vittorio Gassman (*Fabio Stolz*), Catherine Deneuve (*Sofia Stolz*), Danilo Mattei (*Tano*), Anicée Alvina (*Lucia*), Gino Cavalieri (*Versatti*), Michele Capnist (*The Duke*), Ester Carloni (*Annetta*). Produced by Pio Angeletti and Adriano de Micheli for Dean Film (Rome)/Les Productions Fox Europa (Paris). 101 mins.

1977
LA STANZA DEL VESCOVO / THE BISHOP'S ROOM. Script: Leo Benvenuti, Piero De Bernardi, Piero Chiara, DR, from the novel by Piero Chiara. Direction: DR. Photography (Telecolor): Franco Di Giacomo. Editing: Alberto Gallitti. Music: Armando Trovaioli. Art Direction: Luigi Scaccianoce. Players: Ugo Tognazzi (*Temistocle Orimbelli*), Ornella Muti (*Matilde Scrosati*), Patrick Dewaere (*Marco Maffei*), Gabriella Giacobbe (*Cleofe Orimbelli*), Marcello Turilli (*Berlusconi*), Katia Tchenko (*Charlotte*), Karin Verlier (*Germaine*), Lia Tanzi (*Landina*), Francesca Juvara (*Martina*), Pietro Mazzarella (*Brighenti*), Franco Sangermano (*The Judge*), Renzo Ozzano. Produced by Giovanni Bertolucci for Merope Film (Rome)/Carlton Film Export, Société Nouvelle Prodis (Paris). 110 mins.

1978
I NUOVI MOSTRI / THE NEW MONSTERS / VIVA ITALIA. Film in 14 episodes. Script: Age and Scarpelli, Ruggero Maccari, Bernardino Zapponi. Direction: DR, Mario Monicelli, Ettore Scola. In this portamanteau film DR did not sign the episodes he directed, including:

JOHNNY DORELLI AND GLORIA GUIDA IN *SESSO E VOLENTIERI*

SENZA PAROLE / NO WORDS. Players: Ornella Muti, Yorgo Voyagis. **MAMMINA MAMMONE.** Players: Ugo Tognazzi, Nerina Montagnani. **TANTUM ERGO.** Player: Vittorio Gassman. Photography (colour/Technospes): Tonino Delli Colli. Editing: Alberto Gallitti. Music: Armando Trovaioli. Art Direction: Luciano Ricceri. Produced by Pio Angeletti and Adriano De Micheli for Dean Film. 115 mins.
PRIMO AMORE / FIRST LOVE. Script: DR, Ruggero Maccari. Direction: DR. Photography (Eastmancolor): Tonino Delli Colli. Editing: Alberto Gallitti. Music: Riz Ortolani. Art Direction: Luciano Ricceri. Players: Ugo Tognazzi (*Ugo Cremonesi*), Ornella Muti (*Renata Mazzetti*), Mario Del Monaco (*Hospice's Director*), Caterina Boratto (*Lucy*), Ricarrdo Billi (*Augustarello*), Luigi Rossi (*Rossi*), Alberto Pastorino (*Hospice's Guest*), Louis Lambert (*Singer*), Marina Fraiese (*Polish Girl*), Fiona Florence, Enzo Maggio, Augusto Caverzasio, Tonino Bernardi, André Hildebrand, Palmira Zaccardi, Annunziata Pozzaglio, Nino Lembo, Vittorio Zarfati, Venantino Venantini. Produced by Pio Angeletti and Adriano De Micheli for Dean Film. 115 mins.

1979
CARO PAPA' / DEAR FATHER. Script: Bernardino Zapponi, Marco Risi, DR. Direction: DR. Photography

(colour, Technospes): Tonino Delli Colli. Editing: Alberto Gallitti. Music: Manuel De Sica. Art Direction: Luciano Ricceri. Players: Vittorio Gassman (*Albino Millozza*), Julien Guiomar (*Parrella*), Aurore Clément (*Margot*), Andrée Lachapelle (*Giulia Millozza*), Stefano Madia (*Marco Millozza*), Joanne Coté (*Laura*), Piero del Papa (*Duilio*), Clara Colosimo (*Myrta*), Josette Vaillant, Sergio Ciulli, Giuseppe Ferrera, Pietro Tordi, Ileana Fraia, Nguyen Duong Don, Andrew Lord Miller, Bruno Rosa, Mila Stanic, Antonino Maimone. Produced by Pio Angeletti and Adriano De Micheli for Dean Film (Rome)/ AMLF (Paris)/Prospect Films (Montreal). 106 mins.

1980
SONO FOTOGENICO / I AM PHOTOGENIC. Script: DR, Massimo Franciosa, Marco Risi. Direction: DR. Photography (colour): Tonino Delli Colli. Editing: Alberto Gallitti. Music: Manuel De Sica. Art Direction: Ezio Altieri. Players: Renato Pozzetto (*Antonio*), Edwige Fenech (*Cinzia*), Aldo Maccione (*Pedretti*), Julien Guiomar (*Carlo Simoni*), Michel Galabru (*Del Giudice*), Gino Santercole, Massimo Boldi, Livia Ermolli, Paolo Baroni, Eolo Capritti, Salvatore Campochiaro, and Ugo Tognazzi, Barbara Bouchet, Vittorio Gassman, Mario Monicelli (all playing themselves). Produced by Pio Angeletti and Adriano De Micheli for International Dean Film (Rome)/Marceau Cocinor (Paris). 117 mins.

1981
FANTASMA D'AMORE / GHOST OF LOVE. Script: Bernardino Zapponi, DR., from the novel by Mino Milani. Direction: DR. Photography (Technicolor): Tonino Delli Colli. Editing: Alberto Gallitti. Music: Riz Ortolani. Art Direction: Giuseppe Mangano. Players: Marcello Mastroianni (*Nino Monti*), Romy Schneider (*Anna*), Wolfgang Preiss (*Count Zini*), Eva Maria Meineche, Victoria Zinni, Michael Kroecher. Produced by Pio Angeletti and Adriano De Micheli for International Dean Film (Rome)/AMLF (Paris)/Roxy Film (Munich). 93 mins.

1982
SESSO E VOLENTIERI / SEX AND VIOLENCE. Film in 10 episodes. Script: Bernardino Zapponi, Enrico Vanzina, DR. Direction: DR. Photography (Technicolor): Sandro D'Eva. Editing: Alberto Galliti. Music: Fred Bongusto. Art Direction: Beppe Mangano. Players: Johnny Dorelli (in 10 disguises), Laura Antonelli (in 4 disguises), Gloria Guida (in 5 disguises), Yorgo Voyagis, Pippo Santanastaso. Produced by Pio Angeletti and Adriano De Micheli for International Dean Film. 111 mins.

Andrei Tarkovsky

by Marcel Martin

One of the greatest cineastes of our time, Andrei Tarkovsky is also one of the least recognised on account of his being so difficult to grasp. Five feature films in twenty years amount to very little, but are sufficient to assure him a prominent place in the history of the cinema. Most of his films have hit the headlines as a result of the difficulties they have encountered in seeing the light of day and in reaching the West. This air of *scandale* has not made their proper appreciation any easier. On the other hand, their considerable thematic range has not helped the public and the critics to acknowledge this director as an *auteur* and not just as a mere director. Finally, the secretive side of the man himself, and his reluctance to expatiate on the meaning of his films have certainly contributed to this disregard of his work by large audiences and even by enlightened critics. Thus, not until now has he figured among the "Directors of the Year" chosen annually by IFG since 1964.

The Italian historian, Giovanni Buttafava, one of the leading authorities on Soviet cinema, has written that the "Thinking Ocean" of *Solaris* is also "the ocean of cinema on which the island of Solaris is floating."[1] This metaphor may be equally well applied to Tarkovsky's entire *œuvre*, which is in some way drifting, without any apparent home port or precise destination, on the ocean of world cinema. A close study of these films allows one to escape from this perplexity and discover the global pattern of Tarkovsky's work.

ANDREI TARKOVSKY was born on April 4, 1932, in Moscow. His father, Arseni, was a well-known poet, some of whose verse is declaimed in *Mirror*. Tarkovsky himself takes up the story: "How did I come to the cinema? During my high school period I attended the School of Music, and I did some painting. In 1952 I enrolled in the Institute of Oriental Languages, where I studied Arabic. All this wasn't for me. Then I worked as a geological prospector in Siberia. And in 1956 I entered the State Institute for Cinema (VGIK), under Mikhail Romm. I left in 1960. My diploma work at the end of my course was the medium-length *The Steamroller and the Violin*,

which was very important for me because it was then that I met the cameraman Vadim Yusov, and the composer Vyacheslav Ovchinnikov, with whom I have continued working."[2]

This first student effort already contains the major themes of Tarkovsky's future work. The protagonist is a young violinist, just twelve years old, who is unfulfilled by his studies and dreams of becoming a steamroller driver. Beneath this anecdote (which one imagines may be autobiographical) lies concealed the ideological metaphor for a reflection on the creative artist, a rather sceptical comment on art as an end in itself and as the meaning of life, and on the privilege the artist enjoys, of creating in an ivory tower and by means of a sort of divine grace reserved for an elite. This rejection of elitism is also the key to the ideological message of *Andrei Rublev*.

In 1961, Tarkovsky made his first feature film, *Ivan's Childhood*, which won the Golden Lion at Venice the following year and became the shining symbol of a renaissance in Soviet cinema. Once again a child of twelve is at the centre of the drama: when his mother is killed by the Nazis, the young Ivan joins up to fight against the invading Germans and volunteers for the most dangerous assignments. One evening he leaves on a mission and fails to return. Later, in the ruins of Berlin, his commanding officer finds a file reporting his having been condemned to death and hung.

In a famous and neglected text, Sartre offered a penetrating analysis of the character: "Ivan is mad, he is a monster. He is a little hero. In truth, he is the most innocent and touching victim of the war. This boy, whom one cannot help but like, has been forged by violence . . . Isn't there here, in the narrowest sense of the term, a significant *criticism* of the positive hero?"[3] And to describe the style of the film, Sartre employs the term "socialist surrealism," already used by the poet Voznesensky. And it is true that one finds in *Ivan's Childhood* a kind of collage of episodes drawn with the most sober realism, and others marked by a feverish aestheticism.

With *Andrei Rublev*, the cineaste achieved

STILL FROM *THE STEAMROLLER AND THE VIOLIN*

complete mastery of plastic expression at the same time as he was clearly formulating his intellectual message, which he described in the following terms: "Whether he wants to fly before he is able to, or cast a bell before he has learned to do so, or paint an icon in a style never seen before – all these actions demand that a man, as the price of creation, absorbs himself into his work, gives himself utterly . . . Creation requires the integral gift of being." Naturally, in making this comment on the characters, the director is also referring to his personal problems with the film: completed in 1967, officially screened at Cannes in 1969 (where it won the International Critics' Prize), *Andrei Rublev* was released in Moscow only in 1971, along with minor cuts approved and accepted by the director himself. More than the great icon painter of the Russian Quattrocento (who retreats into silence and inactivity because he feels that his art cannot help people to live), it is the bell-founder's son who is the real hero of the story in

that he builds a masterpiece because he is literally *inspired* by popular enthusiasm. While it is true that the artist has in him some "divine spark," he can only really create in so far as he is the *medium* for his people's genius.

After the prolonged vicissitudes of the "affair" stirred up by this film, Tarkovsky appeared to take refuge in science fiction with *Solaris*, as though to escape his earthly problems. However, he declared with regard to this new production: "The idea I had during the shooting was of transferring the entire plot to Earth. I did not succeed." It is without doubt Tarkovsky's most poorly received and worst-understood work. The idea, nevertheless, is simple. On the planet Solaris, surrounded by a "Thinking Ocean," some scientists perceive the materialisation of their fantasies and suffering. One, for instance, sees the double of his wife, whom he always loved but who has recently committed suicide, with him to blame. These men are at grips with an obsessive past, shameful even, from which they cannot free themselves.

The moral behind the adventure is that everyone must assume responsibility for his past and before the collective mass. Also that Man must take into consideration the problems that he will have to confront in the future as a result of scientific progress; this moral message precisely recalls Antonioni's famous dictum, a decade earlier: "Man, who has no fear of the scientific unknown, is afraid of the moral unknown." It's a matter here of "moral fiction" rather than science fiction, which is why the director would have liked to transfer to Earth a problem concerning each and every one of us. But among these obsessive memories there can also be sudden moments of happiness, like the one at the close of this sombre film: the sociologist sees himself again as a child with his father in front of the family *izba* (cottage), and this

image, floating on the surface of the "Thinking Ocean," recalls the picture of Ivan among the ruins of the Reich's Chancellery.

Thus we return to the theme of childhood, evoked by the final image of *Solaris*, and stressed by the opening sequence of *Mirror*, in which an inhibited adolescent boy is convinced by a psychologist that he can talk like everyone else and thus free himself from the intolerable past. This mirror reflects a fragmented autobiography, a memoir bursting out in all directions according to the whims of reverie. "It's the story of my mother and thus of a part of my own life," Tarkovsky has said. "The film contains only genuine incidents. It's a confession." The mother's life is refracted by the memories of the child, against whom is superimposed the adult he has become through the figure of his father, just as the image of his mother is superimposed on that of the director's wife.

STILL FROM *ANDREI RUBLEV*

STILL FROM *SOLARIS*, WITH NATALYA BONDARCHUK AND DONATAS BANIONIS

The unspoken cause of these disturbing recollections was the separation of the parents in 1935, with the mother remaining alone with the young Tarkovsky. The poems of Arseni, read offscreen by the writer himself, are like a reflection of the father, superimposed by the grown-up Andrei on the fleeting images of the offspring himself. The silent adolescent of the opening sequence is clearly the cineaste himself, locked, like Rublev, in the silence that precedes a fresh creative spell. This reputedly "difficult" film is in fact its director's most secretive, the film in which he liberates himself metaphorically from the shock brought about by the split-up of his parents. Prior to this point he had referred to his childhood only through that of other individuals. *Mirror* is a parable in which Tarkovsky lets it be known that he is recovering his powers of address by exorcising the ghosts of his childhood, while the voice of his father, the poet, guides him along the road towards artistic creation.

With *Stalker*, he returns to science fiction, but without relinquishing his regular thematic concerns. As in his previous films, it is once again a child who is the true protagonist, for she is the bearer of despair: the deformed daughter (who, in the novel by the brothers Strugatsky, is a little monkey, produced by mutation) seems to be the sole excuse for the Stalker to persist with his dangerous missions, as though he had been tempted to use the powers of the "Wishing Room" to effect her cure. But he cannot formulate this wish, because hope is indispensable to Man who, in the words of another Russian author, "does not live by pain alone." And the moral of the film is that the source of all hope is Man and not some superior power.

This journey into the Zone is merely a

metaphor for a descent into our inmost selves. The Stalker is not just a guide but a real medium. He is an enlightened believer: "One must have faith," he says, and he regrets that "people think only of gorging themselves." But the possible mystical interpretation of the film conflicts with Tarkovsky's agnosticism. "I have no organ through which one may feel God again," he has declared. But he has also spoken of the "spiritual crisis" through which Man is passing. The conclusion is that the cineaste should be a *humanist moralist*, who reckons that Man must believe in universal values and who emphasises that faith in these values is in the process of being lost in our materialist societies. And if the Scientist refuses to place his atomic bomb in the "Wishing Room," it is because he is finally convinced that hope, however false, is vital for Men in order that they may continue living.

Are the films of Tarkovsky mere stages in a difficult and unwearying quest for the absolute? Yes, but for an absolute that belongs to humanistic belief, the belief that each person is capable of finding in himself the strength and the genius for acting for the common good, in particular by means of artistic creation. If certain of his films have fallen victim to chicanery on the part of the Soviet authorites, it is because the ideology they express does not spring from orthodox Marxism, but rather from a kind of existentialist philosophy inherited from traditional Russian thinking, from writers such as Tolstoy and Dostoyevsky. Besides, these films, often criticised for their hermetic nature, do not constitute a simple meal for the mass public even if they escape the charge of being elitist. Everyone can find in them some stimulus for his own moral and intellectual consideration. Tarkovsky demands a great deal from the viewer, but if he refuses to vulgarise both his style and his content, it is because he honours the public by believing it capable of participation and a sympathetic response.

[1] *Film URSS 70* (Marsilio Editori, Venezia/Mostra Internazionale del Nuovo Cinema, Pesaro, 1980).
[2] Quoted in an interview with Luda and Jean Schnitzer, in *Andrei Rublev* (Editeurs Français Réunis, 1970).
[3] "Discussion sur la critique à propos de *L'enfance d'Ivan*" (in *Situations, VIII*, Gallimard, Paris, 1965).

ALISA FREINDLIKH IN *STALKER*

TARKOVSKY FILMOGRAPHY

1960
KATOK I SKRIPKA / THE STEAMROLLER AND THE VIOLIN. Script: Andrei Mikhalkov-Konchalovsky, AT. Direction: AT. Photography (Sovcolor) Vadim Yusov. Music: Vyacheslav Ovchinnikov. Production Design: S. Agoyan. Players: Igor Fomchenko (*Sasha*), Vladimir Zamansky (*Sergei*), N. Arkhangelskaya (*Small Girl*). Produced by Mosfilm Children's Film Unit. 50 mins.

1962
IVANOVO DETSTVO / IVAN'S CHILDHOOD. Script: Vladimir Bogomolov, Michael Papava, from the story *Ivan* by Bogomolov. Direction: AT. Photography: Vadim Yusov. Music: Vyacheslav Ovchinnikov. Art Direction: V. Chernyaev. Sound: E. Zelentsova. Players: Kolya Burlyaev (*Ivan*), I. Tarkovskaya (*His Mother*), Valentin Zubkov (*Captain Kholin*), Y. Zharikov (*Lieutenant Galtsev*), V. Malyavina (*Masha*), D. Milyutenko (*Old Man*), S. Krylov (*Katasanov*), N. Grino (*Gryaznov*). Produced by Mosfilm. 95 mins.

1966
ANDREI RUBLYOV / ANDREI RUBLEV. Script: Andrei Mikhalkov-Konchalovsky, AT. Direction: AT. Photography (scope, part colour): Vadim Yusov. Music:

Vyacheslav Ovchinnikov. Art Direction: Yevgeni Chernyaev. Sound: I. Zelentsova. Players: Anatoli Solonitsyn (*Andrei Rublev*), Ivan Lapikov (*Kirill*), Nikolai Grinko (*Daniel the Black*), Nikolai Sergeyev (*Theophanes the Greek*), Irma Raush (*Deaf-and-Dumb Girl*), Nikolai Burlyaev (*Boriska*), Rolan Bykov (*Buffoon*), Yuri Nikulin (*Patrikey*), Mikhail Kononov (*Fomka*), Yuri Nazarov (*Grand Duke*), Nikolai Grabbe, S. Krilov, Bolot Beizhenaliev, B. Matisik, A. Obukhov, Volodya Titov. Produced by Mosfilm. 146 mins. in UK (185 mins. originally in U.S.S.R.).

1972
SOLYARIS / SOLARIS. Script: AT, Friedrich Gorenstein, from the novel by Stanislaw Lem. Direction: AT. Photography (Sovcolor, scope): Vadim Yusov. Music: J. S. Bach, Eduard Artemiev. Art Direction: Mikhail Romadin. Players: Natalya Bondarchuk (*Hari*), Donatas Banionis (*Kris Kelvin*), Yuri Jarvet (*Snauth*), Anatoli Solonitsyn (*Sartorius*), Vladislav Dvorzhetski (*Burton*), Nikolai Grinko (*Father*), Sos Sarkissian (*Gibaryan*), Sergei Paradzhanov. Produced by Mosfilm. 165 mins.

1975
ZERKALO / MIRROR. Script: AT, Alexandr Misharin. Direction: AT. Photography (part colour): Georgi Rerberg. Editing: L. Feiginova. Music: Eduard Artemiev, J. S. Bach, Giovanni Battista Pergolesi, Henry Purcell. Art Direction: Nikolai Dvigubsky. Sound: Semyon Litvinov. Players: Margarita Terekhova (*Alexei's Mother/Natalya*), Filip Yankovsky (*Alexei, aged 5*), Ignat Daniltsev (*Ignat/Alexei, aged 12*), Oleg Yankovsky (*Father*), Nikolai Grinko (*Man at Printing Shop*), Alla Demidova (*Lisa*), Yuri Nazarov (*Military Instructor*), Anatoli Solonitsyn (*Passer-by*), Innokenti Smoktunovsky (*Voice of Alexei, the Narrator*), L. Tarkovskaya (*Alexei's Mother, as an Old Woman*), Tamara Ogorodnikova, Y. Sventikov, T. Reshetnikova, E. del Bosque, L. Correcher, A. Gutierres, D. Garcia, T. Pames, Teresa del Bosque, Tatiana del Bosque. Produced by Mosfilm Unit 4. 106 mins.

1979
STALKER. Script: Arkadi Strugatsky, Boris Strugatsky, from their story *Roadside Picnic*. Direction: AT. Photography (colour): Alexandr Knyazhinsky. Editing: L. Feiginova. Music: Eduard Artemiev. Art Direction: AT. Sets: A. Merkulov. Sound: V. Sharun. Players: Alexandr Kaidanovsky (*Stalker*), Anatoli Solonitsyn (*Writer*), Nikolai Grinko (*Professor*), Alisa Freindlikh (*Stalker's Wife*), Natasha Abramova, F. Yurna, E. Kostin, R. Rendi. Produced by Mosfilm Unit 2. 161 mins.

THE VOYAGERS IN TARKOVSKY'S *STALKER*

WORLD SURVEY

Afghanistan

by Lyle Pearson

The Third World Film Festival in Paris extended an invitation to Afghanistan's most popular director, Toryali Shafaq, again in 1982 and for some weeks it appeared that he might be able to attend. Several telexes had been received from the French Embassy in Kabul: Shafaq had agreed to enter his three feature films, *Mujesama Makandad* (*The Statues Are Laughing*, 1976), *Ghulam Ishq* (*The Slave of Love*, 1979), and *Janayat Karan* (*Criminals*, 1981). But a few days before that festival, in March, a final telex announced, "*Affaire annullée* (It's finished)." Shafaq could not, apparently, obtain a temporary visa to leave Afghanistan. Shafaq is now at work on his fourth feature film as a solo director, *Wattan Paniman* (*My Country Hides Me*), a script which he had previously discarded. He remains working for his own company, Shafaq Films, in Kabul.

Another source imparts that all other private production companies in Kabul also remain active. Aparcine Films' *Gharatgaran* (*Thieves*), Afghanistan's first 35mm colour (Fujicolor) film, is complete and the same company is preparing two new films. Gulistan Films' *House No. 555* is also complete. Aryana Films, headed by the director, producer and cinematographer Engineer Latif, remains open but the fate of its *Achtar Maskara* (*Achtar the Clown*) is unknown.

Some other film-making personalities, somewhat surprisingly, also remain in Kabul. Abdullah Shadan, the hero and one of the five co-directors of the 1974 *Rabhi Balkhie* (*Rabhi of Bakh*), is now the President of Afghan Television. (Afghanistan has had TV, in colour, only since 1978, government operated, on only one channel.) Film directors Latif and Abbas Shaban remain in private production but Daoud Farani, again one of the co-directors and co-stars of *Rabhi Balkhie*, has gone to Germany. A leading actress, whose name is unknown at this writing, has according to the above source, been "killed here in Kabul."

What is most surprising in Afghan cinema at the moment is that the government's Afghan Films has, after six years of rejection, apparently taken up the production of what could be the country's true revolutionary epic, *Tora* (a name). The script of *Tora* has been read on Afghan radio (also government operated), some sort of presentation has been made of it on TV, and the film itself, while "not yet finished," is under production. Tora, a revolutionary hero of several decades ago, was a Robin Hood-figure who trod on landowners for the sake of the poor. Perhaps a second Tora is needed to liberate Afghanistan from Soviet control. National independence, in the eyes of some observers, always involves an armed struggle. The situation for (not *of*) film-makers in Afghanistan in 1982 is none too clear.

While films continue to be made in Afghanistan less and less information comes from Afghanistan as time progresses. While it is known that the above film-makers are at work the details of their films, at least in the West, are not known. Marxism, in at least the commercial capital of Kabul, seems to be winning its battle over Islam.

A country which used to produce a revolution

as often as a film, Afghanistan continues to make films but has not had a revolution since the Soviet-backed coup of 1979. If there is not another revolution Afghanistan's films may never be shown in the West.

Given the feudal state of Afghan society before 1979 it is not surprising that some film producers have the financial strength to continue work. But with an audience available only in large

cities and the only other possibility of presenting their films in Soviet bloc countries, those producers must continue to work at least reluctantly (if not clandestinely) under an unpopular government.

Another revolution may come, but not from Kabul. Unlike its films, that revolution will come from the peasants. In its desire to compromise Afghan cinema may harm itself. Apparently, and unfortunately, it is not about to fight the Russians.

Argentina   by Alberto Tabbia

By the end of May 1982, Argentinian cinema could only be defined by its contradictions. On the one hand, costs had sky-rocketed under the ever-present economic crisis; on the other, the film institute (Instituto Nacional de Cinematografía), so far subordinate to the Secretary of Information, had been placed under the control of the Secretary of Culture. This hopeful move could ease the weight of censorship and military control.

Before this development, some films had already dared to tread on (by local standards) delicate ground. On a more realistic level *Plata dulce* and on a level of fable *El agujero en la pared* dealt critically with the period 1977-1980, when financial speculation was rife and local industries were liquidated. One wonders how far the adaptation of Manuel Puig's novel, *Pubis angelical*, will

dare go in alluding to the previous (and partially overlapping) period of the anti-terrorist crusade, missing persons and exiles – an "untouchable" subject, if any.

Adolfo Aristarain's *Tiempo de revancha*, with its first run of twenty-two weeks in 1981 (a success no other Argentinian film has had for a long time), seems to have done more than any political measure to attract more demanding audiences, usually reluctant to patronise Argentinian films, and to lead wary producers to try their luck at more ambitious projects. The war in the South Atlantic has only worsened the economic situation: but Argentina's film workers do not despair – "situation desperate but not serious" has been the diagnosis of the local industry for too long, and they have all learned to be survivors.

Focus on Adolfo Aristarain

Aristarain is undoubtedly the revelation of the past few years in the Argentinian film scene. A professional in the Hollywood tradition, he approached direction after years of work as an assistant with a first film of unusual promise – *La parte del leon* (*The Lion's Share* – see IFG 1980). After this remarkable debut, he directed two quickies in a series of musicals on hit parade LPs before being allowed to embark on his two most recent major films, one of which (*Tiempo de revancha*) has been the only ambitious local film to attract a large audience in recent years. It may, therefore, prove to be a landmark as well as a healthy influence on

present production trends. Aristarain's three main films show a devotion to *film noir* that goes way beyond European exercises. In this world of masculine loneliness and unreliable love affairs, of conspiracy as the only apparent world order, Aristarain has found a metaphor for the way of feeling in Buenos Aires – as witness both the popular music and high literature of that vast, crowded, featureless city.

Born in Buenos Aires in 1943, Aristarain started as an assistant in 1965. In 1968 he left for Spain, where he also worked as a 2nd Unit director in such co-productions as Lewis Gilbert's *The*

Adventurers, Gordon Flemyng's *The Last Grenade* and Melvin Frank's *A Touch of Class*. "When I left," he recalls, "I already knew my way around a set. What I learned in those films was how to work with much larger means. I watched everything – from conventional shooting with two or three cameras, where the editor is trusted to shape it up, to the freer approach of more imaginative directors. I used to shoot mentally the next day's work and then check if the director's way coincided with my ideas; if he didn't I tried to see which were the best solutions for that particular scene. I learned a lot from the Spanish director Mario Camus, who also became a friend."

Aristarain returned to Argentina in 1974, where he worked as an assistant for four years before his remarkable debut as a director. "*La parte del leon* was an old idea of mine. Nobody would have trusted me with a big budget but this screenplay had been tailored for a four-week shooting period and the film cost $80,000 at a time when the average Argentinian product cost $200,000. That's how I managed to break in." About his love-affair with *film noir*, Aristarain prefers to be modest. "If you choose it, you start with many advantages – suspense, action, a certain dose of erotic tension. You have to be really bad to lose the audience's attention with such elements!" But he also admits that "*film noir* is so appropriate to the cinema because it is the realm of understated emotion. Also, the genre's feeling of impending violence is so close to everyday reality."

Aristarain's notion of cinema is as recreation, not as an immediate reflection of life. "Directors like Hawks or Walsh invented an image of reality that, for me, is closer to real life. I always found the everyday types and situations of Neo-realism flat and uninteresting. On the screen, reality is invented, put together, has a logic of its own. I would like to achieve something close to what they did. I hate films 'with a message'; I just want to give the most truthful and critical images possible of the world I know."

Aristain's films to date are: *La parte del leon* (*The Lion's Share*, 1978); *La playa del amor* (*Love Beach*, 1979); *La discoteca del amor* (*Love Disco*, 1980); *Tiempo de revancha* (*Time for Revenge*, 1981); *Ultimos dias de la victima* (*Last Days of the Victim*, 1982).

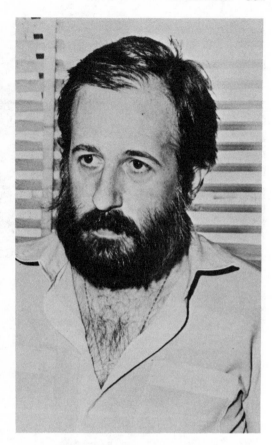

ADOLFO ARISTARAIN

TIEMPO DE REVANCHA
(Time for Revenge)

Script and direction: Adolfo Aristarain. Photography: Horacio Maira. Music: Enrique Kauderer. Editing: Eduardo López. Producers: Héctor Olivera and L. O. Repetto. Players: Federico Luppi, Haydée Padilla, Julio de Grazia, Rodolfo Ranni, Ulises Dumont, Aldo Barbero, Enrique Liporace, Joffre Soares, Arturo Maly. An Aries Cinematográfica Argentina Production.

Bengoa, a middle-aged technician in explosives with a compromising political record as an unionist, manages to get a "clean file" and finds work in a quarry in the far south. Isolated in a Patagonian settlement where cards, booze and the whorehouse

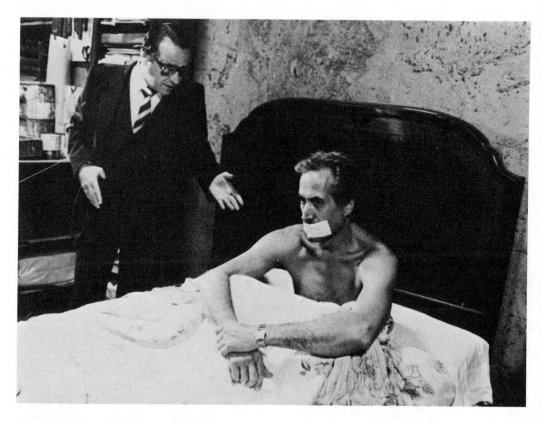

JULIO DE GRAZIA AND FEDERICO LUPPI IN *TIEMPO DE REVANCHA*, DIRECTED BY ADOLFO ARISTARAIN

are the only amusements, he discovers the multi-national company he works for violates security regulations. A companion proposes a plan to cheat the company – fake an accident and simulate having been struck dumb by the shock in a way that cannot be checked clinically. Bengoa goes ahead but, when his friend dies in the accident, he takes over the scheme. Speechless, he goes back to Buenos Aires, does not accept the large settlement proposed by the company, and goes out to expose the violation of security regulations. The company tries to expose his fraud but after a year Bengoa wins at court and the company is investigated. Reunited with his wife, he searches his apartment for hidden microphones, fills it with every possible source of noise, takes his wife under the shower and speaks into her ear – a story which is also inaudible for the audience. Next day he gets a tape from the company in which his words to his wife are clearly audible. He cuts off his tongue.

A triumph of narrative precision and astringency, there is not one overwritten line of dialogue or an empty atmospheric moment in this film. It never sacrifices its thriller structure to the possible allegorical readings of its fable. These may be negative virtues but there is also the question of the film's impact. For the first time in a very long while, an Argentinian film has conveyed to its audience something of the reality in which they live – beyond recognisable characters and milieux, a shared longing for hitting back at the impunity of power and a pervading feeling of frustration.

ALBERTO TABBIA

MÓNICA GALÁN, ULISES DUMONT AND FEDERICO LUPPI IN *ULTIMOS DIAS DE LA VICTIMA*

ULTIMOS DIAS DE LA VICTIMA
(Last Days of the Victim)

Script: A. A. and José Pablo Feinmann, based on the latter's novel. Direction: Adolfo Aristarain. Photography: Horacio Maira. Music: H. Emilio Kauderer. Special effects: Alex Mathews. Sound: Daniel Castronuovo. Editing: Eduardo López. Producers: Héctor Olivera and Luis O. Repetto. Players: Federico Luppi, Soledad Silveyra, Julio de Grazia, Ulises Dumont, China Zorrilla, Mónica Galán, Arturo Maly, Enrique Liporace, Noemí Morelli, Elena Tasisto, Carlos Ferreira. An Aries Cinematográfica Argentina Production.

Mendizábal, a professional killer, is given a new assignment – to keep an eye on and gather information about an intended victim. He moves to a boarding-house room whose windows face the victim's apartment. He contacts his ex-wife and son and develops a kind of family relationship with them. Later, he spies on the victim's encounters with a couple of women, and starts to tail these. When urged to go ahead with the killing, he breaks into the apartment and finds only one of the women; trying to make her release some information about the victim's whereabouts, he kills her. He asks his employers for an extension but instead is paid a token sum and taken off the job. Back in the boarding house he sees a light in the victim's apartment but finds it empty except for a gun pointing at him amid walls covered with hundreds of photographs of himself. He is shot. The intended victim arrives, collects Mendizábal's belongings and leaves under his identity in a series of shots almost identical to the opening ones in the film.

The narrative pace and economy, the gift for capturing dialogue and behaviour with precision – all rare in Argentinian films – are as strong here as in Aristarain's *Time for Revenge*. However, his new film shows an even stronger visual sense and discovers a new Buenos Aires, devoid of the usual tango nostalgia and colourful minor characters. The uneasy balance between fantasy and a recognisable realistic surface is so perfect that each element of fiction seems to echo in the experience and imagination of the audience. The killing of the victim's mistress – in a crescendo of violence leading to an orgiastic outburst of gunfire – is the most powerful sequence in the film and carries the traditional misogyny of *film noir* to unprecedented heights. Besides some outstanding performances by Julio de Grazia and Ulises Dumont (both regular actors in Aristarain's films), two newcomers also make an impact – Mónica Galán and Noemi Morelli, who have the kind of screen presence, at the same time intense and unaffected, that coincides with the director's approach.

ALBERTO TABBIA

LA INVITACION
(The Invitation)

Script: Rodolfo Mortola, Gustavo Bosset and Manuel Antín, based on the novel by Beatriz Guido. Direction: Manuel Antín. Photography: Alberto Basail. Editing: Enrique Murzio. Art Direction: Ponchi Morpurgo. Players: Graciela Alfano, Rodolfo Bebán, Pepe Soriano, Ulises Dumont, China Zorrilla, Boy Olmi, Elida Gay Palmer, Roberto Antier. Produced by Inversiones Cinematográficas.

The idiosyncratic fictional world of Beatriz Guido – the best-selling novelist who contributed so much to the best films of her late husband, Leopoldo Torre Nilsson – comes back to life in Manuel Antín's new film, his first since the adaptation of W. H. Hudson's *Far Away and Long Ago* in 1977. There is, again, an isolated, aristocratic manor, like in *The House of the Angel* – now a country state in the Andes forests. This time, the lonely over-sensitive daughter discovers that her father's mysterious guest is really a gun-runner and that the father himself is involved in the business. She goes to bed with the visitor and talks him into not making the delivery. Later, during the deer hunt which was the pretext for the invitation, the father has his unfaithful partner shot.

The year in which all this happens is 1973, when Perón returned to Argentina with support from young left-wing militants, many of whom were massacred at the airport by the old, hard-line, right-wing Peronists. This historical focus brings Guido's perennial "loss of innocence" theme into sharper, almost brutal contact with a gruesome page from recent Argentinian life. Antin's gift for poetic atmosphere and evocative lyricism are strengthened this time by an assured handling of the dramatic elements. There are some very good performances in the cast – from China Zorrilla as the grandmother, Elida Gay Palmer as the mother, and newcomer Boy Olmi as one of the young sons. The camerawork of Alberto Basail is, like all his work, sensitive and imaginative.

ALBERTO TABBIA

other films

PLATA DULCE (Easy Money). Dir: Fernando Ayala. Script: Oscar Viale, Jorge Goldenberg, from a story by Héctor Olivera. Players: Federico Luppi, Julio de Grazia, Flora Steinberg, Marina Skëll. A satirical comedy on the recent (1977–80) period of financial speculation. In a middle-class family, some members are more sensitive than others to the lure of a quick fortune but most ape the

GRACIELA ALFANO IN *LA INVITACION*

American way of life . . . The film includes week-end shopping sprees in Miami, colour TV-sets as hand-luggage on the flight back to Buenos Aires and other typical situations of an embarrassingly recent past. The authors call it "an attempt at self-criticism."

VOLVER (Coming Back). Dir: David Lipszyc. Script: Aída Bortnik. Players: Héctor Alterio, Graciela Dufau, Rodolfo Ranni, Hugo Arana. An Argentinian business man who "made it" in the U.S.A. is back home with a very special mission – liquidating a national firm on behalf of a multi-national conglomerate. In Buenos Aires he meets not only his ex-wife but also his own past and the whole question of national identity.

PUBIS ANGELICAL. Dir: Raúl de la Torre, based on the novel by Manuel Puig. Players: Graciela Borges, Silvia Pinal, Alfredo Alcón. An Argentinian exile in Mexico is torn between two men, a husband who only wants to own her and a terrorist lover who wants to kidnap the husband. As she fights for her life in the cancer ward, she tries to understand the political experiences of the early Seventies in Argentina. Her emotions and ideas are counterpointed by two other women's destinies on a dream stage – Hedy Lamarr's enslavement by the Hollywood star-system and a woman's enslavement in a futuristic society where sex and love have been banished.

SENORA DE NADIE (Nobody's Wife). Script and dir: María Luisa Bemberg. Players: Luisina Brando, Rodolfo Ranni, Julio Chávez, China Zorrilla, Susú Pecoraro. An upper-class married woman refuses to put up any longer with her husband's infidelities and leaves to set up house with a homosexual friend. A rather unexpected glimpse into the ways of female independence, the emotional, glossy film includes outstanding performances from veteran China Zorrilla and newcomer Susú Pecoraro.

LA CASA DE LAS SIETE TUMBAS (The House of the Seven Tombs). Dir: Pedro Stocki. Script: Atilio Polverini, Fernando Real. Players: Miguel Angel Solá, Soledad Silveyra, Cecilia Cenci, María Leal, María Rosa Gallo. An isolated attempt at horror and fantasy, including a lonely dark manor, rural eccentrics, a woman afraid, and large doses of madness and sex. A dim-witted girl gets her kicks from wallowing in the pigsty and playing around with the pigs. A treat for connoisseurs.

EL AGUJERO EN LA PARED (The Hole in the Wall). Script and dir: David José Kohon. Players: Alfredo Alcón, Mario Alarcón, María Leal. Bruno, a frustrated middle-aged man earning his living as a party photo-grapher, meets a character straight out of Buenos Aires picaresque fiction. His new friend seems to have "connec-tions" and leads Bruno from swindling aspiring film stars into shadier deals on the stock exchange, where he seems to have unaccountable "good tips." When Bruno wants to leave, his friend discloses a chilling, though perhaps not unexpected identity. Remember Faust?

LOS PASAJEROS DEL JARDIN (Garden Travellers). Dir: Alejandro Doria, based on a novel by Silvina Bullrich. Players: Graciela Borges, Rodolfo Ranni, Julio de Grazia, María Leal, Olga Zubarry. Two Argentinians meet in Paris, fall in love and are separated by cancer (his). She goes on touring and remembering past hap-pinesses in beautiful settings. One of Argentinian cine-ma's curiously few tries at the work of this domestic best-selling author of women's fiction.

¿SOMOS? (Are We?). Dir: Carlos-Hugo Christensen, based on a short story by Eduardo Gudino Kieffer. Players: Olga Zubarry, Silvia Kutika. A motherless teenager in search for his identity in a peculiar Buenos Aires neighbourhood – that of La Recoleta, where an aristocratic cemetery is surrounded by expensive res-taurants, fashionable night spots and Via Veneto-like cafe terraces.

FRANCISCO FLOR Y ARCILLA (Francisco, Flower and Clay). Dir: Carlos Procopiuk. Script: Juan Raúl Rithner. Players: Osvaldo Terranova. A first feature, shot on Super-8 but with a professional actor in the leading role, this story of the friendship between an older man (a widowed potter) and a fourteen-year-old boy, who would like to live close to nature, also explores the striking scenery of El Bolsón in Patagonia.

Australia

by David Stratton

The past year has seen the best of times and the worst of times for the Australian film industry. As noted in IFG a year ago, production has been booming as a result of the tax concessions intro-duced by the federal government; but more films do not usually mean better films, and general standards seem to have fallen in almost direct proportion to the increase in quantity. Though there have been a couple of excellent films, there have also been disappointing ones (some from established directors) and there has been a great deal of trash.

Meanwhile, as the Americans belatedly dis-covered Australian cinema (Ronald Reagan reportedly loved *Breaker Morant*; "Time" did a cover story; *Gallipoli* was released by Paramount and had rave reviews), Europeans, and especially the British, became more and more disenchanted. *Gallipoli* opened the 1981 London film festival but the film had mainly lukewarm reviews from the critical establishment; and the spring 1982 issue of "Sight and Sound" carried a briskly dismissive column about the Australian cinema.

Back home some local films continued to do

LISA PEERS AND NONI HAZLEHURST IN *MONKEY GRIP*

good business at the box-office, with some of the past year's greatest commercial successes from any source being *The Man from Snowy River*, *Gallipoli*, *Mad Max 2*, *Puberty Blues* and *Starstruck*. Others did terrible business; and many more still await distribution (and will probably wind up being shown only on television). The immediate prospects for future production are rather alarming. At last count more than 50 features were in active preparation for production during the next financial year (starting July 1, 1982) – far, far more than the industry can possibly handle. Furthermore, a rider to the tax concessions law requiring that films must be completed and earning money in the same year the money is invested, means (a) that productions will be rushed if summer (December–February) shooting is required, and (b) that no films at all will go into production from March–

July, hardly a satisfactory state of affairs.

Australian films and series (such as *A Town Like Alice*) capture consistently high ratings on local television. Even vintage classics – like the Ken Hall films of the Thirties which the multi-cultural TV station 0/28 played during Anzac Day week – capture huge viewing audiences.

One ugly note in the past year has been the anachronistic attempts of chief film censor Janet Strickland to bring censorship back to the bad old days of the Sixties. Her motives remain obscure, but there is no doubt that – without apparent community support, save for the lunatic Right – she has been tightening the screws. Her attempt to ban the Brazilian film *Pixote* from screening at the Sydney and Melbourne film festivals in June (the first time since 1970 that there has been an attempt to censor the festivals) was greeted with almost

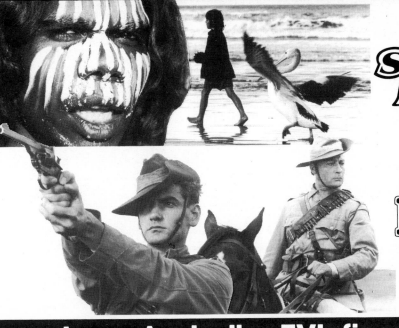

THI
FILM

In Australia, the New South Wales Film Corporation plays a major role in developing, packaging, marketing and investing in motion pictures.

Through the Australian Films Office Inc., its North American subsidiary, it has a Los Angeles base to take its films into the international marketplace.

And you'll find the corporation's representatives at the major selling events around the world – the American Film Market in Los Angeles, the Cannes Film Festival and the London Multi-Media Market.

Since 1976, it has put money into 19 feature films.

They include some of the breakthrough Australian movies of the last few years – such as Gill Armstrong's **My Brilliant Career** and Phil Noyce's **Newsfront.**

These are the films in which it has invested:

Crosstalk	Dimboola
Goodbye Paradise	Cathy's Child
The Best of Friends	My Brilliant Career
Hoodwink	Tim
The Club	The Odd Angry Shot
Stir	The Money Movers
The Last of the Knucklemen	The Night The Prowler
Maybe This Time	Newsfront
Thirst	The Picture Show Man
The Journalist	

NEW SOUTH WALES CORPORATION

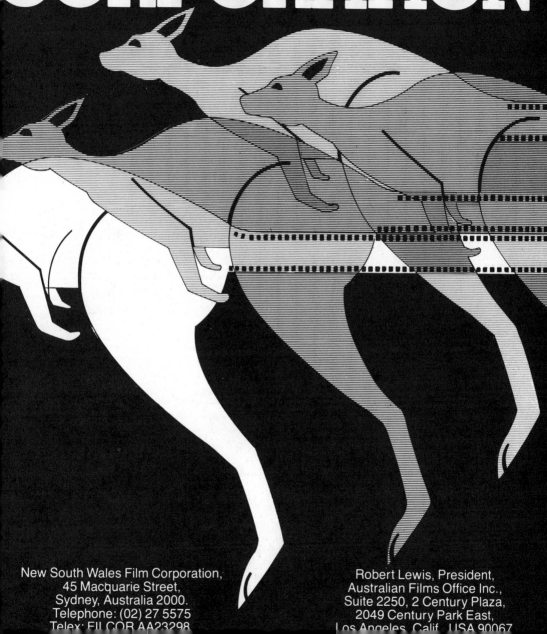

New South Wales Film Corporation,
45 Macquarie Street,
Sydney, Australia 2000.
Telephone: (02) 27 5575
Telex: FILCOR AA23298

Robert Lewis, President,
Australian Films Office Inc.,
Suite 2250, 2 Century Plaza,
2049 Century Park East,
Los Angeles, Calif., USA 90067

We're in the business of moving pictures

The Australian Film Commission was established to assist in the development, financing and marketing of the Australian film industry.

The AFC has offices in the United States and the United Kingdom to assist in the international marketing and distribution of Australian feature films, documentaries and television programmes.

Our representatives are available to advise you on all aspects of the Australian film industry.

Australian Film Commission

AUSTRALIA
David Field
(Director of Marketing),
Australian Film Commission,
8 West Street,
North Sydney,
N.S.W. 2060, Australia.
Telephone: (02) 922 6855
Telex: 25157

LONDON
Ray Atkinson
(UK European Representative),
Australian Film Commission,
Victory House,
99/101 Regent Street,
London W1, England,
Telephone: 439 1031
Telex: 28711 AUSFILM-G

AMERICA
Mike Harris
(North American Representative),
Australian Film Commission,
Suite 720,
9229 Sunset Boulevard,
Los Angeles,
California 90069, U.S.A.
Telephone: (213) 275 7074
Telex: 691355

universal condemnation from the film industry, the media, and politicians alike. The ban was over-ruled by the Appeal Board but the incident will not be forgotten easily.

There have been several good feature films this past year but certainly no masterpieces. The two highlights have been George Miller's *Mad Max 2* (re-titled *The Road Warrior* in the U.S.A.) and Ken Cameron's *Monkey Grip*. The two could not be more different. *Mad Max 2* is an energetic sequel to Miller's successful first feature and, aided by a much larger budget, an even greater success. This futuristic fantasy, spectacularly shot in the desert around Broken Hill, is virtually a cowboys-and-indians western in new guise. Miller proves himself again to be a dazzling technician and has cheerfully filled the film with bits of Australiana (including a lethal boomerang) as well as some spectacular stuntwork.

Monkey Grip, a first feature from former

MEL GIBSON AT THE WHEEL IN *MAD MAX 2*

schoolteacher Ken Cameron (who previously made some prize-winning short films), is taken from a popular counter-culture novel by Melbourne author Helen Garner. It is the story of a single mother (Noni Hazlehurst) and her infatuation with a young actor (Colin Friels) who is also a heroin addict. Although the film was made in Sydney, it manages to capture the atmosphere of the inner-Melbourne suburb of Carlton with considerable accuracy; several of its characters are seemingly based on (or inspired by) prominent Carlton citizens. Dominated by a glowing performance from Noni Hazlehurst, the film overcomes its slight narrative and presents a fascinating group of people – friends, lovers, rivals, victims. It is a credit to all concerned, especially talented producer Patricia Lovell (who co-produced *Gallipoli* with Robert Stigwood).

The biggest commercial success of the past year has been *The Man from Snowy River*, directed by (a different) George Miller. It is an unsatisfactory, clichéd piece of work but a very crafty commercial package. Its very title (one of Australia's best-loved poems) is almost a guarantee of across-the-community acceptance. With the added insurance of an extraneous American star (Kirk Douglas in a fatuous dual role) and cigarette-commercial style photography, it is the closest thing to an American film in style and look – yet with plenty of local Australian colour. Jack Thompson's part is miniscule but newcomer Tom Burlinson (as The Man) is a good find. Despite its clichéd dialogue and glossy look, it has the advantage of one of the better Australian scores written so far.

Gillian Armstrong's *Starstruck* is her first

JUDY DAVIS AND TUI BOW IN *HEATWAVE*

feature since *My Brilliant Career* and is another story of an ambitious young woman who, in this case, wants a brilliant career as a punk rock singer. Although commercially successful and handsome to look at (photography by Russell Boyd), the film is disappointing: its structure is awkward (especially the first reel in which the main characters are introduced) and the choreography is uninspiring. Jo Kennedy, who plays the ambitious teenage singer, is energetic but surprisingly clumsy, and Ross O'Donovan as her fourteen-year-old manager is singularly charmless. However, there is at least one excellent musical number and some good comic invention in the families of the two kids who run an old pub beneath Sydney's Harbour Bridge.

Phil Noyce's *Heatwave*, his second feature after *Newsfront*, is also rather uneven. Noyce again shows considerable talent as a director, and his story (based on real events) of the murderous tricks used by city developers and organised crime to evict people from old areas of Sydney is always interesting. However, Judy Davis proves this time to be an unappealing lead as an activist who rather unconvincingly starts an affair with the architect hero; and the film's climax – a shooting in a nightclub on New Year's Eve – is botched.

Donald Crombie's *The Killing of Angel Street* has an almost identical plot to *Heatwave*, but treats the subject more soberly. Despite good performances from Liz Alexander and John Hargreaves (as the owner of a threatened house and a communist unionist respectively) the film fails to spark, though there are a couple of genuinely scarey moments as the heroine finds herself in mortal danger. Crombie's second feature of the year, *Kitty and the Bagman*, is a jolly look at female gangsters in inner-Sydney in the Twenties. An impeccable production, told with plenty of bawdy humour and peopled with eccentrics almost worthy of Fellini, the film (like *Angel Street*) has a serious underlying theme of wholesale corruption both in the police force and in much of the Establishment.

A similar story is told in Kevin Dobson's *Squizzy Taylor*, the biography of a notorious Melbourne gangster of the early Twenties. Squizzy is played by actor-dancer-choreographer David Atkins who is very good as a rather nasty little punk. The modestly budgeted, but exceedingly handsome, production has some flat spots but is certainly one of the classier films of the year.

A promising debut was made by director Michael Caulfield with *Fighting Back*, the story of a schoolteacher's efforts to help a deeply disturbed 13-year-old boy. Though the character of the teacher is under-developed, that of the boy is presented in-depth; and there is an amazingly tough performance from young Paul Smith in the role.

John Duigan made two very good films during the past year: *Winter of Our Dreams* and *Far East*. Both star Bryan Brown, in the former as an ex-radical of 1968 (now settled into a trendy middle-class lifestyle) who forms a relationship with a young prostitute (Judy Davis). *Far East* is a loose re-working of *Casablanca*: Brown is a former soldier who fought in Vietnam and then stayed on in an (unnamed, but presumably the Philippines) Asian country where he runs a bar for visiting Australians. Enter an ex-flame (Helen Morse) and her journalist husband (John Bell) and, while sexual passion between Brown and Morse is re-kindled, Bell is arrested by the fascist police and has to be rescued by the resourceful Brown. A good, old-fashioned, entertaining movie, slightly marred by unnecessary use of slow motion during the final shoot-out.

Bruce Beresford left for the U.S.A. after completing *Puberty Blues*, the beautifully titled adaptation of a book by two teenage girls about the surfie-groupie scene on Sydney's southern beaches. The film rings true as a very accurate and well scripted look at a singularly charmless lifestyle; it is also well acted – Beresford is good with actors – by its mostly young cast.

Finally, and in some contrast, there is a 16mm feature worthy of attention. Ned Lander's *Wrong*

Side of the Road is a well-made drama about a travelling Aboriginal rock band and explores rural racism in Australia forthrightly and unflinchingly.

recent and forthcoming films

STARSTRUCK. Script: Stephen MacLean. Dir: Gillian Armstrong. Phot: Russell Boyd. Players: Jo Kennedy,

NORMAN KAY AND WENDY HUGHES IN *LONELY HEARTS*

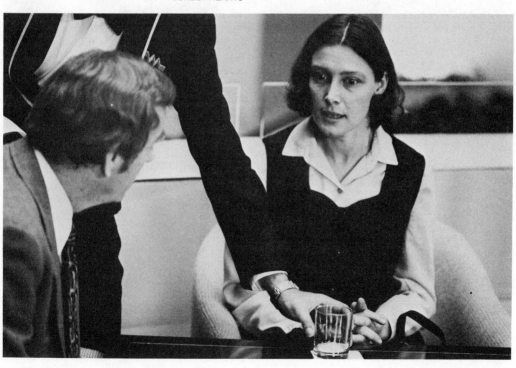

JACKIE KERIN IN *NEXT OF KIN*

Ross O'Donovan, Pat Evison, Margo Lee, Max Cullen, Ned Lander, Melissa Jaffer, John O'May, Dennis Miller. Prod: David Elfick, Richard Brennan, for Palm Beach Pictures.

KITTY AND THE BAGMAN. Script: Phillip Cornford, John Burnie. Dir: Donald Crombie. Phot: Dean Semler. Players: Liddy Clark, Val Lehman, John Stanton, Gerard McGuire, Collette Mann. Prod: Anthony Buckley, for Forest Home Films.

FAR EAST. Script and dir: John Duigan. Phot: Brian Probyn. Players: Bryan Brown, Helen Morse, John Bell, Bill Hunter, Raina McKeon, Sinan Leong. Prod: Richard Mason, for Alfred Road Films.

SQUIZZY TAYLOR. Script: Roger Simpson. Dir: Kevin Dobson. Phot: Dan Burstall. Players: David Atkins, Jacki Weaver, Alan Cassell, Steve Bisley, Kim Lewis, Cul Cullen, Michael Long. Prod: Roger Le Mesurier, for Simpson Le Mesurier Films.

FIGHTING BACK. Script: Michael Cove, Tom Jeffrey. Dir: Michael Caulfield. Phot: John Seale. Players: Lewis Fitz-Gerald, Paul Smith, Robyn Nevin, Kris McQuade. Prod: Sue Milliken, Tom Jeffrey, for Samson Productions.

WRONG SIDE OF THE ROAD. Script: Graeme Isaac, Ned Lander (in association with the cast). Dir: Ned Lander. Phot (16mm): Louis Irving. Players: No Fixed Address, Us Mob (rock groups). Prod: Ned Lander, Graeme Isaac, for INMA Productions.

A DANGEROUS SUMMER. Script: David Ambrose, Quentin Masters. Dir: Quentin Masters. Phot: Peter Hannan. Players: Tom Skerritt, James Mason, Ian Gilmour, Wendy Hughes, Kim Deacon, Ray Barrett, Guy Doleman. Prod: James McElroy, for McElroy & McElroy. Action drama in which an attempt to swindle an insurance company starts a massive bush fire. (Previously titled *A Burning Man*.)

THE PIRATE MOVIE. Script: Trevor Farrant. Dir: Ken Annakin. Phot: Robin Copping. Players: Kristy McNicol, Christopher Atkins, Gary McDonald, Bill Kerr, Ted Hamilton. Prod: David Joseph for JHI Produc-

tions. A musical updating of "The Pirates of Penzance."
THE SEVENTH MATCH. Script: Yoram Gross, Elizabeth Kata. Dir: Yoram Gross. Phot: Jenny Osche. Animated film about small child during a European war.
LONELY HEARTS. Script: John Clarke, Paul Cox. Dir: Paul Cox. Phot: Yuri Sokol. Players: Wendy Hughes, Norman Kaye, Julia Blake, Jon Finlayson. Prod: John B. Murray, for Adams Packer Films. A tragi-comedy about a love affair between two mature people.
FREEDOM. Script: John Emery. Dir: Scott Hicks. Phot: Ron Johanson. Players: Jon Blake, Jad Capelja, Candy Raymond, Charles Tingwell, Max Cullen, Reg Lye. Prod: Matt Carroll, for South Australian Film Corporation. An unemployed youth steals a car and goes off on an extended joy-ride with a girl hitch-hiker.
GOODBYE PARADISE. Script: Bob Ellis, Denny Lawrence. Dir: Carl Schultz. Players: Ray Barrett, Robyn Nevin, Janet Scrivener, Kate Fitzpatrick, Lex Marinos, Guy Doleman. Prod: Jane Scott for Petersham Pictures. An ex-policeman investigates a girl's disappearance in a winter holiday resort and uncovers a strange conspiracy.
RUN, REBECCA, RUN! Script: Charles Stamp. Dir: Peter Maxwell. Phot: Phil Pike. Players: Henri Szeps, Simone Buchanan, Adam Garnett. Prod: Brendon Lunney, for Independent Productions. The story of a girl who tries to help an illegal immigrant.
EARLY FROST. Script: Terry O'Connor. Dir: none credited. Phot: David Eggby. Players: Diana McLean, Jon Blake, Jan Kingsbury, Guy Doleman, Joanna Samuel. Prod: David Hannay, Geoff Brown, for David Hannay Productions. A killer stalks the streets in a Sydney suburb. (Previously titled *Something Wicked*.)
CROSSTALK. Script: Linda Lane, Mark Egerton (uncredited: Keith Salvat). Dir: Mark Egerton. Phot: Vincent Monton. Players: Gary Day, Panny Downie, Kim Deacon, John Ewart, Brian McDermott, Peter Collingwood. Prod: Errol Sullivan, for Wall to Wall Productions. A variation on *Rear Window*: a computer expert is confined to his Sydney apartment and his computer sees a murder. (Previously titled *Wall to Wall*.)
BREAKFAST IN PARADISE. Script: Morris Dalton. Dir: John Lamond. Phot: Ross Berryman. Players: Barbara Parkins, Rod Mullinar. Prod: John Lamond, for Motion Picture Enterprises. A romance in Paris for two professional people.
DOCTORS AND NURSES. Script: Morris Gleitzman, Doug Edwards, Robyn Moase, Tony Sheldon. Dir: Maurice Murphy. Phot: John Seale. Players: Pamela Stephenson, Bert Newton, Graeme Blundell, Andrew McFarlane, June Salter. Prod: Maurice Murphy, for Universal Entertainment Corporation. Child actors play hospital staff, adults their patients.
DUET FOR FOUR. Script: David Williamson. Dir: Tim Burstall. Phot: Dan Burstall. Players: Mike Preston, Wendy Hughes, Diane Cilento, Michael Pate, Gary Day, Vanessa Leigh, Sigrid Thornton, Rod Mullinar. Prod: Tom Burstall, Tim Burstall, for Burstall Productions. The personal problems of a Melbourne toy manufacturer. (Previously titled *Partners*.)
THE CLINIC. Script: Greg Millen. Dir: David Stevens.

Phot: Ian Baker. Prod: Robert Le Tet, Bob Weis, for The Film House. Comedy set in a VD clinic.
MOVING OUT. Script: Jan Sardi. Dir: Michael Pattinson. Phot: Vincent Monton. Players: Peter Sardi, Luciana Catenacci. Prod: Jayne Ballantine, for Pattinson Ballantine Pictures. The experiences of a teenage migrant boy in Melbourne.
NOW AND FOREVER. Script: Richard Cassidy. Dir: Adrian Carr. Phot: Don McAlpine. Players: Cheryl Ladd, Robert Coleby, Carmen Duncan, Christine Amor. Prod: Treisha Ghent, for Now and Forever Film Partnership. A marriage is shattered when the husband is accused of rape.
ON THE RUN. Script: Mende Brown, Michael Fisher. Dir: Mende Brown. Phot: Paul Onorato. Players: Rod Taylor, Paul Winfield, Beau Cox, Ray Meagher. Prod: Mende Brown, for Pigelu.
THE YEAR OF LIVING DANGEROUSLY. Script: David Williamson. Dir: Peter Weir. Phot: Russell Boyd. Players: Mel Gibson, Sigourney Weaver, Phipps Hunt. Prod: Jim McElroy for Wayang Productions and M-G-M. A strange triangular affair set in Djakarta during a time of political upheaval.
DUSTY. Script: Sonia Borg. Dir: John Richardson. Phot: Alex McPhee. Players: Bill Kerr, Noel Trevarthen, Carol Burns, John Stanton. Prod: Gil Brealey, for Dusty Productions. Adaptation of a classic novel about a sheepdog.
GINGER MEGGS. Script: Michael Latimer. Dir: Jonathan Dawson. Phot: John Seale. Players: Gary

WENDY HUGHES AS THE INVESTIGATOR IN *A DANGER-OUS SUMMER*

McDonald, Coral Kelly, Paul Daniel, Harold Hopkins, Gwen Plumb. Prod: John Sexton, for John Sexton Productions. A film version of a famous newspaper comic strip.
MIDNITE SPARES. Script: Terry Larsen. Dir: Quentin Masters. Phot: Geoff Burton. Players: James Laurie, Gia Carides, Max Cullen, Bruce Spence, David Argue. Prod: Tom Burstall, for Wednesday Investments. Action film about young people caught up in car stealing.
NEXT OF KIN. Script: Michael Heath, Tony Williams. Dir: Tony Williams. Phot: Gary Hansen. Players: Jackie Kerin, John Jarratt, Charles McCallum, Gerda Nicholson. Prod: Robert Le Tet, for The Film House. A thriller set in an old family home.
THE RETURN OF CAPTAIN INVINCIBLE. Script: Andrew Gaty, Stephen de Souza. Dir: Phillipe Mora. Phot: Mike Molloy. Players: Alan Arkin, Christopher Lee, Kate Fitzpatrick, Bill Hunter, Graham Kennedy, Michael Pate. Prod: Andrew Gaty, for Seven Keys. A flying super-hero and his comedy adventures.
RUNNIN' ON EMPTY. Script: Barry Tomblin. Dir: John Clark. Phot: David Gribble. Players: Terry Serio, Deborah Conway, Richard Moir, Max Cullen, Grahame Bond. Prod: Pom Oliver, for Film Corporation of Western Australia. A young factory-worker is obsessed with cars.
THE DARK ROOM. Script: Michael Brindley, Paul Harmon. Dir: Paul Harmon. Phot: Paul Onorato. Players: Alan Cassell, Anna Jemison, Svet Kovich. Prod: Tom Haydon, for Nadira Productions. An unstable young man discovers his father is having an affair with an attractive young woman.
DEAD EASY. Script and dir: Bert Deling. Phot: Mike Molloy, Tom Cowan. Players: Scott Burgess, Rosemary Paul, Tim McKenzie, Max Phipps, Tony Barry. Young people become involved with crime.
LADY, STAY DEAD. Script and dir: Terry Bourke. Phot: Ray Henman. Players: Chard Hayward, Louise Howitt, Deborah Coulls, Les Foxcroft. Prod: Terry

Bourke, for Ryntake Productions. Battle-of-wits between a young woman and a killer.
NORMAN LOVES ROSE. Script and dir: Henri Safran. Phot: Vincent Monton. Players: Carol Kane, Tony Owen, Warren Mitchell, Myra de Groot, David Downer. Prod: Henri Safran, Basil Appleby, for Norman Films. A young Jewish boy falls in love with his sister-in-law.

Listed last year and to date unreleased: **We of the Never-Never, Turkey Shoot, Double Deal.**

Projects

As mentioned earlier, some fifty films are projected for the year July 1982 to June 1983, and it will be interesting to see how many are made and released. Two of the more interesting projects are *Time's Raging*, to be directed by Sophia Turkiewicz from a script by her and Frank Moorehouse, and produced by Joan Long; and *For Love Alone*, to be directed by Stephen Wallace and produced by Margaret Fink. There is still talk of making films about the explorers Burke and Wills and about some strange events of 1915 (*The Battle of Broken Hill*).

Focus on Shorts

One or two outstanding short films brightened up the scene. Notable was Gil Scrine's *Home on the Range*, a powerful indictment of CIA meddling in Australian affairs, particularly in relation to the 1975 sacking of the Whitlam government. This film won the documentary section of the 1982 Greater Union Awards at the Sydney film festival. Also of consequence is *Greetings from Wollongong*, by Mary Callaghan, winner of the 1982 Rouben Mamoulian Award, a dramatic featurette about unemployed youth in a large industrial centre. Martha Ansara made *Changing the Needle* in Vietnam, a film about a drug rehabilitation programme. Stephen Wallace made an excellent short fiction film, *Captives of Care*, about patients in a home for the disabled who are agitating for better treatment. Andrew Pike's *Angels of War* is an exemplary documentary about the way native New Guineans helped Australian soldiers during the Second World War. And Rivka Hartman's *A Most Attractive Man* is a sardonic feminist comedy about a woman involved with a man who takes advantage of her at every turn.

PETER COUSENS AND CATHRIN LYNCH IN THE SOUTH AUSTRALIAN FILM CORPORATION'S PRODUCTION OF *UNDER CAPRICORN*, MADE FOR TELEVISION

1981 Australian Film Awards

Best Film: *Gallipoli*
Best Director: Peter Weir (*Gallipoli*)

Best Actor: Mel Gibson (*Gallipoli*)
Best Actress: Judy Davis (*Winter of Our Dreams*)
Best Supporting Actor: Bill Hunter (*Gallipoli*)
Best Supporting Actress: Judy Davis (*Hoodwink*)
Best Photography: Russell Boyd (*Gallipoli*)
Best Screenplay: David Williamson (*Gallipoli*)
Best Sound: Don Connolly, Greg Bell, Peter Fenton (*Gallipoli*)
Best Editor: William Anderson (*Gallipoli*)
Best Music: Grahame Bond, Rory O'Donoghue (*Fatty Finn*)
Best Art Direction: Herbert Pinter, Wendy Weir (*Gallipoli*)
Best Costumes: Norma Moriceau (*Fatty Finn*)
Best Documentary: *Stepping Out* (Chris Noonan)
Best Short Fiction: *Captives of Care* (Stephen Wallace)
Best Experimental: *Drink the Moon* (Mark Foster)
Jury Prize: Ned Lander for *Wrong Side of the Road*
Longford Award: Phillip Adams

1982 Greater Union Awards

Best General: *Shadows* (Royden Irvine)
Best Documentary: *Home on the Range* (Gil Scrine)
Best Fiction: *Last Breakfast in Paradise* (Meg Stewart)
Rouben Mamoulian Award: *Greetings from Wollongong* (Mary Callaghan)

Austria   by Goswin Dörfler

One year after the legislation for film encouragement came into force, the production situation has not changed drastically. It is true that 14 Austrian films were premiered in 1981 (7 of these were co-productions: 4 with Germany, 2 with the U.S.A., and 1 with Britain), as against 6 films in 1980, but this increase – indeed this doubling of the production figures – might well have nothing to do with the legislation as the preparatory work for these films had begun before the new law. The practical effects can only be judged in two or three years, when the whole system is running smoothly. There have been subsidies from the state or from Vienna in the past; to what extent the new law will help Austrian film, only the future will show. So let us stay with the past year's actual events instead of trying to forecast the future.

The Vienna Film Week (the Viennale) took place last year for the 21st time (November 3-12, 1981) in the Künstlerhauskino in Vienna. The programme consisted of 31 Austrian and foreign films (from 15 countries); there was also a Hungarian film week and a Portuguese season. As a curiosity, there were screenings of nine of the Worst Films of All Time, for which Harry Medved, co-founder of the Golden Turkey Award, had come from California. The Viennale programme was mainly selected from films unknown to the Viennese public, films that would have little commercial chance in Austria. The most important films were Rosi's *Tre fratelli*, Truffaut's *Le dernier métro* and *La femme d'à côté*, Godard's *Sauve qui peut (la vie)*, Blier's *Beau-père*, Menzel's *Postřižiny*, Varda's *Mur murs*, and Loach's *Looks and Smiles*. The press rightly acknowledged the efforts of the organisers to treat film-makers and buffs to a spectrum of representative, interesting films that were worthy of discussion.

The Austrian Film Days (Österreichischen Filmtage) took place for the fifth time on September 30-October 3, 1981, once again in the small industrial town of Kapfenberg in Styria. There were guests from eight countries, all of whom took great interest in the festival. The festival is becoming more and more a review of Austrian cinema – as Pula, for instance, is for Yugoslav films – and the film-buff can see a comparatively full survey of Austrian film in the course of a year.

Finally, the summer exhibition and retrospective organised annually by the Austrian Film Archive at Laxenburg near Vienna, the former summer residence of the Hapsburg family, took place for the 11th time on June 13-October 18, 1981. This year the theme was "Film – Cinema – Advertising," accompanied by slide, video and film shows. The retrospective "Film Stars from Europe, as shown by France and Italy" showed an interesting selection of 38 feature films. The events were comparatively well-attended, and yet this type of retrospective is slowly becoming less useful. If the organisers do not take more care over their selection, and do not find more original, attractive retrospectives, then Laxenburg Castle with its beautiful park (in which the Empress Maria Theresia used to stroll) will become more attractive than the event itself.

Some 304 films were premiered in Austria from January 1 to December 31, 1980; in 1981 there were 331 films, from 22 different countries. Most of them – 119, in fact – came from the U.S.A. Some 52 were from West Germany, 40 from France, 36 from Italy, 26 from Hongkong, 17 from England, 11 from Austria itself, 6 each from Spain and Switzerland, 5 from Canada, 2 from the U.S.S.R. and one each from Australia, East Germany, Hungary, Israel, Jamaica, Japan, Mexico, the Netherlands, Panama, Poland and Sweden. Of those 331 features, 14 were shown in their original language (10 in English, one each in French, Italian, Russian, and Swedish); 322 films were in colour, 9 in black-and-white.

Filmgoing statistics for 1981 were as follows. In 1980 there were 17,533,899 admissions (of which 6,044,432 were in Vienna); in 1981 the total was 18,297,133 (6,263,033 in Vienna). By the end of 1981 the total number of cinemas had risen again to 521 (from 510 in 1980), of which 91 were in Vienna (82 in 1980). By December 31, 1981, the number of TV licences issued was 2,232,814 (up from 2,226,754 a year earlier).

Austrian films of 1981

DER SCHÜLER GERBER (The Pupil Gerber). Script: Friedrich Torberg, Werner Schneyder, Wolfgang Glück, based on the novel "Der Schüler Gerber" by Friedrich Torberg. Dir: Wolfgang Glück. Phot (colour): Xaver Schwarzenberger. Music: Franz Schubert. Players: Gabriel Barylli, Werner Kreindl, Paola Loew, Oskar Willner, Eduard Linkers, Michael Toost, Helmut Janatsch. Prod: Arabella/Almaro/Satel Film, Vienna/FRG. Released January 16, 1981, in Vienna. *Gerber, a talented, mature high-school student, suffers because his father is ill and because of his own unhappy love-affair. Faced with the unjust, sadistic behaviour of his teacher, Gerber finally breaks down and, after passing his examinations, commits suicide. Friedrich Torberg's novel has been filmed with great sensitivity and authentic period atmosphere, and with exceptional performances. One of the best Austrian films of recent years.*
DER BOCKERER (The Obstinate Man). Script: Kurt Nachmann, H. C. Artmann, based on the play "Der Bockerer" by Ulrich Becher and Peter Preses. Dir: Franz Antel (=François Legrand). Phot (colour): Ernst Kalinke. Music: Gerhard Heinz. Players: Karl Merkatz, Marte Harell, Hans Holt, Ida Krottendorf, Gustav Knuth, Alfred Böhm, Sieghardt Rupp, Klaus-Jürgen Wussow, Heinz Marecek, Georg Schuchter. Prod: Neue Delta, Vienna/TIT, FRG. Released January 19, 1981, in Vienna. *How an honest Viennese butcher – naively at first and then, as his political awareness grows, with great cunning – obstinately manages to struggle through the occupation of Austria from 1938 to 1945 by the Nazis, to whom he was opposed. Not particularly original as a film subject, but this biting "tragic farce" shows such an accurate portrait of typical Austrian behaviour during the Anschluss that it is worth seeing for that alone.*
WAS KOSTET DER SIEG? (What Price Victory?). Script: Walter Bannert, Klaus Kemetmüller. Dir: Walter Bannert. Phot (colour): Hanus Polak. Music: Hans Kann. Players: Heinz Peter Puff, Nikolas Vogel, Dieter Manhardt, Wilhelm Herzog. Prod: Cinnecoop, Vienna. Released January 30, 1981, in Vienna (October 1980 in Kapfenberg). *A high-school football team become Austrian champions in the school league table but the path to victory is not without problems for school and pupils. The subject is an interesting one but the film itself is weak and confused. Though photography and music are admirable, dialogue and the acting (of the pupils) are not of a very high quality, and the film falls short of international standards.*
DER TRAUM DES SANDINO (The Dream of General Sandino). Script: Rudi Palla, Margareta Heinrich. Dir: Rudi Palla, Margareta Heinrich. Phot (colour, 16mm): Rudi Palla. Commentary: Manfred Kaufmann, spoken by Johanna Tomek, Linde Prelog and Günter Peiritsch. Prod: Extrafilm, Vienna (16mm). Released March 27, 1981, in Vienna. *A two-hour documentary about social conditions in Nicaragua in 1980 which shows the misery of the people after the cruel regime of the dictator Somoza. Emphasis is placed on the fight against illiteracy*

in this developing country. Despite a rather florid commentary and rambling format, the film nevertheless often aroused the audience's emotions.

DIE REVOLUTION IST GRÜN (The Revolution Is Green). Script and dir: Werner Grusch. Phot (colour, 16mm): Bernd Neuburger. Prod: Afro-Dok Films, Vienna/England. Released May 8, 1981, in Vienna (in two parts on Austrian television in 1980). *This film takes Libya as an example of a poor, underdeveloped country which has been changed into a technologically highly specialised industrial state, geared to Western consumer ideologies. The confrontation of Bedouin families with the "green" revolution of Colonel Gaddafi, and the schism arising from the centuries-old way of life and tradition, is shown through interviews with nomads, but this only succeeds partially because of the excessive amount of talk. The film remains not entirely convincing or interesting.*

TROKADERO (Trocadero). Script: Jörg Graser. Dir: Klaus Emmerich. Phot (colour): Peter Gauhe. Music: J. M. Bertl, Ludwig Hirsch. Players: Franz Xaver Kroetz, Ludwig Hirsch, Elisabeth Stepanek, Werner Asam, Beatrice Richter, Lisi Mangold. Prod: Satel, Vienna/Solaris/Bayerische. Rundfunk, Munich/FRG. Released May 15, 1981, in Vienna. *Two unsuccessful con-men (portrayed by Bavarian playwright Kroetz and Viennese singer Hirsch) try to make money out of an old rural inn by offering "striptease in the country." Their chaotic scheme fails because of the well-ordered bureaucracy on the one hand and people's cliche-ridden thinking on the other. A crude comedy, more Bavarian than Viennese, with a few farcical moments and hardly a trace of social criticism.*

SHE DANCES ALONE. Script: Paul Davids, from an idea by Robert Dornhelm. Dir: Robert Dornhelm. Phot (colour): Karl Kofler. Music: Gustavo Santaolalla. Players: Kyra Nijinsky, Max von Sydow, Bud Cort, Patrick Dupond, Walter Kent, Sauncey le Sueur. Prod: D.H.D./U.S.A. and ORF/Vienna. Released May 31, 1981, in Vienna. *This interesting U.S.-Austrian coproduction gives us a psychological portrait of the 68-year-old daughter of the Russian dancer Nijinsky. Magnificent dancing, the fascinating self-depiction of Kyra Nijinsky, and a most interesting cinematic style make this film essential viewing for all film lovers and ballet enthusiasts.*

DEN TÜCHTIGEN GEHÖRT DIE WELT (The Uppercrust). Script: Helmut Zenker, Peter Patzak. Dir: Peter Patzak. Phot (colour): Walter Kindler. Music: Stravinsky, Brahms, Waits, etc. Players: Nigel Davenport, Broderick Crawford, Franz Buchrieser, Frank Gorshin, Bibiana Zeller, Walter Davy, Fred Schaffer, Pavel Landovsky. Prod: Satel/ORF, Vienna, Baytide-Film, San Francisco/U.S.A. Released September 18, 1981, in Vienna. *A very confused film. A police inspector investigates a strange case of murder in which a Viennese building industry mafia is involved. Through the lack of style – at one moment the film is a gangster movie, then a parody of a ganster movie, then social criticism – the end result is very feeble, and the many prominent actors in the cast are powerless to help.*

ANIMA – SYMPHONIE PHANTASTIQUE. Script and

VOLKER SPENGLER, LYDIA KREIBOHM AND KARINA FALLENSTEIN IN *OBSZÖN – DER FALL PETER HERZL*

dir: Titus Leber. Phot (colour): Titus Leber, Mike Gast. Music: Hector Berlioz, Hans Possega. Players: Mathieu Carrière, Charo Lopez, Bruno Anthony, Marquis de Frigance, Hans Klein, Ghislaine Dumas, Christian Renaud. Prod: Clasart/Titus, Vienna. Released September 23, 1981, in Vienna. *An experimental film filled with a mass of detail and dissolves to the music of Berlioz's "Symphonie fantastique," whose programme is extended through philosophical and poetic themes. The audience is faced not only with an over-abundance of sometimes incoherent impressions, but also has to listen to wooden and over-literary dialogue of philosophical abstruseness. At best, an experimental film for buffs.*

KOPFSTAND (Headstand). Script and dir: Ernst Josef Lauscher. Phot: Toni Peschke. Music: Karl Ratzer. Players: Elisabeth Epp, Christoph Waltz, Ingrid Burckhardt, Alfred Solm, Heinz Petters, Pavel Landovsky. Prod: Götz Hagmüller, Vienna. Released October 3, 1981, in Kapfenberg. *Because of a misdemeanour, a barber's apprentice falls into the hands of the police, and then into a psychiatric asylum, where he is systematically destroyed by tablets, injections and electro-shock treatment. A humane lady doctor finds a way for him to regain his liberty; he finds a new job and also a spare-time occupation as a social worker, looking after an old lady. Equally impressive in style and content, this film is one of the best Austrian productions of recent years, and should find an appreciative international audience.*

DIE TOTALE FAMILIE (The Total Family). Script: Ernst Schmidt Jr., Günther Janicek, based on the novel "Die Merowinger oder Die totale Familie" by Heimito von Doderer. Dir: Ernst Schmidt Jr. Phot (colour): Helmut Pirnat. Players: Armin Akermann, John Weiler, Valie Export, Johann Kirchberg, Franz West. Prod: Signal-Film, Vienna. Released October 16, 1981, in Vienna. *This film, which could be described as an experiment, is from a well-known Austrian novel by Heimito von Doderer. It is the farcical, fantastic story of a nobleman who regards himself as a descendant of the*

Merovingian kings, and works out a system of marriages and adoptions that make him his own father, grandfather, son-in-law, and father-in-law. An attack, exaggerated into the realms of parody, on certain social classes and their mode of behaviour.

OBSZÖN – DER FALL PETER HERZL (Obscene – the Peter Herzl Case). Script: Alfred Paul Schmidt, Hans Christof Stenzel. Dir: Hans Christof Stenzel. Phot (colour): Rudolf Blahacek. Music: Bach, Schubert, Ambros Seelos. Players: Volker Spengler, Lydia Kreibohm, Karina Fallenstein, Heinz Schubert, Hanno Pöschl, Monica Bleibtreu, Hans Peter Hofmann, Dieter Seefranz. Prod: Intertel, Vienna/GK Filmprodukton, Vienna and Salzburg/Rapid Film, Munich/GT, Berlin. Released October 29, 1981, in Hof (Germany). *A harmless German citizen is pursued in Vienna as a suspect terrorist by a ridiculously mysterious organisation from his own country and by the Vienna police. Most of the film then takes place in the underworld of whores and pimps, portrayed both visually and verbally in a very coarse manner. The confrontation with the decadence, perversity and stupidity of the organs of state power – the film's alleged target – fails for lack of intellectual substance and wit.*

EIN WENIG STERBEN (To Die a Little). Script: Mansur Madavi. Dir and phot (colour): Mansur Madavi. Players: Alfred Solm, Maria Martina, Axel Klingenberg, Kurt Kosutic, Heribert Sasse, Inge Toifl. Prod: Unger/Madavi, Vienna. Released November 12, 1981, in Vienna (Viennale). *In this socially critical drama an old man has to give up the flat he has lived in since childhood* because the block is to be demolished. He resists with every means available, finally even with a weapon. In a showdown between the old man and the implacable, soulless, merciless bureaucracy, the weaker is bound to be defeated by the power of the state. The old man is removed from the building in a strait-jacket ... The simple story is told in a series of calm, studied pictures, and is brought to life by its detail, its many truthful touches, and the magnificent performance by the leading actor, Alfred Solk. A simple but beautiful film.*

ZECHMEISTER. Script and dir: Angela Summereder. Phot (colour, 16mm): Hille Sagel. Music: Franz Lehár, Christian Geerdes, Fritz Mikesch, Ursula Weck. Players: Herbert Adamec, Asher Mendelssohn, Claudia Schneider, Peter Weibel, Gernot Klotz, Frank Hofer (and Maria Zechmeister). Prod: Studio-Film, Vienna (16mm). Released November 30, 1981, in Vienna. *A farmer's wife from Upper Austria, Maria Zechmeister, was sentenced to life imprisonment in 1949 for having murdered her husband, although the deed could not be proved. After 17 years, she was pardoned. Her trial has now been reconstructed and re-staged with actors, from the court reports. Witnesses from the time tell how they see the case today; Maria Zechmeister herself talks about her life. Whether the husband really was a victim of poisoning, whether his wife was a victim of a terrible miscarriage of justice, remains open. The only thing proved is the risk of prejudice and the danger of circumstantial evidence. A somewhat bewildering experimental film with an interesting theme.*

Belgium   by Paul Davay

As in some other countries, the phenomenon of rising attendances has been confirmed in Belgium, albeit modestly, and allowing for the fact that the cinemas benefit from screening super-productions (mostly American) and/or French films, whether helped by a glittering cast or exploiting a certain pseudo-humorous vulgarity with no connection to the *esprit français*, which vanishes daily ever further into legend and myth. Releases that for economic reasons simply do not benefit from a major publicity campaign – often those therefore that do not chime with the mood of a very large public – rarely have the chance of being held over. The problem for these films is especially acute in the Walloon areas, where people are allergic to original versions, the excuse being that reading subtitles tires the eyes, while in the Flemish provinces there is never any difficulty of this kind. And while on the subject of exhibition, one can report also a slight increase in the number of cinemas, with the big circuits steadily closing or rebuilding the old theatres, and replacing them with duplexes and triples etc.

It goes without saying that in this situation the *cinéma d'art et d'essai* keeps going as best it can. However, to take but one example, if a duplex shuts its doors in the centre of Brussels, then in an offbeat district of the capital another may have opened, complete with bar, bookshop, and meeting area. There is no doubt that it is in the Flemish towns such as Antwerp, Ghent, and Leuven that the so-called difficult films most excite the curiosity of movie buffs. Nevertheless, outside the art houses, this category of audience has begun to express a certain disillusionment in the face of various marginal films. It's true that the same applies to several other concerts and entertainments. The exceptions are the screenings organised by the Belgian Cinémathèque (Prix L'Age d'Or and "Cinédécouvertes"), where monetary awards are dispensed to the distributors of films selected by the jury, while in Ghent the "Filmgebeuren" enjoys mounting success. Clearly – but here one returns to the purely "commercial" level – the film event that attracts the largest audiences is the Brussels Festival, which in 1981 was almost on the point of refusing admission to those involved in the film branch.

As for the national production, it continues to hover at around a dozen features per annum. The political gulf, more and more pronounced, between the Dutch-speaking and the French-speaking populations, render a "Belgian film industry" a complete mirage. And as cultural aid programmes are extremely restricted, it seems absolutely clear that our provinces will never yield anybody other than journeyman directors, some of whose international reputations may marginally exceed that of Val Saint Lambert glass, or FN hunting rifles. Some energetic and perseverent film-makers also manage to shoot a production every two or three years, and we have reached a point at which we tend to hail just about every film that is actually completed.

The most distinguished films of 1981 were without doubt *Le grand paysage d'Alexis Droeven* (Jean-Jacques Andrien) and *Tijd om gelukkig te zijn* (Frans Buyens), both reviewed separately. Apart from these two fiction movies, there were a couple of very interesting documentaries. The first, *Du Zaïre au Congo* (Christian Mesnil) consists of an excellent dialectical montage of animated and still pictures (newsreels, reportage, etc.), mingled with a protest song by Pierre Akendengue, who describes the history of colonialism, de-colonisation, and neo-colonialism in the former Belgian dependencies of Central Africa.

The second, *La mémoire fertile* (by Michel Khleifi, a graduate of one of our film schools), follows the lives of two separate Palestinian women, the one influenced by Israeli policies, the other by Muslim traditions.

Two other productions were worthy of note. First *21:12 Piano Bar* (by Mary Jiminez), steeped in a filmic style that stems from, among others, Marguerite Duras, but which is in the circumstances so cerebral that it can reach only a very

JAN DECLEIR AND EVA KANT IN *TIME FOR BEING HAPPY*

limited public. Then *Bruges-la-Morte*, an adaptation in Dutch of a symbolist novel written in French in 1892 by Georges Rodenbach. Using a sober screenplay by the noted film critic Théodore Louis, the ever audacious Roland Verhavert has made of this a film of considerable plastic beauty. However, this story of a man obsessed with his religious scruples has left Belgian audiences cold, especially the younger generation.

Even in the short film, which for so long has garnered international awards and a wide reputation for Belgium, the harvest is rather poor, even though on a technical level there has been enormous progress. In this area what deserves most note is the proliferation of independent studios (particularly on the French-speaking side), which are supported financially by the official authorities. For the moment, the most interesting results have come from CAB (Centre Bruxellois de l'Audiovisuel), of which Henri Storck is the guiding light, and the Atelier de Création, headed by Jean-Claude Batz and which allows students recently graduated or in their final year at the INSAS Film School in Brussels to make a semi-professional film, in order to help them at the start of their career. A studio of a similar kind is linked to IAD, the film school attached to the Catholic university at Louvain-la-Neuve.

Finally, there is considerable activity in the realm of non-commercial animation, the best example of which during the past year has been *Alephah*, a new cartoon by Gérard Frydman, who previously made *Scarabus* and *Agulana*.

TIJD OM GELUKKIG TE ZIJN
(Time for Being Happy)

Script and Direction: Frans Buyens. Photography (Fujicolor): Alain Derobe. Music: "More Vibes with Sadi." Production Design: Philippe Itterbeek. Players: Jan Decleir, Eva Kant, Noëlle Fontaine, Bert André, Marcel Dossogne, Alex Willequet, Jan Moonen. Produced by Iris Films Dacapo (Brussels). 103 mins.

Frans Buyens is a socially-committed director who, although extremely active, has produced some rather uneven work, in the sense that his documentaries, whether shorts or features, are simply too dense from a human angle and too superficial, while up to now his fiction films have been in one way or another disappointing, in spite of certain successful moments. So much so that in this area at least he has been the man from whom a surprise has been awaited. Now we have it, with *Time for Being Happy*, the first production in which he shows himself concentrating from start to finish, and not merely in the concise and ever accurate dialogue, which reminds one that Buyens,

before going behind the camera, was a writer and man of the theatre.

What then is this "time that allows one to be happy," that he refers to so ironically? It's the time at the disposal of a forty-year-old man, abruptly thrown out of work, and who is not just reduced to a punctilious routine of leisure activity, but also to recognising the futility of his relationship with a married woman who is a "terrible" bourgeoise. This unemployed man, looking vainly for work, and demoralised by idleness, is fortunate enough to make friends with a young woman who gives him a fresh insight into life. This is a film by turns serious and satirical, which ends with the unfortunate hero saying farewell with a mocking laugh. Although it takes place in Brussels, this fundamentally critical film uses both Dutch and French dialogue, which is quite normal for the capital city, but which displeased the Flemish authorites. Some weaknesses in performance are almost completely overcome by the magnificent playing of Jan Decleir, whose sheer presence and brio confirm him as the greatest actor in Belgium at the moment.   PAUL DAVAY

LE GRAND PAYSAGE
D'ALEXIS DROEVEN

Script and Direction: Jean-Jacques Andrien. Photography (Eastmancolor): Georges Barsky. Photography (monochrome): Michel Baudour. Music: Richard Wagner, Claudio Monteverdi, J. F. Maljean. Production Design: Philippe Graff. Players: Jerzy Radziwiłowicz, Nicole Garcia, Maurice Garrel, Jan Decleir. Produced by Films de la Drève (Brussels), RTBF (Liège)/Radio-Cinés (Paris). 88 mins.

Jean-Jacques Andrien made *Le fils d'Amr est mort!* (which won the Grand Prix at the Locarno Festival of 1975), a rather austere film, all in long shot-sequences. He had to wait five years before being able to start on his second feature, which is quite typical of the Belgian cinema situation, above all when a really national subject is being dealt with, which obviates foreign co-producer participation. Years of reflection and maturity have led Andrien to select situations and circumstances that are not invented and that he himself knows well. In itself, the screenplay is very simple. It opens with the death of the agricultural distributor, Alexis

Droeven. His son, Jean-Pierre, who has not been back to the countryside for several years, and his aunt Elizabeth, who is a lawyer in Liège, attend the funeral. Jean-Pierre, the only direct beneficiary, dreams of selling the farm and its land. His conversations with the aunt, and her own memories, summon up an image of what Alexis was like: a man who deeply loved his native soil, his "countryside," where he fought both to preserve the Walloon heritage called into question by the Flemish politicians, and for the survival of the peasant class which was being threatened by the industrialisation process in agriculture. This struggle is described by the use of newsreel footage showing disturbances and rather violent demonstrations in the Fourons region (where the film is set), and in Brussels itself. While the portrayal of life and rural customs is always close to reality, the most beautiful parts of the film are those in which Jean-Pierre realises that he must continue his father's work, and in which the subtle psychological relationship grows between the son and his aunt whom he has not seen for so long, and whom

MAURICE GARREL IN *LE GRAND PAYSAGE D'ALEXIS GROEVEN*

he in some way rediscovers rather as he does the image of his dead father. The actors, led by Radziwiłowicz (from *Man of Iron*), are remarkably well directed. And it should be noted that for his work on this film, Georges Barsky won the prize for the Best Cinematography at the Berlin Festival.

PAUL DAVAY

recent films

HET BEEST (La Bête). Script and Dir.: Paul Collet. Phot (Eastmancolor): Ralf Boumans. Mus: Egisto Macchi Art Dir: Ludo Bex Players: Willem Ruis, Hedie Meyling, Anouk Collet, Ward De Ravet, Cara Van Wersch, Josée Ruiter, Harry Kümel. Dutch language. Prod: Showking Films (Brussels).

BRUGGE-DIE-STILLE (Bruges-la-Morte). Script: Théodore Louis, Roland Verhavert, from a novel by Georges Rodenbach. Dir: Roland Verhavert Phot (Eastmancolor): Walther Vanden Ende. Mus: Claude Debussy. Art Dir: Ludo Bex. Players: Idwig Stephane, Eve Lyne, Chris

Boni, Caroline Vlerick, Herbert Flack, Philippe Vervoort, Cecile Fondu. Dutch language Prod: Visie (Brussels).

DU ZAÏRE AU CONGO. Script: Christian Mesnil, Hubert Galle, Yannis Thanassekos. Dir: Christian Mesnil Phot (black-and-white, and colour): Michel Baudour, Raymond Fromont, Dominique Brabant, Bruno Muel, Jacques Gurfinkel, Gilbert Lecluyse. Mus: André Stordeur, Pierre Akendengue. French language. Prod: NIP and CBA (Brussels) Les Films 2001 (Paris).

HOTEL MEUBLE. Script: Jean Van Hamme, from a novel by Thomas Owen. Dir: Marc Lobet Phot (Eastmancolor); Ken Legargeant. Mus: Alain Pierre. Art Dir: Luc Monheim. Players: Anny Duperey, Bernard Giraudeau, Roger Dutoit, Idwig Stephane, André Bernier, Pierre Fabien, Marie-Ange Dutheil, Alexandre von Sivers, Daniel Emilfork, Eva Ionesco. French language. Prod: Odec (Brussels) Babylone Films (Paris).

LES JOURS DE NOTRE VIE. Script: Maurice Rabinowicz, Yvette Michelems Dir: Maurice Rabinowicz. Phot (Gevacolor): Ken Legargeant. Mus: Marc Herouet. Art Dir: Luc Monheim, Guy Derie Players: Marie Dubois, Roger Van Hool, Claire Wauthion, Bruno Sermonne, Maureen Dor, Frank Aendenboom, Irene Vernal, S.

Excoffier, F. Nicolaï, G. Pirlet. French language Prod: F3 (Brussels), RTBF (Liège) Babylone Films (Paris).

LE LIT. Script and Dir.: Marion Hänsel, from a novel by Dominique Rolin. Phot (Eastmancolor): Walther van den Ende. Art Dir: Daniel Scahaise. Players: Natasha Parry, Heinz Bennent, Johan Leysen, Francine Blistin, Patrick Massieu, Yvette Merlin. French language. Prod: Man's Films (Brussels).

LA MEMOIRE FERTILE. Script and dir.: Michel Khleifi. Phot (Eastmancolor): Yves van der Meeren, Marc-André Batigne. Mus: Jacqueline Rosenfeld, Jean-not Gillis. Players: Farah Hatoum, Sahar Khalifeh – Arabic language. Prod: Marisa Films (Brussels) ZDF (Mainz) NCO, NOVIB, IKON (Holland).

MENUET. Script: Hugo Claus, from a novel by Paul-Louis Boon. Dir: Lili Rademakers. Phot (Eastmancolor): Paul van den Bos. Art Dir: Philippe Graff. Players: Hubert Firmin, Carla Hardy, Alkemay Marijnissen,

Theu Boerman, Ingrid Pollet, Vivian de Munck, Pol Wuts. Dutch language. Prod: Iblis Films (Brussels) Fons Rademakers (Amsterdam).

NEIGE. Script: Marc Vilard, Juliet Berto. Dir: Juliet Berto, Jean-Henri Roger. Phot (Eastmancolor): William Lubtchansky. Mus: Bernard Lavilliers, François Breant. Players: Juliet Berto, Jean-François Stevenin, Robert Leinsol, Patrick Chesnais, Jean-François Balmer, Paul Le Person, Raymond Bussière, Yvette Merlin, Michel Lechat. French language. Prod: F3 and Odec (Brussels) Babylone Films, Odessa Films, Marion's Films (Paris).

21:12 PIANO BAR. Script and Dir: Mary Jimenez Phot (Eastmancolor): Michel Houssiau. Mus: Ramon de Herrera, Alain Marchal. Art Dir: Françoise Hardy – Players: Lucinda Childs, Carole Courtoy, Anne Guerrin, Jean-Marc Turine, Philippe Marannes, Claude Zaccai, Alain Marchal. French language. Prod: Productions de la Phalène (Brussels).

Belgian Specialised Distributors

Bevrijdingsfilms
332 Koningsstraat
1030 Brussel.

Cinélibre
5 rue de la Filature
1060 Brussel.

Cinevog Films
10 rue des Palais
1030 Brussel.

C.N.C.
259 rue Royale
1030 Brussel.

Film International
12/6 Lange Brilstraat
2000 Antwerpen.

Fugitive Cinema
38a Keizerstraat
2000 Antwerpen.

Ossessione Films
32 Cuylitsstraat
2000 Antwerpen.

Progrès Films
243 rue Royale
1030 Brussel.

Toekan Films
263 Koningsstraat
1030 Brussel.

Official Bodies

Ministère de la Communauté Française
(Emile Cantillon, head of Film Promotion Section)
7 Galerie Ravenstein
1000 Bruxelles.

Ministerie voor Nederlandse Cultuur
(Juul Anthonissen, head of Film Department)
29–31 Koloniëstraat
1000 Brussel.

Ministère des Affaires Etrangères
(Gerard Legros, head of Film Service)
2 rue des Quatre-Bras
1000 Bruxelles.

Ministère de l'Education Nationale
7 Quai du Commerce
1080 Bruxelles.

Trade Associations

Chambre Professionelle Belge de la Cinématographie
32 avenue de l'Astronomie
1030 Bruxelles.

Association Belge des Auteurs de Films et de TV
266/6 rue Royale
1030 Bruxelles.

Union Nationale des Producteurs Belges de Films
30 rue Léon Frédéric
1040 Bruxelles.

Art House Associations

Association Belge Francophone du Cinéma d'Art et d'Essai
(Paul Davay, Chairman)
10 avenue Jeanne
1050 Bruxelles.

Vlaamse Verenigung van Kunstfilmtheaters
(Jos Rastelli, Chairman)
63 Hoornzeelstraat
1980 Tervuren.

Brazil

by Luis Arbex

In 1981 Brazilian film production totalled 105 features, 8 more than in 1980, but the increase did not produce better-quality pictures. Only three or four were up to international standards where contemporary problems and technique were concerned. The majority of them continued to range from low-budget pictures to sexploiters.

Liberalisation in censorship of both domestic and foreign pictures is not going ahead as expected. *Prá frente Brasil (Onward Brazil)*, the winner at the Gramado festival, was banned for exhibition. Pasolini's *Salò* continues to stay on the shelf.

Embrafilme, which finances almost 60% of Brazilian film-making, is going through economic difficulties. Its policy remains unchanged and its productions repeating the same formulas – fewer now but with guaranteed box-office returns. Exhibitors demand a certain amount of sexual content to finance a production, unless a film has a guaranteed box-office return.

The high price of importation (paid in dollars), the closing of domestic distributors, and an increase in the price of theatre tickets have made film a very expensive form of entertainment. Only super-productions or films with erotic content have a certain success. *Eu te amo (I Love you)* was given the highest publicity budget ever for a Brazilian film.

It has become the rule for prints of foreign films to be struck locally, but the general quality is poor. *Excalibur*, *Kagemusha* and *Man of Marble* were ruined by bad processing, but *The Elephant Man* (black-and-white) was a tremendous hit. The import of foreign pictures continues to subside dramatically, notably from Italy, as predicted in IFG 1982. Happily, Gaumont read our appeal in IFG last year, and French films have gained a new impulse here.

In 1978 admissions totalled 220,000,000. By 1981 the figure had dropped to 160,000,000. A further reduction is expected for 1982. The average budget of a domestic film is 15,000,000 cruzeiros; at least 600,000 admissions are needed

to make the film break even. In 1981, some 71 Brazilian films were sold abroad for a total income of $4,500,000–5,000,000. The main foreign market was Latin America which produced an income of $365,300, compared with $310,400 from East Europe, $83,300 from the U.S.A., and $65,400 from the rest of the world. The Foreign Chamber of Commerce expects to export around 15 films a year if Embrafilme solves its financial difficulties; in the first half of 1982 it recorded a loss of 107,000,000 cruzeiros.

The main handicap of the Brazilian industry is the lack of producers who are willing to finance prestigious films; most having a hard time raising the money for their next production. In such a crisis, producers only risk financing *pornochanchadas*, but audiences are already saturated with them after 11 years of boom. Embrafilme was set up to gain 10% of the market for foreign films in the U.S.A., with an expected yearly gross of $10 millions, after the box-office successes of *Bye Bye Brazil*, *Pixote* and *Gaijin*. They hope to open new doors with *Gabriela*, financed with M-G-M. But after the affair of *Prá frente Brasil* it will be very difficult for a producer to finance a political film in Brazil.

All cinemas are obliged to devote 133 days a year to showing Brazilian films (including shorts of questionable value). They get their percentage every time they are screened – the ones selected to run in a double-bill with *Raiders of the Lost Ark* . . . The remaining days of the year are filled with American films or European super-productions with a guaranteed box-office return. There is no room for the "art film."

Footnote: after 30 years away, this correspondent returned to live in the city of Belo Horizonte (population: 3,000,000). Twenty cinemas had closed and three new ones opened. Dolby stereo is unheard of; two exhibitors decide what the population sees. Fortunately, two unsatisfactory theatres have been transformed into Art Houses – the Pathé and Roxy.

CRISTINA ACHÉ IN *O HOMEM DO PAU BRASIL* (ABOVE)

STILL FROM *ASA BRANCA – UM SONHO BRASILEIRO*

recent films

PRÁ FRENTE BRASIL (Onward Brazil). Script and dir: Roberto Farias. Phot (Eastmancolor): Dib Lufti. Edit: Roberto and Mauro Farias. Music: Edberto Gismonti. Players: Antônio Fagundes, Reginaldo Farias, Elizabeth Savalla, Nathalia do Vale, Maurício Farias, Paulo Porto, Carlos Zara, Claudio Marzo, Luis Mario Farias.

Unanimously acclaimed as the best domestic picture at the Gramado festival, it was then banned by the authorities. It is a courageous and opportune film in Costa-Gavras style, dealing with a painful period of repression in Brazil. It is perhaps the most outstanding film made in Brazil, bringing the audience to the one same harrowing thought – "that could have happened to me." The film caused a minor scandal in the press since Roberto Farias was a former Embrafilme director.

ELES NÃO USAM BLACK TIE (They Don't Wear Black Tie). Dir: Leon Hirszman, from the play by Gianfrancesco Guarnieri. Script: Hirszman, Guarnieri. Phot (Eastmancolor): Lauro Escorel Filho. Edit: Eduardo Escorel. Art Dir: Marcos Weinstock, Jefferson de Albuquerque. Music: Radamés Gnatalli. Players: Fernanda Montenegro, Gianfrancesco Guarnieri, Carlos Alberto Ricelli, Bete Mendes, Milton Gonçalves, Rafael de Carvalho, Lélia Abramo, Anselmo Vasconcelos, Francisco Milani.

The action ot Guarnieri's original play has been transplanted to São Paulo 1980 from Rio 1954. A family of four lives in a modest house: the father and eldest son are labourers, and the youngest a teenager. There arises a conflict between the generations: the fear of unemployment, urban violence, and the struggle and anxieties of the wife looking for a better social position. The small family functions as a microcosm of Brazil's problems. The father is dogged and constant. The son cannot understand the values defended by his father and blames them for their misfortunes. He thinks only of saving money to get married to his pregnant fiancée, who little by little comes to the conclusion that she disagrees with his way of thinking. The wife is afraid that if her husband is arrested again it will destroy her home. Violence explodes in the streets; repression is tough. Both women react in different ways. The girl is disillusioned and refuses to get married; the wife relies on the husband and the son leaves home for good. (Awarded six major prizes at Venice in 1981, besides other prizes at Nantes, Valladolid and Havana. Voted as best picture at the Brasilia festival in 1981.)

O HOMEM DO PAU BRASIL (The Man of the Brazil-Tree). Dir: Joaquim Pedro de Andrade, based on the works of Oswald de Andrade. Script: Andrade, Alexandre Eulálio. Phot (Eastmancolor): Kimihiko Kato. Art Dir: Helio Eichbauer, Adão Pinheiro. Edit: Marco Antônio Cury. Music: Rogério Rossini. Players: Itala Nandi, Flávio Galvão, Regina Duarte, Cristina Aché, Dina Sfat, Dora Pellegrino, Grande Otelo, Othon Bastos, Paulo José, Antônio José Pitanga, Fábio Sabag, Arduino Colassanti, Paulo Hesse, Riva Nimitz, Etty Frazer, Marcos Fayad, Wilson Grey, Isa Kopelman.

When the Portuguese discovered Brazil in 1500, they found a tree that "bleeds" with a brazier-like oil. Its wood turned out to be sought-after in Europe. The tree was also a phallic emblem among the natives. The country's name derives from this tree. Oswald de Andrade (1890–1953) was one of the most polemic modernists. Scenes from his life and satirical works are recreated with total freedom. The poet and novelist's personality is shared between two players (Flávio Galvão and Itala Nandi), who perform side by side or alternatively. The film is about Andrade's adventures and the women he loved in São Paulo, Rio and Paris, during the transition of Art Nouveau to Art Déco: his first wife, a Parisian poet, an astronomer who discovers the sideral Eiffel Tower, the Divine Isadora, the ill-fated Al Capone, and his subversive and Marxist friends. After Oswald-male was devoured by Oswald-female, a new civilisation was to be founded, with the creation of the Woman of the Brazil-Tree – leader of the revolution that would install a man-eating matriarchy in Brazil. That was called The Caribbean Revolution.

GABRIELA. Dir: Bruno Barreto. Novel: Jorge Amado. Players: Marcello Mastroianni, Sônia Braga (replacing Sophia Loren). Prod: M-G-M.
TIETA DE AGRESTE. Dir: Lina Wertmüller. Novel: Jorge Amado. Players: Sophia Loren, Marcello Mastroianni.
AO SUL DO MEU CORPO (South of My Body). Dir: Paulo Cesar Saraceni. Story: Paulo Emílio Salles Gomes. Players: Ana Maria Nascimento, Paulo Cesar Pereio.
ASA BRANCA – UM SONHO BRASILEIRO (White Wing – A Brazilian Dream). Dir and script: Djalma Limongi Batista. Phot: Gualter Limongi Batista. Edit: José Motta. Music: Mário Valério Vasconcelos. Art Dir: Jefferson Albuquerque Jr., Felipe Crescenti. Players: Edson Celulari, Eva Wilma, Walmor Chagas, Gianfrancesco Guarnieri, Regina Wilke, Garaldo D'El Rey, Vivian Buckup, Mira Haar.
RIO BABILÔNIA (Rio Babylon). Dir: Neville D'Almeida. Players: Joel Barcelos, Denise Dumont, Cristiane Torloni, Jardel Filho, Norma Bengell.

BETE MENDES IN *THEY DON'T WEAR BLACK TIE*

forthcoming films

TENSÃO NO RIO (Tension in Rio). Dir: Gustavo Dahl. Players: Anselmo Duarte, Lilian Lemertz, Dina Sfat.
DAS TRIPAS CORAÇÃO. Dir: Caroline Nabuco. Players: Antônio Fagundes, Dina Sfat, Xuxa Lopes. (Shown at Cannes.)

Art House Focus

The most notable events of the year took place at the Museum of Modern Art in São Paulo and Rio. A World Cinema Forum included 27 films not released on the commercial circuit, among them *Deutschland bleiche Mutter, Salò, Ziemia obiecana, Woyzeck, Prova d'orchestra, Nikola Tesla, Adoption*. German films included *Die dritte Grad, Lena Rais, Die letzten Jahre Der Kindheit, Die Hamburger Krankheit, Die Kinder aus Nr. 67, Der mond ist nür a nackerte Kugel*. A Yugoslavian programme of 8 films included *Tajna Nikole Tesle, Sreca na vrvici, Ljubavni život Budimira Traiković, Živi bili pa vidjeli, Petra's Crown, Special Education*. A Spanish programme comprised *Mama cumple cién años, El nido, El setiembre función la noche, Maravillas, Opera prima, El corazón del bosque, Mater amantissima, La mano negra, El crack*. A French festival comprised *Hôtel des Amériques, La femme d'à côté, Beau-père, Garde à vue, Coup de torchon, Le grand patron, Tout feu tout flamme, Eaux profondes*. And there was also the first Italian festival for 20 years . . .

Burma

by Fred Marshall

The Burmese Government does not issue film permits so easily; consequently very little of the region has been seen on motion picture film outside the country, although portions of *The Bridge on the River Kwai* were made in Burma. One of the great stories of the Second World War, *The Purple Plain*, was about Burma and starred a local actress Win Min Than opposite Gregory Peck. Many other war stories about Burma have been made on Hollywood back lots.

The country is still a virgin territory for foreign film-makers. Burmese films on the other hand are a sociological necessity for the recreation of the worker. They are not for export and their contents are realistic and melodramatic, as they depict life styles of the Burmese.

In order to stimulate interest among the local film industry the U.S. Information Service, in conjunction with the American Embassy, presents seminars and discussions for local film-makers with film critics from time to time. They also have 16mm and video cassette screenings on a monthly basis.

The cost of film admission is about US75¢. Theatres are old, but the worker has developed a built-in habit of seeing films in his own language, therefore in his own way he supports the industry and patronises the Burmese films which are now being made with colour processing. Imported films are purchased by the State, though they are heavily censored and usually the last place in Asia to get the print.

Altogether there are some 420 theatres which are occupied on the average once a week by the 32 million who constitute the population. The Burmese have an extremely high literacy rate of 70%. Just over 50% of the total population speak English.

All foreign films are shown in original English versions without subtitles. In this manner the local Burmese film benefits, as it is the only way in which audiences can hear their own language spoken.

The industry is supported by the Ministry of Culture and many actors are working in both TV and film industries. The newspapers carry daily announcements of films and colourful advertising displays cover the theatre exterior. People queue to purchase tickets for the two nightly performances except on holidays and weekends.

Colour film-making has come to Burma with the opening of a new colour film lab two years ago. This has cut the quota of films in half with producers emphasising quality in their productions.

Bulgaria

by Ivan Stoyanovich

The wave of films started by the thirteen hundredth anniversary of Bulgaria is still rolling. In the space of six months Lyudmil Staikov's giant spectacular *Khan Asparoukh* was seen by 11,000,000 people. Bulgaria's population is only about 8,700,000, so this must be a national – perhaps even a world – record in terms of per capita attendance. Georgi Dyulgerov's *Measure for Measure*, an original interpretation of historical events is already approaching the 2,000,000 mark. Due for release shortly are Georgi Stoyanov's *Constantine the Philosopher* (about the creators of the Slavonic alphabet) and Borislav Sharaliev's *Boris I* (about the Bulgarian tsar who helped to spread the new alphabet and converted Bulgarians to Eastern Orthodox Christianity). All these films combine high artistic standards and profitability.

Among films on contemporary subjects, there are at least two whose box-office success is assured: *The Racket* and *A Dog in a Drawer* are typical representatives of their respective genres. The first is an exciting thriller about heroin smuggling across Bulgaria; the second deals with the feelings of children emotionally involved in the fate of a stray dog. *The Avalanche*, a well-made film by Hristo Piskov and Irina Aktasheva, offers a wealth of literary and visual metaphors.

Ivan Andonov's *White Magic* is noteworthy

ABOVE: STILL FROM *THE RACKET*

ABOVE: STILL FROM *WHITE MAGIC*

BELOW: STILL FROM *THE WARNING*

for its kaleidoscopic portrait of Bulgarian country life in an unspecified era. A wide variety of national characters are seen in a melee of tragi-comic fairground elation – perhaps a final desperate indulgence in the face of the impending, but as yet unperceived threat, of the violence of the Twenties and Thirties. As a philosophical parable, a blend of the absurd and the real, *White Magic* is deserving of attention.

The Warning also deserves particular mention. It is an impressive co-production by Bulgaria, the U.S.S.R. and East Germany but the Bulgarian contribution predominates. Two names attract attention immediately: the historical figure Georgi Dimitrov, a leader of the international workers' movement who at the Leipzig Trial of 1933 won a moral victory over Nazism, and the contemporary Spanish film director Juan Antonio Bardem, who was inspired by the personality of Dimitrov and decided to direct the picture. Using documentary sequences, recreating scenes of the historic duel, and with a good physical likeness in actor Peter Gyurov, Bardem creates an epic panorama of the world movement for peace and unity against emergent Fascism. Many of the film's characters are true historical portraits. *The Warning* was Bulgaria's entry at the 1982 Karlovy Vary Festival.

Bulgaria has also taken part in the Oberhausen, Lille (two prizes), Los Angeles, Kraków, Zagreb and Leipzig festivals; in all, Bulgarian films were shown at some forty festivals in 1981/82. Special programmes of Bulgarian films were also shown in France, where a Bulgarian Film Month was held; in New Delhi where, after *The Unknown Soldier's Patent Leather Shoes* won the Golden Peacock award, a large retrospective of Rangel Vulchanov's films was arranged; and in Sienna, where a retrospective of director, actor and animator Ivan Andonov was held. Much business was also transacted in 1982 by Bulgarian representatives at the markets in West Berlin, Monte Carlo, Cannes, Tashkent, Karlovy Vary and MIFED.

Several important festivals are regularly held in Bulgaria: the National Film Festival, a biennial review of Bulgarian feature films, was held in October 1981 in Varna; the International Festival of Balkan Cinematography, was held in November in Sofia; and there is also the National Animated

Film Festival in Tolbukhin, where directors such as Donyo Donev, Stoyan Doukov, Todor Dinov, Henri Koulev, Hristo Topouzanov, Pencho Bogdanov, Ivan Vesselinov and Roumen Petkov will attend.

Bulgarian animated films have gained much international popularity, and have recently enjoyed a real boom in video-cassette form all over Europe. In 1981 the Stockholm-based Swedish company Frekvensia Ge Te bought the video rights

for Europe of seventy-two animated films. And that was just the beginning: other films, including features, are being bought and marketed all the time.

In 1982 the "Vreme" Popular Science and Documentary film Studio celebrates its thirtieth birthday – a fitting occasion to note the development of the Bulgarian short film and its regular success at many prestigious international events.

Canada

by Gerald Pratley

At the 1982 Canadian Film Awards (now called by the trite name of "Genies"), Alan Arkin was deemed Best Foreign Actor for his performance in Eric Till's *Improper Channels*. In accepting the award he remarked that "he didn't feel like a foreign actor" playing in the film. There was no reason why he should: like nine out of ten Canadian movies, the film was set in the U.S.A. and told an American story, in which Arkin played an American. Like its many counterparts, *Improper Channels* received limited exhibition and deservedly disappeared.

Since the introduction of the Capital Cost Allowance (CCA) plan just over five years ago, more than $650,000,000 has been spent on some 400–500 feature films. Only $50 million has been recovered by investors and the state has lost more money in taxes than it would have done had it directly subsidised indigenous Canadian films through a properly-constituted Canadian Film Development Corporation (CFDC).

Few individuals – other than anti-cinema elements in government and business – would complain unduly about this loss if they could at least point with pride to several hundred genuine Canadian films which, like most other nations' films, were about the country and its people. Instead, it is difficult to find ten such titles among the mass of pseudo-American monstrosities. By manipulating the liberal points system set up by the CCA – supposedly to guarantee the "Canadian" nature of enterprises submitted for approval – producers, brokers and investors managed to churn out such monstrosities on inflated budgets and with great profit. Hundreds of technicians found work; but few actors, directors and writers

benefited from this ugly burst of Hollywood North activity because the so-called creativity came from outside the country – usually in the form of cast-off material and talent from Los Angeles.

Now the bragging and belching is over. The sickness has all but passed as production comes to a standstill and everyone is out-of-work again. Even if the recession had come about after a genuine renaissance of Canadian films, film-makers could at least have consoled themselves that they had worked on material they were proud of and would become an important part of Canadian film history. But the period yielded nothing of worth and not a single actor, director, cameraman or writer became established as a result of it. Such material, deliberately contrived to be "international" in appeal, found a few successes in the U.S.A.; the rest was consigned to the rubbish bins of the European and South American markets.

Few individuals in government film departments, the trade or the media want to recognise this. "The films turned out not to be very good," they murmur. "We did too much too soon," they mutter. "We were inexperienced," they moan. No one will admit that (with few exceptions) everybody wanted imitation American movies. Even after this debacle, people still think American rather than Canadian when talking of film production. The provinces (except Québec) spend thousands of dollars on attempting to attract American producers to film in their "marvellous mountains and lovely lakes and bustling cities" but the last thing their film departments think of doing (unlike the Australian states) is to make money available to local film-makers with ideas.

Alberta now plans to build a $20,000,000

Canadian Film Development Corporation

Société de développement
de l'industrie cinématographique canadienne

C.P. 71, Tour de la Bourse
Montréal, Québec H4Z 1A8
(514) 283-6363
Telex: 05-25134 MTL

111 Avenue Road, Suite 602
Toronto, Ontario
M5R 3J8
(416) 966-6436

1176 West Georgia Street, Suite 1500
Vancouver, British Columbia
V6E 4A2
(604) 684-4829

Canada

studio complex which no one needs – on the dubious premise that, because *Superman* used locations there, the next *Superman* will be filmed in its entirety there instead of at Pinewood studios! Nothing is said about making funds available to Alberta's film-makers – who can hardly be called such as no money is forthcoming for them to make films. Toronto and Montréal are well equipped with facilities to carry out regular work and are not exactly pressed for business.

So desperate is the trade, the government and certain areas of the media to claim successes in production that there is now the absurd spectacle of proponents of non-Canadian movies jumping with excitement over such successes as the ridiculous *Quest for Fire*, the simple-minded *Atlantic City*, and the reprehensible *Porky's* – on the grounds that because Canadian money was invested in them they are true Canadian film achievements. Some rocky location work was done in Canada for *Quest for Fire*; what few Montréal- and Toronto-based actors are in them are only gnawing on bones – as usual.

Co-productions are the new white hope, the latest rage, the next rainbow to chase; and the C.F.D.C., which is not in a position to develop anything these days, cheerfully talks about "co-productions" as though they are the answer to Canada's difficulties of presenting itself to the world. Those so far have been of no benefit to Canada and its film community.

Now Pay-TV is around the corner. The winners of the licences to operate this potentially lucrative service have fallen over themselves promising Canadian films and programmes. CRTC regulations are supposed to make sure they live up to their promises. No one expects that they will; no one expects that the CRTC will compel them to do so. Television stations are past-masters at evading content rules. Pay-TV companies will not be involved in production themselves; they will commission producers to provide them with programmes and motion pictures. And it is the same hustlers who are lining up at the doors.

Perversely, Québec – the province which gives Canada the most difficulties over political and cultural matters – has given Canada its one distinguished film in the past year. The once exasperatingly obscure Jean-Pierre Lefèbvre, who turned the corner in his discovery of the human psyche with *Les dernières fiancailles* (*The Last Betrothal*), is back again with *Les fleurs sauvages* (*The Wild Flowers*). This was invited to the Directors' Fortnight at Cannes, where it won a FIPRESCI Award for its "poetry, warmth and human tenderness."

Canadian Film Development Corporation

Investments in French and English-track production from the Canadian Film Development Corporation (CFDC) will not increase in 1982/83 if the federal government does not inject capital into the corporation's finance pool, a report to the House of Commons Standing Committee on Communications and Culture says. Because it can no longer finance productions in French on an equity basis, the CFDC says its 1982/83 budget for Québécois projects has been almost entirely committed, leaving little funds for ventures late in the summer or for generating new ones. Three major films are set to shoot in Québec with budgets totalling almost $13,500,000, but only one is now shooting. Another 13 are in development, but cannot start without proper financing.

The CFDC says its budgetary situation is just as serious for English-track projects, except for those able to make use of the corporation's interim financing fund. "The fact remains, however, that, with commercial financing now scarce, the CFDC is the only source of high-risk funds. The back-up of production exists," the brief says, adding that "22 projects are in development and could go into production this year." Unfortunately, the CFDC is simply financially incapable of responding to the demand.

The prospect for any kind of substantial production is diminished, says the corporation, by the future application of a 50% CCA over one year. "The continuing advantage of the 100% CCA is not recognized by the financial and investment community," it says. "The lowering of marginal tax rates and the limitations on interest deductibility contained in the November budget, compounded by high interest rates, have caused hesitation within financial circles."

In response to small increases in its operating

budget and a need to develop an industrial base of Canadian production through new financing strategies, the CFDC says its medium-term plans (1982–86) will include a de-emphasis of feature films in comparison to TV and short films within the total Canadian private sector production; an increase of Canadian film sales here and abroad through the CFDC's Film Canada operations in collaboration with other federal agencies, the provinces and the private sector; a working relationship with provincial governments and agencies to decentralise the private sector and promote regionally-based production and distribution, and promotion of Canadian cinema and its creators, performers and craftsmen through industry support programmes.

The objectives of new approaches to financing production are to diversify and decentralise the production base of Canada's private sector industry, says the CFDC, adding that its strategy includes the development of "packages" of films to be sold to investors under the CCA and the 1982

and 1983 (Half-year Convention) rules; stimulation of other forms of production, especially lower-budgeted production and regional projects; the encouragement of co-productions as a means to expand the industry's base, and "the development of competence within the financial community to finance culturally important projects with a guaranteed return through activities such as banking or discounting distribution contracts."

The CFDC says it wants to "package" three fiction features in collaboration with the Institut Québécois du Cinema with its participation of $500,000 equity and to help financially with script and project development in features and documentaries. On the English-track production side, the CFDC says "packages" of five or six productions with budgets of between $750,000 and $2,000,000 are needed, with its participation on an equity as well as interim level. Script and project development, including made-for-TV productions and a low-budget feature programme with CFDC equity is also needed, it says.

notable films

LES FLEURS SAUVAGES (The Wild Flowers). Dir: Jean-Pierre Lefèbvre. A gentle, understanding and perceptive look at family life observed during the summer when, for a week, the wife's mother comes on her annual visit. The little irritants, tensions, misunderstandings, joys and delights are all accurately conveyed, together with the moments of happiness, the sadness of time passing, the sudden awareness at the end of the day of the need to find some meaning to those things in life which become increasingly unimportant. It is acted with perfect naturalism by Marthe Nadeau, Michèle Magny, Pierre Curzi, Eric Beausejour, Claudia Aubin. Prod: Cinak. 152 mins. Colour.

others

ESCAPE FROM IRAN (The Canadian Caper). Dir: Lamont Johnson. A hurried job of telling the true story of how the Canadian ambassador to Iran at the time of the revolution assisted American embassy officials in escaping from the country. Gordon Pinsent, R. H. Thomson, Chris Wiggins. Prod: Canamedia Productions. 96 mins. Colour.

HUMONGOUS. Dir: Paul Lynch. Another version of the "dreadful something" hiding in the basement – this time in an old house on an island. Janet Julian, David Wallace, Janit Baldwin. Prod: Humongous Productions. 93 mins. Colour.

SCANDALE. Dir: George Mihalka. Low budget "quickie" made to cash in on the reputed use by the staff of the Quebec Legislature of video equipment to make a

LES BEAUX SOUVENIRS (The Old Memories). Dir: Francis Mankiewicz. A strange, brooding yet compelling narrative, told in fragments which finally come together, about a young woman who returns to her family home outside Québec city only to find that her father ignores her in favour of her sister, who has moved into her former bedroom and removed all traces of their mother. Her sister is also possessed by a strange passion for her father. The past slowly reappears and the various pieces make up an absorbing family study. Monique Spaziana, Julie Vincent, Paul Herbert, R. H. Thompson. Prod: National Film Board. 113 mins. Colour.

porno picture. At first a funny spoof, it turns sour when hard-core pornography is introduced. Sophie Lorain, Alpha Boucher, Gilbert Comtois. Prod: RSL Films. 90 mins. Colour.

UNE JOURNEE EN TAXI. Dir: Robert Menard. Frustrating taxi ride through Montréal with a prisoner on parole who is determined to kill the friend who betrayed him. Jean Yanne, Gilles Renaud. Prod: Videofilms (a French-Canadian co-production). 90 mins. Colour.

forthcoming films of note

The Grey Fox (d. Phillip Borsos); The Wars (d. Robin Philips); War Story (N.F.B.); Lupus (d. Bahman Farmanara, Script by George Woodcock).

National Film Board

The N.F.B. has struggled through another year coping with budget cuts and criticism of its role in the trade, its spending, the nature and quality of its work, and its very necessity to cultural life. Much to its surprise, it found itself in a glare of publicity over a documentary on pornography called *Not a Love Story* which, typically for a Canadian film, is about pornography not so much in Canada but in New York. Because it was made by two women film-makers, Bonnie Sherr Klein and Anne Henderson, and reflects the feminine point of view, it received well-deserved support. Yet because the film itself lacks shape, consistency and is somewhat naive, male critics who found it lacking were severely castigated by women's groups for not being sympathetic to the way women feel – and were further accused of exhibiting male superiority! The film was banned for commercial exhibition in Ontario.

One of the best documentaries made by the NFB for many years is *A War Story* (82 mins.), directed by Anne Wheeler, in which she tells the story of her father, Dr. Benjamin Wheeler, and his years in a Japanese PoW camp in Taiwan. Wheeler was a doctor with the British-Indian army sent to Singapore at the time of the Japanese invasion. After the surrender, he and hundreds of British soldiers suffered dreadfully at the hands of the Japanese; many more would have died had it not been for Wheeler's care and devotion. The film is a clever amalgam of archive footage with re-enacted scenes; Donald Sutherland reads excerpts from the doctor's diaries written to his wife and sons. It is a moving and authentic film, reminding us of a subject little dealt with since *The Bridge on the River Kwai*.

Barry Greenwald, who received critical acclaim for his first student film, *Metamorphoses* (1979), has made a one-hour documentary for the NFB entitled *Taxi*, which looks at the taxi business in Toronto and the lives of the drivers. It is funny and concerned, lively and revealing.

The International Division of the NFB sold 215 titles in 30 countries during the last quarter of fiscal 1981/82 (January–March 1982). *Black Ice*, a documentary on the sport of iceboat racing produced in Toronto, was sold in Czechoslovakia,

Norway, Sweden and the U.S.A. The quarter included a major sale of Norman McLaren films to the U.K.'s new Channel Four. Following is a list of those sales.

Austria *Bead Game;* **Czechoslovakia** *Black Ice; Laugh Lines; This is an Emergency;* **Denmark** *Earthware; Lady Fishbourne's Complete . . . ; Metal Workers; Threads; Wax and Wool;* **Finland** *Cannabis; Aucassin and Nicolette; How Death Came to Earth; Story of Christmas; Wind; Every Child; Children of the Tribe; Hard Oil; Wolf Pack;* **France** *Le pays de la terre sans arbre;* **West Germany (incl. West Berlin)** *Volcano;* **Iran** *Beginning; After Life; Lines Horizontal; Icarus; Cycle; The Street; Neighbours; Above the Horizon; The Wind; Metamorphoses; Estuary; The Sea; Man: The Polluter; Element 3; Best Friends; 60 Cycles; Mindscape; Deep Threat; Satellites of the Sun; Zea; Path of the Paddle; Doubles Basic; It's Snow; Cycling: Still the Greatest; Magic Flute; Paradise Lost; Nails; Buster Keaton Rides Again; Why Me; Paddle to the Sea; Notre univers; Air; What Is Life; Lion and Mouse; Face of the Earth; Sky; Harness the Wind;* **Israel** *Boomsville; Monsieur Pintu;* **Italy** *Getting Started; This Is Your Museum Speaking; About Puberty and Reproduction;* **Japan** *Cosmic Zoom; Hunger; Street Music;* **Korea** *Games of the XXIst Olympiad;* **New Zealand** *Rusting World; Decline;* **Norway** *Christmas Cracker; Sea Dream; Black Ice; Day Off; Blowhard; Delta Plane; Easter Eggs; The Egg; Faces; The Hometown; The Horse; Lady Francis Simpson; Log Driver's Waltz; Love on the Wheels; The Performer; Beginnings; La Plage; S.P.L.A.S.H.; Trees;* **Singapore** *Mr. Symbol Man; Danny and Nicky; The Ross Family Mystery; Fixes in Time; A Victorian Album; Kurelek; This Was the Beginning Parts 1 and 2; Name of the Game Is Volleyball; Diving; No Place for Cowards; Cycling: Still The Greatest; Maud Lewis; A World without Shadows; Images Stone B.C.; Pictures Out of My Life; Garden of the Great Spirit; Haida Carver;* **South America (10 countries)** *About Flowers; Balablok; Climates of North America; Development of a Fish Embryo; High Arctic; Tchou Tchou; A Tree Is a Living Thing; Under the Rainbow;* **Sweden** *Premiers Jours; Beginnings; Black Ice; Every Child; Jacky Visits the Zoo; Lady Fishbourne's Complete . . . ;* **Switzerland (Italian)**

D'ou vient la Vie; **Taiwan** *North China Commune; Un mois à Woukang; China: A Land Transformed;* **United Kingdom** *59 Films by and about McLaren; Boomsville; Bow and Arrow; Town Mouse and Country Mouse; Bate's Car; Doctor Woman; Bravery in the Field; Fiddlers of James Bay; Flight of the Snows; Horse Drawn Magis; Sandcastle; Why Men Rape;* **U.S.A.** *Images of the Wild; The Hoarder; Paradise Lost; The New Alchemists; Sun Wind and Wood; Child Behaviour: You; Mr. Symbol Man; Symbol Boy; Doctor Woman; North China Factory; Why Men Rape; Continuum; For Land's Sake; Getting Started; Black Ice; Melvin Arbuckle: Famous Canadian; S.P.L.A.S.H.; The Town Mouse and the Country Mouse;* **Yugoslavia** *Beautiful Lennard Island; Benoit; Gurdeep Singh Bains; I'll Find a Way; Kevin Alec; My Friends Call Me Tony; My Name is Susan Yee; Veronica; Best Friends; The Drag; King Size.*

ONTARIO

We service the province through our regional film theatres and Festival Ontario.

FILM

We show the old and the new from the entire international spectrum.

INSTITUTE

We provide comprehensive information and archival services.

Ontario Science Centre, 770 Don Mills Road, Don Mills, Ontario, M3C 1T3, 416/429-4100

Government of Ontario / Ministry of Culture

Specialised Film Showings

Le Cinéma Parallèle, a non-profit organisation dedicated to the showing of historic and experimental films as part of its distribution body, La Coopérative des Cinéastes Indépendants, and which is responsible for the annual Festival International du Nouveau Cinéma, Montréal; the Ontario Film Theatre (Ontario Film Institute), Toronto, with regional programmes in Windsor, Brockville, Sarnia; the National Film Theatres (National Film Archive), Ottawa, Edmonton, Kingston; the Cinémathèque Québécois, Montréal, the Conservatory of Cinema Art (Concordia University), Montréal; the Pacific Cinémathèque, Vancouver; the Funnel (experimental films), Toronto; and the first-run and repertory cinemas, Fine Arts, Festival, Revue, Cineforum, in Toronto; Outremont, Seville, in Montréal, Underground (Edmonton); Varsity (Vancouver).

Figures (Dominion Bureau of Statistics)

Regular Theatres	1979: 1,070
	1980: 1,037
Net Receipts	1979: $239,349,000
	1980: $271,128,000
Paid Admissions	1979: $86,010,000
	1980: $88,980,000

(*Latest figures available*)

Publications

Canadian Film Digest Yearbook
(Exhibition, Distribution, Production etc,)
Film Publications of Canada Ltd
175 Bloor St. East
Toronto, Ontario, M4W 1E1
$12.00 per copy. Extremely useful reference book on all aspects of trade matters and related activities.

Canada's American Films

The latest group of "Stars and Stripes" pictures – in which Canadian towns are often used for cities or unnamed places in the U.S.A. and which employ American actors – include: **The Class of 1984** d. Mark Lester – a thoroughly revolting picture which cynically exploits the issue of crime and violence in schools (Perry King, Merrie-Lynn Ross, Roddy McDowall, Timothy Van Patten); **Death Bite** d. William Fruet – a horror film about snakes (Peter Fonda, Oliver Reed); **Hank Williams: "The Show He Never Gave"** d. David Acomba – a musical in which the singer tells his story (Sneezy Walters, Dixie Seatle); **If You Could See What I Hear** d. Eric Till – tiresome tale of the life of blind American singer, Tom Sullivan (Marc Singer, R. H. Thomson); **Julie Darling** d. Paul Nicolas (shot mostly in Germany) – tired story of teenage daughter who loves daddy and murders second wife (Anthony Franciosa, Isabelle Mejias); **Kings and Desperate Men** d. Alexis Kanner – confused and pretentious kidnap melodrama (Patrick Macnee, Margaret Trudeau, Alexis Kanner); **Paradise** d. Stuart Gillard (shot in Israel) – feeble re-working of *The Blue Lagoon*, supposedly taking place in the Middle East (Willie Aames, Phoebe Cates); **Porky's** d. Bob Clark (shot in Florida) – gross sex-comedy about students in the Fifties (Kim Cattrall, Dan Monahan); **Sneakers** d. Joseph L. Scanlon (shot in Florida) – two thirteen-year-old tennis players and the pressures in their lives (Susan Anton, Carling Bassett); **Visiting Hours** (formerly *Fright*) d. Jean-Claude Lord – psychopath on the loose (Lee Grant, William Shatner).

A SCENE FROM *TED BARYLUK'S GROCERY*, A SHORT FILM FROM THE NFBC SHOWN IN COMPETITION AT THE CANNES FILM FESTIVAL 1982

Chile

by Malcolm Coad

The division of Chilean cinema into that produced at home and that made in exile became even more apparent this year. While the country's near economic collapse reduced production in Chile itself even further than that described in recent editions of the IFG – only one film was made this year, and that a 40 minute short – exiled directors from Finland to Costa Rica, the USSR to Canada, made a total of 18 films. Of the 105 films made by Chilean directors since the 1973 military coup brought about this division, 90 have been made in exile.

In Chile the effects of the country's deepening economic crisis could be seen in the closure of yet more cinemas, particularly in the capital, Santiago. Audiences continued to decline, despite an increase in the number of films premiered from 220 in 1980 to 265 in 1981 (mostly from the U.S.A.). The effect on production was even more damaging. In Chile the national audience is considered too small to provide a major return for commercial investors and under the military government all state protection for local production has been abolished. The handful of independent producers must therefore rely almost entirely on the profits from making television commercials to finance their projects. Production of these, however, fell by half this year, with the inevitable result. One film was made, the 40-minute documentary *Domingo de Gloria (Glorious Sunday)* by the brothers Juan Carlos and Patricio Bustamante. This is a contemplative montage of aspects of life in the Chilean countryside, described by its makers as "an excursion beyond the well-known, into those regions of our reality where nothing can truly be narrated, from which one returns with fragments of memory and emotion."

However, economic problems – and others, such as severe censorship and blacklists of supporters of the pre-1973 government – have not dampened the will of those concerned with cinema to maintain the country's film culture. For the first time since 1973 seasons of Chilean cinema were organised inside the country. The first was in a major Santiago cinema, the Sala Bandera. Its success led in September 1981 to a week's season

of some ten films on the television channel run by the University of Chile, Canal 11. While these seasons ignored both exile production and the boom in film-making under the Popular Unity government overthrown by the military, they were nevertheless important reaffirmations of the talents of Chilean film-makers.

Meanwhile, longstanding projects were edging towards completion, held up by lack of finance, and others were being planned. Carlos Flores's *Identicamente Igual (Identically the Same)* still awaits money for final editing. Christian Sanchez's *Los deseos concebidos (Desires Conceived)* was due for release at about the time this edition of the IFG went to press. Carmen Neira and Jaime Alaluf, two of the makers of the acclaimed short *Invernadero (Wintering)*, shown at Lille in 1981, were working on a medium-length documentary examining Chile's particular cultural identity, *Talca, París y Londres (Talca, Paris and London)*. Their former partner, Benjamin Galemiri, was also preparing a project with a group of young actors and film-makers. The Bustamante brothers were looking for backing for a feature to follow *Domingo de Gloria*, for which a script is ready. Silvio Caiozzi was planning a feature with the well-known writer Jorge Edwards.

One of the most significant developments in the past year has been an upsurge in the use of video as an alternative to more expensive film projects. Such is the interest in the medium – 15 projects are already on tape – that a video exhibition hall was opened in April 1982 in a Santiago theatre, the Teatro La Comedia. Several of Chile's leading film-makers are now working in video. Carlos Flores and Guillermo Cahn (whose production company, Foco Film, has been a major force in keeping the country's cinema alive) are making a series of tapes on Chilean writers, involving new shooting and the re-working of material already on film. The writers will be Nicanor Parra, Jose Donoso and a third so-far un-named. The sculptor and expert on pre-Colombian art, Hernan Puelma, has begun work on a series of 15 tapes on the art of Chile's pre-Colombian peoples. And one of the country's leading theatre companies, Ictus, has thrown itself with enthusiasm into video production, so far making no fewer than ten tapes, including theatre pieces, sketches and documentaries, the latter on subjects such as the influence of the mass media, homelessness and life in Santiago. Two of these productions were directed by Silvio Caiozzi.

A further project was that of Hernán Castro and Victor Misa, who made a 25-minute tape on the situation of Chile's Mapuche indian people. The programme, called *Ngillatun*, was made together with the Mapuches' own cultural organisation, the Centros Culturales (Cultural Centres).

In exile, the past year was one of intensified activity. Miguel Littin, Chile's best-known director, shot a major feature in Nicaragua. Called *Alcino y el Condor* (*Alcino and the Condor*), the film was reputed to be a return from his recent "grand frescoes" to the lower-key style of his first feature *El Chacal de Nahueltoro* (*The Jackal of Nahueltoro*), made in 1969. Patricio Guzmán, director of the mammoth documentary *La Batalla de Chile* (*The Battle of Chile*), filmed his first major feature *La Rosa de los Vientos* (*Rose of the Winds*). A Spanish/Venezuelan/Cuban co-production, the film is a magic evocation of Latin America's struggle for political and cultural independence from the Spanish Conquest to the days of space travel and high technology. It features the Spanish singing star Padxi Andión, the Chilean actors and actress Nelson Villagra, Hector Noguera and Coca Rudolphy, the Venezuelan actor Andrubal Menendez, and has special participation by the veteran Argentinian film-maker Fernando Birri.

In Europe, Raul Ruíz made two features, *El Techo de la Ballena* (*The Roof of the Whale*) in Holland, and *Les Trois Couronnes Danois de Matelots* (*The Three Danish Matelots' Crowns*). In September 1981 a full retrospective of Ruíz's work was presented at the National Film Theatre, London, preceded by a scaled-down package at the Edinburgh Film Festival. This was the first time that the considerable body of his work, both in Chile and in exile, had been brought together almost complete, and provided a unique insight into the career of one of the most remarkable film-makers in the world today.

Elsewhere, features were made by Claudio Sapiain in Sweden, Sebastian Alarcón in the U.S.S.R., and Dunav Kúsmanich in Colombia. The latter director merits special mention as his two films were long in the gestation and made in difficult circumstances in a country where there is very little production. Valeria Sarmiento followed up her *Gens de partout, gens de nulle part* (*People from Everywhere, People from Nowhere*) with the humorous but uncompromising essay on Latin American *machismo*, *El Hombre cuando es Hombre* (*A Man When He's a Man*), shot in Costa Rica. Chile's other two women directors, Angelina Vasquez and Marilú Mallet, made three films.

The solidarity of Chilean film-makers with events in Nicaragua was pointed up not only by Miguel Littin's and Angelina Vasquez's work there, but by that of Wolfgang Tirado, a founder member of the production company Tercer Cine (Third Cinema) in Managua, Nicaragua's capital. His documentary *Gracias a Dios y la revolución* (*Thanks to God and the Revolution*) documents the participation of Nicaraguan Catholics in the revolution in their country.

Useful Address

Association des Amis de la Cinémathèque Chilienne
c/o Confluences
15 Passage Lathuile
75018 Paris.

China

(*see* People's Republic of China)

Denmark

by Claus Hesselberg

The Danish Film Act, once described as the best of its kind in the world, has now been revised and recently passed by parliament. Compared with the former act, there are no major changes apart from the fact that the committee has stressed the importance of Denmark producing at least 15–20 films a year to keep the business alive. Far fewer than that have been made in recent years: the Film Institute has been under siege by many talented film-makers, only eight of whom have been able to make a feature.

The revised act is accompanied by an economic framework to subsidise the above-mentioned number of films. Without such support from the government via the institute, no features at all would be made in Denmark. One may, therefore, hope that the institute and its advisers are able to initiate the above plan – they have had some years to learn the tricks of the trade.

Although we now have the new act – and peace on the film battlefield – there is still a long way to go. Many cinemas, especially in rural districts, have closed down; others are barely alive. Help is needed fast, and it may come from local communities.

The system of selecting worthwhile projects has not been revised under the new act. The Danish Film Institute is still the body through which financial guarantees are given; projects to be supported are selected by advisers. In spite of the

expertise, it is not an easy task – some mistakes have been made and will be made again. Also, because of the paucity of local films, each opening attracts much attention from both the media and the public. A failure is neither easily hidden nor forgotten. And we cannot "afford" too many failures.

Peter D. Ringgaard's *Truck Driver* was not received very favourably by critics, but surprisingly enough it had good results at the box-office. Though the script has its faults, it is an honest account of the lives of people trucking from Denmark to Italy. *Cry Wolf*, directed by Jens Ravn, was expected to be much better than it turned out. A thriller, based on a best-seller, with two of the best Danish actors in the leads and an experienced director and crew: how could it go wrong? However, the quality of the ingredients is not always a guarantee – the mixing is what produces good results.

Have You Seen Alice?, a first feature by Brita Wielopolska, describes a group of Copenhagen youngsters living in the underbelly of the city, away from home and involved in petty crime and drugs. A weak script mars a film based on documentary evidence and facts.

One of the few short-films to have won the Danish film prize Bodil was Hans-Henrik Jørgensen's grim and moving *The Story of Kim Skov* about a boy who when his family moves from the

OTTO BRANDENBURG AND PETER SCHRØER IN *RUBBER TARZAN*

STIG RAMSING AND HELLE RYSLINGE IN *STAB IN THE HEART*

The Tree of Knowledge

The new film by Nils Malmros
presented
by Per Holst Filmproduction

 KERNE FILM ApS

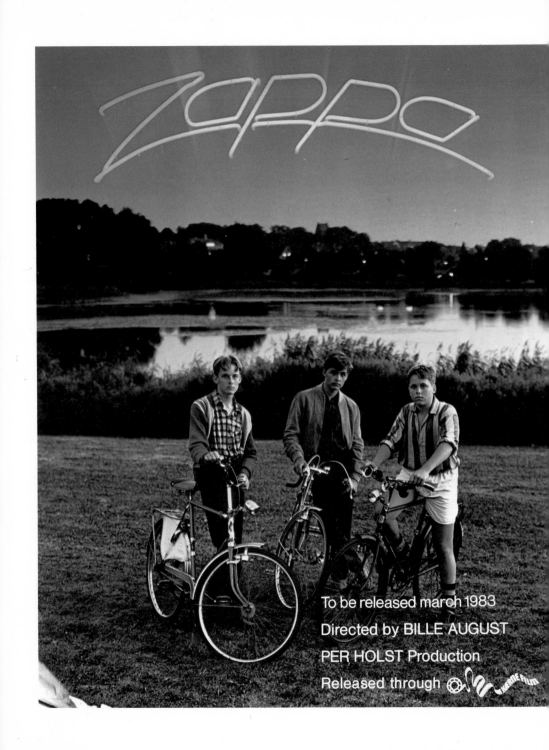

ZAPPA

To be released march 1983
Directed by BILLE AUGUST
PER HOLST Production
Released through KÆRNE FILM

countryside to the city, becomes a born victim of bullying and teasing.

A UNICEF award winner at the Berlin film festival, and a local as well as international success last year, was *Rubber Tarzan*. It is about a small boy, his dreams and fantasies, and the way he discovers that life is just a matter of finding out what you are good at.

The famous Olsen Gang series is finally at an end – so says the production company Nordisk. It made two films with the popular gang in one year – the thirteenth being the last.

Another film praised for its quality was *The Tree of Knowledge*, directed by Nils Malmros. The film was selected for the "Un Certain Regard" section at Cannes and a great number of Danes also thought the film was well worth a look.

Two respected TV reporters made *Your Neighbour's Son*, a dramatised documentary about the former military junta in Greece. Interviews with former henchmen alternate with reconstructed scenes in prisons and training camps. It is a cruel and gripping film with perhaps more television than cinema potential.

Lene and Sven Grønlykke, who in the Sixties made *The Ballad of Carl Henning*, returned with *The Ballad of Linda*, a love story set during the construction of the Danish railways around 1910. A disappointing film to some, but praised highly by others.

Henning Carlsen wrote and directed the thriller *Your Money or Your Life* without gaining the expected success, and Søren Melson and Hans-Erik Philip did a more conventional crime story based on a best seller by the late Frits Remar, *The Parallel Corpse*.

Waiting for release as of summer 1982 is Erik Clausen's *Felix*. After his successful start in films with *Casablanca Circus* everyone is looking forward to Clausen's new venture. Children – and their parents – are looking forward to the Bertram films, now in production at Nordisk Film Studio.

Newcomer Claus Ploug is directing *The Imprudent Lover*, based on the novel of the same title by Leif Panduro. And Bille August is shooting *Zappa*, based on a Bjarne B. Reuter best seller.

Jørgen Leth, famous for *A Sunday in Hell*, *Peter Martins – A Dancer* and *Good and Evil*, is on location in Haiti shooting a story about a foreign correspondent with the working title *Interference*.

HEIDI ZAHLE THOMSEN IN *HAVE YOU SEEN ALICE?*

The Danish Film Institute
is subsidizing, producing,
showing, promoting and selling

DANISH FILMS

For further information,
please contact:

 The Danish Film Institute
Store Søndervoldstræde - DK-1419 Copenhagen K.
Phone: (01) 57 65 00 - Telex: 31465 - Cable: Filminst.

Morten Arnfred has also begun shooting a film about farming life, *What a Charming Country*.

With just enough money to pull through, Danish cinema is not dead yet. Thumbs up, we wait for some box-office hits in the near future.

recent and forthcoming films

DET PARALLELLE LIG (The Parallel Corpse). Script: Søren Melson, Hans-Erik Philip, from a novel by Frits Remar. Dir: Søren Melson, Hans-Erik Philip. Phot (colour): Henning Kristiansen. Editor: Grete Møldrup. Players: Buster Larsen, Agneta Ekmanner, Jørgen Kiil, Masha Dessau, John Hahn-Petersen. Prod: Panorama Productions. 116 mins.
PENGENE ELLER LIVET (Your Money or Your Life). Script: Henning Carlsen. Dir: Henning Carlsen. Phot (colour): Claus Loof. Edit: Lizzie Weischenfeldt. Players: Dick Kaysø, Pauline Rehné, Ole Ernst, Henning Moritzen, Ghita Nørby, Lise Ringheim. Prod: Dagmar Filmproductions. 93 mins.
THORVALD OG LINDA (The Ballad of Linda). Script: Lene and Sven Grønlykke. Dir: Lene and Sven Grønlykke. Phot: Claus Loof, Jesper Høm. Edit: Lars Brydesen. Players: Stina Ekblad, Carsten Bang, Aksel Erhardtsen, Erik Paaske, Otto Brandenburg, Jesper Klein. Prod: ASA Filmproduction. 89 mins.
KUNDSKABENS TRAE (The Tree of Knowledge). Script: Nils Malmros, Fred Cryer. Dir: Nils Malmros. Phot (colour): Jan Weincke. Editor: Janus Billeskov-Jansen, Merete Brusendorff. Players: Eva Gram Scholdager, Jan Johansen, Line Arlien-Søborg, Gitte Iben Andersen. Prod: Per Holst Filmproduction. 110 mins.
FELIX (Felix). Script: Erik Clausen. Dir: Erik Clausen. Phot (colour): Morten Bruus. Edit: Lizzie Weischenfeldt. Players: Tove Maës, Poul Bundgaard, Allan Olsen, Erik Clausen, Katrine Jensenius. Prod: Casablanca 80 Productions.
OTTO ER ET NAESEHORN (Otto the Rhino). Script: Rumle Hammerich, Mogens Kløvedal. Dir: Rumle Hammerich. Phot (colour): Dan Laustsen. Edit: Niels Pagh. Players: Axel Strøbye, Kirsten Rolffes, Birgit Sadolin, Judy Gringer, Leif Sylvester Petersen. Prod: Metronome Productions.
KIDNAPPET/TRE ENGLE OG FEM LØVER (Kidnapping/Three Angels and Five Lions). Script: Sven Methling, from stories by Bjarne B. Reuter. Dir: Sven Methling. Phot (colour): Claus Loof. Edit: Finn Henriksen. Players: Otto Brandenburg, Lisbeth Dahl, Jesper Langberg, Michael Nezer, Elin Reimer, Axel Strøbye. Prod: Panorama Productions. Two features with similar casts and crews. Each approx. 90 mins.
DER ER ET YNDIGT LAND (What a Charming Country). Script: Jørgen Ljungdahl, Morten Arnfred. Dir: Morten Arnfred. Phot (colour): Dirk Brüel. Edit: Anders Refn. Players: Ole Ernst, Karen-Lise Mynster, Ingolf David. Prod: Metronome Productions.
DEN UBETAENKSOMME ELSKER (The Imprudent Lover). Script: Claus Ploug, from a novel by Leif

Panduro. Dir: Claus Ploug. Phot (colour): Dan Laustsen. Edit: Lars Brydesen. Players: Dick Kaysø, Karen-Lise Mynster, Pia Vieth, Peter Steen, Ghita Nørby. Prod: Crone Film/Gunner Obel. 100 mins.
INTERFERENS (Interference). Script: Jørgen Leth. Dir: Jørgen Leth. Phot (colour): Alexander Gruszynski. Edit: Kristian Levring. Players: Hanne Uldal, Henning Jensen. Prod: HTM Films.

Statens Filmcentral

When the Danish film critics were distributing the annual awards, the "Bodils," they chose to nominate three films in the drama-documentary genre: Hans-Henrik Jørgensen's *Historien om Kim Skov* (*The Story of Kim Skov*), Jon Bang Carlsen's *Hotel*

STILL FROM *YOUR NEIGHBOUR'S SON*

of the Stars and Wagner's, Flindt Pedersen's and Stephensen's *Din Nabos son* (*Your Neighbour's Son*). All three films have a running time of around one hour and have assumed the motto of seeking a "creative treatment of actuality" – to use a John Grierson statement.

Hans-Henrik Jørgensen's film, which was awarded the Bodil, describes the sad lot of *Kim Skov*. The boy moves with his parents from the country into a suburb and thus into another school with other friends. Kim is a contemplative type, who is exposed to mobbing by the other children, and who must – in order to survive in the new, harsh and dull world – become one of the mobbers. Hans-Henrik Jørgensen wrote in co-operation with Ulla Ryum, the writer, the script of the film based on research in the Danish school world, where "survival of the fittest" is often a reality. The film was produced in co-operation between Statens Filmcentral and the Danish Film Institute, and it is already in great demand in 16mm from Statens Filmcentral.

The talented Jon Bang Carlsen returned to his investigation into the documentary film language with his *Hotel of the Stars*, which is a documentary comedy on the extras of a Hollywood hotel. The extras are waiting for their chance in show business, the first step being to get a speaking part.

Din Nabos son (*Your Neighbour's Son*) has already gained international applause. The film is a fascinating description of the making of a torturer – as it could have happened all over the world to your neighbour's son. The film is based on specific documentary material gathered by Amnesty International on the training of Greek youth during the Junta period. Reconstructed scenes are mixed with interviews with victims and ex-torturers – constituting the TV journalists Jørgen Flindt Pedersen's and Erik Stephensen's first medium-length documentary produced for Ebbe Preisler Film/TV, the Danish Film Institute, The Danish Radio, The Swedish Radio and Statens Filmcentral.

With *66 scener fra Amerika* (*66 Scenes from America*), the well-known Jørgen Leth returned to experimentation within the short film genre. Leth – and his colleague Ole John – have in 40 minutes given *their* impression of the United States of America, an impression based on a fascinating and aesthetic point of view on an America quite

STILL FROM *THE STORY OF KIM SKOV*   PHOTO: STATENS FILMCENTRAL

different from that given daily by the news media. Statens Filmcentral produced the film.

Another veteran is Jannik Hastrup, who – having worked for many years with the animated children's series on the Nordic thralls – returned to his previous satiric style with a new animated interpretation of a Hans Christian Andersen tale, *Hvordan det videre gik den Grimme Ælling (The Further Adventures of the Ugly Duckling)*. The film, produced by Statens Filmcentral and Jannik Hastrup himself, tells the story of the duckling, where a visit to the psychiatrist is one of many procedures taken by the unlucky figure.

Two other talented animation workers were asked by Statens Filmcentral to make a film for young people on the dangers of too much alcohol . . . Flemming Quist Møller and Anders Sørensen introduced for this purpose a new figure *Det Usynlige Pattebarn (The Invisible Baby)*, the one always pleading for more and more. The film is intentionally made in a non-moralising way, the philosophy being that this is the best way to further a discussion among the youngsters.

Also ironic in its style is another Statens Filmcentral film directed by Jørgen Vestergaard, *Danmark dit og mit (Denmark Yours and Mine)*, which is a study of twenty years' political and architectural planning in Denmark. Many things have gone completely wrong, the film says, because of our desire for a country based on material welfare.

Statens Filmcentral sent two film debutants to Nicaragua, Michael Mogensen and Helle Toft Jensen. They made a film about the young nation, which set out to create democracy after the revolution. *Revolutionens børn (The Children of the Revolution)* portrays the participation of the young people in building up above all the anti-illiteracy campaign among the older people.

Producers

Foreningen af Danske Filmproducenter
c/o A/S Nordisk Films Studier
Mosedalvej
DK-2500 Valby.
Chairman: Bent Fabricius-Bjerre.
ASA Film Production
8, Gammel Torv
DK-1457 Copenhagen K.
Phone: (01) 11 00 87.
Telex: 19 853 piret dk.
A-S Panorama Film
Lindegården, Gl. Tølløse
DK-4340 Tølløse.
Phone: (03) 48 55 80.
Telex: 44 147 asapan dk.
Cop. Casablanca 80
c/o Det danske filmstudie
Crone Film
c/o Det danske filmstudie
Dagmar Film produktion
c/o Det danske filmstudie
Det danske filmstudie
52 Blomstervaenget
DK-2800 Lyngby
Phone: (02) 87 27 00.
Telex: 37 798 studio dk.
Filmforsyningen
12A, Gammeltoftgade
DK-1355 Copenhagen K.
Phone: (01) 12 06 55.
Focus Film
c/o Nordisk Films Kompagni
Mosedalvej
DK-2500 Lyngby
Phone: (01) 30 10 33.
HTM Film
8, Gl. Torv
DK-1457 Copenhagen K.
Phone: (01) 11 00 87.
Telex: 19 853 piret dk.
Kollektiv Film
20. Valkendorfsgade
DK-1151 Copenhagen K.
Phone: (01) 12 69 96.
Kosmorama Film
1, Lille Kirkestraede
DK-1072 Copenhagen K.
Phone: (01) 14 22 66.
Laterna Films
50, Klampenborgvej
DK-2930 Klampenborg.
Phone: (01) 63 33 11.
Merry Film Produktion
30 Reventlowsgade
DK-1651 Copenhagen V.
Phone: (01) 31 71 21.

Metronome Productions
31, Vibevej
DK-2400 Copenhagen NV.
Phone: (01) 19 01 12.
Telex: 27 204 metror dk.
Nordisk Films Kompagni
Mosedalvej
DK-2500 Valby
Phone: (01) 30 10 33.
Telex: 15 286 filmko dk.
Obel Film
31, Storegade
DK-7700 Thisted.
Phone: (07) 92 10 33.
Per Holst Filmproduktion
17, Livjaegergade
DK-2100 Copenhagen Ø.
Phone: (01) 26 42 00.
Telex: 19 430 kaerne dk.
Vester Vov Vov Filmproduktion
27, Gl. Kongevej
DK-1610 Copenhagen K.
Phone: (01) 31 31 05.

Short Films and Documentaries

For information about all Danish
short films and documentaries,
please contact:
Statens Filmcentral
27, Vestergade
DK-1456 Copenhagen K.
Phone (01) 13 26 86.
Cable: Statfilm.

Distributors/Importers

Foreningen af filmudlejere i Danmark
(The Association of Danish Film
Distributors)
73 Bredgade
DK-1260 Copenhagen K.
Phone: (01) 14 88 61.
Alliance Film
Postboks 66
27, Gl. Vartovvej
DK-2900 Hellerup.
Phone: (01) 62 58 74.
ASA-Panorama-Palladium
Lindegaarden, Gl. Tølløse
DK-4340 Tølløse.
Phone: (03) 48 55 80.
Telex: 44 147 asapan dk.
Bellevue Films
451, Strandvejen
DK-2930 Klampenborg.
Phone: (01) 63 64 00.
CHS Films
32, Sct. Pederstraede
DK-1453 Copenhagen K.
Phone: (01) 13 37 20.

Columbia-Fox
16, Søndermarksvej
DK-2500 Valby.
Phone: (01) 17 22 66
Telex: 19 497 unique dk.
Constantin Film
8, Gl. Torv
DK-1457 Copenhagen K.
Phone: (01) 12 01 24.
Dan-Ina Film
55, Rådmandsgade
DK-2200 Copenhagen N.
Phone: (01) 83 63 62.
Filmselskaberne
Dansk Svensk Film – Europa Film
Teatrenes Film Kontor
28, Reventlowsgade
DK-1615 Copenhagen V.
HTM Film
8, Gl. Torv
DK-1457 Copenhagen K.
Phone: (01) 11 00 87.
Telex 19 853 piret dk.
Jesper Film
36, Frederiksberggade
DK-1459 Copenhagen K.
Phone: (01) 11 55 77.
Kommunefilm
Ballerup Centret
DK-2750 Ballerup.
Phone: (02) 65 62 62.
Kaerne Film
17, Livjaegergade

DK-2100 Copenhagen Ø.
Phone: (01) 26 42 00.
Telex: 19 430 kaerne dk.
Nordisk Films Kompagni
7, Axeltorv
DK-1609 Copenhagen V.
Phone: (01) 14 76 06.
Telex: 15 286 filmko dk.
Obel Film
31, Storegade
DK-7700 Thisted
Phone: (07) 92 10 33.
Regina Film
1A, Frederiksberggade
DK-1459 Copenhagen K.

Phone: (01) 13 09 75.
Toofa Film
404, Brovejen
DK-5500 Middelfart
Phone: (09) 41 42 42
United International Pictures
13, Hauchsvej
DK-1825 Copenhagen V.
Phone: (01) 31 23 30
Telex: 22 402 cicas dk.
Warner & Metronome Film
16, Søndermarksvej
DK-2500 Valby.
Phone: (01) 46 88 22.
Telex: 19 497 unique dk.

KUNDSKABENS TRÆ
(The Tree of Knowledge)

Script: Nils Malmros and Fred Cryer. Direction: Nils Malmros. Photography (colour): Jan Weincke. Editing: Marete Brusendorff, Janus Billeskov-Jansen. Music: none. Players: Eva Gram Schjoldager, Jan Johansen, Line Arlien-Søborg, Marian Wendelbo, Gitte Iben Andersen. Produced by Per Holst Film Production for Kaerne Film release. 110 mins.

In recent years, the Scandinavians have become pre-eminent in the field of films for and about children, and no director has laboured more perceptively than Nils Malmros, who until now has not received due recognition abroad. But *The Tree of Knowledge* should change all that, for various reasons. The first is that it deals with kids somewhat older (in 8th and 9th grade) than the ones featured in Malmros's earlier work, and that adults can therefore relate to their own adolescence much more immediately. The second is that

the film takes place at the close of the Fifties, at a period when even public schooling still contained an element of discipline and formality, so that much of the children's development evolves *within* the framework of the class and its ritual excursions. The other factors contributing to the film's considerable impact are those we know already: Malmros's wonderful way of letting his young subjects unravel their emotions behind the backs of their elders, his unforced use of symbols (the fish, for example, passed round the table at summer camp), and his innate sense of humour that time and again disperses any hint of pedagogy. As they dance in fumbling nearness to the recorded music of Chris Barber, and stray near the illicit pleasures of sex and smoking, these boys and girls grow both physically and psychologically, emerging from the chrysalis of childhood to the quirkish individuality of their teens.

PETER COWIE

ABOVE: ANDERS TOENSBERG WITH RIKKE BONDO IN *ZAPPA*

ANDERS TOENSBERG, PETER REICHHARDT, AND MORTEN HOFF IN *ZAPPA*

STILL FROM *FELIX*   PHOTO: ROALD PAY

STILL FROM *TRUCK DRIVER*

Eire   by Liam O'Leary

For the cinema in Eire it has been the best and the worst of times. The Minister for Industry and Energy, with rather indecent haste, and worse timing closed the National Film Studios of Ireland, just after the very successful Third Festival of Films from Celtic Countries at Wexford and on the eve of the public hearings of the Government-sponsored Irish Film Board. The former, organised locally by Donald Taylor Black, the Cultural Adviser of the Cork Film Festival, brought many diverse film elements together. At the hearings of the Film Board very full and representative attendances covered every aspect of Irish Film activities and of course strong exception was taken at the ill-advised Ministerial action in removing one vital facility for Irish film-making.

The Ardmore Studios have had a chequered history since they were opened by Emmett Dalton and Louis Elliman in 1958. Here were made Robert Altman's *Images*, Francis Coppola's *Dementia 13*, Martin Ritt's *The Spy Who Came in from the Cold*, Peter Glenville's *The Lion in*

Winter, and more recently John Boorman's box-office success, *Excalibur*. It is ironic that the studios that helped make this multi-million grossing film should be closed down as a commercial failure. John Boorman himself was a director of the Studios and fought valiantly for their survival in the face of Government procrastination and penuriousness. He was also a member of the Irish Film Board from which understandably he has resigned. The case for survival is being fought on the grounds that this facility is vital for Irish film-making. It is pointed out that the losses incurred by the Studios were minimal compared with those of other Government-subsidised white elephants, and also that concealed assets included influx of money into the country, touristic prestige and advertising.

The Irish Film Board under its experienced Chairman, Muiris MacConghail, is the outcome of a Government Committee inspired by John Huston in 1968. It has a meagre £4,000,000 to spread over the next four years. Previously the Arts Council awarded large sums towards the production of winning scripts, the latest grant being to Miss Pat Murphy in the nature of £60,000 for a film on the Irish heroine Anne Devlin. Her *Maeve* – assured of world-wide distribution – ironically drew meagre attendances at the Irish Film Theatre, causing one letter-writer to ask if Ireland really wanted an Irish film industry.

Reaction to the cinema in Ireland has always been ambiguous. The inferiority complex is perhaps a corollary to the enormous Irish literary success and the deficiencies of Irish visual culture. But Ireland has a film tradition, if a somewhat fragmented one. From 1910 the Kalem Film Company in Killarney made Irish films and we would have had a Film Studio but for the intervention of War in 1914. The genuinely native Film Company of Ireland made features of considerable interest from 1916 to 1920. The recent death of Tom Cooper of Killarney reminds one of his remarkable sound film *The Dawn* of 1935, made under extraordinary circumstances. The passing of Miss Annie O'Sullivan some months previously breaks a link with that same Kalem Company which included Sidney Olcott, Gene Gauntier and Robert Vignola.

Today Ireland has young and talented film-makers. This year saw *Maeve* by Pat Murphy and *Angel* by the young writer, Neil Jordan, both of which reflect the Ulster tragedy and its confusion. These promising films are however flawed by obliqueness of narrative which weakens their impact. With the Arts Council, the Irish Film Board and, let it be added, the practical encouragement of the British Film Institute, Irish film-making will continue. The vital impetus of a National Film Archive is however lacking and many an Irish film would have perished but for the fact that the National Film Archive of Britain sheltered it.

The National Film Institute of Ireland under its new energetic director Malachy O'Higgins has now become the Irish Film Institue with ambitious plans for development including a Film Archive.

The Irish Film Theatre, with excellent Winter Festivals, has however been having a falling off in attendances and suffered the collapse of its Limerick Theatre. It has to some extent been hoist with its own petard as its efforts to secure audiences on a short-term basis and by rather dubious appeal has not paid off.

The Federation of Irish Film Societies under its director Michael O'Dwyer has gone from strength to strength and branches proliferate all over the country.

R.T.E., the Irish Television authority has been one important source of film-making and the two-hour film by Sean O'Mordha, *Is There One Who Understands Me?*, made for the James Joyce Centenary, and Trish Barry's compassionate *Victims of Violence* were prize-winners at the Festival of Films from the Celtic Countries. Following the success of the serial *Strumpet City*, a new historical series *The Day of the French*, shot in Ireland and France and featuring Jean-Claude Drouot, has just been completed.

The commercial cinema in Eire is going through a crisis following the advent of the video-tape market. In Dublin attendances are being affected by the incidence of violence in the depopulated inner city which makes people hesitant about stirring out at night.

In spite of the tribulations there is still a solid core of young Irish people who want to make films and a larger group which feels that late in the day as it is – 90 years after Lumière to be precise – Ireland should have its own film industry.

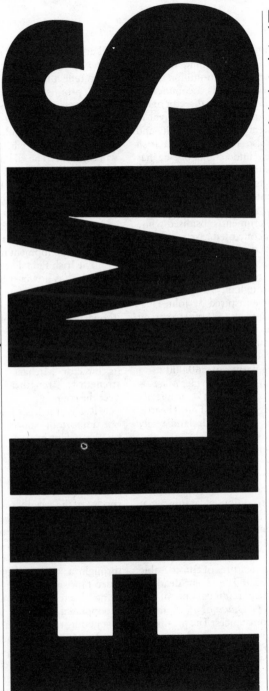

FILMS

We Know How To Finance / Produce / Distribute / Export / Import

Jörn Donner Productions, Pohjoisranta 12, SF-00170 Helsinki 17
Phone International +358 0 661212, Telex 123439 jdp sf.

Finland

by Kari Uusitalo

About a year ago we looked at the state of film theatres in Finland and found that the boom was over. However, so far the downward trend has not been too steep: there was only a 2.03% drop in attendance figures in 1981 compared with the previous year. The total audience in 1981 was 9,762,000, i.e. a 2.03 per capita figure. Viewings of Finnish films accounted for 12% of the total, which is more or less the same as the average for the previous decade.

This was the third consecutive year when the number of theatres increased. The net increase was 2.84% and the total number of theatres in operation at the end of 1981 was 362. The total number in operation is not likely to rise above this figure.

The most popular film in Finland in 1981 was a James Bond story, *For Your Eyes Only* (379,427 people). *The Marital Crisis of Numbskull Emptybrook* came second (371,032) and the American film *Seems Like Old Times* (286,864) third. The next were *Private Benjamin* (269,787) and *The Blue Lagoon* (208,419), followed by the Finnish *Milka – A Film about Taboos* (202,091) and the American Oscar winner, *Ordinary People* (174,413).

Of the new Finnish films, *Ramses and the Dreams*, *Gotta Run!* and *Sign of the Beast* are dealt with separately below. *That Kiljunen Family*, a family entertainment film based on a popular Finnish children's book, was directed by Matti Kuortti and produced by Filminor. It was an appropriate continuation to the good-natured comedy movies first made in the mid-Seventies by

the company's late chief director, Risto Jarva. Tapio Suominen, who directed *Right on, Man!*, a film well-received by critics and audiences alike, has made a new study of the problems of the young in their late teens called *Gunpoint*. However, he did not attain the same momentum and artistry as in his previous film, even if his description of life in the depressed areas of the country was extremely persuasive in its sense of desperation.

Fugitives of All Kinds by Visa Mäkelä, *The Village of Simpletons* by Pertti Reponen etc. and the *P . . . P . . . Pill* by Frank Siponen were all poor quality farces, uninspiring and easily forgettable. *The Marital Crisis of Numbskull Emptybrook* by Ere Kokkonen brought to the screen the leading Finnish anti-hero of the last decade for the sixth time, interpreted by Vesa-Matti Loiri. As the movie proved another box-office hit, these films will no doubt continue.

The Saimaa Gesture by Aki and Mika Kaurismäki and the *Rock 'n' Roll Digger* by Jouko Lehmuskallio were both musical movies featuring live recordings and leading Finnish light music bands in main roles. *i+i* and *I'm Scared* by Pekka Hyytiäinen were movies from a director whose will to make films was stronger than his technical know-how.

A great number of fictional shorts is a characteristic and very interesting feature of Finnish film production. The 60-minute *Liar* and *Rainy Season*, which were both shown in 1980, were already indicative of this trend and at the Tampere Short Film Festival in February 1982 there were more

FINANCING
Finnish Films at Home

PROMOTING
them abroad

Finnish Films
in Competition at Major Festivals 81

Berlin MILKA
Cannes FLAME TOP
Moscow NIGHT BY THE SEASHORE

The Finnish Film Foundation
Salomonkatu 17 b SF-00100 Helsi
phone +358-0-6941255
cable SESFINN Helsinki telex 12

STILL FROM *THAT KILJUNEN FAMILY*, A FILMINOR PRODUCTION

fictional Finnish shorts than normally during a whole decade. The determined efforts made by the Finnish Film Foundation during the last couple of years to back this type of movie production have borne rewarding fruit. The first prize in the Finnish series at the Tampere Festival was won by Janne Kuusisto for his interesting apprentice work, *Breakthrough*, and the 50,000 mark Risto Jarva Award went to Tapani Lundgren's short, *Visit*. Several other new fictional shorts would have deserved an award.

The Finnish Film Foundation was reorganised under the direction of its new chairman, Jörn Donner, in 1981. Perhaps the most visible sign was the invitation to Veikko Korkala, previous head of production at the Foundation, to become the Foundation's first managing director as of June 1, 1981, for a two-year period.

AJOLÄHTÖ
(Gotta Run!)

Script: Matti Ijäs, Mikko Niskanen. Direction: Mikko Niskanen. Photography: (Fujicolor) Henrik Paersch. Editing: Tuula Mehtonen. Music: Mikko Alatalo, Harri Rinne, Martti Luoma. Players: Timo Torikka, Tero Niva, Heikki Paavilainen, Sanna Majanlahti, Paavo Pentikäinen, Leena Uotila, Lis Laviola. Produced by Mikko Niskanen for National-Filmi Oy. World Sales: Jörn Donner Productions Oy. 109 mins.

Mikko Niskanen, 53, the famous director of *Boys* and *Under Your Skin*, has produced one disappointment after another with his films during the last decade. After *Eight Deadly Shots*, a television serial completed in 1972, Mikko Niskanen has not been able to put his all into a movie as he used to. With this background in mind it is a

1912-1982

FINLAND'S OLDEST AND BIGGEST BRANCH-COMPANY

FINLAND'S LEADING INDEPENDENT DISTRIBUTOR

FINLAND'S LARGEST CIRCUIT OF CINEMAS

ADAMS FILMI OY

**MIKONKATU 13 · 00100 HELSINKI 10 · FINLAND
PHONE: 176440
CABLES: ADAMSFILM · TELEX: 123321 ADAX SF
DIRECTORS: FELICIA ADAMS · THOMAS ADAMS**

pleasure to note that Niskanen's eleventh feature film, *Gotta Run!*, marks a triumphant return to the conscientious, disciplined, and artistically successful cinematic art of this miracle man of the Sixties.

Despite his age, Mikko Niskanen has pre-served a warm heart for the young, in particular, and their problems. The main characters in *Gotta Run!* are three 21-year-old youths from the same village, who are just out of the army. Their joy in returning home quickly changes into everyday

STILL FROM MIKKO NISKANEN'S VERY SUCCESSFUL *GOTTA RUN!*

O.Y. KINOSTO

FOUNDED 1920

CINEMA CIRCUIT

1 9 CINEMAS WITH 2 4 SCREENS
IN 8 LARGEST CITIES.
TOTAL NUMBER OF SEATS 9416.

DISTRIBUTION

INDEPENDENT AMERICAN AND
EUROPEAN FILMS.

FINNISH FILMS.

IN ALL APPR. 1 5 RELEASES PER YEAR.

O.Y. KINOSTO

Kaisaniemenkatu 2 b
00100 Helsinki 10
Cables: Kinosto
Telex:122964 kinos sf
Telephone: 65 00 11
Bank: Union Bank of Finland

cares, the search for jobs, longing to be far away, and disputes with their families. Without illusions, but maintaining a sense of humour, Mikko Niskanen depicts the feelings, experiences and lives of the main characters during the first months after they get out of the army. They split up, their paths cross later, they unite for a moment and then go their separate ways again. The fatherland has three more rootless citizens.

Mikko Niskanen has demonstrated a keen sense of direction in casting Timo Torikka, Tero Niva and Heikki Paavilainen in the main roles. This time he has avoided the foibles of the films immediately preceding *Gotta Run!* by restraining himself, and not taking the lead role.

KARI UUSITALO

RAMSES JA UNET
(Ramses and the Dreams)

Script: Heikki Partanen, Riitta Rautoma. Researcher: Rostislav Holthoer. Direction: Heikki Partanen. Photography (colour): Henrik Paersch. Editing: Riitta Rautoma. Music: Antti Hytti. Produced by Heikki Partanen for Partanen & Rautoma. World Sales: Partanen & Rautoma Films. 83 mins.

Ramses and the Dreams, a new film by Heikki Partanen and Riitta Rautoma, is an odd combination, a feature documentary with a focus remote from Finland, that is, Egypt and the distant past. The filming in Egypt took several weeks and produced 25 hours of basic material. The final motion picture uses 83 minutes of this. The main character in *Ramses and the Dreams* is the artist Sennezem, a man who lived 3,100 years ago, at the time of the assassination of Ramses III. Sennezem's well-preserved tomb was found at the end of the Nineteenth Century. His tale, illustrated by means of ancient art, stems from confused musings triggered by the murder of the pharoah. Man slays his brother, the slaves rise in revolt, and signs of decadence are in evidence everywhere.

The extensive ancient art of Egypt arose from belief in an after-life, in the journey to the Land of the West, where the dead were able to continue their life in their own image and mummy for eternity. The more complete the provisions and things placed in the burial chamber, the more

STILL FROM HEIKKI PARTANEN'S POETIC DOCUMENTARY ABOUT ANCIENT EGYPT – *RAMSES AND THE DREAMS*

secure the life on the other side. With love and care Heikki Partanen and Riitta Rautoma have recovered the past of Egypt from its hiding places in the pyramids and the Cairo Museum. Special permission was also obtained to open tombs. The narration is composed primarily of dialogue translated directly from the hieroglyphics and is palpable evidence of how little man's innermost emotions have changed over three millenia. The primitive methods of the village potter – still used today – and child labour are further indications of this.

The key to the success of the motion picture is cameraman Henrik Paersch, whose work skilfully brings this age-old art to life. The music of Antti Hytti, which was composed before the final editing, also makes an important contribution. The jazz-like melodies mesh well with the events of the motion picture. On the whole, *Ramses and the Dreams* is an interesting and challenging journey to Egypt and its ancient art, a film that requires an alert mind to detect all the messages transmitted on different wave-lengths.

KARI UUSITALO

HANNU LAURI AND ESKO SALMINEN IN *SIGN OF THE BEAST*

PEDON MERKKI
(Sign of the Beast)

Script: Timo Humaloja, Jaakko Pakkasvirta, Arvo Salo. Directing: Jaakko Pakkasvirta. Photography (Eastmancolor): Esa Vuorinen, Pertti Mutanen. Editing: Jaakko Pakkasvirta. Music: Henrik Otto Donner. Players: Esko Salminen, Irina Milan, Tom Wentzel, Hannu Lauri, Vesa-Matti Loiri. Produced by Matti Penttilä for Filmityö Oy. World Sales: Filmityö Oy. 120 mins.

Olavi Paavolainen (1903–64) was a Finnish writer of the Thirties who wanted to attract attention with his works, and also succeeded in doing so. Jaakko Pakkasvirta (b. 1934) is a Finnish film director of the Seventies who seeks to attract attention with his films, and has also succeeded. Here in Finland all his previous films have been the subject of lively debate: *Green Widow* (1968), *Summer Rebellion* (1970), *Home for Christmas* (1975) and *Poet and Muse* (1978). Now the same interest is focused on the director's most recent work, *Sign of the Beast* (1981).

The basis for *Sign of the Beast* is Olavi Paavolainen's last work, *A Gloomy Monologue* (1946), based on entries in the author's war-time diaries. The scriptwriter decided to divide the writer of *A Gloomy Monologue* into two persons, Kaarlo and Olavi in the film, both of whom are authors in the service of the intelligence section of the supreme command. The third role is that of a German liaison officer, who during the war marries the woman Kaarlo loves. And there is even more profound symbolism involved: The Maid Finland is allied in war with Germany, and turns her back on Western civilisation. As in *Poet and Muse*, Esko Salminen plays Kaarlo, the lead male role in *Sign of the Beast*. The German liaison officer is Tom Wentzel, and the woman who deceives Kaarlo is Irina Milan. *Sign of the Beast* is more impressive proof that Jaakko Pakkasvirta knows how to make a film that is rich in detail, skilful in its character descriptions, provocative in terms of the way the plot is handled. The final line of the film is as relevant today as it was four decades ago, Olavi's letter to his friend Kaarlo ends with this question: "Do you still believe in people?"   KARI UUSITALO

recent and forthcoming films

YÖ MEREN RANNALLA (Night by the Seashore). Dir: Erkko Kivikoski. Players: Pertti Palo, Sirkku Grahn, Pauli Virtanen, Eeva Eloranta, Mauri Heikkilä. Prod: Anssi Mänttäri for Filmiauer Oy.
ROKKIDIGGARI (Rock 'n' Roll Digger). Dir: Jouko Lehmuskallio. Players & music: Mistakes, Hurricanes, Sleepy Sleepers, Kojo, Falcons. Prod: Art Films Only.
SAIMAA-ILMIÖ (The Saimaa Gesture). Dir: Aki Kaurismäki and Mika Kaurismäki. Players & music: Juice Leskinen Slam, Eppu Normaali, Hassisen Kone, Juhani Leskinen, Ismo Alanko. Prod: Villealfa Film-productions Oy.
SYÖKSYKIERRE (Gunpoint). Dir: Tapio Suominen. Players: Kimmo Liukkonen, Markku Toikka, Esko Nikkari, Jorma Markkula. Prod: Jorma K. Virtanen for Sateenkaarifilmi Oy (Rainbow-Film Ltd.).
KILJUSEN HERRASVÄKI (That Kiljunen Family). Dir: Matti Kuortti. Players: Jukka Sipilä, Marja-Sisko Aimonen, Jouni Lukus, Kai Lemmetty, Tuija Ahvonen, Paavo Piskonen. Prod: Kullervo Kukkasjärvi for Filminor Oy.
AIDANKAATAJAT (Overthrowers). Dir: Olli Soinio. Players: Martti Kainulainen, Erkki Pajala, Toivo Tuomainen. Prod: Sateenkaarifilmi Oy.
ARVOTTOMAT (The Worthless). Dir: Mika Kaurismäki. Players: Matti Pellonpää, Pirkko Hämäläinen, Jukka Hirvikangas. Prod: Villealfa Filmproductions Oy.
ISO VAALEE (Big Blond). Dir: Veikko Kerttula. Players: Kirsti Otsamo, Kimmo Tuppurainen. Prod: Sateenkaarifilmi Oy.
JON–KERTOMUS MAAILMAN LOPUSTA (JON – A Story about the End of the World). Dir: Jaakko Pyhälä. Players: Kari Väänänen, Vesa-Matti Loiri, Matti Geschonneck. Prod: Tambur Ltd Tamburfilm.
MUUKALAINEN (A Stranger). Dir: Markku Lehmuskallio. Players: Jouni Labba, Jukka Häyrinen, Eeva-Maija Haukinen, Mauri Vakkilainen. Prod: Giron-Filmi Oy.
PESSI JA ILLUSIA (Pessi and Illusia). Dir: Heikki Partanen. Players: Jorma Uotinen. Prod: Partanen & Rautoma Films.
SATU KUNINKAASTA JOLLA EI OLLUT SYN-DÄNTÄ (The King Who Had No Heart). Dir: Liisa Helminen and Päivi Hartzell. Prod: Neofilmi Oy.
ULVOVA MYLLÄRI (The Howling Miller). Dir: Jaakko Pakkasvirta. Players: Vesa-Matti Loiri, Eija Ahvo. Prod: Filmityö Oy.

State Institutions

Taideteollinen korkeakoulu, Kuvallisen viestinnän laitos, Elokuva-ja tv-linja – University of Industrial Arts, Faculty of Visual Communication, Film and TV Studies. Founded 1959. Aesthetically based educational institution giving courses in the fields of film and television. Address: Ilmalantori 1 D, SF-00240 Helsinki 24.
Valtion elokuvatarkastamo – State Board of Film Censorship and **Valtion elokuvalautakunta** – State Film Board. Founded originally in 1919. Entrusted with the

task of censoring films in advance. Address: Jaakonkatu 5 B, SF-00100 Helsinki 10.
Valtion elokuvataidetoimikunta – State Motion Picture Art Commission. Founded 1964. Duties include promoting creative and performing arts connected with films, knowledge of and interest in such arts and timely research of significance from the standpoint of the arts. Address: Mariankatu 14 D 27, SF-00170 Helsinki 17.
Valtion audiovisuaalinen keskus – **State AV-Centre.** Founded 1976. Together with the Finnish education authorities the State Audiovisual Centre is responsible for distributing audiovisual study aids and promoting their use throughout Finland. Address: Hakaniemenk. 2, SF-00530 Helsinki 53.

Organisations

Elokuva-ja televisiokasvatuksen keskus– Centre of Film and TV Education in Finland. Founded 1958. Address: Yrjönkatu 11 D 10, SF-00120 Helsinki 12.
Elokuva-ja tv-opiskelijat – Films and TV Students. Founded 1972. Address: Kamerataiteen laitos, Ilmalantori 1 D, SF-00240 Helsinki 24.
Mainoselokuvatuottajain liitto – Advertising Film Producers' Association in Finland. Founded 1966. Address: Kaisaniemenkatu B 29, SF-00100 Helsinki 10.
Nordic Film Festival, The, c/o Walhalla, Mannerheimintie 18 A, 6th floor, SF-00100 Helsinki 10.
Suomen elokuva-arkisto – The Finnish Film Archive. Founded 1957. Address: P.O. Box 216, SF-00181 Helsinki 18 (Lönnrotinkatu 30 C, SF-00180 Helsinki 18).
Suomen elokuvakerhojen liitto – The Federation of Finnish Film Societies. Founded 1956. Address: Yrjönkatu 11 A 5a, SF-00120 Helsinki 12.

Suomen elokuvakontaki – The Finnish Film Contact. Founded 1970. Purpose: to promote the production and distribution of non-commercial films. Address: Yrjönkatu 11 E 10, SF-00120 Helsinki 12.
Suomen elokuvasäätiö – The Finnish Film Foundation. Founded 1969. Address: Salomonkatu 17 B 6, SF-00100 Helsinki 10.
Suomen elokuvateatterinomistajain liitto – Finnish Cinema Owners' Association. Founded 1938. Address: Kaisaniemenkatu 3 B 29, SF-00100 Helsinki 10.
Suomen elokuvatoimistojen liitto – The Finnish Film Distributors' Association. Founded 1937. Address: Kaisaniemenkatu 3 B 24, SF-00100 Helsinki 10.
Suomen elokuvatuottajat – The Finnish Film Producers. Founded 1973. Address: c/o Mia Seiro, Iso-Roobertinkatu 3–5 A 25, SF-00120 Helsinki 12.
Suomen elokuvatyöntekjät – The Association of Finnish Film Workers. Founded 1972. Address: Maneesikatu 4 c, SF-00170 Helsinki 17.
Suomen filmikamari – Finnish Film Chamber. Founded 1923. Central business organisation of the Finnish film industry. Address: Kaisaniemenkatu 3 B 29, SF-00100 Helsinki 10.
Suomen filmivalmistajien liitto – The Finnish Film Producers' Association. Founded 1945. Address: Kaisaniemenkatu 3 B 29, SF-00100 Helsinki 10.
Suomen kaitaelokuvaajien liitto – Finnish Society of Amateur Film-Makers. Founded 1955. Address: Keijukaistenpolku 11 B 17, SF-00820 Helsinki 82.
Tampereen elokuvataide – Society for Film Art in Tampere. Founded 1969. Organises, among others, the Tampere International Short Film Festival annually in February. Address: PO Box 305, SF-33101 Tampere 10.

Production Companies

Amusement Films Oy &
Funny-Films Oy & Filmituotanto
Spede Pasanen Oy
Veneentekijänt. 14
SF-00210 Helsinki 21.
Arctic-Filmi Oy
Siltak. 12 A 5
SF-33100 Tampere 10.
Art Films Only
Liisank. 19 B
SF-00170 Helsinki 17.
Atelje Seppo Putkinen & Kni
Risukallio
SF-83100 Liperi.
Cine-Art Oy
Höyläämönt. 5
SF-00380 Helsinki 38.
Curly-Produktion &
Filmproduktion Visa Mäkinen
Iso Uusik. 10 B
SF-28100 Pori 10.

Oy Epidem Ab
Kalevank. 34 D 9
SF-00180 Helsinki 18.
Fennada-Filmi Oy
Kulosaarent. 27
SF-00570 Helsinki 57.
Filmiauer Oy
Katajanokank. 6
SF-00160 Helsinki 16.
Filmi-Jatta Oy
Eerikink. 5
SF-00100 Helsinki 10.
Filminor Oy
Laivastok. 8-10 D 33
SF-00160 Helsinki 16.
Filmiryhmä Oy
Kruunuvuorenkatu 5 f
SF-00160 Helsinki 16.
Filmityö Oy
Luotsik. 3 C 19
SF-00160 Helsinki 16.

Finn Co-Producers Oy
c/o Filmi-Jatta Oy
Eerikink. 5
SF-00100 Helsinki 10.
Giron-Filmi Oy
SF-99320 Kätkäsuvanto.
Jörn Donner Productions Oy
Pohjoisranta 12
SF-00170 Helsinki 17.
Kari Kekkonen & Pekka Pajuvirta
Jaakkimant. 24 D
SF-02140 Espoo 14.
Kinotuotanto Oy
Katajanokank, 6
SF-00160 Helsinki 16.
Erkko Kivikoski
Nuuksio
Märstrand
SF-02820 Espoo 82.

Käpy-Filmi Oy & National-Filmi
Oy
Iso Roobertink. 35-37 G 88
SF-00120 Helsinki 12.
Lähikuva Oy
Jämeräntaival 11 C
SF-02150 Espoo 15.
Markku Lehmuskallio
Forselleksent. 5-7 C 23
SF-02700 Kauniainen.
Neofilmi Oy
Korkeavuorenk. 2 b G
SF-00140 Helsinki 14.
Partanen & Rautoma Films
Kasarmik. 4 c
SF-00140 Helsinki 14.

Per-Olof Strandberg
Vänrikki Stoolink. 9 A 22
SF-00100 Helsinki 10.
P-Kino Oy
Katajanokank. 6
SF-00160 Helsinki 16.
Reppufilmi Oy
Katajanokank. 6
SF-00160 Helsinki 16.
Riitta Nelimarkka & Jaakko Seeck
Niittyranta 22
SF-00930 Helsinki 93.

Sateenkaarifilmi Oy
Albertink. 27 A 8
SF-00180 Helsinki 18.
Suomi-Filmi Oy
Bulevardi 12
SF-00120 Helsinki 12.
Tamburfilm Oy
Nervanderink. 12 A 4
SF-00100 Helsinki 10.
Villealfa Filmproductions Oy
Kristianink. 15 B
SF-00170 Helsinki 17.

Film Distributors

Adams Filmi Oy
Mikonkatu 13
SF-00100 Helsinki 10
Oy Cinema International
Corporation Ab
P. Esplanadi 33 A
SF-00100 Helsinki 10.
Cine-studio Oy
Mannerheimintie 6
SF-00100 Helsinki 10.
Diana-Film Oy
Vyökatu 8
SF-00160 Helsinki 16.
Eini Carlstedt
Hakakuja 2 C
SF-02120 Espoo 12.
Filmari Ky
Ari Tolppanen
c/o Nordfilm Oy
P.O. Box 1026
SF-00101 Helsinki 10.
Oy Fox Films Ab
P. Makasiinikatu 7 A 4
SF-00130 Helsinki 13.
Kamras Film Agency
Albertinkatu 36 D
SF-00180 Helsinki 18.

Kasetti-TV Oy
P.O. Box 284
SF-00101 Helsinki 10.
Kino-Filmi Oy
Itäinen teatterikuja 5 A 1
SF-00100 Helsinki 10.
Oy Kinosto
Kaisaniemenkatu 2 B
SF-00100 Helsinki 10.
Kosmos-Filmi Oy
Annankatu 41 G
SF-00100 Helsinki 10.
Lii-Filmi Oy
Kaisaniemenkatu 1 B
SF-00100 Helsinki 10.
Lunaris Oy
P.O. Box 284
SF-00101 Helsinki 10.
Oy Magna-Filmi Ab
Kalevankatu 32 E
SF-00100 Helsinki 10.
Ky Marten Kihlman
Laivurinkatu 33 C 69
SF-00150 Helsinki 15
Nordfilm Oy
P.O. Box 1026
SF-00101 Helsinki 10.

Republic-Filmi Oy
Kaisaniemenkatu 1 B
SF-00100 Helsinki 10
Ruusujen Aika Oy
Yrjönkatu 11 D
SF-00120-Helsinki 12.
Suomi-Fimi Oy
Bulevardi 12
SF-00120 Helsinki 12.
Tralag Oy
P.O. Box 284
SF-00101 Helsinki 10.
Oy United Artists Films Ab
P. Makasiinikatu 7 A 4
SF-00130 Helsinki 13.
Oy Valio-Filmi Ab
Kasarmikatu 48 B
SF-00130 Helsinki 13.
Walhalla – Forum for Nordic Films
in Finland
Mannerheimintie 18 A
SF-00100 Helsinki 10.
Oy Warner-Columbia Films Ab
P. Esplanadi 33
SF-00100 Helsink 10.

France   by Michel Ciment

In the autumn of 1981 there was an atmosphere of optimism among French exhibitors: audience attendances had risen and, probably because of the high quality of several local films, the French cinema seemed to attract filmgoers. The first three months of 1982 confirmed this trend and showed the best box-office results of the past fifteen years. However, producers were worried because their ally French TV – which co-finances many ambitious projects – had been paralysed by the reforms of the new socialist government. Furthermore, French TV seemed to want to disengage itself from cinema productions.

However, Minister of Culture Jack Lang, whose budget has almost doubled due to Mitterrand's desire to boost culture's position in French life, has shown an interest in the future of the cinema. Besides having a new head of the Cinémathèque Française – film-maker Costa-Gavras – to develop and modernise the institution, Lang also plans to restructure the teaching of cinema. He plans to have a major new film school with equipment and collaborators which IDHEC so poorly lacks.

He has also charged Jean-Denis Bredin to write a report on French cinema suggesting plans for the future. The report looks reformist but is certainly not revolutionary – understandable in a period of economic crisis. To attack the big trusts directly would endanger the production of expensive films and their export possibilities. Since one of the aims is to conquer foreign markets, the Bredin report does not attack the three major groups – Parafrance, Gaumont and UGC. Its proposals have nothing comparable to the Paramount decree of 1948 in the U.S.A. On the other hand, it proposes the dissolution of the Pathé-Gaumont combination, a partial fight against monopolies through encouragement to the regions, the creation of a fourth TV channel to co-operate with the film industry, a doubling of financial help for ambitious projects (avance sur recettes), and a return to working in the studios through a plan for their modernisation.

Nevertheless, French cinema had a difficult spring in 1982, and showed definite signs of inflation (parallel to the nation's economy). The agency Artmedia, which has a quasi-monopoly on all major film artists, is directly responsible for rising production costs by asking high salaries for its clients.

A total 231 feature films were made in 1981 (against 189 in 1980) – an all-time record. Of them, 186 were 100% French, the rest co-productions. The total does not include X-rated films without access to financial help. Production costs totalled 1,000,380,000 francs – or an average budget of 4,490,000 francs per film. Only seven films had a budget of over 20,000,000 francs; the cost for commercially ambitious films was between 5,000,000–8,000,000 francs (35 films came within this bracket).

Some 688 films were released in Paris during 1981 (against 527 in 1980). Audiences mostly chose local product, as witness the ten biggest grossers of the year (number of Paris admissions in brackets): 1 – *La chèvre* (comedy; Francis Veber; with Pierre Richard and Gérard Depardieu) 1,404,540; 2 – *Raiders of the Lost Ark* (Steven Spielberg) 1,258,285; 3 – *Le professionnel* (thriller; Georges Lautner; with Jean-Paul Belmondo) 1,192,085; 4 – *Quest for Fire* (Jean-Jacques Annaud) 1,128, 135; 5 – *Rox and Rouky* (Walt Disney) 1,089,342; 6 – *For Your Eyes Only* (James Bond) 908,090; 7 – *Les uns et les autres* (Claude Lelouch) 850,720; 8 – *Garde à vue* (thriller; Claude Miller; with Lino Ventura and Michel Serrault) 726,359; 9 – *Coup de torchon* (Bertrand Tavernier; with Isabelle Huppert and Philippe Noiret) 693,591; 10 – *Viens chez moi l'habite chez une copine* (comedy; Patrice Leconte) 680,436.

This popularity of French films made even more ridiculous a manifesto for the defence of cultural identity signed by several intellectuals; it was published in various newspapers and asked for the defence of France against the cultural imperialism of the U.S.A. In fact, of all the major European industries French cinema seems to have best survived and shown real continuity. Though several observers pretend that New Wave directors are

BEATRICE ROMAND AND ANDRE DUSSOLIER IN ROHMER'S *LE BEAU MARIAGE*

now doing the films that they criticised in their youth (not altogether true – *vide* Godard), it is nevertheless interesting to notice that the past year has seen accomplished new works by the five major New Wave film-makers.

Le beau mariage by Eric Rohmer, less daring than *La femme de l'aviateur*, is a brilliant comedy (and brilliantly acted by André Dussolier) about a young girl from the provinces who studies in Paris and decides to get married. She attempts to seduce a middle-aged lawyer and fails. The scheme is typical Rohmer; and so is the intelligence of the dialogue and the paradoxical morality play. *Le Pont du Nord* by Jacques Rivette, with Bulle Ogier and her daughter, is an adventure film (in the style of *Fantomas* or *Alice in Wonderland*) set in Paris – a discovery of the city as a maze or chessboard, against the background of a spy story. It fails to capture the playful spirit of *Céline et Julie vont en*

bateau, showing the limitations of improvisation, but it has some felicitous moments.

La femme d'à côté stands on the romantic side of Truffaut's personality. It is more captivating and surprising than the flawless, charming but a little mechanical *Le dernier métro*. Fanny Ardant and Gérard Depardieu have been lovers in the past; they are now married and by chance live as neighbours. She draws him into a new affair that he accepts half-willingly and which leads to tragedy. Claude Chabrol's *Les fantômes du chapelier* marks a return to form after the highly disappointing *Cheval d'orgueil*. Leaving aside all attempts at a sociological reconstruction (though it is adapted from Simenon), Chabrol concentrates on the relationship between his two main characters. Charles Aznavour, a shopkeeper, observes his neighbour Michel Serrault: he knows his secret (the murder of his wife) but does not reveal it,

ABOVE: BULLE AND PASCALE OGIER IN RIVETTE'S *LE PONT DU NORD*

ABOVE: CATHERINE DENEUVE AND YVES MONTAND IN *LE CHOIX DES ARMES*. BELOW: FANNY ARDENT AND GERARD DEPARDIEU IN *LA FEMME D'A COTE*

fascinated as he is by the assassin. Serrault gives an extraordinary performance, full of invention and fantasy; and Chabrol confirms himself as the legitimate heir of Hitchcock and Lang.

In *Passion* Godard is the heir of nobody except himself – and too much so according to many people. He remains at 52 the eternal child, breaking his toys, destroying classical narration, in his parallel stories of a factory strike and the shooting of a film about living paintings. The two "passions" of Godard – politics and make-believe (i.e. art) – are combined in a work with stunning visual moments, some exasperating passages, and a mixture of wry humour and emotion.

If one adds the return of Agnès Varda, with her charming and brilliant documentary on the murals of California, *Muvs murs*, one can see how a twenty-year-old movement still shows signs of vitality. Less energetic were the younger disciples of the New Wave. André Téchiné, with his melodrama *Hôtel des Amériques*, had a beautiful Catherine Deneuve and visual flair (with the help of Bruno Nuytten) to recreate the atmosphere of provincial Biarritz, but on the whole showed a rather sterile aestheticism: Jean-Louis Comolli, in *L'ombre rouge*, tries to evoke the bickerings of the Left during the Spanish Civil War but fails to bring life to its ideological and human conflicts.

One of the best French films of the year was signed by Michel Deville. *Eaux profondes*, from a Patricia Highsmith novel, does not have the boldness of his former *Dossier 51* and *Voyage en douce*, but it certainly shows dramatic control of the growing tension between an unfaithful wife (Isabelle Huppert) and murderous husband (Jean-Louis Trintignant). The Prix Delluc went this year to Pierre Granier-Deferre, an uneven and modest professional director who made a fascinating study in possession – *Une étrange affaire*, in which a businessman (played with devilish grace by Michel Piccoli) takes control of a company and mesmerises one of his employees.

The new generation of film-makers has struck box-office gold while confirming its talent. Bertrand Tavernier's *Coup de torchon*, from a Jim Thompson novel, is an evocation of French colonial Africa in the Thirties, with a macabre and grotesque tone new to the director's career. While it refers to French popular films of the period (full of exotic and colonial stories), it turns their themes upside down in a biting social critique, helped by remarkable players like Philippe Noiret, Eddie Mitchell and Stéphane Audran. More conventional in its subject-matter but a tour de force of *mise en scène*, Claude Miller's *Garde à vue* confirms Miller as a top director. The confrontation between a judge and a suspect (terrific acting by Lino Ventura and Michel Serrault) in one room allows Miller to build up a stifling sense of atmosphere and psychological suspense of the highest quality. Less successful was Alain Corneau in *Le choix des armes*, in which the brilliance of some sequences does not hide an easy acceptance on the director's part of tired clichés.

ABOVE: LINO VENTURA, GERARD LANVIN, AND MICHEL SERRAULT IN *GARDE A VUE*

The names mentioned so far have not suggested any distinct rejuvenation. However, the production year witnessed the appearance of original works, sometimes by newcomers. In fact, the French selection at the Cannes festival – although highly debatable (particularly since it eliminated Rohmer's and Chabrol's new films) – at least tried to suggest the existence of another cinema. Peter del Monte's *Invitation au voyage* was a sophisticated story about incest between a brother and the dead body of his sister, a tour through France with the aroma of *fin-de-siècle* decadence. Gérard Guérin's *Douce enquête sur la violence*, a post-Godard collage on politics, was awkward and ludicrous. Robert Kramer's *A toute allure*, on the contrary, captured in less than sixty minutes all the chaos of a generation, through the story of two young roller-skaters living in the modern outskirts of Paris and dreaming of making it to America.

ABOVE: PHILIPPE NOIRET AND ISABELLE HUPPERT IN *COUP DU TORCHON*. BELOW: MICHEL PICCOLI (LEFT) IN *UNE ETRANGE AFFAIRE*

Three films that were not in competition at Cannes broke new ground. Two are more or less autobiographical. Romain Goupil's *Mourir à trente ans* is about a generation and a friendship. Goupil has devoted a feature to his friend Michel Recanati, who committed suicide at the age of thirty and was a militant with him in the Trotskyite movement. Goupil had kept private films about their youth and he uses them with militant films and archive footage to record ten years of French political life (before and after May 1968). It is moving and lucid without ever being nostalgic or contemptuous. In *Cinq et la peau* Pierre Rissient – whose first feature, *One Night Stand*, has been on the shelf for five years because of the producer's

HAYDEE CASTILLO IN PIERRE RISSIENT'S *CINQ ET LA PEAU*

bankruptcy – has probably made the most original film of the season. It is a poem, an essay, a private diary combined – about a man drifting through Manila and confessing his thoughts and feelings about women, solitude, poverty and death. It is beautifully shot, with a sensuousness and sense of existential angst, and with a subtle relationship between image and commentary.

Finally, Catherine Binet's *Les jeux de la comtesse Dolingen de Gratz*, a first feature, is an astonishing puzzle. It mixes the character of Countess Dolingen de Gratz (from *Dracula*), a little girl's experience, and a divided couple with a mysterious husband who sets a trap for a burglar's visit. Based on a short story by Unica Zurn (Hans Bellmer's wife), it is a fascinating exercise in reality and fiction, pictorially stunning and with a complexity of narrative structure that will enchant partisans of dream-like cinema. At a time when world production is particularly conservative, such new winds on the French scene are particularly welcome.

LES FANTOMES DU CHAPELIER (The Hatter's Ghosts)

Script and direction: Claude Chabrol, from the novel by Georges Simenon. Photography (Eastmancolor): Jean Rabier. Editing: Monique Fardoulis. Music: Mathieu Chabrol. Art Direction: Jean-Louis Poveda. Players: Michel Serrault, Charles Aznavour, Monique Chaumette, Aurore Clément, Christine Paolini. Produced by Philippe Grumbach for Horizons Productions/Films A2/SFPC. 120 mins.

Chabrol in Simenon country offers greater promise than his recent efforts. Certainly this is his best film for some time, although without quite equalling the achievements of the early Seventies. The setting is a small Breton town: the "hero" is a respected hat merchant who has murdered his nagging wife and constructed an elaborate charade (involving a dummy woman in a wheelchair) to assuage the suspicions of his neighbours, notably the little tailor who lives opposite. From the opening shots of streets, windows and furtive figures darting down night alleys, it is clear that we are being offered a beautifully crafted, classical piece of narrative film-making.

Aided by regular cameraman Jean Rabier, Chabrol creates a world from these cluttered interiors, local restaurants and bars which constantly switches from everyday reality to the interior hysteria of a mind on the verge of disintegration. Apart from the murder flashback (done in several sweeping camera movements, ending with a mirror reflection), the tone is surprisingly quiet, even matter-of-fact; yet, except towards the end, Chabrol rarely lets the inner tension subside. His preoccupation with the strange passions lurk-ing behind the bourgeois facade of everyday meetings and actions, centres (as often before) on a series of elaborate, comic and sinister eating scenes which traverse the narrative like an *idée fixe*. Charles Aznavour adequately fills in the underwritten part of the tailor, but it is Michel Serrault who dominates the film in a performance which is actorish, demonic and perverse in turn. It is rendered with immaculate precision, especially in the moments when his prim, workaday persona changes into the haunted killer, alone in his upstairs room with his life-size mannequin (shades of *Psycho*) and facing his self-made phantoms.

JOHN GILLETT

French Film Producers

Activités Cinégraphiques
95 Champs Elysées
75008 Paris.
Adel Production
4 rue Chambiges
75008 Paris.
Agence Française d'Images
26 rue de l'Etoile
75017 Paris.
A. J. Films
87 av. Mozart
75017 Paris.
Albina Production
39 rue Marbeuf
75008
Alexandre Film
38 rue du Colisée
75008 Paris.
Alpes Cinéma
5 av. Velasquez
75008 Paris.
A. M. S. Productions
2 rue de Lancry
75010 Paris.
Ancinex
88 rue des Dames
75017 Paris.
Apple Films
34 Champs Elysées
75008 Paris.
A. R. C. Films
33 Champs Elysées
75008 Paris.
Argos Films
4 rue Edouard Nortier
92200 Neuilly.

Art Technique Cinématographique
3000
12 rue Chabanais
75002 Paris.
Artichaut Films
13 passage d'Enfer
75014 Paris.
Atya Production
35 rue des Bergers
75015 Paris.
Babylone Films
4 pl. du 18 Juin 1940
75006 Paris.
Basta Films
26 av. Pierre 1er de Serbie
75008 Paris.
Bavaria
31 place St. Ferdinand
75017 Paris.
Bela Productions
10 rue du Chaillot
75116 Paris.
Belstar Production
71 av. F. Roosevelt
75008 Paris.
Bloody Mary
52 rue Monsieur Le Prince
75006 Paris.
Brut Productions
33 av. de Wagram
75017 Paris.
Caméra One
6 av. Gourgaud
75017 Paris.
C.A.P.A.C.
5 rue Lincoln

75008 Paris.
Cap Films
70 Champs Elysées
75008 Paris.
Capi Films
61 rue des Saints Pères
75006 Paris.
Caraibes Productions
8 Impasse Bellevue
92100 Boulogne.
Carthago Films
99 av. du Roule
92200 Neuilly.
Castor Productions
44 Champs Elyseés
75008 Paris.
Cathala Productions
47 rue Pierre Charron
75008 Paris.
Cat's Film
1 rue Séguier
75006 Paris.
Cedra Films
53 rue des Prairies
75020 Paris.
Cerito Films
6 rue Gassendi
75014 Paris.
Challenge
29 Villa Wagram St-Honoré
75008 Paris.
Chloé Production
135 bd Pereire
75017 Paris.
Cinéastes Animaliers Associés
3 rue de Constantine

ZARAH LEANDER, CECILE SOREL, AND JEAN COCTEAU IN PARIS IN 1941. FROM EDGARDO COZARINSKY'S EXTRA-ORDINARY EVOCATION OF THE OCCUPATION PERIOD, *LA GUERRE D'UN SEUL HOMME*

75007 Paris.
Cinéfrance
78 Champs Elysées
75008 Paris.
Cinémag
19 rue Montrosier
92200 Neuilly.
Cinéphonic
21 rue Jean Mermoz
75008 Paris.
Cinépix
78 Champs Elysées
75008 Paris.
Cinéproduction
52 rue de Ponthieu
75008 Paris.
Cine Tamaris
86 rue Daguerre
75014 Paris.
Cinq Continents
18/20 rue du Pont Neuf
75001 Paris.

Citeca Productions
63 bd Beauséjour
75016 Paris.
Cité Film
58 rue Pierre Charron
75008 Paris.
C.O.F.C.I.
33 Champs Elysées
75008 Paris.
Comex Productions
23 rue de Maubeuge
75009 Paris.
Corona Films
44 av. Georges V
75008 Paris.
Courcelles Investissements
72 bd de Courcelles
75017 Paris.
Credo
53 bd V. Hugo
92200 Neuilly.
Critère Films

39 av. F. Roosevelt
75008 Paris.
Cythère Films
18 rue Marbeuf
75008 Paris.
Dargaud Films
12 rue Blaise Pascal
92200 Neuilly.
Diagonale Films
33 rue Danton
94270 Le Kremlin-Bicêtre.
Diam's Films
26 rue de la Croix Nivert
75015 Paris.
Dimage
70 rue de Ponthieu
75008 Paris.
Dovidis
42 bis, rue de Lourmel
75015 Paris.
Editions Thanatos
12 av. de Wagram

75008 Paris.
E. I. Productions
15 rue Sarrette
75014 Paris.
Elefilm
36 rue Reinhardt
92100 Boulogne.
Elephant Productions
122 Champs Elysées
75008 Paris.
Elisa Production
40 rue des Francs Bourgois
75003 Paris.
Eurocine
33 Champs Elysées
75008 Paris.
Europa Films
99 rue de Courcelles
75017 Paris.
Europrodis
116 bis Champs Elysées,
75008 Paris.
Famous French Films
33 Champs Elysées
75008 Paris.
Farena Films
39 rue d'Assas
75006 Paris.
F.D.R. Productions
127 Champs Elysées
75008 Paris.
Fichier Electronique du Spectacle
25 rue St Didier
75116 Paris.
Fideline Films
10 av. George V
75008 Paris.
Fides
32 rue Washington
75008 Paris.
Fildebroc
58 rue Auguste Buisson
92250 La Garenne-Colombes.
Filmad
18/20 pl. de la Madeleine
75008 Paris.
Filmedis
4 rue Balzac
75008 Paris.
Filmel
9 rue Lincoln
75008 Paris.
Film-Film Uziel-Perez
11 rue d'Abbeville
75010 Paris.
Filmodie
135 rue de la Roquette
75011 Paris.
Films ABC
6 rue l'Alboni
75016 Paris.

Films Aleph
18 rue Marbeuf
75008 Paris.
Films Ariane
44 Champs Elysées
75008 Paris.
Films Armorial
223 bd Pereire
75017 Paris.
Films Christian Fechner
29 av. de Friedland
75008 Paris.
Films Concordia
32 av. George V
75008 Paris.
Films de la Chouette
44 Champs Elysées
75008 Paris.
Films de la Commune
1 rue de Fleurus
75006 Paris.
Films de la Drouette
91 rue de Monceau
75008 Paris.
Films de l'Alma
68 bd Malesherbes
75008 Paris.
Films de L'Arquebuse
12 rue de l'Echequier
75010 Paris.
Films de la Tour
30 av. de Messine
75008 Paris.
Films de l'Epée
8 rue Jean Goujon
75008 Paris.
Films de l'Equinoxe
18 Galerie Vero Dodat
75001 Paris.
Films 2001
7 rue de Solférino
92100 Boulogne.
Films du Canivet
2 rue du Canivet
75006 Paris.
Films du Carrosse
5 rue Robert Estienne
75008 Paris.
Films du Grain de Sable
206 rue de Charenton
75012 Paris.
Films du Griffon
122 Champs Elysées
75008 Paris.
Les Films du Jaguar
69 bd Berthier
75017 Paris.
Films du Jeudi
95 Champs Elysées
75008 Paris.
Films du Livradois

Residence Ste-Claire
78170 La Celle St-Cloud.
Films du Losange
26 av. Pierre 1er de Serbie
75116 Paris.
Films du Nautile (Les)
35 rue Vineuse
75016 Paris.
Films du Pelican
70 rue de Ponthieu
75008 Paris.
Films du Prisme
72 bis, rue de la Tour
75000 Paris.
Films du Rhinoceros (Les)
6 rue des Martyrs
75009 Paris.
Films du Sabre
24 rue d'Armaillé
75017 Paris.
Films du Sioux
12 rue Chabanais
75002 Paris.
Films du Soleil et de la Nuit
44 Champs Elysées
75008 Paris.
Films du Triangle
34 Champs Elysées
75008 Paris.
Films Espace et Mouvement
13 av. Victor Hugo
92220 Bagneux.
Films Feuer et Martin
47 av. George V
75008 Paris.
Films Français (Les)
43 Fg St Honoré
75008 Paris.
Films Galaxie
3 av. de Friedland
75008 Paris.
Films Jean Image
5 rue Laure Surville
75015 Paris.
Films Montfort
11 rue de Sance
78490 Montfort L'Amaury.
Films Noirs
24 rue Condorcet
75009 Paris.
Films Number One
16 av. Hoche
75008 Paris.
Films Princesse
19 rue de Bassano
75008 Paris.
Films 7
4 Chemin du Val des Vignes
95450 Avernes.
Films 66
7 av. Mac Mahon

75017 Paris.
Films Soleil O (Les)
72 bis, rue Philippe de Girard
75018 Paris.
Films 13
15 av. Hoche
75008 Paris.
Films 21
12 rue Marbeuf
75008 Paris.
Films Willemetz
9 rue d'Artois
75008 Paris.
Forum Films
26 rue du Cdt Mouchotte
75014 Paris.
Francos Films
17 rue de la Trémoille
75008 Paris.
French Movies ad Creation
277 rue St Honoré
75008 Paris.
Gaumont
30 av. Charles de Gaulle
92200 Neuilly.
Gerland Production
5 rue Lincoln
75008 Paris.
Gibe Films
44 av. George V
75008 Paris.
Ginis Films
19 rue de Berri
75008 Paris.
G.M.F. Production
57 bis, rue de Varenne
75007 Paris.
Gold Production
3 rue de l'Arrivée
75015 Paris.
Greenwich Productions
25 rue François Ier
75008 Paris.
Guilmain (Claudine)
192 rue Lecourbe
75015 Paris.
Hamster Films
12 bis, rue Keppler
75116 Paris.
Indémedia
9 rue Lincoln
75008 Paris.
ISA Films Production
16 bd de Magenta
75010 Paris.
Japhila Production
19 rue de la Trémoille
75008 Paris.
Jivaros Films
8 chemin Scribe
92190 Meudon.

J.K.L. International
2 rue Constantin Pecqueur
75018 Paris.
J.P.L.L. Production
2 rue Gervex
75017 Paris.
Junior Productions
23 rue Laugier
75017 Paris.
K.G. Production
244 rue St Jacques
75005 Paris.
Kuiv Productions
8 rue Jean Goujon
75008 Paris.
Lambretta
12 ter, rue Louise Michel
92300 Levallois.
Laura Production
1 av. de l'Abbé Roussel
75016 Paris.
Link Production
43 fg St Honore
75008 Paris.
Lira Films
103 rue Fbg St Honore
75008 Paris.
Little Bear Production
66 Bd Malesherbes
75008 Paris.
Lyric International
26 av. Pierre 1er de Serbie
75116 Paris.
Madeleine Films
7 rue des Dames Augustines
92200 Neuilly.
Magyar Productions
8 rue Jean Goujon
75008 Paris.
Maki Films
23 rue d'Artois
75008 Paris.
Mallia Films
20 rue des Champs Elysées
94250 Gentilly.
Manufacture d'Images (La)
33 rue Paul Doumer
78140 Velizy.
Marianne Productions
1 rue Meyerbeer
75009 Paris.
Marifilms
19 rue Galilée
75116 Paris.
**Mars International Production
(M.I.P.)**
1 rue Lord Byron
75008 Paris.
Méditerranée Cinema
72 rue d'Antibes
06400 Cannes.

Melody Movies
88 av. Wagram
75008 Paris.
M. Films
3 rue de Beaune
75007 Paris.
Midas
9 rue St Romain
75006 Paris.
Mondex Films
44 Champs Elysées
75008 Paris.
M. Production
7 rue du Disque
75013 Paris.
Multimedia
163 rue du Fg St Honoré
75008 Paris.
Nadja Films
57 rue de Clichy
75009 Paris.
Newin Productions
16 bis, rue Lauriston
75116 Paris.
Neyrac Films
133 rue du Théâtre
75015 Paris.
Nouvelles Editions de Films
15 rue du Louvre
75001 Paris.
Odessa Film
29 av. Th. Gautier
75016 Paris.
Oeil en Boîte (L')
7 pl. Franz Liszt
75010 Paris.
Oliane Productions
44 rue du Colisée
75008 Paris.
Open Films
6 rue du Pont de Lodi
75006 Paris.
Panoceanic Films
92 Champs Elysées
75008 Paris.
Paris Film Production
79 Champs Elysées
75008 Paris.
Paris Inter Productions
26 av. Pierre 1er de Serbie
75116 Paris.
Partners Productions
62 rue La Boétie
75008 Paris.
Phenix Productions
11 rue d'Artois
75008 Paris.
Philippe Dussart
99 av. du Roule
92200 Neuilly.
Pierson Production

59 rue des Trois Frères
75018 Paris.
Port-Royal Films
10 rue Royale
75008 Paris.
Primavera
13 rue Jean Beausire
75004 Paris.
Procinex
62 av. de la Grande Armée
75017 Paris.
Productions Artistes Associés
25 rue d'Astorg
75008 Paris.
Productions Audiovisuelles (Les)
11 rue d'Artois
75008 Paris.
Productions Belles Rives
88 bd de Courcelles
75017 Paris.
Productions de la Guéville
16 rue de Marignan
75008 Paris.
Productions du Danou
9 rue Daunou
75002 Paris.
Productions du Delta Rouge
10 bd des Batignolles
75017 Paris.
P.E.C.F.
18/20 rue Troyon
75017 Paris.
Productions Jacques Roitfeld
19 rue de Bassano
75116 Paris.
Productions Jelot-Blanc
64 rue de la Condamine
75017 Paris.
Productions Marcel Dassault
9 Rond-Point des Champs Elysées
75008 Paris.
Productions Roc
70 rue de Ponthieu
75008 Paris.
Productions Werlaine and Co
44240 La Chapelle-sur-Erdre.
Progefi
9 rue du Boccador
75008 Paris.
Promedifilm
67 rue St. Jacques
13006 Marseille.
Promocinéma
76 rue Denfert Rochereau
92100 Boulogne.
Promundi
16 bd Pereire
75017 Paris.
Prospectacle
26 rue du Renard
75004 Paris.

Radeau Production Distribution
39 rue Volta
75003 Paris.
Radio Cines
32 av. de l'Opéra
72002 Paris.
Reggane Films
14 rue du Château
92250 La Garenne Colombes.
Renn Productions
10 rue Lincoln
75008 Paris.
Requins Associés (Les)
18 rue Beffroy
92200 Neuilly.
Rosa Production
5 rue d'Artois
75008 Paris.
Rush Productions
2 rue Toulouse Lautrec
75014 Paris.
Sara Films
78 Champs Elysées
75008 Paris.
Sedif
25 rue Quentin Bauchart
75008 Paris.
Selta Films
36 av. Hoche
75008 Paris.
Seve (Groupe)
65 av. Marcel Cachin
92320 Chatillon-sous-Bagneux.
Shangrila Production
95 bis rue de l'Admiral Mouchez
75013 Paris.
Silke Production
22 rue de Bellechasse
75007 Paris.
Simar Films
10 av. George V
75008 Paris.
**Société Nouvelle de
Cinématographie**
5 rue Lincoln
75008 Paris.
Société Nouvelle de Doublage
27 rue Desportes
93400 Saint-Ouen.
Sofracima
36 rue de Ponthieu
75008 Paris.
Solstice Production
138 rue du Théâtre
75015 Paris.
Sonimage
99 av. du Roule
92200 Neuilly.
Soprofilms
12 bis rue Keppler
75016 Paris.

Stephan Films
71 av. Franklin Roosevelt
75008 Paris.
Tanagra Productions
23 rue d'Artois
75008 Paris.
Technisonor
10 rue Magellan
75008 Paris.
Telecip
89 bd Auguste Blanqui
75013 Paris.
Télé-Hachette
161 rue du fg St Honoré
75008 Paris.
Top No. 1
26 bis, rue François Ier
75008 Paris.
Trinacra Films
42 av. Ste Foy
92200 Neuilly.
U.G.C.
5 av. Velasquez
75008 Paris.
**Union des Producteurs de Cinéma
et de Télévision**
70 rue de Ponthieu
75008 Paris.
Uranus Productions France
1 rue Meyerbeer
75009 Paris.
V. Films
10 av. George V
75008 Paris.
Viaduc Productions
10 rue Jean Giraudoux
75116 Paris.
V.M. Productions
15 rue du Louvre
75001 Paris.
Whodunit
18 rue Marbeuf
75008 Paris.
Woog Robert
23 rue Auguste Renoir
78160 Marley-le-Roi.
Zenith Productions
11 rue de la Trémoille
75008 Paris.

French Film
Exporters

Albatros Films
74 Av. de la Grande Armée
75017 Paris.
American European Film Service
34 av. Hoche
75008 Paris.

Boris Janowski
9 av. Ingres
75016 Paris.
Carlton Film Export
51 bis, av. Ste Foy
92200 Neuilly.
Celia Films
33 Champs Elysées
75008 Paris.
Ciné 7
116 bis, Champs Elysées
75008 Paris.
Cinéthèque
16 av. Hoche
75008 Paris.
Cinévision
20 rue de l'Hôtel de Ville
92200 Neuilly.
Cinexport
78 Champs Elysées
75008 Paris.
Compagnie Jean Renoir
10 rue Pergolèse
75782 Paris Cédex 16.
Compagnie Méditerranéenne de
Films
53 av. George V
75008 Paris.
Consortium d'Achats Audiovisuels
5 av. Velasquez
75008 Paris.
Cravenne Robert
183 place Haute
92100 Boulogne.
Davis Films
116 bis, Champs Elysées
75008 Paris.
Eureka Productions
11 rue de Douai
75009 Paris.
Europex
92 Champs Elysées
75008 Paris.
Exportation Française
Cinématographique
39 av. Franklin Roosevelt
75008 Paris.
Félix Film
7 rue du Commandant Rivière
75008 Paris.
Filmcontact International
14 rue Sainte-Anne
75001 Paris.
Films Cosmos (Les)
25-27 rue d'Astore
75008 Paris.
Films du Scorpion
54 av. Marceau
75008 Paris.
Films Jérôme Deprez
4 rue Marbeuf

75008 Paris.
Films Max Linder
78 Champs Elysees
75008 Paris.
France Cinéma Production
14 rue de Marignan
75008 Paris.
France Inter Cinéma
7 rue de Naples
75008 Paris.
Gaumont
30 av. Charles de Gaulle
92200 Neuilly.
Gerviac
6 rue Lincoln
75008 Paris.
Goldman et Cie
31 Champs Elysées
75008 Paris.
Hexatel
9 av. Hoche
75008 Paris.
Interama
10 rue du Mont-Thabor
75001 Paris.
Inter Ciné TV
9 rue Jean Mermoz
75008 Paris.
International Film Development
4 rue Marbeuf
75008 Paris.
Interpix
118 rue La Boétie
75008 Paris.
Investissement et Commerce
27 bd de Courcelles
75008 Paris.
Jacques Barigant Productions
116 bis Champs Elysées
75008 Paris.
Joker-Films
8 rue Lincoln
75008 Paris.
La Guéville Etranger
16 rue de Marignan
75008 Paris.
Ofer-Omni Films
122 Champs Elysées
75008 Paris.
Office Central Cinéma et
Television
4 rue du Marche St. Honore
(Tuileries) 75001 Paris.
Orcine Films
1 rue Lord Byron
75008 Paris.
Paris Asia Films
34 av. des Champs Elysées
75008 Paris.
Piloix Laurence
8 rue Auguste Renoir

78400 Chatou.
Pictural Films
16 av. Hoche
75008 Paris.
Plazza Films
60 rue Pergolèse
75116 Paris.
Procidis
35 rue Marbeuf
75008 Paris.
Pyrine Films
32 rue de la Princesse
78430 Louveciennes.
Roissy Films
10 av. George V
75008 Paris.
Sami Films International
78 Champs Elysées
75008 Paris.
Seawell Films
45 rue Pierre Charron
75008 Paris.
Sergyve Films
365 rue de Vaugirard
75015 Paris.
Société Nouvelle Outremer Films
78 Champs Elysées
75008 Paris.
S.O.G.E.A.V. Club 70
16 bis, rue Lauriston
75116 Paris.
Stoumon Liliane
125 Champs Elysées
75008 Paris.
Studio 72 Films Christiane Kieffer
45 rue de Ponthieu
75008 Paris.
Suède Films
125 Champs Elysées
75008 Paris.
Teledis
11 av. Victor Hugo
75116 Paris.
Union Africaine de Cinéma
5 av. Velasquez
75008 Paris.
Vauban Productions
9 av. Franklin Roosevelt
75008 Paris.
Wettstein (Ernest)
1 rue Lord Byron
75008 Paris.
World Marketing Film
8 rue Lincoln
75008 Paris.

French Specialist Distributors

Action
9 rue Buffault
75009 Paris.
Argos Films
4 rue Edouard Nortier
92200 Neuilly.
Cinémas Associés
67 rue Monsieur le Prince
75006 Paris.
Clef Distribution (La)
21 rue de la Clef
75005 Paris.
Films de la Marguerite (Les)
30 av. Ch. de Gaulle
92200 Neuilly.

Films Molière (Les)
71 rue de Monceau
75008 Paris.
Films Saint-André-des-Arts
30 rue St. Andre des Arts
75006 Paris.
Gaumont
30 av. Charles de Gaulle
92200 Neuilly.
Grands Films Classiques (Les)
49 av. Théophile Gautier
75016 Paris.
MK 2 Diffusion
55 rue Traversière
75012 Paris.

NEF Diffusion
35 bd. Malesherbes
75008 Paris.
Olympic Distribution
10 rue Boyer Barret
75014 Paris.
Pari-Films
18 rue Vignon
75009 Paris.
Ursulines Distribution
1 bd St. Michel
75006 Paris.

STILL FROM CATHERINE BINET'S *LES JEUX DE LA COMTESSE DOLINGEN DE GRATZ*

German Democratic Republic (G.D.R.)

by Dieter Wolf

A small output like DEFA's, with sixteen features a year (four of those for children from six to twelve), cannot offer sensations every year. The recent increase of interest in films is not exclusively due to a few titles which scored box-office successes; the range of films has become more colourful, more varied in subject-matter, with markedly different styles. This was the impression of foreign guests at the second National Film Festival in Karl-Marx-Stadt in 1982 and the most recent productions seem to confirm this trend.

Apprehension, directed by Lothar Warneke, triggered lively discussion, as the film does not follow the entertainment recipe with which some film-makers hope to keep people away from TV. A middle-aged woman, self-confident and emancipated, working as a psychologist at a welfare centre, is faced with a suspected malignant disease. One day before she is to be operated on, she asks herself and the people around her about the meaning of life, about the value and strength of human relationships. She comes closer to her young son and breaks off with a married man. The meaning of life is substantiated in an unsentimental way, both for the woman and the audience. With this work Warneke returns to the documentary style of his first films.

The film was shot by a small crew in actual

SYLVESTER GROTH IN *THE STAY*   PHOTO: DEFA-LÜCK

CHRISTINE SCHORN IN *APPREHENSION*
PHOTO: DEFA-KUHRÖBER

locations, and features many amateur players. Christine Schorn has risen to among the top actors in this country by her deeply moving central performance, and the amateurs help to bring the film an unmistakable whiff of reality. Thomas Plehnert, a young documentary cameraman, has won praise for this his feature debut. By using black-and-white stock and doing without technical effects, he gains much greater authenticity.

Roland Gräf, also one of the middle-aged generation of directors, has produced quite a different surprise, entitled *Exploring the Marches of Brandenburg*. This is a contemporary comedy, with an excellent cast. Almost by chance two men meet who are very different in every respect: the self-confident, famous professor of literature, living in the capital, and the agile but completely unknown teacher at a village school.

Both are following the tracks of a German writer, who set many problems between the French

HERMANN BEYER IN *EXPLORING THE MARCHES OF BRAN-DENBURG*   PHOTO: DEFA-PATHENHEIMER

PETRA LÄMMEL IN *SABINE KLEIST – SEVEN YEARS OLD*
PHOTO: DEFA-SKOLUCA

Revolution and German Romantic poetry. The discoveries made by the amateur in the country do not suit the image of a hero established by the city theorist. This elevated subject is the cause of a fierce quarrel about truth, in the course of which human virtues and moral qualities are tested. This adaptation of a novel by Günter de Bruyn is a filmic pleasure of a special kind. And it is much closer to the medium than a lot of other original scripts.

Among children's films, one directed by Helmut Dziuba stands out for its professionalism. *Sabine Kleist – Seven Years Old* is about an orphan who flees from the well-kept order of a home and goes for a day to Berlin, to see what the city is like. Writer/director Dziuba offers a lot of everyday observation, and casts a critical eye at the world of grown-ups. The film not only glances beneath the surface of things but also into the very soul of a child. The director has an ideal cast.

A new film on an anti-fascist theme deserves special attention. From a novel by Hermann Kant,

Wolfgang Kohlhaase wrote *The Stay* for director Frank Beyer, whose previous films have included some of DEFA's best anti-fascist productions, such as *Five Cartridge Cases*, *Naked among Wolves* and *Jacob, the Liar*. *The Stay* concerns a young German, just old enough to be involved in the war, who is suspected of war crimes while in Polish captivity. During detention pending trial, he encounters the hatred of Polish prisoners – a hatred not only for the SS jacket which he was given by the warden. Later, in a cell of German civilians, Gestapo as well as officers of all ranks and kinds, he is welcomed as a fellow-countryman. However, very soon he is treated as an outsider and potential collaborator because he does not submit to the old "German order" that still exists there, and because he puts unpleasant questions to the real guilty persons. At the eleventh hour the Polish investigation absolves him and saves him from his own people.

The director has strikingly cast this strange

film with a talented newcomer in the lead, and with excellent German and Polish actors. The film gives a vivid description of a grave chunk of history, and of a nation's self-contradictory relations with its neighbours.

German Federal Republic (BRD)

by Edmund Luft

"The old film is dead. We believe in the new!" The text of the legendary Oberhausen manifesto – with which, twenty years ago, young German film-makers outlined their aims – ends with this once laughed-at rallying cry in the best *Sturm und Drang* tradition. Since then film production in West Germany has changed considerably. Through renewed activity, a different generation, and stronger socio-political awareness, an entertainment industry of little international significance and modest profits has been transformed into today's publicly subsidised New Cinema, in which profitability is now longer the only valid criterion. Films are still being produced which one is glad to see vanish into the vaults; but there are also quite a few German films which arouse great interest around the world.

The money which sustains production totals more than DM80,000,000 a year in prizes, bonuses, subsidies and loans. This has incurred the opposition of EEC officials in Brussels, who allege that such subsidies create unfair competition for other EEC members. most German writers, producers and directors see this as an attack on their cultural independence and, as Alexander Kluge puts it, "a misunderstanding of the realities of film-making."

Most West German productions today possess a notably high cultural level. Only a few gamblers long nostalgically for the days when production was dominated by films of dubious merit. The present system of selection and promotion acts as a counter-balance to the commercial market when a few hits dominate the scene and lead to stagnation of content and style in the films on offer.

In fact, the vitality and diversity of the industry are due to its active part in and increased awareness of social and cultural movements of our times. Whether by Fassbinder, Herzog, Petersen, Geissendörfer, Schlöndorff or Schroeter, West German films are unerringly hitting their international targets. They often make greater profits abroad than at home; one exporter told me they make between DM300,000–1,500,000 and another quoted much higher figures. Comparisons are difficult because, when home market profits are calculated, the often high production costs have often already been deducted from the total revenue.

Attendances have increased by 25% in 4 years, and are now approximately 150,000,000 a year. However, figures vary according to the season, so there are sometimes alarming reports about the situation. Attendance for foreign films is now dropping, and not only the market analysts are worried about this. Whatever the reasons, the industry no longer has to be satisfied with only 10% of the market. It is estimated that German films' share of ticket sales is now 17%, and for a long time American films have had less than 50%. The big box-office hits are still films like *For Your Eyes Only*, *The Aristocats* and *The Cannonball Run*. But to this list can also be added Ulrich Edel's drug drama *Christine F*, Wolfgang Petersen's submarine epic *The Boat*, Fassbinder's melodrama *Lili Marleen*, and a few others.

Where do we go from here? The struggle for progress, growth and affluence has gone as far as it can, and the authors of the latest wave, the thirty-year-olds, are making their protest against further exploitation and destruction of our world. *No Runway West – A Region Resists*, produced by a Frankfurt team, is directed against any extension of West Germany's largest airport. *Neon City*, a portmanteau socio-critique by graduates of the Munich film school, shows the senseless life in the city's concrete tower-blocks. Isolation, prom-

iscuity and discomfort form the theme of Marianne Lüdcke's *Casual Relations* (*Flüchtige Beziehungen*), and the same theme of impermanency is found in many variations in other films. Through Adolf Winkelmann's satire *Any Amount of Coal* (*Jede Menge Kohle*), set in the Rhine coal-mining area, the drop-out has become a model which many will follow. Young film-makers are all trying with passion and imagination to show why a growing portion of modern society is exchanging an apparently well-ordered life for a disorganised existence.

DER ZAUBERBERG
(The Magic Mountain)

Script and direction: Hans W. Geissendoerfer. Photography (colour): Michael Ballhaus. Music: Juergen Knieper. Production Design: Heidi and Tony Leudi. Players: Rod Steiger, Marie-France Pisier, Flavio Bucci, Christoph Eichhorn, Hans Christian Blech, Irm Herrmann, Kurt Raab, Charles Aznavour. Produced by Frank Seitz Film (Munich), Iduna Film (Munich)/Gaumont (Paris)/and Opera Film (Rome) in co-production with Zweites Deutsches Fernsehen (ZDF). 150 mins.

Lavish literary adaptations are also taking pride of place in the German cinema and their success nearly always proves that their courageous producers have made the right choice. After Grass's *The Tin Drum* and Bucheim's *The Boat* comes Mann's *Magic Mountain*, a particularly difficult undertaking because its lyrical style and subtle language are essential elements of the work. Thomas Mann was himself sceptical about filming *The Magic Mountain*, written in the Twenties as a portrait of European life before the First World War. He thought that, if tackled boldly, a "remarkable drama" could be made from this story of love, illness and death, a "fantastic encyclopaedia", but that the task made spiritual and material demands which were too great.

The DM 20,000,000 film, tackled boldly by producer Franz Seitz, really has become a "remarkable drama." There are two versions: one lasting 2½ hours, will be shown in cinemas; the other, over 4 hours long, will be serialised on TV in 1984. Directed by Hans W. Geissendörfer, the film is faithful to the novel. Hans Castorp (Christoph Eichhorn), an ordinary young man from Hamburg, visits his sick cousin (Alexander Radzun) in a TB sanatorium in a mountain-top hotel in Davos. At first he is amazed at the hunger for life and love shown by people often mortally ill. Then he is caught up in the all-embracing, cocooning atmosphere of the place, and when he himself falls ill, he is told by the all-powerful senior physician (Hans Christian Blech) that he must stay. Castorp falls in love with a seductive Russian girl (Marie-France Pisier), and when she leaves the sanatorium he determines to wait for her return. In the next few years his spiritual development is influenced by the many conversations between two contrasting intellectuals, who at the end fight a duel because of him. One is an extreme left-wing Catholic ideologist (Charles Aznavour), the other a liberal humanist (Flavio Bucci) who is working on "The Sociology of Suffering." When the Russian girl whom Castorp loves returns to the mountain, she is accompanied by an older man, a Dutch plantation owner (Rod Steiger), who later commits suicide. His visionary, bacchantic manner and mysterious end make a strong impression on Castorp. As a mature adult, he leaves the sanatorium at the beginning of the Great War, emerging in time for the "World Carnival of Death."

Desire, love, disease and death are presented by Thomas Mann as part of an apparently alchemistic transformation, as a way of reconciling all contradictions. In Geissendörfer's film there is little sense of such complex, often encoded philosophical content; he restricts himself to the psychological side, and shows with great pathos a morbid hothouse of seduction, a raging inferno in which people of strong passions talk, laugh, love and die. The painstaking production design, decor and period costumes will help to satisfy that worldwide longing for the past which reflects our fear of the future, a future which started a long time ago.

EDMUND LUFT

Manfred Durniok Productions

Motion pictures and television

We cover the entire range of film-making, from documentary and industrial films to full-length features, television series and specials.
We have shot on location in 80 different countries and won over 45 national and international awards.

Production facilities

We have the most modern cameras, sound and lighting equipment for 35 mm, 16 mm and video, all of which can be fully mobilized for location shooting anywhere in the world.
We have our own editing rooms and studios for sound, special effects and animation.

Import of foreign films

We also acquire licences of films from all over the world for television and cinema release in Central Europe.

Your partner
for international co-productions
and import of films:

Manfred Durniok Productions
Hausotterstraße 36
D-1000 Berlin 51 (West Germany)
Phone 491 80 45
Telex 1–81 717

ROSEL ZECH WITH THE LATE RAINER WERNER FASSBINDER ON THE SET OF *DIE SEHNSUCHT DER VERONIKA VOSS*

DIE SEHNSUCHT DER VERONIKA VOSS
(Veronika Voss)

Script and direction: Rainer Werner Fassbinder. Photography: Xaver Schwarzenberger. Editing: Juliane Lorenz. Music: Peer Raben. Production Design: Rolf Zehetbauer. Players: Rosel Zech, Hilmar Thate, Annemarie Dueringer, Doris Schade, Cornelia Froböss, Eric Schumann, Armin Mueller-Stahl, Peter Luehr, Brigitte Horney. Produced by Laura Film and Tango Film in coproduction with Rialto Film, Trio Film and Maran Film. 105 mins.

Fassbinder shows the desperate spirit of an epoch through particular women. After Petra von Kant and Maria Braun, after Lili Marleen and Lola, we now have the mystery of Veronika Voss, the tragedy of a former UFA star in the Fifties. A reporter (Hilmar Thate) meets a charming former film star (Rosel Zech), who is desperately trying to make a comeback. His interest grows when he realises that the actress is living with a woman doctor (Annemarie Düringer) who treats her with narcotics. Gradually he finds out that the doctor uses these drugs to murder rich, lonely, depressed patients for their money. Her accomplice is an official from the Ministry of Health, and a mysterious American GI is always around. Together with his girl-friend (Cornelia Froböss), the reporter tries to trap the doctor but fails. The actress kills herself with tablets; the girl-friend is murdered. The reporter, now frightened and sensing the futility of trying to fight the might of the Establishment, capitulates.

The authors' imagination was sparked off by the fate of the once popular actress Sybille Schmitz who committed suicide in the Fifties in similar circumstances; but the ideological thrust is aimed – as in *Lola* – at the unmasking of the post-war Adenauer era when West Germany was rebuilding. Many Germans were then starting to regain some confidence in their own lives but the intellectuals of Fassbinder's generation regard the period with repugnance. The conclusion drawn from this story is that the individual is helpless when caught up in the cogs of society; that was the way life was then, and still is today.

Veronika Voss is good old German *Weltschmerz*, portrayed here with bright lights and powerful shadows. In fact, apart from the gripping performances of Rosel Zech and the hand-picked supporting cast, it is the black-and-white virtuosity of Xaver Schwarzenberger's camerawork that gives the film its style. At the 1982 Berlin festival this searingly critical and effective melodrama won the first prize of the Golden Bear.

EDMUND LUFT

FITZCARRALDO

Script and direction: Werner Herzog. Photography (colour): Thomas Mauch. Editing: Beata Mainka-Jellinghaus. Music: Popol Vuh, plus archive recordings. Production Design: Henning von Gierke, Ulrich Bergfelder. Players: Klaus Kinski, Claudia Cardinale, José Lewgoy, Miguel Angel Fuentes. Produced by Werner Herzog and Lucki Stipetic for Werner Herzog/Pro-ject Film. 158 mins.

The prize for best director awarded to Werner Herzog at the 1982 Cannes festival seemed to

STILL FROM *FITZCARRALDO*

STELLAN BENGTSSON IN JOACHIM KRECK'S FILM ABOUT THE SPORT, *TISCHTENNIS*

many to be an award for bravery. The story of how *Fitzcarraldo* was created is as full of adventure as the film itself. Despite immense, time-consuming difficulties with people, material, the forces of nature, and the whims of fate, the determination of this fanatical *cinéaste* prevailed. On the Croisette at Cannes, Herzog was able to say with pride, "Mon film est une œuvre inimitable, destinée à encourager l'être à la folie et la fantaisie."

Fantasy and folly – the film is about the vision of Brian S. Fitzgerald, known as Fitzcarraldo (Klaus Kinski), an admirer of the useless and the beautiful. During the rubber boom on the Amazon, he is obsessed with the desire to bring Caruso to the jungle in great Italian operas. With his lively mistress (Claudia Cardinale), he collects so much money from the other rubber speculators that he is able to equip an expedition into the huge, virgin forests. To get there, hundreds of Indians have to haul a steamer from one river, across a mountain, to another jungle river, which in its lower reaches seems to be impassable. Faced with enormous hardships, they succeed; but in the night Indian medicine-men cut the ship's lines, and it drifts, damaged by the rocks in the rapids, back to the place where they started. Yet Fitzcarraldo still realises his dream by holding a concert on board the festively decorated ship. Opera must be heard.

This heroic study of a latter-day Sisyphus, with Kinski smiling proudly at its happy end, is

H. J. SYBERBERG WITH EDITH CLEVER ON THE SET OF *PARSIFAL*

presented with tranquil, beautiful photography (Thomas Mauch) and dynamic editing (Beata Mainka-Jellinghaus). However, one has the impression that Herzog wanted to tell much more. His film does not have the cohesive atmosphere and compelling power of *Aguirre*; yet as a parable of human audacity it is indeed inimitable.

EDMUND LUFT

SUBSCRIBE . . .

to INTERNATIONAL FILM GUIDE

To be certain of receiving your copy of INTERNATIONAL FILM GUIDE 1984, please send us your name and address immediately. We will then add you to our mailing list and send you an order form a few weeks prior to publication so that you can be sure of delivery promptly.

Write today!

THE TANTIVY PRESS LIMITED,
136-148 TOOLEY STREET, LONDON SE1 2TT, ENGLAND.

SELECTION OFFICIELLE CANNES 1982 "Un certain regard"

ROSA POUR SAUVER LE RÊVE

un film de
CHRISTOFORO
CHRISTOFIS

ANDRZEJ SEWERYN · EVA KOTAMANIDOU · DANIEL OLBRYCHSKI

Musique : ELENI KARAÏNDROU   Photographie : ANDREAS BELLIS

Production : CREATIVITY FILMS HELLAS - GREEK FILM CENTER

Greece

by Andreas Bellis

The change of government was also the year's most important event for the cinema. A lot of things have changed in socialist Greece, and we expect a lot more to change. The perspectives for the development of Greek cinema are more positive than ever, as the responsible positions are now occupied by qualified and well-meaning people. The old, pre-election, supposedly progressive guard was totally replaced after it had proved its incapability and the emptiness of its intentions. Especially spectacular was the failure of well-known director Nikos Koundouros as head of cinema at the Ministry of Culture. His widespread involvement led to misunderstandings, injustices, fights and more "bad scenes" at the National Film Festival in Thessaloniki than at any other time, while his plans for the Film Centre were rejected out of hand.

The new guard has made a lot of promises: tax reductions, an end to censorship, a new proposal for a cinema law, the reorganistion of the Film Centre, and significant financial support. However, censorship is still in operation, the first tax measures were disappointing, and all the important matters are seriously delayed. Nevertheless, these delays – for the first time – do not mean that nothing is going to happen. They mean that the problems which have been piling up are difficult ones and the various parties that deal with them often represent contrasting interests and points-of-view.

Meanwhile, production has steadily increased, despite the problems and the year's decrease in ticket sales. Almost every week one or more new films are released. These films, produced en masse, are dated farces of incredibly low production values. They are shot in two or three weeks and are shown immediately in second-run cinemas mainly outside Athens. It seems that films of this kind will continue to torture us for as long as production remains unprofessional and film theatres are run by reactionary businessmen. But of the year's approximately 40 films, only 5 were a real success; the rest ran all over the country for a whole year to cover their extremely low production costs.

Cinematic interest now lies elsewhere. New Greek Cinema, as it has come to be called, now produces a good number of films of all kinds – from the purely commercial to the totally personal, from experimental to documentary. Its many forms and its solid place in the audience consciousness are guarantees for its future – if, of course, it is supported by the state both in production and in distribution and foreign promotion.

In this last area, the first steps were taken in 1982 with the setting up of a Greek stand at the Cannes festival and the search for persons suitable to undertake the distribution of Greek films in festivals and markets all over the world. In the area of production, the funds announced by the state are larger than before but still insufficient and disorganised: there is no logic, no programme, no allocations in the decisions concerning Film Centre co-productions.

A problem which will seriously occupy Greek cinema in the future is that of film distribution. There seems no chance of more support for new kinds of film. The very same distributors that have no intention of risking money on New Greek Cinema control and exclusively programme most of the theatres in Athens and all theatres outside Athens. Thus, a lot of Greek films end up being shown off-season or sometimes only in clubs.

OLIA LAZARIDOU IN *STIGMA*

Theatre owners do not seem any more to be interested in programming, as long as the existing theatres assure them solid profits; and, worst of all, they do not have the least interest in projection quality, which in 99% of the theatres is absolutely atrocious.

OI ATTEANTI (I APENANDI) (A Foolish Love)

Script: Giorgos Panoussopoulos, Philippos Drakontaidis, Petros Tatsopoulos. Direction: Giorgos Panoussopoulos. Photography (colour): Aris Stavrou. Editing: Giorgos Panoussopoulos. Music: Stavros Logaradis. Art Direction: Nikos Perakis. Players: Bette Livanou, Aris Retsos, Georges Siskos, Dimitris Poulikakos. Produced by Giorgos Panoussopoulos Ltd./Greek Film Centre/ Greka Film M. Lefakis S.A./Stefi Film. 110 mins.

Undoubtedly the most beautiful film of the year, very well received by both audience and critics. It stems from a solid script and good performances by the actors – a very important point for the new Greek cinema which has not, until now, demonstrated any particular interest in these two areas.

The film's main interest arises from the intensely penetrating and sensitive eye of the director, who is also camera operator, as he surveys Athens. The story is set in the present-day capital, a city dominated by Americanised behaviour and lifestyles. But the setting overlaps with the private world of the central character. He is a young man aged about twenty, who lives with his widowed mother in one of the innumerable, nondescript apartments lost in the great concrete jungle that Athens has become.

He wants to study astronomy at the university, and spends most of his time scrutinising the stars and the surrounding world through an ancient telescope, which his grandfather had used long ago to look for mermaids in the Aegean Sea. On the other side of the wide avenue, in a rather similar apartment, dwells Stella with her husband and daughter. Trapped in the dull, mechanical routine of a meaningless marriage, devoid of joy, she feels her youth slipping away and grey middle-age creeping up on the horizon.

The young man, Haris, follows her movements through his spyglass for a whole week. Gradually he drops out of his gang of friends who

BETTY LIVAROU AND ARIS RETSOS IN *A FOOLISH LOVE*

spend every evening playing with death astride their lethal, semi-illegal motorbikes. He drifts more and more deeply into Stella's life; before the week is out he finds himself in love with her. Their only point of contact is the phone. Then one day, Stella makes her decision, prompted by the wild, persistent call of Haris's youth. On Sunday, around noon, she crosses the wide avenue and offers herself to him, with neither fear nor shame.

Before the day is over, this foolish, ill-matched love will have completed a full circle. Stella returns home.

What are the prospects for love in this city?

ANDREAS BELLIS

STILL FROM *THE FACTORY*, THE GREEK ENTRY AT THE LOCARNO FILM FESTIVAL

TO ERGOSTASIO
(The Factory)

Script and Direction: Tassos Psarras. Photography (colour): Alexis Grivas. Editing: Nikos Kanakis. Music: Domna Samiou. Art Direction: Anastasia Arseni. Players: Vassilis Kolovos, Vana Fitsori. Produced by Tassos Psarras/Greek Film Centre. 101 mins.

Greece has just entered the Common Market. Somewhere in Northern Greece, George Papyros, a small-time tanner, faces a major crisis as his traditional workshop, unable to compete with the large up-to-date tanneries in the area, goes into decline. His only hope is to secure a loan from a Greek bank, so that he can modernise his "factory," as he proudly calls his workshop. A typical old-time Greek peasant, Papyros is a real patriarch at home, and a humble vassal of politicians and MPs, as he firmly believes their patronage will help him get his loan from the bank.

The loan remains a remote dream. Disappointment turns to despair. Eventually the members of his family start losing faith in him. Financial ruin is accompanied by social decline. Unable to face the situation created by the big business trusts and the multinationals, George Papyros, a man with an awakening class consciousness, finally takes a job as a worker in the same tannery as his son.

ANDREAS BELLIS

ROZA
(Rosa)

Script and Direction: Christoforo Christofis. Photography (colour): Andreas Bellis. Editing: Georges Triantafillou. Music: Helene Karaindrou. Art Direction: Tassos Zografos. Players: Andrzej Seweryn, Eva Kotamanidou, Daniel Olbrychski, Aleka Paizi, Aliki Georgouli. 110 mins.

The subject of the film is based on a real incident which took place in the Seventies, during the military dictatorship in Greece. In those days, it was a common occurrence for outstanding persons to be arrested and forced to give evidence at the Council of Europe in Strasbourg to the effect that human rights were not violated in Greece. The film begins with the arrest of a professor and then moves to a *pension* in Trieste, where Kyveli, the professor's wife, seeks out Klaus Offenbach, a

ANDRZEJ SEWERYN AND ANNE LIPINSKA IN *ROSA*, SCREENED AT CANNES IN 1982

former pupil of her husband's, who is known to be involved in anti-dictatorial activities in Europe.

Kyveli gradually comes under the spell of the *pension* atmosphere; it turns out to be the meeting-place of various characters, all reflecting at the spirit of revolt and resistance prevailing at the time. For instance, there is a Greek communist couple, living in exile, who keep lashing out at each other, caught in a political dream which both binds and separates them. All the characters in the *pension* are stalking some dream or other. They are preparing the ground for a revolution that will never take place; Rosa Luxemburg is their inspiration and exemplar. Kyveli falls in love with Klaus Offenbach, but the relationship has no future.

We watch the disintegration, one by one, of all the characters living in the *pension*. The Strasbourg trial is cancelled; Kyveli kills Klaus in a dream and leaves the now deserted *pension*.

I DROMI TIS AGAPIS INE NICHTERIN (Love Wanders in the Night). Script and dir: Frieda Liappa. Phot (colour): Nikos Smaragdis. Music: Giorgos Papadakis. Players: Maria Skoundzou, Mirka Papakonstantinou, Grigoris Evagelatos, Maritima Passari. Prod: Electra Films/Greek Film Centre. 90 mins.
Two sisters have left their village some time ago and moved into a flat in Athens. Their only relative is a cousin, a painter who lives in Paris. Tied with an almost pathological affection for each other, they also share a secret infatuation for their cousin. On his coming back to Athens the drama climaxes; the older sister commits suicide while the younger one goes abroad with him.

The starting point of the film is a small newspaper item about the double suicide of two sisters in their late thirties. Two lively, almost fascinating faces. The film tries to narrate a passionate story, avoiding the "realistic" aspect of the situation. So the lust for life of the two heroines changes into deadly anguish in a hostile and menacing city. The characters, both realistic and poetical, try to fulfil their desires in an impossible relationship on the borderline of melodrama.

MATHE PEDI MOU GRAMATA (Go to School, Son).
Script and dir: Theodoros Marangos. Phot (colour): Nikos Malas. Music: Nikos Tatsis. Players: Vassilis Diamandopoulos, Anna Manzourani, Nikos Kalogeropoulos, Christos Kalavrouzos. Prod: Theodoros Marangos. 100 mins.
Periklis is a teacher *cum* school director in a village. His school faces a crisis. It is empty of students, as the village is empty of people and the very few that remain are full of problems and questions. They don't believe in school classes any more. Among them is Sokrates, Periklis's younger son; while the older son is finishing his post-graduate specialisation abroad and returns to the village. Despite his excellent education, he remains unemployed and passes his time at the Kafenion.

The village, for the first time, holds a memorial service for the people executed by the Germans inside the schoolyard, during the occupation. But the name of the village's leftist is missing from the list of names of the executed. Periklis's son dares to protest. The village is turned upside down and the event reaches the court's of justice. The conflict between the two opposite views about the history, the tradition and the future of the place reaches its peak.

Periklis who is a witness for the prosecution, has remained virtually alone. His wife and children realise that truth lies on the other side and drift away from him. In court, the truth-loving teacher testifies lies. A whole world collapses in front of everyone's eyes, and especially in the eyes of Sokrates, who had been nursed with his father's "truths."

ISTORIES MIAS KERITRAS (Stories of a Beehive).
Script, dir and prod: Nikos Vergitsis. Phot: Tassos Alexakis. Players: Thalia Aslanidou, Mitsos Yiannakopoulos, Maria Kondili, Lida Tassopoulou. 80 mins.
Noon. The scenes scheduled for this morning have been shot. The people working in the film (all of them could claim to be leftist) separate. We follow their parallel

STILL FROM *LOVE WANDERS IN THE NIGHT*

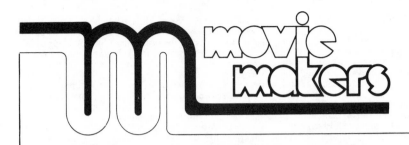

stories, as their personal relations, built on everyday events, begin to reveal a new, sad picture.

As night approaches, their stories reach a common axis. Their behaviour looks identical and each person's work has no further role to play. Late at night, they begin to realise where their way of life is leading them. In the morning, their social conduct will again give the impression that all is well. The atmosphere they collectively create is happy and friendly. There is nothing to indicate that tonight will be like last night, like all nights. There is nothing to idicate that they constitute a beehive with many cells.

STILL FROM *GO TO SCHOOL, SON*

TAXIDI STIN PROTEVOUSA (Voyage to Athens). Script and dir: Takis Papayiannidis. Phot (colour): Alexis Grivas. Music: Thanos Mikroutsikos. Players: Costas Cazakos, Stavros Mermigis, Vassilis Lagos, Costas Chalkias. Prod: Takis Papayiannidis/Greek Film Centre.
A young man, just released from the army after his mandatory service, goes to Athens because the prospects are better there than in his village. The film encompasses the stories of the people he meets and associates with, to become a fresco of the contemporary tendencies of Greek society and of the historical circumstances that played a role in the formation of social strata.

The young man's circle of friends inevitably breaks up at some point, and he returns to his village to become a worker in the new multi-national factory that opens up near his village. But his journey to the big city has changed him. It was a journey into knowledge.

ARIS VELOUCHIOTIS – DILIMA (Aris Velouchiotis – Dilemma). Script and dir: Fotos Lambrinos. Phot (colour): Giorgos Kavayias. Prod: CINE-VIDEO/Greka Film. 100 mins.

A documentary that attracted the audience's interest as it deals with an important figure in the liberation fight of the Greeks during and after the German occupation, and with the events in which he was somehow the hero.

Through the character of ELAS' chief guerilla leader Aris Velouchiotis and through the witnesses of people who lived the most important events of 1941–1945 from the inside, the film tries to analyse the problem of People's power and present the forces that contributed to the victorious people's revolution, which was born and matured in Greece during the German occupation, being lost after the liberation of the country.

In the film participate leaders of the communist party of Greece and of EAM (National Liberation Front), captains and guerillas of ELAS (National Popular Liberation Army), British and German officers, who operated on the Greek mountais during the war and the resistance fight. Old newsreels are also used.

PETROCHIMIKA, I KATHEDRIKES TIS ERIMOU (Petrochemicals, the Cathedrals of the Desert). Dir: Stathis Katsaros, Giorgos Sifianos. Phot (colour): Giorgos Cavadimos. Prod: Agricultural Union of Neochorion. 80 mins.

Polemical documentary that traces the struggle of the people of the town Neochorion to prevent the establishment of heavy industry at the delta of their river, a development that would provoke the pollution of the area. The film examines the environmental problems and the social changes that arise out of heavy industry, and also, the political struggle around the specific case in question. The main interest of the film lies in the fact that it was produced on the initiative and through the sponsorship of the people of Neochorion themselves, and in the fact that the film itself served as a weapon in their fight and as a means of uniting in their aims.

REPO (Day Off). Script and dir: Vassilis Vafeas. Phot (colour): Giorgos Kavayias. Players: Petros Zarkadis,

STILL FROM *ELECTRIC ANGEL*

Anna Makraki, Anna Michalitsianou. Prod: Vassilis Vafeas/Greek Film Centre. 90 mins.
A day in the life of a working man, outside his job, in the strange working areas of middle class Athenian society and in the seemingly familiar environment of his kin. The events of the film create a chain of tragic-comic circumstances and twists that hinder the hero in living a true human relationship.

STIGMA. Script and dir: Pavlos Tassios. Phot (colour): Theodoros Margas. Music: Kyriakos Sfetsa. Players: Olia Lazaridou, Andonis Kafetzopoulos, Dina Konsta. Prod: United Film-Makers. 90 mins.
A young couple gives birth to a hydrocephalous child. In accordance with the Laws and the State, the child must live. Euthanasia is forbidden. Every human creature has the right to live. But this applies for the parents also, and they decide to let the baby die of starvation so that they can save their own lives. But the outcome is quite different. The baby's slow death brings their own breaking up. It is the price of their choice.

EPIKINDINA PECHNIDIA (Dangerous Games). Script and dir: Giorgos Caripidis. Phot (colour): Theodoros Margas. Players: Zoe Laskari, Aris Retsos, Spiros Fokas. Prod: United Film-Makers. 100 mins.
Police thriller. An accountant from Athens goes on vacation to some island and there he gets involved in solving the death of a woman. The case turns out to be much simpler than what his need for adventure had led him to imagine. It is his own emotional involvement in the events that creates suspense.

I DIKI TIS CHOUNDAS (The Trial of the Junta). Dir: Theodossis Thedossopoulos. Music: Giorgos Yiannoulatos. Prod: Christos Mangos. 110 mins.
The year's top commercial success, that surpassed by far the expected attendance of a documentary. This success led to the making of a sequel, *The Trial of the Torturers*, which continues into further events of the first post-junta years in Greece with the trials of the junta leaders. The film deals historically with the 1936–1974 period. It begins with the establishment of the fascist dictatorship of Ioannis Metaxas and ends with the fall of the recent dictatorship. It exclusively uses documents – cinematographic, photographic and historical – that cover the main political, military, economic and social events of the period in question.

STIN ANAPAFTIKI MERIA (On the Cozy Side). Script, dir. and prod: Takis Spetsiotis. Phot (colour): Phillippas Koutsaftis. Players: Nikos Bitjanis, Takis Tsandilis. 80 mins.
Experimental film with references to narrative cinema. Absolutely stylised, it operates by replacing the dialogue with texts narrated off-screen, the theatrical acting of the players, the recycling of the picture in always the same spaces, the peculiar time passages, and with the use of the

cinema camera as moving photographic camera. The aesthetic of still photographs plays the most important role, since stills become the method of presenting the characters, the spaces, and even the text, which has the form of a caption or diary entry. The theme of the film is the peaceful presentation of the life of two authors in the Athens of the Sixties who are dedicated to the worship of art, and who occupy themselves with the external uses of culture, social life and publicity until they suddenly retire, covering the rest of their lives with absolute mystery.

ARPA-COLA (Patchwork – Cola). Script and dir: Nikos Perakis. Phot (colour): Aris Stavrou. Players: Mimis Chrissomalis, Despina Vayianou, Nikos Kalogeropoulos, Ilias Logothetis. Prod: Nikos Perakis, Giorgos Panoussopoulos.

Satire on the cinema itself – especially that of Greece, which presents idiosyncratic conditions. The satire expands into Greek society, as the film's heroes – self-sponsored directors who cannot make the films they want – come face to face with the everyday social problems of today's average Greek. They immediately transform the circumstances they face into imaginary scripts, thus adding to the circumstances their greatest problem, that of personal expression.

STILL FROM *MUSEUM PIECES*

TO EMA TON AGALMATON (**Museum Pieces**). Script: Tony Lycouressis, Stratis Karras. Dir: Tony Lycouressis. Phot (colour): Andreas Bellis. Music: Giogos Couroupos. Players: Vera Krouska, Richard Svare, Giorgos Ninios, Ilias Logothetis, Eva Kotamanidou. Prod: Tony Lycouressis/Greek Film Centre. 120 mins.
Winter in a Greek country town. On the occasion of the opening of the archaeological museum, the local authorities, together with foreign economic agents, plan the industrial rebuilding of the area. Suddenly three young people who have just escaped from the juvenile correction centre hide in the galleries chased by the police. The hold some statues as hostages and threaten to destroy them if their demands are not met and their fellow prisoners are not set free . . .

Hongkong

by Derek Elley

For some years it has been a New Year tradition that the latest comedy of Michael Hui (Hsü Kuan-wen) sets a new box-office record. Yet the HK$18,000,000 grossed by his latest *Security Unlimited* (*Mo-teng pao-piao*) – a thoroughly likeable slapstick comedy about a firm of inept security officers which showed a return to the warmer style of the earlier *The Private Eyes* – was soon surpassed in early 1982 by Tseng Chih-wei's *Aces Go Places* (*Tsui-chia p'ai-tang*), which calmly took HK$26,000,000 in 34 days and proved that anarchic Cantonese comedy is now up for grabs.

It has been a buoyant year for the Hongkong box-office – far more so than in neighbouring Taiwan – with even Shaw Brothers managing to enter the big league once again with a respectable HK$10,000,000 in 22 days for Liu Chia-liang's *Legendary Weapons of China* (*Shih-ba pan wu-yi*), perhaps thanks to its above-average quota of *fantastique* effects, and Golden Harvest's *Dragon Lord* (*Lung Shao-yeh*), shot in Taiwan by director/ star Jacky Chan (Ch'eng Lung), managing HK$11,000,000 in 24 days. The gross for *Dragon Lord* was, in fact, somewhat disappointing in such circumstances (particularly since it confirmed Chan as a director of some talent following his earlier *The Young Master*), but even that figure showed that Hongkong, with an average 62,000,000 admissions a year for the colony's 82 cinemas, is still a film-going town despite the inroads of the video market.

As of early 1982, the latest production of King Hu (Hu Chin-ch'üan) had still not surfaced in Hongkong. *The Juvenizer* (*Chung-shen ta-shih*), premiered in its original Mandarin version in Taiwan in August 1981, is a major departure for Hu – a contemporary comedy set in Taipei about an advertising executive who has to find a wife to secure a contract. The comedy is deftly played by actor T'ao Wei (an ad. executive in real life) and the film's production values are high, especially notable in the sharp editing; but Hu's heart does not really seem to be in the exercise.

Shaws is slowly responding to the changing local market with more comedies but veteran Chang Ch'eh continues to grind out martial arts dramas which are pale copies of his earlier successes. Only the recent *Brave Archer and His Mate* (*Shen-tiao*) showing real style, thanks to the return to his stable of actor Fu Sheng. Veteran Li Han-hsiang has also resumed filming after a break overseas (see IFG 1982).

The much-publicised New Wave of young directors has almost to a man been consumed in the commercial stream. Yü Yün-k'ang (Dennis Yü) followed *The Beast* with the equally exploitation-ary horror item *The Imp*. Hsü K'o, the most gifted of all in terms of technique, has continued to squander his talent, most recently with *All the Wrong Clues (For the Right Solution)* (*Kuei-ma chih-to hsing*) an exceptionally slick Chinese version of *Bugsy Malone* which sets new levels in cultural hybridism. T'an Chia-ming's *Love Massacre* (*Ai sha*), shot in the U.S.A. with Taiwanese actress Lin Ch'ing-hsia, is a pretentious piece of textbook Antonioni.

Curiously, the one young director still going from strength to strength is Ann Hui (Hsü An-hua), who since her first film, *The Secret*, has successively filtered the blander occidentalisms from her style and produced some sensitive portraits of modern Chinese life. Her third feature, *The Story of Woo Viet* (reviewed below), is perhaps her finest to date.

Two other works by young directors have also stood out for their sensitivity and avoidance of Hongkong's growing blood, sex and gore exploitation market. *Father and Son* (*Fu-tzu ch'ing*), by Allen Fong (Fang Yü-p'ing), is an ultimately moving, low-key portrait of a Hongkong youth's love-hate relationship with his father; and *Sealed with a Kiss* (*Liang hsiao-wu-chih*), by Kenneth Yip (Yeh Chien-hsing), avoids most of the cliches of a charming young love story to shape an almost Truffautesque view of the magic of childhood, rudely interrupted by the simmering violence of Hongkong society. The latter features two fine performances by Hsü Chieh (younger sister of Taiwanese actress Hsü Feng) and Ou Jui-ch'iang in the principal roles.

ABOVE: STILL FROM *THE SHAOLIN TEMPLE*

The year's most talked-about film, however, came right out of left field. Chang Hsin-yen's *The Shaolin Temple* (*Shao-lin szu*), directed and produced by the team of the left-wing Great Wall studio (under the banner of Chung Yüan Motion Picture Company), was, on the face of it, little different to any other martial arts picture – apart from the fact that it was shot on actual locations on the Mainland and featured several genuine champion fighters. Its triumphant HK$16,000,000 gross in 42 days (wiping out *Raiders of the Lost Ark*) was later echoed by large takings in other overseas Chinese communities such as Singapore (S$1,500,000 in 27 days). Chang's direction is strictly routine, but the film has an interesting semi-documentary thread and some witty portrayals of its neophyte Buddhist heroes.

HU-YÜEH-TE KU-SHIH
(The Story of Woo Viet)

Screenplay: Chang Chien-t'ing. Direction: Hsü An-hua (Ann Hui). Photography (colour): Huang Chung-piao. Editing: Huang Yi-shun. Music: Chang Hua. Art Direction: Ou Ting-p'ing. Players: Chou Jun-fa, Lo Lieh, Chung Ch'u-hung, T'ang Chin-t'ang, Chin Piao, Lin Ying-fa. For Pearl City Films. 92 mins.

Ann Hui's third feature is a complete change of pace from her glossy thriller *The Secret* and surreal farce *The Spooky Bunch*, and is the most intelligent treatment yet of the plight of Chinese refugees from Vietnam. Hui previously dealt with the subject in her RTHK drama *Boy from Vietnam*; here she deals with social estrangement on a wider scale as we follow Woo, a former South Vietnamese soldier, from Hongkong internment camp to the Chinese underworld of Manila as he tries to reach the United States.

Woo Viet has at times an almost documentary feel and is in marked contrast to several recent exploitation pictures on the same subject. Woo's labyrinthine progress from fixer to fixer, and his ingenuous struggle to rescue a fellow refugee forced into prostitution, form the meat of the tale, and Hui's use of the Manila locations is pleasingly unstereotyped. The story tips over into melodrama in its final moments, but otherwise this is impressive cinema.

DEREK ELLEY

Hungary

by Derek Elley

The cold days of the postwar Rákosi era have always proved a key source of inspiration for Hungarian cinema, but no more so than during the past year. Three of the year's best films chart the period in very personal terms: Péter Bacsó's *The Day Before Yesterday* (*Tegnapelőtt*) examines the loss of political idealism in the days of the People's Colleges of the late Forties; Zoltán Fábri's *Requiem*, in characteristically literary style, shows a young woman coming to terms with the loss of an ideal; and Pál Gábor's *Wasted Lives* (*Kettévált mennyezet*) describes relationships torn apart by the political flux of the early Thaw of 1953–55. The year's fourth major film, from the younger Péter Gothár, starts directly after this era, with the 1956 uprising and the generation scarred by the event: like the other three films, his *Time Stands Still* (*Megáll az idő*) is above all an intensely personal memory.

Possessed of a similar strength was Gábor Koltay's *The Concert* (*A koncert*), the year's surprise from left field. A document – rather than a documentary – of the 1980 reunion concert of Hungary's most famous pop group of the Sixties, it breaks through the restrictive boundaries of its genre to paint a detailed landscape of a vanished decade. The Illés Group, formed in 1965, was more than just another pop group to young Hungarians of the time: it was the first to assimilate the influence of western pop music in recognisably Hungarian terms, with lyrics of strong nationalist connotations by János Bródy (sometimes using the poems of figures such as Sándor Petőfi).

It is difficult for non-Hungarians to pick up all the references in Koltay's film but such is the conviction of the singing (particularly in Zsuzsa Koncz's two numbers, and the final, highly emotive song of the concert), and the skill of assembly, that the picture carries a powerful punch. Into footage of the actual concert (shot by some of Hungary's greatest cameramen – Kende, Ragályi, Andor *inter alios*), Koltay cuts footage from the Sixties charting the group's formation, growth, fall from official grace for a year, and final breaking up. Clips from key youth films of the period (by Mészáros, Bacsó, etc.) build up the portrait of the late Sixties; multiscreen and colour effects are used with restraint to vary the portrayal of the actual concert.

The ever-unpredictable Zsolt Kézdi Kovács failed to impress with *The Right to Hope* (*A remény joga*), a curiously diffuse tale of a 12-year-old boy torn between estranged parents and a cold, if ultimately affectionate, aunt. Kézdi Kovács's outlook is bleak: the adults are more concerned with sorting out their own confused lives than helping the boy adjust his own after the death of his grandfather. The ending offers a glimmer of hope – son and mother reunited? – but ultimately the film is as confused as its subject-matter. Untypically for

SINGER ZSUZSA KONCZ AND LYRICIST JÁNOS BRÓDY IN GÁBOR KOLTAY'S *THE CONCERT*

ANDRE DUSSOLIER AND EDIT FRAJT IN *TEMPORARY PARADISE*

the director, the picture suffers from a lack of overall visual style and few virtues emerge from its oblique exposition; poor delivery of large chunks of English dialogue does not help, either.

In *Mascot* (*Kabala*), János Rózsa deals with a similar kind of alienation, here leading to daughter and younger brother hitting the road on their own. Julianna Nyakó, the leading actress of Rózsa's previous *Sunday Daughters* (*Vasárnapi szülők*), harnesses all her sullen, tomboyish qualities to the role of the daughter determined to reunite her parents. The first half of *Mascot* is impressively constructed, with strong performances all round (Garas and Esztergályos as the mother and father) and some tight exposition; however, Rózsa later has difficulty developing his material. The children's act of rebellion offers intriguing glimpses of the underbelly of modern Hungarian life (gypsy harrassment; black marketeering) but leads nowhere other than a tragic, hopeless act of rebellion.

Following a line similar to fellow-veteran Fábri, András Kovács surprised with an avowedly warmer work, *Temporary Paradise* (*Ideiglenes paradicsom*). Smoothly scored by György Vukán, and with relaxed, sympathetic performances by André Dussolier and Edit Frajt, the film nevertheless has the authentic Kovács atmosphere of political tensions, of inevitable events, closing in on the

characters' lives. Here, a French POW and Hungarian Jewish divorcee meet in an internment camp by Lake Balaton in 1943; what starts as a temporary idyll soon develops into a cat-and-mouse game of life and death in the rapidly worsening climate of 1944 Budapest. The film has a surface gloss which robs it of some atmosphere – several of the year's films show the results of a decision to use brighter colour lighting to aid foreign TV sales – but Kovács responds to his subject with some bravura scenes.

In the case of Miklós Jancsó's The Tyrant's Heart, or Boccaccio in Hungary (A zsarnok szíve, avagy Boccaccio Magyarországon) surface gloss triumphs above all. Shot entirely in the studio, the film has some of the exotic feel of his Italian works (plus a screenplay by Giovanna Gagliardo rather than Gyula Hernádi) but the content is so oblique as to be indecipherable without a detailed synopsis. Dealing with the attempts of a returning prince to discover the truth of his father's death, The Tyrant's Heart exploits its Fifteenth-century setting with truth and illusion games involving a mime troupe of itinerant Italian actors. János Kende's camera roams Jancsó's vast castle set to memorable effect but at times – especially the ending with horsemen, puszta and gunshots – the film comes close to self-parody.

Márta Mészáros's Mother and Daughter (Anna) also sports a high sheen, plunging the viewer into an immaculately crafted metaphysical universe close to women's magazine romance. The French co-production is more Gallic than Magyar in feel: Marie José Nat (emotively dubbed by Ildikó Bánsági) hunts for her long-lost daughter in Budapest and Paris, finally achieving togetherness through a kidney transplant. Mészáros's metaphysical surgeon, the acute social observer of the early Seventies, seems a long way away. In comparison, the far less prolific Géza Böszörményi has lost none of his touch. Despite Czech overtones, Heart Tremors (Szivzür) maintains the verve of his earlier Birdies (Madárkák, 1971) and The Car (Autó, 1974). Casually witty, its portrait of a village community and its put-upon young doctor attains moments of surreal lunacy worthy of its

GRAZYNA SZAPOLOWSKA AND JADWIGA JANKOWSKA-CIEŚLAK IN *ANOTHER WAY*

experienced cast and the cameo presence of Jiří Menzel as a flying carpenter.

To end on a sadder note, the Hungarian film world lost one of its most distinguished members with the death in October 1981 of Zoltán Huszárik. A complete original, drawing together the related worlds of painting and cinema, Huszárik left behind two features quite outside the normal run – *Sinbad* (*Szindbád*, 1971) and *Csontváry* (1979). At the time of his death he was working on a documentary about a state farm.

MEGÁLL AZ IDŐ
(Time Stands Still)

Screenplay: Géza Bereményi, Péter Gothár. Direction: Péter Gothár. Photography (Eastmancolor): Lajos Koltai. Editing: Mária Nagy. Music and musical arrangements: György Selmeczi. Players: István Znamenák, Henrik Pauer, Sándor Sőth, Péter Gálfy, Anikó Iván, Lajos Őze, Lajos Szabó, Josef Kroner, Mária Ronyecz, Ádám Rajhona, Ági Kakassy, Pál Hetényi. For Budapest Stúdió. 97 mins.

With this second feature Péter Gothár establishes himself as the most exciting of Hungary's younger generation of directors. Like his previous *A Priceless Day* (see IFG 1981), the film is infused with a mass of references which strike a responsive chord in Hungarian audiences; yet in *Time Stands Still* his net has widened to embrace not only a historical perspective but also the experiences of a whole generation. Gothár sketches the passions, boredom and petty rebellions of a group of Budapest secondary school youngsters in the heady days of 1963, as Western influences (pop music, Coca-Cola) and the onset of puberty work their way through their collective personality: a "defection" to America gets no further than a wrecked car by Lake Balaton; girlfriends are absorbed into the teenage maw; and porno pictures are trafficked beneath the watchful eye of superiors. Yet the shadow of an older generation hangs heavy over their lives: Dénes's father fled the country in 1956, and it is the legacy of that act (in the form of a returning friend) which eventually shapes the boy's future. Gothár's *mise-en-scène* is notably tighter than in *A Priceless Day*, less in dramatic-realist style – slow motion captures unforgettable moments, and Lajos Koltai's camera roams the streets and school corridors with apocalyptic pre-

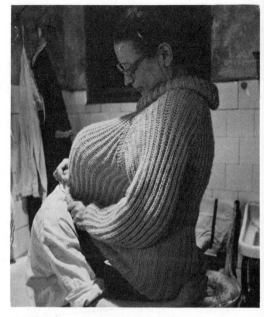

STILL FROM *TIME STANDS STILL*

sence. Sharp cutting and a strong vein of sharp, poe-faced humour drive the film to its ironic postscript on New Year's Eve 1967 – the elders nostalgically celebrating, the youngsters now coping with the trials and responsibilities of adulthood.

DEREK ELLEY

TEGNAPELŐTT
(The Day Before Yesterday)

Script and direction: Péter Bacsó. Photography (Eastmancolor): Tamás Andor. Editing: Mihály Morell. Music: György Vukán. Players: Éva Igó, György Dörner, Károly Nemcsák, Tamás Tóth. For Dialóg Stúdió. 107 mins.

Bacsó's film is an intensely personal return to the period brilliantly satirised in his earlier *The Witness* (1968). As the opening quote from József Atilla stresses, the theme is the loss of integrity: "You have become a false witness at your own trial." In *The Day Before Yesterday* – and the implicit irony of the title is surely deliberate – the integrity is more political than personal, but the

ÉVA IGÓ AND TAMÁS TÓTH IN *THE DAY BEFORE YESTERDAY*

two are shown to overlap with catastrophic effect. In the purposeful days of 1947, young convent-educated Dorottya joins a then fashionable People's College and is swept along on the tide of political fervour; by 1949 her idealism starts to dim as both her lover and early principles come under fire in the changing political climate; in 1951 we find her broken and disillusioned, working as an unskilled labourer in a foundry. "We thought the youth of the world would join together and defeat even the elements," she tells her inquisitor before giving false testimony against her lover; later, she and an old friend ironically sing a revolutionary song of the old days – but as a mournful ballad rather than fiery hymn (György Vukán's main and end title music picks up this strain and segues to menacing fanfares over an insistent side-drum *ostinato*). This is the same territory traversed by Jancsó in *The Confrontation* (1968); but Bacsó, as always, is more interested in

personalities than ritual. Strong ensemble playing from a largely unknown young cast – especially Éva Igó as the bright-eyed Dorottya – ensure that the story's emotional line is not lost amid the tide of events.

DEREK ELLEY

KETTÉVÁLT MENNYEZET
(Wasted Lives)

Script: Endre Vészi. Direction: Pál Gábor. Photography (Eastmancolor): Miklós Jancsó Jr. Music: György Selmeczi. Players: Juli Básti, Jan Nowicki, Edit Ábrahám, Emese Simorjay, Péter Ábel Jr., Éva Almási, Éva Szabó. For Budapest Studió. 102 mins.

There is a magical, at times mystical, strain in Gábor's sixth feature which is new to his work; it is not the strongest element in *Wasted Lives* but it imparts a sense of timelessness to the story which is most appropriate. The time is the shifting thaw of 1953–55, against which is played out a sad love story between a bull-nosed engineer and a young textile mill hand. Unlike in *Angi Vera*, however, the background is relatively unimportant, merely a shifting backcloth against which relationships are formed and broken, so many promising lives wasted. The household into which the young Julia moves has an almost tangible personality of its own, shifting (like the times) from friendship to disdain: Árpád's three children toss the idealistic Julia around like an emotional shuttlecock, the teenage daughters both resenting and accepting her hold over their father, and the young son

JULI BÁSTI IN *WASTED LIVES*

EDIT FRAJT IN *REQUIEM*

communing with the stone spirits of the grounds. György Selmeczi's broken, atonal scraps of melody point up the fragile atmosphere; and Jan Nowicki's cold, somewhat cruel, appeal is finally put to good use opposite the sad beauty of actress Juli Básti. Gábor's lack of attention to period detail is finally unimportant: spirit of place is the concern here, achieved with spell-binding power in the final tableau of father and son left alone in the deserted garden like so much flotsam on the banks of history.

DEREK ELLEY

REQUIEM

Script: Zoltán Fábri, based on a short story by István Örkény. Direction: Zoltán Fábri. Photography (Eastmancolor): György Illés. Editing: Mrs. Ferenc Szécsényi. Music: György Vukán. Players: Edit Frajt, Lajos Balázsovits, László Gálffi, György Kálmán. For Dialóg Studió. 93 mins.

Requiem has all of Fábri's customary precision and control, but the overall emotional temperature is markedly warmer than usual. Expanded from a short story by István Örkény, the film charts an abstract idea – the transference of an ideal (of beauty) from one man to another – with chamber-like economy and refinement. As in Gábor's *Wasted Lives*, the setting – 1952 – is relatively unimportant to the central theme, although the residual atmosphere helps to point up the intensity of the story. At the centre of the emotional whorl is Netti (played with luminous poise by Edit Frajt), who one evening alone is visited by Gyula, former cell-mate of her activist first husband István Hannover. Their tentative conversation is explored subjectively from both sides: from Netti's as she recognises mannerisms similar to István's, and from Gyula's, as he is brought face-to-face with the idealised figure of Hannover's reminiscences. Fábri interweaves time present with the web of István and Netti's own memories, in which Gyula and Ágoston are caught up like helpless flies. *Requiem* is an elegiac poem to a vanished past and a new beginning – for Netti, as the ghost of István is finally exorcised through Gyula. With György Vukán's warm score and György Illés's cut-glass colour images, Fábri's film achieves moments of great intensity – a memory-drama played out between four players. It may finally lack the

consequence of his earlier works, but it bears the stamp of a master-craftsman nonetheless.

DEREK ELLEY

recent and forthcoming films

ÖLELKEZŐ TEKINTETEK (Another Way). Script: Károly Makk, Erzsébet Galgóczi, based on a novel by Erzsébet Galgóczi. Dir: Károly Makk. Phot (Eastmancolor): Tamás Andor. Music: László Dés, János Másik. Players: Jadwiga Jankowska-Cieślak, Grażyna Szapolowska, Jozef Kroner, Gábor Reviczky, Péter Andorai. For Mafilm (Dialóg Studió).

KABALA (Mascot). Script: István Kardos. Dir: János Rózsa. Phot (Eastmancolor): Elemér Ragályi. Music: Levente Szörényi. Players: Julianna Nyakó, Zoltán Jakab, Dezső Garas, Cecilia Esztergályos, Róbert Koltai, Enikő Tóth, János Bán, Miklós B. Székely. For Mafilm (Objektiv Studió).

A REMÉNY JOGA (The Right to Hope). Script and dir: Zsolt Kézdi Kovács. Phot (Eastmancolor): János Zsombolyai. Players: Miklós Varga, Ildikó Bánsági, Maija-Liisa Turkka, István Novák, Gunnar Peterssen, László Szabó. For Mafilm (Objektiv Studió).

SZIVZÜR (Heart Tremors). Script: József Balázs, Géza Böszörményi, Péterpál Gulyás. Dir: Géza Böszörményi. Phot (Eastmancolor): Péter Jankura. Music: Zdenkó Tamássy, György Kovács. Players: Gábor Máté, Dorottya Udvaros, Jiří Menzel, Judit Pogány, Juli Básti. For Mafilm (Objektiv Studió).

A PARTFOGOLT (On Probation). Script and dir: Pál Schiffer. Phot (Eastmancolor): Tamás Andor, Miklós Jancsó Jr. Music: EDDA. Player: János Kitka. For Mafilm (Hunnia Studió).

SZELEBURDI CSALÁD (A Harum-Scarum Family). Script: Ágnes Bálint, György Palásthy. Dir: György Palásthy. Phot (Eastmancolor): Sándor Kardos. Music: Zdenkó Tamássy. Players: Béla Ernyei, Andrea Drahota, Anita Ábel, János Szanyi, László Tóth, Erzsi Máthé, László György, Zoltán Boros, József Hágen, Ádám Szabó, Péter Balázs, Zsuzsa Mányai, Mónika Ulmann, Ferenc Némethy, Anikó Felföldi, László Csákányi. For Mafilm (Dialóg Studió).

RONTÁS ES REMÉNYSÉG (Bewitched by Hope). Script: Domokos Moldován, Miklós Erdély. Dir: Domokos Moldován. Phot (Eastmancolor): Ferenc Pap. Players: Mrs. István Ferkovits, Mrs. Jolán Jakab-Makula, Athina Papadimitriu, László Borbély, Blanka P. Lukács, Péter Imre Horvhát, Dr. Mihály Kádár, Dr. Lajos Mikófalvy, László Somogyi. For Béla Balázs Studió.

A KONCERT (The Concert). Script and dir: Gábor Koltay. Phot (Eastmancolor): János Kende, and Elemér Ragályi, Tamás Andor, Mihály Halász, Miklós Jancsó Jr., Loránd Mertz, Péter Vékás, Sándor Janovics. Players: The Illés Group, Zsuzsa Koncz, The Fonográf Group, The Tolcsvays and the Trio. For Mafilm (Budapest Studió).

NÉMA KIÁLTÁS (Silent Cry). Script and dir: Márta Mészáros. Phot (Eastmancolor): Miklós Jancsó Jr. Players: Zsuzsa Czinkóczy, Jan Nowicki, Ildikó Bánsági,

Mari Szemes, Pál Zolnay. For Mafilm (Budapest Studió).
GYŐZŐ. Script: Mihály Sükösd. Dir: Rezső Szörény.
Phot (Eastmancolor): Péter Jankura. Music: Zdenkó
Tamássy. Players: László Helyey, László Vajda, Erika
Bodnár, Hédi Temessy. For Mafilm (Objektiv Studió).
DÖGKESELYŰ (The Vulture). Script: Ferenc András,
Miklós Munkácsy. Dir: Ferenc András. Phot (Eastman-
color): Elemér Ragályi. Music: György Kovács. Players:
György Cserhalmi, Mária Glatkowska, Hédi Temessy,
Zita Perczel, László Szabó. For Mafilm (Dialóg Studió).
VUK. Script: Attila Dargay, István Imre, Ede Tarbay,
based on a novel by István Fekete. Dir: Attila Dargay.
Phot (Eastmancolor): Irén Henrik. Music: Péter Wolf.
For Pannonia Film Studio. Animated feature.
FEHÉRLOFIA (Son of the White Mare). Script: Marcell
Jankovics, László György, based on Hungarian folk-
tales. Dir: Marcell Jankovics. Phot (Eastmancolor):
Zoltán Bacsó. Music: István Vajda. For Pannonia Film
Studio. Animated feature.

STILL FROM *HEART TREMORS*

Iceland

by Thor Vilhjálmsson

The Icelandic film, which appears only new-born,
has already achieved a certain maturity. Fortunately, it still retains the fresh approach of those
newly initiated in the ritual and craft of this art
and/or industry. Sometimes we call that "blue-
eyed." In other words, those involved mortgage
their belongings, apartments, wives and mistresses, trinkets, and even their children's teddybears
or their husband's mistresses or golf clubs and
salmon rods. This might lead to a certain fractious
climate in the home even if it leads to an enthusiastic climate outside. Thus far the interest and
support of the entire population are required to
save your skin as well as the production. Luckily,
Iceland holds the world record for frequency of
cinema attendance, and still considers this child
prodigy a part of its own family.

Awards from the Icelandic Film Fund may be
the temptation for someone to risk plunging into
the abyss or taking off into outer space.

In some countries television either has played
or does play a decisive role in establishing film
talent (for example, West Germany, Switzerland,
Canada). Icelandic television has been less fortunate even if on rare occasions it has proved ambitious. A regrettable instance was when a TV film

film

Icelandic Drama Distribution
Häaleitisbraut I, Reykjavik
P.O.Box 7103, Telex 2018is

**Icelandic Drama Distribution
Producers and Distributors of
Feature Films**

**Previous Productions:
"Fathers Estate„
"Lilly„**

was launched on Snorri Sturluson, the literary giant of the Saga Age and pivotal politician during the fateful struggles of the Thirteenth Century. Sturluson was assassinated by envoys from the King of Norway, but suffered no less cruel a fate at the glove-clad hands of television.

After such setbacks, it was all the more encouraging to welcome another film about the Saga period. Namely the feature-length production, *The Outlaw*, directed by Ágúst Gudmundsson who, with Hrafn Gunnlaugsson, has been the most prominent member of the Icelandic film wave. Ágúst continues to work in a rewarding relationship with his excellent cameraman Sigurdur Sverrir Pálsson. The second feature to have emerged during the past year is *Jón Oddur and Jón Bjarni*, by Thráinn Bertelsson. Two further features are due within the next few months, both of which have already aroused a certain controversy. The first is *Inter Nos* (*Okkar á milli*), directed by Hrafn Gunnlaugsson, mentioned in IFG 82. Hrafn provoked the entire country's population by getting his crew to tickle the tits of the national pride "Geysir," a phenomenon of nature that has given its name to all the hot springs of the world, and to make it erupt higher than ever before.

The other impending release is a study of sub-culture in Reykjavík: *Rock in Reykjavík*, by Fridrik Thor Fridriksson. It's an agglomeration or medly of pop and punk etc., with embryonic bands thundering away in suburban garages, derelict sheds, or run-down factories, all in the quest for stardom. On one occasion, the filming was interrupted by the police after some gentle prying souls had complained about a flock of hens being summarily massacred by the musicians, while a grunting pig was seated in state on a lavatory stool pontifically awaiting a similarly crimson execution in the service of rock.

Fridrik Thor has just displayed some rare promise in his recent TV film, *The Blacksmith* (*Eldsmidurinn*), a documentary dealing with a natural inventor of the machines he needs for himself, and who approaches life with the delicacy of a Zen master, all beneath the shadow of glaciers in the Icelandic countryside.

A documentary is being made about the celebrated Icelandic ballet dancer, Helgi Tómasson, now engaged at the New York City Ballet. It's

SIGRÍDUR GEIRS AND MARÍA ELLINGSEN IN *INTER NOS*

directed by two young men, Valdimar Leifsson and Haraldur Fridriksson, who quit TV in order to realise their dreams. Many other projects are fermenting in different categories of film-making. And new talent in Iceland is impatient.

Meanwhile the Icelandic Film Festival seems firmly established, and each February in Reykjavík it offers a reasonable display of the most important products of contemporary international cinema, with foreign directors apparently ever more eager to send their work to the festival.

It is too early to try to isolate definite trends in the Icelandic cinema, but so far the outstanding individuals seem to be Ágúst Gudmundsson and Hrafn Gunnlaugsson, who are contrasting personalities. Ágúst is refined and contained in his approach while the aggressively-talented Hrafn seems ready to take considerable risks and grows from film to film with a promise of great achievement, having already behind him various films of uneven quality, with the best being outstanding.

Thorsteinn Jónsson, who some years ago made on his own a remarkable documentary about a farmer who could not leave his doomed smallholding after all his neighbours had departed, is now preparing a feature film based on the famous novel by the Icelandic Nobel Prize-winner Halldór Laxness: *The Atomic Station* (*Atómstödin*), Thorsteinn is also the director of the popular *Dot, Dot, Comma, Dash*, drawn from the popular novel by Pétur Gunnarsson.

ÚTLAGINN
(The Outlaw)

Script and Direction: Ágúst Gudmundsson. Photography (colour): Sigurdur Sverrir Pálsson. Music: Áskell Másson. Players: Arnar Jónsson, Ragnheidur Steindórsdóttir, Tinna Gunnlaugsdóttir. Produced by Isfilm.

The immensely rich heritage of the Saga literature of Iceland from the Twelfth, Thirteenth, and Fourteenth Centuries – a literature of universal importance – seems no less tempting for the artistic film-maker than the Samurai tradition of Japan. These ancient novels are of such dimensions that they have often made Icelanders dream of persuading a Kurosawa or a Kobayashi to come to Reykjavík and film their strange blend of extreme delicacy and grotesque cruelty, both precise and economic in expression. But now our own directors have begun drawing on the sources. Ágúst Gudmundsson has been wise in his approach to this particular Saga. There is many a trap lying in wait, but Ágúst has dealt with the material prudently and the result is a movie that merits international attention. The Saga of Gísli Súrsson is given adequate film expression in *The Outlaw*. The camerawork of Sigurdur Sverrir Pálsson is a delight to watch, lyrical yet soberly resisting the extravagance that the Icelandic landscape can so easily produce with its savage splendour. This was also clear in their previous collaborative effort, *Land and Sons*. Arnar Jónsson is brilliant in the title role, and on the whole the casting is admirable. Since his talented debut film at the London International Film School, *Lifetime to Cathy*,

STILL FROM *THE OUTLAW*

Ágúst's work has borne the stamp of a man of talent and taste who knows his limitations and avoids the pitfalls of film-making.

THOR VILHJÁLMSSON

JÓN ODDUR AND JÓN BJARNI

Script and Direction: Thráinn Bertelsson. Photography: Baldur Hrafnkell Jónsson. Music: Egill Ólafsson. Produced by Nordan 8.

Jón Oddur and Jón Bjarni is a smooth, agreeable example of family entertainment dealing with the pranks and adventures of a pair of twins, delightfully interpreted by real-life twins found by the director, Thráinn Bertelsson, in Reykjavik. It is based on a popular children's book by the versatile

Member of Parliament, Gudrun Helgadóttir. This is a pleasant film, unmarred by any pretensions.

THOR VILHJÁLMSSON

forthcoming films

OKKAR Á MILLI (Inter Nos or Between Us). Script and Dir: Hrafn Gunnlaugsson. Phot: Karl Óskarsson. Sound: Gunnar Smári. Players: Benedikt Árnason, Sigrídur Geirs, María Ellingsen. Prod: F.I.L.M.

ROCK IN REYKJAVÍK. Script and Dir: Fridrik Thor Fridriksson. Phot: Ari Kristinsson. Sound: Jón Karl Helgason. Music: Studio Thursabit. Prod: Hugrenningur.

KONA (Woman). Dir: Helgi Skúlason. Photo and Adapt: Páll Steingrímsson, from a play by Agnar Thordarson. Players: Helga Backman and Thorsteinn Gunnarsson.

SÓLEY. Script and Dir: Róska. Phot: Charles Rose, Gudmundur Bjartmarsson. Players: Rúnar Gudbrandsson and Tine. Prod: Sóley.

BELOW: ONE OF THE GROUPS FEATURED IN *ROCK IN REYKJAVÍK*, THE FIRST ICELANDIC FILM RECORDED IN DOLBY STEREO

BELOW: STILL FROM *JÓN ODDUR OG JÓN BJARNI*

Useful addresses

Kvikmyndasjódur Íslands
(The Icelandic Film Fund)
Hverfisgata 4–6
Reykjavík.
Tel: 25000. Telex 2111-Iskult is.
Félag kvikmyndragerdarmanna
(Association of Icelandic Film-Makers)
P.O. Box 5162
Reykjavík.
I.L.M.
(Icelandic Drama Distribution)
P.O. Box 7103
Reykjavík.
Tel: 22517. Telex 2018
Kvikmyndafélagid Odinn
(Odinn Film Production)
P.O. Box 623
Reykjavík.
Tel: 28155

F.I.L.M.
Feature-film Productions and for co-productions
P.O. Box 7103
Reykjavík.
Tel: 28810. Telex 2018
Isfilm (Icefilm)
Hafnarstræti 19
Reykjavík.
Tel: 19960.
Kvikmyndabladid
(A monthly film magazine)
Vesturgötu 3
101 Reykjavík.
Hugrenningur
Film Production
Vesturgata 3
Reykjavík.
Tel: 13339.

India

by Uma da Cunha

On the world scene, Indian films have been better known for their statistics than for their intrinsic quality. However, in the past year both quantity and quality have come together to gain world attention – and India itself prominence as a location for major international productions.

The golden jubilee of the Indian talkie in 1981 may have triggered the interest. Never before has the history of Indian cinema had such extensive exposure. "Film India" presented over eighty Indian films at the Museum of Modern Art in New York. The event was organised under the auspices of the Indo-US Subcommission on Education and Culture and the Directorate of Film Festivals, Government of India. The package later toured seven American cities. "Film India" had three sections: the first and most popular was the Satyajit Ray retrospective; then there was a brief survey of early Indian cinema; and contemporary Indian cinema. A documentary section paid homage to the work of the late Sukhdev. In Britain, The "Festival of India" celebrations had a comprehensive film section, highlighted by the work of the late Ritwik Ghatak at London's National Film Theatre. This retrospective was later expected to go to Locarno and then to the Nantes festival.

However, none of this prevented a decline – albeit marginal – in foreign sales of Indian films since the major foreign exchange earner is not so much Ray as the song-and-dance Hindi feature film. Solid markets like the U.K., U.S.A. and Middle East wanted considerably less of their accustomed rations. New markets offset some of the decline: Europe, Africa, Latin America and the Far East.

India may now need a new marketing strategy. Video potential, for instance, needs to be borne in mind; and perhaps the low-budget film can play a supporting role alongside the blockbuster. Countries offering better prospects are Peru, Mexico, Singapore, Dubai and East/West Africa.

Within India the film boom continues, despite dire warnings and predictions. Box-office receipts rose by 15% to just over $370,000,000. This has been attributed mainly to an increase in the total number of cinemas – to something over 11,000.

The audience/cinema ratio still remains amongst the poorest in the world: 7.37 seats per 1,000 people. The UNESCO recommendation for India was 30,000 cinemas.

India is still the world's most prolific film producer. The past year, at 737 films, showed a slight reduction (10 less than the previous year). Hindi films are once more at the top of the list (153), followed by Tamil (137), Telugu (132), Malayalam (111), Kannada (65), Bengali (42), Gujerati (34), Marathi (27), Oriya (10), Punjabi (8), Assamese and Bhojpuri (5 each), Manipuri (3), English (2), Rajasthani (2) and Tulu (1). Little-known languages are now venturing into film, among them Konkani, Prithibhasha, Nepali and Maithili. India has 16 official regional languages and over 1,600 dialects. There are still many places and tongues to go for the Indian film.

There is a demand for regional cinema – films made in languages other than Hindi, India's national and most widely understood language. Abroad, following the Nantes festival's presentation of South Indian films, a festival of Marathi pictures toured the U.S.A. The Japan Foundation plans a section on Indian cinema as part of its Panorama of South Asian Films.

Regional cinema is getting better known even within India, due to television showing features every weekend. The main encouragement though comes from state support. A major step forward this past year has been the funding not only of regional cinemas but also of film production. The West Bengal government has taken the lead in producing both feature films and TV featurettes. Shyam Benegal's *Aarohan*, Satyajit Ray's *Sadgati* and Goutam Ghose's *Dhakal* have been the first impressive results, all three winning the nation's top awards.

The National Film Development Corporation (NFDC), the body controlling the government's interest in film production, has also been both innovative and far-sighted. It has begun producing its own films, starting with Bhaskar Chandavarkar's *Atyachar*. It has expanded its distribution network for both Indian and foreign films. Finally, the NFDC has made extensive efforts to buy and

WE UNDERSTAND
THE INDIA YOU NEED

MEDIUS INDIA came into being in 1979 as two needs began keenly to be felt:

*the need among producers outside India for consultancy and production services in the country.

*the need among Indian producers for the same services and promotion of their work outside India.

In meeting both needs for several years now, our services have focused on saving money and time. This may be why we have a record of delivering good work on schedule, on budget.

Consultation/liaison/processing: *Script *official approvals *budgeting *casting *location-hunting *staffing *production. Functioned in one or other of these fields in Satyajit Ray's *The Chess Players*: Euan Lloyd's *The Sea Wolves*; the Granada TV production of Paul Scott's *Staying on*; various BBC and ATV features.

Subtitling: The translation into English and spotting of over 120 Indian films and of a dozen into French *capability in Arabic, Spanish, Russian and most European languages.

PR/Publicity: Ray's *The Chess Players* and short film *Bala*, Benegal's *Ankur*, Sathyu's *Kanneshwara Rama*, Rathod's *Ramnagari*, etc *International Festivals, major and specialised *data collection and compilation *writing; editing four published works on Indian cinema plus monographs.

Contact **Uma da Cunha**

Medius India
Film and Media Services

10 Fairlawn
128 Maharshi Karve Marg
Bombay 400 020
Tel.: 222170

KUNAL KAPOOR IN *VIJETA*

sell films on an international level. It has been organising marketing at major film centres and festivals such as MIFED, Filmex and Cannes. NFDC's import of foreign films has also risen in the past few years.

The only other source of imports into India is a package deal between Motion Picture Export Association of America and India's Ministry of Information and Broadcasting. All import goes through NFDC. The total number of foreign films imported in the past year was 203: of these 117 were from the U.S.A., followed by the U.S.S.R. (39), the U.K. (19), Japan (6), Australia (5), France (4), Italy (3), Sri Lanka and East Germany (2) with one each from Canada, Hongkong, Hungary, Turkey, Czechoslovakia and Netherlands.

Film-making has showed some cautious attempts at change within its formula structure.

The themes are now more varied, the stars more in number – and younger and slimmer. Wild adventure capers are giving way to homespun drama and tender romance. Disco-fever has hit its high point, adapting western tunes with panache and impunity. Hindi film music is now very popular among overseas Indian communities.

The trend for family dynasties to rule over the film world continues to have almost feudal overtones. More ex-stars are launching their sons as instant heroes in their own productions. The latest is evergreen hero Dev Anand, acting with his son Vijay in a film called *Anand and Anand*. Veteran film magnate V. Shantaram is promoting his grandson. But the great and grand Kapoor clan overshadows all others: Shashi Kapoor's son, Kunal, is the youngest to join the fray.

Shashi Kapoor, entrepreneur extraordinary of

STILL FROM *SADGATI*

PHOTO: NEMAI GHOSH

the New Cinema, has been spurred on by the success of *36 Chowringhee Lane*, which won the Manila festival's top prize. He now has two new films in hand – one directed by Govind Nihalani, the other by Girish Karnad. Shyam Benegal has been concentrating on two large-scale documentaries and plans to complete his next feature by the end of 1982. There are other promising newcomers to look forward to this year. The film scene is bright – despite vested interests grumbling about Indian poverty and the negative presentation of superstition in "festival films."

Foreign film-makers have been favouring Indian locales and themes. Richard Attenborough's *Gandhi* (to be released in late 1982) is awaited with much expectation. In people like Shama Habibullah and Suresh Jindal, it has been proved that Indian production managers can match international standards anywhere, along with local technicians. Equipment in India is also of a high standard: it took a large-scale production like *Gandhi* to prove this fact – even to Indians. In

1982 the Merchant-Ivory team also returned to the cradle of their unique partnership 21 years later – to shoot Ruth Prawar Jhabwala's *Heat and Dust*, starring Julie Christie (who was actually born in India). Granada TV's ambitious series on Paul Scott's *Raj Quartet* was filmed in all its glory. David Lean, working in seclusion, has begun the script of E. M. Forster's *Passage to India*. And James Bond will also go Indian this time, in his next extravaganza *Octopussy*.

SADGATI
(Deliverance)

Script and direction: Satyajit Ray, from a story by Munshi Premchand. Photography (colour): Soumendu Ray. Editing: Dulal Dutta. Art Direction: Ashoke Bose. Music: Satyajit Ray. Players: Om Puri, Smita Patil, Mohan Agashe, Gita Siddarth, Bhaiyalal Hedau. 50 mins. Hindi. Inquiries: Doordarshan, Mandi House, Copernicus Marg, New Delhi 110 001.

This TV film concerns a day in the life of a villager

of the Untouchables caste – Dukhi (Om Puri), who comes to ask the village Brahmin priest Ghasiram (Mohan Agashe) to come to his house to fix an auspicious date for his daughter's wedding. The priest agrees but makes Dukhi perform various chores while he has his meals, advises people and enjoys his siesta. Weak from a recent fever, Dukhi dies while chopping wood. This causes a crisis because the corpse prevents the Brahmins from going to the village well and the Untouchables refuse to touch the corpse until the police come. The priest commits the distasteful but permissible act of dragging the corpse away with a rope (thereby not polluting himself by direct contact) and dumping it in a refuse trap. He has retained his sanctity and pre-empted public humiliation.

Ray has stuck to the naturalistic style of the story; those who expect complexity and nuance will be disappointed. The film makes its points briefly, with every act and every word made to count. Any comparison with *Pather panchali* is also misleading. That was an evocation both of an early innocence and of remembered poverty; *Sadgati* is about caste and class. Boldly drawn characters dominate. Smita Patil is completely divested of her sexuality – made to look like any nondescript Harijan woman who looks dully at you in thousands of villages. Her screams at the priest after Dukhi's death are not melodramatic; they are expected of her position in life. Gita Siddarth plays the heavy, sensuous wife of the priest, by turns mean and kind. The priest is not a tyrant – he is a petty exploiter who gets his fee in kind. At the centre of the film is the mind of Dukhi which accepts tradition, however sullenly. It is that which binds him – not force or economic necessity. What kills him is not the Brahmin or the system: it is the hollowness within him created by centuries of brutish existence.

IQBAL MASUD

STILL FROM *BARA*

STILL FROM *RAT-TRAP*

ELIPPATHAYAM
(Rat-Trap)

Script and direction: Adoor Gopalakrishnan. Photography (Eastmancolor): Ravi Varma. Editing: M. Mani. Music: M. B. Srinivasan. Art Direction: Sivan. Players: Karamana, Sarada, Jalaja, Rajam K. Nair, Prakash, Soman, John Samuel, B. K. Nair, Joycee, Thampi, B. Nair. Produced by Ravi for General Pictures (Kerala). World Sales: National Film Development Corporation (Bombay). 121 mins.

The third feature by writer/director Adoor Gopalakrishnan (in Malayalam) is a rarity in Indian cinema in that its formal methods and visual styling (influenced, perhaps indirectly, by the Japanese way of "looking" at a scene) become the primary tools in tracing this study in paranoia. The story itself has a built-in symbolic link: an indolent, selfish landowner exerts a baleful influence on his family who are expected to wait on him hand and foot; when he is left alone, he finds himself unable to face a changing future, trapped like the rats his younger sister catches in a little cage.

Utilising the minimum of dialogue, Gopalakrishnan takes this rather obvious theme and builds a structure of closely interlinked images with extreme concentration on shot details – the house's verandah, open doors, pots, water, drenched streets, hands and eyes.

This breaking down of scenes gives the narrative a slow, dream-like progress allied to changes in climate, all of which is visually enhanced by off-centre framing in certain episodes. The director's skill in sustaining this method owes much to the beautiful colour camerawork of Ravi Varma and some delicate, detailed playing from his cast – notably Sarada, Jalaja and Rajam Nair as the three contrasted sisters representing varying degress of revolt against the old order symbolised by their brother (played slightly too inflexibly by Karamana). Gopalakrishnan also makes a nice contrast between the light and heat of the surrounding countryside and the dark, increasingly claustrophobic atmosphere of the house's interior, backed by a precise application of sound and music. JOHN GILLETT

AROHAN
(The Ascent)

Script: Shama Zaidi. Direction: Shyam Benegal. Photography (colour): Govind Nihalani. Music: Purna Das Baul. Editing: Bhanudas Divkar. Dialogue/lyrics: Niaz Haider. Players: Om Puri, Victor Banerjee, Noni Ganguly, Rajen Tarafdar, Gita Sen. 144 mins. Hindi. Inquiries: Government of West Bengal, Writers Building, Calcutta.

This is perhaps the first Hindi film which is unambiguously about politics seen as a process of perpetual and unending struggle. The case history of Indra Lohar, the Bengal peasant who struggled through courts to establish his claim to a plot of land during a succession of rightist and leftist governments, forms, as Benegal says, "the spine of the film." However, the story of Lohar's filmic counterpart, Hari Mandal, goes further to the urban influx caused by rural poverty. *Arohan* is a documentary in the most literal sense: it documents rather than preaching, condemning or exhorting.

There is no striking of attitudes; Hari Mandal undergoes no radical transformation or catharsis. Things happen to him, he struggles, and there is a slight but heartening change in the social climate. Second, the film explores a specific urban situation (well-known but not grasped fully by New Cinema film-makers) where misery leads not to the joining together of the dispossessed but to their manipulation by fascist elements. Hari Mandal's brother, Bhalai, emigrates to Calcutta, becomes a railway wagon thief, and is promoted to political assassin by a party. This state-of-affairs has been shown on the Calcutta stage but never in Hindi film. Third, and most important, the court scenes in which Hari Mandal wages a never-ending life-and-death battle are the most truthful ever shown on the Indian screen. *Arohan* brings the viewer down to earth, placing him firmly in the dusty, rule-ridden world of the Indian court whose language – as well as "justice" – remains foreign to the people.

IQBAL MASUD

BARA
(The Famine)

Script: Shama Zaidi, Javed Siddiqi, from a story by U. R. Ananthamurthy. Direction: M. S. Sathyu. Photography (colour): Ashok Gunjal. Editing: S. Chakravarty. Art Direction: Bijan Das Gupta. Players: Anant Nag, Lavlin Madhu, Nithin Sethi, Veeraj Byakod, Uma Shivkumar. Hindi and Kannada versions. Inquiries: M. S. Sathyu, B-3 Nehrunagar, Juhu Tara, Bombay 400 049.

The film is set in Bidar, a perennially drought-prone backward district in the southern state of Karnataka. The action centres round the young, idealistic district collector (Anant Nag). His integrity has not been corrupted by the in-fighting between the chief minister and home minister. Bidar is the constituency of the ambitious home minister and he has an extensive power base there. The wholesale grain merchants and the superintendent of police are in his camp. The collector is powerless to bring the hoarded stocks into the open, despite a "surprise" raid. Drought and famine stalk the land, forcing the hungry villagers to flock to the town in search of employment and food. Unless the collector can get the chief minister to declare the area as drought-affected, no aid will

be forthcoming. The chief minister evades the issue, because starting relief works will benefit his political rival who will be given credit by the electorate.

An ambitious and opportunistic political activist with a colourful past insinuates himself into the collector's favour by promising to get the chief minister's help. He incites the masses to loot the food shops, forces the concealed grain into the open and becomes a hero by selling it at fair price. The film chillingly shows how easy it is to engineer communal riots through exaggerated rumours. Bidar has a sizeable Muslim population – mostly poor and backward, and easy prey to religious frenzy.

The film's postscript is ironic. The home minister resigns, taking responsibility for the riots. The chief minister at last declares a famine area, rushing food and money to the parched land blackened by smoke from arson and littered with the innocent dead.

MAITHILI RAO

PHANIYAMMA

Script and direction: Prema Karanth, from a story by
M. K. Indira. Photography (colour): S. Ramachandran.
Music: B. V. Karanth. Players: L. V. Sharada, M. V.
Narayan Rao, Sunder Raj. Hindi. Inquiries: National
Film Development Corporation, 13–16 Regent Chambers, Nariman Point, Bombay 400 021.

An array of new faces refreshes the eye. Phaniyamma, the story of a child widow, unfolds in a
series of close-ups. In the title role is actress L. V.
Sharada. Uncannily like her in physical appearance
is the adolescent Phani, hair shorn and clean
browed: the two little girls playing the child widow
are extraordinarily touching. The film proceeds in
flashback as the aged Phaniyamma watches her
childhood go by. Director Prema Karanth (from
the National School of Drama, making this her
first film) carries off the childhood part of *Phaniyamma* with some flourish.

The second part features the adult widow.
The film is based on the real-life story of Phaniyamma who lived from 1870–1952, and on the
biography written by popular writer M. K. Indira.
Phaniyamma is a person of dignity and charm:
married at the age of nine, her "husband" dies six
months later of a snake bite. The Brahmin elders sit
in conference: with puberty, the young Phani dons
the costume prescribed for the South Indian
Brahmin widow – the shaven head, the bleak dress.
(Brahmin convention did not permit a widow to
re-marry; in the early Twentieth century child
marriage was banned by law.) She stoically accepts
her role and makes her life fruitful by serving
others. In the village of Hebbalige (in the beautiful
Malnad area of Karnataka) a familiar white-cowled figure crosses the landscape, flitting from
house to house, tendering help and advice.

Somewhere in the latter half the screenplay
loses its way – between delineating the figure of the
brave widow and the development of the climax in
which Phaniyamma supports a young widow
refusing to submit to Brahmin orthodoxy.

By all accounts, the New Cinema in Karnataka – heralded by Pattabhi Rama Reddy's *Samskara* more than a decade ago – has recently
flickered out. Prema Karanth's film, promising and
likely to be popular, will hopefully lead to its
renaissance.

RANI BURRA

new and forthcoming films

IMAGI NINGTHEM (My Son, My Precious). Language: Manipuri. Dir: Abiram Syam Sharma. Prod/phot:
K. Ibohal Sharma. Story/scr: M. K. Binodini. Music:
Khundrakpam Joykumar. Players: Leikhendro, Rashi,
Ingodam Mangi, Bhubaneswari, Indrakumar. Inquiries:
X-Cinema Productions, Paona Bazar, Imphal, Manipur.
*A simple, touching story of a schoolteacher who chooses
to work in a village and finds that a withdrawn little boy,
her pupil, is her brother-in-law's illegitimate child. She
tells her sister, who begins to like the boy and forces her
husband to accept him as their son.*
APARUPA. Language: Assamese and Hindi versions.
Prod/dir/edit: Jahnu Barua. Scr: J. S. Rao/Jahnu Barua.
Phot (colour): Binod Pradhan. Music: Bhupen Hazarika.
Players: Suhasini Mulay, Biju Phukan, Sushil Goswamy,
Girish Karnad. Inquiries: National Film Development
Corporation, 13–16 Regent Chambers, Nariman Point,
Bombay 400 021. *A scholarly girl is made to give up her
studies to marry a tea-planter. Her new idle-rich life
distresses her. She then discovers that her marriage had
been arranged in order to settle family debts. A college
friend (an army officer) arrives and provides an opportunity for escape. This is the first film by a Poona Film
Institute graduate.*
AN INDIAN STORY. English narration with subtitles.
Dir: Tapan K. Bose. Prod: Suhasini Mulay. Phot (colour): Salim Shaikh. Edit: Prakash Kothare. 58 mins.
Inquiries: Suhasini Mulay, B-42 Friends Colony West,
New Delhi 110 065. *An unwaveringly honest
documentary on communal atrocities. Based on press
reports and interviews concerning police brutality meant
to control crime in Bihar state, the film is also an
expression of caste and class retribution. The focus is on
the ruthless blinding of low-caste prisoners in Bhagalpur,
an event that has since rocked the country.*
MANJA (The Mist). Malayalam and Hindi versions.
Dir/story: M. T. Vasudevan Nair. Prod: Ravi. Phot
(colour): Shaji/N. Karun. Music: M. B. Srinivasan.
Players: Sangeeta Naik, Shankar Mohan, Dinesh Thakur. Inquiries: General Pictures, Quilon, Kerala. *A
reclusive school teacher, working in a hill-station boarding school, constantly broods over her displaced childhood and memories of a tender, passing love-affair. Her
subsequent liaison with a strange neighbour ends on a
note of tragic irony.*
FATIKCHAND (Fatik and the Juggler). Language: Bengali. Dir: Sandip Ray. Story/script/music: Satyajit Ray.
Phot (colour): Soumendu Ray. Players: Rajib Ganguly,
Kamu Mukherji, Biplab Chatterji, Haradhan Bannerji.
Inquiries: D. K. Films Enterprise, F-36 India Exchange
Place, Calcutta 700 001. *Four crooks kidnap twelve-year-old Bablu. Their car has an accident. Bablu is
knocked unconscious. Two kidnappers are killed, the
other two escape thinking that the boy is dead. Bablu,
now a victim of amnesia, meets a juggler, Haroun, in
Calcutta, who gives him shelter and work. The boy calls
himself Fatikchand. The relationship between the two
forms the basis of the film.*
UMBARTHA (Threshold). Language: Marathi and

STILL FROM *PHANIYAMMA*

Hindi versions. Dir: Jabbar Patel. Prod: D. V. Rao. Story: Shanta Nisal. Script: Vijay Tendulkar, Phot (colour): Rajan Kinagi. Players: Smita Patil, Girish Karnad, Daya Dongre, Kusum Kulkarni. Hindi title: *Subah (Morning)*. Inquiries: Dr. Jabbar Patel, Daound, Pune District. *A social worker defies her upper-class upbringing and leaves her husband's family to work as superintendent of a destitute women's home. The shift in social status creates hardships, an awareness, and confrontation with bureaucracy. Finally, it leads to a rift in her marriage and home life.*

KHARJI (The Case Is Closed). Language: Bengali. Dir/script: Mrinal Sen. Story: Ramapada Choudhury. Phot (colour): K. K. Mahajan. Music: B. V. Karanth. Players: Mamata Shankar, Anjan Dutt, Sreela Majumdar, Indranil Moitra. Inquiries: Neelkanth Films, 158 Lenin Sarani, Calcutta 700 013. *A teenage servant's death near a kitchen oven fills his employers with panic, dread and guilt. They fear a police inquiry. The servant's father leaves without implicating them, which only heightens their guilt.*

ATYACHAR (Atrocities). Language: Marathi. Dir/music: Bhaskar Chandavarkar. Script/dial: Meena/Bhaskar Chandavarkar. Story: Daya Pawar. Phot (colour): S. D. Deodhar. Players: Vibha Jakatdar, Satish Pulekar, Sushma Deshpande, Avinash Ambedkar. Inquiries: National Film Development Corporation, 13–16 Regent Chambers, Nariman Point, Bombay 400 021. *A film about a low-caste community carrying the stigma of earning its living by dissecting dead animals. Despite progressive laws and education in its favour, the community still feels castigated by a more subtle and disguised caste heirarchy.*

KATHA (Story). Language: Hindi. Dir: Sai Pranjpye. Prod: Suresh Jindal. Story: S. G. Sathe. Phot (colour): Virendra Saini. Music: Raj Kamal. Players: Naseeruddin Shah, Dipti Naval, Farooque Sheikh. Inquiries: Devki Chitra, 12A Eden Hall, Dr. Annie Besant Road, Bombay 400 18. *A tenderly observed love triangle set in the overcrowded tenement suburb of Bombay.*

SAMEERA. Language: Hindi. Dir: Vinay Shukla. Prod: K. K. Mahajan/Kashibhai J. Shah. Script: Kamleshwar.

Phot (colour): K. K. Mahajan. Players: Parikshit Sahni, Shabana Azmi, Mithun Chakraborthy, Amol Palekar. Inquiries: Sanket Chitra, 701 Menka, Off J. P. Road, Versova, Bombay 400 061. *An ambitious engineer arrives with his wife in a remote area to build a dam. The neglected wife falls in love with his colleague and later marries him. The second marriage is also endangered by the wife's vulnerability in her closed, empty environment.*
VIJETA (Conquest). Language: Hindi. Dir/phot (colour): Govind Nihalani. Prod: Shashi Kapoor. Story: Dilip Chitre. Script/dial: Satyadev Dubey. Music: Ajit Burman. Sound: Hitendra Ghosh. Edit: Naidu. Players: Shashi Kapoor, Amrish Puri, Rekha, Kunal Kapoor. Supriya Pathak. Inquiries: Filmvalas, Readymoney Terrace, Dr. Annie Besant Road, Worli, Bombay 400 018. *The story of a father and son in search of their true identity. And also the story of growing young men in the air force, attaining manhood, confronting the fear within and the enemy without – and finally, emerging as mature professionals with a deeper understanding of life.*
GRIHAYADHYA (The Crossroad). Language: Bengali. Dir/script/music: Buddadeb Dasgupta. Phot (colour): Sambit Bose. Story: Dibyendu Palit. Players: Anjan Dutt, Mamata Shankar, Gautam Ghose, Manoj Mitra. Inquiries: Director of Film, Dept. of Information and Cultural Affairs, Govt. of West Bengal, Writers Building, Calcutta 700 001. *A thriller based on the murder of the chief labour officer in a steel factory with tragic implications for a group of people used as ploys.*
SATYAJIT RAY – FILM MAKER. Language: English. Dir: Shyam Benegal. Colour. 90 mins. Inquiries: Films Division, Film Bhavan, Peddar Road, Bombay 400 026. *This well-researched documentary deals primarily with Satyajit Ray's twenty-six films – their form, style and structure. In examining his work, it explores the filmmaker's background, cultural influences and inspiration.*

JAWAHARLAL NEHRU. Dir: Shyam Benegal. Colour. Two parts, 90 mins. each. Inquiries: Ministry of Information and Broadcasting, Shastri Bhavan, New Delhi. *An Indian-Soviet co-production dealing with the life, development and contribution of the country's first prime minister, Jawaharlal Nehru. The film studies his life and work in terms of both India and the world.*
Untitled feature. Language: Hindi. Dir: Shyam Benegal. Script: Shama Zaidi, Satyadev Dubey, Shyam Benegal. Music: Vanraj Bhatia. Phot (colour): Ashok Mehta. Players: Shabana Azmi, Naseeruddin Shah, Smita Patil, Om Purim, Nina Gupta, Saeed Jaffrey, Anita Kanwar, Pankaj Kapoor. Inquiries: Blaze Film Enterprises, Lalji Naranji Memorial Building, Veer Nariman Road, Bombay 400 020. *A prostitutes' quarter in a small town is banished to an abandoned village by the municipal authorities on moral grounds. The presence of the prostitutes in the village transforms it into a thriving new town. The newly elected municipality decides to banish them, again on moral grounds, this time to a place twice removed.*
DAKHAL (The Occupation). Language: Bengali. Dir/phot (colour): Goutam Ghose. Story: Sushil Jana. Script: Goutam Ghose, Partha Banerjee. Edit: Prasanta Dey. Music: Goutam Ghose. Players: Mamata Shankar, Robin Sen Gupta, Sunil Mukherjee, Sajal Roy Chowdhury, Bimal Deb. Inquiries: Government of West Bengal, Information and Cultural Affairs Department, Writers' Building, Calcutta 700 001. *A widow with two children is visited by her nomadic gypsy tribe, from which she had been rescued years before by her higher-caste husband. Together they had reclaimed land. He died of a snakebite. The landowner sees an opportunity to usurp her farm by declaring her marriage invalid. Her hut is burnt but she decides to stay on and fight.*

Indonesia

by Fred Marshall

Cinema "Berita" started early in 1982 when the Ministry of Information spearheaded a drive to inform the rest of the world about its talented film-makers. It started by sending out more and better English subtitled prints of their best productions.

This move enabled Indonesian film to reach a larger market and had two purposes. One, to tell others about the existing life of the country, and the other to interest buyers who would eventually

dub the films for their own market. In addition several screenings abroad gave critics, film festival audiences and film buffs an opportunity to pinpoint the social problems of this Third World Asian giant which has become the second largest film-making country in Southeast Asia.

The Ministry of Information brought a delegation of 30 film-makers, writers, producers and artists to the Berlin film festival, where they had a chance to observe, and also have their work seen. The "Berita" movement has been encouraging on both the commercial and artistic sides. The Asian Society of New York soon expressed an interest in showing Indonesian films throughout the United States, within a framework of other Asian films.

In September 1981, the Asian Film Festival and its market in Malaysia along with the Manila International Festival, opened a new door for Indonesian film-makers. Over half a dozen Indonesian "occult" films were sold to European exhibitors. The 1982 Hongkong International Film Festival had a record entry of five Indonesian films, which won plaudits from both the local and foreign press. Elsewhere, Taiwan's Golden Horse Festival showed two outstanding Indonesian films and Tokyo's National Film Library also had a special presentation, paying tribute to Asian film-makers.

West German television is currently showing some of the best works of Teguh Karya and Wim Umboh, and France too has shown interest in talented newcomers like Ismail Subardjo and Slamet Rahardjo.

So it seems that the Cinema "Berita" movement is proving fruitful. With its annual output of some seventy films, the Indonesian industry is starting to aim for quality and not simply quantity. More film-makers are concentrating on doing most of the post-production work within the country, although in many instances the more sophisticated technical work still goes to Japan and Hongkong. The Indonesian motion picture has come a long way since the days of that pioneer film-maker, Usmar Ismail. It is now well developed, and gets no competition from local television and is well protected from the domination of imported American and Asian products by a government import quota.

SERANGAN FAJAR
(The Dawn)

Script and direction: Arifin C. Noer. Photography (colour, scope): M. Soleh Ruslani. Music: Embie C. Noer. Art Direction: Supandi. Players: Dani Marsuni, Amoroso Katamsi, Suwastinah, Suparmi, Antonius Yacobus, Nunuk Khaerul Umam, Jajang C. Noer, Charlie Sahetapy, Abduh Mursyid. Produced by Sumantri and Katam

ABOVE AND BELOW: NUNGKI KUSUMASTUTI AS THE OSTRACISED VILLAGE GIRL IN ISMAIL SUBARDJO'S *THE HIDDEN TRUTH*

LENNY MARLINA AND FRANS TUMBUAN AS WIFE AND HUSBAND IN SOPHAN SOPHIAAN'S *DON'T LET ME DIE*

K. Mihardja for Pusat Produksi Film Negara (PPFN). 190 mins.

The greatest triumph of Arifin C. Noer's ambitious film is that what could so easily have turned out to be a dreary, propagandist plod through a few pages of history has become nothing of the sort. *The Dawn* has its moments of national fervour; but first and foremost Noer's picture is a cinematic interpretation of history, chock-full of magical moments which fully exploit the powers of his chosen medium. The subject is the postwar struggle of the Indonesians to throw off first the Japanese and then the Dutch colonial yokes; the place is Jogjakarta, Java; the time 1945–47. Noer weaves three complementary strands to build up a portrait of those turbulent years: a poor family in a jungle village, an upper middle-class family in Jogjakarta, and the events of history itself. The three strands unite in the famous Dawn Attack (the meaning of the film's Indonesian title) on July 29, 1947, the prelude to the final establishment of independent rule in 1949.

Noer has made enormous strides since his first feature *Suci the Primadonna* (*Suci sang prima-dona*, 1977) and the sheer technical ambition of *The Dawn* dwarfs even his previous work *Yuyun* (1980). With a magical score by his brother, Embie C. Noer, and superb scope compositions by M. Soleh Ruslani, the film wraps the viewer in one enchanting sequence after another. Most of the picture is shot in selected tints, with colour reserved for emotional climaxes: a sunrise, a flag raised in victory, the boy Temon nursing an orphaned bird, a couple in full wedding regalia, and the dawn attack itself. The scenes of village life recall Ray's *Pather panchali* in their simple humanity; those of middle-class life have a more structured character. Throughout the vast three-hour tapestry Temon wanders in childlike awe, like a blank page of history on which great events are written. It is to Noer's credit that, even in the large-scale set-pieces, the viewer is made to share the boy's simple wonder.

DEREK ELLEY

Focus on Directors

ARIFIN C. NOER was born on March 10, 1941, in Cirebon, West Java. He was active in theatre from his teens and in late 1960 went to Jakarta and formed his own group, Teater Kecil (Small Theatre). He began his film career as a scriptwriter, winning awards at the 1974 and 1975 Indonesian Film Festivals for *Rio anakku* and *Melawan badai*. His first film as a director, *Suci the Primadonna* (*Suci sang primadona*, 1977) dealt with the attempts of a stage actress to make a new life for herself when she becomes involved with a free-wheeling youth. Films since then: *The Harmonica* (*Harmoniku*), *Petualang-petualang*, *Yuyun, a Patient in a Mental Hospital* (*Yuyun pasien rumah sakit jiwa*) and *The Dawn* (*Serangan fajar*). He is currently filming *History of the New Government* (*S.O.B. – Sejarah orde baru*).

TEGUH KARYA was born in Pandeglang on September 22, 1937. In 1954/55 he attended the Academy for Dramatic and Film Arts (Asdrafi) in Jogjakarta and later the National Academy for Theatrical Arts (ATNI) in Jakarta, whence he graduated in 1963. In the same year he received a fellowship to study at the East-West Center, Hawaii, where he took a course in stage designing. In 1968, with some friends, he formed Teater Populer. His first film, *Ballad of a Man* (*Wajah seorang laki-laki*, 1971) dealt with the struggle of a young man in Nineteenth-century Dutch colonial Indonesia to escape from the domination of his patriarchal father. Following that he made the contemporary trilogy focussing on young people, comprising *First Love* (*Cinta pertama*, 1973), *The Wedding* (*Ranjang pengantin*, 1974) and *The Elopement* (*Kawin lari*, 1975). Other films: *The Wolves* (*Perkawinan dalam semusin*, 1976), *When the Storm Is Over* (*Badai-pasti berlalu*, 1977), *November 1828* (*Nopember 1828*, 1978), *The Age of 18* (*Usia 18*, 1980) and *The Fan* (*Kipas akar wangi*, 1981). A slow, meticulous worker, he makes only one film a year in between theatre work. All his films star actor Slamet Rahardjo. He is currently shooting *Behind the Mosquito Net* (*Dibalik kelambu*).

SLAMET RAHARDJO was born in Serang, West Java, on January 21, 1949. After finishing high school in 1967, he entered the National Academy for Theatrical Arts (ATNI) where he studied acting and art direction. He was a co-founder with Teguh Karya in 1969 of Teater Populer, Indonesia's most

THE TWO FACES OF HISTORY: DANI MARSUNI AS THE VILLAGE BOY TEMON AND ADVANCING GUERRILLA TROOPS IN ARIFIN C. NOER'S *THE DAWN*

prominent theatre group, and started his acting career in 1971 in Teguh Karya's *Ballad of a Man*. He has acted only in Karya's films. In 1980 he made his debut as a director with the partly experimental *A Time to Mend* (*Rembulan dan matahari*), followed by the family drama *As White As Her Heart, As Red As Her Lips* (*Seputih hatinya semerah bibirnya*, 1981). He is currently filming his third feature, *Honeymoon Bed* (*Ranjang penganten*).

DEREK ELLEY

recent films

BERCANDA DALAM DUKA (The Hidden Truth). Script and dir: Ismail Subardjo. Phot (colour, scope): Tantra Surjadi. Art dir: Suryo Susanto. Music: Franki Raden. Players: Sant Laksana, Nungki Kasumastuti, August Melasz, Nani Wijaya, W. D. Mochtar. For Garuda Film and Bhaskara Indah Cine Prod.

BAWALAH AKU PERGI (Take Me Away). Script: Asrul Sani. Dir: M. T. Risyaf. Phot (colour, scope): Hasan Basri Djafar. Music: Ireng Maulana. Art dir: S. K. Syamsuri. Players: Roy Marten, Marissa Haque, Maruli Sitompul, Roldiah Matulessy, Pong Jarjatmo, Nani Wijaya. For Bola Dunia Film.
JANGAN AMBIL NYAWAKU (Don't Let Me Die). Script: Tatiek Malyati, from the book by Titie Said. Dir: Sophan Sophiaan. Phot (colour, scope): Akin. Art dir: Rizal Asmar. Music: Tri Sutji Kamal. Players: Lenny Marlina, Frans Tumbuan, Rima Melati, Zaina l Abidin, Titiek Qadarsih. For Garuda Film and Sanggar Film.
GADIS MARATHON (Marathon Girl). Script: Sjuman Djaya. Dir: Chaerul Umam. Phot (colour, scope): Akin. Music: Franki Raden. Art dir: B. Benny M.S. Players: Roy Marten, Yenny Rachman, Rachmat Hidayat, Farouk Affero. For Tiga Sinar Mutiara Film.
SANG GURU (The Teacher/Topaz). Script: Parakitri. Dir: Edward Pesta Sirait. Phot (colour, scope): M. Soleh Ruslani. Music: Sudharnoto. Art dir: Edward Pesta Sirait. Players: S. Bagio, Maruli Sitompul, Rahayu Effendi, Bambang Hermanto. For Sanggar Film.
SEPUTH HATINYA SEMERAH BIBIRNYA (As White As Her Heart, As Red As Her Lips). Script and dir: Slamet Rahardjo. Phot (colour, scope): George Kamrullah. Music: Eros Djarot. Art dir: Benny Benhardi. Players: Christine Hakim, Frans Tumbuan, Menzano. For Garuda Film, Interstudio and Darma Putra Jaya Film.

Useful Facts

Seventy domestic features were exhibited in Jakarta during 1982. PT Perfin, which is in charge of the distribution of Indonesian films, reported total admissions of 5,252,166 in 74 first and second run houses. Of the 70, fourteen were comedies, 10 horror pictures, 5 children's films and the remaining adult dramas.

The Indonesian capital has a population of 6.5 million with 2.5 million aged under 17. Features shown in theatres here are classified into three groups; for general audiences, for those aged 13 and over and for those aged 17 and over.

Indonesia has a total population of 145 million.

Useful Addresses

Film Centre Haji Usman Ismail
Jalan H. Rasuna Said, Kuningan
Phone: 584577-584578-584579
Jakarta, Indonesia
Badan Sensor Film
(Board of Film Censor)
Jalan H. Agus Salim no. 60,
Jakarta, Indonesia
Lembaga Pendidikan Kesenian Jakarta
Akademi Sinematografi
(Academy of Cinematography – Institute of the Arts, Jakarta)
Jalan Cikini Raya no. 73,
Jakarta, Indonesia
Asosiasi Importir Film Eropa-Amerika

(Association of European & American Film Importers)
Jalan Jenderal Sudirman no. 2,
Gedung Arthaloka,
Jakarta, Indonesia
Asosiasi Importir Film Mandarin
(Association of Mandarin Film Importers)
Jalan K.H. Samanhudi no. 9,
Jakarta, Indonesia
Asosiasi Importir Film Asia Non Mandarin
(Association of Asian Non-Mandarin Film Importers)
Jalan H. Rasuna Said, Setiabudi Building,
Jakarta, Indonesia

PT. Peredaran Film Indonesia
(Indonesian Film Distributors)
Jalan Menteng Raya no. 62
Jakarta, Indonesia
Indonesian Motion Pictures Producers Association
Pusat Perfilman H. Usmar Ismail
Jl. Raya H.R. Rasuna Said
Jakarta, Indonesia
Kine Klub Jakarta
(Film Society Club)
Jalan Cikini Raya no. 73
Jakarta, Indonesia

Israel   by Dan Fainaru

The Israeli film industry took two major steps forward during the past year, each on a different front but both equally important for its future development. The first one was purely economic, a breakthrough in a policy which seemed in the past to be immovable. Considered as entertainment without any cultural value, the cinema has been always heavily taxed, not so much by the government itself but more by municipalities which, at one time, were taking about half the value of an admission ticket. As long as business boomed, exhibitors complained but did not do much else; but since the advent of television, with audiences steadily diminishing and the economic crisis adding its own burden the industry started to head towards bankruptcy. Cinemas closed several times in protest and finally, after much wheeling and dealing, all taxes on cinema tickets were abolished, except for a symbolic contribution to local production and the usual tax on added value.

Since the share of the exhibitor and distributor has gone up, these people are now prepared to take more chances and consider more adventurous programming. Consequently, films that would never have stood a chance in Israel are now slowly trickling in; some, such as a number of Hungarian imports or the Tavianis' *Padre padrone* have had

surprising success. Even more importantly, the reticence to show Israeli films of anything less than commercial appeal is not as strong as it was in the past. Since local productions enjoy, beyond their share of regular distribution, a subsidy of about $1.00 per ticket for the first 100,000 and an additional 25 cents for the next 100,000, the danger of losing money (at least as far as the distribution and exhibition is concerned) is almost non-existent. This fact is crucial for many of the smaller and more ambitious films which often have a harder time getting shown than actually made.

While on this topic, it is worth noting the growing trend towards smaller cinemas for more selective audiences. The traditional Tel Aviv cinema, with at least 700–800 seats, and quite often over 1,000, which had to attract as many people for three shows a day, was forced to screen only very popular material. As the number of small cinemas has increased (some by splitting up the big ones, others newly built), an entirely new approach can be expected, particularly since the new system seems to be doing much better than the old one.

The second step forward during the past year could be called a psychological one. For many a year, it was almost a tradition that any film with the slightest bit of artistic ambition was doomed to

DORON NESHER AND LIRON NIRGAD IN *REPEAT DIVE*

failure at the box-office. The creation of the Fund for the Promotion of Quality Films a couple of years ago meant that at least such film-making could be pursued through state help, if not by popular demand. The fund invested in several projects, films came out, some were even praised by critics; but the curse of the missing audience could not be lifted. The situation became serious enough for detractors of the fund to start rubbing their hands together with glee.

Two films were responsible for turning the tide. One of them, *Noa at 17*, produced and directed by Isaac Yeshurun, amazed even those who believed in his talents. With a record of two commercial and artistic flops, and a much-acclaimed TV feature *Kobi and Mali*, Yeshurun decided to shoot *Noa at 17* in spite of warnings that he was going to break his neck, not least of all financially. Using a dilapidated house not far from

Tel Aviv, and going ahead with his project even when the fund was still dubious whether to step in or not (finally it did), Yeshurun turned out a highly sensitive film (see review below). However, opinions seemed to differ as to its chances, so it was initially released only in one small cinema. Later, however, other prints were made and *Noa at 17* stands a good chance of being the first fund-assisted film that will make money (not least of all because of the small investment). Yeshurun, who had such a difficult time finding producers in the past, is already at work on his next opus, this time to be fully financed by the film establishment.

Repeat Dive's road to success was less tortuous as Shimon Dotan, a graduate of the Film Department at Tel Aviv University, had a conventional producer who backed the project. Even if work took much longer than expected and went over budget several times, the film finally came out more or less as both expected. Looking much more opulent than Yeshurun's film, and costing more than twice as much, it had an easier time finding release; and its successful performance at the Berlin film festival gave it additional prestige when it reached local audiences.

The success of these two films will hopefully make life easier in future for those who wish to make similar films. With a number of young film-makers already at work, or finishing, their second, third or fourth feature, it seems that a new and different generation of directors has definitely arrived. Michal Bat-Adam is now editing *First Loves*, after *Moments* and *A Thin Line* had international distribution; Daniel Wachsman is preparing the release of *Khamsin*, to follow *Transit*, which represented Israel in Berlin; and Yaki Yosha is starting work on his fourth feature, *Dead End Street*, the first he is doing with commercial producers. Much is expected of *Stigma*, the first feature by Uri Barabash, whose reputation lies in a number of impressive documentaries he made for television; and there is much curiosity concerning Uzi Peres and his special brand of cinema, when the first of the *Human Errors* cycle is released in late 1982.

HAMSIN

Script: Daniel Wachsman, Yaakov Lifshin, Danny Verete. Direction: Daniel Wachsman. Photography: David Gurfinkel. Music: Raviv Gazit. Players: Shlomo Tarshish, Yassin Shoaf, Ruth Geller, Hemda Levy. Produced by Yaakov Lifshin.

A most controversial item, that will doubtlessly shake many Israelis into extreme opinions, pro and against. Daniel Wachsman's second film attacks the most emotional issue in Israel to-day, the relations with the Arab neighbours, and doesn't mince words about it. While he may be more interested in the problems he raises than in the characters putting them across, Wachsman nevertheless reveals, in a very pungent way, the conflict between Jews and Arabs in a northern Jewish settlement, in which young Arabs, coming from a village next door, are hired hands. The increasing climate of violence is fostered by both sides. The Arab nationalism is boosted by the fear that the Israeli government is going to take away lands that

have never been properly registered but by traditions are theirs, and the Jewish suspicion that their workers by day are sabotaging their fields by night, nurture an atmosphere of mutual hatred that grows day by day. This may also be partly blamed on the difference between the older generation, more idealistic on the Jewish side, and more patriarchal on the Arab side, which could have found a common language, and the younger generation, who on the Jewish side is motivated only by sheer profit, and on the Arab side is only concerned with political activism.

There is a love story inserted in all this, between a Jewish girl and an Arab farmhand, its purpose being to point out that even liberals lose their peace of mind when things are happening in their own back yard.

Well shot and well acted, even if some points are taken for granted and others insufficiently clarified, this is a vast improvement for Wachsman himself and a remarkable achievement for the struggling Israeli industry.

DAN FAINARU

LENA

Script and direction: Eytan Green. Photography: Yakhin Hirsch. Music: Itzhak Klepter. Editing: Ira Lapid. Players: Fira Kanter, Dov Glickman, Itzhak Keshet. Produced by Nissim Dayan with the assistance of the Fund for the Promotion of Quality Films.

Eytan Green, a graduate of the Film Department at Tel Aviv University, and now a teacher there and also film critic, has attempted in his first film to follow in the steps of all the directors he admires, particularly Bresson and Rohmer. His story of a Russian woman, Lena, who comes to live in Israel and dedicates her first three years to a public struggle to convince the Soviet government to release her imprisoned husband, is told in a subdued style; it avoids focusing on political or social problems, and instead settles for the woman's personal drama. She has had more than enough of assemblies, speeches and conferences, she refuses to act as a spokesman for a cause anymore, and yearns for her own private life; it is perhaps this yearning that leads her into an affair with her hypochondriac, spoiled Hebrew teacher.

SHLOMO TARSHISH IN DANIEL WACHSMAN'S *HAMSIN*

Green takes up the story at the point where Lena starts flinching after three years of self-denial and concentrates on her relationship with Benjamin, the teacher, and Boris, another immigrant who represent the interests of Lena's absent husband. Camera movements carefully avoid any spectacular effects or superfluous embellishment; the acting

DIRECTOR EYTAN GREEN WITH FIRA KANTER AND ITZHAK KESHET IN *LENA*

is purposely contained; every effort is made to create a sober, clear and unsentimental atmosphere. The problem lies, as always, with these limitations. Being less experienced than his models, Green holds back too much, and what should have been controlled, moulded performances turn out to be far too close for comfort to indifference, both by director and some of the cast. Fira Kantar, in the lead, could have been more persuasive but her performance is still to be commended. She deservedly won the local prize for the best female performance of the year.

DAN FAINARU

NOA AT 17

Script and direction: Isaac Yeshurun. Photography: Isaac Oren, Jacob Saporta. Music: Isaac Steiner. Editing: Tova Asher. Players: Dalia Shimko, Irith Zur, Osnath Offer, Shmuel Shilo, Moshe Havatselet, Adi Neeman. Produced by Isaac Yeshurun with the assistance of the Fund for the Promotion of Quality Films.

Yeshurun has toyed for a long time with the idea of making a film about the split in the labour movement during the early Fifties which seriously shook the ruling establishment and split up old friendships, families and entire *kibbutzim*. He originally planned a much more extensive production, but later decided to concentrate the whole action inside one family, one house, and a limited number of characters. Noa, who is about to celebrate her seventeenth birthday, may well be a symbol of a society moving from childhood and innocence to maturity and strife, but she is much more than that – she is a real person, an adolescent who tries to assert her own personality and define her own needs, in a society which still considers conformism a synonym for equality, and therefore a supreme quality.

Around Noa moves a constellation of characters, each very human and convincing, yet conditioned by political and social forces. Her mother, a domineering and strong-headed woman, is fully committed to a brand of socialism pointing West;

this is why she had convinced her soft-spoken, peace-loving husband, whose one wish is to be a farmer, to leave the *kibbutz* and move into town, which he hates. Her visiting uncle represents yet another stance: he has stayed behind in the *kibbutz*, a staunch believer in socialism Soviet-style, and refuses any compromise that would mean less than his ideals. The arguments tearing the grown-ups apart leave their traces on young Noa, who has to face the rigid morality and strict rules by which her own generation conducts itself in emulation of the adults.

Yeshurun has developed a style that is not too far removed from Cassavetes. He ellicits moving, intelligent performances from all his cast, who manage to incarnate authentic, vibrant human beings. Foreign audiences may have some difficulty with the historical background, and the film is very talky, but this should not detract from its otherwise remarkable qualities.

DAN FAINARU

REPEAT DIVE

Script and direction: Shimon Dotan, based on a short story by Judith Hendel. Photography: Daniel Schneur. Music: Zohar Levy. Editing: Danny Schick. Players: Doron Nesher, Liron Nirgad, Danny Muggia, Yair Rubin, Ami Traub. Produced by Amos Mokadi with the assistance of the Fund for the Promotion of Quality Films.

This is a very personal film, summing up the experiences of Shimon Dotan as a crack diver in a Navy commando unit during his military service. The Judith Hendel story on which he based his script gave him a frame for his plot but the underlying message is definitely his own. In his first feature film, Dotan describes the uneasy romance, culminating in an uneasy marriage, between the widow of a diver killed in action and his best friend, a member of the same unit. There is much ritual in the care and responsibility the late husband's comrades display for the widow, and it is as part of this ritual that the two protagonists are drawn to each other. Behind the bravado of the young divers, all in their early twenties, there is a deep undercurrent of sadness and doom, with death a constant companion. Even more relevant is the discrepancy between the men of action, brilliant performers in daring exploits, and the same

persons' inadequacy in real life, their incapacity to cope with anything beyond the level of military operations. These are adolescents who did not have the chance to grow up emotionally – part of a new generation of emotional cripples.

Dotan does not always manage to overcome the awkward points of his script, and the film seems to lose its impetus towards the middle to gain it back later on; but Doron Nesher and Liron Nirgad are perfect in the two leading parts, and Daniel Schneur's camerawork is of a high quality. All the points Dotan cares about are made with absolute clarity.

DAN FAINARU

Focus on Daniel Wachsman

Born 35 years ago in Shanghai, China, Daniel Wachsman is the son of German refugees who escaped from Nazi Germany and went half across the globe before coming to Israel in 1950. Raised and educated here, he soon started dabbling in cinema, working as an assistant to editors, before going to study at the London Film School. On his return, he directed two shorts, both highly praised by critics. *My Father*, based on his own relationship with his father (a theme that had much to do with his first feature), won a number of awards; his second one, *Elvira*, did almost as well. It was only a matter of time before he started his first feature but, when money proved scarce, he decided to go ahead with a friend of his, Jacob Goldwasser (now directing his first film), as producer. The film, *Transit*, was made under almost underground conditions, with the entire cast and crew working for promises, and the whole project more than once endangered by shortage of cash. With additional investment by the Fund for the Promotion of Quality Films (Wachsman was its first beneficiary), a final print was achieved and indicated Wachsman was a talent to be taken into consideration. Now preparing the release of his second feature, *Khamsin*, whose production was much easier, Wachsman realises its subject may raise a few brows – it deals with relations between Israelis and Arabs at an even more sensitive time than usual.

DF

DANIEL WACHSMAN

Public Organisations

The Israel Film Centre
Ministry of Industry & Trade
30 Agron Street
PO Box 299
Jerusalem.
Israel Television
Broadcasting Authority
Television House
Romema
Jerusalem.
Instructional Television
14 Klausner Street
Ramat Aviv
Tel Aviv.
The Israel Film Service
1 Mendele Street
PO Box 7885
Jerusalem.
The Israel Film Institute
10 Glikson Street
Tel Aviv.
Federation of Independent Film Distributors
84 Hahashmonaim Street
Tel Aviv.

Production Companies

April Films
(Rudi Cohen)
237 Dizengoff Street
Tel Aviv.
Roll Films
(Israel Ringel)
43 Shimon Hatarsi Street
Tel Aviv.
Shapira Films
(David Shapira)
34 Allenby Street
Tel Aviv.
Dan Wolman Production and Direction Services
Givat Beit Hakerem
3/43
Jerusalem.
Yaki Yosha Ltd.
29 Lilienblum Street
Tel Aviv.

STILL FROM *LA NOTTE DI SAN LORENZO,* AWARDED THE SPECIAL JURY PRIZE AT CANNES IN 1982

Italy

The season started in an unexpected way – people once again filling the theatres that they had previously deserted for the daily indigestion of movies on TV. The final official statistics (for the large towns only) showed a 16.9% rise in attendances – 4,776,000 admissions more than the preceding season. It was only a recovery to the figures for 1979/80 (33,000,000 admissions), but the trend made both exhibitors and the few remaining producers very happy. So the summer of 1982 saw a burst of activity Cinecittà and elsewhere, with Fellini back to work (on ... *e la nave va*), Sergio Leone at last shooting his monumental *C'era una volta in America*, Lina Wertmüller directing Sophia Loren in a big epic, and some foreigners using our technical facilities and even reviving our obsolete *peplum* genre.

It was inflation that kept consumers away from more expensive pleasures and that brought about this "instant moviegoing": audiences rushed to a few movies in the city centres and the old system of suburban theatres and of second-run houses continued to decline. The indiscriminate taste of this new audience can be seen in the season's list of hits: (1) *Innamorato pazzo* (starring Adriano Celentano and Ornella Muti, directed by Castellano and Pipolo): 1,649,809 admissions; (2) *Il tempo delle mele* (the French film *La boum* by Claude Pinoteau): 1,531,890 admissions; (3) *Il marchese Del Grillo* (Mario Monicelli, with Alberto Sordi): 1,393,491 admissions; (4) *Culo e camicia* (Pasquale Festa Campanile, with Enrico Montesano and Renato Pozzetto): 913,753 admissions; (5) *Nessuno è perfetto* (Pasquale Festa Campanile, with Renato Pozzetto and Ornella Muti): 875,911 admissions; (6) *Raiders of the Lost Ark* (Spielberg): 741,721 admissions; (7) *Excalibur* (Boorman): 707,595 admissions; (8) *Eccezziunale ...veramente* (by Carlo Vanzina, with Diego Abatantuono): 670,277 admissions; (9) *For Your Eyes Only* (John Glen): 657,153 admissions; (10) *I fichissimi* (Carlo Vanzina, with Diego Abatantuono): 636,037 admissions.

The slump in distribution (259 films compared with 328 last season) paralleled the slump in national production, where the total fell for the first time to under 100. Except for *Il marchese Del Grillo*, all the Italian blockbusters were medium or small-budget comedies in which most of the budget went on one or two stars' high fees.

"The *commedia all'italiana* is finished," said Pasquale Festa Campanile (the most successful and prolific director nowadays) in the columns of "Il corriere della sera" (March 6, 1982). "No more sermonising on the screen about our national faults... The audience is now more mature: it understands humour which is almost completely verbal; it floats on unreal situations, it accepts paradox. A vein of madness runs through the latest comedies. They use colossal metaphors, they twist everyday reality, they refuse to moralise..." Wishful thinking or prophecy? It is undeniable that several young comedians are attracting teenagers' attention with their regional dialects, absurd witticisms, and by identifying with the not so comical despair of the young generation.

Diego Abatantuono, born in Milan to a family who emigrated from the southern Puglie, after working in cabaret exhibitions and some minor film roles, was featured during the past season in four films: the two mentioned above, plus two others by Steno (the veteran director, father of Carlo Vanzina) – *Sballato gasato completamente fuso* and *Il tango della gelosia*. This lion-headed troglodyte speaks a hybrid jargon typical of emigrants pretending to be pure Milanese. Like his fellow new comedians, his repertoire is limited and repetitious – but could be exploited *ad nauseam* by uninventive Italian producers.

Adriano Celentano, the most popular singer of the decade, is not a recent discovery but his appeal is still strong thanks to his perfect blending of crazy mannerisms and simple-minded jokes. Twinned again with the divine beauty of Ornella Muti, in *Innamorato pazzo* (*Madly in Love*), he tries to repeat the all-time record-breaking success of their earlier *Il bisbetico domato* (L17,000,000,000 last season).

Ornella Muti has now outclassed all other Italian female stars, such as Monica Vitti, Laura Antonelli or Eleonora Giorgi. She brilliantly plays a rich princess falling in love with a bus driver in

Innamorato pazzo, and a husband who underwent a sex change in *Nessuno è perfetto* (*Nobody's Perfect*). Previous work with Monicelli, Ferreri, Risi and James Toback (in her ill-fated American feature, *Love and Money*), prepared her for Ferreri's sublime *Storie di ordinaria follia* (20th at the box-office, with 443,278 admissions).

Renato Pozzetto has since 1974 scored some hits every season. But his loony humour is becoming monotous now that he is growing fatter and opting for vulgar gags. In his episode of *Culo e camicia* he plays a gaudy homosexual seduced by a lady. If Celentano, Muti and Abatantuono have overall appeal, Pozzetto as a true Milanese is preferred by northern audiences; that is why the other episode in the same film is astutely given to a mainly southern comedian, Enrico Montesano. Montesano is very Roman and folksy, and has malleable puppet-like features. In *Culo e camicia* he is a stammering TV reporter who is helped by a supernatural cobbler; in *Il paramedico*, directed by Sergio Nasca, he is an unfortunate physician; in *Più bello di così si muore*, by Pasquale Festa Campanile again (his best work this year), he plays a transvestite who cannot revert to his normal sex.

Alvaro Vitali, in *Pierino contro tutti, Pierino medico della SAUB* and *Pierino colpisce ancora*, smashed all records in the sub-genre of *film-barzelletta* (suites of obscene jokes that make up almost *one third* of the Italian production, practically killing all the other genres). A galaxy of starlets, ready for any and all indignities, populate this softcore territory, from Lori Del Santo to Carmen Russo, Annamaria Rizzoli, Edwige Fenech, Barbara Bouchet. Minor – but growing – regional comedians, like Lino Banfi and Pippo Franco, star in their own farces.

What critics admit are the real "New Comics" are the few author/director/actors like Nanni Moretti and Carlo Verdone. Moretti, after years of silence, continued his fictional autobiography with *Sogni d'oro* (*Golden Dreams*), his 8½: as a director shooting a film on Freud's life, he satirises the worlds of cinema and TV and gives a sympathetic performance. In his third work, *Borotalco* (*Talcum Powder*), (after the more personal comedies *Un sacco bello* and *Bianco rosso e Verdone*), Verdone plays just one character – a timid door-to-door book salesman who pretends to be a playboy

in order to win the affections of a colleague (Eleonora Giorgi). This Wilderian comedy confirms Verdone's talent as a keen observer of the squalor and grotesqueness of the middle class. Newcomers like Alessandro Benvenuti, of the Tuscan group I Giancattivi, with *Ad ovest di Paperino*, and Enzo Decaro, of the Neapolitan group La Smorfia, with *Prima che sia troppo presto*, ingeniously but unoriginally followed the same path of these "New Comics" – and that of Lino Troisi, still cashing in on his first and only film, *Ricomincio da tre*, after two years of phenomenal success.

The new, non-comic directors brought a gloomy vision indeed. Salvatore Piscicelli in *Le occasioni di Rosa*, his second work after the much-acclaimed *Immacolata e Concetta*, takes a dark look at the underworld of Naples and shows the decay of a gorgeous girl wanting a place in the sun. His rigid formalism is as annoying as the emptier style of Marco Tullio Giordana in *La caduta degli angeli ribelli* (also a second work), about a neo-romantic couple of adventurer-terrorists. Pier Giuseppe Murgia in *La festa perduta* gives a more realistic treatment to the theme of terrorism, but stuffs his story with all the associated clichés. Peter Del Monte in *Piso Pisello*, greatly helped by a solid script from Bernardino Zapponi, tells the amusing fable of a boy-father who wanders with his precocious child in a dream-world. Other promising film-makers worth mentioning: Giorgio Pressburger, with *Calderon*, an imaginative adaptation of Pasolini's late play; Corrado Franco, with *Al riparo da sguardi indiscreti*, a film buff's self-denunciation produced on the fringe; and Ciro Ippolito, with *Lacrime napulitane*, starring the popular Neapolitan actor Mario Merola, a melodrama in the grand tradition of this once florid genre.

The oldtimers were not very busy. Luigi Comencini employed the shrill gifts of TV entertainer Beppe Grillo in *Cercasi Gesù*, a rather pale parable on the resurrection of a kind of updated Christ. Nino Manfredi removed Alberto Lattuada from *Nudo di donna*, and himself finished this Pirandellian comedy of a husband looking for the ideal opposite to his wife – no signs here of the grace and style of Manfredi's previous *Per grazia ricevuta* (1971). Ugo Tognazzi, his rival and still a

STILL FROM ANTONIONI'S *IDENTIFICAZIONE DI UNA DONNA*

very popular actor, did not save Bernardo Berto-lucci's *La tragedia di un uomo ridiculo* from commercial failure – a displeasing work dealing with a mass of problems, social and private alike. Liliana Cavani persisted with her abominable exercises in pseudo-historical gore with *La pelle*, annihilating Curzio Malaparte's classic study of Naples after its liberation by the American army. At least Lucio Fulci's bloody essays *(Quella villa accanto al cimitero* and *Lo squartatore di New York)* did not show Cavani's pretentiousness.

The advance patrol at the Cannes festival will only be submitted to the public's judgement in the 1982/83 season. Ettore Scola's *Il mondo nuovo* conjures up some forgotten episodes from the French Revolution, seen from a stagecoach in which some emblematic characters meet after the escape of the king to Varennes; too much didactic

dialogue makes this a long journey. Paolo and Vittorio Taviani's *La notte di San Lorenzo*, unani-mously praised at Cannes, may be their best film: a moving and visually glorious tale of the escape of a group of Tuscan peasants from the Nazi invaders. Michelangelo Antonioni's return to his own coun-try – after many experiences abroad and an abortive electronic film – with *Identificazione di una donna* is more than just a reappraisal of his "alienation" period (the film was conceived a long time ago): the "identification" of the title is that of a man's conscience in his relationships with two women. As in Bertolucci's film, the human myster-ies remain unexplained; we are merely dazzled by the director's dilemmas.

One cannot neglect RAI-TV's productions by major directors. Vittorio Cottafavi returned with *Maria Zef*, a moving and naturalistic treatment of

BEN GAZZARA AND ORNELLA MUTI IN *STORIE DI ORDINARIA FOLLIA*, DIRECTED BY MARCO FERRERI

a novel about the tragic destiny of a poor peasant girl who turns against her master; Pupi Avati's *Dancing Paradise* is a nostalgic musical odyssey infused with touches of the fantastic; Gianfranco Mingozzi's *La vela incantata* is the moral tale of two brothers and their travelling cinema during the end of the silent era, engagingly set against a Fascist background; and in the documentary *Venezia, una Mostra per il cinema*, Alessandro Blasetti (born in 1900) masterfully recalls the earliest Venice festivals and the passions of his youth.

Blasetti's two books of collected writings ("Scritti sul cinema," Marsilio Editori, and "Il cinema che ho vissuto," Dedalo Edizioni), from the Thirties to the Eighties were among the highlights of the publishing season, which also included the collected criticism of another old master, Giuseppe De Santis ("Verso il neorealismo," Bulzoni Edi-

tore), the best-selling autobiography of Vittorio Gassman ("Un grande avvenire dietro le spalle," Longanesi Editore), the long interview-cum-confession by Bernardo Bertolucci ("Scene madri," with Enzo Ungari, Ubulibri), the second instalment of Goffredo Fofi's and Franca Faldini's very readable oral history ("L'avventurosa storia del cinema italiano, 1960–1969," Feltrinelli Editore), the third tome of Aldo Bernardini's definitive history of the silents ("Cinema muto italiano, 1910–1914," Editori Laterza), plus two illustrated Citadel-like volumes on the films of "Gina Lollobrigida" and "Vittorio Gassman" (Gremese Editore) and some important works on neglected artists – the poster designer "Anselmo Ballester" (Università di Parma) and Visconti's costumer Umberto Tirelli ("Vestire i sogni," by himself with Guido Vergani, Feltrinelli Editore).

STORIE DI ORDINARIA FOLLIA
(Tales of Ordinary Madness)

Script: Marco Ferreri, Sergio Amidei, from the stories by Charles Bukowski. Direction: Marco Ferreri. Photography (Eastmancolor): Tonino Delli Colli. Editing: Ruggero Mastroianni. Music: Philippe Sarde. Art Direction: Dante Ferretti. Players: Ben Gazzara, Ornella Muti, Tanya Lopert, Susan Tyrrell, Elisabeth Long, Lewis Ciannelli, Cristina Forti, Argento, Carlo Monni. Produced by Jacqueline Ferreri for 23 Giugno (Rome) / Ginis Film (Paris). 107 mins.

An alcoholic poet with a bottle in his hand recites on the stage of a huge old theatre; he talks about "style," those who have it and those who don't, and how to live with it. This striking first scene sets the tone for Ferreri's masterpiece, a stylish attempt to catch the essence of art among the debris of society. Inspired by the gutsy literary work of the American writer *maudit* Charles Bukowski, and by his self-destructive myth (more popular in Italy than in his own country), Ferreri and the late Sergio Amidei conceived this bizarre meandering of a writer named Charles Serking through the jungle of Los Angeles.

It is an obsessive town, where Serking can be sexually devoured by a sadistic blonde (Susan Tyrrell), experience a regression to the maternal womb of a housewife prostitute, or fall for "the prettiest girl in town." This stunning creature on sale (Ornella Muti) cannot dominate her masochistic impulses, nor be more than a fleeting source of inspiration for the poet. The desolation of the artist worsens until he meets a radiant girl on an apocalyptic beach. . .

The stark blue and oozing whites of Tonino Delli Colli's photography pervade Ferreri's limpid film, as pure a distillation of his universe as the previous *La cagna/Liza*. The existential anxiety of Ferreri is memorably conveyed in Ben Gazzara's striking performance as Serking.

LORENZO CODELLI

IL MARCHESE DEL GRILLO
(The Marquis Del Grillo)

Script: Leo Benvenuti, Piero De Bernardi, Mario Monicelli, Tullio Pinelli, Alberto Sordi, from a story by Bernardino Zapponi. Direction: Mario Monicelli. Photography (colour): Sergio D'Offizi. Editing: Ruggero Mastroianni. Music: Nicola Piovani. Art Direction: Lorenzo Baraldi. Players: Alberto Sordi, Paolo Stoppa, Flavio Bucci, Marc Porel, Riccardo Billi, Cochi Ponzoni, Caroline Berg, Elena Daskowa Valenzano, Leopoldo Trieste. Produced by Luciano De Feo for Opera Film Produzione Gaumont. 133 mins.

The character of the Marquis Del Grillo an extravagant joker in corrupt Roman society of the Eighteenth century, is still a very popular legend. Film-makers such as Aldo Fabrizi and Totò several times planned films on him. Adapting the oral and written stories, Mario Monicelli and his co-screen-writers transposed them to Napoleonic Rome of the next century, a period full of contemporary resonances and rarely shown on the screen.

Monicelli's caustic wit, previously evident in historical comedies like *The Great War, The Organiser* and *L'Armata Brancaleone*, this time derides the striking class differences between a decaying nobility and the exploited pariahs. His Marquis Del Grillo makes fun of the Pope, rich Jews, the privileged and the poor, wildly subverting the social rules. In his most audacious trick, the marquis puts a look-alike in his place, a drunken coalman who behaves outrageously and is nearly decapitated. In this double role, Alberto Sordi is at his best and most devilish, casting light on the inner destructive forces of his restless character. In a season full of insipid and outdated comedies, the success of this ambitious satire provides hope that the Italian industry can recapture audiences without abandoning local values and habits.

LORENZO CODELLI

recent and forthcoming films

BOROTALCO (Talcum Powder). Dir: Carlo Verdone. Phot: Ennio Guarnieri. Players: Carlo Verdone, Eleonora Giorgi, Angelo Infanti, Christian De Sica. Prod: Intercapital.

ECCEZZZIUNALE. . . VERAMENTE (Really Exceptional). Dir: Carlo Vanzina. Phot: Alberto Spagnoli. Players: Diego Abatantuono, Teo Teocoli, Massimo Boldi, Stefania Sandrelli. Prod: Cinemedia.

PIERINO COLPISCE ANCORA (Pierino Strikes Again). Dir: Marino Girolami. Phot: Federico Zanni. Players: Alvaro Vitali, Enzo Liberti, Michela Miti, Riccardo Billi. Prod: Filmes International, Dania Film, Medusa Distribuzione.

STILL FROM THE TAVIANI BROTHERS' *LA NOTTE DI SAN LORENZO*

LO SQUARTATORE DI NEW YORK (The New York Ripper). Dir: Lucio Fulci. Phot: Luigi Kuveiller. Players: Jack Hedley, Almanta Keller, Howard Ross. Prod: Fulvia Film.

BANANA JOE. Dir: Steno. Phot: Luigi Kuveiller. Players: Bud Spencer, Marina Langner, Gianfranco Barra, Enzo Bracardi. Prod: Derby Cinematografica.

CERCASI GESÙ (Jesus Wanted). Dir: Luigi Comencini. Phot: Renato Tafuri. Players: Beppe Grillo, Maria Schneider, Fernando Rey, Nestor Garay. Prod: Intercontinental Film Company.

PIÙ BELLO DI COSÌ SI MUORE (You Can't Get More Beautiful). Dir: Pasquale Festa Campanile. Phot: Alfio Contini. Players: Enrico Montesano, Ida Di Benedetto, Monica Guerritore, Vittorio Caprioli. Prod: Filmauro.

BELLO MIO BELLEZZA MIA (My Handsome My Beautiful). Dir: Sergio Corbucci. Phot: Giuseppe Rotunno. Players: Giancarlo Giannini, Mariangela Melato, Stefania Sandrelli, Massimo Mollica. Prod: PLM Film Produzione.

VIENI AVANTI CRETINO (Come On Stupid). Dir: Luciano Salce. Phot: Enrico Menczer. Players: Lino Banfi, Franco Bracardi, Michela Miti, Gigi Reder. Prod: San Francisco Film.

I PREDATORI DEL COBRA D'ORO (The Raiders of the Golden Cobra). Dir: Antonio Margheriti. Phot: Alessandro Mancori. Players: David Warbeck, John Steiner, Almanta Siuska. Prod: Gigo Cinematografica.

IDENTIFICAZIONE DI UNA DONNA (Identification of a Woman). Dir: Michelangelo Antonioni. Phot: Carlo Di Palma. Players: Tomas Milian, Christine Boisson, Daniela Silverio. Prod: Iter Film.

OLTRE LA PORTA (Beyond the Door). Dir: Liliana Cavani. Phot: Luciano Tovoli. Players: Marcello Mastroianni, Eleonora Giorgi, Michel Piccoli. Prod: Futur Film 80.

MORTE IN VATICANO (Death in the Vatican). Dir: Marcello Aliprandi. Phot: Alejandro Ulloa. Players: Terence Stamp, Gabriele Ferzetti, Paula Molina. Prod: Film International Company.

TRENTA MINUTI D'AMORE (Thirty Minutes of Love). Dir: Marco Vcario. Phot: Giovanni Vino. Players: Monica Vitti, Ugo Tognazzi, Fiorenza Marcheggiani. Prod: Laser Film, Italian International Film.

IL MONDO NUOVO (The New World). Dir: Ettore Scola. Phot: Armando Nannuzzi. Players: Marcello Mastroianni, Jean-Louis Barrault, Hanna Schygulla, Harvey Keitel. Prod: Opera Film.

COLPIRE AL CUORE (Strike at the Heart). Dir: Gianni Amelio. Phot: Antonio Nardi. Players: Jean-Louis Trintignant, Tomas Milian, Michele Placido. Prod: Società Antea Cooperativa.

IO SO CHE TU SAI CHE IO SO (I Know That You Know That I Know). Dir: Alberto Sordi. Phot: Sergio D'Offizi. Players: Alberto Sordi, Monica Vitti. Prod: Scena Film.

LA VERITÀAAAAAAAA (The Tru-u-uth). Dir: Cesare Zavattini. Phot: Arturo Zavattini. Player: Cesare Zavattini. Prod: Reiac Film, RAI.

DOMANI SI BALLA (Tomorrow We'll Dance). Dir: Maurizio Nichetti. Phot: Mario Battistoni. Players: Maurizio Nichetti, Mariangela Melato, Paolo Stoppa. Prod: Vides International.

AMICI MIEI ATTO II (My Friends Act II). Dir: Mario Monicelli. Phot: Sergio D'Offizi. Players: Ugo Tognazzi, Philippe Noiret, Adolfo Celi, Gastone Moschin. Prod: Filmauro.

STILL FROM THE SHOCHIKU PRODUCTION, *DAYDREAM*

Japan

by Naoki Togawa

On Movie Day, December 1, 1981, most cinemas throughout the country lowered their prices by 50%. It was an attempt by exhibitors to win audiences back – and it seemed to succeed. Attendances were four or five times the average in almost every cinema. In response, exhibitors are to hold such days at least three times a year. Movie Day originated in 1956 as a memorial day for films.

Nagisa Oshima has finally started his new film *Merry Christmas in the Battleground* after a long preparation period following *Ai no borei* (*Empire of Passion*) four years ago. Shooting will begin on a small New Zealand island in August 1982 and is to finish by the end of the year. The film is scheduled to be shown at the 1983 Cannes film festival. *Merry Christmas in the Battleground* is based on the novel by Lawrence van der Post and stars rock singer David Bowie. Oshima decided to make it a co-production with producer Jeremy Thomas. It is budgeted at $6,000,000 and, as the title indicates, deals with international friendship during the last war – a subject completely different from Oshima's two previous films.

Masaki Kobayashi recently completed the long work of editing his documentary *The Tokyo Trial* (*Tokyo saiban*) – also known as *The Far East Martial Court* – depicting how Japanese war criminals were tried in military court. Footage has come from US government film as well as domestic newsreels of the time. Kobayashi has spent more than three years editing his four hour film from a huge amount of material. The producer Kodansha, one of Japan's major publishing companies, is to release the film in spring 1983 through Toho-Towa.

Akira Kurosawa has spent another year searching for a producer for his next film, *Ran* (*Confusion*), an adaptation of Shakespeare's "King Lear." The cost is estimated at about $10,000,000 – much higher than that of *Kagemusha*.

The past year (1981–82) could be called the Year of New Directors, as several have come out with fresh works. *Doro no kawa* (*Mud River*), directed by Kohei Oguri, was voted one of the best pictures of the year by film magazines and also won a prize at the Moscow film festival. In his first feature film Oguri shows a meditative style which is perfectly fitting for his story of lower-class people. *En-rai* (*Distant Thunder*), directed by Kichitaro Negishi, was also a local prize-winner. After several porno pictures, Negishi has followed his own path. In *En-rai* he shows a brilliant talent for serious drama in his story of young people and their way of life. Toshio Goto's first film, *Matagi* (*A Traditional Hunter*), which was shown at the Berlin film festival, won a minor prize and has a rather square style. But all these film-makers, with little or no experience in film, have shown promise with their independent productions.

Japan Film Library Council (Kawakita Memorial Film Institute) is busy providing programmes to film libraries and other cultural organisations abroad. Among recent projects are a programme on the Japanese Edo period – to be shown in Rome (April–May) and New York

STILL FROM *IREZUMI – SPIRIT OF TATTOO*

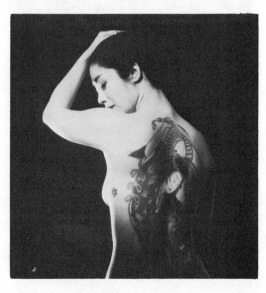

STILL FROM KOHEI OGURI'S *MUDDY RIVER*

(June–August) – and a season of "Unknown Excellent Japanese Masterpieces" – in Hongkong (June–July). All the available films of Ozu are to be shown in New York in autumn 1982.

In the documentary field, remarkable work has been done by Eizo Culture Centre (Nippon Audio-Visual Library), which has been collecting notable films from many countries and showing them in its own (300-seat) hall with the financial assistance of NTV, one of Japan's major broadcasting companies. Parallel with its daily showings, the centre arranges symposia every week on the themes of the programmes by inviting film-makers and other specialists. Last year NAVL invited many prominent documentarists, including Jean Rouch, Monica Flaherty, Guartiero Jacopetti, Eckart Stein, David and Judith MacDougal, and Von Clemens Klopfenstein. Jun-ichi Ushiyama, chief managing director of NAVL, is himself one of TV's most active documentary film-makers. The library, now in its fourth year, has a stock of documentary films from countries including the U.S.A., Canada, France, Britain, Australia and East Germany, with a special emphasis on anthropology.

The National Film Centre also arranged some notable programmes in the past year, including German films of the Twenties, Italian classics and a retrospective of Finnish films (1940–1977). In July 1982 it planned to show programmes devoted to D. W. Griffith, and a retrospective of Yugoslavian films late in November.

KIYOSHI ATSUMI, MIKIKO OTONASHI, AND KAYOKO KISHI-MOTO IN *TORASAN AND A PAPER BALLOON*

recent and forthcoming films

AKURYO-TO (Devil's Island). Script: Kunio Shimizu. Novel: Seishi Yokomizo. Dir: Masahiro Shinoda. Phot: Kazuo Miyagawa. Players: Takeshi Kaga, Sima Iwashita, Hideo Murata, Kayoko Kishimoto. Prod: Haruki Kadokawa.
BOSATSU, SHIMOYAMA JIKEN (Murder Case Shimoyama). Script: Ryuzo Kikushima. Novel: Mikio Yada. Dir: Kei Kumai. Phot: Shun-ichiro Nakao. Music: Masaru Sato. Players: Tatsuya Nakadai, Kei Yamamoto, Yoko Asaji, Daisuke Ryu. Prod: Makayuki Sato. For Haiyuza.
EKI (Station). Dir: Yasuo Furuhata. Script: So Kuramoto. Phot: Daisaku Kimura. Music: Ryudo Uzaki. Players: Ken Takakura, Chieko Baisho, Ayumi Ishida, Setsuko Karasuma. Prod: Juichi Tanaka. For Toho-Eiga.
EN-RAI (Distant Thunder). Script: Haruhiko Arai. Novel: Wahei Tachibana. Dir: Kichitaro Arai. Phot: Shohei Ando. Players: Toshiyuki Nagashima, Eri Ishida, Johnny Okura, Rie Yokoyama. Prod: Hiromi Higuchi. For New Century, ATG.
HAKUJITSU-MU (Daydream). Script and dir: Tetsuji Takechi. Novel: Jun-ichiro Tanizaki. Phot: Akira Takada. Players: Kei Sato, Kyoko Aizen, Takemi Katsuyori, Sae Kawaguchi. Prod: Takechi Productions.

RUMIKO MATSUBARA AND YASUHITO YAMANAKA IN
KURA NO NAKA

RYODU UZAKI IN TOMOAKI TAKAHASHI'S *A MAN WITH
TATTOO*

HOKUSAI MANGA (Hokusai, Ukiyoe Master). Script
and dir: Kaneto Shindo. Novel: Sei-ichi Yoshiro. Phot:
Keiji Maruyama. Music: Hikaru Hayashi. Players: Ken
Ogata, Toshiyuki Nishida, Yuko Tanaka, Kanako
Higuchi. Prod: Kindai Eiga Kyokai, Haiyuza.
HYORYU (Wreckage). Script: Sakae Hirosawa, Shiro
Moritani. Novel: Akira Yoshimura. Dir: Shiro Moritani.
Phot: Kozo Okazaki. Music: Gen-ichi Kawakami. Play-
ers: Kin-ya Kitaoji, Jiro Sakagami, Choei Takahashi,
Keiko Mita. Prod: Tokyo Eiga.
KAGERO-ZA (Theatre Troupe Kagero). Script: Yozo
Tanaka. Novel: Kyoka Izumi. Dir: Seijun Suzuki. Photo:
Kazue Nagatsuka. Players: Yusaku Matsuda, Katsuo
Nakamura, Michiyo Okusu, Reiko Kusuda. Prod:
Cinema Placet.
KEIJI MONOGATARI (Detective Story). Script: Yusuke
Watanabe, Tetsuya Takeda. Dir: Yusuke Watanabe.
Phot: Yukio Yada. Players: Tetsuya Takeda, Hisayo

Ariga, Kunie Tanaka. Prod: Kazuo Kuroi, Kinema
Jumpo.
KOFUKU (Happiness). Script: Shin-ya Hidaka, Ikuko
Oyabu. Dir: Kon Ichikawa. Phot: Kiyoshi Hasegawa.
Players: Yutaka Mizutani, Toshiyuki Nagashima, Rie
Nakahara, Kei Tani. Prod: Yutaka Goto. For Life,
Toho-Eiga.
KURA NO NAKA (In a Warehouse). Novel: Seishi
Yokomizo. Dir: Yoichi Takabayashi. Phot: Muneyuki
Tsuda. Players: Yasuhito Yamanaka, Rumiko Matsu-
bara, Ako, Akira Nakao. Prod: Haruki Kadokawa.
LOVE LETTER. Script: Yozo Tanaka. Novel: Akihiro
Emori. Dir: Yoichi Higashi. Phot: Koichi Tanaka. Play-
ers: Keiko Sekine, Katsuo Nakamura, Mariko Kaga,
Noboru Nakaya. Prod: Gento-Sha.
NOGIKU NO HAKA (Graveyard of Chrysanthemums).
Script: Fukiko Miyauchi. Novel: Sachio Ito. Dir: Shin-
ichiro Sawai. Phot: Fujio Morita. Players: Seiko Mat-

KOICHI SATO IN KOREYOSHI KURAHARA'S *THE GATE OF
YOUTH – II*

STILL FROM KIHACHI OKAMOTO'S *WHY CHARLSTON
DAYS AGAIN?*

TOSHIYUKI NISHIDA AND KEN OGATA IN THE SHOCHIKU RELEASE, *EDO PORN*

suda, Tadashi Kuwabara, Kunio Murai, Miyoko Akaza. Prod: Tokyo-San Music.
NORIKO WA, IMA (Now, Not Handicapped Noriko). Script and dir: Zenzo Matsuyama. Phot: Ken-ichiro Morioka. Players: Noriko Tsuji, Misako Watanabe, Hiroyuki Watanabe, Hiroshi Mikami. Prod: Matsuo Takahashi. For Kinema Tokyo.
ORE TO AITSU NO MONOGATARI (A Story of Me and Him). Script: Yoshitaka Asama, Masao Kajiura. Dir: Yoshitaka Asama. Phot: Mitsuo Hanada. Music: Koichi Morita. Players: Tetsuya Takeda, Ran Ito, Nobuko Otowa, Kei Yamamoto. Prod: Toru Najima.
OTOKOWA TSURAIYO, NANIWA NO KOI NO TORAJIRO (Torasan's Love in Osaka). Script: Yoshitaka Asama, Yoji Yamada. Dir: Yoji Yamada. Phot: Tetsuo Takaba. Music: Naozumi Yamamoto. Players: Kiyoshi Atsumi, Keiko Matsuzaka, Chieko Baisho, Gannosuke Ashiya. Prod: Kiyoshi Shimazu. For Shochiku.
OTOKO WA TSURAIYO, TORAJIRO KAMIFUSEN (Torasan and a Paper Balloon). Script: Yoshitaka Asama, Yoji Yamada. Dir: Yoji Yamada. Phot: Tetsuo Takaba. Music: Naozumi Yamamoto. Players: Kiyoshi Atsumi, Mikiko Otonashi, Kayoko Kishimoto, Chieko Baisho. Prod: Kiyoshi Shimazu. For Shochiku.
THE RAPE. Script: Yoichi Higashi, Yoshi Shinozaki. Novel: Keiko Ochiai. Dir: Yoichi Higashi. Phot: Koichi Kawakami. Players: Yuko Tanaka, Morio Kazama, Masahiko Tsugawa, Mariko Kaga. Prod: Gento-Sha.
RENGO KANTAI (The Combined Fleet). Script: Katsuya Suzaki. Dir: Shukei Matsubayashi. Phot: Yuta Kato. Players: Toshiyuki Nagashima, Hisaya Morishige, Ken-ichi Kaneda, Kiichi Nakai. Prod: Yuko Tanaka. For Toho.
SAILOR FUKU TO KIKANJU (A School Girl with a Machine-Gun). Story: Jiro Akagawa. Dir: Shinji Somai. Phot: Seizo Senmoto. Music: Masaru Hoshi. Players: Hiroko Yakushimaru, Tsunehiko Watase, Yuki Kazematsuri, Rentaro Mikuni. Prod: Haruki Kadokawa.

SEISHUN NO MON, JIRITSU HEN (The Gate of Youth – II). Dir: Koreyoshi Kurahara. Novel: Hiroyuki Itsuki. Phot: Hanjiro Nakazawa. Players: Kaori Momoi, Koichi Sato, Kaoru Sugita, Morio Kazama. Prod: Toei.
SIRIUS NO DENSETSU (A Legend of Sirius). Dir: Masami Hata, Phot: Iwao Yamaki. Music: Koichi Sugiyama. Prod: Shintaro Tsuji. For Sanrio. Animated film.
TATTOO ARI (Man with a Tattoo). Script: Takuya Nishioka. Dir: Tomoaki Takahashi. Phot: Yuichi Nagata. Players: Ryudo Uzaki, Keiko Sekine, Misako Watanabe, Ayako Ota. Prod: Takahashi Pro. For ATG.
TORITATE NO KAGAYAKI (A Brilliant Collector). Dir: Masayuki Asao. Phot: Koichi Suzuki. Players: Yuji Homma, Aiko Morishita, Reiko Takizawa, Hideko Hara. Prod: Mitsuru Kurosawa.

Statistics

Figures for the period January to December 1981, with previous year's figures in brackets.

Number of Cinemas:

total	2,298 (2,364)
for domestic films only	1,041 (1,085)
for foreign films exclusively	689 (701)
for both categories	568 (578)

Number of Films Released:

total	555 (529)
domestic films by major companies	123 (119)
domestic films by independents	209 (201)
foreign films	223 (209)

Box-office:

yearly attendance 149,450,000 (164,422,000)
gross theatre receipts without tax
163,259 million yen (165,918)
average admission fee without tax
1,093 yen (1,009)

Gross Film Rental:

total	61,820 million yen (63,454)
domestic films	33,690 million yen (34,897)
foreign films	28,130 million yen (28,557)

income from export of films
$6,757,148 (6,866,586)

Number of TV Sets Registered:
29,658,000 (29,062,000)

Korea (South)

by Fred Marshall

Korean cinema has now returned to an international level, with many films being shown abroad at film festivals, on European television and in commercial exhibition.

The major pastime for the public is still the cinema, despite inroads made by TV and other software. The import of foreign pictures has been curtailed and the public gets only the best of the West to go along with its own cinema, which consists of pot-boilers, epics, war dramas, historical films, action dramas and tear-jerkers. A greater artistic flavour in the new wave of South Korean films has become evident in the past year, with some products looking more like European instead of Asian cinema.

The cost of admission to a Korean film is about 30% less than to an imported film. South Korean cinema is a reflection of a society which has made marked progress and its content has become more liberal. As only 40 films a year can be imported by local producers, the industry has been trying to find a substitute. The end result is that the South Korean film now looks like something between a European and Japanese film.

There are several TV and film schools which offer opportunities to would-be film-makers. Career training can be given and motion picture techniques can be developed at an early stage, which is one reason why there are many new directors coming up. The Motion Picture Producers' Association of Korea offers film-makers cash prizes with their Grand Bell awards. These come once a year and carry much prestige, especially for fledgling film-makers. Many of the industry's creative people work in TV: there is a great deal of talent to draw from, with Seoul being the centre of all activity.

Censorship is still very strong although it has relaxed in the past year. A film must show the establishment playing an important role in the story's development. Social themes seem to be the most suitable for producers, although they are sometimes worried about letting directors develop original material because of financial risk at the box-office. In short, producers are worried about getting their money back and they require, in most cases, a property that is known or familiar to Koreans.

The old culture of the country comes alive in the cinema and many film-makers show great promise developing their technique with the country's ancient and mystic culture.

Cinematography and lighting are now among the best in Asia. Musical scoring has improved tremendously in the past two years. Modern techniques now plug the gap, and have eliminated many of the long dialogue scenes; this in turn has tightened up the slack moments of dramatic stories.

South Korea has some 447 theatres – more than enough to assure Korean films of a return on their initial investment. Some 80 films were made in the past year by 22 production companies, of which only 11 are active in both import and export. Many local films are sent abroad for Korean audiences in the Middle East, Europe and the U.S.A. Some Korean films are exported to Taiwan, Singapore, Malaysia and Hongkong; and to Africa and South America after being dubbed into English.

Some of the major films shown in the past year were *The Lovemaker, Girl in the Sad Season, The Small Ball Tossed by a Dwarf, The Sparrow Sings at Night, A Rose Swallowed by its Thorn, The Free Woman, They Shot at the Sun, Invited People, A Fine Windy Day, People in Darkness* and *The Parrot Sings with its Own Body.*

Among the leading directors is cameraman/writer/producer Wo Lee-Jin. His first success was *Lovers in the Rain* (1978), described by one international critic in New Delhi as "a European type of motion picture, very stylish and ambitious in content." He followed up on this with *The Sparrow Sings at Night* (1981). He has shown many of his films abroad, is one of the few directors who speaks English, and is a master at portraying Korean emotions blended with local culture.

Another important director is Choi Ha-Won. His *Invited People* dealt with the persecution of the Catholics and was one of the country's most controversial films in the past year. His latest work

(Continued on page 263)

Malaysia

by Baharudin A. Latif

FINAS, the National Film Development Corporation set up in late 1981, has drawn up various development projects for short- and long-term implementation. They include setting up a studio complex along the lines of Universal. Initially to cost M$17 million (£3 million), it will have complete facilities within its 30-acre confines to cope with an expanding company. Equipment will be leased to independents and FINAS itself will have no direct involvement in the projects. This is to prevent its excessive intervention in the private sector.

Plans are also afoot to provide credit facilities to local productions and foreign co-productions. Advisors would be recruited to provide consultancy services to producers. FINAS has also set up workshops for actors, directors, producers, and the like, in a bid to generate more motivation towards quality. However, the sessions attracted only a handful of bored participants, suggesting that FINAS has an identity problem with the very film community whose interests it is supposed to serve.

FINAS is reported to be more interested in creating a body of young, cinema-oriented and academically qualified cineastes rather than pamper to the whims of veteran film-makers with their out-dated ideas and techniques. As such, it is planning five years ahead rather than concentrating on the present situation. However, as FINAS and film-makers do not see eye to eye, it may be difficult to iron out certain problems, and the ambitious masterplan may fall victim to bureaucracy.

The government's tight money squeeze, which has already frozen some prestigious projects and new appointments, may also stunt FINAS's growth, as it is still having problems finding middle-level personnel to fill up artistic, technical and professional jobs. Without them, a major part of FINAS' expansion will unceremoniously grind to a halt.

FINAS director-general Ismail Zain has said that setting up a third cinema circuit is not considered a top priority. This has angered film-

AZNAH HAMID (LEFT) AND NANCIE FOO ASSIST POLICE TO TRACK DOWN THEIR FRIEND'S KILLERS IN *PEMBURU*
PHOTO: BAHARUDIN A. LATIF

makers who feel that the lack of Malay-owned theatres has always been the source of their problems. They feel (and not without justification) that FINAS should concentrate on eventually putting all aspects of production, distribution and exhibition into their hands – or at least 30%, as provided for in the second Malaysia plan (1970–1975).

Production, meanwhile, has been perking up. More films are now being planned or shot than at any other time in the past 50 years – and most are by Malay companies. Jins Shamsudin's *Bukit kepong* is smashing box-office records in spite of its controversial theme. Its success has spawned similar productions. An American-based film company has plans to do a Second World War spectacular, *Penang*, hopefully to star Richard Chamberlain and Jane Fonda.

An interesting note is that three of the top 10 films released on the Cathay circuit in 1981 were local productions – *Abang*, *Dia Ibuku* and *Da di du*. But not surprisingly, *Raiders of the Lost Ark* topped all releases.

recent and forthcoming films

BUKIT KEPONG. Script, dir and prod: Jins Shamsudin. Players: Jins Shamsudin, Yusof Haslam, Hussein Abu-Hassan, A. Rahim, Jamaliah Arshad, ASP Latifi Datuk Ahmad, Seah Lai-Soon, Ng Thin-Hong. For Jins Shamsudin Productions.

LANGIT PETANG. Dir: Shahrom Mohd. Dom. Players: Azean Irdawaty, Dharma Harun al-Rashid, Mahmud Jun, Sidek Hussein, Shasha, Rohaya Rahman, Shamsi, Omar Suwita. A Syed Kechik Production.
KAMI. Script and dir: Patrick Yeoh. Players: Sudirman, Zul Zamanhuri, Osman Zailani, Ho Kwee-Leng, Ibrahim Din, Azizah Muslim, Azmi Mohamad, Sharif Babu. An Indra Film.
PEMBURU. Script and dir: Rahim Razali. Players: Ahmad Yatim, Aznah Hamid, Ahmad Tarmimi Siregar, Nancie Foo, Osman Zailani, Fatimah Yassin, Tamam Idris, Rahim Razali. A Fleet Communications Film.
PENENTUAN. Script and dir: Aziz Jaafar. Players: Zulkifli Zain, Noor Kumalasari, Yusof Haslam, Rubiah Suparman, Raja Noor Baizura, Mozaid, Dayang Sulu. A Pancar Seri Production.
SENJA MERAH. Script and dir: Hussein Abu-Hassan. Players: Yusof Haslam, Jamaliah Arshad, Latif Ibrahim, Ahmad B. Mahyon Zailani, Rose Iskandar, Hasnah Ibrahim, Rokiah Shafie. A Cahaya Jaya Film.
ESOK UNTUK SIAPA. Script and dir: Jins Shamsudin. Players: Jins Shamsudin, Noor Kumalasari, Latif Ibrahim, Fauziah Ahmad Daud, Sharifah Aminah. For ISE Films.
PERTENTANGAN. Script and dir: Salleh Ghani. Players: Rubiah Suparman, Mokhtaruddin, Salina Tun Salleh, Fadillah Wanda, Rahim Zailani, Bob Mustaffa. An EPA Film.
ANAK SULUNG. Script: Ali Azia. Dir: Aziz Jaafar. Players: Zulkifli Zain, Sharifah Hasnor, Malek Selamat,

AHMAD YATIM (LEFT) AS *PEMBURU* (*THE HUNTER*) CORNERS ONE OF HIS VICTIMS PHOTO: BAHARUDIN A. LATIF

Dali Siliwangi, Zainuddin Zimbo, Emilia Surkasih, Norizan, Samsee Said. For Reza Films.
SIKIT PUNYA GILA. Script and dir: Raja Ismail. Players: Hamid Gurkha, Dharma Harun al-Rashid, Ibrahim Pendek, Norlia Ramlee, Yusni Jaafar, Nora Shamsuddin. An Indra Film.
HALIMUNAN HITAM. Script and dir: M. Osman. Players: Che Man Mamat, Rozi Sahar, S. A. Bakar, Azian M. Osman, Zulkifli Osman, A. Wahab. For Roots Film Industries.

Mexico by Tomás Pérez Turrent and Gillian Turner

On March 24, 1982, the National Film Library was destroyed by fire. Two cinemas, a library of over six thousand films (the most important film archive of Latin America), a specialised library of film books, thousands of documents, film records, scripts, photographs, and a hitherto undetermined number of human lives, were all consumed in the flames. This is a catastrophe of incalculable dimensions for the film culture, history and memory of this country.

But this tragic event could also be seen as a metaphor, a symbol of what has been film policy during the present administration headed by Margarita López Portillo, which has lasted now for over five years. Her term of office ends in December 1982 and the results are anything but encouraging: infinitely bad films of scant interest, the only criterion of which has been that they should sell; a film industry in debt and with no

solid base, in which the sections dealing with exhibition and distribution are those with the best profits, in detriment to the production sector.

The previous administration, headed by Rodolfo Echeverría, had left in 1976 a structure permitting State participation in all sectors of the film industry. The State already possessed the main exhibition chain of the country, the most important studios and the national distributing company, in society with the Producers' Association, all of which being managed by the Film Bank.

During Mr. Echeverría's term of office the State-owned production companies became, during 1975 and 1976, the most important both in the number of films produced annually and in their quality. There was no guideline laid down of what national cinema should aim to be, but economic profit was secondary to social and cultural gain. No definitive basis for a healthy industry could be

STILL FROM *MOJADO POWER*

established in this time, and no great cinematographic works were achieved, but the lines to take were indicated, and interesting films were made which could have been the beginning of a real national cinema. All that was needed was to follow up these beginnings.

The administration of Sra. López Portillo needed only a few months to dismantle everything. The Film Bank disappeared, as did one of the State-owned production companies, and the remaining two have made fewer and fewer films.

With the idea of maintaining employment for the thousands of people working in the film industry, the private producers were protected, as they made films of the worst possible quality, and with no greater aim than that of recuperating costs and making quick, easy profits. The censor became stricter, making difficulties for the co-operatives and the independent groups. The results, now that

the present administration is in its final phases, are unfortunate.

The reactions of Sra. López Portillo herself were slow to appear. In April 1982 she spoke out against the producers and the films she had encouraged: "My efforts to achieve good cinema have not been satisfied. And I must express my most profound discontent and disagreement. You have chosen to make easy cinema, of the worst possible kind, with personal gain as your only objective." And further on: "I do not wish to be remembered as the person who protected a denigrating cinema of such bad quality." Against her wishes, she is already remembered as the promoter of the worst moments of Mexican cinema in all its history.

During 1981 a total of 88 films were made, including two completely foreign productions made in Mexico. The private producers made 75, of which the company Televicine, a branch of the

STILL FROM *HOTEL VILLA GOERNE*

huge television monopoly Televisa, made seven. The State produced only seven films, and the four remaining are independent films made in 16mm, and outside industrial channels. Of the seven films produced by the State, only three were completely national: *Mexico 2000* by Rogelio Gonzalez; *Rastro de Muerte* (*A Trace of Death*) by Arturo Ripstein; and *La Derrota* (*The Defeat*) by Fernando Vallejo. The rest were co-productions, two with Spain: *El Niño del Tambor* (*The Boy with the Drum*) by Jorge Grau, and *Mar Bravo* (*Rough Sea*); one with France: *La Cabra* (*La Chèvre*) by Francis Weber; and one multimillionaire super-production with Italy and Russia: *Campanas Rojas* (*Mexico in Flames*) by Sergei Bondarchuk. The showing of this film in Mexico, in March 1982, produced a unanimously unfavourable reaction from the critics, an unprecedented occurrence which could be compared to the American critics' reaction to *Heaven's Gate* by Cimino.

Campanas Rojas is the first part of a film which like *Reds* by Warren Beatty is based on the biography of John Reed (the second part filmed in Russia will be ready by the end of 1982) and has been a complete failure both with the critics and with the general public. This makes evident the disastrous effects of a strategy basing the salvation and the hopes for international prestige on a co-production where the foreign co-producers take all the advantages. In spite of all this, a new co-production has already been started with

France and Spain this time. And as in the case of *Campanas Rojas* it will take the budget of ten nationally produced films. This co-production is *Antonieta*, directed by Carlos Saura, although here the name of Saura guarantees much higher quality than that of Bondarchuk.

MOJADO POWER
(Wetback Power)

Script: Alfonso Arau, Emilio Carballido. Direction: Alfonso Arau. Photography (colour): Angel Goded. Music: Guillermo de Anda. Editing: Alfonso Arau, Carlos Puente. Players: Alfonso Arau, Blanca Guerra, Pedro Damián, Nono Arsu, Isaac Ruiz, Priscilla García, Donald Eldson. Produced by AMX Productions, Inc. Alfonso Arau (1981).

Mojado (wetback) is the name given to workers crossing the border into the United States illegally, in the hopes of finding work. They are so called because at one time they used to cross the border by swimming the Rio Bravo. This film is the story of one of them, a "lumpen" from the city who reaches Los Angeles, and in the face of hostility from the Migration Police and the Chicanos, and with the help of other illegal immigrants, he takes up lodging in an atomic bomb shelter, wins dance contests, and the love of a pretty young Chicano girl, invents all sorts of recognition signs: T-shirts, insignia, buttons and other gadgets with which he unites all his followers, who end by realising that the struggle of the "wetbacks" and that of the Chicanos is one and the same.

Arau returns to his comic character from other films: the man who comes from the masses and through circumstances out of his control becomes a leader. A chain reaction of events is sparked off and ends by provoking a radical change. He keeps the girl and the movement he has provoked continues on its own impetus. Thus, there is a similarity to *l'uomo qualunque* of the Neapolitan tradition, who sets a whole movement in motion quite unconsciously, and with no more arms than those of the picaresque and the comedy. His idea of giving consumer society a dose of its own medicine in this way may be questioned, since by attempting to draw them into the problem he ends by alienating them still more.

The film was made independently, in 16mm

(later blown up to 35mm), and with a small budget. In spite of its technical faults, it is worth mentioning as a proposal for a type of cinema using humour to illustrate a certain type of problem, a spectacle to amuse, and via this amusement to make the spectator think about this problem.

TOMÁS PÉREZ TURRENT

HOTEL VILLA GOERNE

Script and Direction: Busi Cortés. Photography (colour, 16mm): Antonio Diaz de la Serna. Music: José Amozur- rutia. Sound: Antonio Betancourt. Editing: Sonia Fritz. Players: Luis Rábago, Rosa María Bianchi, Judith Arci- niegas, Mari Carmen Cárdenas. Produced by Centro de Capacitación Cinematográfica (1981). 60 mins.

A surprising film made as a graduation piece by a young film student called Busi Cortés. Her work is far superior, even technically, to films made daily in the industry. The story concerns a writer who goes to stay in an old hotel in the provinces, with the idea of writing a novel. The theme of his novel is to be the strange world of the two women in charge of the hotel, and their niece.

The film is surprising for its simplicity, the clarity of the intrigue, its dramatic elements, the film-maker's control of the composition of spaces and time constructions, and her unique mastery of the film technique. But by simplicity we do not refer to the story line. The narration is extremely complex and has various levels of meaning. The function of the characters varies. The writer seems to be the character carrying the action, and is finally seen as a kind of toy manipulated by the three women, especially by the little girl.

Busi Cortés creates brilliantly a deathly, twi- light atmosphere. Reality in the film is surrounded by a mysterious halo, distorting it and evoking phantoms, although one never feels that the direc- tor is playing "at being fantastic." Everything lies in the perversion of that reality so minutely described. Here are to be found the echoes of that Latin American literature defined as "magical realism."

The film is also a meditation on creation, its mechanism and its profound duplicity. The writer tries to create a literary world, transporting reality to his fiction, and thus attempts to manipulate his characters just as he does in his fiction. Little by little his characters begin to manipulate him, and impose themselves upon him, their creator. In the development of this process reality imposes its "creation" on the writer's fiction, and ends des- troying it in an obvious metaphor: in the final scene the little girl makes paper boats from the pages of the writer's future novel.

TOMÁS PERÉZ TURRENT

EL INFIERNO DE TODOS TAN TEMIDO (Hell So Feared by All)

Script: Luis Carrión, Jorge Fons, Sergio Olhovich. Direc- tion: Sergio Olhovich. Photography (colour): José Ortiz Ramos. Music: Raul Lavista. Editing: Rafael Ceballos. Players: Manuel Ojeda, Diana Bracho, Jorge Humberto Robles, Delia Casanova, Abel Woolrich, Isabela Corona, Gabriel Retes. Produced by Conacine (1979).

This film was forbidden for two years because the Mexican authorities considered it "subversive." It is the story of an individual, useless rebellion which becomes a coherent act as soon as it extends and is channelled collectively. The hero is a writer in a state of permanent crisis, a dissatisfied soul who rejects the rules of the society in which he lives. But his rebellion is a solitary one and makes more present his inner phantoms and demons. His response to social aggression is more aggression. His path can only end in an acute narcissism and self-destruction (alcohol, drugs). He is an egoist, an enraged loner.

But although his rebellion is an individual one, it is sufficient to be considered "harmful." He must be reduced to normality, his impulses must be destroyed, all that is dangerous to social order or questions its validity must be annihilated. Here he enters the asylum, and meets institutional psychiatry (electric shocks and drugs) understood as bureaucratic and reactionary control.

The metaphor is obvious. The psvchiatric asylum is a microcosmic representatinn of an opressive and repressive society which an..uls and destroys. But here the character finds the possibil- ity of taking concrete action, exorcising the interior demons and phantoms, burying the romantic myths of self-destruction, overcoming his solitude by way of collective action (the rebellion of the inmates who end by taking over the asylum), fraternity, solidarity.

Olhovich may be reproached for certain obvious faults, such as the abundance of dialogue and an over-academic style. His film style is not an adequate vehicle for the justness, the audacity even, of his ideas. Anyway, this does not stop this film from being one of the most interesting in Mexican cinema in the last five or six years.

TOMÁS PERÉZ TURRENT

new and forthcoming films

TIEMPO DE LOBOS (**Wolf Season**). Script and Dir: Alberto Isaac. Phot (colour): Angel Bilbatúa. Edit: Federico Landeros. Players: Ernesto Gómez Cruz, Gonzalo Vega, Jaime Garza, Patricia Rivera, Miguel Angel Rodríguez, Carmen Salinas. Prod: Colima Films, S.A., Julio Ruiz Llaneza, México, 1981.

EL NIÑO FIDENCIO. Script and Dir: Nicolás Echevarría. Phot (colour): Nicolas Echevarría. Mus: Mario Lavista. Edit: Joaquín Osorio. Research: Guillermo Sheridan. Full-length Documentary. Prod: Centro de Producción de Cortometraje, 1981.
EN LA TORMENTA (**In the Storm**). Script and Dir: Fernando Vallejo. Phot (colour): Xavier Cruz. Mus: Mozart and Latin-American popular music. Edit: Federico Landeros. Players: Carlos Riquelme, Carmen Montejo, Dacia González, Gina Moret, Fernando Balzaretti, Gerardo Vigil. Prod: Conacite Dos, 1981.
ANTONIETA. Script: Jean Claude Carrière. Dir: Carlos Saura. Phot (colour): Teo Escamilla. Players: Isabelle Adjani, Hanna Schygulla, Gonzalo Vega, Carlos Bracho, Ignacio López Tarso, Diana Bracho. Co-production Mexico-France-Spain, 1982.
UNO ENTRE MUCHOS (**One among Others**). Script: Ariel Zuniga, Alberto Cortés. Dir: Ariel Zuniga. Phot: (colour, 16mm): Tony Kuhn. Mus: José Elorza. Edit: Ariel Zuniga, Alberto Cortés. Sound: Bernardine Ligthart. Players: Fernando Castillo, Socorro de la Campa, Scarlett Quiroz, Sebastian Salinas. Prod: Zinc, S.A., 1981.

Morocco   by Lyle Pearson

With a long cultural history, Morocco has yet a short cinematic one. Only two Moroccans had directed independently produced films, Hamid Benani and Ben Barka Souhel, both since 1970. Neither has directed a feature since 1980; now emerges Moumen Smihi, with the most ambitious Moroccan feature film to date.

Quarante-quatre, or *Les récits de la nuit* (*44*, or *The Tales of One Night*) is a fresco of two Moroccan families – one, Arab, from Fez, the other, Berber, from Chaouen – whose lives are observed from 1912 to 1956, an important period in Morocco's history. Through these families Smihi alludes to the two major levels of colonial resistance in Morocco, the nationalistic or Arab resistance (in the major cities), and the tribal or Berber resistance (in the Atlas mountains and the Sahara). History is evoked here as a backdrop, not as a didactic presentation of events. Smihi borrows the narrative structure of *A Thousand and One Nights*, a series of tales, brief or extended throughout the film, mixing themselves, parallel to history. This non-linearity of narration aims at creating a multiplicity of viewpoints on an overturned society, according to Smihi.

Ba-driss is a storyteller, famous throughout the capital of the Sherifian Empire, Fez. He recounts daily the cyclical adventures of the popular heroes of Islam: Antar Ibn Chaddad, Seif Ibn Yazan, etc. A negro, a stranger to Fez, he lives alone in a miserable cave-like room. Often, under the effect of cannabis, he loses himself in pagan and ecstatic dances, recalling his faraway past. Once someone wanted to introduce him into a harem to recount to the women his epics on condition that he be blinded. His stories weave the mythic background of Moroccan society.

El Haj, professor at the ancestral university of Fez, is the incarnation of the past and of tradition. A respected patriarch, he rules a family of wives, children and slaves under one roof. By conviction a reformer, El Haj fights obscurantism in his heart and among his friends. He is attached to the movement of thought which is at the origin of Arab nationalism, Salafia (Islamic reform), yet he is too orthodox to sacrifice prayers, polygamy, or slavery. Near death, El Haj turns to meditation, which brings him a new shock: his own anachronism and the downfall of all his values.

Abdelhaq, the eldest son of El Haj, is the

MARIE-FRANCE PISIER AND NAIMA EL MCHARGI IN *44 – OR THE TALES OF ONE NIGHT*

symbol of the new generation. Enrolled in a French school, his father wants him to study in France for a promising, that is to say "modern," career. Living wounds mark Abdelhaq, from the day that he saw the humiliation of his mother by his father taking a second wife, and physically from his circumcision. But Abdelhaq remembers also the women playing in the courtyard, on roller skates and bicycles, introduced by foreigners for the edification of the "natives." His viewpoint becomes more and more contemporary as he learns to analyse his society. His end, at the end of the film, remains suspended.

Moussa, a Berber from the small Northern city of Chaouen, is the symbol of the lost generation of the colonial night. From a modest family, he studies at the old university, where he is an assistant of El Haj and the tutor of his children; bored with his studies, he becomes friends with the storyteller and participates in a drama group, drama being a new and imported, even unknown,

art. He plays Othello, in Arabic, opposite a boy dressed as Desdemona, the troupe in half-Elizabethan and half-Moroccan costumes. Moussa above all is conscious of cultural disintegration: he loses himself in unanswerable questions of history, culture and being. Later a writer and mystic, refused reentrance into El Haj's home, Moussa dies a beggar. History has availed itself of Moussa, not the opposite.

Iakout is El Haj's favourite slave; the slave market in Fez was closed only in the Thirties. On her back she carries El Haj's second wife to the marriage bed, and she suffers the physical blows of Abdelhaq's anger. Aged, her legs paralysed, she is made guardian of the family steambath, where she cannot sleep, defending herself against the constant assaults of cockroaches and rats. Through her, Smihi attempts to explain the role of women in Morocco.

In certain scenes and occasional titles, printed in Arabic and French, Smihi hints at the following historical events: a long time closed on itself, leading an "archaic" life, the Sherifian Empire underwent a colonisation from 1912 to 1956 which came first militarily under the name of "pacification." French and Spanish troops suppressed the rebel tribes on the authority of the Sultan, the religious and temporal head of Morocco. France and Spain reorganised the Empire, modernised it, and opened it to the commerce and civilisation of the West. Morocco fell into disorder, then took refuge in nationalism. The mountain, nomad and peasant resistances subdued, troops occupied even the edge of the Sahara. In 1930, the Protectorate instituted the Dahir Berber which aimed at separating the Arab population from the Berbers.

During the Second World War, under the Protectorate, Morocco officially supported the Allies. Ben Youssef, Sultan of Morocco, met Roosevelt, who assured him Morocco would be liberated after the War. But the Sultan remained loyal to the nationalists. He was deposed by the French and exiled to Madagascar. Under the pressure of a powerful popular movement (riots, urban terrorism, birth of a Liberation army) Ben Youssef returned triumphantly to Morocco. On March 2, 1956, the political Independence of Morocco was declared.

What, therefore, happened? And how can the cinema show it, asks Smihi. *44* is the act of filming in a culture which has received the cinema as an armoured vehicle which helped impoverish a people. A film which examines this wound, this state of loss, ought to examine itself first on its own function. Every image is, therefore, above all the image of the *ritual* of a society. Smihi uses his landscapes as scenographic space (and not as simple decor), props and costumes as vehicles of opposition, of cultural significance, in colour as in

meaning. He used two guides: the ochre sketches of Delacroix, and Moroccan mosaics and calligraphy. Close-ups of Moroccan objects (plates, woodwork, walls) are as essential to the film as the group compositions. Montage is also essential to the morseled narrative, and the music (sounds, silences, musical instruments) is meant to *listen to itself* just as the film is meant to *see itself*.

If *44* remains intentionally obscure it is even more so, unintentionally, to a Western audience. Another problem, Smihi is better at analysing Morocco than France, and while certain anachronisms are intentional, such as the Othello costumes, others could not have been intended: even the French costumes are sometimes out of sorts. *44*'s obscurity is not compensated for by the use of European stars (Pierre Clémenti as Moussa, Marie-France Pisier as the second wife), even though they play Berbers (a language group, not a race), and extend the sense of anachronism even to the casting.

44 is not as successful as Smihi's 1978 hour-long black-and-white 16mm TV film *El Chergui* (*The Violent Silence*) – the obscurity in *El Chergui* was based clearly on mystic Berber rites. In *44* that obscurity is embedded too far in the technique of the film, mystifying us all. Yet *44* offers many pleasures to the viewer who has the patience to unlock its secrets and forgive Smihi his indulgences.

Moumen Smihi is now at work on a parallel film, on the Berber resistence in the Atlas mountains. *44* was filmed almost entirely in the old city of Fez, south of those mountains. Morocco's first feature film in three years may be the first chapter in a multiple work on the struggle for Independence in Morocco – which had never been touched in fiction cinema before.

Netherlands

by Pieter van Lierop

All those concerned with Dutch cinema are convinced that highly promising developments are taking place in the Netherlands. Over the past twelve months there have been some particularly encouraging signs of this. We have seen a series of films which have been well received by both the public and the critics. The beginning of 1981 saw the premières of *A Flight of Rainbirds* by Ate de Jong and *Charlotte* by Frans Weisz. In the autumn these were followed by *The Girl with the Red Hair* by Ben Verbong, *Two Queens and a King* by Otto Jongerius, and *The Distance* by Van de Velde, Seegers and De Winter, all of which commanded

respect. There were also two unpretentious comedies which were not so well reviewed but nonetheless became huge box-office successes. These were *High Heels, True Love* by Dimitri Frenkel Frank and *Looney Joe* by Guus Verstraete Jr. The end result was that in 1981 Dutch films drew larger audiences in Holland than in any of the previous five years. Some 3,109,714 tickets were sold for Dutch films, as against 1,914,313 in 1980, and receipts amounted to 26,108,592 guilders, as against 14,837,829 guilders in 1980.

The noticeable improvement in quality continued into the new year, and has begun to attract

ERIC CLERCKX AND LINDA VAN DIJCK IN *TWO QUEENS AND A KING*   PHOTO: CONCORDE FILM

Sabine

A film by René van Nie

DESSA FILMS B.V.   RENE VAN NIE
OUDE ZIJDS VOORBURGWAL 219, AMSTERDAM, HOLLAND
TELEPHONE: 020-25 00 93/24 56 02

GERARD THOOLEN AND MARJA KOK IN *A HOT SUMMER NIGHT*

attention in other countries. At the Berlin Festival, Ulrich Gregor, the co-director, spoke of the "new Dutch wave," and no less than nine Dutch films were shown in various sections. In September 1981 the first ever Dutch Film Festival was held in Utrecht at the initiative of the film-maker Jos Stelling, who was born in this city. During the festival week all the Dutch shorts, full-length features, animation films and documentaries made in the previous twelve months were shown. Golden Calf Awards were presented for each category, and competition was fierce, if only because there have been no film prizes in Holland for the last ten years. The prize for the best full-length feature went to *The Mark of the Beast* by Pieter Verhoeff (reviewed in IFG 1982). Marja Kok won the best actress award for her role in this film. The best actor award went to Rutger Hauer for his work as a whole. He has recently become known in Hollywood for his roles in *Nighthawks*, *Blade Runner* and *Eureka*. Kees Linthorst received a Golden Calf for best sound, and the prize for the best short was won by Henri Plaat for *Spurs of Tango*. The Dutch

Film Critics Award was established at the festival and was presented to Ben Verbong for his first film, *The Girl with the Red Hair*, which immediately revealed a highly promising talent.

Initially the media greeted the idea of a Dutch Film Festival with some scepticism, but as the week proceeded enthusiasm grew and it was eventually decided to make it an annual event. It will be held in the last week of September each year and it is hoped to attract foreign visitors. The competition at the second festival promises to be especially interesting since several excellent films have been released in the meantime. *Two Queens and a King* by Otto Jongerius proved to be a moving piece of work which interwove two stories by the Dutch writer R. Peskens. It is set in the picturesque port of Flushing during the Twenties and is based on the author's experience of growing up in poverty. The boy's life is dominated by two women: his anarchist mother, who wages a private guerilla war against the Calvinist middle class in a series of nocturnal sorties, and his libertarian aunt, who initiates him into sex. The film is particularly remarkable for the roles of the two women, played by Kitty Courbois and Linda van Dijck. Three other stories by Peskens have been made into separate episodes of the film *Things Past*, directed by Bas van der Lecq, Bram van Erkel and Roy Logger. Each of these episodes is a fine example of concise story-telling conveying a cynical view of the petit bourgeois and female vindictiveness. The story called *Mevrouw van Putte*, directed by Roy Logger, has the additional ingredient of a special brand of black humour which raises it above the level of the other two episodes.

One of the highlights of the end of 1981 was *The Distance* by the trio of Jean van de Velde, René Seegers and Léon de Winter, whose earlier film *The Demise of Herman Dürer*, inspired by the work of Wim Wenders, received considerable attention. *The Distance* is more original in concept and stronger in dramatisation as well as more sober in style. The film concerns a young man who signs on as a merchant seaman and looks back on his lost youth and in particular his friendship with a boy who has recently died of a heroin overdose. The young man carries his past with him in the form of amateur films he has made. *The Distance* may be seen as a pessimistic comment on the nature of film, which is doomed to remain a voyeur and is never able to alter the course of events.

The films which made the most impression in the first half of 1982 were *The Silence of Christine M . . .* by Marleen Gorris, *The Waves* by Annette Apon, and *A Hot Summer Night* by Frans Weisz and Shireen Strooker. All three are worthy of international attention and should at least be shown on the festival circuit (the first two are reviewed separately). *A Hot Summer Night* is

STILL FROM *THE DISTANCE*

holland
good for features

For general information and inquiries about feature film production, addresses, laboratory-, subtitling-, studio-, video- and sound-facilities,

please contact:

NEDERLANDSE BIOSCOOPBOND
2 Jan Luykenstraat
1071 CM AMSTERDAM
Tel.: 020 - 79 92 61
Secr.: L. Claassen

BENTHE FORRER AND MIKE BURSTEYN IN RENE VAN NIE'S LIVELY AND THOUGHTFUL FILM ABOUT THE GENERATION
GAP – *SABINE*   PHOTO: GOFILEX FILM

based on a stage production by the Werkteater, an alternative theatre group. Two years ago the group won prizes all over the world for *In for Treatment*, the film version of their play about the taboos surrounding cancer and death. In contrast, *A Hot Summer Night* is a comedy which makes gentle fun of the institution of marriage. The action is set in a circus tent where a cabaret show is being performed. As a result of various kinds of marital conflict there is a series of disasters both on and off-stage. With this film, in contrast to *In for Treatment*, the director, Frans Weisz, was allowed to change the original *mise en scène* (by Shireen Strooker). But the theatrical character of the production has been preserved by deliberately creating a glossy, artificial surface and by having adults playing children. This unusually refreshing film was shot entirely in a studio, with the circus tent erected on a set made to look like a city square.

Despite the general improvement in the quality of Dutch cinema, there were of course some less satisfactory and disappointing films. *Come Back* by Jonne Severijn and *Sabine* by René van Nie were not very successful, but did at least combine interesting themes with competent acting. Some controversy was caused by *Lugher*, a wild film made entirely independently by newcomer Theo van Gogh. By showing Fascist behaviour in a rather unsavoury crime story, his intention was to register a protest against neo-Fascism. But the effect of the film remained ambiguous, and as a result some critics regarded it as dangerous. At the same time there was general respect for van Gogh's unmistakable flair and highly individual style.

In the field of documentaries an impressive achievement was *Sacrifice Area* by Ernie Damen and Otto Schuurman. This showed how at various places in the United States the rights of Indian

which Caspar Verbrugge dealt with the subject of paedophilia with admirable delicacy and wit.

* * *

It looks as if there will be fewer short films made in Holland in the future. This is because of the decision by the Ministry of Cultural Affairs, Recreation and Social work to allow the funds concerned to be used for meeting up to 90% of the costs of full-length features not primarily intended for commercial cinemas. This will make available an annual sum of 3,575,000 guilders in addition to the funds already provided by the Dutch Film Finance Corporation, which currently receives 5.2 million guilders from the Ministry and 880,000 guilders from the Dutch Cinema Association. The Film Finance Corporation will meet about 50% of the costs of approved commercial features up to a maximum of about 900,000 guilders.

The implementation of this plan for two film funds is now likely to be delayed as a result of spending cuts by the new centre-left government which replaced a centre-right government in 1981. This is all the more surprising when one remembers that the left-wing governments which recently came into power in France and Greece have both spectacularly increased their support of the national film industries. Dutch film-makers already suffer from high unemployment and concern among them reached such a point that in May of this year protest marches and demonstrations were held. In the middle of May there was a

RIJK DE GOOYER AND MONIQUE VAN DE VEN IN *HIGH HEELS, REAL LOVE*

tribes are still being violated by mining companies in search of coal and uranium on the reservations. *Daughters of the Nile* was a fascinating study of female emancipation in Egypt by Hillie Molenaar and Joop van Wijk. The Amsterdams Stadsjournaal again produced a number of highly informative documentaries, including a particularly disturbing report on the dumping of chemical waste. Paul Driessen confirmed his reputation as the best Dutch animation talent with *Home on the Rails*. The best short film was undoubtedly *De Oppas* in

STILL FROM *THINGS PAST*

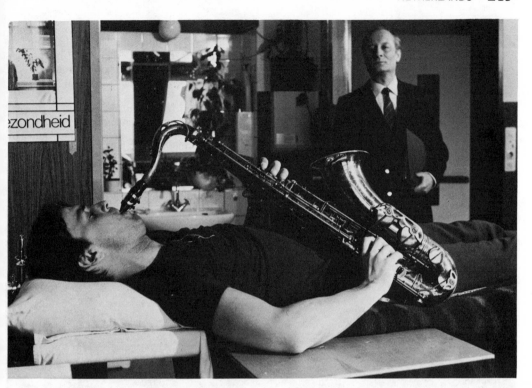

THEO BERMANS AND COR VAN RIJN IN *COMEBACK*

government crisis, bringing the centre-right again to power, but it is doubtful that they will introduce a new policy in cultural affairs. So while Dutch cinema is flourishing in the artistic sense, its economic prospects are sombre. But necessity is the mother of invention, and an attempt is now being made to raise finance for films on the stock exchange. A special share company has been set up and it has already contributed funds to two films, *Passage* by Bas van der Lecq and *The Deep of Deliverance* by Nouchka van Brakel. It remains to be seen how this scheme will work out in future.

Given the economic recession, Dutch cinemas did not do too bad business in 1981. The 553 cinemas which are members of the Cinema Association drew a total audience of 27,934,124, which is 95.5% of the 1980 total. The turnover was only 0.1% less than in the previous year. It is worth noting the success with which the Association has fought against the pirate television stations over the past twelve months. A large part of urban Holland now has cable television and there was a plague of pirate stations breaking into the cable system. The pirates showed commercials and illegally made copies of brand new films. By bringing a dozen court cases against different cable companies, the Cinema Association succeeded in forcing them to take steps against the pirates, and the number of illegal transmitters has dropped sharply as a result.

In 1981 the members of the Association imported 371 foreign films, i.e. 35 more than in 1980. Seven Dutch feature films were shown on the commercial circuit and four of these were among the ten most popular films of the year. The Top Ten were: 1. *For Your Eyes Only*, 2. *A Flight of Rainbirds* (Dutch), 3. *The Blue Lagoon*, 4. *Christiane F.*, 5. *The Girl with the Red Hair* (Dutch), 6.

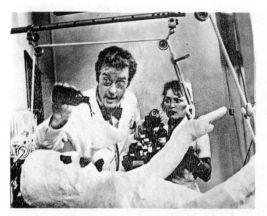

Raiders of the Lost Ark, 7. *High Heels, True Love* (Dutch), 8. *Flying High!* 9. *Looney Joe* (Dutch), 10. *The Blues Brothers*. The public has shown great interest in the products of the domestic film industry and this suggests a hopeful future for Dutch cinema.

Stop Press: the fall of the centre-left government has precipitated catastrophic cuts in subsidies to *both* Dutch film funds, and the Council of Arts resigned *en bloc* in protest at not being consulted. New elections may complicate the issue still further.

ABOVE: ANDRE VAN DUIN IN THE REMARKABLY POPULAR COMEDY, *LOONEY JOE* (ONE MILLION VISITORS WITHIN FOUR MONTHS IN HOLLAND)

BELOW: NOUCHKA VAN BRAKEL WITH RENEE SOUTENDIJK ON THE SET OF MS. VAN BRAKEL'S FORTHCOMING *THE DEEP OF DELIVERANCE*

RENEE SOUTENDIJK IN *THE GIRL WITH THE RED HAIR*

HET MEISJE MET HET RODE HAAR
(The Girl with the Red Hair)

Script: Ben Verbong and Pieter de Vos. Direction: Ben Verbong. Photography: Theo van de Sande. Editing: Ton de Graaff. Music: Nicola Piovani. Players: Renée Soutendijk, Peter Tuinman, Adrian Brine, Loes Luca, Johan Leysen, Chris Lomme, Henk Rigters, Jan Retèl, Maria de Booy. Produced by Chris Brouwer and Haig Balian for Movies Film Productions. 110 mins.

Director Ben Verbong received the Dutch Film Critics Award for *The Girl with the Red Hair*, his first feature. This gives some indication of the quality of the film, which tells the story of Hannie Schaft, a member of the Dutch Resistance during the Second World War. In 1943 she gave up her law studies and joined the Resistance. Shortly before the end of the War she was arrested by the Germans and murdered. Hannie Schaft was posthumously awarded the highest honours by Queen Wilhemina, but during the Fifties she became the subject of fierce controversy over whether or not she was a Communist. The film is largely based on a book with the same title by Theun de Vries, himself a Communist, who portrayed Hannie Schaft as being motivated by Communist ideals. The film does not take this view, but one of its weaknesses is that it does not offer an alternative explanation for her abandoning her legal studies in favour of the most militant form of resistance, which was hardly a matter of course. Her activities were not exactly restricted to distributing underground newspapers. She was often involved in highly dangerous sabotage and in the liquidation of Nazis and collaborators. She became

increasingly reckless and a law unto herself, and she was eventually captured as the result of rather silly mistakes.

There must have been some kind of upheaval going on in the mind of this introverted young student, who was only 24 when she died. In details the film is subtle and psychologically sharply observed, but it leaves her basic motives unclear. It shows movingly that she did not at first take easily to killing her enemies, and how, as a very shy girl from a sheltered background, she was placed under enormous pressure in living a dangerous double life. While she remains to some extent an enigmatic figure, the film is very successful in bringing her to life humanly and emotionally, and this is due in no small measure to Renée Soutendijk's impressive and subtle performance in the leading role. There is also fine acting to be seen in the supporting roles. Another of the film's strengths is the sureness of touch with which the atmosphere of the Occupation is recreated. It is full of a sinister authenticity which owes much to Theo van de Sande's almost monochrome photography, imbuing practically every shot with a sense of unease and oppression.

PIETER VAN LIEROP

DE STILTE ROND CHRISTINE M . . . (The Silence of Christine M . . .)

Script and Direction: Marleen Gorris. Photography: Frans Bromet. Editing: Hans van Dongen. Music: Lodewijk de Boer. Players: Cox Habbema, Nelly Frijda, Henriëtte Tol, Edda Barends, Eddy Brugman, Dolf de Vries, Onno Molenkamp, Hans Croiset, Frederik de Groot. Production: Matthijs van Heijningen, Sigma Films. 95 mins.

Marleen Gorris studied English and dramaturgy before deciding to write a film script. Producer Matthijs van Heijningen and the Dutch Film Finance Corporation were so enthusiastic about her script that they agreed to let her make the film even though she had no experience of directing. Their confidence proved to be well justified. Made on a low budget and given a limited release, *The Silence of Christine M . . .* surprised both critics and public. The film, which might be described as a

STILL FROM *THE SILENCE OF CHRISTINE M . . .*

feminist murder story, concerns three women arrested on charges of killing a boutique owner. We soon learn that they have indeed killed the man, and the film concentrates on examining their motives. The women do not know each other, and their presence together in the boutique turns out to be coincidence. There seems to be no explanation for the exceptional brutality with which the murder was committed. A female psychiatrist is given the task of determining whether the women can be held responsible for their act. She interviews each one: an ordinary housewife, a working-class waitress, and an extremely intelligent private secretary. Initially the psychiatrist takes a purely professional attitude, but this changes into a growing sympathy. In her own marriage to a career-minded lawyer, she comes to recognise more and more of the hostility to her sex which the three women have lived with all their lives. In the end the murder can only be explained as a spontaneous outburst of violence, a response to the war which the women

feel that the men have waged against them for years.

To demonstrate her solidarity with the accused, the psychiatrist declares them to be fully responsible for their act. This causes consternation among the male lawyers at the trial, and leads to uproar in the courtroom. The typically male arguments are greeted with roars of laughter from all the women present, a grotesque display of female solidarity which comes completely out of the blue and ends the film.

It is a pity that this ending has the effect of giving the film an allegorical slant in retrospect, since up to this point it is a highly effective and absorbing tale told in naturalistic terms. Few feminist films have been so successful in combining strong drama with a convincing presentation of the case against a male-dominated society. But the ending makes one feel cheated: all the sympathy inspired by skilled acting and very recognisable characters turns out to have been wasted on the abstract figures of a morality play. This would be less annoying were it not for the excellent overall quality of the rest of the film.

PIETER VAN LIEROP

GOLVEN
(The Waves)

Script and Direction: Annette Apon. Photography: Theo van de Sande. Editing: Ton de Graaff. Music: Louis Andriessen. Players: Aat Ceelen, Thea Korterink, Michel van Rooy, Truus te Selle, Marianne Stieger, Edwin de Vries, Gerardjan Rijnders. Produced by René Scholten for Studio Nieuwe Gronden. 95 mins.

As far as is known, Annette Apon is the first director to attempt a film version of a book by Virginia Woolf, and *The Waves* can certainly not be accused of showing lack of respect for the original. Indeed, what some may find irritating about the film is the prominent place given to the literary text. This is Annette Apon's first full-length feature, and in it she returns to the experiments with form of her earliest short films, having spent

seven years making documentaries with the Amsterdams Stadsjournaal collective.

The Waves is a group portrait of six people about to enter adulthood. Their differing personalities, lost dreams, insecurities, emotions and ambitions are portrayed through their thoughts about Percival, the mysterious seventh figure. We learn about these people through a series of monologues rather than through the images in the film, which are contemporary while the story is set in the Twenties. The film is divided into five segments interspersed with an occasional old photograph or minimal scene. The monologues are first spoken off-screen while we see the obviously contemporary actors trying on their Twenties costumes. Later the texts are read as during a first rehearsal. Then we see how the texts are made applicable to the reality of each actor. This is followed by the dinner scene, which is played in costume but with the monologues again being spoken off-screen. The film ends with the six actors each presenting his own epilogue.

STILL FROM ANNETTE APON'S *THE WAVES*

The idea of structuring the film in this way is to detach the text from the period in which it was written and thus give it a timeless quality. This makes no sense in fact, since good writing is always timeless anyway and does not need to be helped in this way. But it is interesting to see how Apon plays this game and to observe the thoughtfulness and precision with which she makes the most of the possibilities offered by the unusual structure. The result is certainly not the liveliest of films, but the austerity of the form does not rule out imagination or prevent Theo van de Sande from performing several tours de force with the camera.

PIETER VAN LIEROP

The "Free Circuit" Cinema

In addition to the commercial system for distributing and showing films, the Netherlands has an extensive chain of alternative film houses which tend to present socially committed films made by collective groups such as the Amsterdams Stadsjournaal (Amsterdam City Newsreel) and the Rode Lantaarn (Red Lantern) from Utrecht. However, for the most part they rely on films (generally 16mm, but occasionally 35mm) imported by noncommercial distributors such as Fugitive Cinema, Cinemien (women's films), the Verenigd Film Instituut and Film International, the largest of these organisations.

Recently Film International has begun to participate in international productions. It has made financial contributions to films by Steve

BACK NUMBERS . . .

of INTERNATIONAL FILM GUIDE

These tend to vanish rapidly (and we have no copies left at all of the early issues of the GUIDE). Order your missing editions now; remember that every volume has an entirely fresh contents, with different director profiles, filmographies, national reports, reviews, and of course each GUIDE contains upwards of 200 unique photographs.

Volumes available, and prices:

1967	£3.95/$7.95	**1976**	£3.95/$7.95
1968	£3.95/$7.95	**1977**	£3.95/$7.95
1969	£3.95/$7.95	**1978**	£3.95/$7.95
1970	£3.95/$7.95	**1979**	£3.95/$7.95
1971	£3.95/$7.95	**1980**	£3.95/$7.95
1972	£3.95/$7.95	**1981**	£4.95/$9.95
1974	£3.95/$7.95	**1982**	£5.95/$10.95
1975	£3.95/$7.95		

Send cheque/Money Order with order, and add 60p/$1.00 per volume for postage and packing, please.

THE TANTIVY PRESS LIMITED,
136-148 TOOLEY STREET, LONDON SE1 2TT, ENGLAND.

INTERIOR OF "THE MOVIES" CINEMA IN HAARLEM, A MEMBER OF THE INTERNATIONAL CONFEDERATION OF ART HOUSES, AND CONTAINING 165 SEATS. OWNED AND PROGRAMMED BY BIOSCOOPONDERNEMING A. F. WOLFF B.V. OF UTRECHT

Dwoskin (*Outside In*), Juliet Berto (*Neige*) and Raul Ruiz (*Dak van de Walvis*), and has also backed various Dutch films, including those of Van der Keuken (*De Beeldenstorm*), Rijneke (*Pinkel*) and Van der Staak (*Your Garden Plot*).

For the last ten years Huub Bals has been the driving force behind the alternative circuit in general and Film International in particular. In his view, recent cuts in government subsidies pose a serious threat to the continued existence of the alternative circuit. Film International is struggling with a desperate shortage of funds, and was forced to reduce the scale of its 1982 festival in Rotterdam. Nonetheless, it drew almost as many visitors (34,000) over 8 days this year as over 10 days in 1981. Despite this, the festival continues to cost

too much, and this is why this year Film International decided to distribute one of its lead attractions, Ferreri's *Tales of Ordinary Madness*, on the commercial circuit.

This was undoubtedly a blow to the struggling alternative cinemas, who could have expected good box-office receipts for the film. On the other hand, Film International's breakthrough on the commercial circuit might lead to a useful interaction which could help the alternative film houses. For example, they could present second showings of interesting Dutch films which have been commercial failures. This has already been done in the case of Severijn's *Come Back* and Van Gogh's *Lugher*, which have been shown on both circuits. One major difficulty, however, is that the Bioscoopbond, the Cinema Association, which is not subsidised, has strong objections to dealing with Film International, which it sees as a subsidised competitor.

Dutch Feature Film Producers

Castorfilms
Nieuwe Baarnstraat 67a
3743 BP Baarn.
Tel. 02154-17108.

N.V. Cinecentrum/Concept
's-Gravelandseweg 80
1217 EW Hilversum.
Tel. 035-13851.

Cine/Vista
Teylingen 13
1275 CX Huizen (NH).
Tel. 02152-56227.

Curiel Films International
Lijnbaanstraat 7
1061 ST Amsterdam.
Tel. 020-276176.

Joop van den Ende Filmprodukties B.V. i.o.
Keplerstraat 34
1171 CD Badhoevedorp.
Tel. 02968-5751.

De Eerste Amsterdamse Filmassociatie van 1980
Leliegracht 25
1016 GR Amsterdam.
Tel. 020-265613.

Fuga Film Produkties B.V.
Fnidsen 44
1811 NH Alkmaar.
Tel. 072-123656.

Bert Haanstra Films B.V.
Verlengde Engweg 5
1251 GM Laren (NH).
Tel. 02153-82428.

Herlekinj Holland Filmproductions
Kerkdijk 11
3615 BA Westbroek.
Tel. 03460-1444.

Hollandia Filmproducties B.V.
Roemer Visscherstraat 38
1054 EZ Amsterdam.
Tel. 020-122352.

Filmproduktie De Maatschap
Geldersekade 11 hs.
1011 EH Amsterdam.
Tel.020-234628.

Maggan Films B.V.
Lange Voorhout 37
2514 EC 's-Gravenhage.
Tel. 020-649988.

M.G.S. Film Amsterdam B.V.
Singel 64
1015 AC Amsterdam.
Tel. 020-231593/729960.

M.M.C. Film B.V.
Dorpsweg 78
1679 KD Schellinkhout.
Tel. 02293-1682.

Movies Filmproductions
Haarlemmerdijk 163
1013 KH Amsterdam.
Tel. 020-732843.

Nieuwe Gronden
Van Hallstraat 52
1051 HH Amsterdam.
Tel. 020-867913.

René van Nie Dessafilms B.V.
O.Z. Voorburgwal 219
1012 EX Amsterdam.
Tel. 020-250093/245602.

Pan Film B.V.
Sloterweg 1212
1066 CV Amsterdam-Sloten.
Tel. 020-152080.

Fons Rademakers' Productie B.V.
Prinsengracht 685
1017 JT Amsterdam.
Tel. 020-221298.

Frans Rasker Film B.V.
Utrechtsedwarsstraat 102
1017 WJ Amsterdam.
Tel. 020-258817.

Rex Film
Thull 11a

6365 AC Schinnen.
Tel. 04493-1421.

Scorpio Verstappen Films B.V.
Nicolaas Maesstraat 68
1071 RC Amsterdam
Postbus 245
1000 AE Amsterdam.
Tel. 020-764320.

Sigma Films B.V.
Bolensteinseweg 3
3603 CP Maarssen.
Tel. 03465-70430.

Sluizer Films B.V./MGS Films B.V.
Singel 64
1015 AC Amsterdam.
Tel. 020-232593/243181.

René Solleveld Filmproductions B.V.
Keizersgracht 60'
1015 CS Amsterdam.
Tel. 020-266355.

Jos Stelling Film Produkties B.V.
Springweg 50-52
3511 VS Utrecht.
Tel. 030-313789.

Carl Tewes Filmprodukties B.V.
De Rijt 16
1251 JM Laren (NH).
Tel. 02153-10677.

Vasana Filmproductie B.V.
Czaar Peterstraat 96
1018 PS Amsterdam.
Tel. 020-233664.

Verenigde Nederlandsche Filmcompagnie B.V.
Keizersgracht 319
1016 EE Amsterdam.
Tel. 020-249277.

Kooperatieve Vereniging Het Werkteater U.A.
Kattengat 10
1012 SZ Amsterdam.
Tel. 020-226231/228254.

THE LEADING FILM AND VIDEO COMPANIES IN THE NETHERLANDS

cutting rooms
sound studios
lighting equipment
studios
shooting crews

P.O. Box 508 - 1200 AM Hilversum - Holland - tel. 010 31 35 13851 - telex 43226

video **hilversum**

video registration
video tape editing
video casseting

P.O. Box 508 - 1200 AM Hilversum - Holland - tel. 010 31 35 16131 - telex 43226

filmlaboratories
optical arthouse with
rostrum camera
special effects
design studio

P.O. Box 503 - 1200 AM Hilversum - Holland - tel. 010 31 35 47141 - telex 43226
Duivendrechtsekade 83-86 - 1096 AJ Amsterdam - Holland - tel. 00 31 20 930960

TRADE-MARK
OF
INDEPENDENCE

Gofilex film bv

P.O. BOX 334 - 3430 AH NIEUWEGEIN - THE NETHERLANDS
TEL.: (03402) 70922 - TELEX: 47837 filex nl

Laboratories and Studios

N.V. Cinecentrum/Concept
's-Gravelandseweg 80
1217 EW Hilversum.
Tel. 035-13851.

Cineco c.c.
's-Gravelandseweg 80
1217 EW Hilversum.
Tel. 035-47141.
Duivendrechtsekade 83
1096 AJ Amsterdam.
135-47141.
Tel. 020-930960.

Cinetone Studio's
Duivendrechtsekade 83
1096 AJ Amsterdam
Tel. 020-930960.

Color Film Center B.V.
Leeghwaterstraat 5
2521 CM Den Haag.
Tel. 070-889207.

Renovo Film CV
Maziestraat 17a
2514 GT Den Haag.
Tel. 070-605737.

Proca Kleurenfilm techniek B.V.
Prinsengracht 311
1016 GZ Amsterdam.
Tel. 020-242239.

Bert Haanstra Filmproduktie
Verlengde Engweg 5
1251 GM Laren (NH).
Tel. 02153-82428.

Bob Kommer Studio's CV
Riouwstraat 71
2585 GW Den Haag.
Tel. 070-551683.

BV Nederlands Laboratorium voor Filmtechniek
Kerklaan 5
3632 EL Loenen a/d Vecht.
Tel. 02943-1855.

Titra Film Laboratorium NV
Egelantiersgracht 82-86
1015 PP Amsterdam.
Tel.020-266186.

Useful Address

Nederlandse Bioscoopbond
2 Jan Luykenstraat
1071 CM Amsterdam.
Tel. 020-799261.

STILL FROM *THE DISTANCE*

New Zealand

by Lindsay Shelton

New records were set for the New Zealand film industry with the local and international success of Roger Donaldson's second feature *Smash Palace*. Its first screenings were in the market at the Cannes Film Festival, where strong international interest soon led to a substantial U.S. distribution deal (with Thomas Coleman's Atlantic Releasing Corporation). In less than a year the feature had been sold to 45 territories – a record for any New Zealand feature.

Donaldson's *Smash Palace* is the story of the break-up of a marriage and the estranged father's attempts to get his daughter back. The film is highlighted by a stunning central performance from New Zealand actor and musician Bruno Lawrence as the father. *Smash Palace* was New Zealand's official entry at the First Manila Film Festival in January, and the international jury had no hesitation in awarding the Best Actor prize to Lawrence for his role in the film.

In February, *Smash Palace* set box-office records in New Zealand's two biggest cities when its local release began – it ran for three months in main centres, and also recorded substantial business in provincial cities. Producer-director Donaldson is now developing his third feature, *The World's Fastest Indian*, which he plans to shoot half in New Zealand and half in the United States.

Another landmark for the growing New Zealand film industry came when Sam Pillsbury's *The Scarecrow* was selected for the Directors' Fortnight at the 1982 Cannes Film Festival – the first time that a local feature had been chosen for one of the official events at Cannes. *The Scarecrow* was selected by the Quinzaine's *delégué-général*, Pierre-Henri Deleau during a visit to New Zealand organised by the New Zealand Film Commission. He told reporters that the film was charming. "It spoke to me very well about a country I don't know. It had the alchemy which I look for in a movie."

As the reputation of *The Scarecrow* grew (not only for its sophisticated directorial style but also for its stunning central performance by veteran

John Carradine) a United States theatrical deal was being negotiated. New Zealand's success in entering the American market is now much greater than might have been expected from a new film industry – of nine completed features which were assisted by the New Zealand Film Commission, five are now in theatrical distribution in the United States. As well as *Smash Palace* and *The Scarecrow*, other titles recently sold are: *Beyond Reasonable Doubt* (to Satori), *Goodbye Pork Pie* (to the Samuel Goldwyn Company) and *Skin Deep* (to Nu-Image.) Roger Donaldson's first feature *Sleeping Dogs* has also been sold to the United States, and became the first New Zealand feature ever to open in New York – only one month ahead of its director's second feature *Smash Palace*, which was selected for opening night at the annual "New Directors, New Films" season presented by the Film Society of Lincoln Center and the Museum of Modern Art.

JOHN CARRADINE IN *THE SCARECROW*

BRUNO LAWRENCE AFTER HIS RACE WIN IN *SMASH PALACE*

British filmgoers have also had their first opportunities to see New Zealand features. Geoff Murphy's *Goodbye Pork Pie* ran for a month in the Haymarket, at the start of a British release by Brent Walker; *Beyond Reasonable Doubt* was released by Enterprise Pictures; and *Pictures* was ready for distribution by Cinegate. *Pictures*, produced by veteran John O'Shea and directed by Michael Black, won a Moscow Press Award at the Moscow Film Festival, for its contribution to humanism in cinema art.

Intense interest was created as Geoff Murphy started work on his new feature *UTU/Revenge*. The most costly New Zealand feature ever made, this film (to be completed early in 1983) will be set in Nineteenth-century pioneer New Zealand and will tell the story of a Maori rebel who is pursued by a pioneer farmer seeking revenge for a merciless attack on his family. The director has compared his script with elements of *Seven Samurai* and even with Sergio Leone's first Italian westerns.

John Laing, director of *Beyond Reasonable Doubt*, also began work on his next feature – a thriller entitled *The Lost Tribe*. Both directors have written original scripts for their productions.

Geoff Steven, whose first feature was *Skin Deep*, is completing work on *Figures Beyond Glass* (working title) which he co-wrote with the distinguished Czech film writer and designer Ester Krumbachová, who made several visits to New Zealand to work on the film. *Figures Beyond Glass* was shot on locations in New Zealand's central plateau – and on the slopes of Mount Ruapehu, an active volcano. It is a psychological drama about two groups of people travelling in a remote area. The cast includes Nigel Davenport, Judy Morris and Tom Brennan. In the same area, first-time director Derek Morton was shooting *Wild Horses*, an action adventure about a man (played by writer-producer Keith Aberdein) setting out to save a herd of wild horses from slaughter. Other roles were played by Kevin Wilson, who originated the script for the film, and Bruno Lawrence (from *Smash Palace*) who relished his role as an out-and-out villain.

Director John Reid (whose first feature was the comedy *Middle-age Spread*, soon to be seen on BBC-TV) completed his second comedy feature – with a story of two young men and a body. *Carry Me Back* has settings around Wellington and the South Island farming district of Marlborough – its two protagonists, played by Grant Tilly and Kelly Johnson (young star of *Goodbye Pork Pie*) come to Wellington for a big rugby match; their old father accompanies them, but the excitement is too much for him, and after his unexpected death they have to smuggle his body back to the farm in order to inherit the property. Needless to say, events conspire against them.

Producers Rob Whitehouse and Lloyd Phillips of Auckland had considerable success with their first co-production – a futuristic action adventure entitled *Battletruck*, which they pre-sold for American release through Roger Corman's New World Pictures. Directed by American Harley Cokliss, *Battletruck* had a cast which was headed by Americans Michael Beck and Annie McEnroe – Bruno Lawrence and Kelly Johnson were among the local cast.

Wellingtonian John Barnett was rewarded for his co-production role in an American horror film (directed in Auckland by Michael Laughlin) when the *Los Angeles Herald Examiner* named *Dead Kids* as one of the year's ten best films.

The 1983 season seemed set to be New Zealand's busiest-ever production year – *Carry Me Back* and *Figures Beyond Glass* were both shooting in February-March, *UTU/Revenge* began

ABOVE: STILL FROM *WILD HORSES*

shooting in April, and *The Lost Tribe* was set to move on to its locations in June. Plans were also announced by John Barnett to shoot *Prisoner*, starring Tatum O'Neal, for 20th Century-Fox, with work due to begin mid-year. And Aucklanders Whitehouse and Phillips announced a South Pacific pirate adventure named *Savage Islands*, for the second half of the year.

New theatres opened during the year included Kerridge Odeon's Regent triplex in Wellington (opening titles: *The French Lieutenant's Woman*, *Arthur*, and *The Scarecrow*) and Amalgamated's King's Centre (with two cinemas built inside the shell of one larger auditorium.) Also in Wellington, Christchurch independent exhibitor Lang Masters successfully launched the Academy, and made plans for another Academy in Auckland. The

establishment of UIP in Auckland brought New Zealander John Essen back to New Zealand to run the new entity – he was formerly United Artists' general manager in London.

BELOW: STILL FROM *BATTLETRUCK*

TOM BRENNAN AND CTIBOR TURBA AS THE TWO LOST TRAVELLERS IN *FIGURES BEYOND GLASS*

Focus on New Zealand Shorts

The year's most distinguished short film was *A Woman of Good Character*, a 50-minute drama directed by David Blyth, whose first feature four years earlier was *Angel Mine*. *A Woman of Good Character* was premiered at the Eleventh Wellington Film Festival. Another distinctive short film was *A Grasp of Wind*, by film-maker Russell Campbell and a Dutch sculptor and painter who has lived in New Zealand for the past 15 years.

Gaylene Preston completed a classic documentary about young people seeking their first jobs – *Learning Fast*. And Melanie Read looked at street girls in Auckland in her dramatised documentary *Them's the Breaks*. A third woman film-maker, Dell King, took a crew to Thailand to film *Burials in Ban Nadi*, about archaeological discoveries by a New Zealand professor.

And young director Richard Riddiford completed a delightful first film, *Pheno Was Here*, in which two young people leave their dead-end jobs and set out to find freedom.

Norway

by Jan Holst

After ten years of successful development, the peripatetic national film festival reached Oslo this summer, presenting winners from Cannes and other festivals alongside new Norwegian features. This event, held every August in a different town, has proved of great value to local exhibitors, critics, film-makers, film society members, teachers, and the daily audience. Both the festival in Haugesund in 1981, attended by Alan Alda, Fons Rademakers, Dušan Makavejev, Ken Wlaschin and others, and the one in Oslo this August, has made the fixture well-known in Europe and the United States. In 1983 the festival will be held in Bergen, and thereafter Haugesund will be the permanent venue.

In Norway, film politics have been a matter for debate for several years. The former social-democratic government presented a state report about the present and future situation of film politics the day prior to the general election of September 1981. They lost the election (not because of the film report!), and the new conservative government withdrew the white paper and issued a revised version this year. Film producers have been discussing it avidly. The main basis of film production in Norway is a state subsidy of 55% of the box-office take, together with a guarantee for private loans up to almost 100% of the production budget. These costs have increased dramatically in recent years. An average Norwegian feature costs about $1,100,000 in 1982. In 1971 the State Advisory Council proposed to produce 15 films per annum in Norway. In 1982 only seven have been put into production.

Some people expect a better production climate with aid from video rights, domestic and foreign, as well as West German TV rights etc. The box-office has rarely been a safe measure of producing a film in Norway during the past ten to fifteen years, with the exception of comedies. Until now, no "tax shelter" or any other commercial form of production has been tried in Norway. But who knows about the future?

The best films last year were undoubtedly those directed by women: *The Betrayal*, by Vibeke Løkkeberg, and *The Witch Hunt*, by Anja Breien. The latter won two separate prizes at Venice in 1981 and *The Betrayal* was screened to enthusiastic audiences in Berlin, Göteborg, and London in 1982. The setting of *The Betrayal* is Bergen in 1948, amid the reverberations of the past war, the trial of war criminals, the rebuilding of a shattered nation, and the economic and cultural invasion by the United States.

In all this turmoil, two children, aged seven, grow up. One is the daughter of a bankrupt factory owner now making his living as a shoemaker and dreaming of a prosperous new life in North America. The other is a working-class boy. Together they experience home breakups, violence, child beating, and social and emotional humiliation. Together they develop the love and solidarity lacking in both homes. The film is an outstanding example of a rough-cut story seen through the eyes of two children who never experience being the object of parental love. The film was produced by Terje Kristiansen of Ås Film, and won the award of the Film Critics' Association in Norway this year.

The Witch Hunt takes its story from a community in the mountains of Western Norway during the Seventeenth Century. A woman from the outside world arrives and obtains employment at the large local farm, and moves into the cottage from where her family originated. She meets the handsome farmhand and gives him her love, completely and entirely. Such a strong and independent woman leads the people to suspect that she has supernatural powers and is in league with Satan. Strange incidents are linked with her, and even the farmhand believes – in his craving for her – that she casts a spell over him to attract him to her. A manhunt is raised, a new witch is found, with the willing help of the authorities . . .

Within the framework of this exciting story Anja Breien has made an exciting piece of *auteurist* cinema, with scenes that could not be found in any other medium. This summer she was awarded the AAMOT Statuette, the highest award in Norwegian cinema, for her outstanding films.

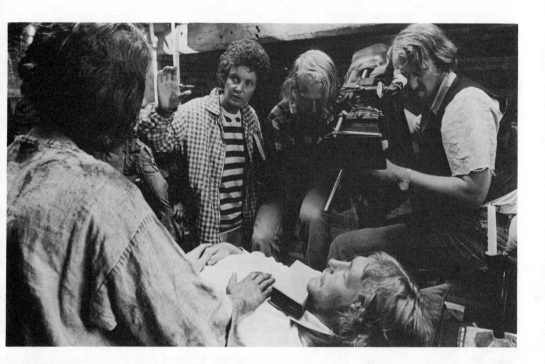

ANJA BREIEN DIRECTING *THE WITCH HUNT*

Partly on account of these titles, the critics changed their generally negative view of the domestic output by comparison with 1980.

Films for children, and featuring children, have also become popular in 1981: *Zeppelin*, by Lasse Glomm, *Silver Mouth*, by Per Blom, *Carl Gustav and his Gang*, by Ola Solum, and *Friends*, by Knut Andersen. None of these films was, however, scripted by its director, and this could represent a trend in the hitherto pro-*auteur* milieu in Norway. The production companies are accepting original screenplays or scripts based on literary sources, for the story values, and assign a skilled director to turn the scripts into film.

For the leading company, Norsk Film, Hans Otto Nicolayssen has directed *Poachers*, a feature in black-and-white scope format, about the conflict between the military forces and the civilian population in a NATO member country such as Norway. The partly humorous, partly ironic, and partly grave story starts with the installation of a military shooting range on what the farmers consider their common grazing grounds. When a sheep is shot dead on the range, the farmers take legal action against the Ministry of Defence. One of the soldiers, whose father happens to be one of the farmers, is faced with divided loyalties: who shall he obey, the community or the officers? The story is based on actual incidents, but Nicolayssen himself has written the screenplay.

The private company Mefistofilm, headed by the busy producer-directors Svend Wam and Petter Vennerød, launched a low-budget comedy in 1982, to follow their *Julia, Julia – A Fairytale*. The new film, entitled *Victoria L.*, studies a widow in her late fifties. She has given up work due to a minor injury, and engages herself in everyone and everything, her family, strangers in the street, those rejected by society, and those less fortunate people in other countries. Suddenly she meets Carl, a young man of 23 with literary ambitions and a long spell in a mental hospital behind him . . . Two

ABOVE: KNUT ANDERSEN DIRECTING *FRIENDS*

the producer-director's yearning for expression outweigh the normal, easygoing wish to make a movie.

Another low-budget enterprise is the full-length documentary, *Prognosis Innerdalen*, an excellent analysis of one of the big disputes in Norwegian politics in recent years: the conflict between hydro-electric developments and the freedom of nature. This is the second time that writer-director-photographer-producer Oddvar Einarson has turned both a political and poetic documentary about this subject (the first being *The Mardøla Contest* in 1971).

Filmgruppe 1, the other state production company, headed from 1982 on by Knut Andersen, launched two films this autumn. The low-budget semi-documentary *Between Wars*, written and directed by Sølve Skagen and Malte Wadman, depicts the generation that became politically conscious at the start of the Sixties, and later took part in anti-Vietnam demonstrations, the events of May 1968, the campaign against the

generations and two attitudes to life in a head-on collision. The film has been made without the normal state guarantee, with the aid of a combination of film-financing institutions. It proves how vivid a low-budget film can be when the story and

JON SKOLMEN AND TOBIAS ASPHAUG IN *SILVER MOUTH*

Common Market, and the general outburst of political interest among students. Since then, passivity has come creeping back and now, twenty years later, the chief character stands out as a loser even in his own private life. This film is something of a production experiment, as it started without a script, just an idea and a contract between Filmgruppe 1's first producer, Kjell Billing, and the two skilled documentarists, Skagen and Wadman. In the interval, hard work has brought to fruition a film that is part-feature, part-documentary. It is photographed by the much-admired Iranian, Bahram Manocheri, who also acted as a camera instructor during his stay in Norway.

The other film from the Gruppe was Oddvar Bull Tuhus's *50/50*, with the action taking place in a young people's musical environment in the year 1981, featuring a gang of youngsters who try to earn their living by playing before obligations and commitments become too binding. After this and his earlier success, *1958*, Bull Tuhus is busy directing his second film for Filmgruppe 1, entitled *Hockey*. These three films by Bull Tuhus (see IFG 82, page 246) have reached an audience far beyond the normal, save only for domestic Norwegian comedies.

Teamfilm, one of the oldest and largest private firms in operation, is well-known for its remakes of the Danish *Olsen Gang* farces. Numbers 11 and 12 have been produced during the last couple of years. Teamfilm has also produced *Henry's Back Room*, which marks the Italian theatre director Gianni Lepre's debut as a film director. For several years, Lepre has been running an experimental theatre in Tønsberg, some two hours' away from Oslo. The main theme of this film is people's lack of identity, focused on a man in his mid-thirties who learns that his only daughter, a drug addict and a prostitute, has committed suicide. The father's monotonous life suddenly acquires a meaning, and he becomes obsessed with the idea of avenging his daughter's death. *Henry's Back Room* is edited by the well-known Italian, Roberto Perpignani.

Marcusfilm has produced its third film, based on a short novel by Espen Haavardsholm, one of the new left-wing generation of writers in the Seventies. The title is *Black Crows*, under the direction of Lasse Glomm, and with Bibi Andersson and Bjørn Skagestad, a popular Norwegian

CONTENTS
A brief survey of Norwegian film
   production and cinema
The Norwegian cinema — a personal
   view, by Thor Ellingsen
Norwegian feature films released
   January 1st 1981 — April 1st 1982
Norwegian feature films in production

NORSK FILMINSTITUTT
ASLAKVEIEN 14 B · TLF. (02) 24 29 94 · POSTBOKS 5 RØA · OSLO 7

Mefistofilm PRESENTS

VICTORIA L

WRITTEN, DIRECTED AND PRODUCED BY WAM & VENNERØD

To be shown at the Berlin Film Festival 1983

Gyldenløves gate 41, Oslo 2, Norway
Tel (02) 41 77 95, cable: "Mefisto"

Mefistofilm 1983

A HYMN TO THE DREAMS
OF THE HUGE AND HOPEFUL GENERATION

A TRILOGY
consisting of three features ready for shooting:

OPEN FUTURE
CASTLE IN THE AIR
ADIEU SOLIDARITÉ
Written by Svend Wam & Petter Vennerød

**TO BE
PRODUCED AND DIRECTED
BY
SVEND WAM & PETTER VENNERØD**

Mefistofilm Gyldenløves gate 41, Oslo 2, Norway
Tel (02) 41 77 95, cable: "Mefisto"

HANS OTTO NICOLAYSSEN DIRECTING *POACHERS*

actor, in the leading roles. The film concerns a Norwegian and a Swedish-French woman who meet during the Frankfurt Book Fair. They become deeply fascinated by each other, physically as well as emotionally. *Black Crows*, however, is primarily concerned with the *man* who, in spite of his modern outlook, cannot unite emotionally with an equally assertive woman.

Elan Film, a small company that began as an ambitious distributor of imported features, produced Svend Wam's first feature in 1973. This year they have produced Laila Mikkelsen's new feature, following her triumph with *Growing Up*. Her new film is based on a novel by the writer Arvid Hansen, who lives in northern Norway, where the film was also shot. Being more a fable than a realistic story, it deals with a tiny community in

northern Norway during the Twenties, where people are linked to one another in both good and bad ways. The period, and the environment are rough, but the people get by with humour and vigour. At the centre of the story is a girl of twelve years old, who tries to prevent a tragedy brought about by the important men in the community. But the story is by no means restricted to a particular time or place.

Besides being a technical producer for small companies like Taurus (with their sardonic semi-documentary about mass-tourism on Sri Lanka – *Destination Paradise*), Norsk Film has also been involved in some successful co-productions with Sweden, notably *Growing Up* and *The Witch Hunt*, with the Jan Troell epic, *The Flight of the Eagle*, about to be released.

recent films

LØPERJENTEN (The Betrayal). Script: Vibeke Løkkeberg· in co-operation with Terje Kristiansen. Dir: Vibeke Løkkeberg. Phot (colour): Paul Rene Roestad. Players: Nina Knapskog, Vibeke Løkkeberg. Prod: Terje Kristiansen for Ås Film A/S.

FORFØLGELSEN (The Witch Hunt). Script and Dir: Anja Breien. Phot (colour): Erling Thurmann-Andersen. Players: Lil Terselius, Bjørn Skagestad. Prod: Gunnar Svensrud for Norsk Film A/S.

ZEPPELIN. Script: Bente Erichsen based on a novel by Tormod Haugen. Dir: Lasse Glomm. Phot (colour): Rolv Håan. Players: Silvia Myhre, Preben Skjønsberg. Prod: Bente Erichsen for Marcusfilm A/S.

DEN GRØNNE HEISEN (The Green Elevator). Script: Avery Hopwood. Adapted for the screen and directed by Odd Geir Sæther. Phot (colour): Harald Gunnar Paalgard. Players: Rolv Wesenlund, Elsa Lystad. Prod: Centralfilm A/S, EMI-Produksjon A/S and Komedieteatret A/S.

OLSENBANDEN GIR SEG ALDRI (The Olsen Gang Never Gives In). Script: Per A. Anonsen, adapted from the original Danish script. Dir: Knut Bohwim. Phot (colour): Mattis Mathiesen. Players: Arve Opsahl, Carsten Byhring, Sverre Holm. Prod: Temafilm A/S.

JULIA JULIA – ET EVENTYR (Julia Julia – a Fairytale). Script, Dir., and Prod: Svend Wam and Petter Vennerød, for Mefistofilm A/S. Phot (colour): Svein Krøvel. Players: Knut Husebø, Gunilla Olsson.

PROGNOSE INNERDALEN (Prognosis Innerdalen). Script, Dir., Phot. and Prod: Oddvar Einarson for Elinor Film. Documentary.

PAKKETUR TIL PARADIS (Destination: Paradise). Script and Dir: Eldar Einarson. Phot (colour): Bjørn Jegerstedt. Players: Erik Søby, Berit Smith Meyer. Prod: Ola Solum for A/S Taurus.

SØLVMUNN (Silver Mouth). Script: Martin Asphaug. Dir: Per Blom. Phot (colour): Erling Thurmann Andersen. Players: Tobias Asphaug, Jon Skolmen. Prod: Norsk Film A/S.

ENGLER I SNEEN (Angels in the Snow). Script: Haakon Sandøy, freely adapted from a novel by Ketil Bjørnstad. Dir: Haakon Sandøy. Phot (colour): Hans Nord. Players: Frøydis Arman, Jon Eikemo. Prod: Haakon Sandøy/Norsk Film A/S.

LEVE SITT LIV (Victoria L.). Script, Dir., and Prod: Svend Wam and Petter Vennerød for Mefistofilm A/S. Phot (colour): Svein Krøvel. Players: Wenche Foss, Pål Øverland.

CARL GUSTAV OG GJENGEN (Carl Gustav and his Gang). Script: Jan Lindvik and Inge Tenvik. Dir: Ola Solum. Phot (colour): Pal Rene Roestad. Players: Frank Arne Johansen, Merethe Andersen. Prod: Regional Film A/S – Norsk Film A/S.

KRYPSKYTTERE (Poachers). Script and Dir: Hans Otto Nicolayssen. Phot (colour): Halvor Næss. Players: Jon Eivind Gulord, Hans Rotmo. Prod: Norsk Film A/S.

FOR TORS SKYLD (Friends). Script: Mathis Mathisen. Dir: Knut Andersen. Phot (colour): Bjørn Jegerstedt. Players: Jacob Ørmen, Monica Sidselrud. Prod: Norsk Film A/S.
50/50. Script and Dir: Oddvar Bull Tuhus. Phot (colour): Rolv Håan. Players: Steinar Raaen, Rune Dybedahl. Prod: Filmgruppe I A/S.
HENRYS BAKVAERELSE (Henry's Back Room). Script and Dir: Gianni Lepre. Phot (colour): Mattis Mathiesen. Players: Svein Sturla Hugnes, Roy Annar Hansen. Prod: Teamfilm A/S.

ETTERKRIGSTID (Between Wars). Script and Dir: Sølve Skagen and Malte Wadman. Phot (colour): Bahram Manocheri. Players: Hildegunn Eggen, Roy A. Hansen. Prod: Filmgruppe I A/S.

forthcoming films

SVARTE FUGLER (Black Crows). Script: Espen Haavardsholm, Lasse Glomm and János Herskó after a

VIBEKE LØKKEBERG, NINA KNAPSKOG, AND HELGE JORDAL IN *THE BETRAYAL*

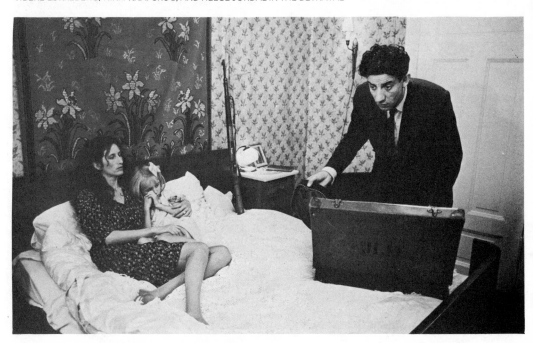

novel by Espen Haavardsholm. Phot (colour): Eling Thurmann Andersen. Players: Bibi Anderson, Bjørn Skagestad. Prod: Bente Erichsen for Marcusfilm A/S.
ELAN PROJECT No. 3. Script: Laila Mikkelsen after a novel by Arvid Hansen. Dir: Laila Mikkelsen. Phot (colour): Rolv Håan. Player: Anneli Drecker. Prod: Elan Film A/S.
PIRATENE. Script: Bjørn Erik Hanssen. Dir: Morten Kolstad. Phot (colour): Halvor Næss. Players: Lars Andreas Larsen, Per Jansen. Prod: Norsk Film A/S.
HOCKEY. Script and Dir: Oddvar Bull Tuhus. For Filmgruppe I A/S.

Focus on Norwegian Directors

Lasse Glomm, one of the owners of the small and successful Marcusfilm A/S, worked for many years as a film critic for the film magazine *Fant* before entering film production as an assistant and later manager at Norsk Film in 1973. He had completed three features prior to *Black Crows* (1982), with *Stop It!* attracting most

LASSE GLOMM DIRECTING BJØRN SKAGESTAD IN *BLACK CROWS*

VIBEKE LØKKEBERG DIRECTING NINA KNAPSKOG IN *THE BETRAYAL*

interest. He has also worked as a co-writer with Anja Breien on her film, *Next of Kin*, and with Oddvar Bull Tuhus on *Strike*, both screened in Cannes.

Vibeke Løkkeberg was known as an actress in Scandinavian films, especially in the two interesting features, *Liv* and *Exit*, directed by Pål Løkkeberg in the early Seventies. Later she started writing and directing short films, as well as TV films, about abortion and the female role as unmarried mother. Her first dramatic short, *Rain*, has much in common with her successful feature film of 1981, *The Betrayal*. Both films see life from the subjective vision of a small girl in the working class milieu of the West Coast town of Bergen, where Vibeke Løkkeberg herself comes from.

Norwegian Producers

Aprilfilm A/S
P.O.B. 52, Hovseter
Oslo 7.
Tel. (02) 17 13 75.

Centralfilm A/S
PO Box 2917 Tøyen
Oslo 6.
Tel. (02) 67 63 93.

Elan Film A/S
PO Box 6821 St. Olavs Plass
Bygdøy Alle 85
Oslo 2.
Tel. (02) 44 81 65.

Elinor Film
Wesselgate 1,
Oslo 1.
Tel. (02) 20 17 09.

EMI Produksjon A/S
Gjøbakken 9
Oslo 3.
Tel. (02) 14 74 85.

Filmforlaget A/S
P.O.B. 1810 Vika
Oslo 1.
Tel. (02) 46 83 01,
(03) 20 23 02.

Filmgruppe 1 A/S
Osterhausgaten 9
Oslo 1.
Tel. (02) 11 50 80.

A/S Fotfilm
Grønland 26
Oslo 1.
Tel. (02) 19 59 05.

Marcusfilm A/S
P.O.B. 3041 Elisenberg
Oslo 3.
Tel. (02) 44 20 60 – 44 96 03.

A/S Mefisto-film
Gyldenløvesgate 41
Oslo 2.
Tel. (02) 41 77 95.

Norsk Film A/S
Wedel Jarlsbergs vei 36
P.O.B. 4
1342 Jar.
Tel. (02) 12 10 70.

A/S Taurus
Ullernveien 42
Oslo 3.
Tel. (02) 55 98 23.

Teamfilm A/S
Keysergate 1
Oslo 1.
Tel. (02) 20 70 72.

Ås-Film A/S
P.O. Box 57
1430 Ås.
Tel. (02) 94 11 84.

Norwegian Distributors

Breien Film
Torggata 25
Oslo 1.
Tel. (02) 20 58 81.

Cinema International Corp. (CIC) A/S
Huitfeldtsgate 5
Oslo 1.
Tel. (02) 56 64 67.

Columbia-Warner I/S
Stortingsgaten 30
Oslo 1.
Tel. (02) 33 02 25.

Europafilm A/S
Stortingsgaten 30
Oslo 1.
Tel. (02) 41 07 75.

Filmco
Waldemar Thranesgate 73
Oslo 1.
Tel. (02) 20 86 68.

Fram Film
Tordenskioldsgate 2
Oslo 1.
Tel. (02) 41 46 15.

Inter-Press A/S Film
Gamle Ringeriksvei 7
1321 Stabekk.
Tel. (02) 53 64 02.

Kommunenes Filmcentral A/S
Nedre Vollgate 9
Oslo 1.
Tel. (02) 41 43 25.

Kontinentalfilm A/S
Stortingsgaten 28
Oslo 1.
Tel. (02) 41 15 17.

Kristen Filmtjeneste
Postboks 6770 St. Olavs Plass
Oslo 1.
Tel. (02) 20 77 45.

Merkur Film A/S
Fr. Stangsgate 41
Oslo 2.
Tel. (02) 56 35 67.

Norenafilm
Stortingsgaten 12
Oslo 1.
Tel. (02) 42 71 45.

Radio film A/S
Stortingsgaten 16
Oslo 1.
Tel. (02) 42 01 65.

Royal Film A/S
Stortingsgaten 28
Oslo 1.
Tel. (02) 41 94 96.

Syncron-Film A/S
Klingenberggaten 5
Oslo 1.
Tel. (02) 41 07 90.

Team Distribution and Export A/S
Keysersgate 1
Oslo 1.
Tel. (02) 20 70 72.

T & O Film A/S
Teatergaten 3
Oslo 1.
Tel. (02) 11 07 04.

Triangel-Film A/S
Pilestredet 15
Oslo 1.
Tel. (02) 20 16 47.

Other Useful Addresses

**Ministry of Cultural
and Scientific Affairs**
PO Box 8030
Oslo 1.
Tel. (02) 11 90 90.

**National Assn. of Municipal
Cinemas**
Lille Grensen 3
Oslo 1.
Tel. (02) 41 27 02.

Norwegian Filmworkers' Assn.
P.O.B. 6824 St. Olavs Plass
Office: Wesselsgt. 4 Oslo 1,
Tel. (02) 20 63 61.

Norwegian Film Council
Osterhausgate 9
Oslo 1.
Tel. (02) 11 14 07.

Norwegian Film Institute
Aslakveien 14b
P.O.B. 5
Oslo 7.
Tel. (02) 24 29 94.

**Norwegian Cinema and Film
Foundation**
Lille Grensen 3
Oslo 3.
Tel. (02) 41 27 02.

State Film Central
Schwensensgate 6
Oslo 1.
Tel. (02) 60 20 90.

Norwegian Assn. of Film Societies
Wesselsgt 4
Oslo 1.
Tel. (02) 11 42 17.

Norsk Film A/S
The Study Centre
Wessels gate 4
Oslo 1.
Tel. (02) 11 31 66.

**Association of Private Cinemas
in Norway**
Postboks 345
4801 Arendal.

Norwegian Film Centre
(Centre for Alternative
Film Distribution)
Office: Wesselsgt 4
Oslo 1
Tel. (02) 20 63 61.

State Board of Film Censors
Klingenberggaten 7
Oslo 1.
Tel. (02) 41 40 38.

**Norwegian Film & Videogram
Producers Association**
c/o Info-Film + Video A/S
PO Box 469
1301 Sandvika.
Tel. (02) 54 25 09.

**Assn. of Norwegian Film
Distributors**
P.O.B. 1812
Vika
Oslo 1.
Tel. (02) 56 64 67.

DIRECTOR OLA SOLUM AND THE CHILDREN IN *CARL GUSTAV* . . .

People's Republic of China   by Wang Wei

Even now, some six years after the fall of the Gang of Four and the resumption of its film industry, China is still traumatised by the legacy of the Cultural Revolution. It has continued to provide a rich source of material for feature films; but the deeper problem of which direction to go forward still remains unsolved. On the one hand, the Chinese film industry is faced with the need to upgrade, modernise and tackle foreign markets; on the other, powerful forces still caution against too rapid a progress. It is a problem afflicting all facets of Chinese life, not simply its film industry; but in a country accustomed to using the medium of film as both political weapon and thermometer, the Chinese film continues to be tossed around like a weathercock, often facing both directions at the same time.

For the past three years or so, there have been major advances in throwing off the Gang of Four's cultural straitjacket. Romances and melodramas, glossily filmed in a style strongly reminiscent of *wenyi pien* from Hongkong or Taiwan, have helped to cater for local needs and at least portray some of the tensions now at work in Chinese society. Indeed, a family comedy like In-Laws (*Xi ying men*) has both strong entertainment value in its own right and a measure of the good life to satisfy everyday aspirations.

The immensely popular The Legend of Tianyun Mountain (*Tianyunshan chuanqi*), glossily directed by Xie Jin, directly confronts the problem of those who "stayed true" during the Cultural Revolution and those who "sold out" but shies away from any precise definition of the two terms. The film reveals Xie Jin as one of the industry's most accomplished technicians, with an almost Sirk-like touch and a love for the colourful image; with Sang Hu, he is one of the few directors whose works measure up to international standards of presentation – although both lack the trenchancy which could make them truly great directors.

It is somehow fitting that Sang Hu's latest work should be an adaptation of Mao Dun's novel Midnight (*Ziye*) set in Thirties Shanghai. As evi-

denced by his recent Twins Come in Pairs (*Talia he talia*), Sang has lost none of the fluency of earlier works like Liang Shan-bo and Zhu Yingtai (1953), the children's film Strange Adventures of a Magician (1962), New Year Sacrifice (1956) or even the revolutionary opera version of The White-Haired Girl (1972). Foreign presentations of Chinese films have revealed the Thirties as one of the peaks of the industry at a time when it was heavily dominated by American imports) and if the Chinese industry is now returning to subjects of that era, Sang Hu is a director to provide the necessary sense of style for corrupt Shanghai life.

The largest overseas presentation so far was the massive retrospective in Torino, Italy, in late February–early March 1982. Many of the 130-odd films came directly from Peking for the event, which was attended by a sizeable Chinese delegation. Films ranged over the entire spectrum, from a couple of Twenties silents to a selection of latest production. It is unlikely that such a comprehensive retrospective of Chinese films will be seen on this scale for some time. The good was allowed to stand beside the bad, the tedious with the exhilarating; and a poll of the many who attended revealed a marked preference for works from the mid-Thirties and 1947–49.

One positive aspect of gradual liberalisation is that some co-productions have actually been going ahead rather than merely being talked about. The huge $22,000,000 co-production with Italy's RAI-TV, Marco Polo, which started shooting in July 1981 under Giuliano Montaldo, is now finished. Also under way are a co-production with the Philippines, The Sultan and the Emperor, and a $7,500,000 Japanese co-production, Unfinished Chess Match, with Daiei International, directed by Junya Sato.

Film exports are gradually rising as Chinese films get more exposure at festivals. Many are pre-PRC classics such as Street Angel, Spring River Flows East and Crossroads; others, from the Fifties and Sixties, include Two Stage Sisters and Uproar in Heaven. In 1981 China Film Export and

AMERICAN ACTOR KEN MARSHALL AS MARCO POLO (ON HORSEBACK) DURING THE SHOOTING NEAR PEKING OF *MARCO POLO*

Import Corporation exported 600 prints, 35% of which were features; some 36 features attended festivals overseas. From 1978–81 the corporation imported about 150 foreign films. Recent titles have included *The Thirty Nine Steps* (1978), *The Sea Wolves*, and *Tess*; from Hongkong have come *Father and Son* and the immensely successful *The Shaolin Temple*, actually filmed in China (see Hongkong section).

Facts and figures

The Ministry of Culture organises film production through a quota and compensation system. Annual production is about 90 pictures, with each studio given a quota. There are 11 major studios: Peking, Shanghai, Changchun, Xi'an, Emei, Pearl River, Guangxi, August 1, Zhejiang, Tianshan and the Youth Studio of the Peking Film Institute. Others include: Peking Children's Film Studio, Central Newsreel and Documentary Film Studio, Shanghai Scientific and Educational Film Studio, Hubei Newsreel and Documentary Film Studio and Central Newsreel and Documentary Film Studio. The main animation studio is Shanghai Animation Film Studio.

Each studio is run by an artistic committee which includes large numbers of Party members. Subject-matter ranges from love stories, melodramas, war films, costume dramas, operas, spy films, historical dramas and regional ethnic productions. A normal budget for a feature is about $400,000 (colour), $285,000 (black-and-white). This budget also includes the cost of about 100 prints.

In 1981 Peking Film Institute graduated 2,100 students in acting, directing, cinematography, sound recording and graphic arts. Over 2,000 rural cinemas were built during the same year.

The Ministry of Culture has given the green light to three American co-productions: *Sun Yatsen*, being prepared by Carl Foreman; *Lady and the Panda*; and an untitled Robert Wise project to star Jane Fonda and Robert Redford. Kirk Douglas has expressed interest in a project on the life of Edgar Snow.

Admissions in 1981 totalled 10,000,000,000.

Foreign festivals attended during 1981 included Cannes, Berlin, Venice, Manila, Oberhausen, Melbourne, Sydney, Hongkong and San Francisco.

FRED MARSHALL
and PENELOPE LIU

The 2nd Golden Cock Awards

Prize of Honour: *In-Laws*.
Best feature: *Neighbours*.
Best script: Zhang Xian (for *The Corner Forgotten by Love*).
Best Director: Cheng Yin (for *Xian Incident*).
Best Actor: Zhang Yan (*The Laughter in Moon Bay*).
Best Actress: Li Xiuming (*Xumao and His Daughters*).
Best Supporting Actor: Sun Feihu (*Xi'an Incident*).
Best Supporting Actress: He Xiaojie (*The Corner Forgotten by Love*).
Best Cinematography: Zhou Jixun (*Xumao and His Daughters*).
Best Special Effects: Ge Yongliang (*Li Huiniang's Revenge*).
Best Costumes: Cao Yinhua (*The True Story of Ah Q*).
Best Make-up: Wan Xizhong (*Xi'an Incident*).

recent and forthcoming films

TIANYUNSHAN CHUANQI (The Legend of Tianyun Mountain). Script: Lu Yanzhou. Dir: Xie Jin. Phot (colour, scope): Xu Qi. Players: Shi Weijian, Wang Fuli, Shi Jianlan, Zhong Xinhuo, Hong Xuemin. For Shanghai.
FATING NEIWAI (In and Out of Court). Script: Chen Dunde, Song Xuexun. Dir: Cong Lianwen, Lu Xiaoya. Phot (colour): Feng Shilin. Players: Tian Hua, Zhou Chu, Lin Moyu, Chen Peisi. For Emei.
BASHAN YEYU (Evening Rain). Script: Ye Nan. Sup. dir: Wu Yonggang. Dir: Wu Yigong. Phot (colour): Cao Weiye. Players: Li Zhiyu, Zhang Yu, Qiang Ming. For Shanghai.
DU SHINIANG (The Beautiful Courtesan). Script: Zhao Menglin, Zhou Yu. Dir: Zhou Yu. Phot (colour): Wang Jishun. Players: Pan Hong. For Changchun.
XI YING MEN (In-Laws). Script: Xin Xianling. Dir: Zhao Huanzhang. Phot (colour): Peng Enli, Cheng Shiyu. Players: Wang Shuqin, Wang Yumei, Yu Shaokang, Zhang Liang. For Shanghai.
ZHIYIN (Intimate Friends). Script: Hua Ershi. Dir: Xie Tieli, Chen Huaiai, Ba Hong. Phot (colour): Nie Jing, Ru Shuiren. Players: Wang Xingang, Zhang Yu, Ying Ruocheng.
MUMAREN (The Herdsman). Script: Li Zhun. Dir: Xie Jin. Phot (colour scope): Xu Qi. Players: Zhu Shimao, Li Xiuzhi. For Shanghai.
SANJIA XIANG (Three Family Lane). Script: Zeng Wei, Wang Weiyi, from the novel by Ouyang Shan. Dir: Wang Weiyi. Phot (colour): Wang Yunhui. Players: Sun Qixin, Ye Yating. For Pearl River.
ZIYE (Midnight). Script: Sang Hu, from the novel by Mao Dun. Dir: Sang Hu. Phot (colour): Fu Jinggong. Players: Qiu Yiren, Li Rentang, Qiao Qi.

STILL FROM *THE TRUE STORY OF AH Q*

ANOTHER STILL FROM THE SAME FILM

Philippines

by Agustin Sotto

In yet another dramatic restructuring of the Philippines' volatile film scene, President Ferdinand Marcos signed Presidential Decree no. 770, dated January 29, 1982, to create the Experimental Cinema of the Philippines (ECP). The new umbrella organisation supersedes all other existing bodies and groups. Alternative Cinema (responsible for film programming at the newly built Film Center), Film Fund (loans to deserving projects at concessional interest rates), Film Production Unit (financing and supervision of films under the ECP's aegis), Board of Standards (tax reductions to deserving films at the end of the year), Film Archives (preservation) and Manila international film festival held every January. The new organisation is chaired by Imee Marcos, daughter of the

president. The Board of Censors and the Film Academy still exist as separate entities.

The year 1982 started out with controversy. The Board of Censors was finally handed over by the military to civilian supervision under former senator Maria Kalaw Katigbak. As soon as the new censors had assumed their posts, they began a wave of indiscriminate cutting of Filipino films already bemoaned for their low level of sex and violence. The dramatic banning of *Boy Condenado* and *Schoolgirls* (for obscure reasons) created insecurity within the industry: producers refused to release completed films or begin new projects due to the censors' unclear and arbitrary guidelines. Production dropped by 40% in the first half of the year. By May, after several rounds of talks,

RICKY SANDICO SITS IN THE ELECTRIC CHAIR AS A TEST OF HIS TRUST IN THE FRATERNITY. FROM MIKE DE LEON'S *BATCH '81*

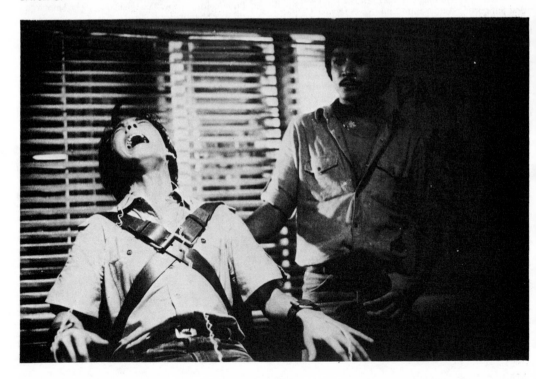

the censors relented and took a more lenient attitude. As of summer 1982 production was returning to normal.

On January 19, 1982, the first Manila international film festival finally opened, despite an accident resulting in the deaths of several workers on the new Film Center, a French boycott, and bomb threats from an American-based anti-Marcos group. The festival was criticised for its lavishness in a period of deep economic crisis, for the meagre participation of Filipino and Asian films, and for the over-emphasis given to Western product.

The objectives of the next festival are being revised along more pro-Filipino and pro-Asian lines. Participation of all Asian industries is being earnestly sought in the hope of successfully projecting an Asian image for the 1983 festival. ECP is producing two Filipino films especially for the occasion: *Himala (The Miracle)* and *Oro, plata, mata (Gold, Silver, Death)*. On June 9, 1982 the industry was saddened by the death of Betty Bantug Benitez, one of the festival organisers, in a car accident.

If the Filipino film went unheralded in its homeland, foreign festivals took up the rallying cry instead. The Nantes-based Festival of the Three Continents (December 1–8, 1981), organised by Philippe and Alain Jalladeau, successfully held a retrospective of Filipino films from 1939–81. Well received were classics like Manuel Conde's *Genghis Khan* (1950), the first Filipino film ever to take part in an international film festival (Venice, 1952) and more recent films such as Eddie Romero's *Ganito kami noon . . . paano kayo ngayon (As We Were)*, Ishmael Bernal's *Nunal sa tubig (Speck in the Water)* and Lino Brocka's films from *Tinimbang ka nguni't kulang (You Are Weighed in the Balance but Found Wanting)* to *Bona*.

The Nantes festival also gave recognition to the late director Gerardo de Leon, who died on July 25, 1981, and was described by "Cahiers du Cinéma" as "a figure of world cinema." Unfortunately, of his 70-plus films, only a few still survive. The screening of four available works showed him to be a great visual artist and a master of foreground composition. On June 12, 1982, De Leon was awarded the status of National Artist, the highest recognition given to Filipino artists.

The Philippines was also the location for many foreign productions. Peter Weir shot *The Year of Living Dangerously*, a thriller set against the downfall of Sukarno. Hongkong director Ann Hui made *The Story of Woo Viet*, about a Vietnamese refugee looking for his girlfriend sold in the brothels of Manila's Chinatown. Vilgot Sjöman's *I Am Blushing* spoofs the filming of Coppola's *Apocalypse Now* but is more concerned with investigating the state of Filipino politics: Bibi Andersson roams the islands to deliver a letter from Amnesty International to an activist who is already dead, and her search explores the myriad colours of Filipino life, from tourist-oriented festivals to sex. Pierre Rissient's fine *Five and the Skin (Cinq et la peau)* looks at a Frenchman's assimilation of Filipino culture and, instead of settling for travelogue, subtly probes the experience on many levels, from personal fantasies on women to miniessays on Filipino artists. The film derives its title from a Chinese wine which extracts the five most powerful perfumes plus the bark itself. Hence, the five senses plus the skin – Rissient's definition of art.

The year 1981 saw 179 new Filipino films and 259 foreign films shown in the Greater Manila area. Art house production was in the doldrums, with the country's top directors primarily doing commercial films. Only Mike de Leon produced two well-received pictures – *Kisapmata (In the Winking of an Eye)* and *Batch '81*. Both films were shown in the Directors' Fortnight at Cannes – the first time that two films by the same director were shown together. *Kisapmata* is based on a real-life incestuous relationship between a retired policeman and his daughter. Using the form of a thriller, Mike de Leon comments on the excesses of the close-knit family system and the over-zealous devotion to Catholic ritual. *Batch '81* exposes the activities of fraternities in Manila's universities; the mental and physical violence becomes a metaphor for the country's master/slave relationships, with allusions to the present dictatorial regime.

Other films of interest are Laurice Guillen's *Salome*, a finely directed and photographed *crime de passion* whose simplicity is obfuscated by an ingratiating *Rashomon*-like structure, and Mario O'Hara's *Bakit bughaw ang langit? (Why Is the*

VIC SILAYAN PLEADS WITH HIS DAUGHTER, CHARO SANTOS, NOT TO LEAVE THE FAMILY, IN MIKE DE LEON'S *KISAPMATA*

Sky Blue?), in which a mentally-retarded basket-ball player becomes the whipping boy for a tenement area's many prejudices.

recent films

BAKIT BUGHAW ANG LANGIT? (Why Is the Sky Blue?). Script and dir: Mario O'Hara. Players: Nora Aunor, Dennis Roldan, Alicia Alonzo. Prod: Four Seasons.
BATCH '81. Dir: Mike de Leon. Script: Mike de Leon, Racquel Villavicencio, Clodualdo del Mundo. Phot: Rody Lacap. Music: Lorrie Ilustre. Edit: Jess Navarro. Art dir: Cesar Hernando. Players: Mark Gil, Jimmy Javier, Dodo Cabasal, Ward Luarca, Ricky Sandico, Prod: MVP Pictures.
KISAPMATA (In the Winking of an Eye). Dir: Mike de Leon. Script: Mike de Leon, Racquel Villavicencio, Clodualdo del Mundo. Phot: Rody Lacap. Music: Lorrie Ilustre. Edit: Jess Navarro. Prod des: Cesar Hernando. Players: Vic Silayan, Charo Santos, Jay Ilagan, Charito Solis, Ruben Rustia. Prod: Bancom Audiovision.
KONTROVERSIAL (Controversy!). Dir: Lino Brocka.

Script: Tony Perez. Phot: Conrado Baltazar. Music: Max Jocson. Prod des: Joey Luna. Players: Gina Alajar, Charo Santos, Phillip Salvador. Prod: Four Seasons.
PLAYGIRL. Dir: Mel Chionglo. Script: Rocky Lee. Phot: Rody Lacap. Prod des: Benjie de Guzman. Music: Max Jocson. Edit: Augusto Salvador. Players: Charito Solis, Gina Alajar, Phillip Salvador, Alicia Alonzo, Joonee Gamboa. Prod: Regal Films.
SALOME. Dir: Laurice Guillen. Script: Ricky Lee. Phot: Romy Vitug. Prod des: Santiago Bose. Music: Ernani Cuenco. Edit: Efren Jarlego. Players: Gina Alajar, Johnny Delgado, Dennis Roldan, Bruno Punzalan. Prod: Bancom-Audiovision.

Useful Addresses

Manunuri ng Pelikulang Pilipino
(Philippine Society of Film Critics)
15-D San Gabriel Street
Cubao, Quezon City.

Philippine Motion Pictures Producers Association (PMPPA)
Suite 413
Regina Building
Escolta, Manila.
Movie Workers Welfare Foundation (Mowelfund)
Cultural Center of the Philippines
Manila.
Experimental Cinema of the Philippines (ECP)
Philippine International Convention Center
CCP Complex
Manila.

Manila International Film Festival (MIFF)
Philippine International Convention Center
CCP Complex
Manila.
Film Institute of the Philippines
35 Cruz Street
Santa Elena
Marikina, Metro-Manila.
National Historical Institute Film Library
National Library
Luneta, Manila.

Poland

by Kjell Albin Abrahamson

Polish feature films had both presaged and taken an active part in the country's democratisation. So the closing down of all the 2,000 or more cinemas on the *Kristallnacht* of December 13, 1981, when the military junta seized power, came as little of a surprise. The official explanation was the ban on popular assemblies. The real reason lay in the cinemas' repertoire, which had been mirroring a reality that was anathema to the junta. When they reopened a couple of months later, all they could offer Polish audiences were severely curtailed programmes, badly mauled by the censor.

The industry's Stalinists, both old and new, found the junta's strangling of the liberalisation process and internment of thousands of workers, intellectuals and artists gave them new air under their wings. Many Polish directors, with their controversial feature films and documentaries, had been forcing the pace towards greater democracy and freedom of expression. When Solidarity was set up, not only had most Polish film workers supported its demands, but nine out of ten had become members. Today a minority are trying to make themselves their mouthpiece.

Only one month after the military coup, Andrzej Wajda, chairman of the film workers' union, was fiercely attacked in the party organ "Trybuna Ludu" by film director Czesław Petelski. "Together with others in the Polish film industry," Petelski declared, "Wajda placed himself at the disposal of extremists within Solidarity."

Poland's film industry is organised in mutually competitive production groups, each with its own character. During the Solidarity period a change came over the groups, whose

leaders were now democratically elected. Two groups – Czesław Petelski's "Iluzjon" and Bohdan Poręba's "Profil" – were dissolved; both were resurrected in February/March 1982, after the junta's takeover.

There are now ten production groups, led by the following: "Aneks" (Grzegorz Królikiewicz), "Iluzjon" (Czesław Petelski), "Kadr" (Jerzy Kawalerowicz), "Perspektywa" (Janusz Morgenstern), "Profil" (Bohdan Poręba), "Rondo" (Wojciech Has), "Silesia" (Ernest Bryll), "Tor" (Krzysztof Zanussi), "Zodiak" (Jerzy Hoffman), "X" (Andrzej Wajda).

Unlike the journalists' union, the film workers' union (under Wajda's chairmanship) has not been dissolved; and the outcome of its tense negotiations with the Ministry of Culture and of its internal conflicts is hard to predict. The far-reaching plans for a reform of Poland's film industry, discussed during the Solidarity period, seem more remote than ever. One was for a clearer distribution of responsibility; another, that the production groups should themselves be in charge of all income from exports. Unlike many other industries, Film Polski has been making profits from exports to the tune of millions of dollars; but only a fraction of this has ever gone back to the production groups themselves.

Poland's economic, political and moral crisis has steadily worsened since the junta's takeover. Many directors and actors now work abroad; others have no work at all, or have taken to other occupations. Although writers, actors and directors are happy enough to work for the film industry, they are boycotting radio and TV. This is

JAN MACHULSKI (AT LEFT) IN JULIUSZ MACHULSKI'S *VA BANQUE*

the most persistent and massive of all protest actions. Those few artists who have declared their support for the junta are being treated with icy scorn and booed by audiences.

The crippling of cultural output has led to a sharp drop in theatre and cinema going. On the thirteenth of each month – the day of the junta's takeover – all theatres, concert halls, art galleries and cinemas remain empty in silent protest. "Tylko same swinie siedzą w kinie" is a phrase dating from the Nazi occupation: "Only swine go to the cinema." Anyone who goes to the cinema on the 13th hears it ringing in his ears.

While looking forward to such films as Andrzej Wajda's *The Danton Case*, Jerzy Kawalerowicz's *Austria* and Tadeusz Konwicki's *The Valley of Issa*, it seems only right to begin with Juliusz Machulski's debut work *Va Banque* (*Vabank*), a comedy-thriller set between the wars. Not unjustly, Polish films have a reputation for being a trifle heavy-handed, loaded with problems, and not easily accessible. This one, however, goes at an exhilarating *vivace con brio* pace and has a

lightheartedness and a humour, a bubbling champagne-like *esprit*, that is totally winning. In its own genre, it is a film of international class. The director's father, Jan Machulski, puts a wealth of imagination into the part of a jailbird, Kwinto by name, who decides to become a law-abiding citizen, but who first has to get his own back on a former punter, now bank manager, who once swindled him. Machulski's complex plot is the fruit of childlike playfulness and adult shrewdness. It is going to be exciting to follow the career of this talented new director. Born in 1955, he began as an actor in 1975, playing the lead in Krzysztof Kiéslowski's *Personnel*. Deservedly, *Va Banque* has been a huge success both with audiences and critics.

A most undeserved box-office success, on the other hand, was Jerzy Hoffman's *The Witch Doctor* (*Znachor*), a monstrous melodrama about a famous surgeon who loses his memory. This corny piece, first filmed in 1937 and even in those days accused of "speculating on the poverty of the masses," leaves no eye dry.

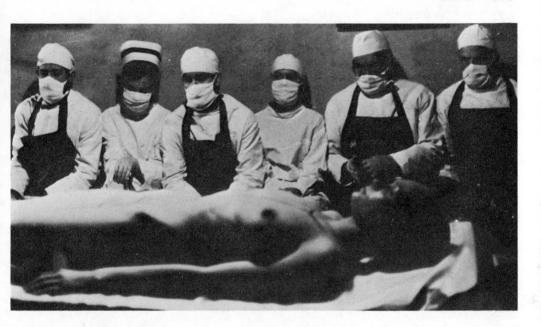

STILL FROM *ANN AND THE VAMPIRE*

One of Polish cinema's main themes in recent years had been the isolation that befalls an honourable individual in a corrupt and mendacious society – the so called "cinema of moral anxiety." Sylwester Szyszko's *Thursdays for the Poor (Czwartki ubogich)* and Roman Zaɫuski's *The Rust (Rdza)* are about, on the one hand, a young doctor and, on the other, an elderly entrepreneur who revolt against society's follies and hypocrisies. Both films make ambitious attempts to extend the range of their enquiries, both in time and space.

A non-event on the Polish film scene is that Ewa and Czesɫaw Petelski have once again flung themselves into the Second World War. This year's production is *Boldyn*, named after the despotic officer who is its main figure.

In his latest film, *Limousine*, the productive Filip Bajon, who moves with tame self-assurance in various periods, places his action in Poznań in 1939. Two brothers, with different ideologies, are the central figures. Despite its heart-rending action, the film still leaves one largely indifferent, perhaps because Bajon has overloaded his subject matter.

One film that at least is sociologically interesting is Janusz Kidawa's *Ann and the Vampire (Anna i wampir)*. A police film, it shares its western counterparts' inexhaustible admiration for the forces of law and order. The unusual thing about it, for an East European production, is that it is based on a true story about a psychopath who eluded the police for seven years, during which time he managed to murder no fewer than fourteen women.

Piotr Szulkin's *Golem* (1979) is a highly selfconscious piece of work. It has carried off several festival prizes and suggests that he is the uncrowned king of Polish SF-films. Certainly Piotr Andrejew, in his tragi-comic vision of the future, *Tender Spots (Czuɫe miejscz)*, is not a patch on him. Admittedly the film contains some brilliant passages; but for the most part it is mannered and pretentious. Szulkin's latest SF-film is entitled *The War of the Worlds – Next Century (Wojna światow – następne stulecie)*, in a country and an age poisoned with lies and hypocrisy. That the film has been banned by the censors is hardly a coincidence. Szulkin has dedicated his film to Wells

– both H. G. and Orson. And one can hear them saying: "Didn't we tell you?"

Also banned is *The Interrogation* (*Przesłuchanie*), a first film by Ryszard Bugajski. It is about a Polish prison during the height of the Stalinist terror. Krystyna Janda plays the lead.

Krzysztof Kieślowski's films are always of a high quality, but this has not prevented his two most recent products from being banned. *The Chance* (*Przypadek*) gives three different versions of a train journey that never started; *A Short Day's Work* (*Krótki dzień pracy*) is an account of the workers' revolt at Radom in 1976, as seen from the window of the local party secretary.

The list of films banned by the censor is depressingly long. Yet, even under this stranglehold, Polish cinema has a range and a brilliance shared by few other industries. If the Polish struggle for democracy is to succeed, international public opinion must be made aware of what is going on there. Here Polish cinema is of inestimable help.

KO-NO-PIEL-KA
(Konopielka)

Script: Witold Leszczyński, based on the novel by Edward Redliński. Direction: Witold Łeszczyński. Photography: Zbigniew Napiórkowski. Editing: Łucja Ośko. Music: Wojciech Karolak. Art Direction: Maciej Putowski. Players: Krzysztof Majchrzak, Anna Seniuk, Jerzy Block, Marek Siudym, Tomek Jarosiński, Joanna Sienkiewicz, Franciszek Pieczka, Anna Milewska. For "Perspektywa" Unit. 92 mins.

It is quite a while since Witold Leszczyński made the overwhelmingly beautiful *The Days of Matthew* (1968), after which he lost his way among a series of trivial films. He now makes a grandiose comeback with *Konopielka*, a film about the tree of knowledge of good and evil which overflows with warmth, insight and humour.

A young teacher (Joanna Sienkiewicz) arrives in a god-forsaken corner of the Polish countryside. She rents a room from a sullen peasant called Kaziuk (Krzysztof Majchrzak), who rules his family with a heavy hand. Kaziuk feels both

STILL FROM PIOTR SZULKIN'S *THE WAR OF THE WORLDS*

KRZYSZTOF MAJCHRZAK AS THE PEASANT KAZIUK IN WITOLD LESZCZYŃSKI'S *KO-NO-PIEL-KA*

threatened by and attracted towards the newcomer and her novel ideas. Her presence breaks down the barriers which have cut Kaziuk off from all contact with desire and passion. Previously he only found freedom in his fantasies (not least the erotic ones) but at the cost of ever greater solitude and humiliation. When he finally makes an open break with habit and tradition, he finds the whole village against him.

Any resemblances to the Russian director Andrei Mikhalkov-Konchalovsky's *The First Teacher* are merely superficial. Leszczyński is a poet who creates myths and an artist who, far from being horrified by the backward life-style of the countryside, finds it fascinating. In the same way as in *The Days of Matthew*, *Konopielka* couples Scandinavian melancholy with Slavonic emotionalism. *Konopielka* is a philosophical, religious, mythic film which, despite all its ballast, never seems artificial or speculative. Although the film's visual style is ritualistic and often stiffly framed, it is ingeniously suitable for its purpose. *Konopielka* is even shot in black-and-white – anything else

would have been unthinkable. For foreigners *Konopielka* may be as impenetrable as its title. Yet no one will be able to resist the enchanting beauty of this modern fairytale in mediaeval trappings.

KJELL ALBIN ABRAHAMSON

RYŚ
(The Smile of the Evil Eye)

Script: Stanisław Różewicz, based on the short story "The Church in Skaryszew" by Jarosław Iwaszkiewicz. Direction: Stanisław Różewicz. Photography (Eastmancolor): Jerzy Wójcik. Editing: Urszula Sliwińska. Music: Lucjan Kaszycki. Art Direction: Tadeusz Wybult. Players: Jerzy Radziwiłowicz, Franciszek Pieczka. Piotr Bajor, Ryszarda Hanin, Janusz Paluszkiewicz, Henryk Machalica, Hanna Mikuć. For "Tor" Unit. 84 mins.

The tales of Jarosław Iwaszkiewicz (1894–1980) have been the basis for some of Polish cinema's most remarkable productions: Jerzy Kawalerowicz's *Mother Joan of the Angels* (1961), Andrzej Wajda's *The Birchwood* (1970) and *The Maids of Wilko* (1979). Now yet another can be added to

JERZY RADZIWIŁOWICZ AS FATHER CONRAD, AND FRANCISZEK PIECZA AS THE CARTWRIGHT IN STANISŁAW RÓŻEWICZ'S *THE SMILE OF THE EVIL EYE*

the list: Stanislaw Różewicz's *The Smile of the Evil Eye*, based on Iwaszkiewicz's novel *The Church in Skaryszew*. The time is the Second World War, the place a little Polish town, the main character a priest. Lynx, a mysteriously precocious child, is a partisan with a bad conscience. He has been ordered to kill the town's carriage-maker, who is said to be collaborating with the Nazis. To save Lynx from everlasting damnation, Father Konrad voluntarily takes upon himself this act of terrorism – but his victim turns out to be innocent. Father Konrad wants to put an end to the devil and all his temptations – to Lynx – once and for all, but instead his bullet shatters the church's image of Christ.

Iwaszkiewicz's short story is a legend, fraught with mysticism and allusions. Różewicz's adapta-tion, though concrete, tries to convey an evasive, almost demonically intense, atmosphere. Its moral dilemma is timeless: do dogmas (political, religious, ethical) stand in the way of human action? Can anyone be good in an evil age? Can anyone take over the dilemmas of someone else's conscience? Or as Father Konrad puts it: to save a human being is much, but to save a human soul is more. To save it at the price of one's own soul – that rarely happens to anyone. This struggle between doubt and faith, between words and actions, in war-torn Poland has a superb interpreter in the actor Jerzy Radziwiłłowicz. In the film's last scene Father Konrad and the carriage-maker both go off into the woods to join the partisans. Their struggle is just.

KJELL ALBIN ABRAHAMSON

Portugal

by Fernando Duarte

The year 1981 is the year of *Francisca*, by Manoel de Oliveira, based on a book by Agustina Bessa Luís, voted best film of the year by the magazine "Celulóide" and the critics of "Cahiers du Cinéma". The year saw the opening of six new feature films in Portugal, not including *Velhos são os trapos* (*Old Rags*, 1980), by Monique Rutler, which was first shown on TV in 1980 and premiered commercially on March 13, 1981. *Kilas, o mau da fita* (*Kilas, the Bad of the Picture*), by José Fonseca e Costa, opened on February 27; *Cerro-maior*, based on a book by Manuel da Fonseca, directed by Luís Filipe Rocha, opened on April 24; *A culpa* (*The Guilt*), original story and direction by António Vitorino de Almeida, opened on May 7; *Oxalá*, by António Pedro Vasconcelos, opened on May 8; *Bom povo português* (*Portugal's Good People*), by Rui Simões, a documentary history of Portugal from April 25, 1974 to November 25, 1975, premièred on April 22 in Paris and opened in Lisbon on November 18; and *Francisca*, by Manoel de Oliveira, with Teresa Menezes as Fanny Owen, Diogo Dória as José Augusto Pinto de Magalhães and Mário Barroso as Camilo Castelo Branco, was first shown in Cannes and Venice in May and September, and opened in Lisbon on December 3.

The year 1982 has been dominated by comedy in the form of *A vida é bela!?* (*Is Life Beautiful?*), directed by Luís Galvão Teles with the comic Nicolau Breyner; the rock film *Chico fininho*, by Sério Fernandes; and the presentation in Cannes of *A ilha dos amores* (*The Island of Loves*), by Paulo Rocha, a biography of writer Venceslau de Morais set in the Orient, Macao and Japan.

The Portuguese Cinémathèque has moved to new quarters at 39 rua Barata Salgueiro, Lisbon, following a serious fire. It presents programmes at the Gulbenkian Foundation, including a complete Alfred Hitchcock retrospective and a season devoted to Portuguese director Leitão de Barros (1896–1967), director of the classic *Maria do Mar* (1930).

recent and forthcoming films

CONVERSA ACABADA (The Other One). Scr and dir: João Botelho. Phot (colour): Acácio de Almeida. Dialogue: Helena Domingos. Sets: Ana Jotta. Music: Jorge Arriaga. Sound: Joaquim Pinto and Vasco Pimentel. Edit: Manuela Viegas. Players: Fernando Cabral Martins

STILL FROM *CONVERSA ACABADA*

(*Fernando Pessoa*), André Gomes (*Mário de Sá-Carneiro*), Juliet Berto (*Helena*), Jorge Silva Melo (*Speaker*). Producer: António Pedro Vasconcelos. Production: VO Filmes. 100 mins.

The director João Botelho was born in Lamego on May 11, 1949. Film club activity in Coimbra and Oporto. In 1974 leaves fifth year of mechanical engineering to attend Cinema School of National Conservatory in Lisbon. Writes as a film critic in newspapers and founds the film magazine "M". In 1978 is co-director with Jorge Alves da Silva, of a short film, *Alexandre e Rosa*. Director of *Conversa Acabada* (*The Other One*), about writers Fernando Pessoa and Mário de Sá-Carneiro. The film is the story of their poetic meeting: texts, friendship and death. Between Sá-Carneiro's voluntary exile in Paris (October 12, 1912) and his death on April 26, 1916 (his suicide at Hôtel de Nics).

A ILHA DOS AMORES (The Island of Loves). Scr and dir: Paulo Rocha. Players: Luís Miguel Cintra (*Venceslau de Morais*), Paulo Rocha (*Camilo Pessanha*), Zita Duarte. Production: IPC and Gulbenkian Foundation.

The director Paulo Rocha was born in Oporto on December 22, 1935. Film club activity in Oporto. University. Paris, IDHEC. Assistant to Jean Renoir and

Manoel de Oliveira. Filmography: 1963: *Verdes anos*; 1966: *Mudar de vida*; 1970: *Sever do vouga*; 1971: *A pousada das chagas*.

O CRIME DE SIMÃO BOLANDAS (Simão Bolandas's Crime). Dir: Jorge Brum do Canto, based on "Raízes ocultas" (Occult Roots), a novel by Domingos Monteiro. Phot (colour): João Moreira. Players: José António Dias, Sandra Barsoti, Virgílio Teixeira, Rui Luís de Castro, Benjamin Falcão, Cunha Marques, Madalena Braga, Delfina Cruz. Prod: Arthur Bourdain de Macedo. Production: IPC.

The veteran director Jorge Brum do Canto was born in Lisbon on February 10, 1910. Film critic in newspaper "O Seculo" and in film magazine "Cinéfilo" (1929–39). Assist. of directors Leitão de Barros and Chianca de Garcia. Filmography: 1929: *A dança dos paroxismos*, experimental film; 1931–38: documentaries; 1938: *A canção da terra*; 1940: *João Ratão*; 1942: *Lobos da serra*; 1943: *Fàtima, terra de fé*; 1944: *Um homem às di reitas*; 1946: *Ladrão precisa-se*; 1953: *Chaimite*; 1962: *Retalhos da vida de um médico*; 1964: Fado corrido; 1968: *A cruz de ferro*.

DINA E DJANGO (Dina and Django). Scr and dir:

TERESA MENESES AND DIOGO DORIA IN MANOEL DE OLIVEIRA'S *FRANCISCA*

Solveig Nordlund. Photography (colour): Acácio de Almeida. Music: Paulo Brandão. Players: Maria Santiago, Luís Lucas, Benvinda Bento, Sinde Filipe, Manuela de Freitas, João Perry.

Crime thriller. In 1974 two youths – Dina and Django – murder a taxi-driver while trying to rob him; but he had only 370 escudos on him. Django was 23, Dina 17. The trial did not take place until 1977.

PASSAGEM OU A MEIO CAMINHO (Passage or the Middle of the Road). Scr and dir: Jorge Silva Melo. Players: Luís Lucas, Teresa Crawford, Glicínia Quartin, Isabel de Castro, Cremilda Gil.

Film based on the life of the the German writer Georg Buchner (1813–37), especially his activity as a political agitator and pamphleteer. Not a biopic.

UM S MARGINAL (One Marginal S). Scr and dir: José de Sá Caetano. Photography (colour): Moedas Miguel. Sound: Carlos Pinto and J. P. Jacobetty. Music: Rui Cardoso. Players: Sinde Filipe, Françoise Ariel, Diogo Dória, Joaquim Leitão, João Lagarto, Rui Morrison, Arthur Schmidt, Eurico da Fonseca. Production: Filmform.

The director José de Sá Caetano was born in 1933. Studied architecture at university, cinema at London School of Film Technique. TV and films. Director of *As ruínas no interior* (1976).

In Portugal, in the near future, preparations are being made to install along the coast a network of oceanic and solar energy plants. The ecological balance is seriously disturbed, and some animal species run away from the towns and revert to a wild state. On receiving news of his sister's death, the son of a well-known Portuguese lawyer tries to warn his father who is about to leave for an isolated place. A recent liaison with the wife of a foreign diplomat makes him take the maximum precautions so as not to be followed. After a day searching, father and son fail to meet. The father and his mistress are in an isolated house by the sea, surrounded by a pack of wild dogs.

Festivals

Four festivals will be held during 1983; the 13th festival of Figueira da Foz; a festival of *film fantastique* in Oporto; an international film festival at Espinho devoted solely to animation; and a festival devoted to children's films in Tomar.

Romania

by Manuela Cernat

Compared with the brilliance of the 1980 season, when most of the top directors were present with first-class works, the 1981 one seemed much less rewarding, partly because of the 28 features from period reconstructions to thrillers, from comedies to melodramas – stood definitely for entertainment. Even Dan Piţa, former spearhead of the new generation of directors, returned with the funny *Oil, the Baby and the Transylvanians*, the western series he started some years ago. There were full houses for *Blackmail*, in which Geo Saizescu, specialist in film comedies, handles with much humour and irony a thriller, with the part of the detective unexpectedly entrusted to a woman, the explosive middle-aged Ileana Stana Ionescu. Also unexpected was the way in which Stere Gulea's *The Castle in the Carpathians* interpreted Jules

Verne's novel. Integrating the original plot into the restless atmosphere of Nineteenth-century Transylvania oppressed by the Hapsburg Empire. Gulea deals with destinies painfully seeking their course.

In his second feature, Tudor Mărăscu – who came to cinema from a successful career in theatre and TV – firmly handled the story of a boxing champion deserted first by fame and subsequently by wife and friends, yet strong enough to give up alcoholism and start a new life for the sake of his son. Carefully avoiding the traps of melodrama, Mărăscu wittily recalls the psychological background of the boxing would as well as the social background of the so-called "obsessive" Fifties.

Also making his second feature, Nicolae Mărgineanu, formerly one of the most eminent camera-

MIRCEA DANELIUC (AT RIGHT) DIRECTING *CROAZIERA*

men of the new generation, reasserted in *Luchian*, a superb biography of one of the greatest Romanian painters (1868–1916), his unusual gift for creating a visual symphony of high aesthetic content. Backed by Călin Ghibu's sophisticated camerawork, Mărgineanu recreated on screen not only the tormented world of Luchian's splendid paintings but also the picturesque atmosphere of the Bucharest *belle époque*. Luchian was affected by paralysis but still went on painting till the very last minute of his life, with the brush tied to his fingers and his hand moved by one of his assistants.

In *Saltimbancii (The Clowns)* Elisabeta Bostan developed an impressive discourse about the artist's place in society. The film is a colourful saga of a Romanian circus family at the beginning of the century, of their ups and downs, of their dramas and sorrows and, above all, of their efforts in taming a polar bear. Up to now Elisabeta Bostan had made herself a reputation as one of the world's specialists in films for children; this time she proved that she is simply a great director, no matter what the audience she aims for.

However, if *Saltimbancii* was the top entertainment movie of the season, the top intellectual one was Mircea Daneliuc's *The Cruise* (see Focus below).

recent films

SALTIMBANCII (The Clowns). Scr: Vailica Istrate. Dir: Elisabeta Bostan. Phot (Eastmancolor): Ion Marinescu, Nicolae Girardi. Art dir: Dumitru Georgescu. Cost: Nely Merola. Music: Temistocle Popa. Edit: Iolanda Mîntulescu, Alex Petrescu. Players: Carmen Galin, Octavian Cotescu, Gina Patrichi, Adrian Vîlcu, Violeta Andrei, George Mihăiță. For Casa de Filme 5.
STEFAN LUCHIAN. Scr: Nicolae Mărgineanu, Iosif Naghiu. Dir: Nicolae Mărgineanu. Phot: Călin Ghibu. Art dir: Nicolae Drăgan. Cost: Nicolae Drăgan, Cătălina Iacob. Music: Lucian Mețioanu. Edit: Christina Ionescu. Players: Ion Caramitru, George Constantin, Maria Ploae. For Casa de Filme 3.
INVINGĂTORUL (The Winner). Scr: Dumitru Furdui. Dir: Todur Mărăscu. Phot: Valentin Ducaru. Art dir: Nicolae Schiopu. Cost: Hortensia Georgescu. Music: Dinu Petrescu. Players: Marian Culiniac, Tora Vasilescu. For Casa de Filme 1.

SANTAJ (Blackmail). Scr: Rodica Ojoc Brasoveanu, Geo Saizescu. Dir: Geo Saizescu. Phot: Nicolai Girardi. Art dir: Mircea Ribinschi. Cost: Lidia Luludis. Music: Temistocle Popa. Edit: Magareta Anescu. Players: Ileana Stana Ionescu, Sebastian Papaiani, Silviu Stănculescu, Ion Besoiu. For Casa de Filme 1.
CROAZIERA (The Cruise). Scr and dir: Mircea Daneliuc. Phot: Gabor Tarko. Art dir: Magdalena Mărăşescu. Cost: Daniela Codarcea. Edit: Maria Neagu. Sound: Horea Murgu. Players: Tora Vasilescu, Nicolae Albani, Mircea Daneliuc, Ioana Manolescu.

Focus on Mircea Daneliuc

A graduate of the Bucharest Film Institute (after an M.A. in French literature from Bucharest University), Mircea Daneliuc (b. 1943) has enjoyed a sparkling rise to the position of the present number one Romanian director. Within a few years and only four films – *Long Drive* (1975), *Special Issue* (1978), *Microphone Testing* (1980) and *The Cruise* (1981) – he has achieved the unique honour of winning unanimous praise from local and international critics and the total support of the public at large. Always an enemy of feeble conformism, he has always aimed at making people re-think. His taste for reform originated in his school short *Dus-întors (Aller-retour)*, a brilliant piece of cinema: the love game of a married woman and a young "wolf" while swimming, which ends in a struggle to avoid drowning. In his first feature, *Long Drive*, an ordinary plot of two lorry drivers and a pretty hitchhiker is turned in Daneliuc's hands into a tender, ironic insight into people's souls, beyond that everyday shield of routine gestures which often hide unhealed wounds or broken dreams. In the rather dull landscape of Romanian films of the time, *Long Drive* brought a breath of fresh air, opening the path for the long series of contemporary movies by the young directors of the Seventies. *Special Issue* raised a commonplace thriller to the level of an art movie (see IFG 1979). The following year, *Microphone Testing*, the stormy romance of a TV reporter and a flapper (see IFG 1981), was rated in Romania as one of the most exciting topical movies of the

MIRCEA DANELIUC

decade – and definitely the most original in stylistic approach.

The same concern for shaking up tired conformism is also to be found in the daring *The Cruise*, a biting parable of a boat journey organised as a reward for good conduct and good work results, for the benefit of a huge group of young people of different backgrounds and professions. Building, as always, on small details and gestures, Daneliuc X-rays with remarkable keenness a portrait of two generations – the older one, that of the organisers of the cruise, full of long-acquired inhibitions and constraints, and the younger one,

that of the cruisers, no longer willing to accept or submit to taboos of an "over-organised" life.

Most controversially received was Daneliuc's *Fox Hunting*, an ambitious version of the Seventies best-seller "Nişte ţrani" (*Some Peasants*) by Dinu Săraru, which recalls the stormy years of the speedy socialisation of agriculture. In his search for novel structures Daneliuc opts to tell the story in an anti-epic way, the film progressing not in a logical way but from the point-of-view of the various characters. Notwithstanding his less firm grasp of the subject-matter, Daneliuc's rare gift for cinema manages to provide many a fine moment.

(*Continued from page 198*)
had the backing of the Motion Picture Producers' Association of Korea, a war drama called *War Reporter's Diary*. He also made the successful *People in Darkness*, a social drama. Though much of his work has yet to be seen outside the country, Choi is a name to watch in the future.

Another successful film-maker is Lee Chang-Ho who had two smash hits in a row. His first was *Fine Windy Days*, and his latest a film called *Lovemaker*. The latter was a European-style erotic drama, with TV superstar Chung Yoon-Hee in the title role. This film is to be shown abroad at festivals and film weeks, and fits very nicely into the mould of new Korean art cinema.

Next comes director Lee Doo-Yong, who enjoyed much success with *Pee-mak (House of Death)* at Nantes. A French critic referred to it as "sheer eloquence in imagery." A master of the occult, Lee demonstrated his versatility by turning to social commentary in *The Doctor and the Woman Doctor*, which had only limited success. However, Lee next made an exciting thriller called *The Last Eye Witness*, which showed him back in form as one of the country's most promising directors.

Lee Won-So directed the unusually titled *The Small Ball Tossed by a Dwarf*. This was a powerful portrayal of a poor family and how it tries to adjust to the country's economic growth. This enabled Lee to become one of the most powerful of the new directors.

One of the past year's most successful directors, Kim Soo-Hyoung returned with three ordinary films – *Woman Has Two Faces*, *The Haughty Pretty Girl* and *Cheers! Byung Tae*. Kim returned to form with *The Man I Abandoned*, an interesting portrait of a middle-aged man who falls in love with the victim of a car accident. Another successful director was Kwon Taek-Lim, whose *Mandala (Two Monks)* received critical acclaim in France and Venice though not successful commercially. This young director also made *Tears of High School Life*, about young people, which was a commercial success.

South Korean locations are not often seen in Western films though there have been a few low-budget productions like *Escape to Seoul* with Chris Mitchum and *North of Seoul* with Jack Palance. The biggest film ever made in the country was funded by the "Moonie" cult and opened at the 1982 Cannes festival – *Inchon*. A record budget of $40,000,000 was spent over a period of 5 years, and it now looks as if the film will find its way to international screens. Terence Young's motion picture of the Korean War is one of the most elaborate war films ever made, with Laurence Olivier, Jacqueline Bisset, Richard Roundtree, the late David Janssen and Toshiro Mifune. Young used many Korean actors and technicians during location filming.

South Korea has meanwhile made its presence felt at many festivals during the past year. Large delegations of Koreans travelled abroad to increase the popularity of the Hanil film. The Motion Picture Association of Korea has gone all out to help film-makers raise standards. Manila, New Delhi, Cannes, La Rochelle, Venice, Taipei, Mannheim, Berlin, Nantes, San Sebastian and Kuala Lumpur are just some of the places which have successfully shown South Korean films.

Facts and figures

Since 1979, when the government established the Korean Public Performance Ethics Committee (a civilian organisation for the censorship of films), the committee has been in charge of censorship of domestic films as well as foreign ones. The committee consists of thirteen members chosen by the Minister of Culture and Information. The committee also rates and selects quality films in accordance with the Motion Picture Law.

The government assigns the quotas for foreign feature imports to producers who have made quality feature films. Imports of foreign cultural films are allowed without quotas, but the total usually cannot exceed ten in a year. The quota for foreign feature films is about 25 a year. Films imported are mostly from the U.S.A.

The total number of cinemas in Korea is 472. Of these 300 are in city areas, the rest scattered elsewhere. In 1979 audiences at the 300 theatres in city areas was 65,519,000 and the total income was 46,844,135,600 won. An average of one person went to see a motion picture about twice a year. Since 1970 (the beginning of the depression of the industry) the size of audiences and number

of cinemas have been decreasing and it seems this trend will continue in the Eighties.

Every production company has its own cameras, studio and other equipment as stipulated in the Motion Picture Law. Korea Film Production (a state-run film organisation) has its own processing and sound recording facilities. Motion Picture Promotion Corporation has up-to-date recording equipment, processing facilities, editing equipment and a special effects studio. All these facilities are used by producers at cost charge. There are also four processing companies, two sound recording companies for feature films, and several small processing and sound recording companies.

STILL FROM CHOI WON'S *INVITED PEOPLE*

Production Companies

Dae Yang Film Co.
P.O. Box 7513
58-1 Kyonam-dong
Jongro-ku, Seoul.

Dae Yung Films Co.
36-3, 5-ka, Choongmoo-ru
Chung-ku
Seoul.

Dong-A Cinema Corp.
211 Sejong-ro
Jongro-ku
Seoul.

Dong-A Exports Co.
P.O. Box 2268
120-1, 1-ka, Changchoong-dong
Chung-ku
Seoul.

Dong Hyuep Corp.
P.O. Box 9005
41-7 Dongja-dong
Yongsan-ku
Seoul.

Film Korea,
3-236 Hyochang-dong
Yongsan-ku
Seoul.

Han Jin Enterprises Co.
62-15, 3-ka, Pil-dong
Chung-ku
Seoul.

Han Lim Cinema Corp.
98 Waryong-dong
Jongro-ku
Seoul.

Hap Dong Films Co.
P.O. Box 1535
59-7 Kwan Soo-dong
Jongro-ku
Seoul.

Hwa Chun Trading Co.
Bowon Bldg.
490, 5-ka, Jong-ro
Jongro-ku
Seoul.

Hwa Poong Industrial Co.
130-30, 3-ka, Namsan-dong
Chung-ku
Seoul.

Hyun Jin Film Co.
P.O. Box 1251
269 Chungjin-dong
Jongro-ku
Seoul.

International Movie Co.
801 Ho Kamri Bldg.
64-8, 1-ka, Taipyong-ro
Chung-ku
Seoul.

Nam-A Pictures Co.
98-78 Woonyee-dong
Jongro-ku
Seoul.

Sam Yung Films Co.
33-4, 3-ka, Choongmoo-ro
Chung-ku
Seoul.

Se Kyoung Enterprise
P.O., Box 4108
69-6, 2-ka, Jeo-dong
Chung-ku
Seoul.

Shin Han Art Film Co.
59-7, 3-ka, Choongmoo-ro
Chung-ku
Seoul.

Southern Asia Enterprises Co.
P.O. Box 2552
Seoul.

Tai Chang Enterprises Co.
P.O. Box 3460
146-14 Sangrim-dong
Chung-ku
Seoul.

Woo Jin Films Co.
56-24, 3-ka, Choongmoo-ro
Chung-ku
Seoul.

Woo Sung Enterprises Co.
56-24, 3-ka, Choongmoo-ro
Chung-ku
Seoul.

Yun Bang Films Co.
28-9 Mook-jung-dong
Chung-ku
Seoul.

Associations

Federation of Theatre Owners in Korea
411 Central Youth Bldg.
27-1, Soopyo-dong
Chung-ku
Seoul.

Film Distributors Association
59-8, 3-ka, Choongmoo-ro
Chung-ku
Seoul.

Senegal

by Lyle Pearson

In a race for *auteurs* a national cinema may take a back seat to a director who has made his mark on the international scene, as with Ingmar Bergman in Sweden and Satyajit Ray in India. In small, impoverished Senegal, the Western-most country in Africa (independent from France since only 1960, with a population of 4,000,000, one-fifth that of Afghanistan in a land area one-third its size) similar effects have been even more negative: they almost wiped out cinema completely.

The first Black African feature film is certainly by Ousmane Sembene, either his 1966 fifty-minute *La noire de . . . (The Black Girl from . . .)* or his 1968 true feature length *Mandabi (The Money Order)*. But in the same years several other Senegalese directors were beginning to make films, usually short, some in 16mm and some in 35mm. The first Black African cineaste was really Pauline Vieyra, whose *Afrique sur Seine (Africa on the Seine)* was made while he was an IDHEC student in Paris a year or two before Sembene's first short film; it is considered by Georges Sadoul as the first true Black African film. Other Senegalese directors of the late Sixties and early Seventies included Djibril Diop Mambetty, Mahama Traore, Tidane Aw, Momar Thiam, Thierno Sow, Africa's first female director Safi Faye, and perhaps the only director of a feature film in Senegal since Sembene's 1977 *Ceddo (The People)*, Babacar Samb. (Sarah Maldoror does not really qualify as an African director as she is from the Caribbean island of Martinique.)

To be sure, it was not entirely the *auteur* policy that set back what was in 1970 the most unusual cinema movement in the world – the Senegalese government helped. By 1974, when Sembene completed his hit *Xala (Impotence)*, many of these directors had also made feature films but unlike Sembene most of them worked in 16mm; Sembene, Traore and Samb were among the most socially engaged. Both Traore's *Lambaaye* (the name of a resort town), an improvisation on Gogol's *The Inspector General*, and Samb's *Codou* (the name of a girl) were shown at the semi-annual Carthage Cinema Days in Tunis in

1972. *Codou*, in 35mm, black-and-white, concerns a young woman who goes insane after finding certain African rituals distasteful: modern psychiatric practices fail to return her to sanity but older African methods do. Samb said of *Codou* at that time.

"Each time someone has tried to graft a culture on our own, it has been a failure. We have our feet in the middle ages and our head in the modern world. To want access to the modern world without taking account of the middle ages is no more viable.

"In my film, I affirm that it is necessary to assume one's own culture to gain access to the modern world."

This thought was expressed well in *Codou*, and it remains one of the major concerns of Black African cinema – the value of African tradition versus the imposed culture of Europe on a people who do not understand that culture. Although Traore (who often satirised Sembene), Samb, Sembene and the rest weren't solving this problem they were stating it clearly in a variety of styles ranging from knockabout farce to objective dissections of mental processes. This was the golden period for cinema in Black Africa and possibly the most important cinema movement of the last two

STILL FROM *JOM*

BABACAR SAMB DIRECTING *JOM*

decades. Oumarou Ganda was active in Niger, Philippe Mory in Gabon and, among others, in Nigeria Ola Balogun was beginning to make a mark. In *Film Quarterly* for Spring of 1973 I compared Traore to Paul Morrissey – their work seemed parallel in technique, the one as engaging as the other in its originality.

But something ruinous happened in 1973, probably with no ill intent. Senegal, realising its new cinema industry was in disarray, nationalised it. In late 1973 Traore and others, with government loans, made their first (and only) 35mm films. (Samb, occupied with other duties, did not begin another feature film until 1977.) Partly now also because of an automatic censorship factor operating as script approval, and disapproval of criticism of Islam at African festivals (the other festival important for African cinema is in Ouagadougou, in Upper Volta), and because there simply is no distribution network in Africa controlled by Africans, most of these new 35mm Senegalese features failed financially. It is possible that they were also not quite so good as the earlier films: Traore's feature, *N'Gangane* (*Student*) while as caustic as *Lambaaye*, also seemed a little emptier. In any case no Senegalese director has gone back to 16mm and

apparently few have made features since Sembene completed *Ceddo*. Not until Samb completed his second feature, *Jom* (*Dignity*), in 1982; although it is not as accomplished a film as *Ceddo*, it updates the concerns of Black African cinema politically.

Jom, which also means the origins of virtues, courage and respect, begins in 1978, when a strike occurs in a factory. The strikers are supported by Khali, a troubadour, who tells them tales of *girot*, or the African past, in flashbacks to the turn of the century, on the fight against colonialism. As the strikers organise a march Khali addresses them, "I say that riches as much as poverty can bring about *jom*, and it does not belong to any one person." Political struggle and faith in *jom* and *girot* are mixed, says Samb, revising the comments he made at the time of *Codou*: here he affirms a right to strike through the analogy of legitimate struggle against repressive colonial regimes. This appears almost as an eternal statement, even a principle, in relation to the history of Senegalese cinema since its origin around 1968.

Jom skips from period to period, rather than actually mixing periods as Sembene did so effectively on the soundtrack of *Ceddo* by alternating traditional African music and modern jazz. The camera remains rather stationary in *Jom*, lacking the mobility of Traore at his most daring. But *Jom* has its fine moments, particularly the languid Victorian ladies – all of them black – with parasols, strolling past horse carriages, perhaps with an intended sense of immobility about them. There is an effectual use of pastel colours throughout.

Jom should be shown widely (it has already been to the Third World Film Festival in Paris) for no new Senegalese appears about to complete a feature, Ganda of Niger has died prematurely of a heart attack, and Balogun in Nigeria has been slowed by the recent drop in world oil prices. Sembene's co-production with West Germany may not be completed until late this year.

Jom is, if by default, the best Senegalese film of 1982. It is refreshing. It is possibly also the only Senegalese feature film of the year.

South Africa

by Lionel Friedberg

Younger film-makers certainly seem to be coming to the fore in what until now has been a very staid, unexciting and boringly predictable industry in South Africa. Despite great difficulties in raising finance for films, and equally great difficulties in getting films released, many fresh and imaginative talents are emerging. Helena Nogueira's feature-documentary, *Fugard's People*, is a penetrating examination of the work of Athol Fugard, South Africa's most internationally respected play-wright. Featuring Athol Fugard, Yvonne Bryce-land, Marius Weyers, Sandra Prinsloo, Bill Curry and Judy Vivier, the film contains numerous interviews and clips from Fugard's films and plays, including his recent *Statements after an Arrest under the Immorality Act*, in which Sandra Prins-loo gives one of the most stunning performances of her career. Miss Nogueira deserves much respect and acknowledgement for this, her first attempt at a feature film.

Recognition is also due to Kevin Harris for his hour-long documentary, *This We Can Do for Justice and for Peace*, which he directed for the South African Council of Churches. To quote Mr. Harris, the film was made as "a cry for justice in the face of apartheid, and is a desperate plea for change to ensure the prospect of a peaceful South African future." The controversial film was origi-nally banned by the Publications Control Board but after certain minor cuts were made the film was eventually allowed to be shown to the general public. This was largely due to Harris's tenacious fight against the P.C.B.'s ruling. The film is a bold attempt to honestly reflect the political realities of this country, and the tasteful and sensitive manner in which it was handled heightens the film's credibility and it is in no way offensive to anyone. It is hoped that it will stand as an example of how pertinent and controversial topics can be trans-lated to the screen, and it will be interesting to see whether anybody else is going to be bold enough to follow in Harris's trailblazing footsteps!

Awake from Mourning is another hour-length documentary worthy of mention. Directed by Chris Austin, the film was made in memory of the black children who died during the 1976 Soweto riots, and is about the self-help movement known as the Maggie Magaba Trust which was started by four black women to aid the development, self-respect and dignity of women in general within the various black communities of South Africa. A compelling and remarkable film, *Awake from Mourning* transmits its message with impressive restraint.

Jans Rautenbach's much-awaited *Blink Ste-faans*, a romantic comedy featuring Regardt van den Berg and Jana Cilliers, was released towards the end of 1981. Rautenbach, a truly gifted and original film-maker, now makes less films than he used to in previous years, and it is hoped that we shall be seeing his work more regularly in future. Daan Retief's *Beloftes van more (Promises from Tomorrow)* is a delicate love story with a hospital setting, and includes some good performances by Elize Lizamore, Mieder Olivier and Magda Beukes. *Nommer asseblief (Number Please)*, directed by Franz Marx, was a most successful comedy film inspired by the locally produced television series of the same name. At the time of writing, a sequel was already being planned. John Hookham's *Sky Blue* was due for completion during the middle of this year. Based on the life of Hugh Dent, the young author-artist who lived in Natal and helped start the now legendary Wilder-ness Leadership Schools, *Sky Blue* features Ian Roberts as Hugh Dent, and Wilson Dunster, Danny Keogh, Barry Trengrove, Elise Cawood, Nomse Nene and Timmy Kwebalana in major roles.

Dirk de Villiers's enterprising new production company, C Films, in Cape Town, has pioneered film making of a different sort. The company has already completed work on its first all-puppet production. Utilising sophisticated electronics, the puppets are remotely controlled and are amazingly lifelike. *Interstar*, a science-fiction series for tele-vision, was also completed earlier this year, and an ambitious series based on African myths, legends and folklore will be completed by August. A separate division within the company is concentrating on animated children's films utilising purely linen, felt and cotton cut-outs, and another department specialises in clay and plasticine animation. Under the expert attention of young Romanian immigrant, Ted Berendson, new techniques and systems have been developed for this challenging field of production and *Dr. Clayman*, a 13-part series for television is due for completion later this year. Cape Town has always been a centre for interesting and noteworthy experimental theatre, music and dance, and it is gratifying to see that a similar vitality and freshness are now being manifested in the professional film industry there.

Most of the country's production output is now geared to serving the S.A.B.C's two television channels, and with a third channel going on the air in January 1983 most of South Africa's technical and creative talents will be hard pressed to ensure a constant flow of local programming, which now amounts to approximately 60% of all the material televised. The feature film industry has experienced a drastic decline in production during the past twelve months and even the more attractive benefits offered by the government's restructured film subsidy system has not yet proved sufficiently enticing to lure investors back to the feature fold. Apart from this lack of interest and investment, the situation has been further worsened by the prevailing general economic slump, the fall in the international gold price and a spiralling inflation rate. Creatively, however, the industry still contains within its grasp a tremendous amount of promise and potential. Talented writers such as André Brink, Michael McCabe, John Cundill, Nadine Gordimer, Alan Paton, Ahmed Essop, Lionel Abrahams, Barney Simon, Adam Small, Pieter-Dirk Uys, Johan Beukes, Tony Fridjohn and many others are writing prolifically for other media and the cinema has yet to draw upon this extraordinarily rich source of material.

It is anachronistic to see the box-office success of a film like Michael Raeburn's excellent *The Grass Is Singing* or Bruce Beresford's *Breaker Morant*, both of which concerned South African subjects, and yet nothing approximating these two films have yet been made within South Africa. Many local film-makers gaze longingly at the Australian film industry and forlornly wonder why a similarly successful situation has not yet been developed here. Wherein lies the problem? It is not easy to find the answer, but if South Africans are ever going to make feature films acceptable on the world market they are going to have to do some very serious probing and soul-searching to find the magical key. The blame cannot be laid entirely at the feet of the investors, and it is the film-makers themselves who are going to have to find the major part of the solution to their ever-growing frustration.

Criticism has been levelled at various sectors of the industry, but one section that has consistently been overlooked are the film critics. They perhaps can do much to bring about a new, dynamic and quality-conscious film industry. On the whole, film criticism in South Africa is of an appallingly low standard. It is all very well for critics to write eloquently in their respective journals and newspapers and damn, pan and slate almost every local film they see with a smug stroke of their pen, while all too infrequently offering anything in the form of *constructive* criticism. Few critics know anything about film-making anyway, and it may well be time for the various creative and technical associations to get together to offer a crash course in film aesthetics, technique and production to those self-styled "critics" who sit in judgement of that for which many of them are obviously totally unqualified.

On a more positive note, film distributors have done very well during the past twelve months. Approximately 600,000 admission tickets are sold every week at the country's 480 four-walled cinemas and 140 drive-in theatres. The tax on cinema tickets was finally abolished by Finance Minister Owen Horwood during his Budget Speech presented to parliament in March. While this does not necessarily mean that admission prices will be reduced it will at least allow distributors and theatre owners to maintain their very high standards. South Africa can undeniably boast to have some of the finest cinemas in the world, most of which offer a superlative standard of projection, sound reproduction, comfort and cleanliness.

Production facilities – particularly in the Johannesburg area – are constantly being expanded and improved. Irene Film Laboratories have opened a second processing laboratory and optical effects facility in the city, and S.A. Film & T.V. Centre recently opened additional sound mixing studios and shooting stages. With all these facilities and a film industry with a solid and sophisticated infrastructure it is both infuriating and lamentable that South Africa just does not seem able, competent or motivated to produce the kind of films that are expected of it. Who knows? Miraculously and hopefully we *may* be able to report differently next year.

Spain
by José Luis Guarner

It does not look as though 1981 was a vintage year for Spanish cinema. However, it will go down on record as the year of the greatest Spanish money-making film in history. *El crimen de Cuenca* (*Cuenca's Crime*), by Pilar Miró, was seen – according to official sources – by 1,972,000 people, the overall box-office take amounting to 370 million pesetas (about $4 million). The long ban imposed on the film, and the threat of military proceedings against Ms. Miró, have played a decisive role in that success, which has exceeded that of the American hits of the year (*Superman II, The Blue Lagoon, Raiders of the Lost Ark*). After *Gary Cooper que estás en los cielos* (*Gary Cooper Who Art in Heaven*), Ms. Miro has just finished *Hablamos esta noche* (*Tonight We Talk*), a movie dealing with the crisis in the life of a nuclear engineer who breaks with his female partner, finds a new woman, and lives through an ethical and professional conflict.

According to figures from the Ministry of Culture, the production of films increased during 1981: 137 features, the highest level for ten years. Quality, however, has not run alongside quantity. Most of the ambitious productions of the year have proved disappointing, whether the work of seasoned directors, or others having recently joined the profession. Among them, Carlos Saura's *Dulces horas* (*Sweet Hours*), Jaime de Armiñán's *En Septiembre* (*In September*), Manuel Summers's *Tó el mundo es güeno* (*Everybody Is Good*), Antonio Mercero's *La Próxima estación* (*The Next Season*), José Luis Garcí's *Begin the Beguine*, Carles Mira's *Jalea Real* (*Royal Jelly*), Jordi Cadena's *Barcelona Sur* (*Barcelona South*), Cayetano del Real's *La Cripta* (*The Crypt*), Juan Antonio Gonzalo's *Demasiado para Gálvez* (*Too Much for Gálvez*), Alberto Bermejo's *Vecinos* (*Neighbours*), etc. Also rather disappointing was *Tac-Wac*, the first Spanish feature by Luis Alcoriza, one of the main collaborators of Buñuel in México. On paper, the most interesting project of the year, *Reborn*, by Bigas (*Bilbao*) Luna, met with a lukewarm reception at the San Sebastián Festival, and has yet to be released.

A characteristic of an industry in transition was, for yet another year, a considerable number of new directors. The year's most intriguing, though controversial, debut was that of Oscar Ladoire, script-writer and star of *Opera Prima*, the sleeper of Spanish cinema in 1980, with *A contratiempo*, an unusual road movie combining *Messidor, Lolita, Viaggio in Italia*, and *I Was a Male War Bride* among others. Joan Minguell stands out among other new names with *La batalla del porro* (*The Joint's Battle*), the third Spanish hit of the season.

HILDE VERA AND VICTORIA ABRIL IN *LA CASA DEL PARAISO*

1982 may, after all, be a stimulating year for the domestic cinema. Among films recently completed are several promising titles: Fernando Trueba's *Chicho, o mientras el cuerpo aguante* (*Chicho, Or As Long as the Body Can Stand It*) Roberto Bodegas's *Corazón de papel* (*Paper Heart*), Javier Aguirre's *Perra vida* (*A Dog's Life*), and Pedro Almodovar's *Laberinto de pasiones* (*Labyrinth of Passions*). And shooting has begun on new films by Berlanga – *Nacional 3* (*National 3*), which includes his characters from *The National Rifle* and *National Heritage* – and Gutierrez Aragon – *Demonios en el jardín* (*Devils in the Garden*).

But the most fascinating project of the year is *Victoria: la gran aventura d'un poble* (*Victoria: The Great Adventure of a Nation*), by the Catalonian film-maker, Antoni Ribas, previously known for *The Burnt Town*. It endeavours to draw a picture (in three films with a total duration of eight hours) of the social and political life in Barcelona in the three first days of June 1917, which preceded a bloody general strike. After 150 days of shooting, neither the film is finished, nor its financing completed. To cover the budget, the director has already placed tickets for the film on sale, a method not used in world cinema since Jean Renoir's *La Marseillaise*.

At the industrial level, the year's event is the commencement of a policy of co-production between film producers and Spanish television (RTVE), similar to that being practised in Italy and West Germany. RTVE has invested 700 million pesetas (about $70 million) in various projects of series and feature films. Among the features already released is Francesco Betriu's *La Plaça del Diamant* (*Diamond Square*), a disappointing adaptation of a very good novel by Merce Rodoreda; it is to be screened later as a mini-series in four parts. RTVE has also produced Mario Camus's *La Colmena* (*The Beehive*), one of the most important Spanish novels, written in 1950 by Camilo José Cela, about Franco's Madrid of the Forties. In the process of shooting is Antonio Betancor's *Crónica del Alba* (*Chronicle of Dawn*), from the excellent book by the late Ramón Sender. It may be objected that this policy, strongly based on literary works, may favour a *cinéma de qualité*, cold and impersonal. But for the time begin it allows Spanish film-makers to carry out their most important projects, both in terms of ambition and budget, for a long time.

ASESINATO EN EL COMITE CENTRAL
(Murder in the Central Committee)

Script and Direction: Vicente Aranda, from a novel by Manuel Vázquez Montalbán. Photography (colour): José Luis Alcaine. Players: Patxi Andion, Victoria Abril, Héctor Alterio, Conrado San Martín, José Vivó. Produced by Carlos Durán and José Antonio Pérez Giner for Morgana Films-Warner Española.

Aranda has distinguished himself in his recent films by the elegance with which he succeeds in producing personal works starting from rather sensationalist premises. This time it is a polished thriller, in the realm of political fiction, built around what might happen in Spain if the Secretary General of the Communist Party were murdered at a meeting of the Central Committee. As the Party mistrust the State Police, a very peculiar private eye of previous leftist affinities is hired. Aranda has concocted a double line of inquiry: to find out, not

ABOVE RIGHT: INSPECTOR VERSUS PRIVATE EYE IN THE SAME FILM

BELOW: VICTORIA ABRIL AS A COMMUNIST MILITANT IN *ASESINATO EN EL COMITE CENTRAL*

A RALLY OF SPANISH FASCISTS IN MADRID, IN *DESPUES DE* . . .

who the murderer is, but who are, what are, today's Communist militants. The director achieves a sarcastic documentary on Madrid, capital of Spain, and a satire on the State Police, such as has not been seen previously in the Spanish cinema. And the plot is used as a platform for an indirect comment on political disillusionment.

JOSE LUIS GUARNER

DESPUES DE . . .
(After . . .)

Script and Direction: Cecilia and José Juan Bartolomé. Photography: José Luis Alcaine (colour). Produced by P. C. Ales SA and Rafael Carbonell.

The subject of this unusual documentary is what has happened in Spain since Franco. The political transition is the main theme. It lasts three hours and is shown in two parts. In the first segment, the characters, treated always in groups, are like the chorus in a tragedy: the *leit-motiv* is the changing of hope to disillusion of those who feel that changes are neither sufficient nor apparent; the other face of disillusion is presented by those who, succumbing to the nostalgia of Francoism, disown democracy and demand a return to the past. The second segment, more classical in structure, analyses the crisis in Spanish reform, the erosion of political parties, the unease of the militants, the escalation of terrorism, the uncertainty of the Army. The shooting of this material began in 1979 and was completed in January 1981. The military coup of February has enhanced its remarkable value as a documentary. But this controversial film has scarcely been shown, and seems to have touched an Establishment nerve – the legal State grant accorded to all Spanish movies has been refused.

JOSE LUIS GUARNER

EMILIANO REDONDO AND VICTORIA ABRIL IN *LA CASA DEL PARAISO*

LA CASA DEL PARAISO
(The House of Paradise)

Script: Santiago San Miguel, R. L. Picón, Angel Guana. Direction: Santiago San Miguel. Photography (colour): Hans Burmann. Players: Victoria Abril, Tina Sainz, Perla Vonasek, Emiliano Redondo, Hilda Vera, Gustavo Rodríguez. Produced by Producciones Zeta (Barcelona)/ Films 80 C.A. (Caracas).

A group of men and women live in voluntary confinement within a strange mansion, an almost Sartrian *huis clos*. Its owner is a mysterious character who knows the past of each member of the group, and exerts a despotic hold over them. The arrival of a visitor, a young and attractive woman, unleashes tensions and violence among the repressed inhabitants of the house. The decor and circumstances, midway between realism and allegory, are typical of an Iberian tradition established by Buñuel (and later imitated by Saura). San Miguel, a Basque film-maker residing in Venezuela, succeeds in giving the film a brilliantly forceful and personal treatment, sharing the aggressiveness of Buñuel, but rejecting the simplification of symbol customary in Saura's work. One of the few really interesting productions of the year, and only the second feature by its director.

JOSE LUIS GUARNER

new and forthcoming films

A CONTRATIEMPO (On the Offbeat). Script: Oscar Ladoire, Fernando Trueba. Dir: Oscar Ladoire. Phot (colour): Angel Luis Fernández. Players: Oscar Ladoire, Mercedes Resino, Paco Lobo, Beatriz Elorrieta, Juan Cueto, Gonzalo Suárez. Prod: Opera Films S.A.
LA BATALLA DEL PORRO (The Joint's Battle). Script: Francesco Bellmunt, Joan Minguell, Miguel Sanz, Juanjo Puigcorbé. Phot (colour): Tomás Pladevall. Players: Victoria Abril, Paul Naschy, Joan Borrás, José María Cañete, Jaume Sorribas. Prod: Profilmar PC, Producciones Zeta S.A., Germinal Films.
BEGIN THE BEGUINE. Script and dir: José Luis Garcí. Phot (colour): Manuel Rojas. Players: Antonio Ferrandis, Encarna Paso, José Bódalo, Agustín González. Prod: Nickel Odeon S.A.

LA CRIPTA (The Crypt). Script: Eduardo Mendoza, Cayetano del Real, Francisco Suirana. Dir: Cayetano del Real. Phot (colour): Jaume Peracaula. Players: José Sacristán, Rafaela Aparicio, Blanca Guerra, Carlos Lucena, Marta Molins. Kaktus PC, Fígaro Films S.A. (Barcelona)/Fígaro Mex (México).

CHICHO O MIENTRAS EL CUERPO AGUANTE (Chico, or As Long as the Body Can Stand It). Script and dir: Fernando Trueba. Phot (colour): Angel Luis Fernández. Players: Chicho Sánchez Ferlosio. Prod: Opera Films S.A.

DULCES HORAS (Sweet Hours). Script and dir: Carlos Saura. Phot (colour): Teo Escamilla. Players: Assumpta Serna, Iñaki Aierra, Alvaro de Luna, Jacques Lalande. Prod: Elías Querejeta PC (Madrid)/Les Productions J. Roitfeld (Paris).

EN SETIEMBRE (In September). Script: Jaime de Armiñan, Ramón de Diego. Dir: Jaime de Armiñan. Phot (colour): Teo Escamilla. Players: Carmen de la Maza, Amparo, Baró, María Massip, María Luisa Merlo, Paula Martel. Prod: A. Punto E.L.S.A.

FUNCION DE NOCHE (Late Performance). Script: Josefina Molina, José Sámano. Dir: Josefina Molina. Phot (colour): Teo Escamilla. Players: Lola Herrera, Daniel Dicenta. Prod: Sabre Films S.A.

JALEA REAL (Royal Jelly). Script and dir: Carles Mira. Phot (colour); Fernando Arribas. Players: Mario Pardo, Berta Riaza, Mapi Sagaseta, Luis Ciges, Joan Monléon. Prod: Lima PC and Nickel Odeon S.A.

LABERINTO DE PASIONES (Labyrinth of Passions). Script and dir: Pedro Almodóvar. Phot (colour): Angel Luis Fernández. Players: Imanol Arias, Cristina Sanchez Pascual, Ana Trigo, Concha Gregory, Cecilia Roth, Fabio de Miguel. Prod: Musidora S.A.

LA LEYENDA DEL TAMBOR (The Legend of the Drum). Script and dir: Jordi Grau. Phot (colour): Fernando Arribas. Players: Andrés Carcía, Mercedes Sampietro, Jorge Sanz, Álfredo Mayo. Prod: Nuevo Cine S.A. (Madrid)/Conacine (México).

LA PLAÇA DEL DIAMANT (Diamond Square). Script: Gustau Hernández, Benet Rossell, Francesc Betriu. Dir: Francesc Betriu. Phot (colour): Raúl Artigot. Players: Silvia Munt, Lluis Homar, Joaquim Cardona. Prod: Televisión Española S.A.

LA PROXIMA ESTACION (Next Season). Script: José A. Rodero, Horacio Valcárcel, Antonio Mercero. Dir: Antonio Mercero. Phot (colour): José Luis Alcaine. Int: Alfredo Landa, Lola Herrera, Carmen de la Maza, Agustín González, Cristina Marcos. Prod: Bridas S.A. de Cinematografia.

TAC TAC. Script and dir: Luis Alcoriza. Phot (colour): Carlos Suárez. Players: Amparo Soler Leal, Héctor Alterio, Beatriz Elori, Fiorella Faltoyano, Angel Alcázar. Prod: Películas Trío S.A. (Madrid)/Alcion Films (México).

TO EL MUNDO ES GÜENO (Everybody is Good). Script: Manuel Summers, Guillermo Summers. Dir: Manuel Summers. Phot (colour): Antonio Cuevas Jr. Players: No professionals. Prod: Kalender S.A., Paraguas Films, and Lima S.A.

Sri Lanka

by Amarnath Jayatilaka

For the first time since the present government came to power five years ago, President J. R. Jayawardhana (under whose purview is the National Film Corporation) met local film producers on March 23, 1982, to discuss their problems. This meeting followed representations made by popular film star Gamini Fonseka.

Fonseka presented a fourteen-point programme, drafted by the eminent film-maker Lester James Peries, which outlined proposals for the encouragement of Sri Lankan cinema. The proposals were as follows:

☐ An increase of 25–50% on the ticket prices of all foreign films.

☐ The extra revenue to form the basis of a film production fund to produce local films.

☐ A minimum 33⅓% subsidy (not a loan) for productions.

☐ Alternatively, 33⅓% of the production costs of a film as prize money for the ten best films of the year, with the legal stipulation that the money is ploughed back into production.

☐ A reduction in customs duties on film equipment (e.g. raw stock, now at 50% duty, should be reduced to 5% as in the past).

☐ The immediate restoration of the extra 5% for fifth-circuit films.

☐ The restoration of publicity as a free service (up to a total R 25,000) by the NFC.

☐ A rebate either of the entertainment tax on quality films or from tickets sold on all locally produced films.

☐ The liberalisation of the censorship code to allow expression of political dissent, social and political criticism and the treatment of sexual matters.

☐ Much greater discipline imposed on exhibitors who kill local films by sabotage, bribery, under-

AN

Historical Relation

Of the Island

CEYLON,

With an ACCOUNT of the Detaining
in Captivity the AUTHOR and divers other
Englishmen now Living there, and of the
AUTHOR's Miraculous ESCAPE.

STILL FROM *ARUNATA PERA*, DIRECTED BY AMARNATH JAYATILAKA

hand dealing and open violation of the basic rights of audiences. Cinemas with sub-standard equipment should also be penalised.

□ Rupavahini should devote 20% of its air-time to Sinhala made-for-TV films, such as half-hour serials and one-hour featurettes.

□ The establishment of a benevolent fund for artists and of insurance and social security for all film industry workers.

□ The modernisation of studios and the abolition of antiquated equipment. Even the GFU and NFC studios have ruined soundtracks at great cost to producers and to the total indifference of studio management.

After talks with the film delegation, the president instructed well-known film-maker D. N. Nihalsinghe, former general manager of the film corporation, to submit a report on the shortcomings of the local film industry. Having agreed to consider the fourteen-point programme, the president said he would meet film industry personnel for further talks after Nihalsinghe's report was submitted. Before the end of the present government's term of office in July 1983, a comprehensive scheme is expected to be implemented to develop the local cinema.

Focus on Sumitra Peries

Sumitra Peries is the first woman in Sri Lanka to gain a reputation as a serious film-maker. Having trained in London and Paris, she joined the celebrated Lester James Peries while he was making his second film, *Sandesaya*, in 1960. She later married him and was editor on almost all his films. Sumitra's first film was based on the popular novel *Gehenu lamai* (*The Girls*) and was shown at many festivals. Her second film, *Ganga Addara* (*River Bank*), was a big commercial hit. Her current film, *Yahalu yeheli* (*Friends*), was chosen, along with Lester James Peries's *Kaliyugaya*, for the Directors' Fortnight in Cannes in May 1982. Sumitra has just finished her latest film, *Maya* (*Illusion*), based on a novel by Manel Abayaratna.

SUMITRA PERIES

ARUNATA PERA
(Before the Dawn)

Script: Amarnath Jayatilaka, Kumara Karunaratna. Direction: Amarnath Jayatilaka. Photography: Suminda Weerasinghe. Editing: Elmo Halliday. Music: Makuloluwa. Art Direction: Joe Dambulugala. Players: Wijeratna Warakagoda (*Banda*), Chandi Rasika (*His Wife*), Denawaka Hamine (*His Mother*), Joe Dambulugala (*Landlord*).

Jayatilaka's film focuses on a maligned family in colonial Ceylon and shows a fate that is as tragic as in the best of Steinbeck. *Arunata pera* is the first movement in an eventual trilogy that will turn full circle to the present day. The most compelling aspect of the film is its almost pastoral quality – a quality that throws into sharp focus both the privations and the joys of simple village life in that harsh era before 1945.

This is perhaps the first time that Sri Lankan cinema has examined critically, yet sympathetically, that unhappy time where the peasant was a mere pawn in the hands of the wealthy landlord. Jayatilaka tells his story with no trimmings and without once straying into melodrama or bathos. There are moments that recall Jayatilaka's mentor Satyajit Ray, but the progress of the film is never affected as a result: it moves ahead smoothly, like a well-equipped long-distance runner.

A virtually untried cast is very effective. Chandi Rasika, in her first leading role, squeezes much feeling from her character, and Wijeratna Warakagoda immerses himself in the central role of the persecuted peasant. The craggy charms of Denawaka Hamine bring a tragic air to the fated grandmother who has to helplessly watch her family disintegrate. *Arunata pera* exerts its own kind of magic – totally winning, totally refreshing. The Jayatilaka children were mainly responsible for heightening the tragedy from the "Wings" – so to speak, and with Somalatha Fernando and Joe Dambulugala brought to the screen finely controlled performances that gave "Arunata pera" a lot of smooth running room.

NALIN WIJESEKARA

Sweden

by Peter Cowie

Like the gambler who stakes his all on a make-or-break throw, the Swedish film industry has this year completed two enormous productions, Bergman's *Fanny and Alexander* and Troell's *The Flight of the Eagle*, that between them will have cost around 50 million Swedish crowns.

That sum represents five times as much as the entire revenue of the Swedish Film Institute a mere dozen years or so ago.

Can a country like Sweden, with just 8 million inhabitants, afford such spectacular effusions for its two most gifted directors?

The answer, of course, is rather complicated. For a start, the Swedes are not paying the entire 50

million crowns. Jörn Donner, executive producer on both films on behalf of SFI, managed to secure substantial investment from abroad – from Gaumont in Paris, and from TV stations in West Germany, Britain, and other Nordic countries.

Secondly, Bergman and Troell are the exceptions who prove the rule. It is unlikely that a pattern of megaproductions will emerge in Stockholm. But both *Fanny and Alexander* and *The Flight of the Eagle* are bound to be remarkably enduring in terms of quality and income; they are also likely to restore the tarnished prestige of Swedish cinema around the world.

Furthermore, the Swedish Film Institute is not

INGMAR BERGMAN ON THE SET OF *FANNY AND ALEXANDER*, WITH ERLAND JOSEPHSON AT RIGHT
PHOTO: ARNE CARLSSON

DARVILL ASSOCIATES LIMITED, 280 CHARTRIDGE LANE, CHESHAM, BUCKS HP5 2SG.   TEL. CHESHAM (0494) 783643.

Memo

Buying or selling for video or T.V.? Contact Peter Darvill, your largest Scandinavian distributor in the U.K. of films for theatrical, non-theatrical, video and television presentations.

HANS ALFREDSON (ABOVE), DIRECTOR OF *THE SIMPLE-MINDED MURDERER*. BELOW, STELLAN SKARSGÅRD IN THE SAME FILM

the only producer in Sweden. Svensk Filmindustri has done well with Hans Alfredson's *The Simple-Minded Murderer* and the distribution of the Swedish spin-off from the Danish "Olsen" series, *Beware of the Jonsson Gang*. Europa Film continues to hit the jackpot with domestic comedies – last year *The Charter Trip*, this year *Who Pulled the Plug?*

But nothing is sure any longer in Sweden. The new Film Law, which makes the Institute heavily dependent on revenue from the video boom for its income; the departure of Jörn Donner, and his replacement as Managing Director of SFI by Klas Olofsson; and the death of Olle Hellbom, the architect of many economic triumphs at Svensk Filmindustri – all these events, combined with the uncertain future after the September 1982 elections, have made it more hazardous to predict the future of Swedish cinema.

The number of films in production has declined dramatically, with virtually all the seed money diverted to Bergman and Troell. Many of the gifted directors of yesteryear are either inactive or working for television. Video has made such inroads into the leisure spending of ordinary Swedes that cinema attendances are being adversely affected. And the so-called "serious" films have flopped with such catastrophic regularity that there is a danger of the industry's retreating into the mood of the Thirties, when domestic comedies ruled the roost and genuine artists like Alf Sjöberg were ostracised.

Last year, in these columns, I complained of the sovereign hold that the *auteur* principle exerted over the Swedish film world. To some extent, that criticism still holds true. Only the Swedes could have allowed a film so self-indulgent, so pretentious, and so naive as *Our Life Is Now* to have been completed; as much a scandal in 1982 as *Love* was the previous year. Vilgot Sjöman's long-awaited *I Am Blushing* was also a great disappointment, and something of an escapade. Even *The Painter*, selected for the Critics' Week in Cannes against formidable competition, proved obstinately anti-commercial, although its use of music and long-held shots confirmed the talent evinced by Göran du Rées and Christina Olofson in *The Tent – Who Owns This World?* (1977).

BROKEN SKY, DIRECTED BY INGRID THULIN. ABOVE: SUSANNA KÄLL. BELOW LEFT: AGNETA ECKEMYR. BELOW RIGHT: SUSANNA KÄLL AND THOMMY BERGGREN

On the positive side, there were two achievements. Ingrid Thulin's *Broken Sky*, an evocation of her own childhood in the far north of Sweden, received a mixed reception. The Swedes found the dialogue banal and the characters implausible. Foreign critics, protected perhaps by subtitles from these dimensions of the film, liked the calm, neo-lyrical manner in which Ms. Thulin summoned up the past, without recrimination. Seldom has a film communicated so acutely the feelings of an only child growing up in a pastoral environment – the walks beside the lake, the skiing across the fields to see the old grannie, with whom Ms. Thulin's *alter ego* has more rapport than she does with her parents. Thommy Berggren and Agneta Eckemyr are too healthy and sympathetic to play such bickering adults as they do in *Broken Sky*. In the final analysis, however, it is hard to fault the direction – clean, honest, and perceptive.

Hans Alfredson, known as a comedian whose previous work has been produced chiefly in tandem with his friend Tage Danielsson, scored a mighty triumph with *The Simple-Minded Murderer*, with Stellan Skarsgård winning the Silver Bear for Best Actor at the Berlin Festival for his role as the simpleton with the hair-lip who is exploited by an evil magnate and who eventually slaughters him at the bidding of three "Angels."

Now the Swedes are rather good at moralities. Sjöberg's *The Road to Heaven* (1942), and Bergman's *The Seventh Seal* (1956) spring to mind. Alfredson has made *The Simple-Minded Murderer* with an obvious conviction and a magisterial control both of pace and players. But the Swedes themselves are impressed by the film's condemnation of that most besetting of Nordic sins – humiliation. For the outsider, there may be too unrelenting a stress on the "evil" of the rich factory

DRUNKEN REVELRY IN *THE SIMPLE-MINDED MURDERER*

GÖSTA EKMAN IN THE IMMENSELY SUCCESSFUL *BEWARE OF THE JÖNSSON GANG*

owner (the time is the Thirties, and Höglund is as clear a Nazi as was the schoolmaster in *Frenzy*), too condescending a view of the "Idiot", and altogether too credulous a concept of the "Angels," who, as they march with wings rampant through the streets of a modern town, seem to be straight from the groves of Monty Python.

This said, it is always agreeable to have a quality film that is both hailed by the critics and accepted by the public in Sweden. One looks forward to Alfredson's next film secure in the knowledge that he need take lessons in direction and technique from none of his Swedish peers.

Approval too for a film that, while Finnish in content, was produced through Bergman's own Cinematograph company, and was shot in Swedish: *The Farewell*, directed by Tuija-Maija Niskanen and based on the daunting life of a prominent woman writer and theatrical personality. An excellent period piece, with something of Bergman's own secretion of guilty memories. A prominent final role, too, for Carl-Axel Heiknert, who died just after shooting had finished.

The new Film Law will mean an end to the quality awards dispensed for the past twenty years by the Swedish Film Institute's jury. With almost every film entered being given some kind of monetary prize, the system had perhaps become top-heavy in any case. For the record, the leading money-winners according to this quality rating were: *Children's Island* (790,033 Skr.), *Sally and Freedom* (771,799 Skr.), *The High Jumper* (482,374 Skr.), and *REFUSE* (424,489 Skr.). The Gold Bugs, Swedish equivalents of Academy Awards, were given to Kay Pollak as Best Director and Ingvar Hirdwall as Best Actor (both for *Children's Island*), Gunn Wållgren as Best Actress (in *Sally and Freedom*), and a fourth to the

HANS MOSESSON IN *THE PAINTER*, SELECTED FOR THE CRITICS' WEEK AT CANNES IN 1982

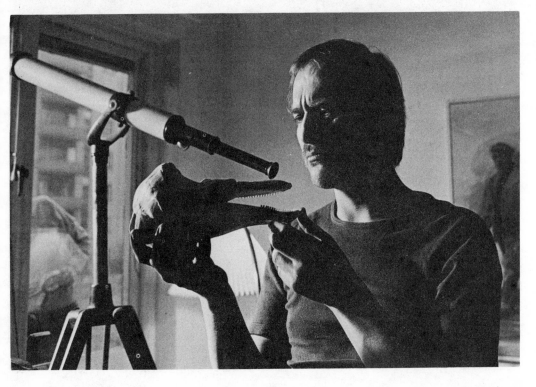

ABOVE: LARRY HAGMAN, GUNNAR HELLSTRÖM AND BIBI ANDERSSON IN VILGOT SJÖMAN'S *I AM BLUSHING*

BELOW: GUNNAR HELLSTRÖM AND BIBI ANDERSSON IN *I AM BLUSHING*

Göteborg Film Festival for its sterling work in establishing a new event in Sweden with comparatively little official aid.

new and forthcoming films

KLIPPET (The Sham). Dir: Janne Halldoff. Prod: Greyhound Film/Europa Film.
LIMPAN (Loafy). Dir: Staffan Roos. Player: Allan Edwall (also script). Prod: Svensk Filmindustri.
MOD ATT LEVA (Courage to Live). Dir: Ingela Romare and Märit Andersson. Prod: Ingela Romare Film/Svensk Filminstitutet.
MAMMA (Our Life Is Now). Dir: Suzanne Osten. Player: Malin Ek. Prod: Moviemakers for Svenska Filminstitutet.
BLUE COLLAR AMERICA. Dir. Anders Ribbsjö and Inger Marklund. Prod: Svenska Filminstitutet.
DEPARTEMENTET (The Ministry). Script and Dir: Carl-Henrik and Stefania Svenstedt. Prod: Svart & Rött Prod. for Svenska Filminstitutet/Sveriges Television, TV1.
DEN ENFALDIGE MÖRDAREN (The Simple-Minded

Murderer). Script and Dir: Hans Alfredson, based on his own novel. Phot: Jörgen Persson. Players: Stellan Skarsgård, Hans Alfredson, Maria Johansson, Per Myrberg, Lena Pia Bernhardsson. Prod: Svensk Filmindustri/Svenska Ord/Svenska Filminstitutet.
GÖTA KANALEN (Who Pulled the Plug?). Script and Dir: Hans Iveberg. Phot: Petter Davidsson. Players: Lars Amble, Kim Anderzon, Janne Carlsson, Nils Eklund. Prod: Drakfilm/Triangelfilm/Rifilm/Sveriges Television, TV2/Europa Film.
SNACKA GÅR JU . . . (Talk's Cheap . . .). Script: Lars Björkman, Sigvard Olsson. Dir: Ulf Andrée. Phot: Petter Davidsson. Players: Carl-Gustaf Lindstedt, Håkan Serner, Margaretha Krook, Berndt Lundquist. Prod: Drakfilm for Svenska Filminstitutet/Europa Film.

RIGHT: MAGNUS HÄRENSTAM IN *THE ROOSTER*

Documentaries for Hire

The Swedish Institute has a wide variety of short and documentary films available on 16mm for hire from embassies and distributors throughout the world (Darvill Associates in Britain, for example, and Audience Planners Inc. in New York, Chicago and Los Angeles). The organisation issues an imposing and informative catalogue in English which this year also includes an article on animated film in Sweden. Some recent film titles are:
MAMA . . . PAPA . . . This is a touching funny film; the situations are everyday ones but grotesquely distorted. A family quarrel at the dinner table becomes a cruel farce. The never-ending lugging around of the daily shopping bags is out of all proportion. The vacuum cleaner and the TV compete with one another, until the sound becomes infernal. The garbage in the streets swells into a river. In this grotesque world, the child is the only human being who is alive and real. In the face, of adult demands and principles, she is stubborn, healthily selfish: "I can do as I like." Dir: Marie-Louise De Geer-Bergenstråhle. 30 mins.
THE STORY OF THE *WASA*. In this new film about the warship *Wasa*, we observe the salvaging and restoration of this naval vessel, which lay hidden at the bottom of Stockholm harbour for 333 years. Dramatic reconstructions provide a glimpse of life on board the doomed ship when she sank in August 1628 and also depict the subsequent trial. The *Wasa* was designed to be the most impressive ship in the fleet of Sweden's King Gustavus Adolphus, who played a pivotal role in the Thirty Years' War. The vessel was decorated with hundreds of gilded sculptures. Together with 14,000 other pieces of the ship recovered from the murky harbour waters, they have once again been put in place. Dir: Anders Wahlgren. 25 mins.
THIS IS A HOLD-UP. Four disabled young persons show how they fight their life-long predicament. Their handicaps are all different. But their lives contain the same mixture of drama, longing and ambition. This film endeavours to picture their confrontations with the life they would so much like to be a part of. In the end, the essence of the film is condensed in a poem written by a young disabled girl. The two key lines are: "I have so many things . . . but I don't want to be alone!" Dir: Leon Flamholc. 28 mins.
VICTOR SJÖSTRÖM – A FILM PORTRAIT. Victor Sjöström (1879–1960) is, internationally speaking, the most outstanding name in Swedish films prior to Ingmar Bergman. Sjöström's pioneering days were from 1913 to 1927 in the era of the silent film. After a long career as actor and stage director he entered the film world in 1912, and in 1913 made his first masterpiece *Ingeborg Holm*. His international breakthrough came at the latter end of the 1910 decade with *Terje Vigen* and *The Outlaw and His Wife*. In 1923 Sjöström was invited to America. There is no doubt that Sjös-

BERGMAN DIRECTING EWA FRÖLING AND ALLAN EDWALL IN *FANNY AND ALEXANDER*   PHOTO: ARNE CARLSSON

tröm, alongside with Chaplin, Lubitsch and Stroheim, came to be recognised as one of the leading directors of serious American films of the Twenties. Dir: Gösta Werner. 65 mins.

Swedish Specialised Distributors

Apollo Film AB
Kungsgatan 15
S–11143 Stockholm.
Tel: 08–212502.

AB Europa Film
Box 20065
S–16120 Bromma.
Tel: 08–987780.

Filmarkivet
Box 43
S–20022 Malmö
Tel. 040–931110.

Film Centrum
Box 2068
S–10312 Stockholm.
Tel: 08–232750.

Föreningsfilmo
Box 3167
S–10363 Stockholm.
Tel: 08–233610.

Minerva Film AB
Tjädervägen 7,
S–181 40 Lidingö.
Tel: 08–765 7629.

Pallas Film AB
Box 1522
S–11185 Stockholm.
Tel: 08–142925.

Sandrew Film & Teater AB
Box 5612
11486 Stockholm.
Tel: 08–234700.

Features from all phases of cinema history.

Shorts of every style.

And videocassettes!

Stockholm Film
Box 1327
S–111 83 Stockholm.
Tel: 08–232105.

AB Svensk Filmindustri
Box 576
S–10127 Stockholm.
Tel: 08–221400.

Svenska Filminstitutet
Box 27126
S–10252 Stockholm.
Tel: 08–630510.

Useful Addresses

Sveriges Förenade Filmstudios
(Swedish Federation of Film
Societies)
Box 27126
S–10252 Stockholm.
Tel: 08–630510.

Svenska Institutet
(The Swedish Institute)
Box 7434
S–10391 Stockholm.
Tel: 08–223280.

Statens Biografbyrå
(Board of Film Censors)
Oxtorgsgatan 5, pl 5
S–11157 Stockholm.
Tel: 08–24 34 25.

Svenska Filminstitutet
(Swedish Film Institute)
Box 27126
S–10252 Stockholm.
Tel: 08–630510.

**Föreningen Sveriges
Filmproducenter**
(Swedish Federation of Film
Producers)
Box 3147
S–103 62 Stockholm.
Tel: 08–20 45 71.

ALLAN EDWALL AND ERIK LINDGREN IN *RASMUS PÅ LUFFEN*, THE LAST FILM DIRECTED BY OLLE HELLBOM BEFORE HIS DEATH IN 1982

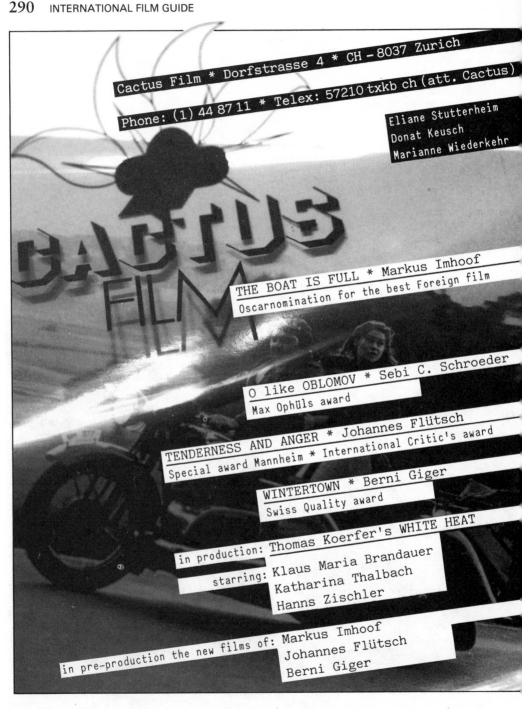

Cactus Film * Dorfstrasse 4 * CH – 8037 Zurich

Phone: (1) 44 87 11 * Telex: 57210 txkb ch (att. Cactus)

Eliane Stutterheim
Donat Keusch
Marianne Wiederkehr

THE BOAT IS FULL * Markus Imhoof
Oscarnomination for the best Foreign film

O like OBLOMOV * Sebi C. Schroeder
Max Ophüls award

TENDERNESS AND ANGER * Johannes Flütsch
Special award Mannheim * International Critic's award

WINTERTOWN * Berni Giger
Swiss Quality award

in production: Thomas Koerfer's WHITE HEAT
starring: Klaus Maria Brandauer
Katharina Thalbach
Hanns Zischler

in pre-production the new films of: Markus Imhoof
Johannes Flütsch
Berni Giger

Switzerland

by Felix Bucher

Swiss cinema in 1982 tells two stories. The first concerns the established film-makers whose work is a Swiss export, proven with success and bolstered with optimism (because the years 1981 and 1982 were, in a complete contrast to other aspects of the Eighties so far – the years of Swiss cinema).

Light Years Away, by Alain Tanner, and *Matlosa*, by Villi Hermann, stand for this kind of film-making, films in warm colours, containing rather curious individualists, and still nourishing some dreams of Utopia.

The second story concerns the newcomers, under the influence of the "hot" Zürich summer of 1981 and of the *triste vie*, which shows itself in monochrome compositions, full of resignation and gloom. Empty apartments, dead pubs, and cold cities are the tokens of this realism which has

nothing to do with the Super 8mm and video films made on the double. Many of these debut pictures have as their theme the lost dreams *and* the inner life of their characters as manifested in the world about them.

German-speaking Swiss film-makers are primarily responsible for the fact that documentaries are not considered as mere sociological celluloid. In 1981/82, a certain stagnation was apparent even in this genre: He who does not trust the image, must talk a lot, and he who does not trust the words must write a lot. But when a cineaste makes a documentary about a prisoner and a guardian with such intriguing and silent persistence as does Urs Graf in *Wege und Mauern*, he then demonstrates his true ability and his thrust into the image as such.

JEAN-LUC GODARD DIRECTING ISABELLE HUPPERT IN *PASSION*

Cinéma SUISSE

Centre Suisse du Cinéma
Schweizerisches Filmzentrum
Swiss Film Center

CH-8001 Zürich, Münstergasse 18
Telefon 01/47 28 60, Telex 56289 SFZZ CH

I would choose as specific Swiss "film of the year" Mathias Knauer's *Die unterbrochene Spur*, an inquiry into the Swiss asylum policy during the Nazi period and showing how the Swiss helped those who were working illegally for their socialist aims in exile. The impact and message of the film are heightened by Knauer's method of counterpointing original footage with the present-day interviews with those involved.

But there is also another notable Swiss title worthy of mention: *Transes*, by Clemens Klopfenstein, the "story" of a Bernese who travels for six months in cars and trains throughout Europe. It is exciting cinema, with subjective camerawork, the real, exhilarating story of an escape.

Other releases of note include two astonishing and exasperating documentaries which were first screened at the opening of the Cinémathèque Suisse at their new (and beautiful) premises at the Casino de Montbenon in Lausanne – *Lettre à Freddy Buache*, by Jean-Luc Godard, and *Inventaire Lausannois* by Yves Yersin. Then there is the appealing and restrained TV production, *Mérette*, by Jean-Jacques Lagrange, which takes place in

serene and tranquil Neuchâtel during the Nineteenth Century, and depicts the tragic story of a young girl in Protestant surroundings. And finally the tale of another long journey, from Geneva to South America, the encounter of a Swiss ethnologist and a Brazilian girl, the meeting of two cultures, in *Transit*, directed by Hans-Ulrich Schlumpf. At once a documentary and an extremely interesting feature film.

With *Das Boot ist voll* (*The Boat Is Full*), nominated for an Academy Award, Markus Imhoof has again raised the issue of the Swiss granting asylum during the Second World War. But the film, which enjoyed widespread success both in Europe and in the United States, has aroused debate on the Swiss rules and attitudes towards foreigners in general.

Some essential facts: 4.1 million Swiss francs is now given by the government in the form of aid to the cinema, and while in Zürich the experiment of a "communal" cinema was torpedoed for lack of funds, perhaps the "wreck" survives all the same!

STILL FROM *O WIE OBLOMOV*   PHOTO: CACTUS FILM

PETER HASSLINGER IN *WINTERSTADT*
PHOTO: CACTUS FILM

recent films

ZUR BESSERUNG DER PERSON (For the Improvement of the Individual). Script and Dir: Heinz Bütler. Phot (colour): Hansueli Schenkel. Players: Johann Hauser, Ernst Herbeck, Edmund Mach. Prod; Heinz Bütler.

WEGE UND MAUERN (Ways and Walls). Script: Urs Graf, Walter Brehm, Claudio Raveane. Dir: Urs Graf. Phot (colour): Rob Gnant. Prod: Filmkollektiv Zürich.

DIE UNTERBROCHENE SPUR (Interrupted Tracks). Script and Dir: Mathias Knauer. Phot (colour): Rob Gnant. Music: Roland Moser. Prod: Filmkollektiv Zürich.

DAS FLUGJAHR (Hard Time Family). Script and Dir: Markus Fischer. Phot: Hansueli Schenkel. Players: Hans Heinz Moser, Rosemarie Fendel, Alex Duda. Prod: Markus Fischer Filmproduktion/Filmkollektiv Zürich/ Stella Film (Munich).

WINTERSTADT (Winter City). Script and Dir: Bernhard Giger, Phot: Pio Corradi. Players: Peter Hasslinger, Gisèle Ratzé, Janet Haufler, Lorenz Hugener. Prod: Cactus Film.

PASSION. Script and Dir: Jean-Luc Godard. Phot (colour): Hans Liechti, Raoul Coutard. Players: Isabelle Huppert, Hanna Schygulla, Jerzy Radzilowicz. Prod: Sarafilm, Sonimage, Antenne 2 (France)/Film et Vidéo Productions (Switzerland).

MATLOSA. Script: Angelo Gregorio, Villi Hermann, from the novel by Giovanni Orelli. Dir: Villi Hermann. Phot (colour): Carlo Varini. Players: Omero Antonutti, Francesca de Sapio, Flavio Bucci, Nico Pepe. Prod: Imagofilm/SSR-RTSI.

SCHÜLERFILM. Script and Dir: Nino Jacusso, Franz Rickenbach. Phot: Pio Corradi, Patrick Lindenmaier. Players: girls and boys from the canton of Solothurn. Prod: Odyssee Film.

DER HUNGER, DER KOCH UND DAS PARADIES (Hunger, the Cook and Paradise). Script and Dir: Erwin Keusch, Karl Saurer. Phot (colour): Pio Corradi. Players:

Dieter Moor, Erika Eberhard, Fredy Meier. Prod: SRG, Cactus Film.

TRANSES. Script and Dir: Clemens Klopfenstein. Phot: Clemens Klopfenstein, Prod: Ombra-Film.

E NACHTLANG FÜÜRLAND (Tierra del Fuego, a Whole Night Long). Script and Dir: Clemens Klopfenstein, Remo Legnazzi. Phot: (colour). Clemens Klopfenstein. Players: Max Rüdlinger, Christine Lauterberg, Adelheid Beyeler. Prod: Ombra-Film.

DIE ZEIT IST BÖSE (Evil Times). Script and Dir: Beat Kuert. Phot (colour): Hansueli Schenkel, Beat Kuert. Player: Monika Kissling. Prod: Gruppe Ansia.

KASSETTENLIEBE (Cassette Love Affairs). Script: Rolf Lyssy, Georg Janett, Emil Steinberger. Dir: Rolf Lyssy. Phot (colour): Fritz E. Maeder. Players: Emil Steinberger, Franziska Oehme, Hilde Ziegler, Buddy Elias. Prod: T & C Film.

O WIE OBLOMOV (O for Oblomov). Script and Dir: Sebastian C. Schroeder. Phot (colour): Hans Liechti. Players: Erhard Koren, Olga Strub, Daniel Plancherel. Prod: Sebastian C. Schroeder.

STILL FROM *KASSETTENLIEBE*   PHOTO: EDUARD RIEBEN

L'AMOUR DES FEMMES. Script and Dir: Michel Soutter. Phot (colour): Hans Liechti. Players: Heinz Bennent, Pierre Clémenti, Jean-Marc Bory, Jean-Pierre Malo. Prod: Film et Vidéo Productions, TSR (Switzerland)/LPA (France).

PARTI SAN LAISSER D'ADDRESSE (No Forwarding Address). Script: Jacqueline Veuve, Eric de Kuyper. Dir: Jacqueline Veuve. Phot: (colour): Philippe Tabarly. Players: Jacques Zanetti, Emmanuelle Ramu, Mista Prechac. Prod: Aquarius Film Production.

Useful Addresses

Federal Office of Cultural Affairs
Sektion Film
Postfach
CH-3000 Bern 6.
Tel. 031/61 92 71.

Federal Department for Foreign Affairs
Kultursektion
Gurtengasse 5
CH-3003 Bern.
Tel. 031/61 35 14.

Swiss Film Center
Münstergasse 18
CH-8001 Zürich.
Tel. 01/47 28 60.
Telex 56 289.

Foundation Pro Helvetia
Hirschengraben 22
CH-8001 Zürich.
Tel. 01/251 96 00.
Telex 56 969.

Solothurn Film Days
Postfach 1030
CH-4502 Solothurn.
Tel. 065/22 01 01.

International Film Festival Locarno
Case postale 186
CH-6601 Locarno.
Tel. 093/31 82 66.
Telex 846 147.

International Film Festival Nyon
Case postale 98
CH-1260 Nyon.
Tel. 022/61 60 60.

International Festival of Films for Children and Teenagers
60, Avenue d'Ouchy
CH-1000 Lausanne 6.
Tel. 021/27 73 21.
Telex 24 833.

International Festival of Film Comedies
5, Place de la Gare
CH-1800 Vevey.
Tel. 021/51 82 82.
Telex 451 143.

Swiss Cinémathèque
6, avenue de Monbenon
case ville 2512
CH-1003 Lausanne.
Tel. 021/23 74 06.

Swiss Association of Film-Makers
Scheideggstrasse 125
CH-8038 Zürich.
Tel. 01/45 98 07.

Cinélibre
Swiss Association of Film Societies and Non-Commercial Screening Organisations.
Postfach
CH-4005 Basel 5.
Tel. 061/33 38 44.

Swiss Interassociation for Film and Audiovision
Kirchgasse 26
CH-8001 Zürich.
Tel. 01/252 64 44.

Swiss Association for Feature and Documentary Film
Seestrasse 41a
CH-8002 Zürich.
Tel. 01/202 36 22.

Swiss Association of Motion Picture Technical Industries
Regensbergstrasse 243
CH-8050 Zürich.
Tel. 01/311 64 16.

Swiss Animated Film Group
c/o Ernest Ansorge
CH-1037 Etagnières.
Tel. 021/91 14 50.

Swiss Association of Film Technicians
Josefstrasse 106
Postfach 3274
CH-8031 Zürich.
Tel. 01/42 60 65.

Swiss Association of Film Critics
c/o Felix Bucher
Töpferstrasse 10
CH-6004 Luzern.
Tel. 041/51 21 95.

Swiss Cinematographic Association
Effingerstrasse 11
Postfach 2674
CH-3011 Bern.
Tel. 031/25 50 77.

French-Swiss Cinematographic Association
5, Place Riponne
CH-1005 Lausanne.
Tel. 021/22 77 55.

Swiss Association of Motion Picture Distributors
Schwarztorstrasse 7
Postfach 2485
CH-3001 Bern.
Tel. 031/45 64 44.

Taiwan

by Derek Elley

The official figures for film production in Taiwan have revealed little change over the past few years: some 264 in 1979, 275 in 1980 and 242 in 1981. These show impressive activity by any measure, although the totals include Hongkong-registered production companies using Taiwan facilities. The local market, however, as reported in IFG 1982, has been increasingly affected by dwindling overseas sales: Hongkong is virtually a closed market (although the two industries still exchange talent), and both Singapore and Malaysia are experiencing their own difficulties. In addition, video during the past year has begun to bite deep into the local market, as elsewhere in the world: new films are mysteriously becoming available on video prior to release and cinema attendances are falling.

Yet the past year has seen several new directions emerge. Three new *genres* – the so-called "Mainland," "student" and "social realist" *genres* – have helped to vitalise an industry urgently seeking fresh initiatives to stave off the growing dominance of exploitation films modelled on Hongkong's recent taste for explicit sex and violence. Wang T'ung's *If I Were for Real* (reviewed below), Pai Ching-jui's *The Coldest Winter in Peking* – both banned officially in Hongkong, and unofficially in countries like the UK, after Mainland Chinese pressure – and Wang Chü-chin's *On the Society File of Shanghai* are all set in post-1949 China and reflect in varying degrees a Taiwanese perspective of Mainland life. Lin Ch'ing-chieh's *Student Days* (reviewed below) initiated a string of films set amongst high-school or university students. The third genre, of "social realism," embraces a wide number of dramas protraying contemporary life from a more objective stance than the Ch'iung Yao-influenced *wen-yi p'ien*.

Pai Ching-jui's *The Coldest Winter in Peking* (*Huang-t'ien hou-t'u*) is for the most part an objective portrayal of China during the year of the Cultural Revolution and just afterwards, shown through the story of a medical student returning from overseas study. The film suffers from an excess of characters and some necessarily shallow development given its abbreviated two-hour running time; but Pai's direction shows great style,

especially in the large set-pieces, and an uncommon restraint in the use of melodramatic devices. (Despite its English title, the film has no connection with Hsia Chih-yen's famous 1977 novel, smuggled from the Mainland and published in Japan.) Pai's subsequent *Offend the Law of God* (*Nu-fan t'ien-t'iao*) showed a further return to his more discreet earlier style of *Goodbye, Darling* (*Tsai-chien, A-lang*, 1970), especially in the scenes of comradeship between two ageing gangsters (K'o Chün-hsiung and the excellent Liang Hsiu-shen) reconciling their past lives under the Japanese occupation with today's changed society.

Wang Chü-chin's *On the Society File of Shanghai* (*Shang-hai shih-hui tang-an*) is more an offbeat crime story than an examination of Mainland society, and lacks the experimental verve of his earlier two features (see IFG 1982). Yet in the final trial sequence, and in Lu Hsiao-fen's powerful performance as a tough female delinquent, *Shanghai* often packs a powerful punch. The year's other picture in a Mainland setting, Liu Wei-pin's *The Ordeals of Daniel* (*Tan-ni-erh-te ku-shih*), was a gentler portrait of a Eurasian doctor caught between East and West, and confused by the changing winds of Mainland politics during the past 25 years. Overall it lacks the subtlety which distinguishes *If I Were for Real*.

The "social realist" vein ran fitfully through

CHIA LING AND LIU YUNG IN CHANG P'EI-CH'ENG'S *A MAN OF IMMORTALITY*

ABOVE: K'O CHUN-LIANG'S IMPRESSIVE *MY GRANDFATHER*
BELOW: LIN CH'ING-CHIEH (CENTRE) DIRECTING *STUDENT DAYS*

PHOTOS: DEREK ELLEY

some films, such as Sung Hsiang-ju's *The Up Train* (*Shang-hsing lieh-ch'e*) set among a group of train stewardesses, and more thoroughly through the impressive *Sailing for Tomorrow* (*Ming-t'ien chih yu wo*). The latter is harmed by director Li Li-an's routine direction and lack of a thoroughgoing style, but the simple rooftop settings, emotional tensions and performances of Ch'en Ming and Wang Ch'eng as two friends trying to make a success in an aggressively commercial society all strike receptive chords. Most accomplished in this *genre*, however, was *My Grandpa* (*Wo-te yeh-yeh*), a movingly simple and unvarnished portrait of a loving but strained relationship between a daughter and her senile father-in-law. Excellent playing by Chang Ai-chia and director K'o Chün-hsiung, and the unadorned setting of everyday, unglossy Taipei life, makes *My Grandpa* one of the year's major discoveries.

Chang Ai-chia, with Ch'en Chün-t'ien, was also producer of a series of eleven short features for TTV, collectively entitled *11 Women* (*11-ko nü-jen*), which gave many young directors their first chance and/or freedom from commercial restraints. The results were uneven but the series produced several jewels, notably Liu Li-li's *A-kuei*, Chang Ai-chia's *Tzu-chi-te t'ien-k'ung*, Yang Te-ch'ang's *Fu-p'ing* and, most accomplished of all, veteran Sung Ts'un-shou's *Tung-hsien ko*. All were low-budget productions, shot on video; only Chang Yi-ch'en's ambitious *Hsien meng* attempted true experiment, but the series could well be as important a first step for young Taiwanese talent as *Below the Lion Rock* was for some of Hong-kong's New Wave several years ago. The important thing was that it took place.

Other moves to help strengthen younger interest in the industry included the Government Information Office-sponsored College Film Festival which toured Taiwan universities in April 1982 showing recent Mandarin production with directors and stars in attendance. GIO also promoted two overseas presentations in 1982 – in Edinburgh and Denver. The government-backed Central Motion Picture Corporation has also put into production a portmanteau film to be directed by four young overseas-trained directors – the biggest gamble a major studio has yet undertaken.

The past year has also seen several achieve-ments in the commercial field. Though heavily influenced by Hongkong's blood-and-gore *genre*, Chiang Lang's psycho thriller *The Third Face* (*K'ung-pu-te ch'ing-jen*) showed much promise, especially in its *Cape Fear*-like finale. Chang P'ei-ch'eng's *A Man of Immortality* (*Ta-hu ying-lieh*) again demonstrated the director's gift of taking a well-tried subject (anti-Japanese resistance fighters in 1911) and drawing fine central performances (Chia Ling, Liu Yung) from his cast, notably in the early and later sequences. Yang Chia-hün's *Unsinkable Miss Calabash* (*Hsiao Hu-lu*) also turned the *wen-yi p'ien* genre on its head with spunky playing from newcomer Ying Ts'ai-ling and dependable veteran Wang Lai. And both Sung Hsiang-ju's *The Helpless Taste* (*San-chiao hsi-t'i*) and Ho Fan's *Taipei My Love* (*T'ai-pei, wu ai*) showed touches of originality within essentially commercial genres.

(Grateful acknowledgement to Chu Ch'üan-pin for additional information.)

HSÜEH-SHENG-CHIH AI (Student Days)

Script: Lin Ch'ing-chieh, Li Lien-mao. Direction: Lin Ch'ing-chieh. Photography (colour, scope): Lin Hung-chung. Editing: Ch'en Hung-min. Music Supervision: Li Lin, T'ang Lin. Players: Li Mu-ch'en, Lin Nan-shih, Ch'in Ch'an-ming, Wang Hsing, Hsin Chia-chen, Chang T'ien-kang, Yüan Sen, Li Wei, Hsien Wan-yi. Produced by Lung Chieh. 87 mins.

There is a freshness of approach in *Student Days* which is unlike anything in recent Chinese cinema. Drawing its strength from pacing and observation rather than sheer narrative drive, Lin Ch'ing-chieh's portrait of a motley group of high-school students is often Truffautesque in its compassion for youthful follies; but such European parallels in no way compromise the essentially Chinese content and character of *Student Days*. Lin's film is shot through with autobiographical references, nowhere less than in the hapless Li Mu-ch'en who drifts with bruised pride from one brush to another; Li's silent enrapturement with a girl who daily travels on the same train is handled (and cut) with deft humour. These train sequences punctuate the action at regular intervals, giving the film an

LI MU-CH'EN (RIGHT) IN LIN CH'ING-CHIEH'S *STUDENT DAYS*

exhilarating rondo structure which knits together the succession of vignettes.

Lin Ch'ing-chieh (b. 1944, Yilan) spent some fourteen years writing film and TV scripts before directing his first feature, *Problem Students* (*Wen-t'i hsüeh-sheng*), in 1979. *Student Days* is his second feature, and the first on which he was allowed a free directorial hand; Lin continues the story in *Fellow Students* (*T'ung-pan t'ung-hsüeh*), his third feature.

DEREK ELLEY

CHIA-JU WO SHIH CHEN-TE (If I Were for Real)

Script: Sha Yeh-hsin, Li Shou-ch'eng, Yao Ming-te, adapted by Chang Yung-hsiang. Direction: Wang T'ung. Photography (colour, scope): Lin Hung-chung. Editing: Hsieh Yi-hsiung. Music: Ch'en Hsin-yi. Art Direction: Wang T'ung. Players: T'an Yung-lin, Hu Kuan-chen, Hsiang Ling, Ko Hsiang-t'ing, Wei Su, Lei Ming, Ch'ang Feng, Chang Shih-yü, Chang Ping-yü, Ma Chia-li, Ts'ui Fu-sheng. Produced by Yung Sheng. 98 mins.

Adapted from an original (banned) script by three young Mainland writers, *If I Were for Real* is in marked contrast to *The Coldest Winter in Peking*. Where *Coldest Winter* offers panoramic spectacle, *If I Were for Real* wraps its critique of post-Gang of Four China in a more intimate story of one young man's attempt to get himself transferred from the countryside to live with his pregnant girlfriend in Shanghai. To do so, he impersonates the son of an absent party official – and briefly experiences the privileged upper stratum of Mainland life.

In his first feature Wang T'ung brings some ten years' experience as an art director to paint a convincing portrait of everyday Mainland life (using locations in Japan and South Korea). Essentially a theatre piece, the film's script develops its characters with surprising depth and compassion, and Wang's measured, calmly composed direction is all the better for its eschewal of grand emotional statements. Hongkong actor T'an Yung-lin hits just the right note of improvised knowingness in the central role, and he is supported by a strong and experienced cast. An accessible, often slyly humorous drama (reputedly based on a true event) which announces a major directorial talent.

DEREK ELLEY

Golden Horse Awards

The 1981 Golden Horse Awards attracted a record eighty entries of Mandarin productions from both Taiwan and Hongkong. For the first time the ceremony, held in conjunction with a week-long festival of international films, took place in the southern city of Kaohsiung, on October 30. Foreign guests included George Cukor, Alain Delon and Charles Bronson. The awards included: Best Feature – *If I Were for Real*; Best Director – Hsü K'o for *All the Wrong Clues (For the Right Solution)* (*Yeh lai hsiang*); Best Actor: T'an Yung-lin for *If I Were for Real*; Best Actress: Chang Ai-chia for *My Grandpa*; Special Award: *The Coldest Winter in Peking*.

recent and forthcoming films

WO-TE YEH-YEH (My Grandpa). Script: Lin Huang-k'un. Dir: K'o Chün-liang (= K'o Chün-hsiung). Phot (colour, scope): Lai Wen-hsiung. Players: K'o Chün-hsiung, Chang Ai-chia, Lo Chiang. Prod: T'ai Yüan.
K'U-LIEN. Dir: Wang T'ung. From the novel by Pai Hua.
CH'IEN CHIANG YÜ SHUI CH'IEN CHIANG MING. Dir: Li Hsing. From the novel by Hsiao Li-hung.
LAO-SHIH, SZU-TI-YEH-K'A (Goodbye, My Teacher). Dir: Sung Ts'un-shou. Prod: CMPC.
NU-FAN T'IEN-T'IAO (Offend the Law of God). Script: Dir: Pai Ching-jui. Players: K'o Chün-hsiung, Kuei Ya-lei, Hu Hui-chung, Liang Hsiu-shen. Prod: First Films.
CHUNG-KUO K'AI-KUO CH'I-T'AN. Script and dir: Wang Chü-chin. Players: Ts'ung Jui-li, Ch'en Chih-yung. Prod: Ta Fa.

Thailand by Michael Denison and Knit Kounavudhi

The past two years have not been good ones for the Thai film industry. Many of Thailand's top directors are either not making feature films or are doing commercials for theatres and TV. Audience taste has swung towards formula romances and comedies and ghost stories. The expected influx of higher-quality Western films, following the readjustment of Thailand's extremely high import duty on films, never happened. There have been almost no films made in the past two years to match the quality of *Red Bamboo* and *The Mountain People*, which were reviewed in IFG 1981. Although much publicity was generated about a few international co-productions recently shot in Thailand, mostly with television actors, these films did poorly at the local box-office and interest in co-productions has waned. *Angkor* and *Gold, Part II* are examples of these.

The star system still dominates the industry, although some of the stars have changed. Most audiences want to see their favourite stars as often as possible and, therefore, any film that wants a guaranteed return on its investment must use one or more of the currently hot stars. The stars, including relative newcomer Charunee and others, still work on several films at the same time, sometimes only being available for shooting a few days, or a few hours, for each film. This traditional system makes for the most films possible featuring the particular star, but few good ones.

The industry currently lacks good writers also. Because of this lack of creative writers, producers rely on the popular formula romances and comedies. A few producers have begun digging into Thailand's historical past and its literature for ideas. Chert Songsri, director of Thailand's biggest-ever hit *The Scar*, which was a period film, is now at work on *Puen Paeng*, a love story based on a well-known short story.

Kit Suwannasorn, one of Thailand's younger directors, is now at work on *Ai Noongthang Luang*, a story about 10-wheel truck drivers who supply Bangkok with food and goods from upcountry. Next year, he plans to do a film based on the true story of a Western woman who came to Bangkok and fell in love with an uneducated

rickshaw driver. He hopes to get Ornella Muti for the role.

Prakorn Prompitak who, like Kit Suwannasorn, works for Saha-Mongkol Films, is now at work on *Kow Nit*, a story about a woman trying to fight prejudice during the reign of King Rama VII, during the Thirties. Permpol Chuaroon, who directed the very successful *Red Bamboo* two years ago, had another success in *Raya* this year. Vichit Kounavudhi, who directed *The Mountain People* two years ago, is now shooting *Son of the North-east*, a story about destitute North-Eastern farmers. The lead is being played by the same actor (then an amateur) who appeared in the black-and-white short feature *Tong-Phan* a few years ago.

Perhaps the most interesting of recent films is *On the Fringe of Society* by Manop Udomej, a relative unknown. The film was shown at Nantes

CHERT-SONGSRI, THAILAND'S INDEPENDENT DIRECTOR

and a few other festivals and is about factory workers, farmers and other exploited classes in Thailand. During Thailand's "democracy experiment" from 1973 to 1976, a German stage director imported by the Goethe Institute did a stage play based on similar material.

The three biggest film companies in Thailand – New Five Star, Saha-Mongkol, and Apex-Pyramid – continue to control most of the action, through ownership of theatres and control of the best directors and stars. Most of the established and accomplished directors work for New Five Star or Saha-Mongkol, although Saha-Mongkol is now trying out some newer and younger directors. Apex-Pyramid concentrates now solely on distribution of independent Thai films and Western blockbusters. Among their hits over the past year were: *The Sea Wolves*, *The Spy Who Loved Me*, *Grease*, *Kramer vs. Kramer*, *The Black Hole*, *King Kong*, *Superman II*, and *Smokey and the Bandit*.

Thailand lost one of its most dynamic film figures when Kiat Iampuengporn, the head of New Five Star Company, was murdered. There was some suspicion that he was killed by business rivals who wished to stop him from taking over still more of Bangkok's first-run theatres. Top movie star Jatuporn Phooaphirom was also killed in 1981, in a car accident.

As bad as the past two years were, there is still some hope for the future, regardless of the fact that the Thai government is again threatening to step in to "help" the ailing industry. There is a rumour that the Thai government may pass a law saying that all Thai films must use local labs for processing, printing and all other lab work. In most cases, this would make little difference to the overall

quality of the film. The best of Thailand's directors, however, may suddenly find the quality of their work compromised. These few artists have been using labs in Japan and Hong Kong for the past few years.

Hope for improvement comes, surprisingly, from the local TV industry. At least two local channels have established schools for actors and technicians and there have been enormous improvements in the quality of local television lately, which is having a spin-off effect on the film industry. Increased ticket prices are keeping more and more people at home in front of their TV sets, where they are seeing high-action Chinese-made Kung-Fu and period epics. Over the past year, there have also been several Thai-made series of vastly improved quality. The better quality acting, stories, technique and sync-sound that viewers are being served on TV have made them less tolerant of the sloppily made formula pictures they are continually served in the theatres. Because advertising revenues are so high on television, TV producers can also afford to pay for top film stars and, soon, directors also. This means that, in order to be able to compete with television, Thai films are, somehow or another, going to have to improve their product. While government meddling and big promises made during publicity campaigns have done little to improve Thai films in the past, real competition from television, which threatens to actually take money away from film producers and distributors, may do the trick. All this will take time, of course, but there are real hopes that the new film-television competition will bring about a Renaissance in the Thai film industry and pull it out of the Dark Ages which exist now.

Turkey

by Vecdi Sayar

The National Film Festival in Antalya which takes place in September/October each year has always been a good indicator of the general atmosphere of the Turkish scene. It was the mainstay of progressive film-makers during the Seventies. And in 1979 the festival came to an end without distributing any awards due to the protest of the film-makers

and jury members against censors who banned three of the competing films. The following year, the organisers announced that the films of both years would be taken into competition, but this intention was never realised. On September 12, 1980, just a day before the festival, the army took over and the festival was cancelled. In 1981 the festival survived, but with a distinctly official after-taste. *Sürü* (*The Herd*), by Zeki Ökten, was expelled from the competition and important films like *Bereketli Topraklar Üzerinde* (*On Fertile Lands*) and *Hazal* were punished by not being given prizes.

Today, the problems facing the Turkish cinema are harder than ever. Under the rule of generals there is an increase in cinema attendance, but the industry's crisis shows no signs of improvement. The number of productions decreased from 195 (1979) to 70 in the years 1980 and 1981, the main cause being inflation and its effect on production costs. The mainstream of the industry is the production of musical melodramas (so called "arabesque" films) which are produced under poor technical conditions. Still lacking any kind of state support, the industry does not have any real capital accumulation. But for the generation of young cineastes the lack of freedom of expression is a greater danger. Censorship is as strict as ever and to produce quality films with a social comment is nearly impossible, since any film facing a problem with censorship suffers a lot from the distributors. Film theatres are decreasing in number and the surviving ones are being bought up by chains, preventing the distribution of films by independent producers (mostly directors or actors).

One of the main problems of Turkish cinema had always been the inabilty to enter the foreign market. In the last two years a good deal of improvement has taken place in this direction. Zeki Ökten's *Sürü* was sold to many countries. This international success was followed by three young directors. Ali Özgentürk's opera-prima, *Hazal*, was first shown at Cannes in 1980 and won awards at San Sebastian (best film) and Mannheim. This film tells the story of an impossible love taking place in an underdeveloped village and under the pressures the feudal traditions. As such, the film reflects the present contradiction between the progressive and conservative forces in the country. Özgentürk's second film *At* (*Horse, My Horse*), shown at Cannes (Quinzaine) and Locarno in 1982, is the story of an Anatolian villager who came to the city to earn his living and to be able to send his son to school. The film depicts his working days as a peddler submerged in an atmosphere of terror.

YILMAZ GÜNEY AT CANNES 1982 PHOTO: B. HUBSCHMID

Erden Kıral's second film, *Bereketli Topraklar Üzerinde* (*On Fertile Lands*), one of the best films of the Turkish social-realist tradition, a prizewinner at the Strasbourg European Festival and the Nantes-Festival of Three Continents was selected as the best film of the 1980–81 season by Turkish critics. Kıral is now completing his third film, *Hakkari'de Bir Mevsim* (*A Season in Hakkari*), which is an adaptation of a Turkish novel. The script is by Onat Kutlar, one of the best writers in the Turkish cinema, who also wrote *Hazal* and *Yusuf ile Kenan*. The film tells the story of a young writer who goes to a remote village in the most underdeveloped part of the country as a teacher, his struggles with natural difficulties, lack of interest of government officials, local ethics, poverty and illness during a winter season. This important work will probably have its premiere at Berlin in 1983.

Ömer Kavur, who had a successful *début* with *Yatık Emine* (*Emine*), continues his career without damaging the hopes he created with his first work. His second feature, *Yusuf ile Kenan* (*Yusuf and*

Kenan), earned the Best Film award at the 1980 MIFED Children's Film Festival. Kavur has finished two films since then. *Ah Güzel İstanbul* (*O, Lovely İstanbul*), the love story of a truck driver and a whore, enjoyed a good reception from the public as well as from the critics. In his third picture *Kırık Bir Aşk Hikayesi* (*A Broken Hearted Love Story*) which has not opened yet, he criticises the ethics of the provinces. The film can be regarded as his most mature work. Kavur is now working on his new film, *Göl* (*The Lake*).

While most of the directors of the older generation (Lütfi Akad, Metin Erksan and Halit Refiğ) are now working for TV, Atıf Yılmaz remains as an exception to the rule as a prolific cineaste. After *Adak* (*Sacrifice*), he made *Talihli Amele* (*The Lucky Worker*), a social comedy about exploitation created by mass-media and advertising, and *Deli Kan* (*Hot Blood*), a melodrama about changing morals. More recently he has produced *Dolapbeygiri* (*Workhorse*), a comedy about an honest and naïve villager fighting corruption in the city and an adaptation of a play called *Mine*, dealing with the plight of a beautiful woman surrounded by conservative pressures in a conservative town.

It seems that Turkish cineastes are gradually leaving the village (one of the exceptions being Türkan Şoray's adaptation of Yaşar Kemal's famous novel *Yılanı Öldürseler* [*To Kill the Snake*]) and moving to the provincial town as their new location. Without doubt, cities will be the next focal point. Feyzi Tuna has already shifted his attention towards the city. He portrays the depression of a bourgeois lady in *Seni Kalbime Göndüm* (*Buried in my Heart*). He is now working on a literary adaptation, *Üç İstanbul* (*Three İstanbuls*) for TV. Another important adaptation for TV is *Yorgun Savaşçı* (*The Tired Warrior*), a story about the Turkish War of Independence, shot by Halit. Refiğ.

Following a fallow period after *Düşman* (*The Enemy*), Zeki Ökten – director of *Sürü* – is now preparing for his new feature about bankers who go bankrupt and the effects on the suffering silent majority. This film will probably be named *Hücum* (*Attack*). Şerif Gören (who completed *Endise* [*Anxiety*] after Yılmaz Güney's imprisonment in 1974) shot *Yol* (*The Way*), written by Güney in prison. Editing, mixing and dubbing of the film

was done by Güney himself after he fled from prison. Gören is now working on two projects, an adventure story called *Tomruk* (*The Log*) and a literary adaptation, Sabahattin Ali's *Gramofon Avrat* (*Lady Gramophone*); while Güney – who is no doubt the forerunner of the generation of young Turkish cineastes – has to continue his work outside his country and it is very likely that he will have a great deal of opportunities after the Golden Palm award he received for *Yol*. This has proved the greatest international success of Turkish cinema to date (the first international success had come with *Susuz Yaz* [*The Dry Summer*] by Erksan, which took the Golden Bear in Berlin in 1964).

One of the promising young directors entering the scene is Sinan Çetin. His opera prima *Bir Günün Hikayesi* (*The Story of a Day*) had to be radically changed and re-shot so that it could get past the censors. It is a sincere first work and an interesting case – being a political work transformed into a love story. His second feature, *Çirkinler de Sever* (*Uglies Can Love Too*), is the story of a poor villager in love with a famous film star – Müjde Ar playing herself – and his third feature, *Çiçek Abbas* (*Abbas the Flower*), is a comedy about a mini-bus driver whose dream in life is to own the car he drives and get married to the girl he loves.

Nowadays, due to the crisis in the national market, co-productions are regarded as a means of survival by Turkish cineastes. Gören's *Yol* is a co-production with a Swiss company, Kıral's and Özgentürk's latest films are co-productions with a German company and the first feature of Tuncel Kurtiz *Gül Hasan* (*Hasan the Rose*) is a co-production with the Swedish Film Institute.

To conclude this overall view we must note that the great majority of imported films are as usual American productions, and that the organisations such as the Turkish Cinémathèque, the Film Workers' Union and Film Critics' Association are still closed down and merely anticipate the promised democratic developments in the country.

new and forthcoming films

AH GÜZEL İSTANBUL (Oh, Lovely Istanbul). Dir: Ömer Kavur, Script: Füruzan-Ömer Kavur (from Füruzan's story). Phot: Taner Öz, Music: Melih Kibar,

STILL FROM *A BROKEN HEARTED LOVE STORY*

Players: Müjde Ar, Kadir İnanır, Hakan Tanfer, Nuran Aksoy, Sümer Tilmaç, Prod: Alfa Film.
AT (Horse, My Horse). Dir: Ali Ozgentürk. Script: Işıl Özgentürk. Phot: Kenan Ormanlar. Music: Okay Temiz. Players: Genco Erkal, Harun Yeşilyurt, Ayberk Çölok, Erol Demiröz, Yaman Okay, Macit Koper, Güler Ökten. Prod: Asya Film/Kenter Film, Munich).
BIR GUNUN HİKAYESİ (The Story of a Day). Dir: Sinan Çetin. Script: Mehmet Günsür-Sinan Çetin. Phot: Ertunç Şenkay. Music: Cem Usal. Players: Fikret Hakan, Nur Sürer, Nizamettin Ariç, Şerif Sezer. Prod: Belge Film.
ÇİÇEK ABBAS (Abbas the Flower). Dir: Sinan Çetin. Script: Yavuz Turgul-Sinan Çetin. Phot: Çetin Tunca. Music: Cahit Berkay. Players: İlyas Salman, Şener Şen, Ahmet Mekin, İhsan Yüce. Prod: Kök Film.
ÇİRKİNLER DE SEVER (Uglies Can Love Too). Dir: Sinan Çetin, Script: Sinan Çetin. Phot: Ertunç Şenkay.

Players: İlyas Salman, Müjde Ar, Atilla Türköz, Tunga Uyar. Prod: Barış Prodüksüyon.
DELİ KAN (Hot Blood). Dir: Atıf Yılmaz. Script: Atıf Yılmaz (from Zeyyat Selimoğlu's novel). Phot: Taner Öz. Music: Yeni Türkü-Selim Atakan. Players: Tarık Akan, Müjde Ar, Makil Sönmez, Aliye Turagay. Prod: Yeşilçam Filmsilik-Atıf Yılmaz.
DOLAPBEYGİRİ (Workhorse). Dir: Atıf Yılmaz. Script: Suphi Tekniker-Atıf Yılmaz. Phot: Salih Dikişçi Music: Melih Kibar. Players: İlyas Salman, Şener Şen, Yaprak Özdemiroğlu, Ayşen Gruda, Şevket Altuğ. Prod: Uzman Film.
GOL (The Lake). Dir: Ömer Kavur. Script: Selim İleri. Phot: Salih Dikişçi. Music: Atilla Özdemiroğlu. Players: Müjde Ar, Hakan Balamir, Talat Bulut, Ferda Ferdağ, Mehmet Esen. Prod: Alfa Film.
GUL HASAN (Hasan the Rose). Dir: Tuncel Kurtiz.

STILL FROM *HORSE, MY HORSE*

Script: Nuri Sezer-Tuncel Kurtiz. Phot: Şalih Dikişçi. Players: Tuncel Kurtiz, Müjdat Gezen, Özcan Özgür, Hasan Gül, Nuri Sezer, Savaş Dinçel, Yaman Okay. Prod: Çiçek Film/Swedish Film Institute (Stockholm).
HAKKARİ'DE BİR MEVSİM (A Season in Hakkari). Dir: Erden Kıral. Script: Onat Kutlar (from Ferit Edgü's novel). Phot: Kenan Ormanlar. Music: Timur Selçuk.

Players; Genco Erkal, Erkan Yücel, Serif Sezer, Rana Cabbar, Berrin Koper, Erol Demiröz. Prod: DATA A.S./Kenter Film (Munich).
HERHANGİ BİR KADIN (Any Woman). Dir: Şerif Gören. Script: Ahmet Soner. Phot: Kaya Ererez. Music: Cahit Berkay. Players: Tarık Akan, Hülya Koçyiğit, Cihan Ünal. Prod: Gülşah Film.
KIRIK BİR AŞK HİKAYESİ (A Broken Hearted Love Story). Dir: Ömer Kavur. Script: Selim İleri-Ömer Kavur. Phot: Salih Dikişçi. Music: Cahit Berkay. Players: Kadir İnanır, Hümeyra, Halil Ergün, Mamuran Usluer, Güler Ökten, Neriman Köksal, Özlem Onursal. Prod: Alfa Film (Ö.Kavur-Necip Sarıcıoğlu.
MİNE (Mine). Dir: Atıf Yılmaz. Script: Necati Cumalı'Atıf Yılmaz (from Necati Cumalı's play). Phot: Salih Dikişçi. Players: Türkan Şoray, Cihan Ünal, Hümeryra, Kerim Afşar, Selçuk Uluergüven, Orhan Çağman, Çelile Toyon Uysal. Prod: Delta Film (Atıf Yılmaz–Ömer Kavur).
TOPRAĞIN TERİ (The Sweating Soil). Dir: Natuk Baytan. Script: Mehmet Soyarslan-Bülent Oran. Phot: Kaya Ererez. Music: Mehmet Soyarslan. Players: Fikret Hakan, Güngör Bayrak, Bulut Aras, Erol Taş, Esra Bora. Prod: Ozen Film.
YILANI ÖLDÜRSELER (To Kill the Snake). Dir: Türkan Şoray. Script: Yaşar Kemal-Işıl Özgentürk-Arif Keskiner-Türkan Şoray (from Yaşar Kemal's novel). Phot: Güneş Karabuda-Muzaffer Turan. Music: Zülfü Livaneli. Players: Türkan Şoray, Mahmut Cevher, Ahmet Mekin, Aliye Rona. Prod: Umut Film.

AT
(Horse, My Horse)

Script: Isil Ozgentürk. Direction: Ali Ozgentürk. Photography (Fujicolor): Kenan Ormanlar. Editing: Yılmaz Atadeniz, supervised by Zeki Ökten. Music: Okay Temiz. Players; Genco Erkal, Harun Yesilyurt, Ayberk Golok, Güler Okten, Erol Demiroz, Selçuk Uluerguven, Macit Koper. Produced by Asya Film (İstanbul)/Kentel Film (Munich). World Sales: Kentel Film. 115 mins.

The second film of Ali Ozgentürk (who made *Hazal*) is another major work from the embattled socialist Turkish cinema, the director having recently undergone a prison sentence on an undetermined charge. In many ways, it is a harsher re-working of *Bicycle Thieves*: a peasant and his son arrive in İstanbul to earn enough money to give the boy an education. The father gets a job selling merchandise from a cart and learns that the son can only get into a special school if the father is dead. When the cart is confiscated, their fate takes a downward spiral, ending with the father's death and funeral.

Ozgentürk captures the "big city" aspects of his story with admirable economy, shooting on location with an all-seeing, mobile camera and achieving images which are both naturalistic and surreal (somewhat akin to the best of the mid-Seventies Iranian cinema). Although the script lets in a few clichéd, sentimental touches in the characterisation of the little group of workers huddled in their courtyard, the harsh monotony of daily life as the men take their carts through the cluttered streets to the city market is observed with a keen, documentary authenticity. Then, as their plight worsens, Ozgentürk introduces several hallucinatory sequences (including a witty parody of the commercial Turkish cinema) which lead to the magnificent closing passages. After the father's death in the market, the funeral car speeds through the shimmering streets as the soundtrack rises in an impassioned cry of anger and pain at the sight of so much human waste.

JOHN GILLETT

YOL
(The Way)

Script: Yılmaz Güney. Direction: Şerif Gören. Photography (Fujicolor): Erdoğan Engin. Editing: Yılmaz Güney, Elisabeth Waelchli. Music: Sebastian Argol, Kendal. Players: Tarik Akan, Serif Sezer, Halil Ergün, Meral Orhonsoy, Necmettin Cobanoğlu. Produced by Güney Film/Cactus Film (Zürich). 111 mins.

The award of the Palme d'Or at Cannes (shared with *Missing*) symbolises both the political courage and the film-making gifts of Yılmaz Güney, now living in Western Europe after absconding from Isparta Prison in October 1981. Although Şerif Gören actually directed the film, Güney's screenplay and editing play the dominant role in the final version of *Yol*, which is by far the most fluent and assured of his productions. For someone confined to jail by the Turkish military authorities for so long, Güney's intimate understanding of the social and economic problems of his country is extraordinary. *Yol* offers a relentless condemnation of the patriarchal system of values on which Turkey still depends, and the tragedy of three of the five men who are on leave from prison is as much the tragedy of the women in their lives. What they hoped and assumed would be a week's taste of liberty turns bitter: a wife's infidelity, a brother killed by the gendarmes, rejection on account of a brother-in-law's death in a robbery that failed . . . Güney recounts these disasters with an impassioned discipline, never succumbing to sentimentality, never lingering on the merely exotic and ethnographic elements of village life. His eye lights on memorable images, such as the children puffing on cigarettes, or a prisoner's kissing the soil of his beloved Kurdistan. Running like a filigree of pain through the entire film, however, is the sense of anguish and exasperation on Güney's part at seeing a land he cherishes so deeply being gradually throttled by its own rigid customs.

PETER COWIE

STILL FROM GÜNEY'S *YOL*, WHICH WON THE PALME D'OR AT CANNES IN 1982

United Kingdom

by Peter Cowie

A delinquent correspondent's failure to deliver copy for this section using the excuse that too much was going on in the British film world for it to be properly assimilated into a concise article, seems to sum up the sorry predicament of the cinema here.

Nobody has placed his finger so accurately, or with such painful wit, on the pulse of the problem as did Lindsay Anderson in *Britannia Hospital* – a film of Swiftian brilliance that was greeted with the defensive disdain native to these shores. The fact is that in spite of all manner of little fires being sparked by intelligent and talented film-makers throughout the U.K., they have yet to unite into one great blaze that will sustain a revival of the British cinema. The triumph of *Chariots of Fire* in winning both the American and British Academy Awards was one such spark; Anderson's movie another; Colin Gregg's top award at Taormina with *Remembrance* (about sailors on leave) yet another. The Venice committee selected *The Draughtsman's Contract* for competition, and *Gregory's Girl* was sensibly acquired by Samuel Goldwyn for U.S. release, where it won excellent notices.

But the top British directors all gravitate towards Hollywood. It began in the late Sixties, when John Boorman made *Point Blank* and Tony Richardson was persuaded to film Faulkner's *Sanctuary* in America. Virtually all save the uncompromising Lindsay Anderson fled to the sunshine and gentler taxes of California. John Schlesinger, Peter Yates, and now a younger generation – Alan Parker, Ridley Scott, and Michael Apted – have become assimilated into the U.S. system. They point out, with justification, that Britain no longer possesses the necessary finance or studio infrastructure to afford them the challenges and budgets they require. How ironic it is that, behind the scenes, British craftsmen labour superbly on the special effects for such megaproductions as *Star Wars* and *Superman*.

Successive attempts to change the situation have briefly lit the horizon. The Rank Organisation returned to production – and failed (although Nicolas Roeg's *Bad Timing* was a fairly honour-able defeat). EMI co-financed one or two major American productions such as *The Deer Hunter* and *Convoy*, but then plunged too deep with *Honky Tonk Freeway*. Lew Grade's ITC stumbled to humiliating defeat this year in the wake of a series of disastrous international productions. Don Boyd has tapped the punk culture for a number of slick if uneven productions, all of which lack the professionalism of their American counterparts. And Goldcrest has tried in vain since the euphoric reception for *Chariots of Fire* to raise outside money for future projects involving the indefatigable David Puttnam.

Talent does not grow in barren fields, however, and any survey of the film industry in Britain today must come to a gloomy conclusion. Consider attendances – dropping at a faster rate than in almost any other civilised country. Mamoun Hassan, managing director of the National Film Finance Corporation, has been quoted as believing that total admissions could fall this year by 40%. Between 1980 and 1981 they declined from 102 million to a mere 86 million. A vicious spiral ensues: prices at individual cinemas are absurdly high – higher even than on Broadway; screening conditions are often ghastly, with the audience subjected still to that unleavened diet of advertisements and travelogues before the main feature. In desperation, West End cinema moguls launched a scheme whereby admission on Mondays would be reduced to £2 ($4 at the time of its

introduction), and then expressed dismay at the public's lukewarm support. Had the exhibitors shown the courage of their American counterparts, and reduced prices to £1 or even 50 pence, then they would have seen the queues they craved.

Habitually cautious in accepting new technology, Britain has once again reacted to the video revolution with quixotic glee. Overtaking even Sweden in its eagerness to rent both hardware and cassettes, the U.K. was soon leading western nations in its conversion to the home video medium. By August 1982, it was estimated that some 730,000 people were renting about 1,250,000 cassettes each week. The British fondness for hiring their TV sets has of course helped to foster such figures, but they are still extraordinary.

And yet the cinema, instead of outwitting the video boom, stands before it transfixed with fear, increasing admission prices instead of lowering them and even in the case of one group of art houses in London having the temerity to charge a "membership fee" of 50 pence atop the £3 ticket for a single movie.

Consequently, attendance figures are so impoverished as to remove the economic basis on which theatrical production may be built. Perhaps the salvation lies with television, and in particular with the new Channel 4, headed by a man, Jeremy Isaacs, who is strongly disposed towards the creativity of the cinema. But the very nature of television precludes the "long run" that is so endearing and valuable a part of commercial film release. If one is abroad on the night a new TV play or movie is screened, or simply otherwise engaged, one has scant chance of glimpsing it again.

And so the British cinema survives in pockets of resistance, akin to some guerilla organisation that refuses to succumb and can still startle the population with the occasional spectacular sortie or muffled explosion. Films like Chris Petit's *An Unsuitable Job for a Woman*, David Gladwell's *Memoirs of a Survivor*, and the ineffably distinguished productions of those quasi-British heroes, James Ivory and Ismail Merchant, continue to emerge, to excite some admiration, and then generally to expire without recovering more than a meagre profit, if that. Even when the N.F.F.C. and the British Film Institute do make an effort to put up finance, certain projects cannot attract the necessary private funding (e.g. Bill Douglas's *Heroes*).

LEONARD ROSSITER IN *BRITANNIA HOSPITAL*

BRITANNIA HOSPITAL

Script: David Sherwin. Direction: Lindsay Anderson. Photography (Technicolor): Mike Fash. Editing: Michael Ellis. Music: Alan Price. Production Design: Morris Spencer. Players: Leonard Rossiter, Graham Crowden, Joan Plowright, Jill Bennett, Marsha Hunt, Malcolm McDowell. Produced by Davina Belling and Clive Parsons for EMI Films. 116 mins.

Once again Lindsay Anderson demonstrates his almost uncanny grasp of British society's flaws and unwritten regulations. And once again he has succeeded in rousing the ire of the domestic critics, who shrink from his attack on sacred cows such as royalty and the trade unions, and from the Swiftian savagery of his wit. Every "hospital" is a micro-cosm, and Anderson's is at once celebrating its 500th year-jubilee and writhing in its death-throes. A manic surgeon occupies one wing, bent on creating a brain that can rule the world and resuscitate the greatness of mankind, while staff in other quarters gird up their loins for a royal visit. A strike, naturally, is in progress, while that other staple of the British social diet, a demonstration, hurls invective at the private wing, where retired generals and an African president enjoy those fruits of comfort beyond the reach of National Health patients. Anderson flings all these dispa-rate, yet related, elements into his bowl of cunning and stirs them into passion, while the media covers the chaos with unerring idiocy as always. The result is as hilarious a satire as any yielded by the English cinema since the heyday of Ealing, and if the tone of Anderson's voice sounds darker and more misanthropic than that of Michael Balcon's studio, it is because the prospects for any improve-ment in British life seem gloomier than ever before. In a year of royal marriage and birth, and of the Falklands escapade, *Britannia Hospital* fixes with deadly skill on that peculiar blend of seething resentment and zest for pomp so endemic to Shakespeare's "demi-paradise."

PETER COWIE

MOONLIGHTING

Script and Direction: Jerzy Skolimowski. Photography (colour): Antony Pierce. Players: Jeremy Irons, Eugene Lipinski. Produced by Mark Shivas and Jerzy Skolimowski for Michael White.

Working at high speed in the wake of the declaration of martial law in Poland, Skolimowski has produced his finest film since *Deep End*. Like that haunting predecessor, *Moonlighting* presents a vision of London viewed through the far end of a telescope; the details may be awry, but the mood is authentic. Four Poles are sent to London by their boss to refurbish his home in Onslow Gardens (an unlikely conceit, but one more witty than confusing). Only their leader, saturnine and disgruntled, speaks English, and he treats his colleagues with disdain. As they demolish the walls of the retreat in Onslow Gardens, and play havoc with the plumbing, they find communications with Poland equally chaotic. Finally, the leader learns of the Jaruzelski takeover, and strives to shield the others from the truth. Money runs out; he is forced to shoplift until, down to their last pennies, the contentious band faces a six-hour walk to Heathrow Airport.

Skolimowski has fashioned a disturbing, if always diverting allegory from this slender material. The *minutiae* of the thefts from a local supermarket are nicely registered, and the cameo portraits of English people have a wicked accuracy, but the character of Jeremy Irons's "leader" grows more disturbing and ambivalent with each reel. Tearing down "Solidarity" posters, hectoring the unfortunate Poles in his care, and evincing no sign of sympathy for his beleaguered countrymen back home, he emerges as a kind of Jaruzelski himself, while at the same time succumbing to the consumer temptations of the West, calmly stealing groceries without a shred of moral discomfort.

PETER COWIE

recent and forthcoming films

THE ANIMALS FILM. Script: Victor Schonfeld. Dir: Victor Schonfeld, Myriam Alaux. Phot: Kevin Keating, Chris Morphet, Nic Knowland, Jeff Baynes, Roger Deakins. Music: Robert Wyatt. Documentary narrated by Julie Christie. Prod: Pegeen Fitzgerald, Victor Schonfeld, Myriam Alaux for Slick Pics International (USA/UK).

GRAHAM CROWDEN AS THE MAD SURGEON IN *BRITANNIA HOSPITAL*

THE APPOINTMENT. Script and dir: Lindsey C. Vickers. Phot: Brian West. Players: Edward Woodward, Jane Merrow, Samantha Weyson. Prod: Ken Julian, Tom Sacks for First Principle Film Prods.
ASCENDANCY. Script and dir: Edward Bennett. Phot: Clive Tickner. Players: Julie Covington, Ian Charleson, John Phillips, Susan Engel. Prod: Penny Clark for BFI.
BETRAYAL. Script: Harold Pinter. Dir: David Jones. Phot: Michael Fash. Players: Jeremy Irons, Ben Kingsley, Patricia Hodge. Prod: Horizon Pictures (Sam Spiegel).
BRIMSTONE AND TREACLE. Script: Dennis Potter. Dir: Richard Loncraine. Phot: Peter Hannan. Players: Sting, Denholm Elliott, Joan Plowright, Suzanna Hamilton. Prod: Pennies From Heaven Prods (Kenith Trodd) for Namara Films (Naim Attallah)/Sherwood Prods (Alan E. Salke, Herbert F. Solow).
CHANEL SOLITAIRE. Script: Julian More from the novel by Mme Claude Delay. Dir: George Kaczender. Phot: Ricardo Aronovich. Players: Marie-France Pisier, Timothy Dalton, Rutger Hauer, Karen Black. Prod: Eric Rochat, Larry G. Spangler for Gardenia Films/Todrest (France/UK).
COMBAT ZONE. Script: Bobbie Bauer, Jeremy Lee Francis. Dir: Lindsay Shonteff. Players: Lawrence Day, Thomas Pollard, Luis Manuel. Prod: Elizabeth Gray for Lindsay Shonteff Film Prods.
COMING OUT OF THE ICE. Dir: Waris Hussein. Phot: Richard Kline. Players: John Savage, Willie Nelson, Francesca Annis, Ben Cross, Peter Vaughan, Bernice Stegers, Frank Windsor, Steven Berkoff. Prod: Chris Pearce for Konigsberg Prods (Frank Konigsberg).
COUNTRYMAN. Script: Dickie Jobson, Michael Thomas. Dir: Dickie Jobson. Phot: Dominique Chapuis. Players: Countryman, Hiram Keller, Carl Bradshaw. Prod: Stephan Sperry, Chris Blackwell for Island Pictures.
CRYSTAL GAZING. Script and dir: Laura Mulvey, Peter Wollen. Phot: Diane Tammes. Music: Lora Logic.

Players: Gavin Richards, Lora Logic, Mary Maddox, Jeff Rawle. Prod: BFI.

CURSE OF THE PINK PANTHER. Script: Blake Edwards, Geoffrey Edwards. Dir: Blake Edwards. Players: Ted Wass, David Niven, Joanna Lumley, Capucine, Robert Loggia, Herbert Lom, Burt Kwouk. Prod: Jonathan Krane, Tony Adams for Blake Edwards Entertainment/MGM-UA.

DESTINATIONS. (Formerly DESTINATIONS: UNKNOWN. See IFG 1982.)

THE DISAPPEARANCE OF HARRY. Script: Joseph Despins, Howard Wakeling. Dir: Joseph Despins. Phot: Phil Meheux. Players: Annette Crosbie, Cornelius Garrett. Prod: Chris Griffin, Joseph Despins for Labrahurst Prods/Channel 4.

EL SALVADOR: PORTRAIT OF A LIBERATED ZONE. Dir: Michael Chanan, Peter Chappell. Phot: Peter Chappell. Documentary. Prod: Michael Chanan, Peter Chappell.

ELECTRIC BLUE – THE MOVIE. Dir: Adam Cole. Players: Marilyn Chambers, Joanna Lumley. Prod: Tony Power, Roger Cook, Adam Cole for Stripglow.

EMMANUELLE IN SOHO. Script: Brian Daly, John M. East. Dir: David Hughes. Phot: Don Lord. Players: Mandy Miller, Julie Lee, John M. East. Prod: John M. East for Roldvale Film Prods (David Sullivan).

EUREKA. Script: Paul Mayersberg. Dir: Nicolas Roeg. Phot: Alex Thomson. Players: Gene Hackman, Theresa Russell, Rutger Hauer, Jane Lapotaire. Prod: John Foreman, Jeremy Thomas for Peerford Ltd/M-G-M-UA.

FIVE DAYS IN SUMMER. Script: Michael Austin from the story "Maiden, Maiden" by Kay Boyle. Dir: Fred Zinnemann. Phot: Giuseppe Rotunno. Music: Carl Davis. Players: Sean Connery, Betsy Brantley, Lambert Wilson, Isabel Dean, Anna Massey. Prod: Fred Zinnemann for the Ladd Co. (Peter Beale)/Warner Bros.

4D SPECIAL AGENTS. Script: Harold Orton, Peter Frances-Browne. Dir: Harold Orton. Phot: Ray Orton. Players: Bryan Marshall, Lisa East, Dexter Fletcher. Prod: Harold Orton, Caroline Neame for Eyeline Films/Children's Film Foundation.

FRIEND OR FOE. Script and dir: John Krish from the novel by Michael Morpurgo. Phot: Ray Orton. Players: Mark Luxford, John Holmes, Stacey Tendetter. Prod: Gordon L. T. Scott for Children's Film Foundation.

FUNNY MONEY. Script and dir: James Kenelm Clarke. Phot: Johnny Wyatt. Players: Derren Nesbitt, Gareth Hunt, Annie Ross, Vladek Sheybel. Prod: Greg Smith for Norfolk International.

GIRO CITY. Script and dir: Karl Francis. Phot: Curtis Clark. Players: Glenda Jackson, Jon Finch. Prod: David Payne, Sophie Balhetchet for Silvarealm Ltd.

GOLD. Script: Lindsay Cooper, Rose English, Sally Potter. Dir: Sally Potter. Phot: Babette Mangolte. Art director: Rose English. Music: Lindsay Cooper. Players: Julie Christie, Colette Lafont, Jacky Lansley, Hilary Westlake, David Gale. Prod: BFI.

GUAMBIANOS. Script and dir: Wolfgang Tirado, Jackie Reiter. Phot: Wolfgang Tirado. Documentary. Prod: Tirado-Reiter Prods (Colombia/UK).

HEAT AND DUST. Script: Ruth Prawer Jhabvala. Dir:

James Ivory. Phot: Walter Lassally. Players: Julie Christie, Greta Scacchi, Shashi Kapoor, Christopher Cazenove, Nicholas Grace, Barry Foster, Julian Glover. Prod: Merchant Ivory Prods (Ismail Merchant).

THE HUNCHBACK OF NOTRE DAME. Script: John Gay from the novel by Victor Hugo. Dir: Michael Tuchner. Phot: Alan Hume. Players: Anthony Hopkins, Derek Jacobi, Lesley-Anne Down, Robert Powell, John Gielgud. Prod: Rosemont Prods (Norman Rosemont) for Columbia/CBS.

THE HUNGER. Script: James Costigan. Dir: Tony Scott. Phot: Stephen Goldblatt. Players: Catherine Deneuve, David Bowie, Susan Sarandon, Zoe Wanamaker. Prod: Richard Shepherd for Peerford Ltd/M-G-M-UA.

THE ISLAND OF ADVENTURE. Script: from a story by Enid Blyton. Dir: Anthony Squire. Phot: Alec Mills. Players: Norman Bowler, Wilfred Brambell, Catherine Schell. Prod: Stanley O'Toole from Ebe Films.

IVANHOE. Script: John Gay from the novel by Sir Walter Scott. Dir: Douglas Camfield. Phot: John Coquillon. Players: James Mason, Anthony Andrews, Sam Neill, Michael Hordern, Olivia Hussey. Prod: Rosemont Prods (Norman Rosemont) for Columbia/CBS.

THE JIGSAW MAN. Script: Jo Eisinger from the novel by Dorothea Bennett. Dir: Terence Young. Phot: Freddie Francis. Editor: Peter Hunt. Players: Michael Caine, Laurence Olivier, Susan George, Robert Powell, Charles Gray, Michael Medwin, John Clements Prod: S. Benjamin Fisz, Robert Porter for Evangrove Film Prods.

KRULL. Script: Stanford Sherman. Dir: Peter Yates. Phot: Peter Suschitzky. Production designer: Stephen Grimes. Players: Ken Marshall, Lysette Anthony, Francesca Annis. Prod: Ted Mann, Ron Silverman for Columbia.

THE LAST HORROR FILM. Dir: David Winters. Players: Caroline Munro, Joe Spinell, Judd Hamilton. Prod: David Winters, Judd Hamilton for Shere Prods.

LOCAL HERO. Script and dir: Bill Forsyth. Phot: Chris Menges. Players: Burt Lancaster, Peter Riegert, Denis Lawson, Peter Capaldi, Fulton Mackay. Prod: Enigma Prods (David Puttnam) for Goldcrest Films International/Warner Bros.

MENAGE A TROIS. Script: Bryan Forbes, Gwen Davis. Dir: Bryan Forbes. Phot: Claude Lecomte. Players: David Niven, Art Carney, Maggie Smith, Kimberley Partridge, Lionel Jeffries. Prod: David Niven Jr, Jack Haley Jr for Sunrise Film Prods/Golden Harvest (Raymond Chow).

THE MISSIONARY. Script: Michael Palin. Dir: Richard Loncraine. Phot: Peter Hannan. Players: Michael Palin, Maggie Smith, Trevor Howard, Denholm Elliott, Michael Hordern, Graham Crowden, Peter Vaughan. Prod: Michael Palin, Neville C. Thompson for Hand-Made Films (George Harrison, Denis O'Brien).

MONTY PYTHON LIVE AT THE HOLLYWOOD BOWL. Dir: Terry Hughes. Documentary of the stage production written and performed by Graham Chapman, John Cleese, Terry Gilliam, Eric Idle, Terry Jones, Michael Palin. Prod: The Monty Python Begging Bowl Partnership for HandMade Films (George Harrison, Denis O'Brien).

NIGHTSHIFT. Script: Robina Rose, Nicola Lane. Dir: Robina Rose. Phot: Jon Jost. Players: Jordan, Anne Rees-Mogg, Yvonne Munro, Heathcote Williams. Prod: Mary Rose.

PINK FLOYD – THE WALL. Script: Roger Waters from the l.p. by Pink Floyd. Dir: Alan Parker. Phot: Peter Biziou. Production designer and director of animation: Gerald Scarfe. Players: Bob Geldof, Kevin McKeon, David Bingham, Christine Hargreaves. Prod: Steve O'Rourke, Alan Marshall for Tin Blue Ltd.

REMEMBRANCE. Script: Hugh Stoddart. Dir: Colin Gregg. Phot: John Metcalfe. Prod: Colin Gregg Film Prods for Channel 4.

THE RETURN OF THE SOLDIER. Script: Hugh Whitemore from the novel by Rebecca West. Dir: Alan Bridges. Phot: Stephen Goldblatt. Music: Richard Rodney Bennett. Players: Alan Bates, Julie Christie, Glenda Jackson, Ann-Margret, Ian Holm, Frank Finlay, Jeremy Kemp. Prod: Skreba Films (Simon Relph, Ann Skinner) for Brent Walker Pictures (George Walker, Edward Simons, John Quested. J. Gordon Arnold)/Golden Communications.

SCRUBBERS. Script: Roy Minton, Jeremy Watt, Mai Zetterling. Dir: Mai Zetterling. Phot: Ernest Vincze. Songs: George Harrison. Players: Amanda York, Chrissie Cotterill, Elizabeth Edmunds, Kate Ingram. Prod: Boyd's Co. (Don Boyd) for HandMade Films (George Harrison, Denis O'Brien).

AN UNSUITABLE JOB FOR A WOMAN. Script: Elizabeth McKay, Brian Scobie, Christopher Petit from the novel by P. D. James. Dir: Christopher Petit. Phot: Martin Shafer. Players: Pippa Guard, Billie Whitelaw, Paul Freeman, Dominic Guard. Prod: Michael Relph, Peter McKay for Boyd's Co. (Don Boyd)/NFFC/Goldcrest Films International.

VOICE OVER. Script and dir: Chris Monger. Phot: Roland Denning. Players: Ian McNeice, Bish Nethercote, John Cassady. Prod: Chris Monger for Chapter Film Workshop.

WAGNER. Script: Charles Wood. Dir: Tony Palmer. Phot: Vittorio Storaro. Musical director: Sir Georg Solti. Players: Richard Burton, Vanessa Redgrave, Gemma Craven, John Gielgud, Ralph Richardson, Laurence Olivier, Joan Plowright, Franco Nero, John Wells, Arthur Lowe, Richard Pasco, Prunella Scales. Prod: Derek Brierly, Alan Wright for London Cultural Trust Prods/RM Prods/Wagner Film/Magyer Televizio (U.K./West Germany/Austria/Hungary).

WHAT ARE SCHOOLS FOR? Script and dir: Patricia Holland. Phot and music: Dixie Dean. Players: Joyce Coakley, Paul Stratford, David Shavreen. Prod: Patricia Holland for The Corner House Bookshop.

Arts Council Films

The Arts Council has been making films for over fifteen years on fine arts subjects. In 1976, the scope of the film section was extended to include all arts topics – music, dance, drama, community and ethnic arts. The film production budget was subsequently increased and the Council's own film sales and distribution office was set up.

An average of twelve documentaries are completed each year, which are sold primarily to the television and educational markets, though some have cinema distribution. The films are usually on 16mm, and many are entered in international festivals worldwide. Awards have been won at the Cannes, Berlin, Chicago, Ottawa Animation, Zagreb, Paris, Melbourne and American film festivals, besides the many selections for competitive festivals of international repute.

In the United Kingdom, all the films are available through the Arts Council Film Library in association with Concord, for hire on 16mm to the educational, gallery and museum sectors. The library also contains other arts films and television programmes from producers in the U.K. and abroad.

This year, a major initiative was taken by the Sales Office to launch Arts Council films on videocassette. Aimed at the educational market, and started initially with twenty titles, Arts Council Video marks the beginning of a new dimension in sales and distribution. Another area of activity covered by the film office is the subsidy of avant-garde and experimental film and video work. This includes support for production, exhibition, distribution and capital equipment for individual artists and their representative organisations.

For information on the Film Library, contact Pat Dawson at the Arts Council, 105 Piccadilly, London W1 (tel. 01 629 9495). For information on the avant-garde and experimental film section contact David Curtis at the same address. For information on applying for Arts Council film production grants, contact Rodney Wilson as above.

For information on sales and distribution of Arts Council films, contact Mary Barlow at Arts Council Film Sales, 9 Long Acre, London WC2E 9LH (01 379 7113) or telex 8952022 AMEC CTYTEL G.

Importer and Distributor of Foreign Films to the USA

GU
ND

George Gund, 1821 Union St.
San Francisco, California 94123
Tel: (415) 921–4929
Cable address: GUNWEST S.F., California
Telex: 356–414

U.S.A. by Diane Jacobs

This past year has been very much the year "after" *Heaven's Gate* in Hollywood, with no conspicuous disasters (in retrospect, even Coppola's *One from the Heart* seems a gentle, if costly disappointment) or triumphs and many modest pleasures. For several of the major film-makers this was a hiatus year: Paul Mazursky's *Tempest*, Woody Allen's *A Midsummer Night's Sex Comedy*, and Martin Scorsese's *King of Comedy* are still in production as we go to press. On balance, it was a good time for the low-budget, naturalistic film. *Diner* won box office as well as critical attention, and the even lower budget, wonderfully wry *Chan is Missing* (made for $20,000) was picked up by New Yorker Films on the strength of its enthusiastic reception at Filmex and the New Director's Festival. On the other hand, it was a black year for film lovers everywhere which saw the close of Robert Altman's Lions Gate Productions and the defection of this most gifted "auteur" from the industry. Hopefully, Altman's justified break with Hollywood will be short-lived.

Curiously, the year's two most-anticipated films were among its least memorable. Though marked by intelligence, Warren Beatty's *Reds* wants a personal style, social vision, and, more crucial still, the compelling focal point. While many of its minor characters stick in the mind – Maureen Stapleton's unflappable Emma Goldman, the witnesses, Jack Nicholson's raffish and vulnerable O'Neill – the central love story is exasperatingly flawed. And though a far more personal work, Miloš Forman's *Ragtime* is also stronger in parts than as a whole. Here too there's a crucial problem of skewed emphasis. In its deftly interwoven opening sequences, *Ragtime* discovers the perfect visual equivalent for Doctorow's prose. But no more than forty minutes into the film, the tapestry approach is forsaken, as Forman and screenwriter Michael Weller fix on the least original aspect of Doctorow's plot, the melodramatic Coalhouse Walker incident.

More successful *auteur* works came from Sidney Lumet, Arthur Penn, Blake Edwards, Robert Altman, and Louis Malle in his two collaborations with American playwrights. Parti-

cularly in light of his earlier and more straightforward *Serpico*, Lumet's *Prince of the City* is an impressive study in moral ambiguity. Those who accused Lumet of television theatricals missed his consciously detached and often discomfitingly honest approach. The anti-hero here is Danny, a loyal police detective and friend who agrees to expose police corruption to the Knapp Commission, with the stipulation that he never be asked to betray a former partner. Government officials agree and shower him with praise and protection, but by film's end, these same officials (or their replacements) have forced Danny to inform on

SUSAN BERMAN IN *SMITHEREENS*, PRESENTED IN COMPETITION AT CANNES IN 1982 AND MARKETED THROUGH AFFINITY ENTERPRISES INC.

NEW YORKER FILMS

PAST, PRESENT, & FUTURE EXCELLENCE IN WORLD CINEMA.

IN 1979:
Rainer Werner Fassbinder's **THE MARRIAGE OF MARIA BRAUN**
Ermanno Olmi's **THE TREE OF WOODEN CLOGS**
Diane Kurys' **PEPPERMINT SODA**

IN 1980:
Maurice Pialat's **LOULOU**
Jean-Luc Godard's **EVERY MAN FOR HIMSELF**
Joseph Losey's **DON GIOVANNI**

IN 1981:
Andrzej Wajda's **MAN OF MARBLE**
Federico Fellini's **CITY OF WOMEN**
Louis Malle's **MY DINNER WITH ANDRE**

IN 1982:
Paolo and Vittorio Taviani's **THE MEADOW**
Claude Goretta's **A GIRL FROM LORRAINE**
Margarethe von Trotta's **MARIANNE AND JULIANE**

16 West 61st Street, New York, N.Y. 10023
(212) 247-6110 Telex: 238282 **NEW YORKER FILMS**

himself and his closest friends. Though finally exonerated, the broken protagonist returns to a mistrustful police department and a life of self-doubt – as hero, villain, and victim.

A dark and gripping, but scrupulously dispassionate film, *Prince of the City* is more closely allied to Martin Scorsese's vision of heroism in *Mean Streets* and *Raging Bull* than to Lumet's own perceptions in *Serpico*. Where Serpico was a maverick, Danny is committed to his job and police friendships. As with Scorsese's heroes, Danny's moral impulses evolve out of a mixture of guilt, violence, faith, and self-destructive whim: they make for a fine, increasingly dark moral drama.

Though the first-rate film that directly confronts the issues, moral and otherwise, of the American Sixties is yet to be made, both Arthur Penn (with screenwriter Steve Tesich) and Louis Malle (with Wally Shawn) made provocative films *around* that era this year. One of Penn's strongest works ever, *Four Friends* was dismissed as melodramatic and sentimental. Not so. Its unearned climactic violence notwithstanding, *Four Friends* offers a fresh, incisive view of the American Dream sustained through a troubled, idealistic decade. Some of the best moments are wistful glimpses of the protagonist's immigrant childhood with a proud, embittered father. Clearly drawing from Tesich's own experiences, these well-observed scenes deepen the film's impact, placing the "revolutionary" goals of the Sixties and the American Dream itself within the chastening perspective of history.

While *Four Friends* was underrated, *My Dinner with Andre* – also obliquely concerned with the Sixties and their legacy – became the year's most unlikely triumph, justly championed by critics and public alike. A bare description of Wally Shawn's scenario – two off-off Broadway theatre people discussing mysticism and mid-life crisis over a quail dinner – sounds unpromising in the extreme, not to mention quintessentially uncinematic. Yet, despite the mostly static camera, *My Dinner with Andre* is continually alive with conversation between suave experimental director Andre Gregory, still a wide-eyed seeker after the Truth, and the rumpled, sceptical playwright/actor Wally Shawn. While Gregory's been to India, Shawn has plodded

away at home, grateful for such occasional pleasures as the electric blanket he and his girlfriend
Debbie received for Christmas. *My Dinner with
Andre* is as engaging as its two colourful characters
whose goals and commitments are finally, and not
unpredictably, revealed as intensely similar.

While the exploitative horror film shows no
sign of falling from favour, comedy and film noir
were also strong forces in the market place this
year. *Arthur* proved that the *Easy Living* high
comedy is still viable (though, to this viewer's
mind, that film was notable only for Gielgud's fine
performance – its script can't hold a candle to the
Thirties' works it feeds off). Blake Edwards followed last year's *10* with two very different comic
statements. The sardonic *S.O.B.* proves him a
fitting heir to Billy Wilder and ranks among the
most malicious – and, one suspects, true – indictments of Hollywood ever. Two recurring gags are
classic: the one involves a hole in the floor, the
other a solitary loyal citizen in movieland – a dog.
Though extravagantly praised, Edwards's second
film, *Victor, Victoria* is more problematical:
depending on tired routines and the not especially
funny or – with Julie Andrews in the lead role –
credible premise of a down-and-out woman singer
finding stardom as a man playing a woman singer
in "gai" Thirties' Paris.

By far the most outstanding comic work of the
year was Robert Altman's *Health*. And the ways of
Hollywood are, indeed, mysterious when an over-
blown political farce like Richard Brooks' *Wrong
Is Right* gets released with fanfare, while Altman's
fresh, distinctive, and, above all else, funny *Health*
must sit two years on the shelf and then sneak into
the art house circuit. Set in an all-pastel Florida
convention hotel, which looks a cross between
Disneyland and a baby's bedroom, *Health* is
Altman's most amiable film in years. All the
familiar themes are here, presented – as always –
through similarly infelicitous alternatives. Though
its apparent subject is a political campaign – for
President of a mythical national health organisation – between the Eisenhower-like Esther Brill
(Lauren Bacall) and the Stevenson figure, Isabella
Garnell (Glenda Jackson), the conflicts are as much
sexual as political – between intellect and flesh,
male and female, cheerful indifference and painful
desire. The true subject is, of course, America, with

FREDERIC FORREST IN WENDERS'S *HAMMETT*

its peculiar and not unloveable ability to turn
almost any ingredients to cotton candy: to make
sit-coms of its myths, business of its ideals, media
celebrities of its heroes and heroines, and vice
versa. Where else in the world could political
"medicine" be delivered by chorus girls in pink and
white capsule hats, or campaign debates conducted around a plastic water melon?

Of new American film talents, Lawrence
Kasdan attracted the most attention, first as
screenwriter on *Raiders of the Lost Ark* and then
as writer/director of the much-touted film noir
Body Heat. As is so often the American way, praise
for this gifted young man's first works was hyper-
bolic. Though an enjoyable thriller, there's nothing
especially adventurous about *Body Heat*, which
unashamedly mingles two classic James Cain plots
(for *Double Indemnity* and *The Postman Always
Rings Twice*) in its tale of lust, murder, and heat
wave in southern Florida.

The far more extraordinary crime film of the year was Ulu Grosbard's *True Confessions*, from a script by John Gregory Dunne and Joan Didion, which pushes beyond the genre context and formula thematic concerns. As much as it is about murder, *True Confessions* is about middle age. As much as it is about the elusiveness of good and evil, it is about the strain of compromise. Though its most spectacular crime has nothing to do with the Church per se, *True Confessions* is especially concerned with routine corruption within the Catholic hierarchy and with a spectrum of Catholic wrongdoers, ranging from a bright-eyed young girl who "has to get married" in an opening sequence to an Irish Mafia leader.

In keeping with a trend toward smaller productions, the "ordinary people" film was very much with us this year, now with homosexual relationships (explored in *Personal Best* and *Making Love*) and divorce as popular subject matter. Divorce films were especially prevalent. *Too Far To Go*, based on John Updike's "scenes from a marriage" Maple stories, chronicles the break-up of a long marriage with children, as does Alan Parker's *Shoot the Moon*, from a script by Bo Goldman. The latter is noteworthy for its performances, particularly Diane Keaton's unusually graceful and understated evocation of the mother figure (this in felicitous contrast to her abrasive Louise Bryant in *Reds*). Yet, while both films have fine, telling moments, each suffers from a preference for the obvious: the pretty child in tears, the pink sunset fading. (By stressing the oblique detail, New Zealand film-maker Roger Donaldson wrings far greater emotional impact from similar material in *Smash Palace*.) What is most interesting about these films, from an historical perspective, is their underlying assumptions about family life, as contrasted to the assumptions of comparable films a decade ago.

For in such films as *The Graduate*, *Five Easy Pieces*, *The Landlord*, and *Next Stop, Greenwich Village* family is either irrelevant or a pernicious influence – parents (and especially mothers) are parodied, while the nuclear family is perceived as an encumbrance which must be jettisoned if the protagonist, usually a young man, is to achieve "self-fulfilment" and adulthood. Superficially, the "ordinary people" film of today remains sceptical

about the nuclear family as well. Divorce is, after all, a stated inevitability in *Kramer Vs. Kramer* as well as *Shoot the Moon*, *Too Far to Go*, and *Smash Palace*. But now the film-makers' *unstated* vision of the family is quite different. Being alone is presented not as a prerequisite for fulfilment, but as a depressing and hopefully temporary condition and a mark of failure. Nor is sexual passion romanticised in these current films. Where the "new" lover is perceived as a kind of salvation in the early Seventies film (the elusive blonde in *American Graffiti*, Katharine Ross in *The Graduate*), the alternative to the discarded wife – or husband – is now an "ordinary" person him or herself, often considerably less attractive than the original spouse. Indeed, the deserted husband in *Smash Palace* sums up a general attitude when he tells a friend he doesn't want to meet new women: "The only woman I'm interested in is eight years old" (his daughter). So these films which are, apparently, about the impossibility of marriage and family commitments are also paeans to their sacred claims.

No round-up of the year would be complete without mention of the out-and-out failures. Though beautiful to look at, Coppola's *One from the Heart* is a hollow work, reflecting only on a most superficial level themes profoundly explored elsewhere. Paul Schrader's *Cat People* is also painfully flawed, at once too coarse and too mild and proving once again that the dearest camera effects can't buy visual poetry or a compelling vision – kinky or otherwise – of sensuality and death.

The year's pleasant surprises were again small productions: notably *Diner*, Barry Levinson's funny, rueful, refreshingly *un*nostalgic recollections of the ever-narrowing options for young middle-class men in the American Fifties. *Chan Is Missing* also introduces a provocative new film-maker. Though less technically proficient than *Shadows*, this episodic first film by Chinese-American Wayne Wang strongly recalls the early Cassavetes. Wang's characters are fresh and ironically drawn, his situations well-observed, and a conceptual sophistication about the Chinese-American dilemma goes a long way toward compensating for clumsy editing and cinematography. (Besides, what can we expect on a $20,000 budget?)

(U.S. section continues on page 371)

Flyaway Dove

Edmond Séchan, Academy Award-winning director of *The Golden Fish* and cameraman for the classic film *The Red Balloon*, again displays his rare feeling for human nature and incomparable talent for aerial cinematography in this 18-minute non-verbal tale about a young circus performer, a beautiful white dove, and a prince's magic palace.

Learning Corporation of America
1350 Avenue of the Americas, Dept. NP
New York, New York 10019
(212) 397-9360
Cable: LEARNCOAM NEW YORK

Ron Wyatt and Tony Cattaneo together with a few of their famous campaigns.

WYATTANEO

22 Charing Cross Road, London WC2. Tel: 01-379 64444. Telex: 24224. Ref. 501.

Animation

Zagreb Festival 1982   by Prescott Wright

In days where the media is replete with headlines of confrontations, multiple warheads, inflation, and the amorality of youth, it is a very pleasant relief to get away from it all and into the fantastic medium of animation. In a warm week in June, some 300 people involved in one way or another with animation gathered in the Yugoslavian city of Zagreb with another several hundred residents to celebrate the currency of this special art and information form. There were Russians, Poles, Chinese, Americans, Canadians, Australian and guests from 29 countries and the talk was solely about animation and how to make more of it. This is Zagreb's fifth year in hosting this international event which included the traditional competitive events, informational screenings, retrospectives of the works of Jerzy Kucia of Poland; Winsor McCay, the pioneer animator; a good round-up of the production of the Zagreb "school" of animation; and three roundtable discussions about the art, craft, and trade of animation.

For Sherie Pollack, a novice animator from Richmond Heights, Missouri, this was her first international class festival attended by a wonderland of personalities she had only read about or whose films she had seen. There was Daniel Szczechura from Poland, John Canemaker from New York, the indomitable John Halas from Britain, three animators from Shanghai, almost all of the Yugoslavian crew including Majdak, Dragić, Marusić, Gasparović, Kolar, Štalter, Dovnicović, Žaninović, and many others whose cleverly manipulated perspectives of life have given the world a laugh, a tear, or a thought. And, the bit of

icing on the cake was the appearance of the jovial Disney "old men" Frank Thomas and Ollie Johnston and their charming wives who came to introduce their new book about working at Disney called *Illusion of Life*.

For those of us who are old hands at animation festivals, the proof was in the pudding and indeed, a not unpleasant surprise. After a rather dour festival at Annecy, France last year (see *IFG*

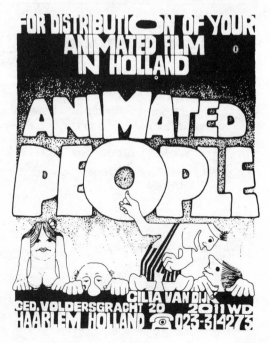

1982, p. 336) many had feared that the world's declining economy had taken its toll of the short animated film which, more typically than not, is one more art form which rarely recoups its production costs, it being more a medium for personal expression in its most creative form rather than a cornucopia of glittering coins. But, here at Zagreb, there were many fine films and a marked increase in the use of electronic forms to realise the motion of drawings. While the classic drawn cel or paper character was still the most popular form, at least ten of the 52 films presented "In Competition" used computerised animation stands, computer generated or assisted video images, or computer controlled devices to generate the usually laborious "in-between" drawings. It is surely a bit too early to develop parameters of criticism for these new images because they must be encouraged to fly before they are fettered by words. The hope from most of the critics at Zagreb was that the animators won't stop deploying these devices just to save time or money for traditional forms, but rather that they will use these new tools, new palettes, new cybernetic extensions of the mind, to discover fresh and differently delightful styles and techniques. Hopefully the explorations of the late Peter Foldes (*La Faim*) will be advanced to find a new beast in these machines, to excite us and extend our realms of experience.

The big surprise at Zagreb was that there was no Grand Prix awarded. Saul Bass, the noted designer, as chairman of the Jury stated, "Despite the fact that a number of excellent films were seen which had impressive qualities of either meaningful content or new forms, not one could be singled out which combined these qualities, so as to merit the high distinction of a Zagreb Grand Prize." And from those of us who spend a great deal of our lives reviewing and marketing animation there was a quiet, if not surprised "Amen," as well as a mini-novena for the courage of the Jury and the festival organisers to take such an important stand.

FIAPF, the international association of independent film producers, which sponsors the major film festivals, has a rule which states that a festival must award an announced prize. This is, of course, foolish and in the name of protecting the filmmakers, unfairly asks a festival and jury to award a

CEL FROM THE PRIZE-WINNING NATIONAL FILM BOARD OF CANADA PRODUCTION, *E*

prize despite the fact that, in their well-considered opinion, there is no film deserving of such merit. But then it is also FIAPF which, by its regulations, limits short film festivals to awarding only seven prizes. These days, life will stride beyond those who seek to nail it in place.

The prize winner in the "up to 5 minutes" category was Nedeljko Dragić's new short *Way To Your Neighbor* which borrows the title from the theme of the Oberhausen Short Film Festival. In Dragić's traditionally wry social commentary, a man is seen in his toilette doing just about everything to himself that you'll find in the pages of a popular magazine. Then he gets into his vehicle and goes out into the night. As it is a "one-liner" the punch-line cannot be revealed here, but the audience took a couple of seconds, got it, and went

wild. In the "five to twelve minutes" group, veteran Czech animator Bretislav Pojar won First Prize for his *E* which he produced at the National Film Board of Canada. Far from a Sesame Street sequence, Pojar, using familiar Eastern European styles and characterisations, tells of the dominating king who insisted on his pronunciation of "*E*" at all costs. "From twelve to thirty minutes" category was topped by the Finns Antti Kari and Juka Ruohomaki's *The Lost World* which is part of an experimental series based on the ballad of the same name by the Finnish poet Eino Leino. The realisation of dark and moody thoughts was accomplished with optical effects, rostrum camera work and computer animation in which they did some 700 drawings in two days. For the eye more used to the ingenuity of hand-drawn images, this

CEL FROM *PIG BIRD*, WHICH WON A MAJOR AWARD AT ZAGREB FOR THE NATIONAL FILM BOARD OF CANADA

piece felt as though it was machined, though certainly a touch-piece of things to come from computers.

In the "First Film" category, the prize was taken by Támas Baksa of the renowned Hungarian Pannonia Filmstudio in Budapest. Now this gets all international juries into the dilemma of comparing "first films" made by artists who have come up in a major production studio like Pannonia (with all the support of such a production house) against those economical films made by individuals who sort letters or drive trucks during the day to earn the money to tediously and laboriously piece together a short personal film on which they have all the credits including, in some cases, even developing the film in pails in the basement. But, we have faith in juries and ultimately if the heart of the film isn't there and visible on the screen, then no end of production values will make it work. In this case, Baksa takes a simple and not unknown ploy of man vs. creaking door and writes and times it into a nicely crafted and blessedly appropriate three minute episode in which man probably doesn't really win; a speciality of Pannonia's many fine animators.

A nice surprise was Emily Hubley's *Delivery Man* which is a roughly hewn narrative of a young woman who talks about her pending operation and her fears stemming from her mother's previous illness and her father's death during an operation.

It is an appropriate subject these days but made all the more poignant for those of us who knew her father, John Hubley.

And not to discount its world reputation for broad-mindedness in an otherwise dour world, the Zagreb festival's Selection Committee made up of Nicole Salomon of France, Witold Giersz of Poland, and Vatroslav Mimica of Yugoslavia, included in the competition a rather graphic and intimate account of Red Riding Hood's sex life. You can just imagine that there's not much left to the imagination in this brief, bizarre, and barely useful film by Cassandra Einstein of San Francisco. Many were outraged, but others were tickled by this outrageous diversion from the serious that Tex Avery might have liked.

For those who look for patterns in the some 140 animated films presented at Zagreb '82 there was a small but interesting one. Two animators from Zagreb Film Studio have treated modern health concerns in similar ways, i.e. that special delicate political humour that has made Zagreb famous. Nedeljko Dragić worried about the psychological effects of going "cold turkey" in his self-explanatory *The Day I Stopped Smoking*, where his character goes through all sorts of extended fantasies, and his colleague Borivoj Dovniković depicted the fantasies of some heavy drinkers which, while delicately amusing were nonetheless pointed in their message. Neither are the new breakthrough we were hoping for in animation but both were very well crafted and still witty and effective as understated messages.

In the "Educational Film Category" the far-and-away winner with a huge ovation was Richard Condie's *Pig Bird*, an unlikely little beast which a couple tries to smuggle through customs and which turns out to be infested with voracious bugs which devour everything. The interesting note about this three minute production from the National Film Board of Canada was that it was financed by the CP Air airline as an informational film. The NFBC is partially financed by the Canadian government but they are now more actively plying their fine talents in income-producing ways to help hold back austerity. A similar understanding was evident from the retrospective of commercials produced at the Zagreb studios and it was delightful to see those talents and skills used in a perhaps less personal but broader delivery system. Lest it be a secret, the vast majority of quality animators all over the world pay dues in one form or another and at some time or another producing commercials, informational films or educational films in order to find time to do the films that come from their fantasies, nightmares, egos or ids. And, while we can easily identify these "personal" films, we are rarely aware of the artistry that goes into the highly compressed commercials where you have 30 seconds to tell how oil is made or how much feeling goes into the making of a hamburger. Nonsense of course, but it takes all of the special skills of an animator to manipulate the phenomenal world into a brief message, and he or she does it with great understanding and command of colours, characterisation, movement, design, and above all, timing. Unhappily this year, the Zagreb Festival did not have a competitive category for commercials. Six categories are probably enough, but this special area of animation needs recognition for its artistry, craftsmanship and unique method of communication.

ALL THE HABITUAL BRILLIANCE OF NEDELJKO DRAGIĆ IS EXPRESSED IN THIS CEL FROM *THE DAY I STOPPED SMOKING*

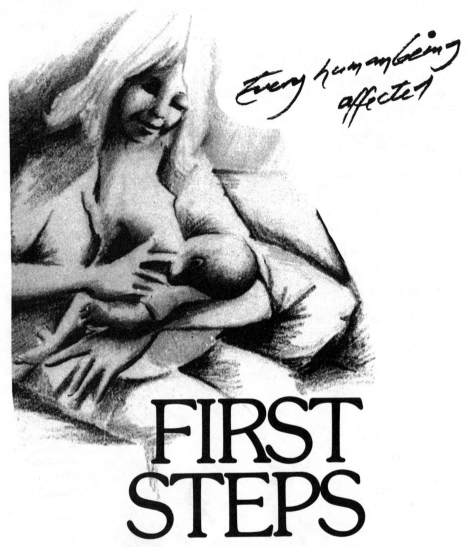

Every human being affected

FIRST STEPS

A film about caring for the very young

PRODUCED BY
EDUCATIONAL FILM CENTRE
3/7 Kean Street, London W.C.2.
Telephone: 01-836 5108 Telex: 269496
in U.S.A.
SCREENSCOPE INC.
3600 M Street N W — Suite 204, Washington DC 20007.
Telephone: (202) 965 6900

To continue with the awards, Category E was for "Children's Films" (films for children). Sam Weiss directed *Hug Me*, a classically and simply animated film from Nick Bosustow's production house in Santa Monica, California. Now certainly there is a good margin of story for messages when two porcupines learn how to hug each other. . . carefully, and for this type of film it works well. The Weiss-Bosustow combination has produced many fine polished educational films taking an Oscar one year for *Is It Always Right to be Right?*. But, another film competing in this category which did not have the same compression, writing, and timing, but which endeared itself to the Zagreb audience was *Jacob and Johanna*, by Kine Aune of Norway. Its eleven minutes were perhaps just a bit too long in comparison with the more slick productions but, using classical cel animation with nice backgrounds, some multi-plane dimensional effects, and with two appealing children, Aune deals very tenderly with a little girl who has no feet and a boy who is at first fascinated and then friendly. In the sometimes pointed way children do, the two explore each other's advantages and handicaps. Each child is unique and their differences and fascination with their specialities bring them to a better understanding of each other. This is not a dogmatic morality film, but rather a carefully fashioned bit of humanity.

There were other edges to the offerings, as so often happens at this historic crossroad of the world. Max Banneh, an animator working in veritable isolation in Queensland, Australia presented his nicely-wrought round-shaped man and wife characters *Violet and Brutal* in a tale of traditional marital combat. And from the National Film Board of Canada Bettina Maylone presented her sequel to her 1979 *Home Town* which was created and animated totally with pieces of cloth, embroidery, and hours of stitching. *Distant Shore*, while less naive, is more complex with elements of her cloth-muraled world now moving like the keys of a sewn piano shifting up and down. Ultimately, she demonstrates that the art of animation is a relationship between things being cleverly moved and our being able to identify via these movements with the thoughts and feelings of their mover. And that's animation.

The jury for Zagreb '82 was most distinguished, being chaired by the world-renowned designer Saul Bass. It included the ex-Disney animator who made his own name in Spain, Bob Balser; Miloš Macourek of Hungary whose *Bird's Life* got the woman out of the kitchen and into the trees; the famed Juri Norstein whose *Tale of Tales* has intrigued festival audiences the last two years; and Boris Sajtinac of Yugoslavia whose mind-bending animation helped to put Yugoslavian animation on the screens around the world. Once again, the organisation of the Zagreb Festival was masterly, making everyone welcome and feeling that they were a part of the festival, not just visitors. Finally, in these days of down-sided festival economics, a kind word must go to the progressive-thinking backers of the Zagreb '82 Festival from Zagreb, Croatia, and the core of the Zagreb Film Studio. A trip to this medieval city in June of 1984 to see what's happening in modern communication is highly recommended. And, don't be afraid to bring a funny hat.

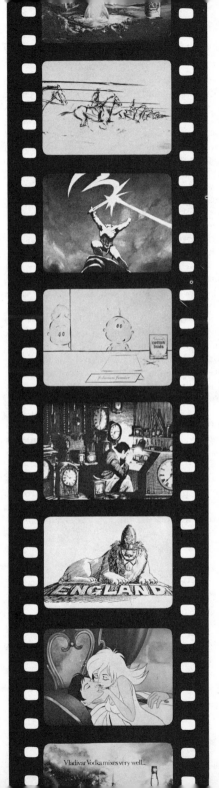

YOU CAN TASTE THE HOPS
IN BEN TRUMAN

BEN TRUMAN "Barge"
30 Second TV Commercial

SHELL "Moonshot"
60 Second TV Commercial

THE PRINCIPALITY
BUILDING SOCIETY

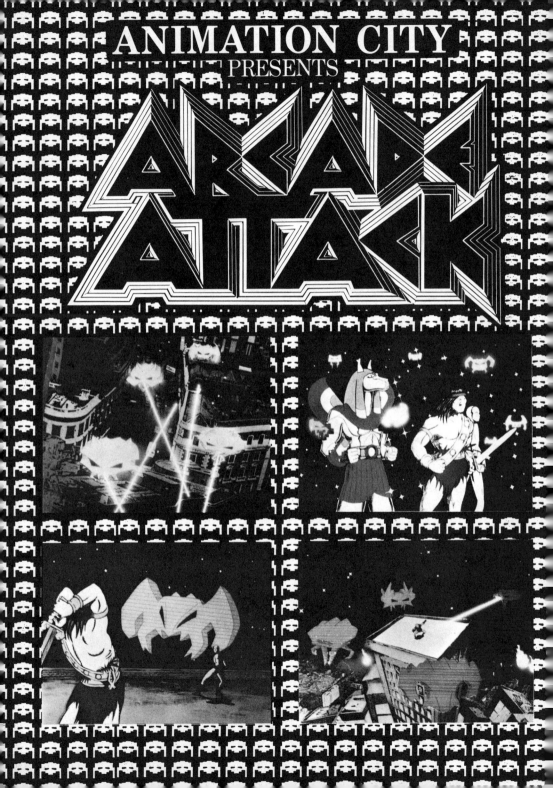

THE SECRET OTHER POLICEMAN'S ∧ BALL

ON CITY · 16-18 BEAK ST · W1 · 01·437·4

B.M.ANIMATION LTD.

26 SOHO SQUARE, LONDON W1V.6BB   TEL, 01-437 1257

CELS FROM TV COMMERCIALS CREATED BY BM ANIMATION. ABOVE: A 20 SECOND SPOT FOR SAMO OF BELGIUM. AT RIGHT: A 30 SECOND SPOT FOR ICI – WEEDOL

Zagreb Round-Up
by Ronald Holloway

Even though the mainstay of the Zagreb Animation Studio, Dušan Vukotić, has turned again to the feature film as his chief interest (*Visitors from a Galaxy*), and despite the growth of cartoon talent in other republics (Slovenia, Serbia, Macedonia), the Zagreb Studio continues to hold its own against mounting competition. One reason for its home supremacy in the field is the biannual Zagreb Festival of Animation Films, but another is that the studio with the flying red horse on its emblem serves as a beacon for maturing talent elsewhere in the Balkans. Thus, Veljko Bikić's *The Bus Stop* (Dunav Film) and Stefan Živkov's *The Flood* (Neoplanta Film), both Oberhausen entries last April, appear to have borrowed freely from, respectively, Nedeljko Dragić and the patented Zagreb mini-cartoon. And no wonder: Dragić frequently designs Oberhausen's "Way to the Neighbour" motif.

One of the studio's successful cartoons (also screened at Oberhausen) was *Leda II*, an Ivan Tomičić fantasy beginning with a lone female 'cello-player on an empty stage and drifting thereafter into erotic Freudian associations amid splashes of colour. Along the same lines is Damjan Slijepčević's *Francesca*, based on the passage in Dante's *Inferno* (Canto 10) about the illicit love of Francesca Polenta for her brother-in-law Paolo Malateste. Another cartoon with a dense graphic design is Zdenko Ricijaš's *The Pill*, with ecology as its theme.

The studio thrives on its individual talent. Borivoj Dovniković prefers a comic-strip style with a "little man" as his hero: *A Day in His Life* is about a factory labourer who steps out of routine on one occasion when he meets an old friend on the street – they end up in a bar for a night of carousing. The subtle twists of a line, the sharp observation of human nature, the pace of the story – these "Bordo" trademarks make for pleasant viewing. But the punch-line is missing, and with that the cartoon fizzles.

Zlatko Grgić is as prolific as ever – he's still the Chuck Jones of the European cartoon. He scripted, together with Pavao Štalter, *Fata Morgana*, directed by Zlatko Pavlinić and Vladimir Jutriša, and *The Vacuum Cleaner*, directed by Štalter and Leo Fabiani; both are whacky nonsense cartoons featuring a blackbird whose main difficulty is getting off the ground in the first place. Grgić and Milan Blažeković wrote the screenplay too for Fabiani's *Cash Register*, containing more bird-nonsense, and *Dad*, directed by Zlatko Pavlinić and Grgić himself with a worm in the middle of things. Grgić and Štalter were back together again in a parody on *Hansel and Gretel* (*Ivica i Marica* is Serbo-Croatian), directed by Pavao Štalter. And the able veteran did the script too for Nevan Petričić's *A Fable*, in which the story twist is how to make an absurd cartoon featuring two typical creatures from the world of Grgić. By the bye, the writer-designer-animator was offered a permanent position at the National Film Board of Canada, and undoubtably Grgić could have found a similar position in the United States ("he's more American than the Americans"), yet he chose Zagreb for a number of personal reasons.

The team of Aleksandar Marks (designer) and Vladimir Jutriša (animator) keeps turning out folklorica based on fables and legends. Their latest is *The Blackbird*, about a naïve farmer and his wife trying to save a wheat crop from scavengers of the air by whatever destructive means possible. The always dependable Jutriša directed a rare cartoon by himself: *The Carp* (screenplay by Zlatko Bourek), about an overgrown fish menacing a cake-shop, of all places.

CEL FROM THE ZAGREB PRODUCTION OF *CASH REGISTER*

Leopold Fabiani has now established himself as another regular at the Zagreb Studio – an all-around talent for most any style and genre. Besides those listed above, he directed and animated *A Winter's Wish*: it's the story of Santa Claus restoring balance to the world of nature after Man has spoiled it to the extent of robbing children of the privilage of the sun.

Dragutin Vunak contributed a script for a grotesque tale, *The Ballad of Podravina*, directed by Željko Nemec in a poetic, surrealistic vein. Rudolf Borošak's *The Picture*, a fantasy on life-styles, is lovely to behold without musing on a story-line (there's any to speak of); there is little doubt that Borošak ranks with Aleksandar Marks as an ace in the design department.

A new name at Zagreb, Joško Marošić, has made *Skyscraper* and *Fisheye*, both dealing with modern society and social problems. *Skyscraper* ties together a string of gags about day-to-day existence in a stifling fortress, while *Fisheye* looks to the benefits of nature in a traditional fishing-village setting. Marošić does everything on his

ABOVE: CEL FROM *LEDA II*, DIRECTED BY IVAN TOMIČIĆ FOR ZAGREB FILM

ABOVE: CEL FROM *THE BLACKBIRD*, DESIGNED, ANIMATED AND DIRECTED BY ALEKSANDAR MARKS AND VLADIMIR JUTRIŠA

cartoons from start to finish, the strength of the artist lying in the graphic work.

The story cartoon is a popular genre, more than at other studios in Socialist countries – for the simple reason that Zagreb seeks partners for both production and pre-sales. Zlatko Pavlinić's *The House of the Plague* is based on a poem by August Senoa, a cartoon of fantasy and imagination. For the young audience there's Radivoj Gvozdanović's *Marko Was Struck by Lightning* and *Glasses*, whose morals are geared to the level of schoolchildren.

ANIMATORS AND ALL FRIENDS OF ANIMATED FILMS:
WE EXPECT YOU AT OUR NEXT GATHERING IN ZAGREB

— JUNE 1984!

For all information please contact:

ZAGREB '84
Festival Office
Nova ves 18
41000 ZAGREB
Yugoslavia

phone: 041/276636   telex: 21790   cable: FESTANIMA Zagreb

Silver Jubilee at TVC

Hard to believe that twenty-five years have run by since John Coates and the late, great George Dunning founded TV Cartoons Limited, better known by its initials TVC. The company produced animated TV commercials from the start, and still does, but TVC has also been a germ cell of imaginative design and animation work. Highpoints of the quarter-century have included the Beatles' cartoon movie, *Yellow Submarine*, in which nearly a hundred artists and animators were involved, and George Dunning's own trail-blazing experiments such as *The Flying Man*, *The Apple*, and *Damon the Mower*. One of the brightest moments came in 1967, when in the Canadian pavilion at the Montreal EXPO, TVC's multiscreen movie, *Canada Is My Piano*, was shown to visitors.

In recent years, TVC has contributed animated sequences to such films as *The Lion, The Witch and the Wardrobe* and *Heavy Metal*, and its latest feat is a sophisticated hour-long American TV special called *Castle*.

Funded from the National Endowment for the Humanities, *Castle* uses live-action and animation in tandem to show how a medieval castle was conceived, constructed, used, and defended. The actual castle is named Aberwyvern, but is a composite of many famous Welsh castles, and especially Harlech. This dramatic documentary, factitious though it may be, brings to rich and entrancing life the excitement that must have attended the building of a major fortress, and the design work of Jack Stokes has contributed to the success of the project.

Now TVC's new associate company, Snowman Enterprises, is preparing a 25-minute animated film from Raymond Briggs's children's story, *The Snowman*. Already purchased by Channel 4 in the UK, this delicate tale should enable TVC to pursue its ceaseless quest for new styles in animation.

Wyatt Cattaneo

After 17 years of partnership, Ron Wyatt and Tony Cattaneo can look back on a remarkable run of achievement in the TV commercial field. Many of the characters that have evolved from their talented pens have become household names in Britain and abroad: the Typhoo Gnu, Home Pride Flour Graders, the Crest Toothpaste Kids, and many others. Wyatt Cattaneo restrict their studio's output to around thirty commercials a year. By resisting the temptation to become a mega-factory, they can continue to offer that personal involvement so many animation companies have long abandoned.

Both Ron and Tony actually *work* on storyboards and cels, watching a project through from conception to execution, proffering ideas and comments at every stage. "Animation is now recognised as a medium in its own right, just like live-action," says Ron Wyatt. "So the agencies know the problems and challenges of the craft, and come to us with those in mind. We help the agencies create the script and sometimes even the copy platform, as well as designing the characters."

The studio spreads its net wide, catering for agencies in France, West Germany, Spain, Holland, Denmark, Belgium, Ghana and Saudi Arabia, Hongkong and Singapore, as well as handling a high proportion of British TV animation. A video single-frame camera has enabled Wyatt Cattaneo to improve the shape and structure of each commercial, visualising the storyboard at a stroke, and providing the agency with a timing concept at a very early stage.

*   *   *

Warmth, and quality of service, are the watchwords at Wyatt Cattaneo. Their characters are immediately engaging, and strongly identified with their product, as the 54 commercials they made for Home Pride Flour attest.

Both Ron and Tony began life at the Pearl and Dean Company as commercial artists, then worked with Richard Williams before branching out on their own. Together they have survived in a partnership that is the envy of British animation and a byword for dependability among ad agencies.

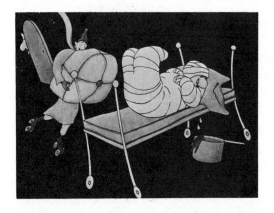

ANIMATION FROM FINLAND: CEL FROM RIITTA NELI-MARKKA AND JAAKKO SEECK'S *BIG AND SMALL*

ANIMATION FROM FINLAND II: CEL FROM SEPPO PUT-KINEN'S *KARELIAN TALES*

JOHN GATI ON SET, ANIMATING A TV COMMERCIAL FOR PEOPLE'S NATIONAL BANK AND TRUST COMPANY

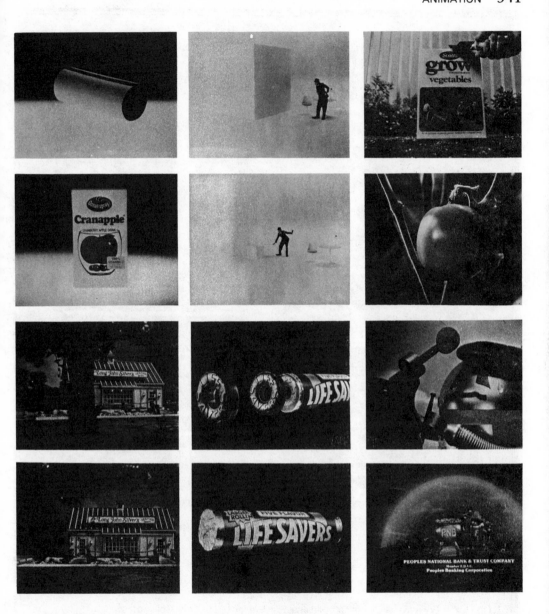

AN IMPRESSIVE ARRAY OF SHOTS FROM VARIOUS STOP-MOTION AND PUPPET-STYLE COMMERCIALS DESIGNED BY THE GIFTED JOHN GATI

Note: the number of film festivals seems to increase annually, and we try here to list only those events that occur regularly and are conducted on a serious basis. (N.B. Festivals not taking place during the next twelve months have been omitted.) There is also an appendix of other significant festivals.

American Film Festival
May 1983

For over twenty years the American Film Festival has stood at the centre of educational film activities in the United States (see our "Films for Young People" section for complete coverage of the event). Jurors in 42 categories assign the traditional Blue and Red Ribbon awards and meetings and screenings are held in the Grand Hyatt Hotel, New York City. Video is also now included in the festival's coverage of educational media. *Inquiries to*: Educational Film Library Association, 43 West 61st Street, New York, NY 10023, U.S.A.

Berlin
February 1983

Berlin is generally recognised to be the most efficiently-organised of the world's major festivals, under the leadership of Moritz de Hadeln and Ulrich Gregor. The Eastern European bloc now participates fully in the Berlinale, and the Film Market puts emphasis on the Nordic countries. In addition to the competitive programme and information section, there is a Retrospective, screenings of all new West German films, and of course the Forum of Young Cinema, directed by Ulrich Gregor, where many of the most imaginative films are screened. *Inquiries to*: Berlin International Film Festival, Budapester Strasse 48–50, 1000 Berlin 30.

AWARDS 1982
Golden Bear (features): **Die Sehnsucht der Veronika Voss** (West Germany), Fassbinder.
Silver Bear (Special Jury Prize): **Dreszcze** (Poland), Marczewski.
Silver Bear (Best Direction): Mario Monicelli for **Il Marchese del Grillo** (Italy).
Silver Bear (Best Actress): Katrin Sass for **Bürgschaft für ein Jahr** (G.D.R.).
Silver Bear (Best Actor): Michel Piccoli for **Une étrange affaire** (France) and Stellan Skärsgård for **Den enfaldige mördaren** (Sweden).
Silver Bear (Screenplay): Zoltán Fábri for **Requiem** (Hungary).
FIPRESCI Prize (competition): **Dreszcze** (Poland), Marczewski. *(Forum)*: **Pastorale** (U.S.S.R.), Ioseliani, and **Lebensläufe** (G.D.R.), Junge.
Golden Bear (shorts): **Loutka, pritel cloveka** (Czechoslovakia), Renc.

Cannes
May 1983

The spectacular new Palais will await festivalgoers at Cannes in May 1983, and the event should be able to accommodate the changes, as it has so many in the past, without disturbing its image and character as the world's leading film festival. Cannes is divided into various categories, enabling the busy distributor or critic to pick his screenings: Competition, Critics' Week, Directors' Fortnight, Un Certain Regard, Market, plus sidebar events like the Scandinavia, West German, and French screenings. Press facilities have been notably improved since the chaotic days of the Sixties. *Inquiries to*: Festival International du Film, 71 rue du Faubourg Saint-Honoré, 75008 Paris, France.

AWARDS 1982
Palme d'Or (ex aequo): **Missing** (U.S.A.), Costa-Gavras, and **Yol** (Turkey), Güney.
Special Jury Grand Prix: **La notte di San Lorenzo** (Italy), Taviani brothers.

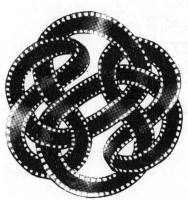

The Fourth International Festival of Film and Television in the Celtic Countries

TO BE HELD IN

SCOTLAND

20 to 25 March 1983

SCREENINGS/SEMINAR/MARKET PLACE/AWARDS

Michael W Russell

SECRETARY GENERAL AND FESTIVAL DIRECTOR
ASSOCIATION FOR FILM AND TELEVISION IN THE CELTIC COUNTRIES
INVERNESS LIBRARY
FARRALINE PARK, INVERNESS, SCOTLAND IV1 1LS
TELEPHONE: INVERNESS (0463) 226189 TELEX: 75670

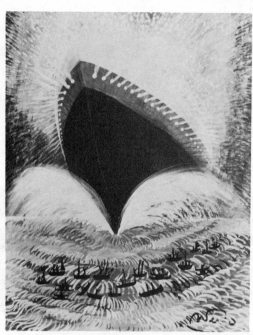

35ᵉ FESTIVAL INTERNATIONAL DU FILM

CANNES   14-26 MAI 198

FEDERICO FELLINI'S POSTER FOR THE 35TH
ANNIVERSARY OF THE CANNES FILM FESTIVAL

Special 35th Anniversary Prize: Michelangelo Antonioni
for **Identificazione di una donna** (Italy).
Best Actress: Edwiga Jankowska in **Another Way** (Hun-
gary).
Best Actor: Jack Lemmon in **Missing**.
Best Director: Werner Herzog for **Fitzcarraldo**.
Best Screenplay: Jerzy Skolimowski for **Moonlighting**.
Palme d'Or (shorts): **Merlin or the Gold Rush** (France),
Joffe.
FIPRESCI Prize: **Yol** (Turkey), Güney. Plus special
awards to **Another Way** (Hungary), and **Les fleurs
sauvages** (Canada).
Caméra d'Or: **Mourir à trente ans** (France), Goupil.

Cracow
June 1983

Since 1972 money prizes of 40,000, 30,000,
25,000 and 15,000 złotys have been awarded at
Cracow, which began its career over a dozen years

ago. All directors, producers, critics, and short film fans are welcome at the mid-summer event, which is Poland's only international festival and a much respected short film showcase. Note that the maximum length of films at Cracow is 30 minutes. *Inquiries to*: Festival Bureau, Pl. Zwyciestwa 9, PO Box 127, 00–950 Warsaw, Poland.

Delhi
January 1983

Every two years, the Indian authorities hold an international competitive festival in New Delhi. In addition to the competition (which is recognised by FIAPF), there are retrospectives, information sections, and a Film Market, as well as a panorama of recent trends in new Indian cinema (with a booklet that follows each festival). *Inquiries to*: Directorate of Film Festivals, Vigyan Bhawan Annexe, New Delhi 110011, India.

Dutch Film Days
September 1983

Now established as an important occasion during which the entire output of Dutch film-making may be assessed, in the attractive old town of Utrecht. In 1981 no fewer than 100 films were screened, and there is a Grand Prix worth a financial award and a "Golden Calf." Useful for festival directors, film buffs, distributors, and critics. *Inquiries to*: Stichting Nederlandse Filmdagen, Hoogt 4, 3512 GW Utrecht, Holland.

Edinburgh
August–September 1983

This lively festival, although one of the oldest in the international calendar, has an enviable "running free" image, with several offbeat screenings, seminars, and retrospectives each year. Jim Hickey has now managed to reinstate the two-week schedule of the past, and the facilities at the lavish Film-house development have contributed to the increasing success and reputation of the Edinburgh event. *Inquiries to*: The Film House, 88 Lothian Road, Edinburgh EH3 9ZB, Scotland.

ULRIKE S. AND LOTHAR LAMBERT, PROVOCATIVE GUESTS AT THE GÖTEBORG FILM FESTIVAL IN 1982

Film International
February 1983

This is the twelfth annual festival organised by the Rotterdam Arts Foundation. Under the direction of Hubert Bals, its aim is to create a focal point for directors, festival programme heads (Rotterdam being one of the earliest events of the season), and the Dutch public. There are no awards, but a distribution guarantee is given to the film regarded as best in a poll among critics and public. Rotterdam is an immensely friendly and informal festival, where guests can talk to visiting directors and personalities in pleasant conditions. *Inquiries to:* Film International, Westersingel 20, 3014 GP Rotterdam, The Netherlands.

Göteborg
January 1983

Now in its fifth year, this is the only festival in Sweden, and has triumphed until recently with only a modicum of state aid. Attendances have grown steadily, and guests from abroad in 1982 included Mago and Nelly Kaplan. The festival is

FILM

PROD:
SCENE

電影

第七屆香港國際電影節一九八三年三月二十四日至四月八日

The Seventh Hong Kong International Film Festival March 24–April 8, 1983

Information:
Hong Kong International Film Festival
City Hall, Edinburgh Place, Hong Kong
Cable: HKIFF, Cityhall, Hongkong
Telex: 60645 UC USD HX
Telephone: 3-7211923

**Presented by the
Urban Council of Hong Kong**

open to features from all countries, and can often manage to secure Swedish distribution for films screened. *Inquiries to*: Göran Bjelkendal and Gunnar Carlsson, Göteborg Film Festival, Kåren, Götabergsgatan 17, S-411 34 Göteborg, Sweden.

Hong Kong
March-April 1983

Now in its seventh year, this Far East Festival is growing steadily in importance, as a meeting place for buyers from Japan, Hong Kong, the Philippines, Malaysia and southeast Asia generally. There are three key categories: International Cinema, Asian Cinema, and a retrospective. *Inquiries to*: Co-Ordinator, International Film Festival of Hong Kong, City Hall, Edinburgh Place, Hong Kong.

Iberoamerican Film Festival
December 1982

The Spanish resort of Huelva is the site for a valuable survey of films from Latin America and the Spanish peninsula. There is a competition for features, an information section, children's section, and a tribute slot. The event has been in existence for eight years and goes from strength to strength. *Inquiries to:* Iberoamerican Film Festival, Hotel Tartessos, Huelva, Spain.

AWARDS 1981
Colón de Oro (features): **Cerromaior** (Portugal), Rocha.
Colón de Oro (shorts): **El cristal amarillo** (Spain), Galán.
Public Awards: **Mojado Power** (Mexico), Arau (features), and **El cristal amarillo** (Spain), Galán (shorts).

Indonesian Film Festival
August 1983

Festival Film Indonesia (FFI) was first held in 1955 and then, personally financed by film director Djamaluddin Malik, in 1960. In 1973 it returned on an annual basis, rotating through different towns in the Indonesia archipelago. The venue in 1982 was Jakarta; in 1983 it will be held in Medan, North Sumatra. FFI is always a colourful affair, with guests treated to displays of Indonesia's varied culture between screenings. Only local films are eligible for entry and substantial cash prizes accompany the awards. *Inquiries to*: Festival Film

Indonesia, National Film Council, Jalan Merdeka Barat no.9, Jakarta, Indonesia.

AWARDS 1980
Best Film, Best Director: **Serangan fajar** (Arifin C. Noer); *Best Script*: **Bawalah aku pergi** (Asrul Sani); *Best Music*: **Serangan fajar** (Embie C. Noer); *Best Photography*: **Jangan ambil nyawaku** (Akin); *Best Art Direction*: **Serangan fajar** (Supandi).

International Festival of Film and Television in the Celtic Countries
April 1983

Now entering its fourth year, this festival features the best in film and TV from Scotland, Ireland, Wales, and Brittany, both for internal consumption and as a showcase. The aim is to promote strong and healthy film and TV industries in countries where such activity has traditionally been dominated by larger neighbours. Seminars, awards, a market, and screenings in all languages spoken in the various Celtic countries. Scotland will be the host country in 1983. *Inquiries to*: Association for Film and Television in the Celtic Countries, Library, Farraline Park, Inverness, Highland Region, Scotland.

International Tournée of Animation

Now in its 18th annual programme, this unique touring showcase of international short animated films is exhibited in over 100 universities, specialised theatres, and art centres in the United States and Canada. Each Tournée of between 15 and 20 film selections includes prize winners from the Academy Awards and major animation festivals as well as the work of independent animators. It rents as a feature-length package. *Inquiries to*: Prescott J. Wright, International Tournée of Animation, 4530 18th Street, San Francisco, California 94114, U.S.A.

GUESTS AT THE INTERNATIONAL FILM DAYS IN HOF, WEST GERMANY: ROGER CORMAN (ABOVE), AND JOHN WATERS (BELOW)

Besides a retrospective dedicated to Mikio
Naruse and an exhibition "Federico Fellini & Nino
Rota" and a lot of films in and out of
competition, Locarno should once more be an
international meeting-point of film-buffs, film-
makers, film-producers, film-critics, film-fans,
all in line for another Golden Leopard.

36. festival internazionale del film Locarno.
August 1983.

POB, CH-6600 Locarno. Telex: 846147.
Telephone: 093/31 82 66, 093/31 86 33.

BURGESS MEREDITH, GIULIANO GEMMA, AND GINA LOLLOBRIGIDA
AT THE WORLD FILM FESTIVAL IN MONTREAL

Internationale Hofer Filmtage
October 1983

Hof, a small town in Southern Germany (Bavaria), on the border between East and West, has built a fine reputation as a festival for American and German independent directors, and is regarded by many as the most intimate and significant film gathering in West Germany. There is also a full-scale retrospective of films by major directors (past recipients have included John Cassavetes, George Romero and Roger Corman, David Cronenberg, and the irrepressible John Waters). More than twenty features are unveiled during the four days of the festival, plus the annual football match for participants! Hof is non-competitive, and all programmes are open to the public. *Inquiries to*: Heinz Badewitz, Director, Internationale Hofer Filmtage, Postfach 1146, D-8670 Hof, West Germany *OR* Lothstr. 28. D-8000 Munich 2, West Germany.

Locarno
August 1983

Under the direction of David Streiff, Locarno has undergone yet another of its metamorphoses, aiming now to be a meeting point for film-makers from around the world, in a location where new features may be viewed in a peaceful atmosphere. A major retrospective will be devoted to Mikio Naruse in 1983. Locarno awards are much prized. *Inquiries to*: Festival Internazionale del Film, Casella Postale, 6601 Locarno, Switzerland.

AWARDS 1981 .
Golden Leopard: **Chakra** (India), Dharmaraj.
Silver Leopard: **Pixote** (Brazil), Babenco.
Bronze Leopard (Special Jury Prize): Ozualdo Ribeira Candeias for **Opçao, as Rosas da Estrada**.
Bronze Leopard (Technical): Gábor Bódy, for **Narcisz és Psyché** (Hungary).

La Rochelle
July 1983

The presence of Cannes tends to overshadow other French film festivals, but during recent years the reputation of La Rochelle, under the zealous leadership of Jean-Loup Passek, has soared. No

San Francisco International Film Festival

DOUBLE

AMERICA'S OLDEST AND LARGEST FILM FESTIVALS

San Francisco Inquir

3501 California

Suite

San Francisco, CA 94

A CALIFORNIA FILM EXTRAVAGANZ

Los Angeles
International
Film Exposition

EXPOSURE

NOW PRESENTED SIMULTANEOUSLY IN MARCH

FILMEX

Los Angeles Inquiries:

Erwin Entertainment Complex
6525 Sunset Boulevard
Hollywood, USA 90028

Accreditation:

Available for
film professionals &
authorized journalists

FOR FILMBUYERS AND FILMGOERS

7ª MOSTRA SÃO PAULO

INTERNATIONAL FILM FESTIVAL

Museu de Arte de São Paulo Assis Chateaubriand
01310 Avenida Paulista, 1578, São Paulo, Brazil. Cable: Museuarte

AN ALTERNATIVE WAY

October/15-31/1983

prizes, but a series of exquisitely-assembled tributes and retrospectives (in 1982: Boris Barnet, Mrinal Sen, John Schlesinger, Peter Del Monte etc.). In ten years, some 500 films have been screened at the festival, which receives our warm recommendation. *Inquiries to*: 4 rue de la Paix, 75002 Paris, France.

London
November 1983

Ken Wlaschin, with the help of some distinguished colleagues, scours the world for films, making London unquestionably the world's leading "Festival of Festivals." There is a "festival atmosphere" with the NFT Three Clubroom open to visitors and film-makers attending the event. All programmes are open to the public, although members of the British Film Institute have booking preference. As well as the 100 or so features from around the world, there is the regular serendipity of a silent film's being revived with a full orchestral accompaniment (in 1982 both *Flesh and the Devil* and *Show People* were screened in this way). *Inquiries to*: British Film Institute, 127 Charing Cross Road, London WC1.

Los Angeles International Film Exposition (FILMEX)
April 1983

By dint of hard work and programming flair, the Los Angeles International Film Exposition has become an established part of the West Coast cultural scene, with its superb catalogue a worthy visiting card. The event has now combined with the former San Francisco Festival to give Californians an unparalleled opportunity to see the richest selection of world cinema during the year. New films, often making their U.S. *début*, classic revivals, tributes to individual artists, and archive treasures all jostle for attention. A film screened here stands a good chance of being snapped up by a U.S. distributor. FILMEX has introduced a series of Audience Awards, with votes coming from over 9,000 attendees. The winner in 1982 was the West German film, *Das Boot*, with *Diva* (France) winning the award for Best First Feature for Jean-

Jacques Beineix. *Inquiries to*: Gary Essert, Festival Director, FILMEX, 6230 Sunset Boulevard, Hollywood, Los Angeles, California, U.S.A.

Manila
January 1983

At the first festival, on January 19–28, 1982, some two hundred films were shown in four categories: competition, focus on Asia, exhibition and market. The 1983 festival plans a bigger Asian presence, with invitations to every Asian film industry. Manila aims to be the Cannes of the East and to serve as a focal point for Asian film-making. *Inquiries to*: MIFF, Philippine Convention Center, CCP Complex, Manila, Philippines.

AWARDS (1982)
Grand Prize (Golden Eagle): **36 Chowringhee Lane** (India), Aparna Sen.
Best Actor: Bruno Lawrence, **Smash Palace** (New Zealand).
Best Actress: Lyudmila Gurchenko, **The Beloved Woman of Mechanic Gavrilov** (U.S.S.R.).
Best Director: Goran Marković, **Majstori, majstori** (Yugoslavia).
Special Awards: Juliusz Machulski, **Va Banque** (Best First Film); Karel Reisz, **The French Lieutenant's Woman**; Peter Weir, **Gallipoli**.

Mannheim
October 1983

This is an annual competition for first features, long and short documentaries, featurettes and animation films, which are judged by a jury of young film-makers. There is always a retrospective screening too. A Grand Prize of DM 10,000 is awarded for the best feature; the Josef von Sternberg prize of DM 2,000 to the most original film; and there are also awards of five Mannheim Film Ducats, each accompanied by DM 1,500. In 1982 a highlight of the week was the retrospective of 25 major films from China, covering the entire history of Chinese cinema. *Inquiries to*: Filmwochenbüro, 6800 Mannheim, Rathaus, E5, West Germany.

Melbourne
June 1983

The Melbourne Festival is unique among feature film festivals in its equal emphasis on shorts. For almost thirty years, this event has been a touchstone of quality in Victoria and now screens some 60 features and around 100 shorts. A total of $10,000 cash prizes and numerous awards have been given, including $2,000 for films on art. *Inquiries to*: Geoffrey Gardner, Director, Melbourne International Film Festival, 53 Cardigan Street, Carlton, Victoria 3053, Australia.

AWARDS 1981
Grand Prix (shorts): **New York Story** (U.S.A.), Raynal.
Best Australian Film: **Mallacoota Stampede**, Tammer.
Other Prizes: **Amy** (U.K.), Wollen, **Chance, History, Art** (U.K.), Scott, **Down and Out** (U.K.), Sproxton and Lord, **Act of God** (U.K.), Greenaway, **The Cat** (Hungary), Hernadi, **House of Flame** (Japan), Kihachiro, **New Jersey Nights** (Canada), Soul, **Public Enemy Number One** (Australia), Bradbury, **Sydney-Bush** (Australia), Winkler, **Groping** (Australia), Proyas and Silverstein.

MIFED (Milan)
April and October 1983

The International Film, TV Film and Documentary Market, known as MIFED, was opened in 1960. The object was to give film-makers as well as their sales and distribution agencies throughout the world a new, efficient trading organisation. From the outset a superbly equipped centre has been provided twice yearly, and over the years, alongside the growth of the Fair itself, the facilities at MIFED have been improved. Now there are numerous screening studios fitted with the latest technical appliances, including videocassette units, plus four large rooms for special presentations. MIFED also aims to help the small and medium-size film-makers who on their own are often unable to gain recognition, far less to sell to circuits or get a foothold in the market. There is also an annual Cine-TV Festival on the theme "The Child in Our Time." *Inquiries to*: MIFED, Largo Domodossola 1, 20145 Milan, Italy (Telex 331360 EAFM 1).

Montréal
October 1983

This festival seeks to discover and promote films of outstanding quality produced as an alternative to the conventions and commercialism of the established film industries. Films are selected on the basis of their originality and significant contribution to the development of cinematic language in terms of content, structure, and form. There is a quite remarkable profusion of films on display here. *Inquiries to*: Le Cinéma Parallèle/Coopérative des Cinéastes Indépendants, 3684 boul. St-Laurent, Montréal, Québec H2X 2V4, Canada.

New York
September–October 1983

Although it is non-competitive, and although it takes place in a city where more films are screened than anywhere else in the West, the New York Festival has established a name and an image that result in SRO signs almost as soon as the schedule is announced. *Inquiries to*: New York Film Festival, Film Society of Lincoln Center, 140 West 65th Street, New York, NY 10023.

Nordic Film Festival
January 20–23, 1983

The fourth biannual showcase of new films from the Nordic countries (Sweden, Finland, Denmark, Norway, and Iceland), held in the picturesque and well-equipped cultural centre of Hanasaari-Hanaholmen, just outside Helsinki. There are 16 features shown in the main sessions, plus video screenings, press conferences, and seminars.

Inquiries to: Nordic Film Festival, Hanasaari-Hanaholmen Cultural Centre, SF-02100 Espoo 10, Finland.

Nordische Filmtage
November 4–7, 1982

This annual event held in the charming medieval town of Lübeck (north of Hamburg), throws a spotlight on the Scandinavian cinema exclusively, and usually enables members of the Nordic trade, critics, and other visitors, to see the best of the new productions. There is always an excellent Retrospective, devoted in 1982 to Jörn Donner, and seminars and discussions are held. *Inquiries to*: Nordische Filmtage, Senat der Hansestadt Lübeck, Amt für Kultur Rathaushof, D-2400 Lübeck 1, West Germany.

Nyon
October 1983

For more than a dozen years, Nyon has been a focus for the world's documentarists to aim at. There are awards for the best entries, and an indispensable retrospective section as well as informative screenings. *Inquiries to*: Festival International de Cinéma – Nyon, Case postale 98, CH-1260 Nyon, Switzerland.

AWARDS 1981
Golden Sesterce: **Du beurre dans les tartines** (Belgium), Bonmariage.
Silver Sesterces: **A Lady Named Baybie** (U.S.A.), Sandlin; **Ipousteguy – Histoires d'une sculpture** (France), Kebadian; **Zur Besserung der Person** (Switzerland), Buetler.
Best Documentary Short: **Stilt-Dancers of Longbow Village** (U.S.A.), Gordon and Hinto.
Special Prize for "Investigative Cinema": **Against Wind and Tide: A Cuban Odyssey** (U.S.A.), Burroughs and Neshamkin.

Oberhausen
April 18–23, 1983

There is no doubt that Oberhausen is the world's premier short film festival. This revival is due in part to the programming of Wolfgang Ruf, the festival director. Not only is there a wide selection of shorts from all over the world (with special

SYDNEY FILM FESTIVAL   JUNE 1983

Telex AA 22969
Cables SYDFEST
Tel. (02) 6603909

GPO Box 4934
Sydney NSW 2001
Australia

emphasis on productions from the Third World and Latin America in particular), but also an opportunity to attend the "Information Days" devoted to West German short films (April 15–17, 1983). *Inquiries to*: Westdeutsche Kurzfilmtage, Grillostrasse 34, D-4200 Oberhausen 1, West Germany.

AWARDS 1982
Grand Prize of the City of Oberhausen: **Adgilis Deda** (U.S.S.R.), Tschocheli.
Main Awards: **La zona intertidal** (El Salvador), **In een tank kun je niet wonen** (Netherlands), **Bagohegy Boszorkanya** (Hungary), **Presa** (Yugoslavia), **Night on the Town** (U.S.A.), **Dzien dziecka** (Poland).
FIPRESCI Prize: **In een tank kun je niet wonen**, **Bagohegy Boszorkanya**, and **Historia de una descarga** (Cuba).

Pesaro
June 1983

The "Mostra Internazionale del Nuovo Cinema" is particularly concerned with the work of new directors and emergent cinemas – in other words, with innovation at every level of the film world. For the past seventeen years, this Mediterranean resort has been the centre for some lively screenings and debates, and in recent seasons the Director, Lino Miccichè, has devoted the festival to a specific theme – in 1982 the cinemas of Hungary and Yugoslavia. Pesaro also tries hard to arrange commercial distribution for films shown during the festival. *Inquiries to*: Mostra Internazionale del Nuovo Cinema, Via della Stelletta 23, 00186 Roma, Italy.

Santa Fe
April 1983

Launched in 1980 in New Mexico, the Santa Fe Festival concentrates on a different theme each year (1980 was devoted to "New Directors/New Films," 1981 was "The Western Film," and 1982 honoured "Music and the Movies"). Bill and Stella Pence bring to this event the same qualities of enthusiasm and efficiency that they gave to Telluride in its early years. Lillian Gish, Gene Kelly and Miklós Rózsa were among the leading guests in 1982. *Inquiries to*: Santa Fe Film Festival, 1050 Old Pecos Trail, Santa Fe, New Mexico 87503, U.S.A.

São Paulo
October 1983

The Mostra Internacional de Cinema is a cultural event originated and managed by the Film Department of the São Paulo Museum of Art. The organisers themselves select the films to be screened, on both 35mm and 16mm, with one feature from each participating country (save Brazil, with two), one documentary from each country, and produce a most handsome catalogue on the occasion of each year's festival. The Mostra is non-competitive, but there is a prize for the film most appreciated by the public (*Montenegro* in 1981). *Inquiries to*: Museu de Arte de São Paulo, 01310 Avenida Paulista 1578, 01000 São Paulo, Brazil.

Sydney
June 1983

One of the senior events in the world's festival calendar, the Sydney Film Festival nevertheless has a perennially young and adventurous image, thanks to the peripatetic efforts of David Stratton, whose international contacts enable him to premiere the most interesting films often long before they reach the United States and other major territories. Prominent visitors are invited from abroad and many of the films screened are subsequently bought for Australian distribution. *Inquiries to*: David Stratton, Director, Sydney Film Festival, Box 4934, G.P.O., Sydney, NSW 2001, Australia.

Tampere
February 9–13, 1983

For twelve years, Tampere has been the Nordic hub of short film activity. The Finnish winter does not deter enthusiasts from several countries, East and West. The international competition consists of categories for documentaries, animated films, children's films and experimental and short fiction films. In addition there is a full retrospective programme. A Nordic Film Market is also being arranged where short film producers from all the

Keep your agenda open at the end of August
for:

THE MONTREAL WORLD FILM FESTIVAL
A competitive film festival recognized by the I.F.F.P.A.

and

THE INTERNATIONAL FILM MARKET

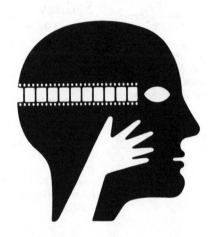

For Information:
The World Film Festival - Montreal
1455 de Maisonneuve Blvd., West
Montreal, Quebec, Canada
H3G 1M8

Telephone: (514) 879-4057
Telex: 05-25472 WOFILMFEST

Nordic countries will present their films for sale. *Inquiries to*: Tampere Film Festival, PO Box 305, SF-33101 Tampere 10, Finland.

Telluride
August–September 1983

Over the past eight years, this friendly gathering in a spectacular location in the mountains of Colorado has become one of the world's most influential festivals, with the town of Telluride virtually doubling in size as famous directors, players, and critics descend on the Sheridan Opera House. The dedication of both organisers and participants liberates Telluride from the shallow ballyhoo that envelops most film events. Each year there are remarkable special events (such as the outdoor screening, in 1979, of Abel Gance's *Napoléon*, in the presence of its creator!). *Inquiries to*: The National Film Preserve Limited, 110 North Oak Street, Telluride, Colorado 81435, U.S.A.

Thessaloniki
September 1983

The International and Domestic Festivals at Thessaloniki take place immediately after the closure of the Thessaloniki Fair. There were 41 shorts from 23 participating countries, three prizes and an honorary distinction. At the 22nd Domestic Festival, several features and shorts were screened, which was one of the most successful from the point of view of feature participation and attendance. Usually, the festival awards some $75,500 in prize money. *Inquiries to*: Film Festival Secretariat, Thessaloniki, Greece.

AWARDS 1981
Best Fiction Short: **Guests of the Maneuvers** (Switzerland).
Best Documentary: **The Lamb** (Bulgaria).
Best Cartoon: **Dilemma** (Britain), Halas.
Best Greek Feature: (ex aequo) **The Factory**, Psarras, and **Petrochemicals, Cathedrals of the Desert**, Katsaros and Sofianos.

Festival International du Cinéma du Tiers-Monde (Third World Film Festival)
March 1983

Partly underwritten by the weekly "Le Nouvel Observateur," the Ministry of Foreign Affairs and the National Cinema Centre, the Third World film festival in Paris has succeeeded in its first four years in two aims: one, to find and create a public interested in the films of Third World countries; and two, to gain an international reputation, as most African, Latin American and Asian countries have participated in it.

The highlights of past festivals have been the cinema of Sri Lanka (particularly that of Lester James Peries), forty Chinese films made between 1937–66, Indonesian, Malay, Mongol, Iraqi, Palestinian, Venezuelan and Syrian cinema, Guru Dutt's Hindi classic *Pyaasa*, fifteen films by Satyajit Ray, several by Shyam Benegal, Ritwik Ghatak's *Ajantrik*, forty films from Black Africa, and many others, most of them unknown to the French public. The 1982 festival included a retrospective of the films of Mexican director Emilio Fernández.

The festival also promotes the distribution of films for commercial, non-commercial and TV showing. It has expanded into the suburbs, where there are immigrant communities and a public which rarely comes into contact with Third World cinema. The fifth festival will take place in March 1983. For entry forms and more information, write to Festival International du Cinéma du Tiers-Monde, 6 rue Saulinier, 75009 Paris, telephone 770 74 71/246 14 11, Telex Hitechs 213 852. LYLE PEARSON

Vancouver
October 1983

A major event focusing on films for young people, with a competitive section, special programmes and retrospectives, an Information showcase, a TV market, and seminars. The Vancouver Festival aims to fill the gap created by the demise of the Tehran Festival for Children and Young Adults and to provide a forum for film-makers to discuss and exchange common experience in this specialised field. There was a retrospective of Karel Zeman's films, a tribute to Walt Disney, and an animation workshop at the first event, with Bahman Farmanara as Director General of the Festival. It is recognised by FIAPF. There is also a jury composed of children alone. *Inquiries to*: 340 Brooksbank Avenue, North Vancouver, BC, Canada V7J 2C1.

Venice
August–September 1983

Going into its 50th anniversary, the Mostra Cinematografica is becoming more rigorous if not more enjoyable. In 1981 a strong injection of American movies (including many classics by Howard Hawks) enlivened the judicious international selection assembled by Carlo Lizzani against the normal pressures of time, money, and politics. Important sidebar events, like the retrospective "Vienna-Berlin-Hollywood," were organised outside the Mostra's official programme. *Inquiries to*: La Biennale – Cinema, Cà Giustinian, 30100 Venezia, Italy.

AWARDS 1981
Golden Lion: **Die bleierne Zeit** (West Germany), von Trotta.
Golden Lion for a First Film: **Sjécaš li se Dolly Bell** (Yugoslavia), Kusturica.
Special Golden Lion (ex-aequo): **Sogni d'oro** (Italy), Moretti, and **Eles não usam black-tie** (Brazil), Hirszman.

Viennale
October 1983

Year after year, the annual Viennale festival, organised with flair and generosity by Edwin Zbonek and Veronika Haschka-Gerlich, has impressed critics and visitors with its programmes of features old and new. Some films are entered at the non-competitive Viennale before they reach the leading festivals; others, passed over by the big events, pop up usefully in Vienna in October. *Inquiries to*: Viennale-Büro, Künstlerhaus, Karlsplatz 5, A-1010 Vienna, Austria.

Wellington
July 1983

The annual Wellington Film Festival, presented by the Wellington Film Society in association with the New Zealand Federation of Film Societies, celebrated its eleventh year in 1982. It is held each July in the independently-owned Paramount Cinema in central Wellington. It selects films of merit as seen in the world's leading film festivals – and offers New Zealand premieres of titles which would not otherwise come to New Zealand. It s non-competitive, and each participating film receives a certificate. *Inquiries to*: Lindsay Shelton (Director), or Bill Gosden (Administrator), Wellington Film Festival, Box 1048, Wellington, New Zealand.

World Film Festival
August 1983

Serge Losique has fought an uphill but successful battle to establish his World Film Festival in Canada at the end of the summer season. Drawing on his close contacts in France and Western Europe generally, M. Losique has forged a bright new link between the old world and the new, and Montréal is the only competitive film festival in America recognised by FIAPF. The event contains the following sections: Official Competition, Hors Concours section, Spanish Cinema of Today (1982), Latin American Cinemas, Canadian Cinema, a Marché, and so on. No fewer than 132,000 people attended the World Film Festival in 1981, and the number of foreign personalities grows each year. Montréal is the ideal location for such an event, with its bilingual facilities and its proximity to all major North American outlets. *Inquiries to*: Serge Losique, Director, World Film Festival, 1455 de Maisonneuve Blvd., West, Montréal, Québec, Canada H3G 1M8.

Other Festivals of Note
Annecy, Journées Internationales du Cinéma d'Animation, 21 rue de la Tour d'Auvergne, 75009 Paris, France. (*Animation – June 1983*.)
Auckland International Film Festival, Box 1411, Auckland 1, New Zealand. (*Features and shorts, non-competitive – July*.)

PHILIPPE JALLADEAU, DIRECTOR OF THE FESTIVAL OF THREE CONTINENTS IN NANTES (LEFT), WITH CARMI MARTIN, ACTRESS, LINO BROCKA, DIRECTOR, AMMY SOTTO, CRITIC (AND IFG CORRESPONDENT), DURING DISCUSSION OF THE PHILIPPINES PANORAMA IN 1982

Biarritz Festival du Film Ibérique et Latino-Américain, Comité du tourisme et des fêtes, Cité administrative, 64200 Biarritz, France. (*Films in Spanish and Portuguese language from Europe and the Americas – September.*)

British Industrial and Sponsored Film Festival, BISFA, 26 D'Arblay Street, London WIV 3FH. (*Annual presentation of awards to best sponsored documentaries produced in Britain – June.*)

Brussels International Film Festival, 32B Avenue de l'Astronomie, 1030 Brussels, Belgium. (*January.*)

Cambridge Film Festival, Arts Cinema, 8 Market Passage, Cambridge, England. (*Features and shorts, non-competitive – late July.*)

Cambridge Animation Festival, 10 City Road, Cambridge CB1 1DP. (*Retrospectives, new animated films, exhibitions, seminars, student films, all under the knowledgeable and enthu-*

siastic direction of Antoinette Moses – September.)

Cape Town International Film Festival, Centre for Extramural Studies, University of Cape Town, Lovers Walk, Rondebosch, Cape, South Africa. (*South African festival arranged on a non-racial, completely integrated basis – April – plus related Documentary Festival in September.*)

Cartagena International Film Festival, Aereo 1834, Cartagena, Colombia. (*Leading Latin American festival. Competitive.*)

Chicago International Film Festival, 415 N. Dearborn Street, Chicago, Illinois 60610. (*Annual event, competitive for features and shorts, with coverage of TV commercials and industrial movies – November.*)

Cork Film Festival, 38 MacCurtain Street, Cork, Ireland. (*Annual, competitive, for documentaries, animation, art films, fiction, and sponsored shorts – October.*)

Announcing
THE SANTA BARBARA
INTERNATIONAL FILM FESTIVAL

The first in a series of annual
gatherings and conferences, alongside
a very select number of screenings.

OCTOBER 1983

Enquiries to: P.O. Box 2095, Goleta, California 93118, U.S.A.

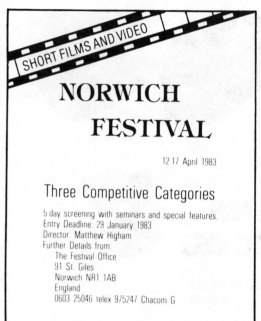

SHORT FILMS AND VIDEO

NORWICH
FESTIVAL

12 17 April 1983

Three Competitive Categories

5 day screening with seminars and special features.
Entry Deadline: 29 January 1983
Director: Matthew Higham
Further Details from:
The Festival Office
91 St. Giles
Norwich NR1 1AB
England
0603 25046 telex 975247 Chacom G

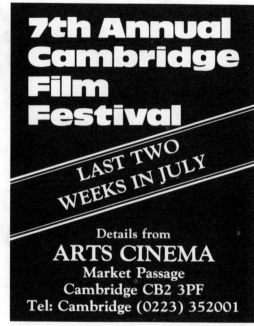

7th Annual Cambridge Film Festival

LAST TWO WEEKS IN JULY

Details from
ARTS CINEMA
Market Passage
Cambridge CB2 3PF
Tel: Cambridge (0223) 352001

Damascus Film Festival, BP 7187, Damascus, Syrian Arab Republic. (*Biannual competitive festival, especially valuable for its coverage of Middle East cinema – October.*)

Dance Film Festival, c/o Cinema/Chicago, 415 North Dearborn Street, Chicago, Illinois 60610, U.S.A. (*Array of dance and ballet films – June.*)

Dance Video and Film Festival, Dance Films Association Inc., 250 West 57th Street, New York, NY 10019, U.S.A. (*16mm and video films on various aspects of dancing – June.*)

Fairytale Film Festival, Rådhuset, Flajhaven, 5000 Odense, Denmark. (*Competitive for cartoons, puppet films etc. – early August 1983.*)

Festival des 3 Continents, B.P. 3306, 44033 Nantes Cedex, France. (*Competitive event open to entries from Africa, Asia, Latin and Black America, plus retrospectives – November.*)

Festival International de Films de Femmes, 1 rue de Florence 1050 Brussels, Belgium (*Focus on women's films.*)

Festival Internazionale Cinema Giovani, Galeria Subalpina, Cinema Romano, 10123 Torino, Italy. (*New festival devoted to young people's films – September.*)

Festival Internazionale del Cinema per i Ragazzi e per la Gioventu, 84095 Giffoni Valle Piana (Salerno), Italy. (*Annual, competitive festival for children's and youth films – August.*)

Festival of Festivals, 69 Yorksville Avenue, Suite 206, Toronto, Ontario M5R 1B7, Canada. (*Annual showcase of international features and shorts, plus a market – September.*)

Festival International du Film Nature, WWF-Genève, CP28, CH-1212 Grand-Lancy, Switzerland. (*Films on 16mm and Super 8, devoted to nature and the environment – November.*)

Festival do Filme Agrícola e de Temática Rural e Meio Ambiente, Cerco de S. Lázaro 51, 200 Santarem, Portugal.

Festival de Cinema da Figueira da Foz, rua Castilho 61–2°, Dt.°, 1200 Lisboa, Portugal.

Festival Internacional de Cinema de Animação, ("Cinanima"), rue 62, No. 251–1°/Apart. 43, 4500 Espinho, Portugal.

la librairie des vrais cinglés de cinéma

LES ZINZINS D'HOLLYWOOD

7 rue des Ursulines.75005 Paris. ☎ 633.48.43
5 rue de Condé.75006 Paris. ☎ 354.66.80

Film International Antwerpen, 437/11 Bisschoppenhoflaan, 2100 Deurne, Belgium. (*Held in conjunction with Film International in Rotterdam.*)

Florence Film Festival, c/o Assessorato alla Cultura, Comune di Firenze, Dipartimento Arti Visive, Via Sant'Egidio 21, 50122 Florence, Italy. (*Review of independent cinema – features only – May–June.*)

Gdańsk Film Festival, c/o Film Polski, Mazowiecka 6/8, 00–048 Warsaw, Poland (*Annual competitive event for Polish features – September.*)

Giffoni Valle Piana, International Festival of Cinema for Children and Youth, 84095 Giffoni Valle Piana (Salerno), Italy. (*Annual survey of young people's features and shorts – July–August.*)

Humboldt Film Festival, Humboldt State University (Theatre Arts), Arcata, California 95521. (*Student event, for films under 60 minutes, and on 16mm, now in its 15th year – May.*)

Hungarian Film Festival, Hungarofilm Báthori utca 10, H-1054 Budapest, Hungary. (*Annually in February, screening all new Hungarian features.*)

International Craft Film Festival, New York State Craftsmen Inc., 27 West 53rd Street, New York, NY 10019, U.S.A. (*For 16mm films dealing with any aspect of traditional or contemporary crafts – December.*)

International Film & TV Festival of New York, 251 West 57th Street, New York, NY 10019, U.S.A. (*Annual competitive survey of film and videotape productions, and with an emphasis on TV and cinema commercials etc. – November.*)

Karlovy Vary Festival, Vaclavske nám 28, Prague, Czechoslovakia. (*Alternates with Moscow as a competitive festival in Eastern Europe – July 1984 next.*)

Knokke-Heist International Film Festival, Zeedijk 581 – bus 16, 8300 Knokke-Heist, Belgium. (*New summer event that seeks to improve distribution chances for foreign films – August.*)

Lausanne – International Festival of Youth Films,

60 Avenue d'Ouchy, CH-1000 Lausanne 6. (*Annual event, with screenings and stands – March.*)

Leipzig Festival, 27 Burgstrasse, 102 Berlin, G.D.R. (*Documentaries and shorts. Competitive.*)

Lille International Festival of Short and Documentary Films, 26–34 rue Washington, 75008 Paris, France. (*Competitive for shorts, with additional panorama of recent French production in the field – March.*)

Moscow Film Festival, 33 Vorovsky Street, Moscow, U.S.S.R. (*Alternates with Karlovy Vary as a competitive festival. Next held in July 1983.*)

Mostra Cinema Mediterrani, Excm, Ajuntament de València, València, Spain. (*Annual festival of "Mediterranean Cinema" – November.*)

Norwegian Film Festival, Norsk Kino- og Filmfond, Lille Grensen 3, Oslo 1. (*The largest single event for the film and cinema trade in Norway, with lively discussions as well as screenings – August 1983 in Bergen, 1984 in Haugesund.*)

Norwich International Festival of Short Films and Video, 91 St. Giles, Norwich NR2 1AB, England. (*Biennial event – next event 1984 – with competitive sections for shorts and video work, plus seminars and market.*)

Ottawa Animation, Canadian Film Institute, 75 Albert Street, Ottawa, Ontario K1P 5E7, Canada. (*Animation – alternate years, next festival probably 1984.*)

Pula Festival, Jugoslavija Film, Knez Mihailova 19, Belgrade, Yugoslavia. (*Annually in July, screening all new Yugoslav features.*)

Rencontres Internationales du Jeune Cinéma, 70 rue Faider, 1050 Brussels, Belgium (*Accent on films for and by young people.*)

Reykjavík Arts Festival, PO Box 88, Reykjavík, Iceland. (*Annual showcase for the best new international features and shorts, immensely popular with the local population – February.*)

Røros/Trondheim Short Film Festival, Filmhuset, Wessels gate 4, Oslo 1. (*Norwegian non-competitive event for domestic and Nordic shorts, plus retrospectives etc. Every November.*)

San Diego International Film Festival, PO Box 441, La Jolla, California 92038, U.S.A. (*Showcase for contemporary and overlooked features, including some U.S. and West Coast premieres.*)

JURY FOR THE FILM FESTIVAL IN OSLO, 1982: (FROM LEFT) GRO JARTO, INGEBORG MORÆUS HANSSEN, NILS KLEVJER AAS, AND GUDMUND HUMMELVOLD

Sanremo, Mostra Internazionale del Film d'Autore, Rotonda dei Mille 1, 24100 Bergamo, Italy. (*Gran Premio worth several thousand dollars – March.*)

San Sebastian International Film Festival, Apartado Correos 397, San Sebastian, Spain. (*Formerly one of the world's leading festivals, now not so prominent. Includes Market – September.*)

Semana Internacional de Cine de Autor, Palacio de Congresos, Torremolinos (Malaga), Spain. (*Annual survey of amateur films, now in its 14th year, in Benalmadena – March.*)

Settimana Cinematografica Internazionale di Verona, Via S. Mammaso 2, 37100 Verona, Italy. (*Features, new and retrospective – June.*)

Solothurn Filmtage, Postfach 92, CH-4500 Solothurn, Switzerland. (*Screenings of all new Swiss films – January.*)

Trieste Festival, Azienda Autonoma di Soggiorno e Turismo, Trieste, Italy. (*July festival, specialising only in fantasy and science fiction films.*)

Trieste Festival of Festivals, Cinema Ariston, Trieste, Italy. (*Eight-month-long competitive marathon for films d'essai.*)

U.S.A. Film Festival, PO Box 3105, Dallas, Texas 75275, U.S.A. (*Collection of new and old American movies – March.*)

Varna: World Festival of Animation, Filmbulgaria, Rakovsky Street 135a, 1000 Sofia, Bulgaria. (*Animated festival under auspices of ASIFA – biannual in October, next gathering 1983.*)

Vevey – Festival International du Film de Comédie, Office du Tourisme, Place de la Gare 5, CH-1800 Vevey, Switzerland. (*Bright new spark on the competitive festival map – devoted exclusively to movie comedy – August.*)

Winter Film Festival, Irish Film Theatre, St. Stephen's Green House, Earlsfort Terrace, Dublin 2, Ireland. (*Now in its fifth year, an annual showcase of new international features – November–December.*)

Internationales Filmwochenende Würzburg, Pleichertorstr. 10, D-8700 Würzburg, West Germany. (*International features and documentaries, noncompetitive – late November*).

"The Way to the Neighbour"

April 18th-23rd, 1983

29th Westdeutsche Kurzfilmtage Oberhausen

"The World's Premier Short Film Festival" – IFG
Director: Wolfgang Ruf. Address: D-4200 Oberhausen, Grillostr. 34
Telex: 0856414

The 15th National West German Short Film Festival will be held 15-17 April 1983

SINEMATEK INDONESIA DIRECTOR H. MISBACH YUSA BIRAN TALKS TO FOREIGN GUESTS AT THE 1982 INDONESIAN FILM FESTIVAL: JERRY W. L. LIU (HONGKONG INTERNATIONAL FILM FESTIVAL), ANGELIKA KETTELHACK (WEST GERMAN TV CONSULTANT), DEREK ELLEY (IFG ASSOCIATE EDITOR) AND KEN WLASCHIN (LONDON FILM FESTIVAL)

U.S.A.
(continued from page 320)

MISSING

Script: Costa-Gavras, Donald Stewart, from the book by Thomas Hauser. Direction: Costa-Gavras. Photography (Technicolor): Ricardo Aronovich. Editing: Françoise Bonnot. Music: Vangelis. Production Design: Peter Jamison. Players: Jack Lemmon, Sissy Spacek, Melanie Mayron, John Shea, Charles Cioffi, David Clennon, Richard Venture. Produced by Polygram for Universal release. 122 mins.

The traditional entertainment dictates of the commercial cinema are usually ignored by political film-makers, with the result that none but the zealous seeks out the message of some ill-shot, po-faced documentary on fascism and injustice. Costa-Gavras, along with Francesco Rosi and Lindsay Anderson, has always turned the popular cinema to his advantage as a committed director. *Missing* sounds, if it does not look, less radical than *L'Aveu*, which summoned up images of persecution in Prague so harrowing that they haunt the screen a decade later. But although made for a major Hollywood studio, Costa-Gavras's new movie compromises only in its image of the Americans, not in its condemnation of the military

COSTA-GAVRAS DIRECTING *MISSING*

dictatorship that succeeded Allende's government in Chile.

Charles Horman disappears from his home in Santiago, where he worked on a "liberal" newspaper. His wife Beth (Sissy Spacek) and father Ed (Jack Lemmon) comb the city in vain for information. They are treated with patronising dispatch by officials at the U.S. Embassy, and Ed – at first exasperated by his daughter-in-law's "anti-establishment paranoia" – by degrees grows as sceptical and sardonic as she. Their quest ends, inevitably, in the revelation of Charles's death, but the fact is less shocking than its ominous concomitants – a National Stadium filled with political prisoners, a morgue overflowing with corpses, the collusion of embassy officials with the new regime, and the bizarre U.S. naval officer who seems to be involved in the anti-Allende coup. If the film falls short of being a masterpiece, it's on account of a tacit, somewhat complacent belief in the capacity and freedom of ordinary Americans to bring baddies to

book. But the vigour and imagination of Costa-Gavras's approach are magnificent and, though obviously set in Chile, the film's resonance extends to Lebanon, Iran, Turkey, southern Africa ... Such is the universal quality of its anguish.

PETER COWIE

SHOOT THE MOON

Script: Bo Goldman. Direction: Alan Parker. Photography (Metrocolor): Michael Seresin. Editing: Gerry Hambling. Production Design: Geoffrey Kirkland. Music: various pop songs. Players: Albert Finney, Diane Keaton, Karen Allen, Peter Weller, Dana Hill, Viveka Davis, Tracey Gold. Produced by Alan Marshall for M-G-M. 123 mins.

Behind the bleakly beautiful, pluvious shoreline of Marin County, a marriage is collapsing, and from the very first shot of this film, with Albert Finney's head slowly emerging in profile from a bedroom, Alan Parker establishes a grasp of the situation that

THE RECONCILING QUARREL IN THE RESTAURANT IN *SHOOT THE MOON*

compounds a European sensitivity with an American vividness of emotion. George Dunlap (Finney) stands at the peak of his career as a writer, yet some irritant has worked its spell upon him to the point at which he leaves wife and cacophanous children for the arms of another woman. Yet even that fails to mollify his deep-seated frustration, which in Finney's perfectly-tuned performance lies always smouldering beneath the burly, hunched-up *macho* exterior. *Shoot the Moon*, leavened with outbursts of farce and genuine feeling, achieves all the goals that Woody Allen's *Interiors* failed to do. Bo Goldman's screenplay allies with Parker's long-established flair for directing kids in presenting a *family's*, not just a wife's, reaction to a marital break-up. And Parker constantly surprises his audience, forcing them to think for themselves, with elliptical cutting that is bold but never ostentatious. Diane Keaton curbs her tendency to take wing and instead presents a meditative, modulated portrait of the wife, and in the scene where she responds to an outsider's seduction technique, projects her meaning with an extraordinary eloquence of smile and stare.

In *Shoot the Moon*, Parker purposely overstates the trivial, understates the essential, and the entire film gives the impression of a carefully reasoned, contemplative study of Western decadence, of a society where money – not sex – may fire a spouse's jealousy, and where children know much of fucking but naught of love. Like Bergman's, Parker's couple may fight and scream, yet remain fettered by an attachment neither quite acknowledges, until in the poignant aftermath of violence at the end, George extends a hand from the pit of his inchoate despair, uttering his wife's name, "Faith!", in a memorable *double entendre*.

PETER COWIE

HEALTH

Script: Frank Barhydt, Paul Dooley, Robert Altman. Direction: Robert Altman. Photography (colour): Edmond Koons. Editing: Dennis M. Hill. Sound: Bob Gravenor. Players: Glenda Jackson, Carol Burnett, Lauren Bacall, James Garner. Produced by Lion's Gate for 20th Century-Fox release. 102 mins.

Altman's most accessible film in years, *Health* is not, as one might suppose, a spoof of the current health craze mentality. Bean sprouts and trendy running outfits are conspicuously missing, and when someone – like Paul Dooley, playing the Independant "Health" candidate – dives into a pool, it's most likely to sink and create a sensation. Altman's parodic model is, rather, the larger and more Middle American world of the business convention; his guests – the metaphorical American electorate – are a plump, ageing, querulous, physically undistinguished and extraordinarily inscrutable bunch. Why are they here, how will they cast their ballots, what are the bright, eccentric candidates to them or they to the candidates?

Where *Nashville* resolves questions such as these with an assassination, *Health* – a gentler and perhaps more cynical film – pushes them aside with a non-violent and altogether anticlimactic election. Every threat here is a red herring. Isabella's (Glenda Jackson's) purported sex "transformation," which might upset her chance to win, is never discovered and probably never occurred. Colonel Coty, who identifies himself as a violent underminer of the democratic process, turns out to be only Esther Brill's (Lauren Bacall's) younger brother. And if there's no real threat here, no violence – as in *Nashville*, *A Wedding*, and most of Altman's earlier works as well, there is no true longing either. When McCabe in *McCabe And Mrs. Miller* says, "Partners is what I came here to avoid"; when Haven exhorts the chaotic audience to sing, at the end of *Nashville*: these earlier Altman characters suggest an albeit betrayed wistful vision of a better America. But when Esther Brill's campaign manager (superbly evoked by James Garner) laments, "And we had such high hopes in the beginning too," he is merely being coy.

Its greater equanimity notwithstanding, *Health* is a first-rate work in fine Altman tradition, with many of its best moments evolving out of inspired characterisations. Virgin Esther Brill exhorts her public to "feel yourself" in a low, sensuous voice. Dick Cavett relaxes after a hard day of Health by switching on the Johnny Carson Show. Ms. Gloria Burbank (Carol Burnett), a White House press secretary susceptible to bouts of nymphomania, leaps into her estranged husband's arms at the sight of a masquerade skeleton. Asked how old Esther Brill's forty-year-old dog would be in human years, Isabella Garnell replies in perfect dead-pan, "In human years, she'd be dead."

DIANE JACOBS

TRUE CONFESSIONS

Script: John Gregory Dunne, Joan Didion, based on the novel by Dunne. Direction: Ulu Grosbard. Photography (colour): Owen Roizman. Editing: Lunzee Klingman. Music: Georges Delerue. Production Design: Stephen S. Grimes. Players: Robert De Niro, Robert Duvall, Charles Durning. Kenneth McMillan, Ed Flander, Cyril Cusack, Burgess Meredith. Produced by Irwin Winkler and Robert Chartoff. 108 mins.

Ulu Grosbard's second film (after the distinguished, unheralded *Straight Time*) was among the strongest and most original of the year. The film's central characters are two brothers: Des (Robert De Niro), a rising young Monsignor, and Tommy (Robert Duvall), the family black sheep turned dissolute cop. Where the classic crime film hints at connections between good and evil, between the socially accepted and condemned, *True Confessions*'s juxtaposition of these two men drums home the analogies. When the film opens, Des, the dignified priest, has risen in the Church by winking at the crimes of his associates. In the film's climax, Tommy, the corrupt police detective, excoriates injustice and (inadvertently) redeems his brother's soul.

Near the end of *True Confessions*, when it becomes clear that Tommy's investigation will ultimately implicate Des, a fellow cop demands, "What are you trying to prove? That [Des is] just like you? Of course, he is, he's your brother." It's an important moment, cementing the odd complicitous relationship between the brothers. But, true to the subtlety of the Dunne/Didion script as well as Grosbard's direction, there's an equally important moment, a few scenes back, where Des walks

quietly into his spare Church quarters and thoughtfully unties his shoes.

True Confessions is that rare film, genre or otherwise, that can integrate a complicated plot, strong themes, and rich characters. On the one hand, it is a reverie on two complex, finally elusive human beings. But like the crime films of yore, it is also a whodunit and a contemplation of moral alternatives. For neither Des nor Tommy is an absolutist, a "catholic" in the secular sense of the word. Though he feels a vocation for the priesthood, Des admits he had no gift for loving God; nor has Tommy a "gift" for loving earthly justice and mankind. By temperament as well as experience, these are worldly men, aware that certain unpleasant means must be employed to achieve desired ends. Intellectually, these middle-aged Catholics have long since made their peace with compromise. And yet, instinctively, they are sick to death of their worldliness, of their intelligent self-interest. And so, impelled by nothing so concrete as a conventional sense of honour (boredom or self-interest would be more accurate descriptions), each brother makes a morally absolute "good" gesture. And *True Confessions*, like *The Big Sleep* and *The Big Heat* and countless other crime dramas, ends with a return to social order and, almost ironically, to Catholicism as well.

DIANE JACOBS

RAGTIME

Script: Michael Weller, based on the novel by E. L. Doctorow. Direction: Miloš Forman. Photography (Todd-AO, Technicolor): Miroslav Ondriček. Editing: Anne V. Coates, Antony Gibbs, Stanley Warnow. Music: Randy Newman. Production Design: John Graysmark. Players: James Cagney, Brad Dourif, Moses Gunn, Pat O'Brien, Elizabeth McGovern, Norman Mailer. Produced by Dino De Laurentiis for Ragtime Productions. 155 mins.

It's easy to see what attracted Miloš Forman to E. L. Doctorow's best-selling *Ragtime*. From his early, socially conscious Czech films, like *The Fireman's Ball*, through his superb adaptations of *One Flew over the Cuckoo's Nest* and *Hair*, Forman has proven himself a strong and subtle film-maker with a gift for fleshing out polemical themes with gently idiosyncratic characters – and *Ragtime* has themes and characters aplenty. During the film's first half hour, Forman seems to have both well under control. In an opening shot, celebrity Evelyn Nesbit (Elizabeth McGovern) and her dancing instructor waltz across what looks like the bottom of an hour glass. It's a seductive image, but something's missing as the following shot makes clear. For now the listless (yes, that was the trouble) couple is gone, replaced by the thick black fingers of a pianist banging out a ragtime score on a black-and-white keyboard. Forman makes his – and Doctorow's – point about American society early and subtly.

And now the threads of Doctorow's narrative begin unravelling above, below, and around these pounding black hands. We see Teddy Roosevelt in an old newsreel; we watch a silent movie and a Houdini trick. Soon we're in a spotless New Rochelle dining room with a not-quite quintessential American family: Father, Mother, Grandfather, a watchful young boy, and Mother's disturbed Younger Brother.

So far, so good. Forman has done nothing extraordinary, but Doctorow's fabulous tapestry is slowly beginning to take shape. And then, no more than forty minutes into a very long film, something strange happens. Forman abruptly turns his back on this melting pot that is at the heart of Doctorow's novel and begins closing in on the book's least authentic, most melodramatic story line. The black man with the musical hands returns, not as a discreet symbol, but as Coalhouse Walker, a "Negro" ragtime player who's seen his car destroyed by bigoted white firemen and is now an embodiment of black wrath. Nothing wrong with this as such. But Walker, as written and as played (by Howard E. Rollins) is not flesh-and-blood, but a soap-opera creation, born of the worst sort of white-liberal guilt: an impeccably noble hero who is, of course, bound for martyrdom in white America.

Ragtime is not quite as simple-minded as a plot summary suggests. There are amusing scenes between Evelyn Nesbit and her various admirers; James Cagney's presence (as the police commissioner) is welcome; Mandy Potenkin's all too infrequent appearances as the feisty immigrant Tateh invariably breath life into the production. Still, from the moment Walker enters the life of the New Rochelle family, most of the wonder goes out of Forman's *Ragtime*.   DIANE JACOBS

CHAN IS MISSING

Script and Direction: Wayne Wang. Photography: Michael Chin. Editing: Wayne Wang. Music: Robert Kikuchi-Yngojo. Sound: Curtis Chong. Players: Marc Hayashi, Wood May. Produced by Wayne Wang. 80 mins.

At one point near the end of *Chan Is Missing*, one of the film's two Chinese American protagonists – Jo – recounts an apochryphal Chinese tale. A businessman offers a woman in his debt a "lady or the tiger" option. There are two doors before her. If she passes through one, she'll find an exit; behind the other is the man's bedroom. "Of course, both doors lead to the man's bedroom," relates Jo, but the lady is smart. She points to the one door and says, 'This door does *not* lead to an exit.' She makes a positive of a negative, you see?" Appropriately, Jo's nephew Steve does not "see" or want to "see" the point to this parable which, in many respects, serves as "key" to Wayne Wang's multi-layered mystery, where superficial negatives – ranging from the film's egregiously low budget to the self styled detectives' dearth of clues – are forever being turned to someone's advantage.

Chan Is Missing is a lively and wise first feature, proving Wayne Wang's strong comic sense, his flair with actors, and a rare ability to pull back from his own most passionate concerns. There's a Resnais-like flavour to the film's unsolved mystery, suggesting things may not be as they appear, absence may imply presence, answers may lie in unresolved contradictions. And then again, the opposite may be true. For Wang Wayne is a Chinese American artist in the most felicitous sense: similarly sceptical of the elusive Chinese and the straightforward Americans, he is vitally involved in both worlds.

DIANE JACOBS

U.S.S.R.

by Ronald Holloway

Those impressive Soviet cinema statistics are well known, but bear repeating. At the beginning of the Seventies, about 130 feature films and an additional 70 TV fiction films were produced annually in all the republics of the Soviet Union. Of the 39 film studios, 19 produce feature films. A round figure of 300,000 employees work at these studios, and of these over 3,000 are classified as "artistic creators." At the beginning of the Eighties, the same 39 studios were turning out more than 150 feature films and approximately 100 TV features, in addition to some 50 feature-length documentaries and up to 500 shorts. The U.S.S.R. produces well over 70 features annually in the scope process.

The most celebrated scope epic has yet to be released: Elem Klimov's *Agonia* (1977), originally produced to celebrate the 60th anniversary of the October Revolution. This historical chronicle of the year 1917 – featuring such personalities as Rasputin the Monk and Tsar Nikolai II – was shelved shortly upon completion, but then turned up suddenly on the last day of the 1981 Moscow international film festival in the Grand Salle. It was then heavily rumoured for the *film surprise* slot at Cannes the following spring, but the necessary compromise with Soviet officials could not be reached in time to guarantee the desired screening.

In the meantime, Elem Klimov has finished another milestone feature film: an adaptation of Valentin Rasputin's critically acclaimed novel, *Farewell to Matjora*. Larisa Shepitko originally started the film but Klimov took over the project when she and members of her shooting crew died in a tragic highway accident in June 1979. *Matjora* will be heavily in demand at future festivals.

The same goes for Gleb Panfilov's *Theme* (*Tema*), also presented on the side during the Moscow festival. Like his other films – *No Ford in the Fire* (1968), *The Debut* (1970) (a New York festival entry), *May I Take the Floor* (1975) (known to several festivals), *Valentina, Valentina* (1980) (based on Alexandr Vampilov's play, *Last Summer in Chulimsk*) – *Theme* is a dialogue tract on the inability of the responsible individual to compromise his ideals. All of his films star, in lead or key bit-roles, the remarkable Inna Churikova;

she is to be seen in *Theme* as a kind of go-between in a story featuring a so-so playwright in a middle-aged crisis. To heal the playwright's spiritual wounds, she suggests he revert to his earlier promise and attempt a play about a local poet in the provinces. The latter turns out to be a disgruntled writer who wishes to emigrate due to a falsification by authorities in his latest publication – a theme far too difficult to tackle than one might imagine at the outset.

With *Agonia* and *Theme* as the highlights of the Moscow festival, and the Academy Award for Best Foreign Film in 1981 going to Vladimir Menshov's *Moscow Doesn't Believe in Tears*, the stage was set for a strong Soviet presence at Berlin and Cannes in 1982. It was not to be: Iskra Babich's sub-par *Fellows* was entered at the Berlinale, and Yuli Raizman's mediocre *A Private Life* was refused at Cannes. Instead, Otar Yoseliani's Georgian masterpiece, *Pastorale*, was programmed as a side-attraction in the Forum of Young Cinema (the director has been living in Paris for nearly two years now) and Andrei Tarkovsky's voice was heard in a festival ball opening the Cannes pageant. Tarkovsky is still at work in Italy on *Nostalgia* and, as of summer 1982, was still questionable for Venice. Another sore note was the protest petition circulated at Cannes for the release of Sergei Paradzhanov, who is reportedly back in prison.

Little has been heard from the Mikhalkov brothers of late. Andrei (alias Andron) Mikhalkov-Konchalovsky has been residing in the U.S.A., seeking support for a project with a title reference to Elvis Presley. Nikita Mikhalkov scored a double hit in American cinemas with *A Slave of Love* (1976) and *Oblomov* (1979) and thereby ranks as the hottest name on the contemporary Soviet film scene, bar none. The presence of Tarkovsky, Konchalovsky, and Yoseliani abroad hints that the U.S.S.R. is ardently seeking co-production partners in the West – thus, *Lenin in Paris* and the derailed John Reed project, originally planned as a U.S. co-production with Sergey Bondarchuk directing. Warren Beatty's *Reds*, three years in the making, reduced John Reed's Kremlin adventures

STILL FROM LEONID KVINIKHIDZE'S *THE HAT*   PHOTO: MOSFILM

to a Marxist love story – the ideological equivalent of Yutkevich's account of Lenin's escapades in Paris.

The return of Grigori Chukhrai to prominence has been most welcome. This Ukrainian-born director made three poignant features on the Great War: *Ballad of a Soldier* (1959), *A Clear Sky* (1961) and *An Untypical Story* (1977), the last never released. *Ballad of a Soldier* depicts heroism on the battlefront; *A Clear Sky* sympathises with the fate of Soviet POWs returning home to Siberian labour camps maintained by an adamant Stalin; and *An Untypical Story* scornfully treats evasion of military engagement on the front lines – it deals with a deserter. These are all autobiographical experiences, the "untypical" example referring to recruits who joined acting troupes for camp enter-tainment to avoid being drafted to the front line. Chukhrai attended festivals in Tashkent, Karlovy Vary, and New Delhi – indication enough that the one shelved film in his career just might surface in a Western festival if diplomatic finesse was exercised by the right person in the right place at the right time. Such an entry at Berlin or Cannes last year would have made an impact.

Veteran screen writers are still in the forefront of quality Soviet films. Yevgyeni Gabrilovich (b. 1899) contributed the human touches in Yuli Raizman's *A Strange Woman* (1977) and Sergei Yutkevich's *Lenin in Paris* (1980), while Alexandr Volodin (pseudonym for Alexander Lifshits, b. 1919) did the same for Nikita Mikhalkov's *Five Evenings* (1978) and Georgi Danelia's *Autumn Marathon* (1979). The new generation of writers

AGONIA
(Agony)

Script: S. Hungin, I. Nusinob. Direction: Elem Klimov. Photography (Sovcolor): L. Casashnikov. Art Direction: Sh. Abdussaldmob, S. Veronkob. Players: N. Petrenko, O. Hine, A. Freindlikh, I. Broneboy. Produced by Mosfilm.

The film was a legend before the first image hit the screen. Begun in 1975 as an official Mosfilm contribution to the 60th anniversary of the 1917 October Revolution, the idea was to capture the atmosphere of that momentous year and, literally, film a page of history. For this purpose, Elem Klimov was allowed access to the Soviet archives to research the facts about the relationship of Rasputin to the family of Tsar Nikolai II. When he finished the film in time for the 1977 celebrations, several buyers appeared on the scene before, during and after the Moscow film festival of that year — among them, it was reported, Dmitri Tiomkin on behalf of a Hollywood interest. In view of the fact that some thirteen feature films had

includes Valentin Rasputin, whose *Farewell to Matjora* has been hailed by many critics as the finest Soviet novel published in the past decade. Rasputin hails from Siberia, the same corner that produced Vasili Shukshin and Alexandr Vampilov.

A children's film at the 1980 Moscow festival won high praise: Viktor Gres's *The Black Hen*, produced by Dovzhenko Studios in the Ukraine. Based on a fairy-tale for adults by A. Pogorelsky, it is set in the Eighteenth century and treats of life in a boarding school for the nobility. The young dreamer in Mozartian dress is an orphaned lad of seven, who imagines mediaeval knights coming to his rescue to fulfil his ardent wishes, receives one day the magic power of memory from an enchanted black hen. The atmospheric polish of this impressively designed and directed period piece owes much to Andrei Vladimirov's photography.

In late June 1982, 30 feature films produced in the 15 republics were to be presented by Sovexportfilm in collaboration with Walter Schobert and the Frankfurt Film Museum. At the Oberhausen short film festival, the grand prix went to a Georgian short feature, Goderdze Chocheli's *Mother of Earth*. The scene is an abandoned village in the provinces and the film, indeed, is a prayerful incantation by an elderly woman.

already been successfully produced on Rasputin and the Empress, *Agonia* in cinemascope was considered box-office gold. Nevertheless, the Soviet authorities decided to shelve the film.

Now, six years after its completion (and one probable cutting session), Klimov's chronicle of that historical year in Russian history is available to buyers abroad. The sketches of Rasputin and Tsar Nikolai will undoubtably capture the attention of most observers, for the former is depicted as the heavy and the latter as a kind of naïve innocent – somewhat the opposite of the account in Marxist revolutionary books. On the aesthetic side, Klimov

has combined black-and-white documentary footage (some stock footage, other scenes from early fiction films) with colour sequences forming the narrative fiction story. The historical backdrop is appropriately eye-catching, particularly the sumptuous decor of the royal quarters. Yet it is the central figures that fascinate: a mild, weak monarch and perverse, evil-soaked monk – this, and the length of time it takes to poison and pump Rasputin with bullets before the scoundrel is finally despatched.

RONALD HOLLOWAY

Yugoslavia

by Ronald Holloway

A long-standing tradition was broken at the 1981 Pula Festival of Yugoslav Feature Films – for the first time in its 28-year history, the festival switched from its regular July 26 to August 2 slot to embrace a 12-day stint at the end of July (in 1982, July 18–29). According to festival director Martin Bizjack (who also happens to be in charge of the Pula Tourist Office), the producers from the various republics clamour to present their films – whether good, bad, or mediocre – in the historical Vespasian arena for a goodwilled and discerning home public of 10,000. Since 26 features were produced for the 1981 event, all but two could be presented in the arena on double-feature billing (the two "outsiders" preferring the modest confines of the Army Club theatre for their low-budget entries). Further, by maintaining a last-two-weeks-of-July profile in the future, Bizjak does not have to worry about sparse hotel space just as the tourist season reaches its height at the beginning of August.

1981 was a bounty year for Yugoslav cinema, a return to the glorious days of the late Sixties when art and box-office satisfied nearly everyone in the jammed arena. Debut directors shared the spotlight with established veterans, while a new production-distribution company – Art Film under the tutelege of Vuk Babić – scored its first success with a pair of satirical comedies: Emir Kusturica's *Do You Remember Dolly Bell?* and

Goran Marković's *Ah, Teachers!* Add to this the respectable shows at Cannes (Rajko Grlić's *The Memory Haunts My Reverie*), Moscow (the award-winning French-Yugoslav co-production, Predrag Golubović's *Peacetime in Paris*), and Venice (Lordan Zafranović's *Fall of Italy* and Emir Kusturica's *Do You Remember Dolly Bell?*, the Debut Prize), and even the most cautious critic

EMIR KUSTURICA'S *DO YOU REMEMBER DOLLY BELL?*

would agree that cinema has returned to the Balkans.

Among the republics, Sarajevo and Skopje have surfaced as important new production centres. Emir Kusturica and his cameraman for *Dolly Bell*, Vilko Filač, were among the last Yugoslav graduates at the famed Czech Film School, FAMU. The Bosnian production recalled the youth of scriptwriter Abdullah Sidran in Sarajevo during the early Sixties, when Pop Music, Italian Vespas, and Western styles flooded the country – as for "Dolly Bell" herself, she was a striptease dancer in a then popular "sensational movie," *Europe by Night*, which in Kusturica's satirical comedy was presented one day at the city's Youth and Cultural Club. If any of this sounds familiar, then picture Emir and Vilko screening the "classics" of the

Czech New Wave as they prepared to begin their own film careers in Sarajevo, the Pop Music Centre of Yugoslavia.

Yugoslav film-makers have become history-conscious. Stole Popov's *The Red Horse* is the best Macedonian feature made to date, following in the same thematic line-of-thinking as the earlier breakthrough film produced in Skopje: Kiril Cenevski's *Black Seed* (1971). Both films are based on the writings of Taško Georgievski, who chronicled the period of the Greek Civil War (1946–49) from the viewpoint of an Aegean Macedonian driven from his country to a forced exile in Uzbekistan in the Soviet Union – others who refused this political solution to end the war were imprisoned on Aegean islands. *The Red Horse* contains some scenes photographed in China, stars the incompa-

STILL FROM *GAZIJA*, DIRECTED BY NENAD DIZDAREVIĆ

rable Bata Zivojinović in one of his strongest roles, and bears all the markings of having been made by a director with style and vision.

Lordan Zafranović's *Fall of Italy* and Rajko Grlić's *The Memory Haunts My Reverie* (Venice and Cannes entries) put Croatia in the forefront of the national film scene. Both films dealt with the troublesome postwar years: the former about the Italians retreating from an island outpost (near Split, where Zafranović was raised), and the latter about the painful Stalinist period (reviewed in IFG 1982). Zafranović and Grlić, both FAMU graduates, were hard pressed in turn by another Stalinist *exposé* tract: Veljko Bulajić's *High Voltage*. The construction of the first power generator in Yugoslavia in 1948 at the very moment of the break with the Soviet Union provides an appropriate symbol, but the complexity of the history lesson is such that the neophyte to Personality Cult films will have trouble interpreting many events of the day. Perhaps Bulajić has purposely left everything open.

As for the Serbian directors, the younger generation is more interested in the present than the past. Yet only one satire from four hits the mark: Goran Marković's *Ah, Teachers!* The setting is a high-school that could just as easily pass for a madhouse, for none of the teachers seem to be able to function as real human beings – particularly on the day a state inspector arrives to investigate a complaint by one of the more distraut members of the staff. Again, the calling-card is the heyday of the Czech Film School, where Marković studied. The three other comedies were also made by born-and-bred Belgrade directors: Dejan Karaklajić's *Erogenous Zone*, Miša Radivojević's *A Promising Lad*, and Branko Baletić's *Plum Juice*.

The costume spectacle has returned to fashion. Vatroslav Mimica's *Banović Strahinja* depicts events in Serbia just before the Battle of Kosovo (1389) against the victorious Turks; the screenplay stems from an earlier project of Aleksandar Petrović, who collaborated with Mimica in getting this international co-production off the ground (Franco Nero and Gert Fröbe play lead roles). Zdravko Velimirović's *Dorotej* is set in Serbia of 1308, when hunger and disease ravaged the country; as in *Banović Strahinja*, a glimpse at the restored churches and monasteries dating from the Middle Ages more than makes up the time

spent on melodramatics. Another costume epic, Nenad Dizdarević's *Gazija*, is based on a brace of Ivo Andrić's short stories; this first film by a young Sarajevo director shows distinct promise.

Lastly, there's Franci Slak's *Time of Crisis*, a remarkable Slovenian *début* by a graduate of the Polish Film School at Lodz. This 16mm experiment for Ljubljana Television has a feeling for people and places: the story, in fact, is constructed from the real-life experiences of the leading actor who went through a similar identity crisis during his university studies.

A sure sign that prosperity has returned to Yugoslav cinema is the presence of foreign actors in both international and national productions. Besides Franco Nero and Gert Fröbe, Yugoslav films starred Daniel Olbrychski, Maria Schneider, and Erland Josephson. And Dušan Makavejev's *Montenegro*, a Swedish entry at Cannes in 1981, was an international hit. Times have certainly changed.

CRVENIOT KONJ / CRVENI KONJ (The Red Horse)

Script: Taško Georgievski, Stole Popov. Direction: Stole Popov. Photography: Branko Mihajlovski. Art Direction: Vlastimir Gavrik. Music: Ljupčo Konstantinov. Players: Bata Zivojinović (*Boris Tusev*), Ilija Džuvalekovski, Dančo Čevrevski, Radmila Zivkovic, Kole Angelovski. Produced by Vardar Film, Skopje, and Makedonija Film, Skopje. 135 mins.

Son of the well-known documentary film-maker Trajče Popov, Stole Popov began his film career in the same genre, won several prizes at international festivals for his documentaries, and then attracted attention at Pula last year with his first feature film. The Red Horse is based on the recollections of writer Taško Georgievski, and it describes a tragic chapter in Macedonian and Greek history: the troublesome Civil War period in Greece, 1946–49, during which some 45,000 people died and several thousands more forced into exile. This is the story of one of those unwilling exiles, Boris Tusev, who is transported with his comrades by freighter and rail to Tashkent in Uzbekistan in accordance with the Yalta Agreement and other diplomatic compromises. After clinging to his ideals over long and bitter years in exile, Boris returns home to his village in Aegean Macedonia, riding into the square on the back of an old red horse.

A combination of Christ and Odysseus so far as national folklore is concerned, Boris is a giant of a man with a gentle heart – without his presence, friends would not pull through the hard times. But as one after another dies or departs to meet his own destiny alone, Boris faces his fate as a worn and tired partisan fighter. He returns home – to find the villagers apathetic and cowed by town bullies, his abandoned home in shambles. With his last strength he steps forward to defend the underdogs, is beaten in a tavern brawl, and awaits his end like a dying elephant. Bata Živojinović plays the lead – it is one of his best performances.

RONALD HOLLOWAY

SJEĆAŠ LI SE DOLLY BELL? (Do You Remember Dolly Bell?)

Script: Abdulah Sidran. Direction: Emir Kusturica. Photography: Vilko Filač. Art Direction: Kemal Hrustanović. Music: Zoran Simjanović. Players: Slavko Štimac, Ljiljana Blagojević, Mira Banjac, Slobodan Aligrundić, Pavle Vujišić, Nada Pani. Produced by Sutjeska Film, Sarajevo, and Televizija Sarajevo. 106 mins.

Emir Kusturica was the last of the Yugoslav directors to study at FAMU, the Prague Film School, graduating in 1978 under Jiří Menzel. After a few credits in Sarajevo television, he made his first feature film and won immediate recognition at both Pula and Venice. This is a warm "human comedy" based on the autobiographical writings of Bosnian poet Abdulah Sidran. The setting is the early Sixties, when Western ways (music, motorbikes, clothes, hair-do styles) seeped into the country to wreak a measure of innocent havoc. The protagonist is a lad of sixteen about to have the first important experiences in life, but the real fun lies elsewhere: the boy's Muslim family with the father's peculiar patriarchal ways. In short, this is a tragicomedy – a refined, perceptive mixture of laughter and tears.

Sarajevo was a sleepy provincial town twenty years ago. Then came government orders to establish a Youth and Cultural Club: chess, dances, amateur band contests, and an occasional movie. The imported film happens to be *Europe by Night*

– there's the lovely Dolly Bell in a striptease act as big as life up on the screen. The house directors struggle to bring "culture" to the youngsters in the meanwhile, which is not always easy as the kids have other things on their minds and no one really knows what culture is in the first place. Then there's the patriarch of the family who readily mixes the Koran with Marx, a long-suffering but lovingly sympathetic mother, and a girl who happens on the scene by chance to spend a few days in the boy's pigeon-coop. A death in the family and a first love provide the climax. The results are so satisfactory that one hopes that the combination of Kusturica-Sidran-Filač will be around for a good time to come.

RONALD HOLLOWAY

new and forthcoming films

BANOVIĆ STRAHINJA. Script: Aleksandar Petrović, Vatroslav Mimica. Dir: Vatroslav Mimica. Phot (colour): Branko Ivatović. Sets: Mile Jeremić. Music: Alfi Kabilja. Players: Franco Nero, Dragan Nikolić, Sanja Vejnović, Gert Fröbe, Rade Šerbedžija, Kole Angelovski. Prod: Jadran Film (Zagreb), Avala Film (Belgrade)/R. von Hirschberg & R. Kalmowicz Filmproduktion, Neue Tele, Contact Filmproduktion (Munich)/Filmska Radna Zajednica (Zagreb), Avala Pro-Film (Belgrade), Zvezda Film (Belgrade).
BERLIN KAPUTT. Script: Antonije Isaković, Mića Milošević. Dir: Mića Milošević. Phot (colour): Aleksandar Petković. Sets: Vladislav Lašić. Music: Vojislav Kostić. Players: Svetozar Cvetković, Milan Gutović. Prod: CFS Košutnjka, OOUR Avala Film (Belgrade).
DEČKO KOJI OBEĆAVA (A Promising Lad). Script: Nebojša Pajkić, Miša Radivojević. Dir: Miša Radivojević. Phot (colour): Božidar Nikolić. Sets: Veljko

FRANCI SLAK IN *TIME OF CRISIS*

Despotović. Music: Koja. Players: Aleksandar Berček, Dara Džokić, Eva Darlan, Rade Marković. Prod: Avala Pro-Film, FRJ "Decko Koji Obecava", RO "Film 41 – Avala Film" (Belgrade).
DOROTEJ. Script: Dobrilo Nenadić, Borislav Mihajlović, Zdravko Velimirović. Dir: Zdravko Velimirović. Phot (colour): Nenad Jovičić. Sets: Vlastimir Gavrik. Music: Vuk Kulenović. Players: Gojko Santić, Gorica Popović, Bata Živojinović. Darko Damevski, Meto Jovanovski, Dančo Cevrevski. Prod: CFS Košutnjak, OOUR Avala Film (Belgrade).
EROGENA ZONA (Erogenous Zone). Script: Dejan Karaklajić, Slobodan Stojanović, Rajko Grlić. Dir: Dejan Karaklajić. Phot (colour): Predrag Popović. Sets: Sava Aćin. Music: Milivoj Marković. Players: Milan Gutović, Marina Urbanc, Bora Todorović, Sonja Divac. Prod: Centar Film (Belgrade).
GAZIJA. Script: Vuk Krnjević. Dir: Nenad Dizdarević. Phot (colour): Tomislav Pinter. Sets: Kemal Hrustanović. Music: Zoran Simjanović. Players: Dušan Janičijević, Pavle Vujišić, Dušica Žegarac, Ante Vican, Abdurahman Šalja, Miralem Zubčević, Jadranka Selec. Prod: Sutjeska Film (Sarajevo).
GOSTI IZ GALAKSIJE (Visitors from the Arkana Galaxy). Script: Miloš Macourek, Dušan Vukotić. Dir: Dušan Vukotić. Phot (colour): Jiří Macak. Sets: Jiri Hlupy. Music: Tomislav Simović. Players: Žarko Potočnjak, Ljubiša Samardžić, Lucie Žulova, Ksenija Prohaska. Prod: Zagreb Film, Jadran Film (Zagreb), Kinematografi Zagreb/Studio Barandov (Prague).
KRIZNO OBDOBJE / KRIZNO RAZDOBLJE (Time of Crisis). Script and Dir: Franci Slak. Phot (colour): Radovan Čok. Sets: Ranko Mascarell. Players: Roberto Battelli, Dušanka Ristić. Prod: Viba Film (Ljubljana), TV Ljubljana, Art Film (Belgrade).
LAF U SRCU (A Great Guy at Heart). Script: Siniša Pavić. Dir: Mića Milošević. Phot (colour): Aleksandar Petković. Sets: Dragoljub Ivkov. Music: Vojislav Kostić. Players: Nikola Simić, Milena Dravić, Irfan Mensur, Danilo Lazović. Prod: RO Film Danas (Belgrade).
LJUBI, LJUBI, AL'GLAVU (Love, Love, But Don't Lose Your Head). Script: Zoran Ćalić, Jovan Marković. Dir: Zoran Ćalić. Phot (colour): Predrag Popović. Sets: Predrag Nikolić. Music: Kornelije Kovač. Players: Dragomir Bojanić-Gidra, Dara Ćalenić, Rialda Kadrić, Vladimir Petrović, Jelena Žigon, Marko Todorović. Prod: Zvezda Film (Belgrade), Union Film (Belgrade), FRZ "Došlo Doba."
MAJSTORI, MAJSTORI (Would You Believe It?). Script: Goran Marković, Miroslav Simić. Dir: Goran Marković. Phot (colour): Milan Spasić. Sets: Marina Milin. Music: Zoran Simjanović. Players: Semka Sokolović-Bertok, Bogdan Diklić, Snežana Niksić, Predrag Laković, Smilja Zdravković. Prod: Radna Zajednica Samostalnih Filmskih Radnika Art Film (Belgrade).
NEKA DRUGA ZENA (Some Other Woman). Script: Dragan Marković, Dušan Perković. Dir: Miomir Stamenković. Phot (colour): Milivoj Milivojević. Sets: Dragoljub Ivkov. Music: Zoran Simjanović. Players: Merima Isković, Dragan Nikolić, Ljubiša Samardžić, Petar Kralj. Prod: Centar Film (Belgrade).

MARIA SCHNEIDER (LEFT) IN *PEACETIME IN PARIS*

PAD ITALIJE (Island Chronicle). Script: Mirko Kovac, Lordan Zafranović. Dir: Lordan Zafranović. Phot (colour): Božidar Nikolić. Sets: Drago Turina. Music: Alfi Kabiljo. Players: Daniel Olbrychski, Ena Begović, Gorica Popović. Prod: Jadran Film (Zagreb), Centar Film (Belgrade).
PIKNIK U TOPOLI (Picnic among the Poplars). Script: Radoslav Pavlović. Dir: Zoran Amar. Phot (colour): Milorad Jakšić-Fando. Sets: Jasna Dragović. Music: Braća Vranješević. Players: Predrag Ejdus, Ena Begović, Danče Cevrebski, Branislav Lečić, Gordana Kosanović. Prod: Radna Zajednica Samostalnih Filmskih Radnika "Film 80" (Belgrade).
RITAM ZLOCINA (The Rhythm of Crime). Script: Pavao Pavličić. Dir: Zoran Tadić. Phot (colour): Goran Trbuljak. Sets: Ante Nola. Music: Hrvoje Hegedušić. Players: Ivica Vidović, Božidarka Frait, Fabijan Sovagović. Prod: Centar Film (Belgrade), Televizija Zagreb.
SEŽONA MIRA U PARIZU (Peacetime in Paris). Script: Predrag Golubović, Ratko Djurović, Vlatko Gillić, Marc Cadiot. Dir: Predrag Golubović. Phot (colour): Milivoj Milivojević. Sets: Milenko Jeremić. Music: Kornelije Kovač. Players: Dragan Nikolić, Maria Schneider. Prod: Centar Film (Belgrade) Albran Film (Paris).
SNADJI SE DRUŽE (Find a Way, Comrade). Script: Joža Horvat. Dir: Berislav Makarović. Phot (colour): Vjenceslav Orešković. Sets: Duško Jeričević. Music: Alfi Kabilja. Players: Miodrag Krivokapić. Prod: Jadran Film (Zagreb), Radiotelevizija Zagreb.
SOK OD SLJIVA (Plum Juice). Script: Branko Baletić, Milan Sećerović. Dir: Branko Baletić. Phot (colour): Živko Zalar. Sets: Miljen Kljaković. Music: Zoran Simjanović. Players: Miki Manojlović, Bata Živojinović. Prod: RO Film Danas (Belgrade).
SESTA BRZINA (Sixth Gear). Script: Dragiša Krunić, Zdravko Šotra. Dir: Zdravko Šotra. Phot (colour): Milan Spasić, Milivoje Milivojević, Nikola Djonović. Sets:

Borislav Nježić. Music: Duško Karuovic. Players: Zoran Radmilović. Prod: CFS Košutnjak, OOUR Avala Film (Belgrade).

ŠIROKO JE LIŠĆE (The Leaves Are Wide). Script: Miroslav Antić, Petar Latinović, Milenko Nikolić. Dir: Petar Latinović. Phot (colour): Dušan Ninkov. Sets: Vladislav Lašić. Music: Zoran Hristić. Players: Jadrinka Selec, Bekim Fehmiu, Mira Banjac, Ivan Hajtl. Prod: Neoplanta Film (Novi Sad).

VISOKI NAPON (High Voltage). Script: Veljko Bulajić, Mirko Bošnjak, Ivan Salečić. Dir: Veljko Bulajic. Phot (colour): Branko Blažina. Sets: Duško Jeričević. Music: Miljenko Prohaska. Players: Božidarka Frait, Vanja Drach, Milan Štrljić, Ljubiša Samardžić, Bata Živojinović, Zvondo Lepetić, Relja Bašić, Ivo Gregurevic, Sanja Vejnović. Prod: Croatia Film (Zagreb).

VLAKOM PREMA JUGU (Southbound Train). Script: Petar Krelja, Vesna Krelja. Dir: Petar Krelja. Phot (colour): Goran Trbuljak. Sets: Zlatko Kauzlarić-Atač. Music: Arsen Dedić. Players: Marina Nemet, Zlatko Vitez, Franjo Majetić. Prod: Zagreb Film (Zagreb), Kinematografi Zagreb (Zagreb).

VREME, VODI / VRIJEME, VODE (Time and Tide). Script: Jovan Strezevski, Branko Gapo. Dir: Branko Gapo. Phot (colour): Ljube Petkovski. Sets: Nikola Lazerevski. Music: Risto Avramovski. Players: Petar Arsovaki, Duško Kostovski, Šišman Angelovski, Nenad Milosavljević, Boris Dvornik, Lidija Pletl. Vardar Film (Skopje), Makedonija Film (Skopje).

STILL FROM GORAN MARKOVIC'S *WOULD YOU BELIEVE IT?*

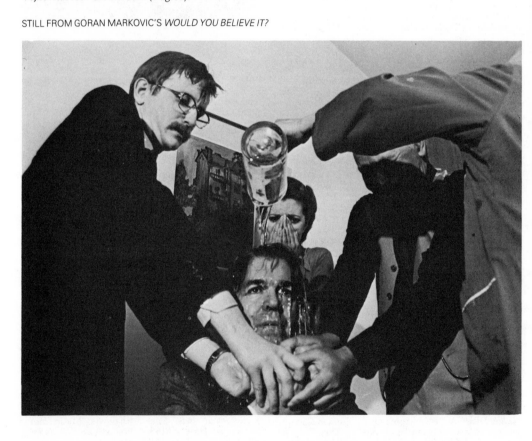

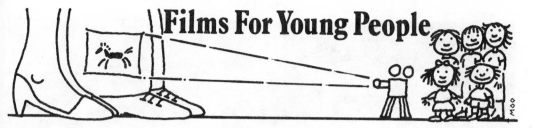

The American Film Festival

During the week of June 14-19, 1982, the American Film Festival (AFF) held its twenty-fourth annual screenings and award presentations. Oldest and largest of the non-theatrical film competitions, its blue and red ribbons in each category, and the two special awards, the Grierson award to a new film maker in the social documentary field, and the Emily award for the highest-ranked film in the festival, are much sought after. Rules require that the entry be in distribution in the U.S.A.; but there are no limitations on place of origin, and productions of many countries turned up in the 1982 festival. In 1983 the Educational Film Library Association, sponsor of the American Film Festival, plans a special programme to celebrate the festival's twenty-fifth anniversary.

Increasingly evident in the entry list are the signs of influence from video. For several years the AFF has accepted video entries as well as 16mm film. In 1982 video was up 35% on the previous year. Total entries were over a thousand; not quite half made it to the finals. There were seventy-five categories, covering all types of subject-matter, with separate categories for film and video, and for long (one hour or more) and short films. One obvious influence of TV is in running times; most films conform to broadcast slots – 27 minutes, 55 minutes, or 84 minutes. However, there are still a few films made to run long enough to do the job well, ignoring the possibility of getting a TV booking.

The top prize-winners were representative of two trends in the 1982 entries. The Grierson award went to Meg Switzgable for *In Our Water*, an account of a community's struggle to track down and stop chemical pollution of its drinking water. It was financed by modest contributions from a number of local organisations and foundations, and is Switzgable's first film. Interest in all aspects of the environment has by no means diminished, in spite of the anti-environmental stance of the Reagan administration. There were enough entries to justify categories in environmental issues, energy, environment features, video environmental issues, and nature and wildlife. Many of these films are getting wide distribution, to school and adult audiences, in public libraries, and through organisations such as the National Audubon Society and Friends of the Earth, as well as public television.

The winners of blue and red ribbons in the energy category dealt with alternative or soft energy – nuclear power has lots its glamour, at least for film-makers. The Blue Ribbon film was *Lovins on the Soft Path*, produced by Nelson B. Robinson, and distributed by Bullfrog Films. It is an example of the triumph of content over technique – it is primarily a record of speeches and workshops conducted by Hunter and Amory Lovins around the country to educate the public on efficient use of renewable energy. But the Lovins are a well-informed and effective couple, and the message gets across. The nature and wildlife winner was an Audubon film, produced by Joel Bennett, and distributed by Learning Corporation, about America's national symbol, the bald eagle. *The Last Stronghold of the Eagles* shows an area in Alaska where more than two thousand eagles gather in winter to feast on late-running salmon, and ends with a plea to protect this unique spot. In the course of the thirty-minute film, viewers can see more bald eagles than exist in the lower 48 states.

Music showed up in a surprising number of categories. The film which received the Emily award was *From Mao to Mozart: Isaac Stern in China* – rather oddly in the category Arts and Crafts. The ninety-minute-long film was produced by Murray Lerner and is distributed by United Artists. It follows the violinist on his 1979 tour of China, made at the invitation of the Chinese government. There are some shots of the Chinese landscape and cities, and street scenes; but most of the film is devoted to the classes, demonstrations, and performances in which Stern shows the young Chinese the fine points of violin playing and Western music. Like an up-to-date Santa Claus, he beams, jokes, plays and charms the students and packed audiences of music-loving Chinese. He also visits classes of gymnasts and rehearsals for Peiping opera. A moving sequence is one in which an elderly professor at the Shanghai Music Conservatoire relates what happened to him and his colleagues during the Cultural Revolution.

Music is also prominent in a winning film in the special education (disabilities) category. *Itzhak Perlman: In My Case Music*, made by Tony de Nonno, uses its famous subject as narrator, as he explains what his disability has meant to him, his family, and his career as a violinist. He entertains disabled children and is an attractive model and inspiration. In *Close Harmony*, blue ribbon winner in the teacher education category, a gifted teacher brings together two widely separated generations. Arlene Symons works with fourth and fifth-graders and with retired people in Brooklyn to establish a chorus in each institution, to develop pen-pal relationships between the children and old people, and finally to present a concert in which they join together. It is a warm and moving film, produced by Nigel Noble, and distributed by Learning Corporation.

The current concern over developments in Central America was reflected in a number of films. *El Salvador, Seeds of Liberty*, produced by Glen Silber and distributed by Icarus Films, won the blue ribbon in the religion and society category. It deals with the killing of missionaries in 1980. *El Salvador: Another Vietnam* examines American involvement in the trouble-torn country. From the same source as the other El Salvador film, it won the international affairs category for features. In

the international events category for short films, the winner was *Americas in Transition*, produced by Obie Benz. It traces the development in this century of dictatorships, Communist influence, and U.S. relations with the Central American nations. A red ribbon (second place) in the war and revolution category went to *From the Ashes: Nicaragua Today*, produced by Helena Solberg Ladd and Glen Silber, and distributed by International Women's Film Project. Blue ribbon winner in that category was a popular choice – *Soldier Girls*, a study of the experience of a group of girls undergoing basic training, produced by Churchill Films. The award was accepted by two of the girls seen in the film.

With all this serious subject matter, it is a pleasure to report that some winning films were just for fun. Ferenc Rofusz's *The Fly*, from Hungarofilm, distributed by Perspective Films, is a short, animated adventure from the fly's point of view. It won the visual essays category. In the humour and satire category, first prize went to Will Vinton for *The Diary*, a clay animation of Mark Twain's wry version of the Creation – as seen by Adam, who is not very enthusiastic about Eve's incursion into his Paradise but comes to appreciate her when they are expelled to face the pioneer experience. It is distributed by Visucom. Second in that category was the animated film *The Sweater*, from National Film Board of Canada, about a small boy whose mother makes him wear a sweater promoting the wrong hockey team. It is a funny, but bitter-sweet, reminder of the pains of childhood. In the children's entertainment category, by coincidence, both winners dealt with frogs. The blue ribbon went to *A Boy, A Dog and a Frog*, produced by Gary Templeton from the popular book by Mercer Mayer, and distributed by Phoenix Films. Tom Davenport won the red ribbon with *The Making of the Frog King*, a documentary about the film he made of the Grimm story, using a turn-of-the-century setting, live actors, and live frogs.

An oddball film which won the social studies award was Stanley Woodward's *Grits!* It is doubtful whether anyone outside the U.S.A. will understand it, and American viewers outside the south have had some difficulty, but it is very attractive in its own way. Shot on grainy black-and-white film,

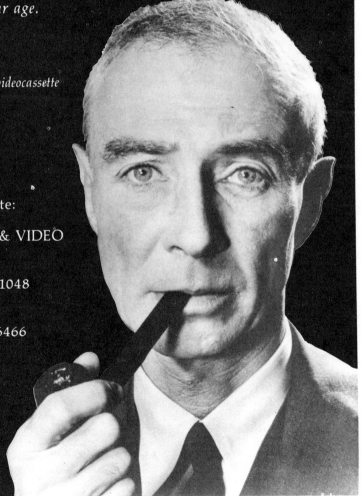

and looking like a *cinéma vérité* film of the Fifties, it interviews a number of people on why they like grits (a kind of cornmeal mush) and how they serve it. The pace, editing, and genial good humour have won it showings on TV.

In 1982 the festival was held for the first time in an educational setting at the well-equipped Fashion Institute of Technology. It lacked some of the glamour that a hotel setting can give but was more efficient for screenings. Glamour was instead provided by the opening evening session, when the Museum of Modern Art presented a special showing of early films made in New York from 1896 to 1912. The screening was followed by a question-and-answer session with the ever-lovely and gracious Lillian Gish, who at eighty can still hold an audience in the palm of her hand. The audience (many of them young people) showed a detailed knowledge of her early films which was impressive.

EMILY S. JONES

The International Scene by Peter Cowie

A sign of changing times was the announcement that, in order to guarantee continued production, the famous Children's Film Foundation of Great Britain would have to extend the distribution of their films to television, and to all the new related media. For decades the CFF has been known to schoolchildren for its Saturday morning matinee screenings up and down the country, and some famous directors have worked on its stream of feature films.

In the States, the Reagan administration's education cutbacks have combined with the video revolution to catch educational film distributors in a wicked pincer grasp. Libraries have ever-shrinking budgets, while pirate prints and cassettes of the more popular titles are somehow smuggled into even the most respectable collections.

Yet video may prove to be a sheep in wolf's clothing. The advantages of the new medium have been underplayed by comparison with its dangers. For example, the storage and shipment of prints, always a costly business for the small distributor, may soon be a chore of the past. Cassettes can be sent through the mail inexpensively, and their storage takes comparatively little space. Teachers are more likely to use cassettes in the classroom, knowing how technically simple it is to set up a screening, or to find a specific passage in a film, when compared with the days of assembling a 16mm projector, etc. Cassettes will be less costly to purchase, with the result that more may be sold, more quickly. Already some of the more enterprising companies, such as Carousel and Pyramid, have built the phrase "and Video" into their actual name.

A new regular competitive festival for young people's films has been founded in Vancouver, Canada, while the Nordic countries continue to be a breeding-ground for excellent features and shorts for children and about children.

As usual, we append herewith a round-up of some of the more interesting commercial producers and distributors.

CAROUSEL FILM & VIDEO

241 East 34th Street, New York, NY 10016. Tel: (212) 683-1660.

The best Carousel films focus on the pressure lines, the incipient flaws in the American dream structure. Typical of this approach are three of the company's most recent offerings: *Just Posing* (33 mins.), *The Wrong Stuff: American Architecture* (13 mins.), and *What Shall We Do About Mother?* (49 mins.).

In *Just Posing*, directed by Lynda Sparrow, a 12-year-old girl falls prey to the greed and callousness of an agent who exploits her as a child star of advertising and TV commercials. Although fictional, *Just Posing* is attuned to the contemporary craze for nymphet advertising, and the sense of a young life distorted and hardened is brought across with unsettling conviction.

Tom Wolfe, the guru of the American intelligentsia, a latterday Max Beerbohm whose pronouncements on art and society are as witty as they are trenchant, rails against the cigar-box syndrome in American urban building. In *The Wrong Stuff*, he demonstrates how the architecture of the past has been dwarfed and suffocated by a style imported from Europe, likening the skyscrapers of Sixth Avenue to German worker tenements of the Twenties. Illuminating and controversial.

What Shall We Do About Mother? is a CBS investigation of the problems faced by ailing parents (and their children) when even a lifetime's savings appear insufficient to provide them with adequate care and shelter. Extremely moving, and all the more pertinent in a society where to be geriatric is a sin.

But the most appealing film of 1982 from Carousel is unquestionably *The Silver Maiden* (12 mins., dir. David Spiel), about two expatriate Chileans who meet by chance in a public park. He (Eli Wallach) is crusty and conservative; she (Jacqueline Brookes) is elegant and liberal. Through the eloquent dialogue of Stephen Whitty, a vanished past emerges from the encounter, and by the close of the conversation two apparently hostile souls have reached out towards each other.

DARINO FILMS

222 Park Avenue South, New York NY 10003. Tel: (212) 228-4024.

Darino is an interesting company in that it offers educationalists a library consisting solely of animation. Many of Eduardo Darino's shorts have won festival awards. *Hello?* (9 mins.), is a hectic, pixillated history of the telephone. *Carousel* (5 mins.), moves delightfully from the realms of geometry to the origins of the carousel and American folk music. *Man the Maker* is a series of five shorts (each 5 mins.), on the major inventions, from the palaeolithic wedge to the supersonic jet, covering the Car, the Train, the Ship, the Airplane, and the Camera. And *The Legend of the Amazon River* (12 mins.), tells the legend of how two little Indians rescued the longest river in the world from inside the old witches' tree. The designs are based on the unique art of the Yagua Indians, while the music and sound effects were recorded on location in the Amazon jungle.

FILMS INC.

733 Green Bay Road, Wilmette, Illinois 60091. Tel: (312) 256-6600.

Thanks to the pioneering efforts of Leo Dratfield, many excellent European shorts have found their way into the Films Inc. catalogues. This awesome giant among non-theatrical organisations is best-known for its feature movies, but the educational side is not neglected either. Carl Sagan's *Cosmos* series is available, as well as a host of titles in such areas as the Social Sciences, Business and Industry, the Humanities, and Science. Several American Film Festival winners and finalists may be found in the 1982 catalogue.

INTERNATIONAL FILM BUREAU

332 South Michigan Avenue, Chicago, Illinois 60604. Tel: (312) 427-4545.

The IFB catalogue covers a wide range of categories, but two particularly interesting recent acquisitions have been two films on American literature, *Herman Melville* and *Nathaniel Hawthorne*. The craft movement is on the upswing in the United States, and *Watching a Woodcarver* covers one intriguing angle of this craft, carving duck decoys.

In the area of conservation and ecology, IFB's three leading releases recently are *The Indiana*

ABOVE: ELI WALLACH (RIGHT) IN CAROUSEL FILM & VIDEO'S *THE SILVER MAIDEN*

BELOW: SUPERB COMPOSITION FROM PYRAMID FILMS' *SEA FLIGHT*

STILL FROM LEARNING CORPORATION'S CAUTIONARY FILM, *BANKRUPT*

BELOW: FROM LEARNING CORPORATION OF AMERICA'S *WHO WANTS TO BE A HERO*

Dunes, dealing with a very special and particular part of the State of Indiana, close to Chicago; *The Guanaco of Patagonia*, dealing with an animal now among the endangered species of the world; and *Fields of Fuel*, which considers the use of alcohol as an alternative fuel for vehicles.

For several years IFB's materials have been available in videocassette format, both ½ inch and ¾ inch, depending on customer requests.

INTERNATIONAL FILM FOUNDATION

200 West 72nd Street, New York, NY 10023.

Although Sam Bryan's famous little operation is no longer originating projects, it still offers to schools and libraries an admirable selection of classic documentaries, many of them "new editions" of standard titles in the IFF repertoire – for example, *Africa: A New Look, Japan, Soviet Union, Israel, Revised Version*, and *Changing Middle East*. Note too more recent titles such as *India: An Introduction*, and *Scandinavia: Unique Northern Societies*.

LEARNING CORPORATION OF AMERICA

1350 Avenue of the Americas, New York, NY 10019. Tel: (212) 397-9360.

The LCA catalogue has mutated over the years into a glittering array of short subjects suitable for viewers of any age or clime. From documentary to animation, from business studies to free-wheeling fiction fantasies, there is something for everyone. All packaged, moreover, with expertise, and available on cassette as well as film.

A touch of Gallic flair illuminates *Flyaway Dove* (18 mins.), directed by the veteran cinematographer, Edmond Séchan. It is a fairytale set in a circus environment, and evokes *The Red Balloon* with its gossamer-light narrative pace, following a small girl and her dove into a world of dreams and wish-fulfilment. This is a non-verbal gem, sure to become an instant classic in its field.

STILL FROM INTERNATIONAL FILM BUREAU'S *HERMAN MELVILLE*

Close Harmony (30 mins.), made by Arlene Symons and Nigel Noble, records a remarkably inspiring symbiosis between the generations, as children and senior citizens join in song and dance at the Friends' School in Brooklyn, New York. Interspersed with the musical activity are interviews with young and old alike, showing their views of each other; everyone seems relaxed, talking freely and sensibly about life and its everyday considerations. *Close Harmony* has won numerous prizes and an Academy Award.

Some of the best LCA productions meld a message with an amiable, movie-like story. *Who Wants to Be a Hero!*, for example, describes a shy high school student's sudden confusion as he rescues a janitor from some hoodlums and becomes both hero (in the eyes of his school friends) and villain (in the eyes of the gang). Coping with pressure and choosing the right moral stance are the issues delineated here with skill and unpretentious verve.

Other excellent additions to the LCA catalogue include *Beyond the Stars* (12 mins.), one of a

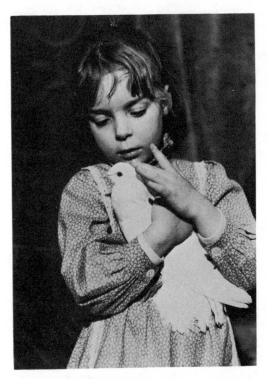

STILL FROM LEARNING CORPORATION OF AMERICA'S *FLYAWAY DOVE*

STILL FROM LCA'S ACADEMY AWARD WINNER, *CLOSE HARMONY*

series of animated shorts entitled *Simply Scientific*, which answers a young child's queries about the sun and the stars; *Stoned* (50 mins.), a TV award-winner about the dangers of drug-taking; *The Electric Grandmother* (48 mins.), a charming live-action fantasy from a story by Ray Bradbury; and some intelligent, articulate documentaries on business and careers being marketed through the LCA Video/Films division.

PYRAMID FILM & VIDEO

Box 1048, Santa Monica, California 90406. Tel: (213) 828-7577.

Always in the forefront of companies when it comes to releasing Academy Award-winners, Pyramid began 1982 with the distribution of

Crac!, the Oscar-crowned animated film from the French side of Canadian television, Société Radio-Canada, with worldwide 16mm non-theatrical rights.

Seaflight presents the brilliant camerawork of Bob and Ron Condon, whose in-the-water camera techniques bring something new to surfing films. A wide variety of new releases are just emerging from the labs – a docudrama of a youth's journey into and out of the Moonie cult, *Moonchild*, a live-action *Peter and the Wolf* in which the orchestra, the forest and the wolf are real players, and *Bypass*, an unusual kind of medical film. *Roller Skate Fever* is playing on the big screens theatrically in Hollywood and Melbourne. The pay TV market is firming up for quality short films, and countries outside the United States are now buying 16mm prints the way the U.S. did during the Seventies.

TEXTURE FILMS

1600 Broadway, New York, NY 10019. Tel: (212) 586-6960.

Although known primarily for their distinguished library of short films, Texture also distribute the occasional feature-length production (e.g. the massive history, *Documentary*), and this year *Clarence and Angel* (75 mins.) heads the company's list. *Clarence and Angel* is an independent film by Robert Gardner, set in a Harlem grade school, and describing the painfully-wrought friendship between a southern migrant black boy, Clarence, and a young Puerto Rican pupil, Angel. The school is viewed as a zone of humiliation, where natural spirits are stifled, and where the staff spend more time haranguing the pupils than trying to understand them as individuals. Clarence cannot read, but he scores well in aptitude and creative tests. Little by little, Angel helps him to master the words . . .

Gardner's film is lively and humorous; his juvenile actors are beyond reproach; and the story is free of physical violence. *Clarence and Angel* has

STILL FROM *CLARENCE AND ANGEL*, RELEASED THROUGH TEXTURE IN THE UNITED STATES

won awards at several festivals in Europe and the United States.

Other additions to the Texture catalogue include two pithy shorts by Carson Davidson, *Granite* (10 mins.), a documentary about the quarrying of granite that conveys the mass and awesomeness of the material; and *100 Watts 120 Volts* (6 mins.), which describes the manufacture

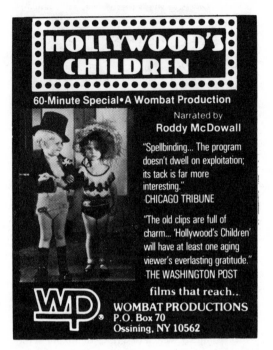
of light bulbs rather in the manner of Bert Haanstra's *Glass*, and is set to the music of Bach.

WOMBAT PRODUCTIONS

Little Lake, Glendale Road, PO Box 70, Ossining, NY 10562. Tel: (914) 762-0011.

Gene Feldman and his wife Suzie actually work on many of the films in their Wombat catalogue, and several of these are aired on television in the United States; others come from film companies and TV stations abroad. *Hollywood's Children* was a one-hour TV special in 1982, narrated by Roddy McDowall and based on the highly praised book of the same name by Diana Serra Cary ("Baby Peggy" in the early Twenties). This was screened by PBS in the States, and received excellent notices.

Other interesting Wombat offerings include *Giustina* (28 mins.), about an Italian American medical student reunited with her family for a birthday celebration and the pressures and divided

loyalties that arise from this. Directed by Rachel Feldman, the film is suitable for junior and senior high college students as well as a general audience. Then there is a beautiful short film (28 mins.) on the *Haiku* poetry of Japan, directed by Seaton Findlay, and *Sandsong* (18 mins.), about the intricate and fascinating "sculpture" thrown up on the beach by a creative digger, and then dispersed by the inevitable tide (directed by Stuart A. Goldman).

In Britain . . .

EDWARD PATTERSON ASSOCIATES

68 Copers Cope Road, Beckenham, Kent. Tel (01) 658-1515.

Bill Orr retains his leadership among British educational film distributors, with several new releases each year. Typical of the catalogue's high quality is the 50 minute documentary, *Mansion of the Sky – A Jordanian Nomadic Experience*, produced by Robert Young. The film examines the tribal structure of the Arab world, the pattern of family life, marriage ceremonies, and the tribesmen's warm and friendly association with their animals, especially the camel.

Confirmation (26 mins.) is a fantasy centring around a young Catholic boy's confirmation service, at once humorous and frightening; *Sandsong* (20 mins.) describes the work of the artist Gerry Lynas and his work in gigantic sand and snow sculpture; and the Edward Patterson Associates catalogue contains other new films from organisations like Wombat, International Film Bureau, and International Film Foundation in the United States.

CONCORD FILMS COUNCIL

201 Felixstowe Road, Ipswich, Suffolk IP3 9BJ, England. Tel: (0473) 76012.

Concord, launched in 1959, is now the largest educational film library of its kind in the United Kingdom. Its enormous catalogue ranges over documentaries, animated films and feature-length productions concerned with contemporary issues, both at home and abroad. Films are selected primarily to promote discussion for instruction and training, not only in schools and colleges but also in the Health Service and other Social Services.

Concord may be regarded as a collection of film libraries, because, in addition to the film titles acquired for the Concord library, the Council also distributes films for over 350 other bodies. The category index at the rear of the catalogue includes some 180 groupings, and this gives an idea of the prodigious wealth of the Concord library. For any producer or film-maker seeking a serious release for a controversial social or political film, Concord may be the answer.

In Scandinavia

FÖRENINGSFILMO

P.O. Box 3167, S-103 63 Stockholm, Sweden. Tel: (08) 23 36 10.

As usual, this remarkably active organisation

MAUREEN STAPLETON (LEFT) IN LEARNING CORPORATION'S *ELECTRIC GRANDMOTHER*

in Sweden offers programmers an enormous selection of films for non-theatrical and TV use, including such recent titles as *Close Harmony* (an Academy Award winner from Learning Corporation of America), *Peter and the Wolf* (from Pyramid), *Honoured and Bruised* and *Love* (from the National Film Board of Canada), as well as two Swedish films (co-produced by Föreningsfilmo) on social issues, *The Fonzie Gang* and *Michael, 18*.

The organisation is geared towards films for young people, but its entertainment catalogue is also impressive, and includes both classics and recent features.

CHS-FILM

Sankt Pedersstraede 32, DK-1453 Copenhagen, K. Tel: (01) 13 37 20.

Scandinavia is the real home of young people's films, and Helge Strunk has carved a place for his CHS-Film, enabling him to reach all the leading film societies and schools in Denmark.

Helge Strunk's expanding company has recently taken on over thirty new titles on 16mm, among them *Max Havelaar*, *Rubber Tarzan* (awarded the UNICEF Prize as the Best Children's Film in the World for 1981), and Karel Zeman's latest Czech film, *The Story of John and Mary*. The emphasis remains on works for children and young people.

STILL FROM *JUST POSING*, LYNDA SPARROW'S BRILLIANT SHORT, FROM CAROUSEL FILM & VIDEO

EL ZORRO IN PETER TORBIÖRNSSON'S *LAND OF THE BURNT HOUSES*, FROM FÖRENINGSFILMO OF STOCKHOLM

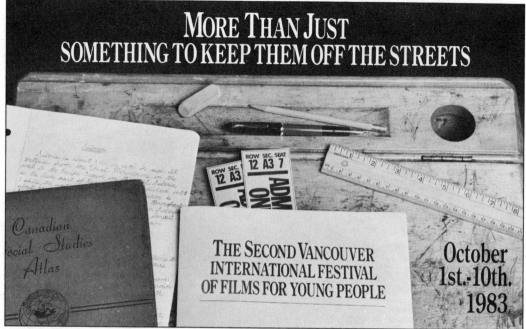

MORE THAN JUST
SOMETHING TO KEEP THEM OFF THE STREETS

THE SECOND VANCOUVER
INTERNATIONAL FESTIVAL
OF FILMS FOR YOUNG PEOPLE

October
1st.-10th.
1983

For Information Contact: Bahman Farmanara, 340 Brooksbank Avenue,
North Vancouver, B.C. Canada V7J 2C1 604·980-7933 Telex 043·52663

STILL FROM *THE STORY OF KIM SKOV*, THE DANISH FILM RELEASED IN SWEDEN BY FÖRENINGSFILMO

Sponsored Films

by Anne Hall

THE ARTS COUNCIL

Film Sales Executive, Arts Council of Great Britain, 9 Long Acre, London WC2E 9LH.

The function of the Arts Films Committee is to receive applications from film-makers for finance of their projects, and if these are judged suitable, then finance to support documentary films on the arts is provided.

One of the most recent and successful of their projects is *The World of Gilbert and George*, in which the two sculptors, Gilbert and George, express their hopes and despairs, their views and passions, the result being a distinctive and highly original film which has evoked a great deal of reaction and comment. *Pastorale*, which can be described as a music theatre piece, has not been released long enough to have received the same kind of attention, but there is no doubt that this extremely unusual film will be the subject of much discussion. Trevor Wishart, who with David Hutt wrote the script, says that for him music is not purely aesthetic, musical structures are actually about ideas, and it is clear that Pastorale is about much more than just the re-telling of the Genesis version of the creation story performed by two musicians, and that this extraordinary composition is packed with ideas, both musical and non-musical.

Another successful and totally different film from the Arts Council is *Return Journey*, which was nominated for BAFTA's Robert Flaherty Award. This film traces the development and usage of the documentary photograph through the work of three photographers, Humphrey Spender, Derek Smith and Jimmy Forsyth. We are treated to a marvellous display of vivid, moving, depressing and touching portraits which capture the harsh realities of life in the North of England in the Thirties. *Return Journey* follows the fascinating story of the rediscovery by Derek Smith of Humphrey Spender's contributions to the Mass Observation project of the Thirties, and his meeting with the amateur photographer, Jimmy Forsyth.

Käthe Kollwitz is the last film which we have space to look at, and it is a film that leaves a deep impression. Brenda Bruce gives a sensitive and moving portrayal of the life and work of the German artist, Käthe Kollwitz. Through her diaries and letters we look back on the life of this extraordinary artist, and the result is a film which is alternatively touching and bleak, hopeful and depressing. Her paintings and etchings, her sculpturing and drawings have a raw, stark quality that shout aloud Käthe Kollwitz's desire for a socialism that lets men live free from death and destruction. It is through her portraits of the working classes that her intense desire to associate and identify herself with the proletariat finds expression. One is left with the unmistakable impression that Käthe Kollwitz was inspired by an intense personal vision. *Käthe Kollwitz* is an unforgettable film and one that deserves to be very successful.

CENTRAL ELECTRICITY GENERATING BOARD

Sudbury House, 15 Newgate Street, London EC1A 7AU. Tel: 01-248 1202.

"The sheer scale is beyond imagination," gasps Faraday, as he is taken from his laboratory into the Eighties and shown what his momentous discovery of 1831 has led to. The Central Electricity Generating Board have "taken the liberty" of transporting Faraday into the present in their new 20-minute film, *The Electric Wave*, and the result is an unusual, lively and informative account of just how vital electricity is to our lives today. Faraday is escorted by the "Future Man" to the farm, into the home, into industry, the office and the school to see what his discovery has prompted, and how electricity is made and transmitted.

The Electric Wave is intended for a wide audience, and although one would really need to have a basic knowledge of how electricity is produced to fully appreciate "Future Man's" explanations, CEGB's new film does show in a

NCB FILMS

N.C.B. Films
National Coal Board
Hobart House
Grosvenor Place
London SW1X 7AE
Tel. 01-235 2020

FUTURE MAN APPEARS IN FARADAY'S LABORATORY IN
THE ELECTRIC WAVE   PHOTO: C.E.G.B.

clear, forthright and entertaining manner the role of electricity in our lives today, and should certainly be of general interest.

Copies of *The Electric Wave* are available on free loan in 16mm film and video from the CEGB Film Library at the above address.

NATIONAL COAL BOARD

Film Branch, Hobart House, Grosvenor Place, London SW1X 7AE.

The NCB film library has an extensive list of films available for loan, their suitability ranging from general interest topics for a wider audience, to those which are aimed specifically at the coal industry. Recent additions include *Noise* which shows the devastating effects that excessive, and sometimes not so excessive, noise can have on our hearing, and it shows what the Coal Board is doing to protect its employees against permanent damage. In a similar vein, *Looking after Your Back* demonstrates how we expose our backs to potential damage every day and it contains some useful hints on how to avoid unnecessary and harmful back strain.

On a totally different subject is *Sea Coal*, which illustrates the tremendous skill and courage of the miners from the Ellington Colliery, an undersea mine several miles from the sea bed. This is a very impressive film that has a strong human interest factor, as we follow the miners on their journey to their work face. Similarly, in *Eyes for the 80's*, we see the day in the life of a new deputy through his eyes, as he undertakes his onerous duties of checking that the mine is completely safe. Although this film does at times seem rather over-contrived and artificial, it does demonstrate once again, the bravery and good humour of the miners.

SAFETY EXERCISE, FROM THE SHELL PRODUCTION, *A TOWN CALLED CHARLIE*

SHELL INTERNATIONAL

Shell International Petroleum Co., Shell Centre, TRF/11 Waterloo, London S.E.1.

The men who live on the Brent Charlie platform, one of the four platforms of the Brent off-shore oil field, have three objects: work, sleep and food. In a new film from Shell, *A Town Called Charlie*, which has been made jointly with Esso, Shell's partner in the Brent Field, we are allowed a glimpse of the lives of the men who inhabit this vast "Las Vegas in the Sea."

We arrive at Brent Charlie with the Off-shore Installation Manager at the start of his week's duty on the rig, and it is through his eyes that we see the workings of this vast complex. This is a film with a strong human interest factor, and through the mens' reactions to their work, to the drilling and pumping of the oil ashore, to the vital safety drills and to their leisure time, we learn a little of the excitements and risks of living in a town called Charlie.

The film contains some extraordinarily spectacular shots, especially of the rig ablaze at night, and one is left with a mixture of admiration and awe for these men who spend such a large part of their lives living in a region fit only for fish and seagulls.

The dramatic question asked in *Time for Energy* is, what will happen when the world's oil supplies run out? There is certainly no shortage of energy in nature, and as this film shows, no shortage of ideas for harnessing them. We see ideas ranging from wind farms in Holland to an ambitious scheme in Brazil where over half of the cars manufactured have engines designed to run on alcohol distilled from sugar cane. The many ideas derived from harnessing the energy from the sun are considered. One example shows a remote Papago Indian village which is totally dependent on the sun for its electricity, and among the many excellent shots in this film, is one particularly eerie futuristic view of a solar power system. The use of coal is considered, and the advantages and disadvantages of nuclear fission, in which the long-term answer to this problem must lie, are discussed. The message of this fascinating film is that while there is obviously no shortage of ideas, there *is* a serious shortage of time, and until these ideas can be developed to their full potential, we have to learn to use the diminishing supplies of oil far more efficiently.

Shell films and videocassettes are available on free loan to interested groups in industry, commerce, education, and to public bodies, associations, societies and clubs.

NUCLEAR POWER STATION IN AYRSHIRE

PHOTO: U.K.A.E.A.

UNITED KINGDOM ATOMIC ENERGY AUTHORITY

11 Charles II Street, London SW1.

The Nuclear Fuel Cycle is a purely factual film in which Michael Rodd, with the aid of diagrams and models, takes us through the nuclear fuel cycle, beginning with the detection of uranium deposits and its mining and enrichment onto the eventual fabrication of fuel and then focuses on the reprocessing and the re-use of uranium and plutonium in fast reactors. This is definitely not a film intended for those with only a limited knowledge of the subject matter, as it is dealt with in a brisk and highly technical fashion.

Of much wider interest is another new film from the UKAEA, *Power from the Atom*, and Michael Rodd is the presenter in this film too. Nuclear fission is explained in much more simplified terms and we are shown how commercial nuclear reactors operate. The emphasis of the film is on the peaceful harnessing of nuclear energy for generating electricity and the film looks to the future of nuclear energy for long term energy supply from fast reactors. We are shown the development of gas-cooled reactor technology in this country, and the enormity of the whole process is shown by some stunning shots of the Hunterston 'B' Nuclear Power Station in Ayrshire. When one considers that one-eighth of our electricity is already being provided by nuclear energy, a proportion which will rise to about one-fifth in the near future, *Power from the Atom* is a very important film and should be shown to as wide an audience as possible.

In addition to the films, slide-tapes, publications, exhibitions, educational materials and talks on nuclear power and energy-related subjects which members of the Nuclear Power Information provide, the Authority's 16mm films are now available to purchasers and borrowers in VHS and Betamax video formats, and other systems by request.

Sponsored Films Round-Up

Esso's comprehensive film catalogue includes the 24-minute colour film *Advance into the Unknown*, made for Esso Germany. It shows various aspects of the research necessary for space flights. On a totally different subject, *Oliver Kite's Fawley* looks at a natural sanctuary of wildlife inside the boundaries of the Esso refinery at Fawley.

De Beers include in their catalogue *One Hundred Million to One*, a 22-minute colour film available in French, German, Swedish, Italian and Dutch versions. It deals with the mining and recovery of alluvial diamonds from the beach deposits off the coast of southwest Africa. *The Magic of Diamonds* shows how diamonds are cut, polished and set.

In the **Post Office**'s *Meet the Royal Mail*, actor and impresario Brian Rix goes on a tour of a modern sorting office and looks at how the Post Office copes with over 30,000,000 letters a day. **National Westminster Bank**'s *Quiet Revolution* outlines the role computers play in helping banks to keep pace with the increasingly complex needs of their customers.

Two of the latest films from **British Airways** are *Speed Bird*, which shows three different flights by Concorde with the passengers talking about the unique appeal the aircraft holds for them; and *Rotor Flight into the Eighties*, which tells the story of the wide range of operations on which British Airways helicopters are engaged today.

In **ICI**'s Films for Schools section, the series *The Foundations of Wealth* takes a look at basic economic concepts. Each film contains a mixture of animation and live footage.

One of the latest and most successful of **Barclays Bank**'s films for young people is *The First Few Years*, in which Dennis Waterman investigates what it is like to work in a bank. The film shows the work young people are expected to undertake in their first few years.

Further details of the films mentioned above and others are available from:

Barclays Bank, *Barclays Bank Film Library, 12 The Square, Vicarage Farm Road, Peterborough PE1 5TS.*

British Airways, *Random Film Library, 25 The Burroughs, Hendon, London NW4 4AT, or Guild, Sound and Vision, Woodston House, Oundle Road, Peterborough PE2 9PZ.*

De Beers, *Public Relations Department, De Beers Consolidated Mines, Saffron House, 11 Saffron Hill, London EC1N 8RA.*

Esso, *Public Affairs Department, Esso Petroleum Company, Victoria Street, London SW1E 5JW.*

ICI, *ICI Film Library, 15 Beaconsfield Road, London NW10 2LE.*

National Westminster Bank, *The National Westminster Bank Film Library, Unit B11, Park Hall Road Trading Estate, London SE21 8EL.*

Post Office, *Royal Mail Film Library, Park Hall Road Trading Estate, London SE21 8EL (16mm and video cassettes), or Royal Mail Film Library, 135 Borden Lane, Sittingbourne, Kent ME10 1BY (8mm sound films).*

Film Theatres Supported by the British Film Institute

BELFAST

Queen's Film Theatre
8 Malone Road
Belfast BT9 5BN.

BIRMINGHAM

Arts Lab
Holt Street
Birmingham B7 4BA

BRADFORD

Bradford Playhouse & Film Theatre
Chapel Street
Leeds Road
Bradford BD1 5DL.

BRISTOL

Arnolfini Cinema
Narrow Quay
Bristol BS1 8JG.

Bristol Watershed
Narrow Quay
Cannon Road
Bristol.

CANTERBURY

Cinema 3 (Canterbury Film Theatre)
c/o Rutherford College
University of Kent
Canterbury
Kent CT2 7NX.

CARDIFF

Sherman Film Theatre
University College
Senghennydd Road
Cardiff.

Chapter Workshops & Centre for the Arts
Market Road
Canton
Cardiff CF5 1QE.

DARTINGTON

The Barn Theatre
Dartington
Totnes
Devon TO9 6EJ.

DERBY

Metro Cinema
Green Lane
Derby DE3 1DT.

DUNDEE

Steps Theatre
Central Library
The Wellgate
Dundee DD1 1DB.

EDINBURGH

Filmhouse
88 Lothian Road
Edinburgh EH3 9BZ.

GLASGOW

Glasgow Film Theatre
12 Rose Street
Glasgow G3.

GRIMSBY

Whitgift Film Theatre
Crosland Road
Willows
Grimsby DN37 9EH.

HULL

Hull Film Theatre
Central Library
Albion Street
Hull HU1 3TF.

IPSWICH

Ipswich Film Theatre
Corn Exchange
Ipswich
Suffolk.

IRVINE

Magnum Theatre
Magnum Leisure Centre
Harbour Street
Irvine
Ayrshire KA12 8PP.

KIRKCALDY

The Adam Smith Centre
Kirkcaldy
Fife
Scotland.

LANCASTER

The Duke's Playhouse
Moor Lane
Lancaster LA1 1QE.

LEEDS

Leeds Playhouse
Calverley Street
Leeds LS2 3AJ.

LEICESTER

Phoenix Arts
6 Newarke Street
Leicester LE1 5TA.

MOLD

Theatr Clwyd
County Civic Centre
Mold
Clwyd.

NEWCASTLE

Tyneside Cinema
10–12 Pilgrim Street
Newcastle-upon-Tyne
NE1 6QG.

NORWICH

Cinema City
St. Andrew's Street
Norwich NR2 4AD.

NOTTINGHAM

Nottingham Film Theatre
Co-Operative Education Centre
19 Heathcote Street
Nottingham NG1 3AF.

New Cinema
The Midland Group
24–32 Carlton Street
Nottingham NG1 1NN.

SCUNTHORPE

Scunthorpe Film Theatre
Central Library Complex
Carlton Street
Scunthorpe DN15 6TX.

SHEFFIELD

The Library Theatre
Central Library
Surrey Street
Sheffield S1 1XZ.

STIRLING

MacRoberts Arts Centre
University of Stirling
Stirling
FK9 4LA, Scotland.

STOKE

Stoke Film Theatre
College Road
Stoke-On-Trent
Staffordshire
ST4 2DE.

STREET

Strode Theatre
Strode College
Church Road
Street
Somerset BA16 0AB.

WARWICK

University of Warwick
Arts Centre
Coventry
Warwickshire
CV4 7AL.

YORK

York Film Theatre
Central Hall
University of York
Heslington
York YO1 5DD.

FILM ARCHIVES

Institutes marked with an asterisk are members of the International Institute of Film Archives (FIAF)

ALBANIA
Arkivi Shtetëror i Filmit i Republikës Popullore Socialiste të Shqipërisë, Rruga Alexandre Moissu Nr-76, Tirana.
ALGERIA
Cinémathèque Algérieene, rue Larbi-Ben-Mhidi, Algiers.
ARGENTINA
*Cinemateca Argentina, Lavalle 2061, Buenos Aires 1051. Curator: Guillermo Fernandez Jurado. Stock: 5,115 film titles, 6,630 books, 312,500 film stills, 5,010 posters. The Cinemateca operates two film theatres with daily screenings from 3 p.m. to 1 a.m. and additional special screenings in one theatre at 1 p.m., and also organises courses and exhibitions on film analysis and the history of the Argentinian cinema. Facilities are available for research and books on the Argentinian cinema have been published.
AUSTRALIA
*National Film Archive, National Library of Australia, Parkes Place, Canberra A.C.T. 2600, Director: Ray Edmondson. Stock: 29,000 film titles, 240,000 stills, 360 film periodical titles, 30,000 posters, 2,000 scripts.
AUSTRIA
*Österreichisches Filmarchiv A-1010 Wien, Rauhensteingasse 5. Film stores and theatre: Laxenburg, Altes Schloss. President: Prof. Dr. Alfred Lehr. Directors: Dr. Walter Fritz, Rudolf Bienert. Stock: 20,800 film titles, 7,051 books, 974 periodicals, 211,000 film stills, 2,270 posters. Regular summer exhibitions and retrospectives are held at Laxenburg Altes Schloss. A viewing service is available for researchers and producers at the archive rooms in Vienna.
*Österreichisches Filmmuseum, A-1010 Wien, Augustinerstrasse 1. Directors: Peter Konlechner and Peter Kubelka. Stock: 6,770 film titles, 5,200 books, subscriptions to 90 periodicals, 200,000 film stills. A non-profit-making organisation, the Museum now has 15,900 members and holds daily screenings at the Albertina Gallery which have created a hungry audience for the cinema despite the unimaginative programming of the commercial cinemas in Vienna. "One of the most active cinematheques in Europe" (*Der Spiegel*).
BELGIUM
*Cinémathèque Royale de Belgique, 23 Ravenstein, 1000 Brussels. Curator: Jacques Ledoux. Stock: more than 10,000 film titles, 20,000 books, 200,000 film stills and a large collection of posters. Publishes useful catalogues and screens three films daily.

BRAZIL
Fundação Cinemateca Brasileira, Caixa Postal 12900, São Paulo. Curator: Carlos Roberto Rodrigues de Souza. Mainly concerned with Brazilian films, this archive has laboratory facilities to preserve and restore films, and all the nitrate material in the country is deposited here. Students and researchers can consult some hundreds of Brazilian and foreign titles at the archive, and catalogues are available at the Documentation Department.
*Cinemateca do Museu de Arte Moderna, Caixa Postal 44 (ZC-00), 20,000 Rio de Janeiro, R.J. Curator: Cosme Alves Netto. Stock: 6,000 film titles, 1,000 books, 2,000 periodicals, 20,000 film stills, 1,000 posters. Daily screenings are held in the archive's 200-seat theatre. The archive also publishes a monthly bulletin, provides facilities for researchers, operates a film school and produces short films.
BULGARIA
Bulgarska Nacionalna Filmoteka, ul. Gourko 36, 1000 Sofia. Director: Todor Andreykov. Stock: 12,920 film titles, 3,127 newsreels, 4,155 books, 1,232 bound volumes of periodicals, 64,400 stills, 16,700 posters, 7,158 unpublished film scripts. The Filmoteka holds four regular screenings a day in its own cinema and organises film seasons and seminars in Sofia and in the provinces as well as Bulgarian film weeks abroad.
CANADA
*National Film, Television and Sound Archives, 395 Wellington Street, Ottawa, Ontario K1A 0N3. Director: Sam Kula. Stock: 29,000 film and video titles, 9,000 books, 1,060 periodicals, 265,000 stills, 7,000 posters. Title index of 225,000 films. Reference dossiers on 88,000 personalities, films and subjects. The collection concentrates on Canadian film and television production and oral history, but the Archives are building up an international collection and expanding facilities available for researchers and students.
*La Cinémathèque Québécoise, 335 boul. de Maisonneuve est, Montréal, Québec H2X 1K1. Tel. (514) 845–8118. Director: Robert Daudelin. Stock: 8,000 film titles, 100,000 stills, 8,000 posters. The Cinémathèque specialises in preserving the work of animators and of Canadian film-makers and this collection is on show at seven screenings a week, together with other aspects of world cinema. Publications include "Copie Zéro" four times a year, "Les Dossiers de la Cinémathèque," a series devoted to film history and a number of brochures and catalogues. The Cinémathèque also has a collection of early cinematographic equipment.
Conservatoire d'Art Cinématographique de Montréal,

THE DANISH FILM MUSEUM

Library Documentation
Exhibition Cinema

Store Sóndervoldstraede DK-1419 Copenhagen Denmark
Telephone 45-01-576500

1455 de Maisonneuve West, Montréal, Québec. Director: Serge Losique. Stock: 3,000 film titles, 1,000 books, 100 periodicals, 2,000 film stills. The Conservatoire screens about six hundred features a year, including major retrospectives, and organises the annual Canadian Student Film Festival.

Ontario Film Institute, 770 Don Mills Road, Don Mills, Ontario M3C 1T3. Director: Gerald Pratley. Several hundred film titles, stills, posters, 9,000 books, 70 magazine titles, card index of 100,000 entries, 2,500 film music recordings, several hundred interviews with film-makers. Ontario Film Theatre screens films four nights a week, arranges film programmes for the Ontario Science Centre, runs regional film theatres at Brockville, Windsor and Niagara-on-the-Lake, Ontario, with special screenings in co-operation with Festival Ontario.

Pacific Cinémathèque Pacifique, 1616 West 3rd Avenue, Vancouver, British Columbia V6J 1K2. Director: Paul Yeung. Most important film activity in West Canada. Maintains an archive of 450 titles, film study collection of over 100 titles, of works by both local and international film-makers; and a reference library comprising 4,000 books, journals, magazines, scripts, indices and catalogues for use by students, teachers, film-makers, and researchers; also runs a regular program of Canadian and international films five nights a week from Sept.–June each year. The Cinémathèque promotes and distributes independent films in the Pacific region, including works such as Fred Cawsey's "The Land is the Culture" and Dennis Wheeler's "Potlatch: a strict law bids us dance;" and organises an annual international film festival for children and young people.

CHILE
*Cinemateca Chilena en el Exilio, Padre Xifré 3, oficina 111, Madrid 2, Spain. Director: Pedro Chaskel. Curator: Gaston Angelovici. The Cinemateca is continuing in exile the work of Chile's principal archive, the Cinemateca Universitaria, which was closed by the military after the coup of September 1973. It has a unique collection of films made during the last years before the coup, the bulk of which have been destroyed inside Chile, as well as copies of films made in exile. Its collection of documentation, stills and other material concerned with the new Chilean cinema is growing steadily. Member of the Union de Cinematecas de América Latina.

COLOMBIA
Fundacion Cinemateca Colombiana, Apartado Nacional 1898, Bogota. Director: Jorge Nieto.
CONGO
Cinémathèque Nationale Populaire, Brazzaville.
CUBA
*Cinemateca de Cuba, Calle 23 n° 1155, Vedado, Havana. Director: Héctor García Mesa. Stock: 5,750 film titles, 110,500 film stills. Member of the Union de Cinematecas de América Latina.
CZECHOSLOVAKIA
*Ceskoslovenský filmový ústav – filmový archiv, Národní 40, 110 000 Prague 1. Deputy Director: Jiří Levý. Stock: about 10,000 features, plus the same number of shorts and documentaries, including newsreels, 81,080 books, 11,000 periodicals, 362,500 stills, 4,000 posters.
DENMARK
*Det danske filmmuseum, Store Søndervoldstraede, DK-1419 Copenhagen K. Director: Ib Monty. Stock: 11,000 film titles, 31,500 books, 380 periodicals subscribed to, 1,185,000 film stills, 12,950 posters. 158-seat cinema used for three daily screenings for members from September to June, also available for private screenings for researchers and students. Permanent exhibition of film equipment. The Museum also publishes a magazine "Kosmorama" and occasional leaflets and books on film.
EGYPT
*Al-archive Al-Kawmy Lil-film, National Centre for Film Culture, 36 Sherif Street, Cairo. Stores: Al-Ahram Studios, Giza. Director: Ahmed Al-Hadary.
FINLAND
*Suomen Elokuva-arkisto, P.O. Box 216, Lönnrotinkatu 30 C, SF-00181 Helsinki 18. Director: Olli Alho. Stock: 3,500 feature film titles, 16,000 shorts and documentaries, 10,950 books, currently subscribed magazines 152 volumes yearly, 4,500 dialogue lists and scripts, 1,075,000 stills, 56,000 posters and documentation on 22,500 titles. The archive arranges "Finnish Film Weeks" abroad, as well as regular screenings in Helsinki and seven other cities.
FRANCE
Cinémathèque Française, Palais de Chaillot, avenue Albert de Mun, 75016 Paris.
*Cinémathèque de Toulouse, 3 Rue Roquelaine, Toulouse. Curator: Raymond Borde.
Service des Archives du Film du Centre National de la Cinématographie, 78390, Bois D'Arcy. Curator: F. Schmitt. Stock: 58,000 film titles, 150,000 stills, 7,300 posters, 24,500 screenplays, 800 apparati. Founded in 1969. Film vaults capable of holding 580,000 reels of film, and laboratory for restoration of old films. Documentation department.
*Cinémathèque Universitaire, UER d'Art et d'Archéologie, 3 rue Michelet, 75006 Paris.
GERMAN DEMOCRATIC REPUBLIC
*Staatliches Filmarchiv der Deutschen Demokratischen Republik, Hausvogteiplatz 3–4, 1080 Berlin. Curator: Wolfgang Klaue. Stock: 40,000 film titles, plus documentation material on about 25,000 titles, 120,000 stills and 8,000 posters. With its own theatre, the Filmarchiv

holds exhibitions and a yearly retrospective on documentaries at the Leipzig festival. Enquiries on production should go to: Staatliches Archiv für den wissenschaftlichen Film der DDR, Breites Gesell 1, 1502 Potsdam-Babelsberg.

GERMANY (WEST)
*****Stiftung Deutsche Kinemathek,** Pommernallee 1, 1000 Berlin 19. Director: Dr. Heinz Rathsack. Stock: 6,000 film titles, 200,000 film stills, 8,000 posters, 30,000 film programmes, 1,800 scripts etc. The Kinemathek's library of books and periodicals is now amalgamated with that of the Deutsche Film- und Fernsehakademie, in the same building. Seminars, screenings and exhibitions are held and viewing tables are available for researchers.
Bundesarchiv – Filmarchiv, Am Wöllershof 12, D 5400 Koblenz. Tel. 0261–3991. President: Prof. H. Booms. Stock: 38,000 film titles, including 36,000 documentary films and newsreels and 2,000 long feature films, mainly of the period 1932–1945. Co-operation with Stiftung Deutsche Kinemathek and Deutsches Institut für Filmkunde in a 1978/79 combined system.
Deutsches Filmmuseum, Stadtverwaltung (Amt 41 DF), Postfach 38 82, 6000 Frankfurt am Main 1. Director: Walter Schobert. Curator: Jürgen Berger. Librarian: Ingrid Tabrizian. Stock: 1,700 film titles, 6,000 books, 70 current periodicals subscribed to, 200,000 stills, 11,000 posters, 500–600 items of cinema equipment, plus musical scores of silent films. The museum is due to open in new premises in 1983 and will incorporate the Kommunales Kino Frankfurt. At present it screens 3 different films a day and publishes books and brochures on cinematic subjects.
*****Deutsches Institut für Filmkunde,** Schloss Biebrich, 6202 Wiesbaden. Director: Dr. Gerd Albrecht. Deputy Director: Eberhard Spiess. Administrative Director: Ulrich Pöschke. Stock: 4,000 film titles, 29,950 books, 260 periodicals, 452,000 film stills, 24,000 posters, 15,250 dialogue lists, 3,420 scripts. Also programmes, newspaper clippings, advertising material.
Arsenal Kino der Freunde der Deutschen Kinematheke. V, Welserstrasse 25, D-1000 Berlin 30. Tel. 213–6039. The nearest equivalent of Britain's NFT. Became a model for all "Communal Cinemas" in the Federal Republic of Germany. Programme Directors: Ulrich and Erika Gregor, and Alf Bold. The Freunde (chairmen: Ulrich Gregor, Gerhard Schoenberner) also run a non-commercial distribution of about 600 films, most of them from the International Forum of Young Cinema, a section of the Berlin Film Festival, created in 1971. The Freunde hold an archive collection of 1,000 films (experimental and third world) and are responsible for an excellent series of brochures which contain material difficult to find elsewhere.

GREAT BRITAIN
*****National Film Archive,** 81 Dean Street, London W1V 6AA. Curator: David Francis. Deputy Curator: Clyde Jeavons. Stock: 45,000 film and television titles, 1,500,000 black-and-white stills, 120,000 colour transparencies, 8,000 posters, 650 set designs. Viewing service for students and researchers, production library for film-makers. Catalogues of the Archive's holdings are

available and copies of stills can be purchased.
The British Film Institute's **Library Services** are part of the **Information Division** and are housed at 127 Charing Cross Road, London WC2H 0EA. Services are available to members. Head of Department: Gillian Hartnoll. Deputy Head: Frances Thorpe. TV Information Officer: Ian Macdonald. Librarian: Sandra Archer. Stock: 30,000 books, 6,000 scripts, 300 current periodicals and a reference index of 250,000 cards.
*****Imperial War Museum,** Lambeth Road, London SE1 6HZ. Keeper of Film Department: Clive Coultass. The museum's collection now includes over 40,000,000 feet of film, the main emphasis being on non-fiction film. The museum encourages a general appreciation of the uses of film in historical studies and has held seminars and conferences on this theme.
Barnes Museum of Cinematography, Fore Street, St. Ives, Cornwall (est. 1963). Curator: John Barnes, MBKS. Superb collection of early apparatus, books, posters, programmes, prints and photographs etc., relating to the history of moving pictures and the photographic image.
Scottish Film Archive, Scottish Film Council, 74 Victoria Crescent Road, Dowanhill, Glasgow G12 9JN. Archivist: Janet McBain. Established in 1976, the Archive is mainly concerned with the filmed history of Scotland. Stock: 750,000 ft. of film, varied collection of non-film material. Viewing facilities for students and researchers.

GREECE
Tainiothiki tis Ellados, 1 Kanari Street, Athens 138. Secretary General: Aglaya Mitropoulos. Curator: Mona Mitropoulos. Director: Theodore Adamopoulos. Stock: 2,000 film titles, 500 books, 1,000 film stills, 1,200 posters, large collection of scenarios. Expanding collection of magic lanterns, praxinoscopes, etc. The archive has a special collection of Greek cinema and holds screenings for the members of its Cinema Club, with screenings every afternoon and evening in Athens. It also runs 47 Ciné-Clubs all over Greece.

HUNGARY
*****Magyar Filmtudományi Intézet és Filmarchivum,** Népstadion ut. 97, 1143 Budapest. Director: Dr. Sándor Papp. Stock: 4,670 feature titles, 6,701 documentaries, 5,275 newsreels, 8,938 books, 2,223 periodicals, 56,444 stills, 7,492 posters. The Institute, besides housing the archive also does research into the history of the cinema and encourages the development of film culture in Hungary. Two periodicals are produced regularly and more than fifty volumes in the series Filmmüvészeti Könyvtár (Library of Film Art) have been published. Currently in preparation is a comprehensive history of the Hungarian cinema, to be published in six volumes.

INDIA
*****National Film Archive of India,** Ministry of Information and Broadcasting, Government of India, Law College Road, Poona 411004. Curator: P. K. Nair. Stock: 5,087 films, 8,873 books, 214 periodicals, 1,341 gramophone records, 14,558 stills, 3,103 posters, 2,688 song booklets, 9,321 scripts, 3,928 pamphlets and folders. Daily screenings for Film & TV Institute students at Poona; weekly public screenings at Poona and Bombay; periodical special screenings at major Indian cities in

collaboration with Federation of Film Societies of India and Film Festivals Directorate. Distribution library of 102 films available to film societies. Holds four-week course in film appreciation annually at Poona and short courses at other centres. Publishes monographs on Indian film-makers.

INDONESIA
Sinematek Indonesia "Pusat Perfilman H. Usmar Ismail," Jalan H.R. Rasuna Said, Jakarta Selatan. Director: H. Misbach Yusa Biran. Stock: about 200 Indonesian film titles (50% negatives). Earliest film dates from 1938. Southeast Asia's first archive, it was established in 1975, building on Biran's personal collection. Now 50% government funded. Large screening theatre.

IRAN
*** Filmkhaneh Melli Iran,** PO Box 262, Tehran.

IRELAND
Liam O'Leary Film Archives, Garden Flat, 74 Ranelagh Road, Dublin 6. Secures preservation of Irish films, and records Irish film history in its widest aspects: native production, films by the Irish abroad, cinemas, personalities, films on Irish themes, Irish literature on film. Source for studies on Irish Cinema – *Rex Ingram, Cinema in Ireland*, etc.

ISRAEL
*** Archion Israeli Leseratim,** 43 Zabotinsky Street, Jerusalem. Director: Mrs. Lia Van Leer. Stock: 2,500 film titles, 3,500 film stills, 3,000 books.

ITALY
Centro Studi Cinetelevisivi (C.S.C.TV), Via IV Novembre 35, 47037 Rimini. Director: José Pantieri. La Fototeca *Charlie Chaplin* has a collection of 2,000,000 stills, and there are other collections of films, stills, and documents, all connected with silent comics like Buster Keaton, Harry Langdon and Mack Sennett, as well as an international museum of comedy.
*** Cineteca Italiana,** Via Palestro 16, 20121 Milano.
*** Museo Nazionale del Cinema,** Palazzo Chiablese, Piazza S. Giovanni 2, 10122 Torino. Tel: 510.370. A 16-room collection covers the history of pre-cinema spectacles, photography and cinematography. Nov–May, the Museum is open 10–12, 3–6.30, and 8.30–11; films screened at 4 and 9.15. June–Oct, open 10–12 and 3–6. Closed Monday.
*** Cineteca Nazionale,** Via Tuscolana N. 1524, 00173 Rome. Director: Dr. Guido Concotti. Stock: 15,000 film titles. 20,000 books and periodicals, 190,000 stills, 2,000 posters. The Cineteca is an adjunct to the Centro Sperimentale di Cinematografia.

JAPAN
Japan Film Library Council, Ginza-Hata Building, 4–5, 4-chome, Ginza, Chuo-ku, Tokyo. Director: Mrs. Kashiko Kawakita. Secretary: Akira Shimizu. Stock: 500 film titles, 3,000 books, 6,000 periodicals, 50,000 film stills, 100 posters. The Council co-operates with archives throughout the world in supplying Japanese films for screening, makes available stills for publication and publishes documentation of its collection.
National Filmcenter, 7–6, 3-chome, Kyobashi, Chuo-ku, Tokyo. Curator: Sadamu Maruo. Stock: 1,500 film titles, 3,600 shorts and newsreels, 2,400 books, 50,000 stills,

1,800 posters, 7,500 scripts. Screenings are held twice daily, except Sunday and national holidays.

KOREA (NORTH)
*** The National Film Archive of the Democratic People's Republic of Korea,** Pyongyang. Director: Pak Sun Tae.

MEXICO
Cinemateca Mexicana, Cordoba 45, Mexico 7 D.F. Director: Jorge Ruz B. Stock: 1,000 film titles, 500 books, 500 film stills, 300 posters. The Cinemateca also has a collection of early apparati dating from 1900, and a special collection devoted to the Mexican film industry from 1930–40.
Cinemateca Luis Buñuel, Calle 5, Oriente 5, Apdo. Postal 255, Puebla, Pue. Curator: Fernando Osorio Alarcon. Established in 1975, this archive has a stock of 100 films, some of them made entirely in Puebla, belonging to the silent period; 300 posters, 500 stills, 200 film books.
*** Filmoteca de la UNAM,** Calle de Filosofía y Letras No. 80, Col. Copilco, Mexico 20 D.F. Tel: 550–46–95 (or Apdo. Postal 70–498). Director: Mtro. Manuel González Casanova. Member of the Union de Cinematecas de América Latina.
Cineteca Nacional, Calzada de Tlalpan 1670, México 21, D.F. Director: Jorge Durán Chávez. Curator: Fernando del Moral G. Mexico's main film archive, supported by the Federal government. Stock: 6,200 film titles and an important collection of documentaries dating from the Thirties, stored in climatic vaults, 10,900 books, 5,300 film stills, 2,000 posters, and a collection of early apparati. The library is open to the public, as are two film theatres where there are approximately nine screenings daily.

NETHERLANDS
*** Stichting Nederlands Filmmuseum,** Vondelpark 3, 1071 AA Amsterdam-W. Director Curator: Jan de Vaal. Stock: about 25,000 film titles, 10,000 books, 175 periodicals, 250,000 film stills, 30,000 posters. The Museum has two theatres, one of 110 seats and a small viewing theatre seating 20. Facilities for researchers are available and the Museum also houses the Joris Ivens archive (films and documentation).
Netherlands Information Service, Film Archive, 76 Anna Paulownastraat, The Hague. Curator: J. A. F. M. van Mierlo. A collection of about 2,000,000 metres of film, mostly of a documetary nature.
B. V. Polygoon, Steijnlaan 5, 1217 JR Hilversum. Director: Ph. Bloemendal. Polygoon has at its disposal a unique collection of newsreels going back to 1921.

NEW ZEALAND
The New Zealand Film Archive, P.O. Box 9544, 150 Wakefield Street, Wellington. Director: Jonathan Dennis. The collection includes New Zealand silent and sound films and some features from 1901 to the present day, as well as a proportion of foreign material. Also held are film stills, posters, books, apparati and special collections. The Archive was jointly established in 1981 by the New Zealand Film Commission, the National Film Unit, Television New Zealand, the Departments of Education and Internal Affairs, the Federation of Film Societies and National Archives.

NORWAY
*Norsk Filminstitutt, Aslakveien 14B, Postboks 5 Røa, Oslo 7. Curator: Jon Stenklev. Stock: 8,200 film titles, 8,500 books, 90 periodicals and a large collection of stills and posters. Also over five hundred pieces of early cinema apparatus and a fine theatre for screening films.
Henie-Onstad Art Centre, 1311 Hovikodden, Oslo. Director: Old Henrik Moe. Curator: Per Hovdenakk. Stock: 200 film titles, 4,000 books and periodicals, 4,000 film stills, 500 posters. A large collection of documentary material on experimental film, with regular screenings.
Kinoteket, an archive theatre run by the Municipal Cinemas in Oslo with assistance from Norsk Filminstitutt (see above), and other archives. Daily performances. Director: Eivind Hjelmtveit. Manager: Jan Erik Holst.

PARAGUAY
Cinemateca Paraguaya, Estrella 496, Oficina 10, Assuncion. Director: Oscar Trinidad.

PERU
Cinemateca Peruana, Apartado 456, Lima. Director: Miguel Reynel Santillana.

POLAND
Filmoteka Polska, ul. Puławska 61, 00–975 Warszawa, skr, poczt. 65. Director: Roman Witek. Stock: nearly 11,300 film titles, 15,500 books plus programmes, leaflets and press cuttings, 955 periodical titles, 200 of which are currently subscribed to, stills from 24,600 films, 40,000 posters, 22,500 scripts, reference indexes

and a collection of early equipment. Regular and comprehensive retrospectives are held at the Filmoteka's cinema "Iluzjon" in Warsaw and at regional centres. The Filmoteka is building up its collection of pre-war Polish films and has rediscovered many "lost" films.

PORTUGAL
*Cinemateca Nacional, Palacio Fox Restauradores, Lisbon. Director: F. Ribeiro. Stock: 850 film titles, 5,500 books, 20,000 stills.

ROMANIA
* Arhiva Naţională de Filme, Bd. Gh. Gheorghiu Dej 65, Bucharest. Director: Marin Pârâianu. Stock: 6,700 feature titles, 21,400 shorts, 5,200 books, 285,000 stills, 19,000 posters, plus a reference index. The Archive also has a collection of clippings, scripts and periodicals.

SOUTH AFRICA
S.A. Film and TV Centre, PO Box 89271, Lyndhurst 2106. Much valuable material dating from the turn of the century is kept in the studio's vaults. Footage available.
South African National Film Archives, Private Bag X236, Pretoria 0001. Director: J. H. de Lange. Enormous variety of 35mm and 16mm footage, as well as stills, scripts, books, posters and other material. The Archive is a State-controlled organisation, dedicated to the classification and preservation of all items relating to the film industry.

SPAIN
*Filmoteca Nacional de España, Carretera de la Dehesa

THE CREDITS OF THE FILM SPECIALLY MADE BY JEAN-LUC GODARD TO CELEBRATE THE MOVE INTO NEW QUARTERS OF LA CINEMATHEQUE SUISSE IN LAUSANNE

de la Villa s/N, Madrid 35. Director: Florentino Soria Heredia. Stock: 6,000 film titles, 6,000 books, 100,000 film stills, 3,000 periodicals and film scripts, 500 posters. Four to five screenings a day in Barcelona and Madrid. Organises film programmes in ten other provinces. Publishes monographs and useful brochures. The Library is open to the public.

Archivo Cinematografico International, Calle Mascaró 26, Barcelona 32. Director: Manuel Ferrer Salvador. Stock: 6,590 books, 30 magazine titles, 20,500 film stills, 25,900 press books, over 90,000 fiches. Publishes two magazines, "Filmguia" and "Filmguia/Documentation."

Roberto de Robert, Archivo cinematografico, c/o Reina Victoria no. 1, Barcelona 21. Archive specialising in American cinema.

SWEDEN

*Cinemateket, Filmhuset, Box 27 126, S–102 52 Stockholm 27. Stock: 8,000 film titles, 25,000 books, 250 current periodicals, 1,500,000 film stills, 30,000 posters, scripts of 1,500 Swedish features. The collection of microfilmed clippings holds 44,000 jackets on individual films, 13,000 jackets on film personalities and 6,000 jackets on general subjects classified under 700 headings.

Asta Nielsen Filmmuseum, Vapenkroken 29, 222 47 Lund. Established in 1946 by G. D. Postén. Film History section at the Dept. of History, University of Lund. This is one of the biggest, private, non-commercial international collections of published, written materials on motion pictures and the film industry. Included in the collection are stills, programmes, books, magazines, posters, historical materials, etc. with the emphasis on the silent screen. Also the most complete collection of material on Asta Nielsen.

SWITZERLAND

*Cinémathèque Suisse, Casino de Montbenon, Case Ville 2512, 1002 Lausanne. Curator: Freddy Buache. Stock: 7,760 features, 6,400 shorts, 20,000 posters, 220,000 film references, 10,000 books, 493,000 stills. The offices, book library, stills collection and viewing equipment were transferred to bright new offices in the Casino de Montbenon in Spring 1981.

Museum des Films, Blauenstr. 49, Basel. The only film museum (open to the public) in German-speaking Switzerland.

TAIWAN
Tien-ying t'u-shu-kuan (Film Library), 4th floor, 7 Ch'ingtao East Road, Taipei. Director: Mr. Hsü. Established by the Motion Picture Development Foundation of the Republic of China in 1978, and formally opened in January 1979, this fledgling archive already has a book library of 4,000 titles, a periodicals collection, a growing print deposit of both Chinese and Western films, a busy screening room and modest information service. Retrospectives have been held on Li Hsing, Sung Ts'un-shou, Pai Ching-jui and Hu Chin-ch'üan, and booklets published on the latter three.

TURKEY
*Sinema-TV Enstitüsü, Kişlaönü, Beşiktaş, İstanbul. Director: Sami Şekeroğlu. Stock: over 3,000 film titles, 30,000 stills, original negatives of early Turkish films, 500 books, collections of major world periodicals, 650 posters, 12 years' collection of press cuttings, 100 scripts, film music tapes. Three theatres, modern film vaults, film and photographic laboratories.

URUGUAY
*Cinemateca Uruguaya, Lorenzo Carnelli 1311, Casilla de Correo 1170, Montevideo. Curators: M. Martinez Carril, Luis Elbert. Stock: 4,300 film titles, 1,500 books, 90 periodicals, 3,500 posters.

U.S.A.
*American Film Institute, John F. Kennedy Center for the Performing Arts, Washington, DC 20566. Administrator: Preservation: Lawrence F. Karr, Motion Picture Archivist: Audrey E. Kupferberg. Stock: 15,000 film titles, 2,500 books, 20,000 stills. The Institute works in close collaboration with the Library of Congress and houses its films at the Library, where many titles are available for study. Screenings are held twice nightly in the Afi Theater at Kennedy Center.
*The Library of Congress, Motion Picture, Broadcasting and Recorded Sound Division, Washington, DC 20540. Stock: 75,000 film titles, 2,000 books, 150,000 stills, descriptive material for more than 150,000 films registered for U.S. copyright since 1912. Much more extensive book and periodical collections in the Library's general collection. Individual screening facilities are available to serious students by appointment.
American Film Institute, Louis B. Mayer Library, 2021 North Western Avenue, Los Angeles, California 90027. Library Director: Anne G. Schlosser. Stock: over 4,500 books, 159 periodicals regularly, over 2,200 scripts, 700 television scripts, oral history and seminar transcripts, clipping files. Primarily for the use of faculty and students of the American Film Institute, the library is also open to outside researchers and members of the entertainment industry.
*Museum of Modern Art, Department of Film, 11 West 53rd Street, New York, NY 10019. Director: Mary Lea Bandy. Curators: Eileen Bowser, Adrienne Mancia. Stock: 8,000 film titles, 2,500 books, 250 periodicals, 3,000,000 film stills. The research and screening facilities of the department are available to serious students only by appointment with the supervisor, Charles Silver.

1,000 of its films are available for rental, sales and lease.
*George Eastman House/International Museum of Photography, 900 East Avenue, Rochester, N.Y. 14607. Film Dept: John B. Kuiper, Director-Curator, George Pratt. Collections: over one million film stills, motion picture collection rich in American and foreign silent films and films of the Thirties, Forties, and Fifties. Researchers and scholars may have access by pre-arrangement. Public served by regular screenings in Dryden Theatre.
*University of California, Theater Arts Library, University Research Library, University of California, Los Angeles, California 90024. Curator: Mrs. Audree Malkin. Stock: 15,000 film titles (housed in the UCLA Film Archive. Theatre Arts Department), 17,941 books, 222 periodicals, 732 posters, 12,516 screenplays, TV and radio scripts, 102,403 stills plus approx. 4½ million stills and negatives from the 20th Century Fox films collection.
*Academy of Motion Picture Arts and Sciences, Margaret Herrick Library, 8949 Wilshire Boulevard, Beverly Hills, California 90211. Library Administrator: Terry T. Roach. Housed on two floors of the Academy's new building, the Library has a book collection of over 14,000 volumes, over 200 periodicals are taken regularly, and there are biography files, general files, and production files containing stills, press-books, posters, etc. from over 50,000 American films.
Pacific Film Archive, University Art Museum, 2621 Durant Avenue, Berkeley, California. The PFA is a lodestone for film-makers and enthusiasts throughout the world. It has a very respectable collection of feature films (especially Japanese) and a study centre, but is best known for the way in which it screens these possessions (and the work of visiting directors) in its own theatre in Berkeley.

U.S.S.R.
*Gosfilmofond, Stantsia Byelye Stolby, Moskovskaya oblast. Director: Mark Strochkov. Stock: 43,790 film titles, 13,388 books, 16,806 periodicals, 171,550 film stills, 40,856 posters. Shows film publicly and has viewing facilities for the serious student.
The Central State Archive of Cinema and Photo Documents of the USSR, Krasnogorsk, near Moscow. Director: O. N. Tyagunov.

VENEZUELA
Cinemateca Nacional, Museo de Ciencias Naturales, Edf. Anexo, Plaza Morelos, Los Caobos, Aptdo. Postal 17045, Caracas. Director: Rodolfo Izaguirre. Stock: 1,012 film titles, 5,000 books, pamphlets and documentation, 12,000 stills, 500-card index. Screenings in the Sala de Proyecciones, National Art Gallery, Tues–Sun 6.30–9pm; children's screenings, Sunday mornings.

YUGOSLAVIA
*Jugoslovenska Kinoteka, Knez Mihailova 19, 11,000 Belgrade. Director: Vladimir Pogačić. Stock: 38,803 films, 12,847 books, 105 current periodicals, 6,580 scripts, reference index of 161,600 cards, 200,000 stills, 10,000 posters. Library is open to the public, screening facilities are available.

Film Schools

AUSTRALIA

Australian Film and Television School, Box 126 PO, North Ryde, NSW 2113. An Australian government authority conducting full-time courses through its Full-time Program and a nation-wide programme of work-shops, short and part-time courses, seminars and lectures through its Open Program. The Open Program also administers the National Graduate Diploma Scheme, which offers a Graduate Diploma in Media for teachers. Full-time Program courses incorporate all aspects of camera, sound, editing and production for film and television, with direction as a third year elective; and a screen-writing course for experienced writers. Facilities include 35mm and 16mm film, four-camera broadcast standard colour television studio, two non-broadcast standard television studios, computer-controlled video-tape editing and a two-camera outside broadcast van. Full-time Program courses are free and students receive a living allowance plus dependents' allowance where applicable. There are no specific educational require-ments but some experience of film or video is necessary and entry is competitive. Approximately 22 students are accepted for the three-year course each year and the equivalent of four one-year terms are offered by the screenwriting course each year. Applications are called in late May and close in early July each year for the course beginning in March of the following year. Applicants must be permanently resident in Australia at the time of application.

AUSTRIA

Hochschule für Musik und darstellende Kunst, Abteil-ung für Film und Fernsehen, Metternichgasse 12, A-1030 Vienna. Director: Prof. Hannelore Götzinger.

BELGIUM

Koninklijke Academie voor Schone Kunsten – Gent, Academiestraat 2, B-9000 Gent. Director: Pierre Vlerick. Animation department, director: Raoul Servais; assisted by Paul Demeyer, Rembrand Hoste and Jo Maes as workshop teachers. The department focusses on the animated cartoon technique, although other animation techniques, such as puppet, pixilation and cut-out anima-tion, are also taught.
Institut des Arts de Diffusion, Rue des Blancs Chevaux 38–40, B 1348 Louvain-la-Neuve, Belgium. Chairman: Jean-Marie Delmée. 140 students and 80 staff. Four-year course in direction or production in film, television, radio and the theatre. Three-year course in photography,

sound, editing and writing. Films made by students include features, documentaries and animated shorts.
Institut National Supérieur des Arts du Spectacle et Techniques de Diffusion (INSAS), Rue Thérésienne 8, B-1000 Brussels. Director: Raymond Ravar. 198 stu-dents and 112 staff. Four-year course leading to a degree, concerned with all aspects of film/radio/television pro-duction, or three-year course giving more specialised instruction in photography, sound, writing or acting. The Institute is equipped with 5 Super 8mm cameras, 7 16mm cameras, 2 sound studios, 1 fully-equipped television studio, 4 portable "U" VTR with cameras, 3 "U" video editing rooms, 3 "U" VTR, 2 VHS–VTR, 8 film editing rooms and 3 processing laboratories.

BRAZIL

Escola Superior de Cinema, Faculdade São Luis, Av. Paulista 2324, São Paulo.
Escola Superior de Cinema, Pontificia Universidade Catolica, Av. Brasil 2033, Belo Horizonte, Minas Gerais.
Instituto de Arte e Communicação Social, Universidade Federal Fluminense, Rua Professor Lara Villela 126, 24.210 – Niterói, Rio de Janeiro.

CANADA

Sheridan College International Summer School of Animation, School of Visual Arts, Trafalgar Road, Oakville, Ontario L6H 2L1. Dean: Scott Turner, Prog-ram Co-ordinator: Tom Halley. This 14-week summer programme, which runs from May until August, is equivalent to one college academic year, and is primarily a foundation devoted to an understanding and applica-tion of basic production techniques. Studies examine both contemporary and traditional approaches to anima-tion. A regular Sheridan College diploma will be awarded after successful completion of three summer sessions. Applicants should have two years post-secondary art school study or equivalent. Competence in English is also required.

CZECHOSLOVAKIA

Faculty of Film and Television (FAMU), Academy of Arts, Smetanovo nábřeží 2, Prague 1. Regular day-study courses in film and TV directing, film and TV photogra-phy, artistic photography, film and TV documentaries, film and TV film editing. Foreign nationals may apply through Ministerstvo školství, zahraniční odbor, Karme-litská 7, Prague 1. Before starting they will take a year's course in the Czech language.

DENMARK
Danish Film School, Danish Film Institute, Store Sønder-voldstræde, DK. 1419 Copenhagen K. Completely reorganised in 1975 under a new director: Henning Camre, the school now offers a series of courses in different aspects of professional film-making. It has an average of 30 students, 8 full-time and 15 part-time staff. Danish-speaking students only.

FINLAND
Taideteollinen korkeakoulu, Kuvallisen viesftinnän laitos, Elokuva-ja tv-linja, University of Industrial Arts, Faculty of Visual Communications, Films and TV Studies, Ílmalantori 1D, SF-00240 Helsinki 24. Chief Instructor: Juha Rosma. Qualifications for admission: matriculation exam and the admission course of two weeks. Foreign students admitted with knowledge of Finnish. Average duration of studies: five years. Main subjects: directing, camerawork, screenwriting, sound, editing. Production on 8, 16 and 35mm films plus video-tape. Production facilities: professional film equipment and mini TV studio and photographic equipment.

FRANCE
L'Institut des Hautes Études Cinématographiques (I.D.H.E.C.), 4 Avenue de L'Europe, 94360 Bry-sur-Marne. President: Jean Delannoy. General Director: C. Kostromine.

Conservatoire Libre du Cinéma Français (C.L.C.F.), 16 rue de Delta, 75009 Paris.
Institut Supérieur de Cinéma, Radio et Télévision (I.S.C.R.T.), 65 Bd. Brune, 75014 Paris.

GERMAN DEMOCRATIC REPUBLIC

Hochschule für Film und Fernsehen der Deutschen Demokratischen Republik, Karl-Marx-Strasse 27, 1502 Potsdam-Babelsberg. Rektor: Prof. Dr. Konrad Schwalbe.

GERMANY (WEST)

Deutsche Film- und Fernseh-Akademie Berlin GmbH, Pommernallee 1, 1 Berlin 19. Director: Heinz Rathsack. Three-year course dealing with all aspects of practical film and television production; direction, photography sound, editing and special effects. Students make films in each of their three years and are encouraged to gain experience in as wide a variety of techniques as possible.
Hochschule für Fernsehen und Film, Ohmstrasse 11, 8000 München 40. Director: Prof. Helmut Jedele. Approx. 100 students, 32 staff. Three-year course providing instruction in the theory and practice of film and television. Normally, students make two short, and one longer, diploma films. Facilities provide for work in 16 and 35mm as well as video equipment. Main professional sectors are film and TV drama, and documentary film and TV journalism. Studies are free. Two-step admission process; ask for details in January each year. Studies begin each autumn.

GREAT BRITAIN

After a long period in which film education in Britain fell severely short of the pace set by the United States, France and West Germany, there are now a considerable number of establishments that cater for formal film training, some of which are described in detail below.

Readers wishing to have further details of these and other establishments should contact the Education Department of the British Film Institute, 81 Dean Street, London W1V 6AA, where two booklets are available: "Film and Television Training" and "Film and Television Studies in Higher Education: a guide to courses."
National Film School, Beaconsfield Film Studios, Station Road, Beaconsfield, Bucks. Director: Colin Young. 75 students at present, 15 full-time teaching staff supplemented by other tutors from the profession. Three years. The emphasis is on the creative aspects of filmmaking including technical instruction, designed to equip the school's graduates for immediate employment in the industry. The admission is described as an open competition among the candidates. The school is fully-equipped and films are made on 16 and 35mm, and on various video formats.
London International Film School, 24 Shelton Street, London WC2 9HP. Director of Studies: John Fletcher. Administrator: Betty Feldman. One-year foundation course followed by a second year of either film, TV, or animation. The latter two may be taken after the second film year if desired. On average, half of each term is devoted to film video production, with tuition, practical

CROYDON COLLEGE

Intermedia
a one-year intensive course in
Film, Television and Animation

Details from: Dick Perry
Intermedia Croydon College
School of Art & Design
Fairfield Croydon CR9 1DX
Tel : 01–688 9271

training, film analysis and theoretical studies occupying the remainder. The school has two viewing theatres, two studios with professional lighting, sound recording with Nagras, fifteen editing rooms, film and sound editing equipment, sound transfer and cameras for 16 and 35mm, and a fully equipped television department. Tuition is by professionals. Entrance requirements are a university degree or technical or art diploma, or five "O" levels and two "A" levels or the equivalent. Applicants must be proficient in English; however, those with special talents, or experience in the industry are sometimes accepted. All applicants must submit samples of their work.
Polytechnic of Central London, School of Communication, 18/22 Riding House Street, London W1P 7PD. Linked MA and Post-Graduate Diploma in Film Studies: three-year and two-year part-time evening courses exploring the intellectual bases of film study and the relationships between general theories of film and specific contexts of production, consumption and analysis. Course leader: Vincent Porter. BA(Hons) Degree in Film and Photographic Arts: Three-year full-time course in the practice and theory of motion-picture and still photography, one-year introductory course is followed by specialisation in either film or still photography. Course leader: Stephen Whaley. BA(Hons) Degree in Media Studies: three-year full-time course examining the dissemination of information by the mass media with the aim of developing "media awareness" through academic study and "media literacy" through practical study. Course leader: David Cardiff.
Royal College of Art, School of Film and Television, Queen's Gate, London SW7. 45 students. Three-year post-graduate course.
Slade School of Fine Art, University College London, Gower Street, London WC1E 6BT. Director of Film Studies: James Leahy.
City of Birmingham Polytechnic, Department of Visual Communication, School of Photography, Dorrington Road, Perry Barr, Birmingham B42 1QR. Head of School: Michael Hallett. One year CNAA M.A. (Graphic Design). Syllabus determined by individual needs in areas of photography, film and television.

THE NATIONAL FILM SCHOOL

The School offers a course of 3 year's professional training to enable its graduates to take positions of responsibility in both films and television and equally to create projects of their own.

ADMISSION: There are no age limits, but most successful candidates will be between 22 and 28. Although it is also expected that many successful applicants will have a high level of academic training, this will not be decisive; applicants will be asked to show proven ability in one or more of the primary areas of instruction — writing, directing, editing, producing, art direction, animation or photography.

Applications can be submitted between January 1st and February 28th 1983 for course commencing October 1983.

All enquiries to:
NATIONAL FILM SCHOOL
Beaconsfield Film Studios
Station Road,
Beaconsfield, Bucks. HP9 1LG.
Tel: (04946) 71234.

Bournemouth and Poole College of Art, School of Photography and Film, Department of Visual Communications, Royal London House, Lansdowne, Bournemouth BH1 3JL. Qualifications for admission: minimum age 18, five GCE passes, two of which must be at "A" level or equivalent, or satisfactory completion of a Foundation course and five GCE "O" levels or equivalent. A three-year course leading to the award of the Bournemouth and Poole College Diploma, the Professional Qualifying Examinations of the Institute of Incorporated Photographers, and Diploma Membership of the Society of Industrial Artists and Designers. Use of extensive film and TV facilities are concentrated into the last two years.

Bristol University, Department of Drama, Radio, Film and Television Studies, 29 Park Row, Bristol BS1 5LT. Director of Film Studies: G. W. Brandt, M.A. Undergraduate courses leading to BA in practical criticism, history, theory and practice of film and TV. Postgraduate: higher degree by dissertation leading to M.Litt and Ph.D.; Certificate in Radio, Film and Television, predominantly practical, provides an introduction to a wide range of technical skills, followed by production of films and TV programmes in the Department's studio and on location. Normally one year; two years in exceptional cases. Film production entirely on 16mm; rostrum facilities available. Close connection with BBC Bristol.

Croydon College, School of Art and Design, Film, Television and Animation Department, Fairfield, Croydon CR9 1DX. Area Director: Eddie Wolfram. Course Directors: Dick Perry, Film and Television; Eileen Baldwin, Animation. Intermedia – An intensive one-year course in Film, Television and Animation designed to provide a practical introduction to these three integrated branches of the media. The course is structured so as to allow a personal selection of the three subjects based on a programme of individual projects and tutorials. Good facilities (16mm synch-sound, U-Matic video, 16mm rostrum camera, etc.). Applicants must normally be diplomates or graduates in related studies, or have appropriate professional experience in TV, film, animation, video, journalism, drama, etc. Overseas students may wish to split options (and gain credits) for their final degree studies (i.e. Junior Year Abroad students). The course has been running successfully for 10 years now in the purpose-built Television and Animation studios of Croydon College, within easy reach of Central London. For full information on the course's structure and facilities, contact Dick Perry.

University of East Anglia, School of English and American Studies, Norwich NR4 7TJ. Offers a B.A. Hons with Film Studies as a Minor Option, and an M.A. in Film Studies. The M.A. course is awarded 50% on coursework and 50% on a dissertation on a freely chosen topic. To some extent the programme can be shaped to students' own areas of interest.

Gwent College of Higher Education, Faculty of Art and Design, Clarence Place, Newport, Gwent NPT OUW. Dean of Faculty: Douglas Halliday ARCA. Course Director, Film: Harley Jones. A two-year vocational course in documentary film-making or animation, aiming to encourage the practical skills of handling film and video equipment.

Harrow College of Higher Education, Northwick Park, Harrow HA1 3TP. Three-year full-time BA(Hons) (CNAA) in Applied Photography Film and Television. After one year of common study, specialisation is possible in film and video, centred around practical documentary and drama projects with accompanying analysis of media, historical, aesthetic and sociological considerations. Emphasis is on the creative application of film and video techniques.

Middlesex Polytechnic, Faculty of Art and Design, Cat Hill, Barnet, Hertfordshire EN14 5HU. Course leader: David Furnham. A one year post-graduate course in Film and Television, designed to offer an integrated programme of study in film and television for graduate students. It combines critical and theoretical study with a considerable amount of practical work, and all students are expected to complete a major project in either film or video. A CNAA diploma awarded to those who successfully complete the course.

University of Stirling, Film and Media Studies, Stirling FK9 4LA. Lecturer in charge: J. J. Izod, B.A., Ph.D. Undergraduate Film and Media Studies is designed at Stirling to give a grounding in the theory and criticism of film, television and radio. Also offers Postgraduate studies in Film.

West Surrey College of Art and Design, The Hart, Falkner Road, Farnham, Surrey. Head of Department of Audio-Visual Studies: Peter Sanger. CNAA BA (Honours) Course in Photography, Film, Video and Animation, with chief studies in each of these areas. The normal intake is 12 students per year each in Film, Video and Animation. Entry requirements, in accordance with CNAA regulations: five "O" Levels *plus* a foundation course in art and design *or* two "A" Levels. Three year course with common first two terms across all chief studies. Excellent facilities with extensive three-camera colour video studio.

HUNGARY

Szinház- és Filmmüvészeti Föiskola, Vas u. 2/c. 1088 Budapest. Rector: Dr. Jeno Simó. General Secretary: László Vadász.

INDIA

Film and Television Institute of India, Law College Road, Poona 411 004. Director: N. V. K. Murthy. 115 students in film wing. Experienced teaching staff. The Institute conducts three-year courses in (a) Motion Picture Photography, (2) Film Editing, (3) Film Direction, and (4) Sound Recording and Sound Engineering. The integrated part of training covers two years for the first three courses and one year for the course in Sound Recording and Sound Engineering. There are also general TV courses for in house training of employees of Doordarshan (Television Authority of India).

Film and Television Institute of Tamil Nadu, Department of Information and Public Relations, Government of Tamil Nadu, Madras, Adyar, Madras – 600 020. 80 students, 20 teaching staff. Three-year courses in direction, cinematography, sound engineering and recording, and film processing. Two-year course in editing. Certificate course of acting for one year. Fully-equipped studios and processing facilities. The Institute also has a production department, where film and production facilities are rented to commercial film producers; this scheme helps students to gain experience of actual film production.

ITALY
Centro Sperimentale di Cinematografica (C.S.C.), Via Tuscolana 1524, Rome. Director: Guido Cincotti.

JAPAN
Nihon University College of Art, Asahigaoka 2–42, Nerimaku, Tokyo 176.. Head of Film Department: Professor Toru Ótake.

NETHERLANDS
Nederlandse Film- en Televisie Academie, Overtoom 301, 1054 HW Amsterdam. Managing Directors: Rens Grott, Hans Klap, Wim van der Velde. 126 students. 22 staff. Four years.

PHILIPPINES
The Film Institute of the Philippines, 35 Cruz Street, Santa Elena, Marikina, Metro Manila. Director: Ben G. Pinga. About 250 graduates each year, staff of 12. Separate specialised courses of varying length, usually between four and ten months, part-time or full-time. Working closely with government media agencies and private institutions, the Institute has recently organised workshops in film direction, writing, motion picture photography, sound effects and animation. Particular stress is laid on work in the field of documentary film-making, in which the Institute has a distinguished record.

POLAND
Państwowa Wyższa Szkoła Filmowa, Telwizyjna i Teatralna, im Leona Schillera, Ul. Targowa 61/63, 90 323 Łódź.

ROMANIA
Institutul de Artă Teatrală şi Cinematografică "I.L. Caragiale," Bd. N. Bălcescu nr. 2 sect 1, cod. 70121, Bucharest. Director: Mircea Drăgan.

SOUTH AFRICA
Pretoria Technikon, 420 Church Street, Pretoria 0002. A 3-year diploma course is offered, covering subjects such as film history, technique, aesthetics, and production. Practical work is done on 16mm and videotape. During the third year students are given the opportunity to receive practical experience within the professional industry.

SPAIN
Ciudad Universitaria, Escuela Oficial de Cinematografía, Carretera dela Dehesa de la Villa s/n, Madrid 25. Director: Professor J. J. Baena Alvarez. 200 students,

teaching staff of 60 and 40 technicians. Three-year course with specialisation in directing, production management, photography, art direction, acting and writing. Students make four films during their three years. Fully-equipped studio, two dubbing theatres, five editing rooms, two projection rooms, 8, 16 and 35mm.

SWEDEN
Dramatiska Institutet (The Swedish Dramatic Institute), Filmhuset, Borgvägen, Box 27090, S-102 51 Stockholm. Principal: post vacant. Administrative Director: Goeran Ingulfson. Head of Film and TV Dept: Janos Hersko. Formed in 1970, the Institute is intended to provide instruction in production techniques for theatre, radio, television and film. A two and a half year course aims to equip students to a professional standard in one of these fields; there is also a one-year course designed for those such as teachers, youth leaders, etc., who require a working knowledge of small scale media techniques in order to widen average citizen media activites. 30 students are accepted each year for the two-year course, 16 for the one-year course. The Institute also runs seminars and shorter courses for further media training throughout the country; it is equipped with film and television studios, 14 editing rooms of 8, 16 and 35mm, sound mixing studios and portable video equipment.
Stockholm University, Department of Theatre and Cinema Arts, Filmhuset, Borgvägen 1–5, Box 27 126 – S–102 52 Stockholm. Stockholm University is the only university in Sweden offering both Theatre and Cinema. Tuition in Cinema Arts is provided for between 300–350 students, and the curriculum offers courses in the history of the cinema, film analysis and mass media studies.

TURKEY
Sinema-TV Enstitüsü, Kişlaönü, Beşiktas, İstanbul. Director: Sami Sekeroğlu. Film and TV school offering applied and theoretical training. 10 students accepted each year. 16 staff. Courses normally last for four years. Undergraduate training is mainly technical and leads to a diploma in one specialised field: camera, editing, sound, or laboratory. Those who prove successful in their first two years may continue to postgraduate level. Excellent facilities.

URUGUAY
Escuela de Cinematografia, 18 de Julio 1265 p. 2, Montevideo. Director: Juan José Ravaioli.

U.S.A.
Information on the many thousands of U.S. film courses is contained in the American Film Institute's **Guide to College Courses in Film and Television,** available from Peterson's Guides, 228 Alexander Street, Princeton, New Jersey 08540 for $11.50 plus postage and packing. The completely updated 1982 edition is now available.

U.S.S.R.
Vsesoyuzni Gosudarstvenni Institut Kinematografii (VGIK) (All-Union State Institute of Cinematography), ulitsa Vilgelma Pika 3, Moscow 129226. Director: Vitali

the london international film school

Courses in Film, Animation, and Television, start in September, January and April.

24 Shelton Street, London WC2 9HP1.

Nikolayevich Zhdan. No. of students: 1500. No. of instructors: 250. Length of courses: actors, economists – 4 years; cameramen – 4½ years; writers, directors – 5 years; designers – 6 years. Specialisation is always taken into account during training. The various disciplines taught can be divided into three groups: socio-economic (e.g. philosophy – 140 hours), general knowledge (e.g. history of Fine Arts – 160 hours – history of theatre, Soviet and foreign literature), and specialist instruction (e.g. for cameramen; 320 hours on operating, 110 on lighting). Practical work undertaken on all courses. The Institute has a training studio (with four stages totalling 1,000 sq. metres and 100 cameras of various types), an information department, its own textbooks and teaching manuals, and also auxiliary instruction quarters for Soviet cinema, foreign cinema, camera operating, direction, etc.

YUGOSLAVIA
Fakultet dramskih umetnosti (pozorišta, filma, radija i televizije), Ho Si Mina 20, 11070 Beograd. Dean: Vladan Slijepčević. Four-year course equivalent to undergraduate level; specialisation in direction, production, photography, dramaturgy, acting or editing. Students make films on 8 and 16mm, and a final diploma film on 35mm; film and television companies often provide facilities for students to gain experience of work under professional conditions.

Film Transporters

AUSTRIA

Frey & Co., *Lindengrasse 43, Vienna.*
Karl Vrablitz, *Neubaugasse 36, Vienna.*

BELGIUM

Import Film Service, *Av. du Castel 58, 1200 Brussels. Tel: 736 39 66.*
Ziegler & Co., *160 Rue Dieudonné Lefèvre, 1020 Bruxelles. Tel: 427 70 60.*

BRITAIN

Bob Burge Ltd., *7 Chalcot Road, London NW1. Tel: 01-586 4411/7.*
D.A.C. Air Services Ltd., *Building 30, London Airport, Hounslow, Middlesex.*
Film Transport Specialists (G.B.) Ltd., *Fairfield House, N. Circular Road, London. NW10. Tel: 01-965 7141.*
Samfreight Ltd., *303/315 Cricklewood Broadway, London NW2. Tel: 01-452 8090.*

DENMARK

Copenhagen Forwarding Agency A/S, *Amager Strandvej 350, DK-2770 Kastrup. Tel: (01) 50 35 55.*
Three out of four Danish film organisations route their films through CFA, which has grown enormously in recent years thanks to the merger with the huge ASC concern, which has an annual turnover of more than $200 million. There are two domestic offices in Århus and Billund, but the film department is still in Kastrup. CFA specialises in transporting physical equipment for TV news crews (not newsreels).

FINLAND

Oy Enroth AB, *Bulevardi 2–4, SF-00120 Helsinki 12. Tel: 649522. Telex: 124729*
Oy Lars Krogius Ab, *Et. Makasiinikatu 4, SF-00130 Helsinki 13. Tel: 171500. Telex: 124640 itahk sf.*

FRANCE

Donot, S.A., *175 rue de Courcelles, 75017 Paris.*
Martini & Cie, *17 Avenue Thiers, Nice. Tel: 88-2961.*
Filminger, *201 avenue Jean Lolive, 93500 Pantin. Tel: 846-3329.*

GERMANY

Hagens Anthony & Co., *Sonninstr. 24, 2 Hamburg 1.*
The oldest firm of transporters on the contenent is – technically – Hagens Anthony & Co. The actual firm was started at the end of the last century, and for many years Hagens Anthony have been IATA agents in air-freight traffic, with a non-stop service at Hamburg Fuhlsbüttel Airport, as well as at Bremen.
Kroll, Franz & Co., *Lindenstr. 39, Berlin. Tel: 251.50.51.*

GREECE

Greca Transport, *86 Academy St., Athens 141.*

ITALY

Cippolli & Zanetti, *Via Nomentana 257, Rome.*

NETHERLANDS

Damco Air, *Vrachstation, Schiphol-Airport Centrum, PO Box 7540. Tel: 020-472191.*

NORWAY

Sundbye Jet Cargo, *Oslo Airport, Fornebu, Oslo. Tel: 02-533407.*

SOUTH AFRICA

Jet Freight Services, *401 Cargo Building, Jan Smuts International Airport. Tel: 975-6818.*
Rennies International Airfreight, *12 Power Street, Isando, Transvaal. Tel: 36-1521.*
South African Airways, *S.A.A. Centre, Johannesburg. Tel: 978-5670.*

SWEDEN

AB Transportkompaniet, *Hornsbruksgatan 28, Stockholm S-10270. Tel: 08-680580.*
AB Transportkompaniet has more than forty years' experience in the handling of film and film units. Crews from abroad can be cleared at the border towns with a minimum of delay. Branch offices are available for clearance at Stockholm, Göteborg, Malmö, Hälsingborg, Trelleborg, Norrköping, Borås, Örebro, Karlstad, and Eskilstuna. Special aiport offices are maintained at the international airports in Stockholm, Göteborg and Malmö.

Film Insurance

Established in 1919, the firm of **Jauch & Hübener**, Katharinenstr. 10, Hamburg 11, West Germany, now look after all the production insurance for the second television channel in Germany, and for a majority of the feature films produced in that country. They have special branches in Berlin, Mülheim, Vienna, Munich, Frankfurt and Zürich so as to maintain direct links with producers, whether in the studio or on location. But Jauch & Hübener do not confine their activities solely to Germany. They work closely with foreign companies and particularly with Lloyd's in London. A useful contact for producers working in Europe.

Subtitling

BELGIUM

LABORATOIRES TITRA S.A., *98 rue des Plantes, 1030 Brussels.*

BRAZIL

TITRA FILM DO BRASIL S.A., *17 rue Sâo Luiz Gonzaga, Rio de Janeiro.*

FRANCE

NEUE MARS-FILM PETERS KG. *4 rue Christophe Colomb, 75008 Paris. Tel: 723.9178.*
LABORATOIRES TITRA S.A., *66 rue Pierre Rimbaud, 92230 Gennevilliers.*
ULTRA TITRES FILMS, *8 rue de Château, 92250 La Garenne-Colombes.*

GERMANY

CINETYP-BERLIN, *Friedrichstr. 235, Berlin 61. Tel: 251.0465.*

NETHERLANDS

TITRA FILM LABORATORIUM N.V., *82-86 Egelantiersgracht, Amsterdam C.*
COLOR FILM CENTER, *Leeghwaterstraat 5, P.O. Box 1083, The Hague. Tel: 88.92.07.*

Found over 75 years ago by the late Willy Mullens, Color Film Center is equipped with the newest available machinery, and provides processing and printing facilities on all current film systems, either negative or reversal. The lab specialises in high-quality jobs to individual customer specifications, and is backed up by a highly sophisticated chemical subtitling department, which handles 35 and 16mm prints, and can guarantee a constant high quality, especially on the more difficult 16mm format. Color Film Center also installs subtitling equipment throughout the world.

WARWICK
DUBBING THEATRE

151-153 WARDOUR STREET, LONDON, W1V 3TB
Telephone 01-437 5532/3

SWITZERLAND

CINETYP-LUCERNE, *Obergrundstr. 101, Postfach, 6005 Lucerne.*
TITRA FILMS S.A., *29 rue de Lancy, 1227 Geneva.*

Studios and Laboratories

AUSTRALIA

CRAWFORD PRODUCTIONS PTY LTD., *1 Southampton Crescent, Abbotsford, Victoria 3067*
THE FILM HOUSE PTY LTD., *159 Eastern Rd. South Melbourne, Victoria 3205.*
PAN PACIFIC PICTURES, *88 Acland Street, St. Kilda South, Victoria 3182.*
   Complete studio complex; editing, recording, and location facilities.
SUPREME SOUND STUDIOS, *11–15 Young Street, Paddington, Sydney.*

AUSTRIA

BERGLAND FILM GmbH, *Baumgarten Studios, Linzerstrasse 297, A.1140 Vienna. Tel: 942276.*
WIEN-FILM GmbH, *Sievering Studios, Sieveringerstr. 135, A.1190 Vienna. Tel: 322153.*

BELGIUM

MEUTER-TITRA LABORATORIES, *69 rue*
Verte, 1030 Brussels. Tel: 218 66 07. Telex: 64 178 B.
STUDIO KLANGFILM, *8 Chaussée de Vleurgat, 1050 Brussels. Tel: 648 51 94. Telex: 64: 178 B.*

BRAZIL

CINEDIA S.A., *Estrada da Soca 400, Jacarepangua, Rio de Janeiro.*
PRODUÇOES CINEMATOGRAFICAS HERBERT RICHERS S.A., *Rue Conde de Bimfim 1331, Rio de Janeiro.*
COMPANHIA CINEMATOGRAFICA VERA CRUZ, *São Bernado do Campo, São Paulo.*

BRITAIN

BRAY INTERNATIONAL FILM CENTRE, *Down Place, Windsor Road, Water Oakley, Windsor, Berks. Tel. (0628) 22111.*
   Close to M4 and Heathrow, with three sound stages, Bray provides modern facilities for film producers, in a rural setting on the bank of the Thames.
CALTON STUDIOS, *Calton Road, Edinburgh. Tel. 031 557 0155.*
CINE-LINGUAL SOUND STUDIOS, *27/29 Berwick Street, London W1V 3RF. Tel. (01) 437 0136/8.*
EDINBURGH FILM STUDIOS, *9 Mile Burn, Penicuik, Midlothian EH26 9LX. Tel. 0968 72131.*
EMI ELSTREE FILM STUDIOS, *Borehamwood, Herts. Tel. (01) 953 1600.*
ISLEWORTH STUDIOS LTD, *Studio Parade, 484 London Road, Isleworth, Middlesex TW7 4DE. Tel. (01) 568 3511.*

LEE INTERNATIONAL FILM STUDIOS LTD, *Kensal Road, London W10 5BN. Tel. (01) 969 9521.*

PINEWOOD STUDIOS, *Iver Heath, Bucks. Tel. (0753) 651700.*

PRODUCTION VILLAGE, *100 Cricklewood Lane, London NW2 2DS. Tel. (01) 450 8969.*

A "mini studio complex", consisting of nine stages plus a variety of offices and other facilities, the Village is run by Samuelsons, and is near their headquarters in Cricklewood Broadway.

SHEPPERTON STUDIO CENTRE, *Studios Road, Shepperton, Middlesex TW17 0OD. Tel. (09328) 62611.*

ST. JOHN'S WOOD STUDIOS, *St John's Wood Terrace, London NW8 PY6. Tel. (01) 722 9255.*

TRILION VIDEO, *36–44 Brewer Street, London W1. Tel. (01) 439 4177.*

Broadcast and standard TV facilities including studios, and complete post-production.

TWICKENHAM FILM STUDIOS LTD, *St. Margarets, Middlesex TW1 2AW. Tel. (01) 892 4477.*

FILM PRODUCTION SERVICES, *82 Holywell Road, Studham, Nr. Dunstable, Bedfordshire. Tel. (0582) 873107.*

This company provides production facilities and technicians for overseas producers filming in this country.

THE FILM STOCK CENTRE, *68-70 Wardour Street, London W1V 3HP. Tel. (01) 734 0038.*

GENERAL SCREEN ENTERPRISES LTD, *97 Oxford Road, Uxbridge, Middlesex. Tel. (89) 31931. Telex. 934883.*

HUMPHRIES FILM LABORATORIES, *71–81 Whitefield Street, London W1A 2HL. Tel. (01) 636 8636.*

Offers a complete service for producers, on every conceivable gauge, with overnight rushes service, total immersion printing facilities, opticals, special effects, titling, etc.

KEN LAILEY STUDIOS, *39 Wyndham Road, Salisbury, Wilts. Tel. (0722) 23099.*

Fully-equipped workshops for the construction of special effects, props and models.

NORMAN'S CINEMA & STUDIO EQUIPMENT LTD, *Norman House, 175 Wardour Street, London W1. Tel. (01) 437 7481.*

STUDIOSOUND, *81–88 Wardour Street, London W1V 3LF Tel. (01) 437 2233 or 734 0263.*

STUDIO FILM LABORATORIES LTD, *8–14 Meard Street, London W1V 3HR. Tel. (01) 437 0831.*

WARWICK DUBBING THEATRE, *153 Wardour Street, London W1. Tel. (01) 437 5532.*

Full range of dubbing services available. Five fully-equipped cutting rooms.

CANADA

CRAWLEY FILMS, *19 Fairmont Avenue, Ottawa 3, Ontario.*

MAGDER STUDIOS, *793 Pharmacy Avenue, Toronto, Ontario M1L 3K3. Tel. (416) 864 9120.*

MERIDIAN FILMS, *175 Bloor Street East, Toronto, Ontario M4W 1E1. Tel. (416) 924 3701.*

TORONTO INTERNATIONAL FILM STUDIOS, *11030 Highway 27, Box 1000, Kleinburg, Ontario. Tel. (416) 851 2201.*

DENMARK

THE DANISH FILM STUDIO, *Blomstervaenget 52, 2800 Lyngby. Tel. (02) 87 27 00.*

A/S NORDISK FILMS STUDIO, *Mosedalvej, 2500 Copenhagen Valby. Tel. 01-30 10 33.*

Owned by Nordisk Film Kompagni.

RIALTO/SAGA STUDIO, *DK–2620 Albertslund. Tel. (01) 64 96 46.*

FINLAND

SUOMI-FILMI OY, *Bulevardi 12, SF–00120 Helsinki 12. Tel. 642112.*

The only complete service house in the Finnish film industry. Film import, export, and distribution. Twenty cinemas throughout Finland; complete film lab; import and wholesale in photography branch. Special facilities for technical stage matters.

FRANCE

STUDIOS ECLAIR, *7 avenue George V, 75008 Paris. Tel. (723) 54 30.*

IMAGES DE FRANCE, *29 rue Vernet, 75008 Paris. Tel (720) 53 17.*

STUDIOS A.P.E.C., *66 rue Mouffetard, 75005 Paris. Tel. (331) 17 27.*
PARIS STUDIO CINEMA, *50 Quai du Pont du Jour, 92100 Billancourt. Tel. (609) 93 24.*
STUDIOS FRANCOEUR, *16 rue Francoeur, 75882 Paris. Tel. (257) 12 10.*
STUDIOS S.F.P., *36 rue des Alouettes, 75935 Paris. Tel. (203) 99 04.*
VICTORINE STUDIOS, *16 avenue Edouard Grinda, 06200 Nice. Tel. 83 10 16.*
LABORATOIRE ANTEGOR, *13 rue Beethoven, 75016 Paris. Tel. (524) 46 10.*
CINETITRES L.T.C., *12 rue Danicourt, 92240 Malakoff. Tel. (253) 36 76.*
C.T.M., *66 rue Pierre Rimbaud, 92230 Gennevilliers. Tel. (794) 99 00.*
ECLAIR, *8 avenue de Lattré de Tassigny, 93800 Epinay. Tel. (821) 63 63.*
G.T.C., *1 Quai Gabriel Péri, 94840 Joinville. Tel. (886) 49 02.*
LABORATOIRES FRANAY, *19 rue Marius Franay, 92210 Saint-Cloud. Tel. (602) 70 25.*
S.F.P., *15 rue Cognacq Jay, 75007 Paris. Tel. (555) 37 33.*

GERMANY

BAVARIA-ATELIER BmbH, *Bavaria-Film-Platz 7, Munich Geiselgasteig. Tel. 47691.*
CCC FILM, *Verl. Daumstrasse 16, Spandau, Berlin.*
STUDIO HAMBURG, *Tonndorfer Haupstrasse 90, 2000 Hamburg 70. Tel. 66881.*
This impressive complex in northern Germany provides German and overseas producers with virtually all the facilities they could hope for. There are 11 studio stages (each 450 to 1,000 square metres), a variety of dubbing and recording studios, rehearsal stages for TV production, 43 film cutting rooms for all gauges, underwater, post-synch, processing and re-wind facilities, mobile TV and VTR units, and post production editing suites.

GREECE

FINOS FILMS, *53 Chiou Street, Athens. Tel. (815) 087.*

HONG KONG/TAIWAN

CENTRAL MOTION PICTURE CO., *34 Chih-shan Road, Section 2, Shihlin, Taipei, Taiwan.*
CHINA MOTION PICTURE STUDIO, *400 Chungyang N. Road, Section 2, Peitou District, Taipei, Taiwan.*
DRAGON FILM PRODUCTIONS, *1/Fl, 2 Conduit Road, Hong Kong. Tel. H228064.*
GOLDEN STUDIOS, *8 Hammer Hill Road, Kowloon. Tel. 3-250136.*
SHAW BROS., *Lot 220, Clear Water Bay Road, Kowloon.*
TAIWAN FILM STUDIO, *292 Mingsheng Road, Chifeng Village, Wufeng Hsiang, Taichung County.*

HUNGARY

MAFILM STUDIOS, *Lumumba utca 174, Budapest XIV.*

IRELAND

NATIONAL FILM STUDIOS OF IRELAND, *Ardmore House, Bray, County Wicklow. Tel. 862 971.*

ISRAEL

UNITED STUDIOS OF ISRAEL, *Hakessem Street, Herzliya.*

ITALY

CINECITTÀ, *Via Tuscolana 1055, Rome.*
Recently modernised, with 10 sound stages.
DEAR INTERNATIONAL, *Via Nomentana 833, Rome.*

JAPAN

TOHO STUDIO, *1–4–1 Seijo, Setagaya-ku, Tokyo 157.*

MEXICO

ESTUDIOS CHURUBUSCO-AZTECA S.A., *Ateltas 2, Mexico 21, DF.*

NETHERLANDS

CINECENTRUM, *'s-Gravelandseweg 80, 1217 EW Hilversum (also at Duivendrechtsekade 83, Amsterdam). Tel. 035–47141.*

With some 300 employees, all experts in their craft, the Cinecentrum Group in Hilversum is the hub of Dutch film technique. There are the Cineco laboratories, a video department (the equipment is right up the the minute with film-to-tape facilities in both colour and monochrome, with the now-famous "Video Train," and a limitless potential for titling and sound amendment), five projection rooms, an editing section, and a massive sound department.

The Cineco laboratories include the "Optical Arthouse," which offers special effects to animators and other film-makers, an impressive service using a Nielsen Hardell rostrum camera and liquid prints. The Audio Visual Centre Wisseloord has a choice of four different sound studios complete with all the most advanced acoustical and technical facilities. Wisseloord is part of the Polygram Group.

CINETONE FILMSTUDIOS, *Duivendrechtse-kade 83-85, P.O. Box 4104, Amsterdam. Tel. 020-930960.*

Founded over 40 years ago, this efficient production centre really came into international importance in about 1972, when the development of the Dutch feature film industry gave Cinetone a solid base for its activities. Located in Amsterdam, 20 minutes from Schiphol Airport, Cinetone now offers a full production service, with two studios and complete facilities, including sound studios, cutting rooms, offices, workshops, and so on.

NORWAY

NORSK FILM A/S, *Wedel Jarlsbergs vei 36, 1342 Jar. Tel. (02) 121070.*

TEAMFILM A/S, *Keysersgt. 1, Oslo 1. Tel. (02) 207072.*

CAPRINO FILM CENTRE, *Mario Caprinos vei 3B, 1335 Snarøya. Tel. (02) 532647.*

CENTRALFILM A/S, *Åkebergun. 56, Oslo 6. Tel. (02) 676393.*

POLAND

ŁÓDŹ FEATURE FILM STUDIO, *Lakowa 29, 90–554 Łódź.*

WROCŁAW FEATURE FILM STUDIO, *Wysta-wowa 1, 51–617 Wrocław.*

WARSAW FEATURE FILM STUDIO, *Chełmska 21, 00–724 Warsaw.*

DOCUMENTARY FILM AND NEWSREEL STUDIO, *Chełmska 21,00–724 Warsaw.*

Besides usual technical facilities, this also has a large library of historical material.

PORTUGAL

MARTRA FILMS, *Lda, Calcad Marqués, Abrantes, 103 Lisbon.*

SOUTH AFRICA

IRENE FILM LABORATORIES, *P.O. Box 15, Irene, Transvaal 1675.*

35mm, 16mm and Super 8 film processing; opticals, animation, dubbing and mixing.

PANORAMA FILMS, *P.O. Box 781754, Sandton 2146.*

S.A.FILM & TV CENTRE, *P.O. Box 89271, Lyndhurst 2106.*

Studio and equipment rental, with sound stage and post-production services.

VIDEO R.S.A., *1 Rockey Drive, Northcliff, Johannesburg.*

Videotape studio and post-production facilities.

LONE HILL STUDIOS, *P.O. Box 70363, Bryanston, Transvaal 2021.*

SPAIN

CINEARTE, *5 Pl. del Conde de Barajas, Madrid 12.*

SWEDEN

EUROPA FILM, *Tappvägen 24, Box 200 65, S–16120 Bromma 20. Tel. 08–987700. Telex 17656 Eurstud S.*

One of the biggest media production plants in

Europe, with two sound stages, a dubbing dept. for both 16 and 35mm, two recording studios, and facilities for video, cassette duplication, and the cutting and master production of discs. Europa are specialists in providing services for advertising and industrial films. No European studio complex is more keenly geared to the future.

SVENSKA FILMINSTITUTET, *Filmhuset, Borgvägen, S–102 52 Stockholm 27.*

Four sound stages, cutting rooms, and other facilities.

SVENSK FILMINDUSTRI, *Box 576, S–101 27 Stockholm.*

SWITZERLAND

CONDOR FILM, *Studio Bellerive, Kreutzstrasse 2, 8034 Zürich.*

U.S.A.

AMERICAN MOTION PICTURE COMPANY, *7017 Fifteenth Avenue Northwest, Seattle, Washington 98117.*

Production specialties include Business documentary, medical, sports, live TV. Services include script-writing, motion picture editing services, AV consultation.

THE BURBANK STUDIO, *4000 Warner Blvd, Burbank 91522.*

HOLLYWOOD GENERAL STUDIOS, *1040 North Las Palmas, California 90038.*

MGM STUDIOS, *10202 West Washington, Culver City.*

PARAMOUNT PICTURES INC, *5451 Marathon Street, Hollywood, California 90038.*

20TH CENTURY-FOX, *10201 West Pico Blvd, Los Angeles, California.*

UNIVERSAL CITY STUDIOS, *100 Universal City Plaza, Universal City, California.*

Films on 16 mm (U.K.)

The 16mm distributors have taken a severe body blow from the attack of video cassettes. Ironically, video has not been so successful in the United States, which in every other area of technology usually outstrips Britain. But the swift success of the cassette rental system has meant that none but the film society stalwarts are prepared to go on threading reels of celluloid on to noisy projectors when they can so easily watch an entire film on a cassette – usually without interruption.

Some companies have been hit harder than others. Contemporary Films, for instance, advertisers in this book for 19 years, were forced to drop out this year because of declining business, while several of the major companies have agglomerated in a desperate attempt to rationalise their activity and slim overheads.

As so often in such a parlous situation, the specialists survive the best. **Curzon Film Distributors,** for example, offer an excellent selection of predominantly French films – *Une Semaine de*

vacances, and *Préparez vos mouchoirs* are recent additions – as well as classics of the past decade such as *Derzu Uzala, The Tree of Wooden Clogs,* and *Violette Nozière.* **Darvill Associates** have long devoted time, patience, love, and money into the establishment of the U.K. finest library of Scandinavian cinema, including most of the Bergman classics, a couple of masterpieces by Arne Mattsson, and Danish and Finnish features of real distinction. A welcome addition this year has been Jacques Tati's overlooked effort, *Parade,* set in a circus.

Cinegate has opened most of its continental releases at one of the Gate Cinemas in central London, with special emphasis on West German cinema (*Lightning over Water* and *Malou* have been added in 1982), but there are also offbeat works such as Águst Gudmundsson's *The Outlaw* and Lino Brocka's *Manila.* The passing of Fassbinder should also draw attention to his films in the Cinegate catalogue. **The Other Cinema,** which has

STILL FROM WERNER HERZOG'S *FITZCARRALDO*, RELEASED IN THE U.K. THROUGH ARTIFICIAL EYE

endured despite all manner of crises over the years, continues to present an audacious selection of fresh releases, among them Arthur MacCaig's *The Patriot Game*, which takes the Republican side on Northern Ireland, and the 1975 Danish film, *Take It Like a Man, Ma'am!* Best of all The Other Cinema's new films, however, is *The Life and Times of Rosie the Riveter* (reviewed in IFG 1982).

Artificial Eye continue to present some of the finest French, Swiss, Italian, German, and Polish films. Among the riches of 1982: *Fitzcarraldo, The Aviator's Wife, Man of Iron, Loulou, Three Brothers,* and *Light Years Away*.

The two big majors are **Harris/Films Ltd** (which incorporates releases from Robert Kingston/Hurlock Cine-World and several other distri-

STILL FROM ÁGÚST GUDMUNDSSON'S *THE OUTLAW*, RELEASED IN THE U.K. THROUGH CINEGATE

butors who are happy to share in the Harris/Films overhead) and **Colombia-EMI-Warner**. Impossible to detail the myriad releases in these catalogues, but for those still using films on 16mm, they will be useful.

Finally, mention of two hardy perennials in the field: the **British Film Institute Film and Video**, which has several very high-quality foreign pictures, including the works of Yılmaz Güney, one of our "Directors of the Year" as well as Ousmane Sembene's *Ceddo* and Max Ophüls's *La signora di tutti*; and **ETV Films Ltd.**, which is Britain's best source of documentaries from Eastern Europe and the Third World, as well as classic features from the U.S.S.R., Czechoslovakia etc.

Non-Theatrical (U.S.A.)   by Stuart Rosenthal

In responding directly and indirectly to the new video technologies, the 16mm non-theatrical film industry has changed so much that it now bears little resemblance to the 16mm rental business of ten years ago. Where we once had a multitude of libraries, each with its own distinctive personality and approach to distribution, we now find a much smaller number of concerns, many of which are virtual movie supermarkets. Many of the more specialised companies have left non-theatrical distribution altogether while others have sold or arranged for rental of their titles through different, larger organisations. Firms once known primarily as outlets for major studio releases today may handle a variety of product from foreign language classics to "experimental" film. Diversification

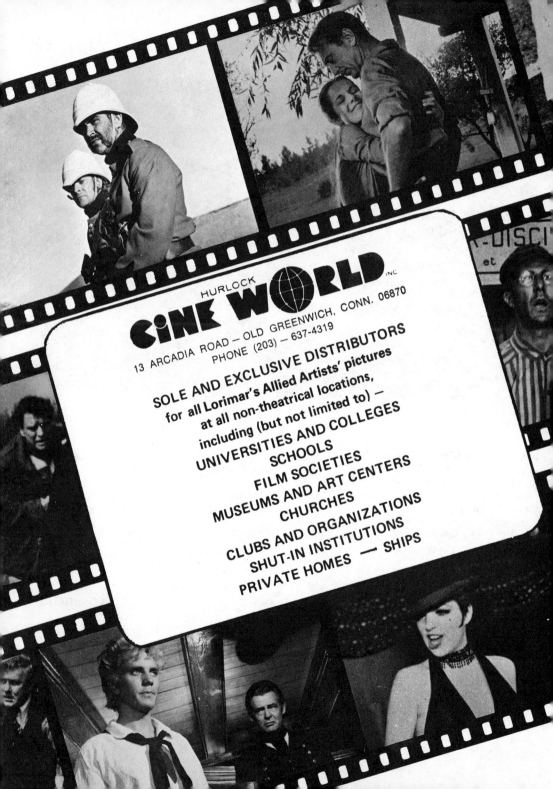

into video formats and the pick-up of theatrical, television and ancillary rights to features by companies that used to be strictly non-theatrical rental establishments further complicate the picture.

It's impossible to predict, at this point, what these changes will ultimately mean to the availability of specialised and foreign language films in the United States. I suspect that – as has already occurred to an extent – many important, though not immensely popular titles will disappear from the marketplace altogether as existing contracts expire and are not renewed. On the other hand, there are still a few aggressive, commercially astute companies which concentrate upon foreign films, carefully taking advantage of all the new markets opened by video to make each acquisition financially viable.

Given the ongoing metamorphosis of non-theatrical distribution, the format used in this section in years past no longer seems workable or appropriate. Instead, what follows is a general description of the products and services of the most important remaining non-theatrical distributors.

CINEMA 5–16mm offers a choice selection of major foreign titles, including the impressive line-up assembled during the company's theatrical heyday in the Seventies. More recently, they have picked up some top independent efforts, among them John Sayle's *Return of the Secaucus Seven*, David Lynch's *Eraserhead*, and Robert Young's eye-opening drama about undocumented Mexican workers, *Alambrista*. Also worthy of mention are such Australian successes as *My Brilliant Career* and Peter Weir's *The Last Wave*. Just for fun, Cinema 5–16mm has George Romero's *Dawn of the Dead*, and *Monty Python and the Holy Grail*. Bookers for the company know the library well, provide thoughtful individualised service and can offer discounts in many cases.

CORINTH FILMS is a major success story in the world of specialised distribution. They began life with the Richard Feiner library and the remnants of the McGraw-Hill Contemporary Films collection. They've expanded their catalogue through a special association with Sovexportfilm, the acquisition of titles like Fellini's *8 1/2* as they expired from other companies' libraries, deals for several old and new French films, and an influx of

Acquaint yourself with the largest and most diversified nontheatrical film distributor in the world.

From American classics to current Hollywood box office hits (*The Grapes of Wrath* to *Star Wars*), the finest in international masterworks (*Rome: Open City, Through a Glass Darkly, Amarcord* and *Breaker Morant*), and the most diverse collection of comedy, drama, musicals and midnight cult favorites, Films Incorporated takes pride in presenting you with the most comprehensive selection of entertainment available. Our expert programming staff will provide you with the film or film package you need—custom-selected to satisfy your audience and your budget.

We've spanned the globe to acquire the finest motion pictures by the most distinguished filmmakers: films from France, Sweden, Italy, Great Britain and Japan, by the most renowned cinema masters of all time, including Francois Truffaut, Ingmar Bergman, Federico Fellini, Alfred Hitchcock and Akira Kurosawa. Films Incorporated makes only the best in worldwide cinema available to our customers.

Call or write us today for our free catalog, instant service or just to talk cinema. Tell us your needs and we'll show you what we can do for you.

Our regional offices are listed below. Get acquainted with Films Incorporated today!

Breaker Morant

Ragtime

West
5625 Hollywood Boulevard
Hollywood, California 90028
213/466-5481

Northeast
440 Park Avenue South
New York, New York 10016
212/889-7910

Southeast
476 Plasamour Drive, N.E.
Atlanta, Georgia 30324
404/873-5101

Central
733 Green Bay Road
Wilmette, Illinois 60091
312/256-6600

Films Incorporated
a division of

PMI
Public Media Incorporated

Films Incorporated

JUTTA LAMPE, GUDRUN GABRIEL, AND JESSICA FRUH IN MARGARETHE VON TROTTA'S *SISTERS OF THE BALANCE OF HAPPINESS*, RELEASED IN THE U.S.A. THROUGH CINEMA 5

Russ Meyer's antic productions. In addition, Corinth is the only source with anamorphic prints of certain American classics. Many titles are available for theatrical or video exhibition.

The venerable Audio Brandon library, after a disappointing sojourn with the Macmillan corporation is now in the capable hands of **FILMS, INC.**, perhaps the largest and most multi-faceted of non-theatrical enterprises. Films, Inc. has ample experience in handling foreign language pictures through its participation in "The Classic Collection" with **Janus Films** (including the great Bergman series) and as a result of their ongoing project with Quartet films. One irony of the Audio Brandon sale is that it returned the post-1948 Paramount Pictures inventory to the Films, Inc. fold. Other major and semi-major distributors releasing in 16mm through Films, Inc. include 20th Century-Fox, Orion, and New World Pictures. Films, Inc. can provide many titles in video and books some of its titles theatrically in 16mm.

HURLOCK CINE-WORLD remains a striking exception to the trend toward bigness in the non-theatrical industry. It still functions with the sort of unique personal attention, efficiency and concern for the customer that one rarely encounters outside smaller, family-run operations. That's because Hurlock Cine-World actually is a family business. Its catalogue describes the best features originally produced and distributed by Allied Artists, ranging from such legendary *film noir* as *Gun Crazy* and *The Big Combo* to box-office hits on the order of *Cabaret* and *Papillon*. Hurlock Cine-World has also acquired rights to some films independently. Rental terms are more than competitive with those of other companies and Hurlock's attention to print quality and their meticulous shipping procedures are unsurpassed.

If you're fed up with the indistinct nth generation dupes of silent films that pervade the market, **THE KILLIAM COLLECTION** is the place to find relief. Working with the best material available

DIANE KEATON IN *SHOOT THE MOON*, NOW AVAILABLE THROUGH MGM/UA ENTERTAINMENT IN THE STATES

Paul Killiam has worked for years to restore silent classics to their original grandeur. Killiam releases most of his titles, including many superb Fox silents, in complete versions with appropriate colour tinting and music tracks.

It would be difficult to overrate **NEW YORKER FILMS'** contribution to the film literacy of American audiences. New Yorker founder Dan Talbot is particularly astute at discovering important film-makers before they have become popular in the United States. The New Yorker catalogues reflect Talbot's early interest in Ozu, Tanner, Godard, Rivette, Malle, Straub, Fassbinder, Herzog and Schlöndorff. New titles of the same calibre as New Yorker's earlier acquisitions continue to swell the company's extraordinary inventory of product. Rental rates are flexible, depending upon the specific exhibition circumstances, and prints are well maintained. A product reel consisting of clips from newer releases is available to non-theatrical customers without charge.

SWANK MOTION PICTURES grew into a giant by working intensively and aggressively in the college "student union" market. Today they are exclusive distributors of many new and old Universal releases (including MCA's pre-1948 Paramount library) and certain films from Columbia, The Ladd Company, Warner Brothers, Cinema Center, AIP, and Embassy. Service is fast and the company welcomes collect calls from customers wishing to order films. Unlike many other distributors, Swank will fill last minute telephone orders and arrange for overnight shipment of prints.

Although **TRANS-WORLD FILM** maintains a selection of classic films for entertainment and film study purposes, the company is especially valuable as a classroom resource, particularly for foreign-language courses. Many films, including some from Trans-World's extensive collections of German, French and Mexican films are available either with or without subtitles. A number of Trans-World's titles are offered for lease as well as for rental at extremely reasonable prices. Under the name **COLLEGE FILM CENTER**, the company operates an animated and documentary educational film library. The firm is also active in acquiring foreign language films for U.S. distribution.

JAMES GARNER, JULIE ANDREWS AND ROBERT PRESTON IN BLAKE EDWARDS'S *VICTOR/VICTORIA*, RELEASED NON-THEATRICALLY THROUGH MGM/UNITED ARTISTS ENTERTAINMENT

As a result of Metro-Goldwyn-Mayer's purchase of United Artists from Transamerica, United Artists: 16mm has become **MGM/UA ENTERTAINMENT**. The entire MGM library, including an ongoing slate of new productions, has been combined with the great United Artists collection which at present includes recent and current UA titles, the output of the old Monogram studios, and the pre-1950 Warner Brothers inventory. Through the activities of United Artists Classics, MGM/UA Entertainment is blessed with an infusion of first rate foreign films, among them key words by Truffaut, Fassbinder, and other major directors as well as such offbeat works as *Ticket to Heaven* and *Diva*. Orders are taken by the experienced staff at the New York office, but prints are shipped from the United Artists facility in Cincinnati where they are expertly cared for and efficiently processed.

Finally, a welcome for one of the most enterprising distributors in the States, **FIRST RUN FEATURES**, an organisation established and directed by film-makers, with a stimulating selection of independent documentaries, comedies, and dramas. Titles such as Victor Nunez's *Gal Young 'Un*, Mark Rappaport's *Imposters*, and Connie Field's *Rosie the Riveter* are worth any programmer's attention.

Book Reviews

HISTORY AND GENERAL

Hollywood and the American Image, by Tony Thomas (Arlington House, Westport, Connecticut, 1981). In a volume distinguished both by the wealth of its design and the urbane relaxation of its style, Tony Thomas casts an affectionate and knowledgeable eye over the movies' image of America. Westerns, musicals, gangster movies, comedies: Thomas selects one or two rewarding yet less conspicuous examples of the genre and evokes them with intelligence.

The Magician and the Cinema, by Erik Barnouw (Oxford University Press, Oxford and New York, 1981). Professor Barnouw is a scholar in many fields – the documentary, the Indian cinema, and now the earliest pioneers of trick effects on film. The research is commendable, the illustrations enchanting, and the text succinct.

René Clair's Grand Maneuver, by Nancy Warfield (Little Film Gazette, New York, 1982). Another of Nancy Warfield's enterprising little pamphlets, devoted this time to one of the most underrated of all European directors – René Clair. The monograph emphasises Clair's development of the sound movie.

Lulu in Hollywood, by Louise Brooks (Alfred Knopf, New York, 1982). Occasional articles have revealed Louise Brooks as a writer of admirable lucidity and penetration, but this elegant album joins her various pieces into a kind of memoir that, though tinged with personal memories, succeeds in repealing much of the history one has simply accepted from more orthodox books. Bogart, Gish, Fields, Wellman, all spring to attention in these pages.

Punch at the Cinema, presented by Dilys Powell (Robson Books, London, 1981). An engaging tombola of whimsy, wit, observation, and the arcane. Extracts, in short, from Britain's most famous humorous weekly from the silent period to the present day. The ideal bedside companion for film buffs.

Suomen Hollywood on kuollut, by Kari Uusitalo (Finnish Film Foundation, Helsinki, 1981). The fifth volume of Kari Uusitalo's definitive history of Finnish cinema, dealing with the period 1956 to 1963 and including such a wealth of reference material, statistics, and listings that it will have an appeal beyond the Nordic area. Profusely illustrated.

Forever Ealing, A Celebration of the Great British Film Studio, by George Perry (Pavilion Books, London, 1981). A splendid tribute to Britain's most idiosyncratic and lovable studio, with details about all the films and a spectacular collection of photographs, both stills and revealing production shots. The design, even to the endpapers, is attractive by film book standards.

Hollywood's Vietnam, From The Green Berets to Apocalypse Now, by Gilbert Adair (Proteus, London, 1981). A wide-ranging, thoughtful, even provocative study, that tackles the major military movies but also such oblique Vietnam statements as *The Edge* and *One Flew Over the Cuckoo's*

Nest. But Adair, like many commentators, spends far too much space denigrating *The Deer Hunter* for its alleged lack of authenticity, denying the metaphorical value of the film.

Le Travail des Ciné-Clubs et le Cinéma en Europe, edited by Jean-Pierre Brossard (Editions Cinediff, La Chaux-de-Fonds, Switzerland, 1981). An admirable survey of film society activity throughout Europe, with detailed texts for each country, extracts from documents, statistics etc.

L'Algérie vue par son Cinéma, edited by Jean-Pierre Brossard (Editions Cinediff, La Chaux-de-Fonds, Switzerland, 1981). Documentation on Algerian cinema in English or French is scanty, and Brossard's little dossier, nicely printed, and accurately presented, will fill a niche.

The Stories Behind the Scenes of the Great Film Epics, by Mike Munn (illustrated Publications Co., London, 1981). A close-up analysis of the making of more than 50 major epic movies, containing some fascinating quotes and statistics as well as a rich crop of photographs (several in colour).

Hollywood, The First Hundred Years, by Bruce T.

Torrence (New York Zoetrope, New York, 1982). A dazzling and nostalgic collection of 300 photographs (richly printed in duotone) evoking the grand days of Hollywood (as well as the seedy sidewalks), with a perceptive commentary by the author.

MONOGRAPHS AND BIOGRAPHY

Show People, by Kenneth Tynan (Virgin Books, London, 1981). A superb memorial to the coruscating, richly-beaded prose of Kenneth Tynan,

JACKET DESIGN FOR A NEW PROTEUS PUBLICATION

whose profiles of Ralph Richardson, Tom Stoppard, Johnny Carson, Mel Brooks, and Louise Brooks, all demonstrate the fading art of good writing. Tynan prances wittily around his subjects, letting them have their say, then slipping in a rapier thrust to bring down their guard; yet he loves them all.

Jane Fonda, by Fred Lawrence Guiles (Michael Joseph, London, 1981). Were it not for Guiles's admirable biography of Marion Davies, one would scarcely glance at his book on Jane Fonda, who has already been extolled in several volumes. Guiles strikes a fine balance between the actress's political commitment, her performances on screen, and her private liaisons. The photographs are carefully chosen, and include several unfamiliar shots.

. . . But We Need the Eggs, The Magic of Woody Allen, by Diane Jacobs (St. Martin's Press, New York, 1982). Diane Jacobs has proved herself one of the more astute analysts of the new American cinema, and her study of Woody Allen covers his stage as well as his movie work, and concludes that while his approach to the cinema has grown darker and more introspective, he has never forsaken his essential love of being the funnyman.

Ingmar Bergman, A Critical Biography, by Peter Cowie (Charles Scribner's Sons, New York; Secker and Warburg, London, 1982). A major study of Bergman by the Editor of IFG, the first biography in English, with emphasis on Bergman's theatre work and life in Sweden and West Germany, as well as long analyses of all the films. Most complete filmography to date, plus over 100 photos.

Betty Grable, The Reluctant Movie Queen, by Doug Warren (Robson Books, London, 1982). A routine biography of the leggy sex symbol who for a while during the Forties was the highest-paid woman in the United States. More illustrations would have brought this book to life.

All the Stars in Heaven, The Story of Louis B. Mayer and M.G.M., by Gary Carey (Robson Books, London, 1982). Carey is a serious historian, and the value of his scholarship here is not so much the biography of the ineffably dull and bullish Mayer as the picture of that miraculous machine, M.G.M., which owed, one suspects, more to Thalberg than to its final M.

Jean Vigo, by Luis Filipe Rocha (Edições Afrontamento, Porto Portugal, 1982). A Portuguese critical biography of the short-lived French director. Paperback, but scholarly.

Blake Edwards, by Peter Lehman and William Luhr (Ohio University Press, Athens, Ohio, 1981). A straightforward monograph, ending with *10* (and thus excluding the delightfully rancid *S.O.B.*).

Bourvil, by Jacques Lorcey (Editions PAC, Paris, 1981). An affectionate and long overdue appraisal of one of France's most popular comedians, whose work never really travelled and yet who became as specifically Gallic a figure as Chips Rafferty was an Australian.

Marguerite Clark, by Curtis Nunn (Texas Christian University Press, Fort Worth, Texas, 1981). Printed and produced with loving care, this Texan tribute to one of the stage and screen's most endearing stars evokes the silent era in all its innocence. Remarkable illustrations.

A GREAT GAP WILL BE FILLED...

TO BE PUBLISHED IN 1983

AMERICAN FILM-INDEX
1916–1920
by
Einar Lauritzen &
Gunnar Lundquist

A COMPANION VOLUME TO THE EARLIER WORK "AMERICAN FILM-INDEX 1908–1915" PUBLISHED by

**FILM-INDEX
KARLAVAEGEN 61
S-11449 STOCKHOLM**

Bogart, by Terence Pettigrew (Proteus, London, 1981). A revised edition of the author's 1977 biography, which relies heavily on newspaper and magazine reviews of the various films but which contains some excellent stills and a comprehensive filmography for all lovers of Bogie.

Peter Sellers, by Derek Sylvester (Proteus, London, 1981). A large-format study of Sellers the man and his films, with stress on the biographical details rather than on the reasons for his being so funny. It was Sellers's tragedy that his life always seemed more interesting than his art.

REFERENCE AND TECHNICAL

The Movies, by Richard Griffith, Arthur Mayer, and Eileen Bowser (Columbus Books, London, 1982). For sheer value, this massive volume would be hard to beat – 1,500 photographs from every phase of film history (with the emphasis, of course, on Hollywood). The text is still almost super-fluous, but the images form an evocative cascade, one pauses before the obese neck of Erich von Stroheim, or the overhead shot of the wagons hurtling across the prairie in *Cimarron* . . .

Maisema taitelun jälkeen, by Markku Tuuli (Finnish Film Foundation, Helsinki, 1981). Behind this Finnish title lies concealed one of the year's most commendable film books – a guide to Polish cinema that even the Poles themselves have acknowledged as being almost without blemish, organised by theme and director, and boasting an 80-page filmographical section that will prove invaluable to any library or student.

Svensk Filmografi 1940–1949 (Swedish Film Institute, Stockholm, 1980). The fourth volume in what promises to be the finest national filmography in the world, assembled with that characteristic Swedish blend of meticulous accuracy and alertness to technological development (the entire project has been set on computer). The Forties included Bergman's early work, the finest films of Sjöberg, the heyday of Hasse Ekman. For each film there are credits, an extended synopsis, and a thorough digest of press reaction. Absolutely indispensable for any serious film library.

Screen World 1981, Edited by John Willis (Frederick Muller, London, 1981). Covers every major domestic and foreign release in the United States, with a cluster of stills, basic credits, and cast lists. The book is intriguing not so much for the omissions of so many European films, as for the inclusion of several features that the majors simply did not feel it worth the trouble of releasing in Europe.

The Illustrated Directory of Film Stars, by David Quinlan (Batsford, London, 1981). 1,600 career entries; the biographical descriptions are tart and succinct, but the filmographies themselves are resolutely complete, which is more than can be said for such rival books as Halliwell and Katz. Quinlan's is a catholic taste, too: all nations, all styles of star and starlet. The portraits are numerous.

L'écran total, pour un Cinéma Sphérique, by Philippe Jaulmes (Lherminier, Paris, 1981). An extraordinarily lucid and resolute defence of what in other countries might be regarded as a gimmick – the "Cyclorama" type screen, well illustrated with diagrams and photographs.

Les Cinémas de l'Amérique Latine, edited by Guy Hennebelle and Alfonso Gumucio-Dagron (Lherminier, Paris, 1981). Without question one of the most significant and invaluable books published on the cinema during the past decade. Over 500 large pages packed with information, history, statistics, opinion, profiles, photographs etc. on 25 separate Latin-American countries. A work of love and scholarship in every sense.

Internationale Filmbibliographie 1979–80, edited by Hanspeter Manz (Filmland Presse, Munich, 1981). Thanks to the enterprise of Klaus Denicke at Filmland Presse, the impressive scholarship of the Swiss book expert, H. P. Manz, has again been put between covers and enables one to turn up virtually every title of interest published on the subject of film during 1979 and 1980. First in a series.

New York Production Manual 1981, compiled, written, and edited by Shmuel Bension (New York Production Manual Inc., New York, 1981). In a thousand pages, this tome covers what New York has to offer as a major production centre, with information on unions, services, production logistics, contract form etc. Invaluable for the private producer thinking of filming on location in NY.

Film i 70'erne, by Claus Hesselberg (Politikens Forlag, Copenhagen, 1981). In two boxed volumes, Claus Hesselberg (our Danish correspondent) provides cast and credits – plus stills – from every feature film screened in Danish cinemas during the period 1968 to 1979. It provides a worthy sequel to the sterling reference handiwork of the late Bjørn Rasmussen.

100 Short Films about the Human Environment, edited by William R. Ewald (ABC-Clio, Santa Barbara/Oxford, 1982). A brilliantly-designed guide to a hundred classic shorts on 16mm for use in senior high school, college and community discussions, edge-indexed by five categories, and profusely illustrated. Invaluable for teachers.

National Film Archive Catalogue of Stills, Posters and Designs (BFI Publishing, London, 1982). No fewer than 37,000 films are listed and annotated in this detailed record of one of the world's greatest collections of memorabilia – alas, not for sale (though stills can be ordered), and cross-indexed by director. One of the BFI's most impressive publications.

The Screenwriters Guide, by Keith Burr and Joseph Gillis (New York Zoetrope, New York, 1982). With just about everyone "at work on a screenplay," this paperback gives practical listings of addresses and sources for the neophyte scriptwriter. Also includes a glossary of terms used in screenwriting.

THEORY AND CRITICISM

Les Conquérants d'un Nouveau Monde, by Michel Ciment (Gallimard, Paris, 1981). A collection of articles ranging over a long period and a diverse number of Hollywood figures (from Welles to Wilder, from Kazan to Malick). Ciment's essays are beautifully modulated, even in temper, judicious in comment, yet courageous in defending the director whose work may have been misunderstood (such as Sternberg) or even ridiculed (Capra).

D'une Image à l'autre, La Nouvelle Modernité du Cinéma, by Youssef Ishaghpour (Denoël/Gonthier, Paris, 1982). An elaborate, somewhat prolix attempt to seize in print the fleeting riches of the more *outré* modern cineastes. Wenders, Straub, Duras, Resnais, Syberberg – these are the talents discussed with lucidity and a degree of humour that leavens the tougher passages.

Film and Dreams: An Approach to Bergman, edited by Vlada Petrić (Redgrave Publishing Company, South Salem, NY, 1981). The yield of a seminar held at Harvard University a year or two back, with such contributors as John Simon and even Dušan Makavejev holding forth on Bergman's deployment of a dream world. Rich in outspoken observation.

The New Italian Cinema, by R. T. Witcombe (Secker and Warburg, London, 1982). For years there has been a need for a sensible study of Italian postwar cinema in English, and Witcombe's book contains sufficient pith of theoretical comment to lift the work out of the reference mould. For all university courses, this will prove a boon, offering the best available introductions to such figures as Olmi, the Tavianis, Petri, and Bellocchio.

Pursuits of Happiness, The Hollywood Comedy of Remarriage, by Stanley Cavell (Harvard University Press, Cambridge, Massachusetts, 1981). There is a streak of irony in the fact that virtually all books about American comedy are inordinately dull and impenetrable. Cavell, a pretentious critic steeped in the humanist tradition, persists in attributing to artifacts such as *The Awful Truth* and *The Philadelphia Story* a weight of social and literary meaning that their structure cannot bear.

Mythologie Profane, Cinéma et Pensée Sauvage, by Yvette Biró (Lherminier, Paris, 1982). One of the most intelligent film theorists of her generation, the Hungarian Yvette Biró discusses the wealth of the cinematic art and its relationship with everyday life. In French, the book is also well illustrated.

Popular Television and Film, edited by Tony Bennett, Susan Boyd-Bowman, Colin Mercer, and Janet Woollacott (BFI Publishing/Open University, London, 1981). A textbook consisting of essays by several prominent critics and commentators. Enough latitude of view to be valuable but somewhat slanted towards semiotics and structuralism. The sections on Genre and on Politics are the liveliest.

American Film-Index 1916–1920

For several years there was an anxious need among film historians and other students of the early American cinema for books cataloguing the works of the silent period, recording both production credits and casts. Even today there are gaps to be filled.

In 1971 appeared the enormous, two-part *American Film Institute Catalog, Feature Films 1921–1930*, covering 6,606 films, and in 1976 came *American Film-Index 1908–1915*, covering both features and shorts with its 23,000 titles, but not supplying story outlines, something the AFI *Catalog* did for all releases.

The authors of *American Film-Index 1908–1915*, Einar Lauritzen and Gunnar Lundquist, promised a companion volume to fill out the period in between i.e. 1916 to 1920. They plan to publish their new book, *American Film-Index 1916–1920*, in 1983, having spent seven years' research on the project in the wake of the praise accorded to their first effort. The AFI *Catalog* is regarded today as an indispensable classic in its field, and it seems possible that Lauritzen and Lundquist's first volume will, with time, fit into this category.

Einar Lauritzen, the former curator of the Swedish Film Archive, is one of the world's foremost film experts, and publisher as well as co-author of the work. His friend Gunnar Lundquist, who took the initiative to start the books, is again the producer. He has written articles for *Films in Review, Classic Images*, and other film magazines. The new volume will contain over 12,000 titles and credits, and a 144-page portrait gallery in duotone of the stars, character actors, directors, and scriptwriters of the period, as well as brief company histories.

Film Bookshops, Posters, Records

AUSTRALIA

Gaumont Book Company, *123 Little Collins Street, Melbourne 3000. Tel. (03) 63–2623.*

Reliable Australian mail-order service for books, posters, and magazines on the cinema. Specialist in locating out-of-print items.

Hollywood & Vine, *Shop 4, 4 Avoca Street, South Yarra 3141. Tel. (03) 267–4541.*

New, antiquarian, and technical cinema books, videocassettes, soundtrack albums, posters etc.

Readings Records and Books, *132d Toorak Road, South Yarra 3141. Tel. (03) 267–1885.*

Impressive range of soundtrack albums; mail order service.

Space Age Books, *305–307 Swanston Street, Melbourne, Victoria 3000. Tel. 663.1777.*

Full range of biographical, pictorial, educational, and critical books, plus magazines, posters, stills, and soundtrack recordings. Also specialising in *Science Fiction*. Catalogues.

Soft Focus, *P.O. Box 98, Ringwood East, Victoria 3135.*

Maureen and Len Gates have opened this new source for movie memorabilia (postal business only), and their first catalogue contains posters as well as books on the subject.

BRITAIN

The Cinema Bookshop, *13–14 Great Russell Street, London WC1. Tel. (01) 637.0206.*

Many conflicting claims are made by the world's various movie bookshops as to size and stock, but Fred Zentner has in the past decade established himself as a key source of books, posters, stills, magazines, memorabilia, etc. that for sheer efficiency and courtesy is hard to beat. His premises may appear small yet there are vast stores of treasure in the basement beneath!

Cine-Search, *24 Cranbourn Street, London WC2H 7 AA.*

A postal business for all collectors of film memorabilia. This firm issues two different catalogues at 75p. each (or eight International Reply Coupons, for overseas readers).

Cox, A. E., *21 Cecil Rd., Itchen, Southampton SO2 7HX. Tel. 0703.447989.*

This long-established dealer specialises in books, magazines, and ephemera on both theatre and cinema; his informative catalogue, "Stage and Screen," has been published for several years, with eight issues per annum, and customers in all parts of the world. Business is either by post or "over the counter" at major Film Book Fairs.

Anne FitzSimmons, *The Retreat, The Green, Wetheral, Carlisle, Cumbria CA4 8ET. Tel. 0228.60675.*

A useful source for second-hand and out-of-print books on the cinema, as well as the theatre, puppeteering, etc.

The Motion Picture Bookshop at the National Film Theatre, *South Bank, London SE1. Tel. (01) 928.3517.*

John Morgan runs a first-class film bookshop, with a wide selection, intelligently displayed and classified, of imported books and magazines as well as the full range of British publications. He also handles mail orders from the NFT.

Movie Finds, *4 Ravenslea Road, Balham, London SW12 8SB. Tel. (01) 673.6534.*

Teddy Green has built this small firm into a

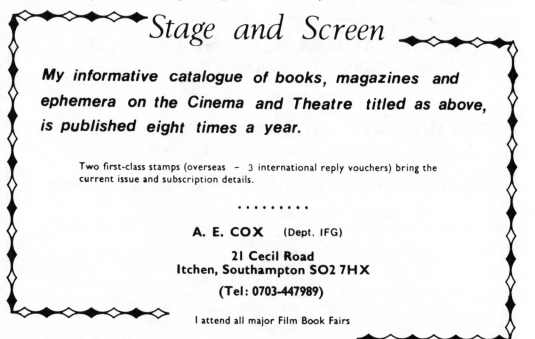

treasure trove of film stills and memorabilia. The range is huge, and the catalogue (£1.00) contains innumerable posters and movie scenes. There is also a "Movie Star Portrait" catalogue (illustrated), also for £1.00.

Movies, *36 Meon Road, London W3 8AN.*

David Henry issues catalogues with a wide range of new and out-of-print books on the cinema.

That's Entertainment, *43 The Market, Covent Garden, London WC2E 8RG. Tel. (01) 240.2227, (01) 379.3490.*

An excellent source of rare soundtrack records, as well as opera and stage show albums. There is a mail order service (address "Wants" and enclose SAE), and a part exchange service for mint records.

Treasures & Pleasures, *18 Newport Court (off Charing Cross Road), London WC2H 7JS. Tel. (01) 734.0795.*

A huge stock of movie memorabilia to browse through here. Prices are low and the management friendly. Worldwide postal service (SAE or two

International Reply Coupons with postal inquiries).

Peter Wood, *20 Stonehill Road, Great Shelford, Cambridge GB2 5JL.*

A stock of new and second-hand books, which covers all the performing arts, with cinema to the fore.

Vintage Magazine Co. Ltd., *39–41 Brewer Street, London W1. Tel. (01) 439 8525*

Magazines, stills, posters, and other movie memorabilia. Mail order service also.

Zwemmer, A., *78 Charing Cross Rd., London WC2. Tel. (01) 836.4710.*

With their window in Charing Cross Road a familiar landmark to all film enthusiasts in London, Zwemmer's have established a peerless reputation among film booksellers, and apart from the stock available to callers, there is a most efficient mail order service.

DENMARK

Busck, Arnold, *Fiolstraede 24, Copenhagen. Tel. 134990.*

Here is a rewarding stock of *second-hand* books on the cinema at very moderate prices. Write to the manager if you are looking for standard works for the prewar era, or if you want to *sell* such items.

FRANCE

Atmosphère, Librairie du Cinéma, *7–9 rue F. de Pressensé, 75014 Paris. Tel. 542.2926.*

Situated in a leisure complex that includes an art cinema and a café. Atmosphère offers a wide

range of film publications, with a special emphasis on science-fiction, fantasy, comics, and pop music as related to the cinema. Also back issues of magazines.

Librairie Contacts, *24 rue du Colisée, 75008 Paris. Tel. 359.1771.*

Visitors to this handsome establishment, just behind the Champs-Elysées, will find a superb selection of film magazines and books, in *all* languages. Write detailing specific wants. If there were a prize for the world's most neatly-arranged film bookshop, then Elaine Michaux-Vignes' "Contacts" would certainly win it.

Les Feux de la Rampe, *2 rue de Luynes, 75007 Paris. Tel. 548.8097.*

Pierre-François Cangardel has contrived, through energy and imaginative stocking, to find a *niche* in the already crowded world of Paris film bookshops. His *forte* lies in magazines, rare book titles, and an encyclopaedic knowledge of the field.

Le Minotaure, 2 *rue des Beaux-Arts, 75006 Paris. Tel. 354.7302.*

For sheer character, Le Minotaure is hard to beat among film bookshops. There are models, optical toys, and other memorabilia as well as long runs of out-of-print magazines, comics, and new items of film literature. The Mecca for any film buff visiting Paris for the first time.

Librairie de la Fontaine, 13 *rue Médicis, 75006 Paris. Tel. 326.7628.*

This long-established French film bookshop has been revitalised by Anne Hortense Lissarague and Philippe Dubuc. In addition to books and magazines, there are film posters, postcards, stills, colour slides, as well as colour portraits of directors and stars (not forgetting some delightful *marionettes* that evoke the era of *Les enfants du paradis!*). Also a range of *video-cassettes.*

Paris des Rêves, 50 *rue Galande, 75005 Paris, Tel.* 633.6756.

Also known as "Aux Visiteurs du Soir," this newcomer to the French movie bookshop scene has a coffee room in the cellar as well as a wide selection of film literature.

Stars-Films, 110 *rue Saint-Honoré, 75001 Paris. Tel. 261.2321.*

A significant source for those searching for rare stills and portraits. Mail-order service.

Le Zinzin d'Hollywood, 7 *rue des Ursulines, 75005 Paris. Tel. 633.4843.*

A treasure trove of over 5,000 stills, posters, books, magazines, and sound track albums, as well as of star portraits.

GERMANY

Buchhandlung Dialog, *Gutleutstr. 15, D-6000 Frankfurt 1. Tel. (0611) 23 52 80.*

Specialists in film books and magazines, and also in *film posters* from Eastern Europe.

Filmland Presse, *Aventinstr. 4–6, D-8 Munich 40.*

Founded in 1977 by H. K. Denicke, this new establishment is now the largest film bookshop in Europe, and circulates lists to 6,500 clients. The speciality is *periodicals* (more than 220 may be subscribed, and back issues of 600 are in stock). There is also an archive open to journalists,

librarians, members of FIAF etc., containing more than 6,500 books on film. Superb!

H. Lindemanns Buchhandlung, *Nadlerstr. 4, D-7000 Stuttgart 1.*

This firm has recently released a fine catalogue containing more than 1,300 items relating to the cinema and photography.

Buchhandlung Walther König, *Breite Strasse 93, 5 Köln 1.*

Useful source for anyone in Europe looking for that out-of-print book or magazine. Write stating wants.

Sautter & Lackmann, *Klosterstern, D-2000 Hamburg 13.*

A North German shop with books and magazines on the cinema as well as on related arts.

Schoeller, Marga, *Knesebeckstr. 33, 1000 Berlin 12.*

The film department of this legendary bookshop (off the Kurfürstendamm) is always worth a visit.

Verlag für Filmschriften Christian Unucka, *Karls-* *bader Ring 54, D-8060 Dachau. Tel. (08131) 13922.*

A mail-order enterprise for all kinds of film literature, with the accent on *original film programmes.*

ITALY

"Il Leuto," *via Di Monte Brianzo 86, 00186 Rome.*

A reliable Italian shop specialising not only in film but also in dance and drama. "Il Leuto" will deal with overseas correspondence. Write with specific wants.

Libreria Editrice Sileno, *Galleria Mazzini 13 rosso, 16121 Genova.*

SOUTH AFRICA

Adams & Co., *West Street, Durban.*

Bookwise, *Strand Street, Cape Town.*

Exclusive Books, *Pretoria Street, Hillbrow, Johannesburg.*

Magazine Centre, *Winchester House, 25 Loveday Street, Johannesburg.*
Page's Bookshop, *Orange Street, Cape Town.*
The widest range of film books in South Africa, and a fair selection of magazines.

SPAIN
Alphaville, *Princesa 5, Madrid 8. Tel. (341) 248 72 33.*
One of Spain's leading art houses has a film bookshop in the main lobby, in which most new titles and magazines, in various languages, are sold.
R. Seriña, *Calle Aribau 114, Barcelona 11.*
A specialist collection of books, photos, magazines, press books, posters and programmes on sale to the public in Spain and abroad.

SWITZERLAND
Filmbuchhandlung Hans Rohr, *Oberdorfstr. 3, 8024 Zürich.*
Hans Rohr's film bookshop is one of the best in central Europe, and not for nothing does business accrue to the firm from many countries beyond the borders of Switzerland. Virtually all books on film, as well as magazines, soundtracks, and many rare items, are available promptly through Rohr whose shop is well-known for its unique catalogue.

U.S.A.
Cinemabilia, *10 West 13th St., New York. NY 10011. Tel. (212) 989.8519.*
Cinemabilia is much more than just a film bookshop. It carries a wide selection of stills, lobby cards, posters, press books, graphics etc. The shop sends free lists of recent acquisitions to readers writing with an S.A.E. A gigantic catalogue devoted to the men and women in front of, and behind, the camera, with lots of cross-indexing, is available, and constitutes a valuable work of reference in its own right. Few booksellers take the time and trouble to issue such catalogues.
Cinema Books, *701 Broadway East, Seattle, Washington 98102.*
Stephanie J. Ogle opens her excellent Northwestern shop each day for business and offers a selection of books, posters, memorabilia and magazines.
Cinema Books by Post, *P.O. Box 20092, Broadway Station, Seattle, Washington 98102.*
This firm issues immaculately-crafted catalogues, including out-of-print titles and film periodicals and newspapers. Susan Favor and Jeremy Ogle travel far and wide searching for new items, and always welcome "wants" lists. Prompt service.
Dayton's Record Store, *824 Broadway at 12th Street, New York, NY 10003. Tel. (212) AL4–5084.*
Also at: *2124 Flatbush Avenue, Brooklyn, NY 11234. Tel. (212) 338–2474.*
Over 100,000 discs are on offer at this remarkable out-of-print record store, with its speciality in the fields of *movie soundtracks* and Broadway shows. Write with specific wants.
Four Continent Book Corporation, *149 Fifth Avenue, New York, NY 10010. Tel. (212) 533–0250.*
For those searching for books in *Russian* on

the cinema (e.g. the writings of Eisenstein, Pudovkin etc.), this is the place to visit.
Gotham Book Mart, *41 West 47th St., New York, NY 10036.*

As its regular "GBM Film Bulletins" will testify, Gotham has achieved a remarkable prominence in the film bookshop field, and has been flourishing since 1920. Philip Lyman, the General Manager, has worked hard to expand the film section.

Hampton Books, *Route 1, Box 76, Newberry, S.C. 29108. Tel. 803.276.6870.*

Each Hampton catalogue represents hundreds of hours of biblio-historical research. This firm specialises in movie, TV, and photography items, but also, note, in aeronautics literature and in material devoted to the Carolinas. Lobby cards, stills, and portraits are available, too – in profusion.

Larry Edmunds Bookshop, *6658 Hollywood Blvd., Hollywood, California 90028. Tel. 213.463.3273.*

In terms of turnover and display of current titles, Larry Edmunds is the world's nearest equivalent to a film-book supermart. The stills collection alone is a goldmine for any film buff.

Limelight Bookstore, *1803 Market Street, San Francisco, California 94103. Tel. (415) 864–2265.*

Roy A. Johnson runs this lively shop for film, theatre, and dance books, and a marvellous collection of screenplays, technical books, and out-of-print items (especially original novels on which famous films were based).

Film Magazines

We survey below a selection of the world's leading film periodicals. Space prevents us from digesting the contents of all but each country's most prominent magazines. New journals, or those omitted through oversight on our part, are invited to submit sample copies for us to evaluate and announce to readers. Abbreviation n.p.a. = numbers per annum.

AMERICAN FILM

Ed: Peter Biskind, American Film Institute, John F. Kennedy Center for the Performing Arts, Washington, DC 20566. 10 n.p.a.: $18.00 ($25.00 abroad). 80pp. approx. Much improved under its new editor, *AMERICAN FILM* recognises the importance of cinematic ideas and creators outside the U.S., and with its immense circulation can afford to print the most exclusive pictures (many in colour) as well as use the most fluent writers. Much coverage of TV and video.

Sep 1981: "Robert Duvall: America's Hard-Boiled Olivier," by Lynde McCormick. Plus a special report on the Independent Feature movement worldwide, and an article on TV's *Hill Street Blues*.

Oct 1981: Report from the set of Coppola's *One from the Heart*. Study of James M. Cain's work as a screenwriter.

Nov 1981: "The Return of the WASP Hero," by Carrie Rickey and Artie West. Special Report: "Hollywood Abroad – Market and Image."

Dec 1981: "Looking for Nicholas Ray," by Jonathan Rosenbaum. Special Report: "The Golden Age of Television."

Jan-Feb 1982: Interview with Rod Steiger. "The Brave New Worlds of Production Design," by Bart Mills. Special Report: "Film and Politics in Poland."

Mar 1982: "Autobiographical Notes," by Akira Kurosawa. "Hollywood's Color Problem," by Michael Dempsey and Udayan Gupta.

Apr 1982: "Milius the Barbarian," by Kirk Honeycutt. "King of Comedy: The Rise of Preston Sturges," by James Curtis.
May 1982: Fascinating report by Michael Goodwin on the location filming of Herzog's *Fitzcarraldo.* "War of the Wizards," by Donald Chase (on special effects in Hollywood).

L'AVANT SCENE CINEMA

Ed: Claude Beylie, 27 rue Saint-André-des-Arts, 75006 Paris. 20 n.p.a.: 285 francs (£25.00 or $48.00). 50pp approx. Serene in its consistency, meticulous in its scholarship, unique in concept, *L'AVANT SCENE* provides readers with the complete screenplay actually checked with the finished film, of one important contemporary or historical classic after another.

Number 273: Ivory's *Quartet.*
Number 274: Doillon's *La fille prodigue.*
Number 275: Fuller's *The Big Red One.*
Number 276: Grémillon's *Le ciel est à nous.*
Number 277: Brusati's *Dimenticare Venezia.*
Number 278: Tacchella's *Le pays bleu.* Plus dossier on Gustav Ucicky, by Goswin Dörfler.
Number 287: Rissient's *Cinq et la peau.*
Number 288: Miller's *Garde à vue.*

CAHIERS DU CINEMA

Ed: Serge Toubiana, Editions de l'Etoile, 9 passage de la Boule-Blanche, 75012 Paris. 11 n.p.a.: 245 francs (£22.25 or $40.00). 64pp approx. This celebrated magazine seems miraculously to prosper, with colour photographs, immaculate design, and acres of text, making it once again an essential concomitant of any cinephile's library.

Number 328: Interview with Manoel de Oliveira and with George Lucas. "Orson Welles: *Monsieur Arkadin*, Un jeu radiophonique," by Charles Tesson.
Number 329: Tribute to Glauber Rocha, and a reassessment of Godard's *Le mépris*, by Alain Bergala.
Number 330: Tribute to Jean Eustache, and interview with Bertolucci.
Number 331: Reportage on the shooting of Syberberg's *Parsifal*, notes on a retrospective of the past decade of American television, and a section on the horror film genre.
Number 332: Second part of a study of the horror film, plus an excellent article on Allan Dwan, by Jean-Claude Biette.

Number 333: Interviews with Edgardo Cozarinsky, Jean-Louis Comolli, and André Téchiné.
Numbers 334/335: Massive, memorable, 130 page issue entitled "Made in U.S.A.," and containing interviews and impressions recorded during a *Cahiers* "voyage en Amérique."
Number 336: Interview with Jean-Pierre Mocky, plus a large dossier on Godard and his *Passion.*

CHAPLIN

Ed: Lars Åhlander, Swedish Film Institute, Box 27 126, S-102 52 Stockholm, Sweden. 6 n.p.a.: 70 Skr. (£6.70 or $12.50). 48pp. The most regular of the Swedish film journals, sponsored by the Swedish Film Institute and covering world cinema as much as Swedish developments.

Number 175: Long studies of *The Postman Always Rings Twice* and Fritz Lang's *The Woman in the Window.* "Spel som dokument. Den massproducerade bildens teknik och stil," by Carl Henrik Svenstedt.
Number 177: Interviews with Andrzej Wajda and George Lucas.
Number 178: entirely devoted to Jörn Donner's account of his years as head of the Swedish Film Institute. Lots of gossip.
Number 179: Report from Berlin Festival. "Bortom gott och ont. En analys av thrillerns moraliska mönster," by Morris Dickstein. "Historier om vardaglig galenskap. Marco Ferreri och hans filmer," by Stig Björkman.

CINEASTE

Ed: Gary Crowdus, Dan Georgakas, Lenny Rubenstein, 419 Park Avenue South, New York, NY 10016. 4 n.p.a.: $7.00 ($12.00 abroad). 64pp. With a spanking new cover and interior layout, this is in many ways the finest anti-establishment movie magazine around, never afraid to put its finger on controversial issues, and never prone to Hollywood worship.

Vol XI, No. 3: A symposium on the documentary film, an interview with Molly Haskell on feminist film criticism, and a re-evaluation of Wajda's *Ashes and Diamonds.*
Vol XI, No. 4: Interviews with Budd Schulberg, Peter Lilienthal, Peter Weir, Péter Bacsó, and a trio of Indian cineastes. "Film Censorship and the New Right," by Edward Benson.
Vol XII, No. 1: Interviews with Satyajit Ray, Costa-Gavras, and Paul Newman. "Bazin before *Cahiers*: Cinematic Politics in Postwar France," by Dudley Andrew.

CINEMA

Ed: Gastron Haustrate, Fédération Française des Ciné-Clubs, 7 rue Cadet, 75009 Paris. 12 n.p.a.: 190 francs (£17.00 or $30.50). 128pp. Too long absent from our columns, *CINEMA* has recovered something of the significance it held during the Sixties, as a middle-of-the-road, broad-based French monthly packed with interviews, reviews, and information.

Number 273: Useful dictionary of French cameramen.
Number 274: Articles on Glauber Rocha, Buster Keaton, Ken Russell, Bernardo Bertolucci, and the Chinese Cinema.
Number 276: Tribute to Jean Eustache and to Abel Gance. Reassessment of the career of Jean Grémillon.
Number 277: Studies of Charles Vanel, Helma Sanders, Douglas Fairbanks, and István Szabó.
Number 278: Interviews with Volker Schlöndorff and Isabelle Huppert.
Number 279: Interviews with George Cukor, Arthur Penn, Jean-Pierre Mocky, and Miou Miou. Plus a valuable dossier on the forgotten film, *L'Etrange M. Victor*, by Grémillon.
Number 280: Interview with Brigitte Fossey, and a study of recent developments in Bulgarian cinema.
Number 281: Dossier on the Austrian cinema, and interviews with Karen Arthur and Jean Mitry.
Number 282: Full re-evaluation of the work of Fritz Lang. Interview with Nathalie Baye.

CINEMA PAPERS

Ed: Scott Murray, 644 Victoria Street, North Melbourne, Victoria, Australia 3051. 6 n.p.a.: $18A (£10.00 or $18.00). 100pp approx. Still the largest film magazine in the world, with its gigantic format permitting splendid photo reproduction, this Australian bi-monthly is a cunning mix of reviews, interviews, news, and hard industry know-how that will be of interest far beyond the boundaries of Australia.

Sep-Oct 1981: Interview with Peter Weir, studies of Blake Edwards and Shohei Imamura.
Jul-Aug 1981: Interviews with Robert Altman and Octavio Cortazar. Full report on the Cannes festival. Television section as usual now.
Feb 1982: Interview with Kevin Dobson, long study of De Palma's *Blow Out*, and report from the Edinburgh Festival.
Apr 1982: Special issue for Cannes, giving valuable details of all the new Australian features. Plus interview with Peter Ustinov, and a study of Carlos Saura.

FILM COMMENT

Ed: Richard Corliss, 140 West 65th Street, New York, NY 10023. 6 n.p.a.: $12.00 ($18.00 abroad). 80pp. approx. A deliciously glamourous magazine, fun to handle and look at, and usually rewarding to read also, especially for its hyper-researched "Midsections." Even the covers look sybaritic.

Jul-Aug 1981: Interviews with Ivan Passer, the ineffable George Lucas, plus a Midsection devoted to "Jews on the Screen."
Sep-Oct 1981: Interviews with Karel Reisz and Lawrence Kasdan, plus an appraisal of five Fassbinder movies by George Morris.
Nov-Dec 1981: Essays on Jacques Prévert and Henri-Georges Glouzot, and a lively interview with Terry Gilliam of *Time Bandits*. Report from the Gdańsk Festival.
Jan-Feb 1982: "Gun-Totin' Women," by Stephen Schiff, plus David Thomson overpraising both *Reds* and *Ragtime*. And a splendid Midsection on Art Direction.
Mar-Apr 1982: The lowdown on who picks the Academy Awards, a study of Roger Corman as independent producer, and an interview with Paul Schrader about *Cat People*.
May-Jun 1982: Steven Spielberg talking about *E.T.* and *Poltergeist*, and a revealing survey of title designers, including some rare frame enlargements.

FILM QUARTERLY

Ed: Ernest Callenbach, University of California Press, Berkeley, California 94720. 4 n.p.a.: $10.00 ($12.00 abroad). 64pp. After more than twenty years in the old square format, *FQ* has changed to a larger page size and an altogether brighter interior design, with more space for the photos. As such, it

QUARTERLY

Film Quarterly is the leading American journal of film analysis. It addresses critical questions of lasting interest as they manifest themselves in experimental and documentary as well as feature films.

It publishes definitive reviews, penetrating theoretical and historical articles, carefully researched interviews, and a yearly survey of English-language film books which is unrivalled in scope.

In short, *Film Quarterly* provides solid reading for people who take film seriously. It's also readable and attractively printed, with many illustrations, and is now in a new, larger format.

Subscriptions are $10.00 in the U.S. and $12.00 elsewhere. Send for a sample copy!

**University of California Press
Berkeley, CA 94720   U.S.A.**

neatly straddles the barrier between the glossy commercial movie magazines and the esoteric, academic journals of the United States.

Fall 1981: "Narrative Pleasure: Two Films of Jacques Rivette," by Robin Wood. "Lost Harmony: Tarkovsky's *Mirror* and *Stalker*," by Michael Dempsey.
Winter 1981/82: "A Musical Comedy of Empire" (on *Flying down to Rio*) by Brian Henderson. "Le Nouveau Godard," by Peter Harcourt. Plus a conversation with Georges Franju, and all the usual reviews.

FILMS & FILMING

Ed: Allen Eyles, Brevet Publishing, 445 Brighton Road, South Croydon, Surrey CR2 6EU. 12 n.p.a.: £12.00 (£16.00/$36.00 abroad). 44pp. Now back under a new publisher, new editor and virtually new team of writers, the new *f&f* (incorporating *FOCUS ON FILM*) bears scant resemblance to its tired old forerunner. Nicely designed and with comprehensive review and listings sections, it also covers vintage areas and video as well as the current scene, and is the only quality British magazine filling the middle area between intellectual excess and popular fan journals.

Oct 1981 (first issue): Interviews with William Wyler and Francesco Rosi. Rank's rejected cinemas.
Nov 1981: Interviews with Michael Powell and Sigourney Weaver. Article on Glauber Rocha.
Dec 1981: Interviews with Brian De Palma, John Travolta and John Carradine. The films of Michael Powell (part one).
Jan 1982: Interviews with Bernardo Bertolucci and George Cukor. Michael Powell (cont.).
Feb 1982: Interviews with Frank Ripploh and Alain Tanner. Article on Claude Rains (part one).
Mar 1982: Sport in the cinema; Claude Rains (cont.)
Apr 1982: Interviews with Timothy Hutton, Pat O'Brien and Richard Williams.
May 1982: Interviews with I. A. L. Diamond (an excellent rare interview) and Arthur Penn and Steve Tesich. Gainsborough Studios (part one).
June 1982: New Zealand cinema. Interview with Mari Törőcsik. Gainsborough Studios (cont.).
July 1982: Interviews with Alberto Lattuada and June Allyson. The Hollywood portrait photographer. Recent sword and sorcery films.

FILMS IN REVIEW

Ed: Brendan Ward, National Board of Review of Motion Pictures, 209 East 66th Street, New York, NY 10021. 10 n.p.a.: $14.00 ($16.00 abroad).

64pp. After decades of stagnation as a fanzine, this monthly has changed formats and editors quicker than the eye can register. The gist remains identical, however: career articles of stars and American directors; interesting, erudite, and sometimes insane letters.

Aug-Sep 1981: "DeMille Centenary," by DeWitt Bodeen.

Oct 1981: "The Two Careers of Melvyn Douglas," part one, by Kevin Lewis. "Ray Harryhausen," by Jon Gartenberg.

Nov 1981: Interviews with Jeremy Irons, Frank Perry, Ulu Grosbard, and Hugh Hudson. "George Cukor," by DeWitt Bodeen. Plus part two (filmography) of the Melvyn Douglas piece.

Dec 1981: "Robert Donat," by DeWitt Bodeen. "Tay Garnett," by John Gallagher.

Jan 1982: "The Australian Cinema," by Charles Sawyer. "Henry Fonda," by Michael Buckley.

Feb 1982: Interviews with Maureen Stapleton and Mark Rydell. "Merle Oberon," by Al Kilgore and Roi Frumkes.

Mar 1982: "James Cagney," by Michael Buckley. "Neil Hamilton," by DeWitt Bodeen.

Apr 1982: "Raoul Walsh," by DeWitt Bodeen. "George Walsh," by Larry L. Holland.

May 1982: "William Wellman," by John Gallagher. Interview with Richard Brooks, and a brief conversation with Francesco Rosi.

ISKUSSTVO KINO

Ed: Yevgyeni Surkov, 9 ulitsa Usiyevicha, 125319 Moscow A-319. 12 n.p.a.: 1 rouble per copy. 192pp. The long-established Soviet monthly, chunky, packed with theory and political discourse and laden with official weight.

Number 8, 1981: Georgian actor Vakhtang Kikabidze talks about his work. Soviet animated films.

Number 2, 1982: Article on cameraman Sergey Urusevsky.

Number 4, 1982: Survey of recent works by Tadzikfilm.

Number 5, 1982: Profile of Luis Buñuel.

KOSMORAMA

Ed: Per Calum, Ebbe Iversen, Jan Kornum Larsen, The Danish Film Museum, Store Søndervoldstraede, DK-1419 Copenhagen K, Denmark. 6 n.p.a.: 100 Dkr. (£7.50 or $13.50). 36pp. Now slightly slimmer, and appearing every other month, *KOSMORAMA* is perhaps the most attractive of the Nordic movie magazines, with particularly splendid emphasis on large photos. In Danish.

Number 154: Interviews with Bob Rafelson and Esben Høilund Carlsen.

Number 157: Introduction to the documentaries of Frederick Wiseman, plus an analysis of *Mephisto* and its implications. And a rehabiliation of *Heaven's Gate*, by Kaare Schmidt.

Number 158: "Miloš Forman og autoriteternes krise," by Peter Schepelern. "Tendenser i ungarsk film," by Ebbe Iversen.

POSITIF

Eds: various, Nouvelles Editions Opta, 1 quai Conti, 75006 Paris. 12 n.p.a.: 260 francs (£22.00 or $40.00). 80pp. approx. By some miraculous alchemy, *POSITIF*, with never so much as a page of advertising, manages to appear monthly, and recently celebrated its thirtieth anniversary! It supplies a ceaseless stream of interviews and reviews in depth.

Number 246: Interviews with Douglas Slocombe, Michael Cimino, and Max Douy.

Number 247: Dossiers on Tarkovski, Boorman, and Buñuel's revived *L'age d'or*.

Number 248: Interviews with Claude Miller and Bernardo Bertolucci.

Number 249: Interviews with Robert Altman, Ray Harryhausen, and (in third person) Tarkovski. Plus a useful survey of films from Southern India.

Number 250: Interviews with Judit Elek and Mrinal Sen.

Number 251: Interviews with Marco Ferreri and Sidney Lumet, and a reassessment of King Vidor.

Number 252: Interviews with Karel Reisz and Arthur Penn, plus analysis of Passer's *Cutter's Way*.

Number 253: Interviews with Agnès Varda and Shohei Imamura. "Tribute to a Good Man: James Cagney ou l'ambivalence de l'Amérique," by Michel Cieutat.

Numbers 254/255: superb 176 page issue to celebrate the magazine's thirtieth anniversary, with voting for the best film of the period etc. (*2001: A Space Odyssey* comes out top). Plus an interview with Georges Wakhévitch.

SIGHT AND SOUND

Ed: Penelope Houston, British Film Institute, 127 Charing Cross Road, London WC2H 0EA. 4 n.p.a.: £5.70 ($14.00). 72pp. *SIGHT AND SOUND* celebrates its Golden Jubilee this year, and Penelope Houston has edited the magazine for more than half that period. The best tribute that can be paid to this most august of British periodicals is that through the years it has assimilated new trends and directors without ever losing sight of the longer view, the historical byways of cinema.

Autumn 1981: "Cannes, Festivals and the Movie Business," by Simon Perry. "Discovering America: Renoir 1941," by Alexander Sesonske. "Sturges' Folly. The Fate of *Unfaithfully Yours*," by E. Rubinstein.
Winter 1981/82: Interview with Andrzej Wajda by Gustaw Moszcz. Interview with Francesco Rosi by Michel Ciment. Richard Quine, by Tim Pulleine.
Spring 1982: "From Nostalgia to Paranoia," by David Nicholls (on French crime thrillers of the Seventies). "*My Dinner with André*," by Wallace Shawn (on how he set up the movie). "Television/France/Socialism," by Jill Forbes.
Summer 1982: "Breathing a Little Harder than Usual," by Nick Roddick (on U.K. production). Ritwik Ghatak, by Derek Malcolm. Interview with Walter Hill, by Michael Sragow. Rodgers and Hart, and Hollywood, by Robert Cushman.

Other Magazines

AMERICAN CLASSIC SCREEN, The Traditions Press, 7800 Conser Place, Shawnee Mission, Kansas 66204. Attractively-produced bi-monthly devoted to the preservation of old films; filled with useful addresses.

ANIMAFILM, Trebacka 3, 00–074 Warsaw, Poland. The ASIFA quarterly, designed to accommodate several languages, and containing distinguished articles by and for animators.

CELUÓIDE, Rua David Manuel da Fonseca 88, 2040 Rio Major, Portugal. Twenty-fifth year of publication. Monthly magazine in Portuguese.

CINE, Focine, Calle 17 No. 7–35 Of. 1405, Bogota, Colombia. South American bi-monthly put together with professional verve, and well-printed.

CINE AL DIA, Apartado 50, 446 Sabana Grande, Caracas, Venezuela. Venezuelan monthly magazine.

CINE CUBANO, Calle 23 no. 1155, Havana, Cuba. Vital information on all Latin American cinema, unfortunately only in Spanish. Often includes interesting theoretical articles.

CINEFANTASTIQUE, P.O. Box 270, Oak Park, Ill. 60303. An enthusiastic, well-written, beautifully produced bi-monthly with a special emphasis on fantasy films. A modern "successor" to the French "Midi-Minuit Fantastique." Most issues have meticulously researched in-depth articles on major attractions (e.g. *Conan the Barbarian*; *Cat People*).

CINEFORUM, C.P. 414, 30100 Venezia, Italy. The official organ of the Italian film society movement. Published ten times per annum.

CINEMA 2002, Ardemans 64, Madrid 28, Spain. First-class Spanish monthly packed with pictures, serious articles and interviews, and a great many news items. Striking covers, and first-class festival reports. Recently printed its fiftieth issue.

CINEMA JOURNAL, Film Division, North-western University, Evanston, Illinois 60201. A scholarly and respected American magazine, now published twice a year and under new editorship.

CINEMA NOVO, Apartado 78, 4002 Porto Codex, Portugal. Bi-monthly Portuguese magazine dealing with international and Portuguese topics. The staff of this magazine is responsible for the organisation of the Oporto International Fantasy Film Festival.

CINEA NUOVO, 67 Via Santa Giulia, 10124 Torino, Italy. Guido Aristarco, the distinguished Italian critic, has edited more than 275 issues of this polemical, academic magazine, which would qualify for our main section were it not for its inclusion of non-film material.

CINEMART (Yin-szu shih-chieh), Flat D, Alpha House, 27–33 Nathan Road, 13/F Kowloon, Hongkong. Monthly glossy survey of Hongkong/Taiwan production, edited by Liu Ya-fo. Somewhat diluted as of late and with less factual back-up. Also runs film distribution outlet, Ocean Films.

CINEMATECA, Florida 1472, escritorio 2, Montevideo, Uruguay. Bright monthly published in collaboration with Cinemateca Uruguaya and Cinemateca Argentina. Readable format, international slant and plenty of factual information.

CINEMATOGRAPHIE, 14 rue du Cherche-Midi, 75006 Paris, France. Monthly including dossiers on major films, interviews, TV coverage, plentiful illustrations.

CINEMA VISION INDIA, 1 Geetika, Swami Vivekananda Road, Santacruz (West), Bombay 400 054. A new independent Indian journal, containing much original and previously unpublished material. Thoroughly researched and illustrated, invaluable to anyone interested in Indian cinema.

CLASSIC IMAGES, PO Box 4079, Davenport, Iowa 52808. Formerly "Classic Film Collector", a good source for film buffs eager to enlarge their library of movies, now with the addition of video news. Issue bi-monthly, and a highly readable paper containing much information. Their "Classic Images Review", comprised of re-runs of material which has appeared in part issues, is published quarterly.

CONTINENTAL FILM AND VIDEO, PO Box 1, Barking, Essex 1G11 8AZ. With a sleek design scheme, CFR probably outsells any other genuine film magazine in Britain. Apart from the appealing pictures, there is often an article of aesthetic or cultural value. Full colour covers.

CTVD, Hampton Books, Rt. 1, Box 76, Newberry, S.C. 29108. A concise digest of foreign-language writing on film, with additional reports by an ever-increasing group of overseas correspondents. Sporadic publication.

DIRIGIDO POR. . . , Pujol 9–1.1, Barcelona 6. This handsomely-produced Spanish monthly throws the spot-light each issue on a particular director of international renown. Very good documentation on all personalities.

LES ECRANS, 7 Boulevard Khémisti, Algiers. Algerian, French-language periodical (ten times per annum) dealing with cinema and TV in Africa, Asia, Latin America, and the Arab world. Tends towards theoretical pieces.

FILM COMMENTARY (Tien-ying p'ing-lun), Chinese Film Critics' Association, Room 403, 4th Floor, 7 Ch'ingtao East Road, Taipei. Twice-yearly paperback digest of criticism and analysis, mostly of international cinema. Includes script excerpts.

F (FILMJOURNAL), Postfach 2749, D-7900 Ulm. An attractively produced, small format, black and white magazine, containing detailed information in German on old and new films, interviews, articles, and high quality stills. Published monthly.

FILM, Zoodohou Pigis 3, Athens. A brave Greek venture, edited by Thanasis Rentzis, aimed at a particularly highbrow readership. Recent special on the image of women in the cinema.

FILM, 81 Dean Street, London W1A 6AA. A tabloid brochure issued on behalf of the British Federation of Film Societies. Indispensable for all film society personnel.

FILM, ul. Paławska 61, 02–595 Warsaw. Popular Polish weekly with international slant, now in a much improved format.

FILM, P.K. 307, Beyoğlu, İstanbul. Turkish monthly, the official organ of the "Sinematek Dernegi."

FILM A DOBA, Václavské nám. 43, Praha 1. The principal Czech film monthly.

FILM AND BROADCASTING REVIEW, 1011 First Avenue, New York, NY 10022. Published fortnightly by the Office for Film and Broadcasting of the U.S. Catholic Conference, this provides reviews of new films, features, and also short and specialist subjects.

FILMAVISA, Filmhuset, Wessels gate 4, Oslo 1. Norwegian quarterly with an analytical approach and including theoretical articles on film history and criticism. One of the best publications on film in the entire Nordic area.

FILM BEOBACHTER, Birkerstrasse 22, 8000 München 19. Issued fortnightly by the Gemeinschaftswerk der Evangelischen Publizistik, contains international coverage of festivals and recent films, and a section on German TV.

FILME CULTURA, Rua Mayrink Veiga 28, ZC 05, Rio de Janeiro, Guanabara. The leading Brazilian film magazine (in Portuguese).

FILM DIRECTIONS, 8 Malone Road, Belfast BT9 5BN. Competent, nicely-printed Irish quarterly.

FILM DOPE, 40 Willifield Way, London NW11 7XT. Not so much a magazine, more a part-work film dictionary, this irregular British quarterly is to be welcomed for its exhaustive research.

FILM EN TELEVISIE, Olmstraat 10, 1040 Brussels. Reliable and informed Belgian magazine (printed in Flemish).

FILM-EN TV-MAKER, Nieuwe Keizersgracht 58, 1018 DT Amsterdam. Dutch organ for the national association of film-makers, with technical news as well as wide-ranging comment.

FILMHÄFTET, Box 16046, S-750 16 Uppsala, Sweden. In terms of seriousness and rigour of analysis, *Filmhäftet* is the best magazine in Sweden. Intelligently illustrated, too. Quarterly.

FILMIHULLU, c/o Suomen elokuvakerhojen

liitto, Yrjönkatu 11A 5a, SF-00120 Helsinki 12. Finnish film and TV magazine with critical approach, appearing eight times a year and published by film consumers' and cultural organisations.

FILM-KORRESPONDENZ, Romanstrasse 20, 8 München 19. Edited by Günther Pflaum, this long-standing German publication contains articles and interviews immaculately typed in stapled form.

FILMKRITIK, Filmkritiker-Kooperative, Kreittmayrstr. 3, 8 Munich 2. Polemical West German magazine, covering the entire range of the visual arts and veering unpredictably from topic to topic. Some 260 issues old.

FILM KULTÚRA, Nepstadion út. 97, Budapest XIV. The major Hungarian film periodical, with articles of a high intellectual calibre, and a useful summary of contents in English.

FILM LIBRARY QUARTERLY, Box 348, Radio City Station, New York, NY 10019. Bill Sloan's editorial flair has kept his educational film quarterly on the shelves of everyone interested in good movies and their classroom use.

FILM LITERATURE INDEX, Box 532 DD SUNY-A, 1400 Washington Avenue, Albany, New York 12222. Some 140 periodicals are indexed in quarterly form, with alphabetical guides by author and subject. Expensive, but comprehensive too.

FILM NEWS, Open Court Publishing Company, 1500 Eighth Street, La Salle, Illinois 61301. The U.S. review magazine of 16mm films, filmstrips, education TV and equipment. An excellent materials source periodical.

FILM NEWS, Ontario Film Institute, 770 Don Mills Road, Don Mills, Ontario, Canada. Up to the minute quarterly tabloid designed for members of the Ontario Film Theatre but useful for non-Canadians too.

FILM OG KINO, Lille Grensen 3, Oslo 1. Excellent Norwegian magazine that ranges more widely than most trade magazines, and contains useful interviews and facts.

FILMOWY SERWIS PRASOWY, ul. Mazowiecka 6/8, 00–950 Warsaw. A mine of information: a Polish MFB with production and trade details.

FILM REVIEW, The Old Court House, Old Court Place, 42–70 Kensington High Street, London W8. Known to scores of thousands of cinema patrons, this monthly is brightly coloured and illustrated and up to the minute with its coverage of new films.

FILMRUTAN, Box 82, S-85102 Sundsvall, Sweden. The magazine of the Swedish Federation of Film Societies, cheerful, well-printed and often containing long and serious articles on world cinema.

FILMS, Thelmill Ltd., 34 Buckingham Palace Road, London SW1. Visually similar to the old-style "Films and filming" (and under its former editor), **Films** is heir to all the previous magazine's weaknesses.

FILM, SZINHÁZ, MUZSIKA, Lenin körút 9–11, Budapest VII. Hungarian popular illustrated weekly, covering local and international cinema (as well as music and theatre).

FILM UND FERNSEHEN, Oranienburgerstr. 67–68, 104 Berlin, G.D.R. Monthly edited by Association of Film- and TV-Makers in the G.D.R. Broad Surveys, extensive interviews, festival reports, historical notes.

FILMVILÁG, Országház utca 20, Budapest I. Popular Hungarian monthly, dealing with both local and foreign films. Summary of contents in English.

FILMWORLD, 70 Snidercroft Road, Concord, Ontario, Canada L4K 1B1. A bright new monthly news magazine for the Canadian trade that will be serviceable for anyone with contracts in that North American market.

FILM WORLD, 8 Horniman Circle, Botawala Building, 2nd Floor, Bombay 400 023. Lively and outspoken Indian monthly, similar to the British "Photoplay."

FRAMEWORK, English and American Studies, University of East Anglia, Norwich NR4 7TJ. English magazine that is steadily improving in looks and likeability. Runs the gamut from Güney to Fellini, Loach to *Dallas*. Translations of material in Italian are especially valuable. Other areas of concern are independent cinema, broadcasting, and marketing and distribution.

GUIA DE FILMES, Rua Mayrink 28–5° andar, Rio de Janeiro, Guanabara. Bi-monthly Brazilian magazine, an equivalent to "Monthly Film Bulletin."

HABLEMOS DE CINE, Libertadores 199, San Isidro, Lima 27. Principal Peruvian film magazine.

HISTORICAL JOURNAL OF FILM, RADIO, AND TELEVISION, Carfax Publishing Company, Haddon House, Dorchester-on-Thames, Oxford OX9 8JZ. An interdisciplinary journal concerned with the evidence provided by the mass media for historians and social scientists.

THE INDEPENDENT FILM/VIDEO GUIDE, EFLA, 43 West 61st Street, New York, NY 10023. New quarterly index to the works exhibited by non-commercial film/video showcases in New York City and New York State (and that's a lot more than one might suspect!).

JUMP CUT, PO Box 865, Berkeley, California 94701, U.S.A. Published four to six times a year, this tabloid contains an extraordinary amount of closely-woven text, with some good, if politically slanted criticism, and extremely comprehensive career pieces.

KINDER JUGEND FILM KORRESPONDENZ, Werner-Friedmann-Bogen 18, D-8000 Munich 50. West German quarterly assemblage of news and interviews on educational films.

KINO, Export-Union des Deutschen Films, Türkenstrasse 93, 8000 Munchen 40. A new monthly

publication, printed in English and financed by the German Federal Film Board, designed mainly to promote German films abroad. Attractively produced, contains much useful information on German cinema generally.

KINO, c/o Holloway, Helgoländer Ufer 6, 1000 Berlin 21. Excellent quarterly devoted to both German and other cinema, with interviews, credits and comment. Recently published a special Polish film issue.

KUVA & ÄÄNI, Ruoholahdenkatu 23, SF-00180 Helsinki 18, Finland. Excellent monthly on technical matters.

A INTERNATIONAL INDEX TO FILM PERIODICALS

These fully-annotated indexes, published annually, cover the world's most important film & TV literature. More than **130 film and TV journals** are indexed to cover articles, interviews, film & programme reviews, festivals, etc.

Each entry includes the name of the author; title of article; full journal citation; inclusion of illustrations, bibliographies, filmographies etc. and a description of the contents of the article. This feature enables researchers to avoid reading irrelevant or repetitious material.

The indexes are divided into four main categories: General subjects (including film & TV producton,

history, social influences, aesthetics etc.); Films & Programmes (articles, reviews & scripts); Biography (covering directors, actors, editors etc.) and Book reviews.

The professional participation of more than **30 film and TV archives** ensures accurate and reliable information.

The indexes appear as annual volumes, or as a card subscription service.

For further information write to:

International Federation of Film Archives (FIAF)
90-94 Shaftesbury Avenue London W1V 7DH

F INTERNATIONAL INDEX TO TELEVISION PERIODICALS

LITERATURE/FILM QUARTERLY, Salisbury State College, Salisbury, Maryland 21801. This quarterly contains many valuable articles on the relationship of the printed word to film, and provides interesting background.

MEDIUM, Friedrichstr. 34, D-6000 Frankfurt, West Germany. Monthly including articles about mass media politics, TV, interviews and portraits of directors, festival reports etc.

THE MILKY WAY PICTORIAL (Yin-ho huapao), Flat C-6, 22/F., Elizabeth House, 254 Gloucester Road, Hong-kong. Much-improved popular monthly covering Hongkong/Taiwan scene, with factual articles. Currently better than **CinemArt.**

MILLIMETER, 139 East 43rd Street, New York, NY 10017. An American technical monthly that covers the spectrum from animation to video, boasts off-beat interviews, and gains from some zestful page design.

MONROE, Postbox 432, SF-33101 Tampere, Finland. Occasional (at least twice per annum) magazine aimed at members of Finland's largest

film society. Put together with love and enthusiasm, knowledge and a dash of elegance too.

MONTHLY FILM BULLETIN, British Film Institute, 127 Charing Cross Road, London WC2 0EA. Provides commendably full and usually accurate credits, synopses and reviews (less objective) of all new films released in Britain. Since the July 1982 issue has had a facelift as well as including a video section.

MOVIETONE NEWS, Seattle Film Society, 5236 18th Avenue NE, Seattle, Washington 98105. Few university film magazines are so prolific, so consistent, and so polemical as "Movietone News," which emerges from Seattle eight times annually to spread across America and attract prominent writers. Foreign libraries should subscribe to this one without question.

NOTAS DEL CINE URUGUAYO, Casilla de Correo No 1191, Montevideo, Uruguay. Domestic publication dealing with technical developments in the cinema from a Uruguayan viewpoint. Apolitical.

PHOTOPLAY, 12–18 Paul Street, London EC2A

4JS. Much improved fan monthly that contains good interviews and useful titbits. Now incorporates the defunct **Films Illustrated.**

PREMIERE, 18 rue Théodore-Deck, 75737 Paris. New glossy, all-colour monthly (11 issues per year), with a pungent editorial style and overall awareness.

PROJEKTIO, Yrjönkatu 11 A 5, SF-00120 Helsinki 12. The magazine of the Finnish Federation of Film Societies, appearing four times a year, with various reviews and articles on world and Finnish cinema.

QUADERNI DI CINEMA, Via Benedetto Varchi 57, 50132 Florence. Wide-ranging Italian quarterly, striving to match cultural politics with an enthusiastic appreciation of film history and current movies.

QUARTERLY REVIEW OF FILM STUDIES, Redgrave Publishing, 430 Manville Road, Pleasantville, New York 10570. An imposing academic journal, which consists in the main of scholarly reviews of several film books.

LA REVUE DU CINEMA, 3 rue Récamier, Paris 7. French monthly that is better known still under the title of "Image et Son," and includes editorial contributions by the staff of the former "Ecran."

LA REVUE INTERNATIONALE D'HISTOIRE DU CINEMA, L'Avant-Scène, 27 rue St.-André-des-Arts, Paris 6. A series of immaculately-produced micro-fiches, issues regularly on a subscription basis, which place information on various subjects at the researcher's fingertips.

SAFTTA JOURNAL, PO Box 41357, Craighall, Transvaal 2024, South Africa. Information-packed biannual publication, containing criticism, technical articles and detailed local coverage.

S.A. FILM & ENTERTAINMENT INDUSTRY, PO Box 41419, Craighall, Transvaal 2024. Gerald Walford's lively monthly trade paper – edited by Selwyn Klass – covers the South African film industry in depth.

SCREEN, 29 Old Compton Street, London W1V 5PL. A once-mild organ put out by the Society for Education in Film and Television, and now a lively debating ground for theoretical issues of all kinds – all highly-respected, notably in the U.S.A.

SEQUENCES, 1474 rue Alexandre-Desève, Montréal 133. French-Canadian quarterly that has an enthusiastic mixture of reviews, comment and production news.

SIGHTLINES, Educational Film Library Association, 43 West 61st Street, New York, NY 10023. Excellent quarterly magazine dealing with film education in the United States, and the various uses of film.

SINEMA TV, Yildiz Yolu, Gayrettepe, Istanbul. Monthly Turkish magazine, the official organ of the "Turk Film Arsivi."

SINCHRONOS KINIMATOGRAFOS, Delphon 4, Athens 144. Attractive and well-produced mixture of serious articles and valuable data, plus criticism designed to improve the state of Greek cinema. Thoughtfully illustrated.

SKOOP, Postbus 11377, Amsterdam, Holland. The well-known Dutch movie magazine, with a spectrum of news, reviews, interviews, and a lavish selection of pictures. Colour covers are always striking.

SKRIEN, Postbus 318, 1000 AH Amsterdam. Excellent Dutch magazine that appears with regularity and enthusiasm. Fine historical articles and recently-improved colour covers.

SOUTHERN SCREEN (Nan-kuo tien-ying), Lot 220, Clear Water Bay Road, Kowloon, Hongkong. Shaw Bros.'s long-running (since 1958) house magazine.

SOVYETSKI EKRAN, ul. Chasovaya 56, Moscow A-319, U.S.S.R. 125319. Popular fortnightly founded in 1925 with up-to-date news of current cinema. Similar to Polish **Film.**

SPEKTRI, Box 142, SF-00101 Helsinki 10, Finland. An independent quarterly aiming at Finnish film buffs. Fresh opinions, no preconceived prejudices. Attractively produced.

SPOTLIGHT, c/o Bo Torp Pedersen, Brunevang 92, DK-2700 Brønshøj, Denmark. Danish magazine that concentrates on special issues, often covering theory and film criticism.

STARS ET CINEMA, 7 place Georges Brugmann, 1060 Brussels. Glossy Belgian monthly with international slant. Similar to the British "Films Illustrated."

STILLS, Cadles Cottage, Sutton, Stanton Harcourt, Oxford OX8 1RU. Oxford University has spawned several important magazines over the years; this latest one covers TV and video as well as films.

TIME OUT. Since coming back on the stands,

London's radical weekly guide has shed some of its more extreme opinions to the overall benefit of its film section.

TRAVELIN, Valázquez 10, Madrid. New Spanish fortnightly that sparkles with colour stills and lively articles on the contemporary world and Spanish movie scene.

TRUE BEAUTY MOVIE MAGAZINE (Chen shan mei tsa-chih), New World Building, 4th floor, Hanchung Street, Taipei, Taiwan. CMPC's house magazine, with some serious criticism and unfamiliar articles on Hongkong/Taiwan scene. Recently much improved in content, and with an attractive face-lift.

24 IMAGES, 169 rue Labonté, Longeuil, Québec, Canada J4H 2P6. Exceptionally attractive French-Canadian quarterly that covers festivals and international cinema with a touch of Gallic verve.

VISION, British Academy of Film and Television Arts, 195 Piccadilly, London W1V 9LG. Formerly "Journal of the Society of Film and Television Arts," a long-established and respected quarterly, containing many articles about the film *industry*.

WHAT'S ON IN LONDON, Onslow House, 60–66 Saffron Hill, London EC1N 8AY. The most established of the London film and entertainment round-ups, recently re-designed and brightened up.

YEDINCI SANAT, P.K., Beyoğlu, Istanbul. Monthly Turkish magazine.

National Organs

BULGARIAN FILMS, Film Bulgaria, 96 Rakovski Street, Sofia. Appears eight times a year, and now is partly in colour. Large format, fully illustrated.

CHINA'S SCREEN, China Film Export and Import Corporation, 25 Xin Wai Street, Peking. Quarterly, colourfully designed, promoting the latest productions of the mainland Chinese industry.

CINEMA, CINEMA, Ministère de la Culture Française, avenue de Cortenbur 158, 1040 Brussels. Neat, stapled newsletter, appearing three times a year and containing "nouvelles du film belge d'expression française." Illustrated.

CZECHOSLOVAK FILM, 28 Václavské námĕsti, Prague 1. Handsomely-illustrated, large format. Short on credits, etc.

HUNGAROFILM BULLETIN, Báthori utca 10, Budapest V. Reliable and comprehensive, including films produced for TV. Appears four or five times a year.

ISRAEL FILM CENTRE INFORMATION BULLETIN, Ministry of Commerce and Industry, 30 Agron Street, Jerusalem. Very high quality glossy bulletin with comprehensive editorial matter.

POLISH FILM, Film Polski, ul. Mazowiecka 6/8, 00-054 Warsaw. This valuable large-format publication also includes coverage of TV films.

THE ROMANIAN FILM, 25 Julius Fucik Street, Bucharest. Now back in a much-improved format, with more credits and information. Large format, in colour.

SCANDINAVIAN FILM NEWS, Swedish Film Institute, Box 27 126, S-102 52 Stockholm, Sweden. Quarterly newsletter distributed by the five Nordic film authorities, giving news and credits for forthcoming films, statistics etc.

SOVIET FILM, Sovexportfilm, 14 Kalashny pereulok, Moscow 103009. Now in its twenty-first year, this handsome monthly continues to be indispensable for students of Russian film. Colour spreads.

SWEDISH FILMS NEWS BULLETIN, Svenska Filminstitutet, Box 27 126, S-102 52 Stockholm. Regularly-mailed information sheets which build up into a comprehensive dossier. A handsomely-produced annual appears every year in addition.

UNIJAPAN FILM QUARTERLY, UniJapan Film, 9–13 Ginza 5-chrome, Chuo-ku, Tokyo 104. This well-printed little booklet is now published only irregularly.

Trade and Technical

AMERICAN CINEMATOGRAPHER, ASC Agency Inc., 1782 North Orange Drive, Hollywood, California 90028. High quality monthly for professionals and cameramen in particular.

AUDIOVISION, PO Box 31720, Braamfontein 2017, South Africa. Lively monthly journal that

deals exclusively with the technical aspects of film and TV.
BKSTS JOURNAL, 110–112 Victoria House, Vernon Place, London WC1B 4DJ. Important monthly specialising in technical trends and developments in Cinema.
BRITISH NATIONAL FILM CATALOGUE, 81 Dean Street, London W1V 6AA. Quarterly that provides essential particulars of all non-fiction films (British and foreign) becoming available in Britain.
LE FILM FRANCAIS, 12 avenue George V, 75008 Paris. The leading French trade weekly.
FILM-ECHO/FILMWOCHE, Wilhelmstrasse 42, 62 Wiésbaden. Regular West German trade paper.
HOLLYWOOD REPORTER, 6715 Sunset Blvd, Hollywood, California 90028. All the news from the Coast. There is also a European edition.
KINOLEHTI, Kaisaniemenkatu 3 B 29, SF-00100 Helsinki 10. Film business organ for Finland, published six times each year, with various articles, reviews, news items, statistics, attractively presented.
MOVIE TV MARKETING, Box 30, Central Post Office, Tokyo, 100–91 Japan. A remarkable monthly enterprise from Japan – in English. Packed with cosmopolitan trade news, statistics . . . but no gossip, thank goodness!
S.A. FILM & ENTERTAINMENT INDUSTRY, PO Box 41419, Craighall 2024. Monthly South African publication, reflecting all sectors and aspects of South Africa's growing industry.
SCREEN INTERNATIONAL, 6–7 Great Chapel Street, London W1. Revamped version of "Cinema TV Today," the British weekly trade paper, still under Peter Noble's energetic editorship. Brightly illustrated, large format, good international news coverage. Known for its daily editions at Cannes, and for its valuable special supplements devoted to different countries.
THEAMATA, Athinon 64, Aharnai Attikis, Greece. Informative fortnightly containing statistics, reviews, news etc.
VARIETY, 154 West 46th Street, New York, NY 10036. Long-established weekly tabloid, and invaluable for anyone interested in films – gossip, statistics, advanced production news, good reviews etc. Covers TV, music, and other entertainment areas too.

Index to Advertisers

Index to Films Reviewed